Causes and Consequences of Human Migration

An Evolutionary Perspective

Migration is a widespread human activity dating back to the origin of our species. Advances in genetic sequencing have greatly increased our ability to track prehistoric and historic population movements and have allowed migration to be described both as a biological and as a socioeconomic process. Bringing together the latest research, *Causes and Consequences of Human Migration* provides an evolutionary perspective on human migration past and present. Crawford and Campbell have brought together leading thinkers who present examples from different world regions, using historical, demographic, and genetic methodologies and integrate genetic, archaeological, and historical evidence to reconstruct large-scale population movements in each region. Other chapters discuss established questions such as the Basque origins and the Caribbean slave trade. More recent evidence on migration in ancient and present-day Mexico is also presented. Pitched at a graduate audience, *Causes and Consequences of Human Migration* will appeal to anyone with an interest in human population movements.

MICHAEL H. CRAWFORD is Professor of Anthropology and Genetics, and Director of the Laboratory of Biological Anthropology, at the University of Kansas, Lawrence, KS, USA.

BENJAMIN C. CAMPBELL is Associate Professor of Anthropology at the University of Wisconsin-Milwaukee, Milwaukee, WI, USA.

Causes and Consequences of Human Migration

An Evolutionary Perspective

MICHAEL H. CRAWFORD
University of Kansas

BENJAMIN C. CAMPBELL
University of Wisconsin-Milwaukee

CAMBRIDGE UNIVERSITY PRESS
Cambridge, New York, Melbourne, Madrid, Cape Town,
Singapore, São Paulo, Delhi, Mexico City

Cambridge University Press
The Edinburgh Building, Cambridge CB2 8RU, UK

Published in the United States of America by
Cambridge University Press, New York

www.cambridge.org
Information on this title: www.cambridge.org/9781107012868

First published 2012

Printed and Bound in the United Kingdom by the MPG Books Group

A catalog record for this publication is available from the British Library

Library of Congress Cataloging in Publication data

Causes and consequences of human migration : an evolutionary
perspective / [edited by] Michael H. Crawford, Benjamin C. Campbell.
  pages   cm
  Includes bibliographical references and index.
  ISBN 978-1-107-01286-8
  1. Human beings–Migrations.   2. Emigration and immigration.
  3. Migrations of nations.   4. Human evolution.   5. Human population
  genetics.   I. Crawford, Michael H., 1939–   II. Campbell, Benjamin C.
  GN370.C38 2012
  304.8–dc23   2012014617

ISBN 978-1-107-01286-8 Hardback

Contents

Contributors

Víctor Acuña-Alonzo
Molecular Genetics Laboratory, National School of Anthropology and History, Mexico City, Mexico

Mark Aldenderfer
School of Social Sciences, Humanities, and Arts, University of California, Merced, CA, USA

Carlos Eduardo Guerra Amorim
Departamento de Genética, Instituto de Biociências, Universidade Federal do Rio Grande do Sul, Brazil

Lindsay Barone
University of Wisconsin-Milwaukee, Milwaukee, WI, USA

Rodrigo Barquera
Molecular Genetics Laboratory, National School of Anthropology and History, Mexico City, Mexico

Ramiro Barrantes
Escuela de Biología, Universidad de Costa Rica, San Pedro de Montes de Oca, Costa Rica

Monica Batistapau
Chemistry Department, University of South Florida, Tampa, FL, USA

K. G. Beaty
Department of Anthropology, University of Kansas, Lawrence, KS, USA

Mwenza Blell
Department of Anthropology, University of Durham, Queen's Campus, Stockton, UK

Benjamin C. Campbell
University of Wisconsin-Milwaukee, Milwaukee, WI, USA

Loredana Castrì
Dipartimento di Biologia evoluzionistica sperimentale, Area di Antropologia, Università di Bologna, Bologna, Italy

Michael H. Crawford
Department of Anthropology, University of Kansas, Lawrence, KS, USA

Bartholomew Dean
Department of Anthropology, University of Kansas, Lawrence, KS, USA

Eric J. Devor
Department of Obstetrics and Gynecology, University of Iowa Hospitals and Clinics, Iowa City, IA, USA

Alvaro Díaz-Badillo
Department of Genetics and Molecular Biology, Centro de Investigación y Estudios Avanzados del Instituto Politécnico Nacional, San Pedro Zacatenco, México D.F., Mexico

Alan G. Fix
Department of Anthropology, University of California Riverside, Riverside, CA, USA

Rocío Gómez
Department of Toxicology, Centro de Investigación y Estudios Avanzados del Instituto Politécnico Nacional, San Pedro Zacatenco, México D.F., Mexico

Carolina Carvalho Gontijo
Departamento de Genética e Morfologia, Instituto de Ciências Biológicas, Universidade de Brasília, Brazil

J. B. Hirbo
Department of Biology, University of Maryland, College Park, MD, and Department of Genetics, University of Pennsylvania, Philadelphia, PA, USA

John M. Janzen
Department of Anthropology, University of Kansas, Lawrence, KS, USA

Anne Justice
Department of Anthropology, University of Kansas, Lawrence, KS, USA

Raquel A. Lazarin
Department of Forensic Sciences, George Washington University, Washington, DC, USA

Philippe Lefèvre-Witier
CNRS, Toulouse, France

María de Lourdes Muñoz
Department of Genetics and Molecular Biology, Centro de Investigación y Estudios Avanzados del Instituto Politécnico Nacional, San Pedro Zacatenco, México D.F., Mexico

Donata Luiselli
Dipartimento di Biologia evoluzionistica sperimentale, Area di Antropologia, Università di Bologna, Bologna, Italy

Lorena Madrigal
Department of Anthropology, University of South Florida, Tampa, FL, USA

Elizabeth Matisoo-Smith
Department of Anatomy, Otago University, Dunedin, New Zealand

Phillip E. Melton
Centre for Genetic Epidemiology and Biostatistics, University of Western Australia, Australia

Igor Mokrousov
Laboratory of Molecular Microbiology, St. Petersburg Pasteur Institute, St. Petersburg, Russia

Felix Moos
Professor Emeritus, Department of Anthropology, University of Kansas, Lawrence, KS, USA

María Concepción Morales-Gómez
Department of Genetics and Molecular Biology, Centro de Investigación y Estudios Avanzados del Instituto Politécnico Nacional, San Pedro Zacatenco, México D.F., Mexico

M. J. Mosher
Department of Anthropology, Western Washington University, Bellingham, WA, USA

Dennis H. O'Rourke
Department of Anthropology, University of Utah, Salt Lake City, UT, USA

Flory Otárola
Departamento de Antropología, Universidad de Costa Rica, San Pedro de Montes de Oca, Costa Rica

Gerardo Pérez-Ramirez
Department of Genetics and Molecular Biology, Centro de Investigación y Estudios Avanzados del Instituto Politécnico Nacional, San Pedro Zacatenco, México D.F., Mexico

Silviene Fabiana de Oliveira
Departamento de Genética e Morfologia, Instituto de Ciências Biológicas, Universidade de Brasília, Brazil

Davide Pettener
Dipartimento di Biologia evoluzionistica sperimentale, Area di Antropologia, Università di Bologna, Bologna, Italy

Christine Phillips-Krawczak
Molecular Bioscience Department, University of Kansas, Lawrence, KS, USA

Eduardo Ramos
Instituto Nacional de Antropología e Historia, Teotihuacan, Edo. de México, Mexico

A. Ranciaro
Department of Genetics, University of Pennsylvania, Philadelphia, PA, USA

Lilian Rebellato
Department of Geography, University of Kansas, Lawrence, KS, USA, and Department of Anthropology, University of Oeste do Pará, Santarém, Brazil

Ernesto Ruiz
Department of Anthropology, University of South Florida, Tampa, FL, USA

Moses S. Schanfield
Department of Forensic Sciences, George Washington University, Washington, DC, USA

Jay T. Stock
Department of Biological Anthropology, University of Cambridge, Cambridge, UK

Mark Stoneking
Max Planck Institute for Evolutionary Anthropology, Department of Evolutionary Genetics, Leipzig, Germany

Eric Sunderland
University of Bangor, Bangor, UK

S. A. Tishkoff
Department of Genetics and Department of Biology, University of Pennsylvania, Philadelphia, PA, USA

Jonathon C. K. Wells
Childhood Nutrition Research Centre, UCL Institute of Child Health, London, UK

Dixie West
Natural History Museum and Biodiversity Research Center, University of Kansas, Lawrence, KS, USA

William I. Woods
Department of Geography, University of Kansas, Lawrence, KS, USA

Kristin L. Young
Carolina Population Center, University of North Carolina at Chapel Hill, Chapel Hill, NC, USA

Preface

We are all products of human migration. Some of us migrated during our lifetimes from one part of the world to another, and had to learn different cultures, languages, diets, and systems of education. Others have parents who were forcibly relocated at different times, particularly during World War II and its sequelae, and experienced displaced persons camps, disease, and violence, and were uprooted to various corners of the world, such as the Americas and Australia. Yet others have ancestors who migrated hundreds or thousands of years ago and have lived in relatively undisturbed households for many generations. Finally, some people originated in Africa and migrated within the continent or were forcibly relocated by wars and the slave trade.

The authors of this volume are migrants and describe the human condition from their unique migratory experiences. Each author has a complex personal history of migration, often occurring in different generations, cultural traditions, and languages. All of the authors currently residing in the Americas are either recent migrants or have descended from ancestors who relocated to the Americas generations ago. Several of the authors have experienced extensive migration and relocation within their lifetimes, as the following examples show.

Felix Moos came to the United States from Germany following World War II. He survived that war only to find himself fighting in the Korean Conflict for his new homeland. As for many of his generation coming from a devastated and exhausted Europe, cultural agility and the will to adapt to new circumstances, different values and life patterns, different education modes, and different languages became essentials to survival and made him, like the multitudes of other migrants throughout history, by definition, more multicultural and multilingual.

Michael Crawford immigrated to the United States as a teenager from China with stopovers in displaced persons camps in Tubabao, Philippine Islands, and in Uranquinty, Australia. He can be viewed as multicultural having grown up speaking Russian, being educated in a French/English school in Shanghai, grade school and high school in Australia and Seattle, Washington, and undergraduate and Ph.D. at the University of Washington.

Lisa Matisoo-Smith's life history illustrates the complexity of migration and ethnic origin. Her father was born in Estonia, but left Estonia as Russians occupied the country in 1944 during World War II; he was a refugee in Germany until after the war when he moved to the United States. Her mother's ancestors were on the first boats arriving in the Americas in the 1600s. Lisa was born in Honolulu, grew up in Japan (8–18 years), moved to mainland United States to go to the University and met her Kiwi husband in London – on her way to an archaeological dig in France. She moved to New Zealand 24 years ago and is now professor, Department of Anatomy, Otago University.

The authors who currently reside in the Americas share a common event – the migration of their ancestors from recent times to several hundred years ago. All of us view the world in terms of our personal history, the movements and origins of our ancestors and families and our common experiences resulting from: religious persecutions, wars, economic incentives, and search for employment, power, and novelty. All humans are the product of this ubiquitous experience that we and our ancestors collectively share.

This volume represents the fruits of an interdisciplinary conference on human migration held at the University of Kansas in Lawrence, Kansas, March 1st and 2nd, 2010, organized by Michael H. Crawford and Benjamin Campbell and funded by several programs and institutions: the Commons Interdisciplinary Research Initiative in Nature and Culture, Center for Gobal and International Studies, College of Liberal Arts and Sciences, Laboratory of Biological Anthropology, Spencer Museum of Art, Latin American Studies and Department of Anthropology of the University of Kansas. Evogen, Inc., a diagnostics company in Kansas City, Kansas, contributed funding for the conference. More than 100 scholars attended the formal portion of this two-day conference. A "brainstorming" session was held on the third day with discussion concerning the development of a migration consortium and an evaluation of potential projects that this multidisciplinary group could initiate and support.

An international group of speakers and participants assembled for this conference, representing 12 countries and 24 institutions worldwide. In addition, this conference featured a strong multidisciplinary approach to human migration with the participation of cultural anthropologists, sociologists, geographers, demographers, biological anthropologists, molecular geneticists, and human biologists. After the conference, a book prospectus was submitted for consideration to Cambridge University Press. Peer reviewers of the book prospectus, solicited by the Press, recommended the addition of several chapters to cover sub-Saharan Africa and Oceania and to consider the disease consequences of migration.

The purpose of this conference was to examine the causes and consequences of human migration from a multidisciplinary perspective. Human migration has figured prominently throughout human history and increasingly so in today's world with transnational migration and the large scale movement of refugees and other forced migrants. The impacts of migration are felt in all aspects of our lives from jobs to the flow of money, development of immigrant communities and kinship, and national politics. As such, migration is a multidimensional process of interest to all of the social and biological sciences, ranging from economics to sociology, political science, anthropology, human biology, and medicine.

BENJAMIN C. CAMPBELL AND MICHAEL H. CRAWFORD

1

Perspectives on human migration: introduction

INTRODUCTION

Migration has a deep history, dating back to the very origins of our species. An evolutionary perspective suggests that an activity as deeply rooted and ubiquitous as migration must be imbedded in our human nature and genes. Thus, the social and cultural factors involved in migration are intertwined within our human biology. Not only are ecological factors such as climate important in the economic push/pull factors that social scientists consider to underlie decisions about migration, but there may be individual variation in our genomes that lead to a propensity to migrating in the first place (see the chapter by Ben Campbell and Lindsay Barone on the variation in dopamine receptors and its association with migration out of Africa).

Furthermore, far from being simply the bearer of ideas and institutions, as sociologists might have it, or job skills and economic goods as the economists may emphasize, migrants represent bodies that carry an imprint of their original surroundings. These include the transmission of disease vectors as well as physiological and behavioral traits that can influence chronic diseases, especially metabolic conditions associated with eating and activity and mental illness (see the chapter by M. J. Mosher on potential epigenetic effects associated with dietary changes in migrant populations). These imprints also include more behavioral and evolutionary factors such as fertility and fecundity patterns that have important demographic consequences in the migrant's new home.

Causes and Consequences of Human Migration, ed. Michael H. Crawford and Benjamin C. Campbell. Published by Cambridge University Press. © Cambridge University Press 2012.

While the primary models for migration include the economic push/pull factors, these factors themselves are subject to other interacting factors and conditions. For instance, climatic changes which affect subsistence have been linked to patterns of migration (Dillehay, 2002), as have social patterns of kinship. The chapter by Michael Crawford and Dixie West examines genetic consequences of climatic changes in the Aleutian Archipelago that stimulated the settlement of the Central and Western Islands, approximately 6000 years ago. Understanding the biological and cultural dynamics that drive human migration will be highly significant in a globalizing world economic system subject to war, political unrest, climatic change, and massive human relocations. Chapters by John Janzen on the migration of Africans to Midwestern United States and by Felix Moos on the massive relocations of Chinese to Peru document how wars and economic incentives currently drive human migration in a global economy.

In terms of the consequences of migration, anthropologists and human biologists have long been aware of the health and demographic consequences of migration. Immigrant populations differ from both the population of origin and their host country in many health measures in ways that may reflect the socioeconomic, physiological, and genetic dimension of migration. Igor Mokrousov, in his chapter on the introduction of the Bejing strain of tuberculosis into Central Asia and Europe, brings a molecular genetic perspective and documents the spread of disease through conquest by Mongolian hordes of Genghis Khan.

This volume is intended to explore the causes and consequences of human migration from its beginning with the origins of the human species (see the chapter by Mark Stoneking on the molecular evidence of hominins migrating out of Africa). Based on the idea that while the scale and scope of migration has changed over time, its fundamental causes have not, this volume gives full attention to migration in the past as the key to understanding current and future patterns of migration. In addition, it stresses genes as one of the most important markers of migration that can be used to link patterns of the past with those of the present.

Thus the first section of the book focuses on the theory, processes, and history of migration relevant to all human populations. This section starts with a chapter by Mark Stoneking "Genetic evidence concerning the origins and dispersals of modern humans" updating the most recent genetic evidence for our growing understanding of the historical origins of human migration. Also included in this section are two chapters that consider migration as a context for selection of the human genotype and phenotype. In "The biology of human migration: the ape that won't commit?", Jonathon Wells and Jay Stock consider the role of migration in promoting a flexible maternal response to the environment so as to maximally benefit fetuses and infants that may be born in different environments experienced by the mother. Ben Campbell and Lindsay Barone in "Evolutionary basis of human migration" take a similar selective perspective and apply it to genes of the dopaminergic system in the brain thought to be related to behaviors and personality traits that would promote individuals to move from one place to another – not only with modern humans, but with their hominid ancestors as well.

Two additional chapters consider the causes and consequences of migration. "Kin-structured migration and colonization" by Alan Fix provides a fundamental understanding of how social relatedness structures the migratory process and contributes to the genetic differentiation of offshoot populations from the parental groups. "The role of diet and epigenetics in migration: molecular mechanisms underlying the consequences of change" by M. J. Mosher suggests mechanisms for genetic change in migrant populations through modification of diets in new environments.

Michael Crawford and Dixie West, in their chapter entitled "Evolutionary consequences of human migration: genetic, historic, and archaeological perspectives in the Caribbean and Aleutian Islands," examine the evolutionary consequences of migration through two distinct examples in highly diverse tropical and Arctic environments. First, they present an evolutionary success story of a triracial hybrid population (Garifuna) and their ability to colonize most of the coast of Central America because of their genetic resistance to malaria – brought from Africa. The second example provides a clear picture of how changes in natural resource abundance have shaped the migratory process for foragers of all stripes. The Unangan (Aleuts) were hunters of sea mammals and foragers and their subsistence and availability of food was dependent on climatic conditions. Thus, population movement was driven by major climatic changes, such as periods of cooling and its subsequent effects on the turbulence of the sea.

The remainder of the volume is divided by geographic regions, including Africa, Europe, Asia, Oceania, the Americas, and the Caribbean. Each section includes case studies, from different disciplinary perspectives. Examples run from the current experience of African migrants in Kansas, displaced by warfare, to the use of tuberculin bacteria to trace human migration in Asia, and to the genetic consequences of migration onto the Tibetan plateau. Special attention is paid to migration in the Americas, both ancient and current because of the richness of the available research and the vast geographical and environmental expanses of the two continents – from the Arctic to the temperate zones to the tropics to the cold of Tierra del Fuego.

Within the section on Africa four chapters are devoted to a variety of widely disparate approaches and topics. These include a discussion of history of population movement and cultural change in North Africa, in a chapter entitled "Human migrations in North Africa" by Philippe Lefèvre-Witier. Based on historical sources, he reconstructs the migrations and conquests from the earliest inhabitants of the Mahgreb to the present day. Jibril Hirbo, Alessia Ranciaro and Sarah Tishkoff in their chapter "Population structure and migration in Africa" consider the relationships among archaeological, linguistic, and genetic data in the examination of migration patterns of sub-Saharan Africa. John Janzen's chapter "Identity, voice, community: new African immigrants to Kansas" tells the story of African migrants to Kansas based on yet another time frame, contemporary United States of America, the here and now, using different methods – primarily oral interviews. Rodrigo Barquera and Víctor Acuña-Alonzo reconstruct the patterns of forced African migration into Mexico due to the slave trade and colonial expansion. The consequences of the African relocation included the presence of specific morphological phenotypes, HLA haplotypes, hemoglobinopathies, glucose-6-phosphate dehydrogenase (A- form and deficiency), Duffy null, and specific immunoglobulins – GM*zabst. Initially, the first Africans were brought as domestic slaves of Moorish, Berber colonists, followed by larger numbers brought for labor in Vera Cruz and Campeche.

The section on Europe contains four chapters mostly based on genetic research within an archaeological and historical framework, tracing population affinities across a number of different groups. These include "Demic expansion or cultural diffusion: migration and Basque origins" by Kristin Young, Eric Devor and Michael Crawford, which examines several theories of Basque origins and possible demic expansions from the Middle East associated with the Neolithic period. The molecular evidence suggests that the Basques represent a Paleolithic population but with more recent Neolithic admixture. "Consequences of migration among the Roma: immunoglobulin markers as a tool in investigating population relationships" by Moses Schanfield, Raquel Lazarin and Eric Sunderland uses immunoglobulin markers to trace the origins and relationships between different Roma groups in Europe. The authors conclude that little can be said about the Roma beyond the fact that they appear to have interbred with local populations. Their geographic origins remain unconfirmed by the immunoglobulin data presented in this chapter. However, recent mitochondrial DNA (mtDNA) analyses have shown specific high-resolution haplotypes that are shared by Indian populations and Roma groups (Pericic Salihovic *et al.*, 2011).

 Two other chapters are featured in this section, "Migration, assimilation and admixture: genes of a Scot?" by Kristie Beaty and "Mennonite migrations: genetic and demographic consequences," by Phillip Melton, consider the histories and European origins of two U.S. populations. Beaty's chapter examines the relationship between social identity and genetics of Scots from the "Highland Clearances" and transplanted to the United States. She finds, on the basis of mitochondrial DNA and Y-chromosome markers, that the Scottish migrants to the Midwest show a greater genetic resemblance to Scottish populations than do the maternally based mtDNA markers. Melton is able to reconstruct the population history of six Mennonite communities through the use of mtDNA markers. He traces the migration of the Mennonites, initially forced by religious persecution, from Switzerland, Germany, and Holland to Ukraine to Midwestern United States. The final leg of the Mennonite relocation to the United States was caused by the loss of the exemption from military service that an earlier Tsar of Russia had offered to attract the pacifist Mennonites to settle in the Molotsniya region of the Crimea.

 The section on Asia includes two genetically based accounts of human population movements in this rather large region of the world, as well as the reconstruction by Felix Moos of current migration of Chinese workers out of Asia and into Peru. "Migration, globalization, instability, and Chinese in Peru" by Felix Moos tells the little-known story of the flow of Chinese workers into Peru, which they often leave to head north to North America. Unfortunately, it is currently not possible to enumerate the flood of emigrants streaming out of the People's Republic of China into the Americas. The numbers are substantial and the economic effects can be seen in Peru and North America. In "Human migratory history: through the looking glass of genetic geography of *Mycobacterium tuberculosis*," Igor Mokrousov uses *M. tuberculosis* genomes to reconstruct human migratory events. The tuberculosis lineages, such as the Beijing strain, are characterized by spoligotyping and its geographic distribution follows the routes of the Mongol invasions from Asia to Europe. By comparing the genomes of the bacteria to the human host, coevolution can be assessed in ancient or modern migration patterns.

Mark Aldenderfer's contribution, "Peopling the Tibetan plateau: migrants, genes, and adaptation," considers the accumulating evidence, both genetic and archaeological, for the movement of humans on to the Tibetan plateau as well as the evidence for adaptation to hypoxia. He concludes that some human groups on the plateau during the Paleolithic would have contributed genes to the modern day Tibetan's ability to work efficiently and, more importantly, reproduce surviving babies at high altitude.

Oceania is represented in a comprehensive chapter by Lisa Matisoo-Smith entitled "The great blue highway: human migration in the Pacific." Matisoo-Smith reviews current theories of human movement through the Pacific based on both genetic and archaeological evidence. She concludes that the peopling of the Pacific is much more complex than merely two migrations: first the Papuans (dating back to 50 000 years ago), chronologically followed by the Austronesians (who migrated 1200 years ago). Many of these reconstruction complications are due to the depopulation following European Contact, contemporary work migration, and forcible relocations.

Migration into the Americas is explored by a series of four chapters. Because of the intensive excavations and genetic analyses conducted in these regions, emphases are placed on Central American (Mexican) and South American (Amazonian and Brazilian) populations. Migration into North America is represented in this volume by the populations of the Aleutian Archipelago, discussed in the chapter by Crawford and West. A fabric of pre-Hispanic migration in Mexico has been woven with archaeological and molecular threads in a chapter entitled "Migration of pre-Hispanic and contemporary human Mexican populations," by María de Lourdes Muñoz, Eduardo Ramos, Alvaro Díaz-Badillo, María Concepción Morales-Gómez, Rocío Gómez, and Gerardo Pérez-Ramirez. They reconstruct the migration patterns using the material culture of the dominant populations of Mexico, initiated by kin migration. They focus on the earliest civilizations of Mexico – Olmecs, the city of Teotihuacan, Toltecs and Aztecs – followed by Spanish colonization.

Amazonian migration is explored in two chapters: "A review of the Tupi expansion in the Amazon," by Lilian Rebellato and William Woods and "Molecular consequences of migration and urbanization in the Peruvian Amazonia" by Anne Justice, Bartholomew Dean and Michael Crawford. Rebellato and Woods compile ethnohistorical, geographic, and linguistic data to examine the origins of the Tupi languages and their expansion throughout the Amazonian lowlands.

The authors pose a significant question in regards to the Tupi speakers: "Does this numerical increase represent an expansion of agriculturalists or are the Tupi migrating?" They conclude that these agriculturalists are obtaining land and expanding through warfare and cannibalism. The chapter by Justice and her colleagues focuses on rural to urban migration in Yurimaguas, a principal city of Amazonia. The application of mtDNA revealed no non-native maternal admixture but that gene flow was directed from surrounding Native American villages.

Carlos Eduardo Guerra Amorim, Carolina Carvalho Gontijo, and Silviene Fabiana de Oliveira's chapter entitled "Migration in Afro-Brazilian rural communities: crossing historical, demographic, and genetic data." They examined the causes and consequences of migration in Afro-Brazilian rural communities. These communities were formed by African slaves and their descendants. As a result of this forced migration, the molecular genetic markers indicate the vast predominance of African ancestry, which contrasts with the majority of such rural Brazilian communities.

In terms of the Caribbean, the focus is on the use of genetic markers in delineating population history. The chapter "Indentured migration, gene flow, and the formation of the Indo-Costa Rican population" by Lorena Madrigal, Monica Batistapau, Loredana Castrì, Flory Otárola, Mwenza Blell, Ernesto Ruiz, Ramiro Barrantes, Donata Luiselli and Davide Pettener uses molecular markers (mtDNA and Y-chromosome) from an Indo-Costa Rican population to measure the genetic effects of migration and marriage patterns. Christine Phillips-Krawczak's contribution "Causes and consequences of migration to the Caribbean Islands and Central America: an evolutionary success story" suggests that genes brought from Africa were protective against malaria and allow for the Garifuna groups to colonize much of the coast of Central America. The indigenous Native American populations on the coast of Central America were ravaged by the introduction of falciparum malaria – carried by African slaves imported to work in the fruit plantations. In contrast to African and Mediterranean populations, Native Americans had not been subjected to natural selection from malaria and at European contact lacked the genetic adaptations against *Plasmodium falciparum*.

Having revealed the deep history of human migration from the beginning of the species and covered the globe with a variety of case studies in migration, the volume concludes with an overview by Dennis O'Rourke.

REFERENCES

Dillehay, T. D. (2002). Archaeology: climate and human migrations. *Science*, **298**, 764–5.

Pericic Salihovic, M., Baresic, A., Martinovic Klaric, I., *et al.* (2011). The role of the Vlax Roma in shaping the European Romani maternal genetic history. *American Journal of Physical Anthropology*, **146**, 262–70.

Section 1 Theory

2

Genetic evidence concerning the origins and dispersals of modern humans

What does genetic evidence tell us about the origins and dispersals of our species, modern humans? This review updates the last review I wrote on this topic (Stoneking, 2008), but it is a substantial update and revision as there is much new information, especially from genome sequences of two extinct hominins, Neandertals (Green *et al.*, 2010) and "Denisovans" (Reich *et al.*, 2010), as well as from more sophisticated demographic analyses of genome-wide data (Reich *et al.*, 2009; Wollstein *et al.*, 2010). In particular, in contrast to previous reviews, we now have a model for human origins and dispersals that has been tested against dense genome-wide data.

MODELS FOR HUMAN ORIGINS

Over the years there have been many ideas about the origins of modern humans, but they basically all fall into the four main categories depicted in Figure 2.1. One of the earliest is the candelabra model, which prevailed for decades. According to this model, the common ancestor of human populations from the major regions of the Old World – Africa, Europe, Asia and Australasia – dates back to the late Miocene, perhaps as much as two million years ago. Since modern humans did not exist at that time, the transformation from our ancestors to modern humans would have occurred independently in four separate regions of the world, at more or less the same time. The candelabra model was most prominently associated with the anthropologist Carleton Coon (Coon, 1962), and fell out of favor when he used

Causes and Consequences of Human Migration, ed. Michael H. Crawford and Benjamin C. Campbell. Published by Cambridge University Press. © Cambridge University Press 2012.

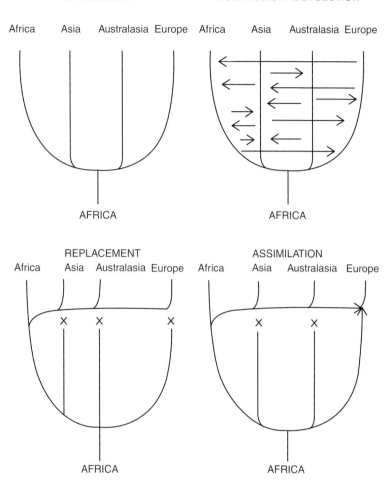

Figure 2.1 Four models of the origin of our species. The horizontal arrows in the multiregional evolution model emphasize the role of migration in this model. The absence of similar arrows in the replacement and assimilation models, prior to the migration out of Africa, are for clarity only, and should not be inferred as indicating an absence of migration during this time period for these models. This figure was redrawn as Fig. 2 of Stoneking (2008).

it to promote racist views. According to Coon, the transformation to modern humans occurred first in Europeans, and hence Europeans have had the most time to evolve from their "primitive"' ancestry, while Africans were the last to transform into modern humans and therefore have had the least amount of time to shed their "primitive" ancestry – and in case you were wondering, Carleton Coon was indeed of European ancestry.

Regardless of the racist implications of the candelabra model, to my knowledge no scientist today regards it as a credible model for human origins for the very simple reason that the biological and genetic changes involved in the transformation to modern humans were too complex to have arisen completely independently in four separate regions of the world. The debate about human origins has therefore revolved around the other three models or variants thereof shown in Figure 2.1, which are based on different interpretations of the same fossil evidence. The fossil evidence indicates that all human evolution (that is, since the human lineage split from that of the chimpanzee) took place in Africa until about 1.5–2 million years ago, and that between 1.5–2 million and 50 000 years ago various waves of migration spread our ancestors or their relatives from Africa across the Old World. There are, however, many different names for various fossil species and just as many arguments for which of these fossils deserve to be called our ancestors. To keep things simple, I will use the term "archaic human" to refer to anything before the appearance of modern humans that might or might not be our ancestor.

The degree to which earlier migrations contributed to modern humans is the main source of contention amongst these models. Multi-regional evolution, at first glance, appears similar to the candelabra model, in that the main lines of descent within each geographic region are from within that geographic region: modern Africans descend mostly from ancient Africans, modern Europeans descend mostly from ancient Europeans, etc. The main argument for multiregional evolution is the contention that the fossil record shows regional continuity over time (Wolpoff *et al.*, 1984). However, the important difference between multi-regional evolution and the candelabra models is that the former includes migration between regions as depicted by the horizontal arrows in Figure 2.1, so any important genetic change would have spread quickly. According to multiregional evolution, our ancestors encompass the entire Old World population of archaic humans, which evolved over the past 1.5 to 2 million years via a complex interchange of species-wide selection for genetic changes that were favorable across all geographic regions, local selection and/or genetic drift influencing traits specific to particular geographic regions, and migration to avoid the problem of independent evolution of modern humans in different regions of the Old World.

By contrast, the replacement model (Figure 2.1) argues that the transformation to modern humans occurred in a single population in Africa, somewhere around 200 000 to 300 000 years ago, which then spread across and out of Africa between 50 000 and 100 000 years ago and replaced completely, without any interbreeding, the archaic populations from earlier migrations from Africa (Stringer and Andrews, 1988). The evidence in favor of this hypothesis is the fact that the earliest fossils of anatomically modern humans come from Africa, and that early modern human fossils from regions outside Africa tend to be more similar to early modern human fossils from Africa than to archaic human fossils from the same region.

The replacement model is the most extreme version of the out-of-Africa models; other versions acknowledge that the transformation to modern humans occurred in Africa, but hold that the spread of modern humans was not a complete replacement event, but accompanied by some degree of interbreeding with non-African, archaic humans (Bräuer, 1989). I refer to these models as assimilation models (Figure 2.1), of which there are various versions that differ in where and how much admixture is postulated to have occurred (Bräuer, 1989; Smith *et al.*, 2005). The fossil evidence cited in favor of a particular assimilation hypothesis is a combination of the evidence for an African origin of modern humans combined with particular traits found in both the modern and archaic inhabitants of a particular non-African region.

It must be emphasized that all of these models were first based on fossil evidence, not molecular evidence. However, I would argue that all of these models are really statements about genes; in particular, they can be distinguished by their predictions for the contribution of African genes to the gene pool of non-African populations of modern humans (Stoneking, 2008). At one extreme is the (discredited) candelabra hypothesis, which predicts that there are no African genes outside Africa: modern Europeans got all of their genes from archaic Europeans, modern Asians from archaic Asians, etc. At the other extreme is the replacement model, which predicts that all of us got all of our genes from our African ancestors. In between these two extremes would be multiregional evolution, which predicts that archaic Asians, Europeans, and Australasians contributed genes to modern humans. Also in between these two extremes, but closer to the replacement side, are the assimilation models, which predict that archaic non-Africans contributed some small percentage of our genome.

Thus, the way to distinguish between these models is to look at our genes. And the current state of the genetic evidence as I write this (in April 2011), can be summarized as follows:

1. *An overwhelmingly strong signal of a recent African origin throughout our genome*. Beginning with the first genetic evidence from

single loci such as mtDNA (Cann *et al.*, 1987; Vigilant *et al.*, 1991) and the Y-chromosome (Underhill *et al.*, 2000), to the current state of genome-wide SNP data (Jakobsson *et al.*, 2008; Li *et al.*, 2008; Lopez Herraez *et al.*, 2009) and genome sequences (Schuster *et al.*, 2010), the message is clear: there is compelling evidence for a recent African origin of our species throughout our genome. A particularly clear indication comes from the astonishingly high correlation between the heterozygosity for a population and its distance from East Africa (Prugnolle *et al.*, 2005); this finding strongly suggests an origin in Africa followed by serial bottlenecks that reduced genetic diversity as humans moved further and further from their African homeland. Although the data would thus seem to support complete replacement, other analyses (Plagnol and Wall, 2006; Wall *et al.*, 2009) suggest instead that replacement alone cannot completely explain patterns of genetic variation in contemporary human populations, and that therefore there must have been some small amount of archaic admixture in our ancestry. However, prior to the availability of the Neandertal genome sequence, this point was hotly disputed (Fagundes *et al.*, 2007).

2. *A signal of genetic contributions from Neandertals to all non-African populations examined to date*. The *tour de force* sequencing of the Neandertal genome (Green *et al.*, 2010) would appear to lay to rest all arguments about which model best explains our origins: all genomes from non-Africans (but no genomes from Africans) examined to date harbor a signal of Neandertal genetic material, on the order of a few percent. While other explanations for this signal are theoretically possible – such as deep structure within Africa – they are much less likely, and rendered even more unlikely by the finding of additional signals of genetic material from Denisovans in some populations, as detailed below. So, the admixture model best explains our origins: we arose as a species relatively recently, then a single population dispersed from Africa, admixed with Neandertals, and then subsequently dispersed around the world. The implications of this Neandertal gene flow for models of single versus multiple dispersals from Africa are discussed in more detail below.

3. *A signal of gene flow from Denisovans to populations from New Guinea*. A complete mtDNA genome sequence obtained from a

fossil bone from Denisova Cave in southern Siberia indicated that it fell outside the range of both modern human and Neandertal mtDNA variation (Krause *et al.*, 2010), suggesting that it came from a previously unknown, extinct hominin. The genome sequence from this bone indicates that the population to which this individual belonged (called "Denisovans") was a sister group to Neandertals (Reich *et al.*, 2010). Intriguingly, a signal of gene flow from Denisovans was found in contemporary human populations from New Guinea and Bougainville, on the order of 4–6%. Given the relatively sparse sampling of populations from Southeast Asia and Oceania in this study, it would be of considerable interest to investigate additional populations from this part of the world for signals of Denisovan gene flow.

SINGLE VERSUS MULTIPLE DISPERSALS FROM AFRICA

Given the overwhelming genetic evidence for a recent origin of modern humans in Africa, was there a single dispersal or multiple dispersals of modern humans from Africa? Based largely on fossil and archaeological evidence, it was proposed that there was a separate, early dispersal of modern humans that migrated via a "southern route" from Africa, along the coast of India, that reached as far as Sahul, the combined Australia–New Guinea landmass (Lahr and Foley, 1994). According to this hypothesis, populations descended from this "early southern route" were then largely replaced by subsequent dispersals from Africa, except perhaps for certain "refugia" populations such as Andamanese, Malaysian and Philippine "Negrito" groups, or aboriginal Australians. The genetic evidence for an early southern route is equivocal. MtDNA and Y-chromosome data have been argued to support the early southern route hypothesis (Macaulay *et al.*, 2005; Mellars, 2006; Thangaraj *et al.*, 2005), while genome-wide SNP data have been argued to support a single dispersal of modern humans from Africa to Asia (Pan-Asian SNP Consortium, 2009).

None of these genetic studies attempted to actually test the strength of support in the data for an early southern route hypothesis versus alternative hypotheses. However, a recent study of genome-wide SNP data from Oceanic populations has now done just that (Wollstein *et al.*, 2010). Using dense genome-wide SNP data and a novel method to correct for ascertainment bias in how the SNPs were chosen for geno-typing, Wollstein and colleagues (2010) tested the following three

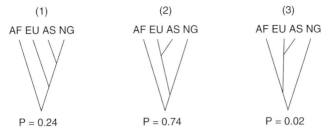

Figure 2.2 Three models of the dispersal of modern humans from Africa, that were tested by comparison to dense genome-wide SNP data (Wollstein *et al.*, 2010). Model 1 assumes a single dispersal of modern humans from Africa, followed by a single dispersal from this non-African source population to Asia and New Guinea. Model 2 is a "modified" southern route hypothesis of a single dispersal of modern humans from Africa, followed by an early dispersal from this non-African source population to New Guinea, and a subsequent dispersal to Asia. Model 3 is the "classic" early southern route hypothesis (Lahr and Foley, 1994) of an early dispersal of modern humans from Africa to New Guinea, followed by a subsequent dispersal from Africa to Eurasia. AF, Africa; EU, Europe; AS, Asia; NG, New Guinea. The P values indicate the relative probability of each model, based on the genome-wide SNP data.

models for human dispersal from Africa to New Guinea (Figure 2.2): (1), a single dispersal of modern humans from Africa, followed by a single dispersal from this non-African source population to Asia and New Guinea; (2) a single dispersal of modern humans from Africa, followed by an early dispersal from this non-African source population to New Guinea, and a subsequent dispersal to Asia; and (3) an early dispersal of modern humans from Africa to New Guinea, followed by a subsequent dispersal from Africa to Asia. Data were then simulated for each model, and the goodness-of-fit of each model to the observed genome-wide SNP data evaluated. As indicated in Figure 2.2, there was strongest support for model (2), some support for model (1), but essentially no support for model (3). Thus, dense genome-wide SNP data indicate that the best-fitting model is a "modified" early southern route hypothesis, with a single dispersal of modern humans from Africa, but multiple dispersals from this non-African source population. Reassuringly, this is exactly the same model that is supported by the signals of gene flow from Neandertals and Denisovans in modern human populations (Green *et al.*, 2010; Reich *et al.*, 2010): all non-African populations have roughly the same amount of Neandertal gene flow, suggesting a single dispersal from Africa; and only populations from New Guinea and Bougainville exhibit a signal of gene flow from Denisovans, suggesting a separate dispersal from the non-African source population in their ancestry.

CONCLUSIONS AND FUTURE PROSPECTS

Genome-wide data – including both ancient genome sequences as well as dense SNP data from contemporary populations – have contributed substantially to our knowledge of human origins and dispersals. In particular, the genetic evidence strongly supports the assimilation model of human origins: there was a recent African origin of our species, followed by a small amount of interbreeding with archaic non-Africans such as Neandertals and Denisovans. The signal of archaic admixture turns out to be an extremely useful marker of population relationships: all non-Africans share a similar signal of Neandertal gene flow that thus strongly supports a single major dispersal of modern humans from Africa; and only populations from Oceania (so far) have a signal of gene flow from Denisovans, supporting a separate dispersal of the ancestors of Oceanians from East Asians. Importantly, both of these conclusions are supported as well by analyses of genome-wide SNP data from contemporary populations, without including any information about gene flow from extinct hominins.

As with any important finding, answering the burning questions about human origins and dispersals has raised even more interesting questions. What other populations, in addition to New Guinea and Bougainville, exhibit signals of gene flow from Denisovans? Where – and when – did the gene flow from Neandertals, and from Denisovans, occur? Are there any signals of gene flow from other extinct hominins in any contemporary populations? Is the genetic material contributed to particular populations by extinct hominins "merely" a neutral relic of the past, or did this genetic material confer traits that were important in human evolution? These – and other – questions are ripe for answering with the new tools that enable the production and analysis of genome-wide data, and I anticipate that the next update on the topic of the genetic evidence concerning human origins and dispersals will add substantially to the preliminary version outlined here.

Note: A recent study (Reich *et al.*, 2011) has found further evidence of Denisova admixture in populations from the Philippines, eastern Indonesia, Australia, and Near and Remote Oceania. Their results support an early southern route dispersal and suggest that the admixture with Denisovans may have occurred in island Southeast Asia.

ACKNOWLEDGMENTS

I thank Michael Crawford for the invitation to participate in a most stimulating meeting, and Sandra Michaelis and Rebecca Carl for producing Figure 2.1.

REFERENCES

Bräuer, G. (1989). The evolution of modern humans: a comparison of the African and non-African evidence. In *The Human Revolution: Behavioural and Biological Perspectives in the Origins of Modern Humans*, ed. P. Mellars and C. B. Stringer, pp. 123–54. Edinburgh, UK: Edinburgh University Press.

Cann, R. L., Stoneking, M., and Wilson, A. C. (1987). Mitochondrial DNA and human evolution. *Nature*, **325**, 31–6.

Coon, C. S. (1962). *The Origin of Races*. New York: Knopf.

Fagundes, N. J., Ray, N., Beaumont, M., *et al.* (2007). Statistical evaluation of alternative models of human evolution. *Proceedings of the National Academy of Sciences of the United States of America*, **104**, 17 614–19.

Green, R. E., Krause, J., Briggs, A. W., *et al.* (2010). A draft sequence of the Neandertal genome. *Science*, **328**, 710–22.

Jakobsson, M., Scholz, S. W., Scheet, P., *et al.* (2008). Genotype, haplotype and copy-number variation in worldwide human populations. *Nature*, **451**, 998–1003.

Krause, J., Fu, Q., Good, J. M., *et al.* (2010). The complete mitochondrial DNA genome of an unknown hominin from southern Siberia. *Nature*, **464**, 894–7.

Lahr, M. and Foley, R. (1994). Multiple dispersals and modern human origins. *Evolutionary Anthropology*, **3**, 48–60.

Li, J. Z., Absher, D. M., Tang, H., *et al.* (2008). Worldwide human relationships inferred from genome-wide patterns of variation. *Science*, **319**, 1100–4.

Lopez Herraez, D., Bauchet, M., Tang, K., *et al.* (2009). Genetic variation and recent positive selection in worldwide human populations: evidence from nearly 1 million SNPs. *PLoS ONE*, **4**, e7888.

Macaulay, V., Hill, C., Achilli, A., *et al.* (2005). Single, rapid coastal settlement of Asia revealed by analysis of complete mitochondrial genomes. *Science*, **308**, 1034–6.

Mellars, P. (2006). Going east: new genetic and archaeological perspectives on the modern human colonization of Eurasia. *Science*, **313**, 796–800.

Pan-Asian SNP Consortium. (2009). Mapping human genetic diversity in Asia. *Science*, **326**, 1541–5.

Plagnol, V. and Wall, J. D. (2006). Possible ancestral structure in human populations. *PLoS Genetics*, **2**, e105.

Prugnolle, F., Manica, A., and Balloux, F. (2005). Geography predicts neutral genetic diversity of human populations. *Current Biology*, **15**, R159–60.

Reich, D., Green, R. E., Kircher, M., *et al.* (2010). Genetic history of an archaic hominin group from Denisova Cave in Siberia. *Nature*, **468**, 1053–60.

Reich, D., Kircher, M., Patterson, N., *et al.* (2011). Denisova admixture and the first modern human dispersals into southeast Asia and Oceania. *American Journal of Human Genetics*, **89**, 516–28.

Reich, D., Thangaraj, K., Patterson, N., Price, A. L., and Singh, L. (2009). Reconstructing Indian population history. *Nature*, **461**, 489–94.

Schuster, S. C., Miller, W., Ratan, A., *et al.* (2010). Complete Khoisan and Bantu genomes from southern Africa. *Nature*, **463**, 943–7.

Smith, F. H., Jankovic, I., and Karavanic, I. (2005). The assimilation model, modern human origins in Europe, and the extinction of Neandertals. *Quaternary International*, **137**, 7–19.

Stoneking, M. (2008). Human origins: the molecular perspective. *EMBO Reports*, **9**, S46–50.

Stringer, C. B. and Andrews, P. (1988). Genetic and fossil evidence for the origin of modern humans. *Science*, **239**, 1263–8.

Thangaraj, K., Chaubey, G., Kivisild, T., *et al.* (2005). Reconstructing the origin of Andaman Islanders. *Science*, **308**, 996.

Underhill, P. A., Shen, P., Lin, A. A., *et al.* (2000). Y chromosome sequence variation and the history of human populations. *Nature Genetics*, **26**, 358–61.

Vigilant, L., Stoneking, M., Harpending, H., Hawkes, K., and Wilson, A. C. (1991). African populations and the evolution of human mitochondrial DNA. *Science*, **253**, 1503–7.

Wall, J. D., Lohmueller, K. E., and Plagnol, V. (2009). Detecting ancient admixture and estimating demographic parameters in multiple human populations. *Molecular Biology and Evolution*, **26**, 1823–7.

Wollstein, A., Lao, O., Becker, C., *et al.* (2010). Demographic history of Oceania inferred from genome-wide data. *Current Biology*, **20**, 1983–92.

Wolpoff, M. H., Wu, X., and Thorne, A. G. (1984). Modern *Homo sapiens* origins: a general theory of hominid evolution involving the fossil evidence from East Asia. In *The Origins of Modern Humans: A World Survey of the Fossil Evidence*, ed. F. H. Smith and F. Spencer, pp. 411–483. New York: Alan R. Liss.

JONATHON C. K. WELLS AND JAY T. STOCK

3

The biology of human migration: the ape that won't commit?

INTRODUCTION

Humans occupied almost all global regions prior to the emergence of agriculture and subsequent technological evolution, emphasizing the extraordinary biological and behavioral versatility of our species. Understanding this versatility may shed light on the past colonizing activities of our species, and on the selective pressures that favored the emergence of such adaptablity. The same plasticity is increasingly appreciated by biomedical research, investigating our present vulnerability to chronic degenerative disease in the expanding obesogenic niche.

The prevailing view in evolutionary anthropology has long been that the primary cause of between-population human phenotypic variability was genetic response to natural selection. As we enter the post-genomic era, it is increasingly common to search for genetic signatures of natural selection using genome-wide scans (Harris and Meyer, 2006; Laland *et al.*, 2010). Comparisons with other apes indicate, however, that contemporary humans are characterized by a relatively high degree of genetic unity, given our unprecedented geographical distribution (Bakewell *et al.*, 2007; Gagneux *et al.*, 1999). Further studies suggest that human genetic adaptation appears to occur less through strong selection on novel alleles, and more through subtle alterations in the frequency of existing alleles (Hancock *et al.*, 2010a, 2010b). There is also mounting evidence that a proportion of the genetic component of human phenotypic diversity can be attributed to

Causes and Consequences of Human Migration, ed. Michael H. Crawford and Benjamin C. Campbell. Published by Cambridge University Press. © Cambridge University Press 2012.

random or neutral evolutionary mechanisms rather than natural selection (Harvati and Weaver, 2006; Roseman, 2004).

Recently, we considered the relative influences of "getting there" versus "being there" on human biology (Wells and Stock, 2007). Genetic adaptation implies a degree of "commitment" induced by relatively consistent environments across generations such that alleles spread under cumulative selection. A lack of genetic sprecialization, as indicated by our genetic unity, suggests that humans evolved a generalized biology, capable of responding to environmental variability across varying timescales. Indeed, the genus *Homo* appears to have followed a more general trend amongst East African mammals, where more specialized species were replaced by more generalized species (Potts, 1996).

There is clear evidence for genetic adaptation amongst humans, such as the independent origin and spread of lactose tolerance (Johnson, 1981) in multiple regions (Tishkoff *et al.*, 2007), with origins in the Neolithic (Burger and Thomas, 2011), and possibly amylase copy number variation as an adaptation to Holocene dietary change (Perry *et al.*, 2007). Whilst further studies may provide additional further evidence for recent genetic adaptation, there is also increasing awareness of a variety of forms of plasticity in human biology, which collectively buffer the genome from selective pressures, and allow a variety of other forms of adaptation (Stock, 2012; Wells and Stock, 2007). From this perspective, we could argue that humans are to some extent the "ape that *doesn't* commit," thus maintaining a relatively homogeneous genome across diverse ecological environments.

In this chapter, we explore evidence for both "genetic commitment" and counteracting plasticity implying "lack of commitment," in order to understand how humans manage to migrate so successfully, and also how regular migrations and colonizations have themselves shaped human biology.

POPULATION GENETIC VARIABILITY: THE EVIDENCE

The recent African origin of our species is well established (Cann *et al.*, 1987; Excoffier, 2002; Ingman *et al.*, 2000; Ke *et al.*, 2001; Kivisild *et al.*, 2001), and there is strong evidence that genetic variation outside of Africa represents a subset of diversity within Africa (Harpending and Rogers, 2000; Tishkoff *et al.*, 1996). Studies of Y-chromosome haplotype frequencies indicate that all non-African lineages coalesce to between 81 and 56 ka (Hammer and Zegura, 2002), and suggest that all non-African populations descend from one or a small number of migration events.

MtDNA haplogroup frequencies place a potential East African origin of mtDNA lineages found outside of Africa between 73 and 55 ka (Kivisild *et al.*, 2000), and approximately 60 ka (Quintana-Murci *et al.*, 1999). Both estimates fit with a chronology of the southern dispersal out of Africa leading to the colonization of Southeast Asia and Australia. Unique derived lineages of the M, N and R haplogroups which coalesce between 70 and 50 ka have been found among mtDNA genomes of indigenous populations of Malaysia, Papua New Guinea, and Australia (Macaulay *et al.*, 2005), as well as the Andaman Islands (Thangaraj *et al.*, 2005). These provide additional support for a rapid southern dispersal of modern humans followed by an extended period of geographic and genetic isolation of some populations. There is some evidence for long-term continuity in populations outside of Africa since these early dispersal events (Metspalu *et al.*, 2004). While genomic analyses indicate one or several ancestral bottlenecks among humans outside of Africa, there is also evidence for some preservation of ancient haplotypes, likely through the process of admixture with archaic hominins both within Africa (Garrigan and Hammer, 2006) and throughout the rest of the world (Green *et al.*, 2010).

The considerable phenotypic diversity within our species lies in contrast to our relative genetic homogeneity compared with other species (Kaessmann *et al.*, 2001). This is partly a reflection of our recent common African origin, but it also suggests that at least some of the tremendous phenotypic diversity in our species is related to biological plasticity in response to environmental variation or other non-adaptive mechanisms. Despite relative homogeneity, it has been noted that humans have a particularly high number of adaptive substitutions when compared with chimpanzees, which can only be explained through a model of very recent differentiation, within the past 40 000 years (Hawks *et al.*, 2007). This has been explained as a recent acceleration of human evolution; however, it corresponds highly with dramatic demographic expansion associated with dispersals out of Africa and subsequent cultural change associated with agriculture. Examining modern human genetic variation in more detail, there is now considerable evidence that many genes, which demonstrate signatures of selection through the identification of long DNA haplotypes associated with particular genes and minor derived alleles, present within specific populations or in frequencies not to be expected under neutral models (Sabeti *et al.*, 2006; Voight *et al.*, 2006). Recently, it has been noted that given the function of many of these genes, their recent selection may relate to cultural change within the Holocene, predominantly after the origins of agriculture. While it is often assumed that cultural change within the Holocene has served to reduce the selective pressure exerted upon our genome by the natural environment, we now see culture as the driving force of recent evolution within our species (Laland *et al.*, 2010; Richerson *et al.*, 2010).

Despite evidence for recent genetic differentiation and selection, we know very little about the factors shaping human genetic diversity within recent history or in contemporary populations. The current methods used to detect selection identify selective signatures of selective events which influenced diversity over thousands of years, but say little about the factors shaping genetic diversity today. In contemporary society, characterized by the demographic transition and increasing urbanization (Mace, 2008), there is increasing genetic diversity, which is likely to counteract local genetic specialization of small populations. The process of urbanization has been demonstrated to result in increasing heterozygosity, which has been linked to improvements in health through heterosis or "outbreeding enhancement" (Rudan *et al.*, 2008). However, modern human genetic variation represents the history and demography of living people today, and it is unclear how recent population interactions, such as disease epidemics and colonial history, may have influenced genetic diversity among small and indigenous populations (Stock and Migliano, 2009).

Overall, human history is characterized by major migrations and diasporas. While there is an increasing number of examples of past selection upon particular genes, many traits which influence phenotypic variation are polygenic, the cumulative product of many small effects (Wells, 2012; Wells and Stock, 2011). The distribution of the developmental control of complex traits throughout the genome may be a form of bet-hedging – increasing phenotypic variance amongst offspring to decrease variance in parental fitness. Bet-hedging offers an explanation for apparently high genetic heritabilities in biological traits (though see below) in the absence of strong local selection (Wells, 2009b).

REDUCING COMMITMENT

In paleoanthropology, systematic climate change remains widely assumed to have represented the key ecological stress to which humans must have adapted. The turnover pulse hypothesis proposed by Vrba in the 1980s suggested that early *Homo*, in common with other species, responded to the emergence of dry savanna habitats in Africa (Vrba, 1985). This view has been challenged by recent work indicating that, notwithstanding any such trends towards greater aridity, the

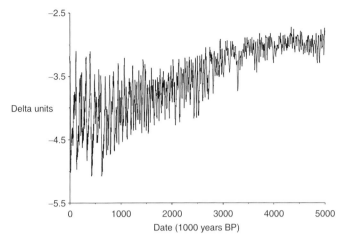

Figure 3.1 Temporal fluctuations in benthic oxygen-18 enrichment, indicating climate fluctuations over the last 5 million years. There has been a systematic cooling, but also an increasing volatility in climate during the period of hominin evolution. (Data from Lisiecki and Raymo, 2005.)

environments of early *Homo* were fragmented and climate was extremely volatile (Potts, 1996). Climatic reconstructions indicate substantial and continual temperature fluctuations, in response to a wide range of predictable cycles relating to the Earth's geophysical properties, in combination with other unpredictable events such as major volcanic eruptions or other sources of ecological change. Figure 3.1 illustrates temperature trends based on benthic oxygen-18 isotope data for the last 5 million years (Lisiecki and Raymo, 2005). The volatility depicted suggests that ecological variability was a key challenge for early *Homo*, inducing complex ecosystem changes, as different species respond on different timescales to physical climate fluctuations (Potts, 1996).

These data suggest that substantial adaptive response through natural selection to a given ecosystem would have been difficult, and even detrimental. Rather, the optimal solution to such volatility would comprise investment in biological processes capable of accommodating environmental change both across and within generations. This helps understand the general trend to generalized biology evident in East African mammals (Potts, 1996).

Human life history appears to represent a key axis of such variability, through which environmental variability is accommodated. Analysis of small-scale societies indicates substantial life history variability between different populations (Walker *et al.*, 2006). Broadly, life history was found to correlate with local ecology, with more favorable conditions associated with faster growth and earlier puberty. Faster growth and development in females was also correlated with increased mortality in females.

Although some of this variability may be genetic, there are good reasons to expect much of the variability to derive from plasticity. Although human life history traits have been proposed to be highly heritable, the data require careful consideration (Wells and Stock, 2011). Heritability calculations based on twin studies may be misleading, for several reasons. First, twin studies may overestimate heritability by failing to incorporate a wide range of environmental variability, which would artificially inflate the genetic contribution to phenotypic variability. Second, monozygotic twins have similar epigenetic as well as genetic profiles, hence their greater phenotypic similarity compared with dizygotic twins may arise from environmental epigenetic effects as well as genomic similarity (Kaminsky *et al.*, 2009), although the relative contributions from genetic and non-genetic sources remain unknown.

Whatever the genetic contribution to life history traits, there is now substantial evidence that they are capable of changing by a standard deviation score over timescales of 3 to 7 generations (Wells and Stock, 2011). These data indicate that there is substantial plasticity in human life history, and that at any given time, traits may be considered norms of reaction (Stearns, 1992), responding to recent ecological conditions. Such transgenerational plasticity reduces the strength of selective pressures on the genome, and hence constrains genetic differentiation.

The polygenetic basis of human life history traits also offers hints as to how they respond to natural selective pressures. For example, approximately 180 genes have been confidently associated with the variability in human stature (Hirschhorn and Lettre, 2009; Lango Allen *et al.*, 2010; Lanktree *et al.*, 2011). For each gene, the magnitude of the effect is relatively small, and much of the genetic basis of heritability may found in the interaction of genes, detected through the analysis of all single nucleotide polymorphisms simultaneously (Yang *et al.*, 2010). Rather than natural selection acting primarily on novel mutations, the genomic basis of life history traits may have been fragmented and distributed across a wide range of different alleles, complemented by enhanced phenotypic plasticity (Wells, 2012).

A key consequence of this genomic fragmentation is that, as the effect of each gene is small, ecological change across generations cannot, directly through gene expression, generate marked change in

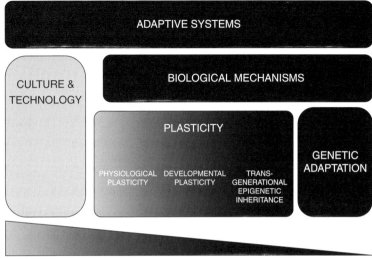

Figure 3.2 A schematic diagram illustrating the range of adaptive systems available to modern humans, and the varying rates at which they allow adaptation. The more unstable and unpredictable the environment, the greater the benefit of "temporary" adaptation through plasticity, rather than commitment to genetic change.

phenotype. We interpret this as suggesting that plasticity in human life history is built on an underlying scaffolding of genomic stability (Wells and Stock, 2011). The polygenic nature of life history traits may represent a form of bet hedging, nudging phenotype incrementally by small amounts rather than demonstrating large-scale discrete effects (Wells, 2009b), and by allowing many minor but cumulative adjustments in the allocation of energy throughout the life course, expressed as life history variation. Thus, human life history appears to offer a striking example of how humans have evaded substantial "genetic commitment" to local ecological conditions, as emphasized in Figure 3.2. This strategy would be favored either in unstable conditions, or in an organism prone to regular migration. However, as discussed below, such life history plasticity coexists with strong canalization of other traits, such as growth of the brain.

THE VALUE OF CAPITAL

Complementary to this polygenic basis, human life history variability appears to be mediated by different forms of "capital." Embodied capital has been defined as resources which may be accumulated across and within generations, and used to invest in fitness (Kaplan *et al.*, 2003). Somatic capital may be represented by physique, and energy capital by both adipose tissue and social relationships (Wells, 2010, 2012).

Life history strategy is generally conceptualized in terms of energy allocation, between the competing functions of maintenance, growth, immune status, and reproduction (Hill, 1993). The principle of allocation assumes that energy allocated to one function cannot be allocated to another, such that fitness is assumed to be maximized by the optimal allocation strategy between these ends. We suggest that the occupation of volatile and unpredictable environments favored the accumulation of energy in two key generalized currencies which facilitate the accumulation of capital from diverse raw sources, enable the delaying of investment decisions, and aid the allocation of energy between competing biological functions (Wells, 2012). Again, the accumulation of such energy capital reduces the need for genetic commitment.

The first kind comprises social capital, and derives from increasing detachment of energetics from individual body size. In most animals, energy expenditure is a function of body size and activity level, each of which affects the ratio of foraging effort to reward. In humans, however, sharing food along with cooperation on subsistence tasks acts to fragment individual energy budgets, and replaces them with pooled budgets which reflect the income and expenditure of a group (Kramer and Ellison, 2010; Reiches *et al.*, 2009). Such pooled budgets are observable in other primate species practicing activities such as hunting (e.g. chimpanzees) or cooperative breeding (e.g. tamarins, marmosets). Humans therefore do not differ radically from other primates, but appear to make substantial use of pooled energy budgets to resolve the costs of reproduction, which occurs at faster rates than in other apes (Wells and Stock, 2011).

Ethnographic evidence from contemporary societies demonstrates substantial variability between and within populations in the relative contributions of ascendant and descendant kin to cooperative breeding, indicating that humans have no specific social adaptation but can rather pursue this strategy regardless of the underlying subsistence regime (Sear and Mace, 2008). What is central to such social behavior is that it represents the accumulation and expenditure of a generalized energy currency, deriving from a wide variety of transactions in food and activity subsidies.

The second kind of capital represents physical capital, in particular energy stored in adipose tissue. Like social capital, adipose tissue represents a generalized store of energy capable of benefiting from either increased food intake or subsidies to the physical activity budget. Adipose tissue is itself able to direct energy to competing functions such as maintenance, growth, and reproduction. Adipose tissue is now understood to be the source of a number of hormonal products, including leptin which signals energy stores to the brain where it contributes to the regulation of both immune function and reproductive function (Wells, 2009c), and cytokines which constitute a fundamental component of the immune system. The link between physical energy capital and immune function may serve in particular to buffer physiological stresses associated with colonization of new environments and exposure to new pathogens.

Both social and physical energy capital confer maximal flexibility on life history "decisions," enabling substantial time delay between the accumulation and expenditure of energy. Once again, the use of capital decreases the need for genetic adaptation to local ecological conditions, because energy may be stored in order to resolve stresses arising in the future. Energy stores, whether located in social relationships or in the body, may be particularly valuable for long-distance migrations, as they reduce the necessity of immediately obtaining total energy requirements upon entry into new, unfamiliar habitats. Many other species demonstrate the accumulation of energy stores prior to migration (Pond, 1998), and this suggests that we might anticipate associations between adipose tissue biology and brain activities associated with migration.

THE DYNAMIC RELATIONSHIP BETWEEN HUMANS AND NICHES

The "natural" environment of human populations is inherently transient not only because humans migrate, but also because we are prone to changing our environments through niche construction (Odling-Smee et al., 2003). Hominins have long inhabited unstable environments, having been exposed to greater seasonality than other apes since the australopithecine era (Foley, 1993), and have evolved a biology that reflects such instability (Potts, 1996; Wells and Stock, 2007). Niche construction represents a solution to such stochasticity, and further buffers the genome from selective pressures.

There are a number of material causes of our colonization success that relate to such niche construction. While early dispersals of the genus *Homo* may have followed game across savanna environments that were broadly comparable (Dennell and Roebroeks, 2005), dispersals into more seasonally variable environments are likely to have been culturally dependent (Gowlett, 2006). The colonization of Europe by Neanderthals and their long evolutionary success in this region was clearly based upon a combination of cultural and biological adapation.

This raises a central question: do humans fit the organism to the niche, or the niche to the organism? On the one hand, we discussed above life history plasticity, whereby populations can adopt appropriate life history strategies in different ecological conditions. On the other hand, the process of niche construction allows humans to transport some of their "ideal" environment with them when they migrate. Humans may be accompanied on their migrations by food resources (e.g. crop or stock species), pathogens (e.g. helicobacter, the flea), and other beneficial organisms (e.g. gut bioflora, domestic dog), as well as by cultural knowledge and material objects (further enhanced through trade and exchange). Thus, we must consider whether migration causes exposure to new ecological stresses, or whether these are buffered by biology and technology. As migrating hunter-gatherers, an emphasis on meat consumption allowed convergence on a common dietary niche: the consumption of grazing and browsing animals provides a substitute for local knowledge of plant resource distribution and availability, whilst also "outsourcing" specialized adaptations to digesting variable plant toxins and forms of cellulose. Reliance on animals also provides raw material for clothing, an important component of environmental manipulation and niche construction in *Homo sapiens*.

Clearly the dispersal of modern humans into novel environments involved more than simple hunting of game, which may have been central to the earlier dispersal of the genus *Homo*. The long-term success and geographic range of modern human dispersals out of Africa seems to have been dependent, largely, on the flexibility of modern human behavior (McBrearty and Brooks, 2000). The precise extent to which modern human origins correspond to cognitive evolution remains controversial, but it may be no coincidence that the successful global colonization of our species is associated with changes in tool technologies towards the use of blades and microliths, the origins of artistic expression and symbolism, and the systematic exploitation of marine resources, which strongly suggest an unprecedented cognitive flexibility of our species (Coolidge and Wynn, 2009). Social identity allows a group to transport cohesive elements of social life and structure between different ecological habitats, thus maintaining a behavioral toolkit that can nevertheless adapt rapidly in any new niche. Technology, culture, and sociality all represent the outsourcing of the means of adaptation from canalized brain "hardware" to variable "behavioral software programs" (Potts, 1996). Increasing use of such adaptive behaviors indicates greater dependence upon niche construction, and again a complementary restraint on genetic commitment.

The subsequent convergent shift towards agricultural subsistence in many global regions from the terminal Pleistocene through the Holocene marks a significant change in the relationship between humans and the natural world (Maher *et al.*, 2012a, 2012b), with increasing control over environmental productivity leading to food surpluses, changes in labor, task specialization, and runaway technological evolution (Stock, 2008; Stock and Pinhasi, 2011). These major cultural shifts suggest a long-term process of shifting environmental adaptability onto cultural mechanisms, which have the potential to profoundly influence our biological adaptations, whether due to plastic or genetic mechanisms. Trade, long-distance exchange networks, and commerce, which follow agriculture and are often an important component of state level society, may provide a means both of risk management and of transporting "fragments of environment" between human populations. This is shown by long-term trends in human health, which for example declined in Egypt with the emergence of agriculture but then improved considerably with the formation of the Dynastic state structure (Starling and Stock, 2007; Stock *et al.*, 2011).

TRANSGENERATIONAL EFFECTS AND TIME-LAGGED CHANGE

Traditionally, adaptation of organisms to ecological stresses has been assumed to occur in response to direct cues from the environment, such as climate (Hancock *et al.*, 2008; Roberts, 1953) or nutrition (Johnson, 1981; Kagawa *et al.*, 2002). However, recent work on mammals has emphasized particular sensitivity during early life (pregnancy and infancy). This suggests that rather than adapting directly to environmental stresses, much of this adaptation is transduced by maternal phenotype (Wells, 2003, 2007b). In turn, adaptations of the offspring may be considered to be targeted at maternal capital, rather than the environment itself (Wells, 2010).

This process generates a time-lag between ecological change and phenotypic change. Maternal buffering of the offspring slows down the rate at which each generation adapts to the local environment, and therefore limits the magnitude of change that can occur in any generation. This buffering effect appears beneficial, as there is increasing evidence that rapid phenotypic change within any single life course is detrimental to health (Misra and Khurana, 2008; Popkin, 2009; Wells, 2007b). Instead, phenotypic change is more beneficially distributed across several generations, manifest as slow secular trends which accommodate broader changes in the availability of food or the presence of predators and pathogens. This mode of adaptation may be particularly important because individual habitats may differ substantially in dietary sources of energy, in rates of energy return from foraging, and in the impact of pathogens on the immune system. Transducing early adaptations under the protective umbrella of maternal phenotype removes acute stresses whilst allowing more coherent transgenerational adaptation to systematic shifts in energy availability (Wells, 2003).

Some have argued that humans develop adaptive metabolic responses in early life in anticipation of ecological conditions likely to be encountered in adult life (Gluckman *et al.*, 2007). We consider such metabolic anticipation implausible in a species prone to regular migration and niche construction such as humans (Wells, 2007a). A recent study showed that exposing caterpillars to malnutrition in early life did not prepare their metabolism for poor energy availability in adult life, but rather increased investment in flight muscles, favoring migration to higher-quality habitats (Saastamoinen *et al.*, 2010). An intriguing hypothesis for humans, therefore, is that early-life adversity induces adaptations likely to promote subsequent migration. This hypothesis could be tested by investigating whether human migrants tend to be those whose phenotypic development early in life proves least suited to the adult environment that subsequently manifests.

NEW METHODS FOR MIGRATION RESEARCH

One of the primary sources of information about phenotypic variability between populations comprises simple measurements of body size and shape. Whilst stature may indicate long-term adaptation to the availability of food, body shape also captures more subtle information about metabolic characteristics and life history strategy. There is increasing recognition that variability in body fat distribution reflects strategic allocation of energy stores between competing regional adipose tissue depots (Wells, 2009a; Wells *et al.*, 2010).

Recently, a new technology has been developed for acquiring detailed information about body size and shape. Known as 3-D photonic scanning, this technology projects visible light onto the body surface, and captures distortions arising from body shape (Wells *et al.*, 2008b). Computer algorithms reconstruct the body surface topography, and provide a highly sophisticated whole-body map (Figure 3.3). Recent studies have highlighted significant variability in body shape between different ethnic groups after adjusting for body size, showing for example that Hispanic Americans have a more central abdominal weight distribution than European Americans (Wells *et al.*, 2008a), while Thais have less central weight distribution than white British (Wells *et al.*, 2012). African Americans have a less central weight distribution than European Americans, though more so in males than females (Wells *et al.*, 2008a).

At present, it is not possible to determine whether such shape variability derives primarily from genetic factors, or from variability in growth and behavioral patterns within the life course; hence further studies will be needed to address these issues. Nevertheless, 3-D photonic scanning offers a powerful opportunity to investigate phenotypic variation in relation to genotype in large population samples. The technology is relatively cheap to apply, can be transported in mobile scanning systems, and has been successfully used in several large national sizing surveys. It may prove ideal for investigating subtle metabolic and tissue allocation variability between populations in the context of migration studies.

Due to the importance of body fat in fueling the immune response, this technique could be used, for example, to test the variable disease selection hypothesis, whereby we have hypothesized that populations differ in their body fat distribution due to different pathogen loads, and hence different optimal allocation of energy stores to different tissues (Wells, 2009a). This hypothesis can be expanded in two ways. First, we hypothesize that non-African populations should have reduced tolerance of infectious diseases, having had fewer generations to adapt to non-African pathogens (McNeill, 1977). According to this hypothesis, we expect greater allocation of energy stores to the central abdominal depot, which is most closely associated with immune function. Second, we hypothe-sized more specifically that south Asians should allocate more fat to the abdomen to protect against gut infections common in the monsoon environment, whereas Africans should allocate more fat to the limbs, storing fat in muscle to provide energy for fevers, which "burn off" pathogens such as malaria which target the blood cells (Wells, 2009a).

Table 3.1 presents preliminary data on shape from several differ-ent populations, supporting both hypotheses although they do not

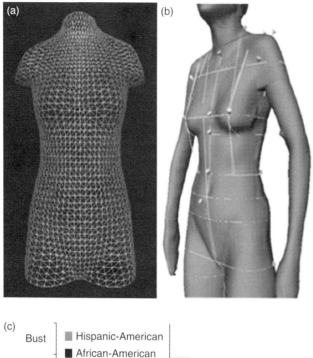

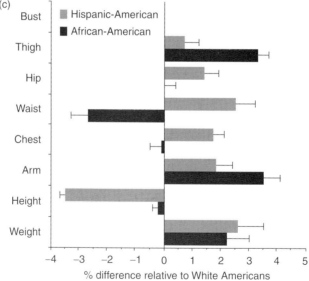

Figure 3.3 Outputs from 3-D photonic scanning, a new technique suitable for large-scale investigations of population variability in size and shape, indexing underlying metabolic adaptations. (a) Reconstructed body surface topography (© Antony Ruto); (b) electronic tape-measure; (c) percentage differences in various body girths between African-American or Hispanic American men and white American men. (Reproduced with permission from Wells *et al.*, 2008a.)

Table 3.1. *Differences in body shape from African individuals (348 male, 583 female),[a,c] adjusting for height and body mass index (BMI)*

Male	n	Arm			Waist			Hip			Thigh		
		Diff	SE	p	Diff	SE	p	Diff	SE	p	Diff	SE	p
Chinese[a]	29	−1.6	0.3	<0.01	3.9	0.9	<0.01	2.2	0.5	<0.01	−1.0	0.5	ns
Thai[b]	2482	−1.3	0.1	<0.01	1.8	0.3	<0.01	−0.1	0.2	ns	−1.1	0.1	<0.01
South Asian[a]	50	−1.5	0.3	<0.01	6.3	0.7	<0.01	0.5	0.4	ns	−2.3	0.4	<0.01
Hispanic[c]	639	−0.6	0.1	<0.01	4.2	0.3	<0.01	1.3	0.2	<0.01	−1.0	0.2	<0.01
White[a,c]	1644	−1.6	0.1	<0.01	6.9	0.2	<0.01	2.6	0.2	<0.01	−2.2	0.1	<0.01

Female	n	Diff	SE	p	Diff	SE	p	Diff	SE	p	Diff	SE	p
Chinese[a]	43	−0.5	0.3	0.8	5.0	0.8	<0.01	−1.1	0.5	0.4	−2.4	0.4	<0.01
Thai[c]	2649	−0.5	0.1	<0.01	1.6	0.2	<0.01	−0.9	0.1	<0.01	−1.5	0.3	<0.01
South Asian[a]	77	−1.0	0.2	0.012	4.3	0.6	<0.01	0.6	0.4	0.7	−1.7	0.3	<0.01
Hispanic[b]	839	0.2	0.1	0.6	4.3	0.3	<0.01	0.9	0.2	<0.01	−3.1	0.1	<0.01
White[a,b]	6920	−0.3	0.1	0.025	4.8	0.2	<0.01	0.9	0.1	<0.01	−2.5	0.1	<0.01

[a] UK National Sizing Survey; [b] Thai National Sizing Survey; [c] US National Sizing Survey.

Diff, mean difference from Africans; SE, standard error; n, sample size.

differentiate between them. Relative to African populations, non-Africans tend to have smaller arm and thigh girths, and larger waist and hip girths. The non-significant results are mostly from the smaller samples. These data indicate a substantially more central pattern of fat deposition in non-African than African populations, and provide preliminary support for the hypothesis that more recent evolutionary exposure to pathogens is associated with greater central adiposity. Further work will be needed to establish whether these shape differences correlate specifically with genetic markers of immune function, or whether adaptation to climate and diet was also important.

A TYPOLOGY OF MIGRATION

From the discussions above, it is clear that migration may influence human biology. To facilitate understanding of this impact, we present a typology of human movement, which has varied in its nature across the evolutionary history of our species, and within and across populations. Such typologies are challenging, as human movements do not fall into neat categories, but rather exhibit a substantial variety along various continuous scales. Movements that begin with one intentionality may drift into another, as social or ecological circumstances change. Thus, our approach is intended only to highlight some of the many forms of variation, and is not intended to be a rigorous or hierarchical framework.

Table 3.2 offers an evolutionary typology of migration, highlighting broad categories of movement that have characterized australopithecines, early *Homo* and *Homo sapiens*. Initial population dispersals amongst australopithecines are likely to have involved regular changes in home range amongst small nomadic populations, linked with reciprocal outbreeding of one sex between neighboring groups as encountered in extant ape species. Group demographics would themselves have been likely to contribute to ecological variability, as subtle changes in group size can substantially alter foraging returns in small-scale human societies (Kelly, 1995).

Such regular movements would likely have been exacerbated by seasonality, which would either have changed the foraging returns in a given territory, or necessitated annual movements between adjacent territories. Organisms exposed to such patterns of movement would have required a certain level of plasticity to buffer regular ecological changes characteristic of every life-course. This plasticity in turn would have aided the opportunistic probing of neighboring territory, or the

Table 3.2. *A typology of migration in human evolutionary history*

Movement	Personnel	Distance	Directionality	Timescale	Magnitude of change
Home range change	Social group	Local	One-way	Hours–days	Small
Seasonal migration	Social group	Local/intermediate	Two-way	Months	Moderate
Colonization	Variable	Intermediate/long	One-way	Months	Moderate–large
"Wave of advance"	Individuals	Local	One-way	Months	Moderate
Exogamy	Young adults	Local	One-way[a]	Hours–days	Small
Invasion	Adults	Local/intermediate	One-way	Months	Small–moderate
Slavery	Adolescents, adults	Local/long	One-way	Years	Moderate–large
Economic migration	Individuals, families	Local/long	Two-way	Years	Moderate–large

[a] But reciprocal between groups.

toleration of unexpected extremes or systematic changes in climatic conditions. We suggested previously that such a dynamic relationship between plasticity and niche-probing could have developed through positive feedback, increasing the capacity to enter and survive in new habitats (Wells and Stock, 2007). Increased plasticity may therefore have been key to the larger dispersals demonstrated by the fossil record for early *Homo erectus*.

Modern humans have clearly been able to benefit substantially from the combination of more sophisticated culture and technology, along with enhanced plasticity, in particular through social behavior. Increasingly, migrations must have involved not just entry into unpopulated territory but also interactions between social groups. Reproductive movements evolved eventually into marriage patterns, whilst population movements incorporated both harmonious assimilation and aggressive invasions, including slavery. In recent history these movements have become possible over increasingly long distances, generating multiple connections between different populations. Many modern migrations highlight ethnic interactions, stressing the importance of social identity as a key component of phenotype for adapting to complex social niches, whilst also impacting in several ways on the gene pool.

Table 3.3 describes a wide range of types of migration amongst modern humans, varying both across and within societies, in order to highlight the diversity of resulting stresses. A few foraging populations still practice nomadic home-range movements linked with seasonality. In sub-Saharan Africa, pastoralists migrate longer distances with their flocks. In populations with greater exposure to the world economy, movements include a range of voluntary and involuntary behaviors. Marriages and relationships may involve voluntary movements of one partner to the other, or unwilling migrations through forced marriages. When invaders impose themselves, refugees may flee or be killed off, again potentially altering the gene pool. For example, famine in Mongolia in the sixth century AD provoked a wave of migrations across the Eurasian landmass, associated with outbreaks of bubonic plague, the fragmentation of the Roman empire and the emergence of diverse temporary population aggregations and centers of power (Keys, 1999). Economic migration may also be imposed by global market forces and declining subsistence opportunities. Marked inequalities in local living costs induce daily or short-term commuting.

In many countries, holiday travel is no longer a luxury but a regular expectation. Whilst leisure activities are seemingly "unimportant" for biology, vacations often result in exposure to new diseases

Table 3.3. *Varieties of migration in contemporary humans, and the resulting stresses faced*

Movement	Typical stresses
Home-range shift	Zoonoses, injury, ecological shocks
Pastoralism	Ecological degradation, injury, zoonoses, territorial competition
Invasion	Death, rape, injury, psychosocial stress, sexually transmitted disease, infectious disease, malnutrition
Economic	Psychosocial stress, infectious disease, non-traditional diet
Colonialism	Oppression, forced labor, injury, psychosocial stress, malnutrition
Rural–urban	Infectious disease, injury, chronic degenerative disease
Marriage	Psychosocial stress, sexually transmitted disease, non-traditional diet
Displacement/ refugee	Psychosocial stress, infectious disease, malnutrition
Commuting	Psychosocial stress, injury, infectious disease
Vacation	Infectious disease, sexually transmitted disease, injury, non-traditional diet

(e.g. malaria, sexually transmitted diseases) and dietary stresses, and also constitute a major global force of change by increasing cross-cultural contact and the flow of genes, pathogens, knowledge, beliefs, and material resources. In the modern world, furthermore, it is not only humans that move between locations but a variety of other species, both beneficial and pathogenic.

It is clear that there is no typical human migration. Rather, our ancestors and contemporaries show an extraordinary range of types of movement across continua of time, distance, climate, ecology, society, and volition, involving exposure to a wide range of stresses, and numerous potential cultural, plastic, and genetic adaptive responses. The migrations that shaped our biology do not map well onto those demonstrated today, in a highly populated world. All that we can say with confidence is that humans have a remarkable tendency to move between locations, and that this has been true for our broader evolutionary history.

SUMMARY

In conclusion, the capacity of *Homo sapiens* to migrate appears to have emerged through the exposure of earlier hominins to highly stochastic environments, favoring increasing plasticity for adaptation and accommodation at the expense of genetic commitment. This biological profile contains some unusual features, such as the tendency for developmental plasticity to track maternal phenotype, introducing a time-lag in the effects of ecological change on phenotype, and the tendency to niche-construct and hence proactively shape the environment encountered. New opportunities are now available in the post-genomic era to link sophisticated phenotypic measurements with the wealth of genomic data, aiding us to understand both the extent to which humans do commit to genetic adaptations, and how they exhibit plasticity when they do not.

REFERENCES

Bakewell, M. A., Shi, P., and Zhang, J. (2007). More genes underwent positive selection in chimpanzee evolution than in human evolution. *Proceedings of the National Academy of Sciences of the United States of America*, **104**(18), 7489–94.

Burger, J. and Thomas, M. G. (2011). The palaeopopulation genetics of humans, cattle and dairying in Neolithic Europe. In: *Human Bioarchaeology of the Transition to Agriculture*, ed. R. Pinhasi and J. T. Stock, pp. 371–84. New York: Wiley-Liss.

Cann, R. L., Stoneking, M., and Wilson, A. C. (1987). Mitochondrial-DNA and human evolution. *Nature*, **325**(6099), 31–6.

Coolidge, F. L. and Wynn, T. (2009). *The Rise of* Homo sapiens: *The Evolution of Modern Thinking*. Chichester, UK: Wiley-Blackwell.

Dennell, R. and Roebroeks, W. (2005). An Asian perspective on early human dispersal from Africa. *Nature*, **438**(7071), 1099–104.

Excoffier, L. (2002). Human demographic history: refining the recent African origin model. *Current Opinion in Genetics & Development*, **12**(6), 675–82.

Foley, R. A. (1993). The influence of seasonality on human evolution. In *Seasonality and Human Ecology*, ed. S. J. Ulijaszek and S. Strickland, pp. 17–37. Cambridge, UK: Cambridge University Press.

Gagneux, P., Wills, C., Gerloff, U., *et al.* (1999). Mitochondrial sequences show diverse evolutionary histories of African hominoids. *Proceedings of the National Academy of Sciences of the United States of America*, **96**(9), 5077–82.

Garrigan, D. and Hammer, M. F. (2006). Reconstructing human origins in the genomic era. *Nature Reviews Genetics*, **7**(9), 669–80.

Gluckman, P. D., Hanson, M. A., and Beedle, A. S. (2007). Early life events and their consequences for later disease: a life history and evolutionary perspective. *American Journal of Human Biology*, **19**(1), 1–19.

Gowlett, J. A. J. (2006). The early settlement of northern Europe: fire history in the context of climate change and the social brain. *Comptes Rendus Palevol*, **5**, 299–310.

Green, R. E., Krause, J., Briggs, A. W., *et al.* (2010). A draft sequence of the Neandertal genome. *Science*, **328** (5979), 710–22.

Hammer, M. F. and Zegura, S. L. (2002). The human Y chromosome haplogroup tree: nomenclature and phylogeny of its major divisions. *Annual Review of Anthropology*, **31**, 303–21.

Hancock, A. M., Alkorta-Aranburu, G., Witonsky, D. B., and Di Rienzo, A. (2010a). Adaptations to new environments in humans: the role of subtle allele frequency shifts. *Philosophical Transactions of the Royal Society of London B: Biological Sciences*, **365**(1552), 2459–68.

Hancock, A. M., Witonsky, D. B., Ehler, E., *et al.* (2010b). Colloquium paper: human adaptations to diet, subsistence, and ecoregion are due to subtle shifts in allele frequency. *Proceedings of the National Academy of Sciences of the United States of America*, **107**(Suppl 2), 8924–30.

Hancock, A. M., Witonsky, D. B., Gordon, A. S., *et al.* (2008). Adaptations to climate in candidate genes for common metabolic disorders. *PLoS Genetics*, **4**, e32.

Harpending, H. and Rogers, A. (2000). Genetic perspectives on human origins and differentiation. *Annual Review of Genomics and Human Genetics*, **1**, 361–85.

Harris, E. E. and Meyer, D. (2006). The molecular signature of selection underlying human adaptations. *American Journal of Physical Anthropology*, Suppl. **43**, 89–130.

Harvati, K. and Weaver, T. D. (2006). Human cranial anatomy and the differential preservation of population history and climate signatures. *Anatomical Record A: Discoveries in Molecular, Cellular, and Evolutionary Biology*, **288**(12), 1225–33.

Hawks, J., Wang, E. T., Cochran, G. M., Harpending, H. C., and Moyzis, R. K. (2007). Recent acceleration of human adaptive evolution. *Proceedings of the National Academy of Sciences of the United States of America*, **104**(52), 20 753–8.

Hill, K. (1993). Life history theory and evolutionary anthropology. *Evolutionary Anthropology*, **2**, 78–89.

Hirschhorn, J. N. and Lettre, G. (2009). Progress in genome-wide association studies of human height. *Hormone Research*, **71**(Suppl 2), 5–13.

Ingman, M., Kaessmann, H., Paabo, S., and Gyllensten, U. (2000). Mitochondrial genome variation and the origin of modern humans. *Nature*, **408**(6813), 708–13.

Johnson, J. D. (1981). The regional and ethnic distribution of lactose malabsorption: adaptive and genetic hypotheses. In *Lactose Digestion: Clinical and Nutritional Implications*, ed. D. M. Paige and T. M. Bayless, pp. 11–22. Baltimore, MD: Johns Hopkins University Press.

Kaessmann, H., Wiebe, V., Weiss, G., and Paabo, S. (2001). Great ape DNA sequences reveal a reduced diversity and an expansion in humans. *Nature Genetics*, **27**(2), 155–6.

Kagawa, Y., Yanagisawa, Y., Hasegawa, K., *et al.* (2002). Single nucleotide polymorphisms of thrifty genes for energy metabolism: evolutionary origins and prospects for intervention to prevent obesity-related diseases. *Biochemical and Biophysical Research Communications*, **295**(2), 207–22.

Kaminsky, Z. A., Tang, T., Wang, S. C., *et al.* (2009). DNA methylation profiles in monozygotic and dizygotic twins. *Nature Genetics*, **41**(2), 240–5.

Kaplan, H., Lancaster, J., and Robson, A. (2003). Embodied capital and the evolutionary economics of the human life span. In *Life Span: Evolutionary, Ecological, and Demographic Perspectives*, ed. J. R. Carey and S. Tuljapurkar, pp. 152–82. New York: Population Council.

Ke, Y., Su, B., Song, X., *et al.* (2001). African origin of modern humans in East Asia: a tale of 12,000 Y chromosomes. *Science*, **292**(5519), 1151–3.

Kelly, R. L. (1995). *The Foraging Spectrum*. Washington, DC: Smithsonian Institution Press.

Keys, D. (1999). *Catastrophe: An Investigation Into the Origins of the Modern World*. London: Century (Random House).

Kivisild, T., Papiha, S., Rootsi, S., *et al.* (2000). An Indian ancestry: a key for understanding human diversity in Europe and beyond. In *Archaeogenetics:*

DNA and the Population Prehistory of Europe, ed. C. Renfrew and K. Boyle, pp. 267–75. Cambridge, UK: McDonald Institute for Archaeological Research.

Kivisild, T., Reidla, M., Metspalu, E., *et al.* (2001). Eastern African origin of the human maternal lineage cluster, ancestral to people outside Africa. *American Journal of Human Genetics*, **69**, 1386.

Kramer, K. L. and Ellison, P. T. (2010). Pooled energy budgets: resituating human energy allocation trade-offs. *Evolutionary Anthropology*, **19**, 136–47.

Laland, K. N., Odling-Smee, J., and Myles, S. (2010). How culture shaped the human genome: bringing genetics and the human sciences together. *Nature Reviews Genetics*, **11**(2), 137–48.

Lango Allen, H., Estrada, K., Lettre, G., *et al.* (2010). Hundreds of variants clustered in genomic loci and biological pathways affect human height. *Nature*, **467** (7317), 832–8.

Lanktree, M. B., Guo, Y., Murtaza, M., *et al.* (2011). Meta-analysis of dense gene-centric association studies reveals common and uncommon variants associated with height. *American Journal of Human Genetics*, **88**(1), 6–18.

Lisiecki, L. E. and Raymo, M. E. (2005). A Plio-Pleistocene stack of 57 globally distributed benthic $\delta^{18}O$ records. *Paleoceanography*, **20**, PA1003; doi:10.1029/2004PA001071.

Macaulay, V., Hill, C., Achilli, A., *et al.* (2005). Single, rapid coastal settlement of Asia revealed by analysis of complete mitochondrial genomes. *Science*, **308** (5724), 1034–6.

Mace, R. (2008). Reproducing in cities. *Science*, **319**(5864), 764–6.

Maher, L., Richter, T., MacDonald, D., Jones, M. D., and Stock, J. T. (2012a). Twenty thousand-year-old huts at a hunter-gatherer settlement in eastern Jordan. *PLoS ONE*, **7**(2), e31447; doi:10.1371/journal.pone.0031447.

Maher, L., Richter, T., and Stock, J. T. (2012b). The pre-Natufian epipalaeolithic of the Southern Levant, developments and transitions to social complexity. *Evolutionary Anthropology*, **21**, 69–81.

McBrearty, S. and Brooks, A. S. (2000). The revolution that wasn't: a new interpretation of the origin of modern human behaviour. *Journal of Human Evolution*, **39**, 453–563.

McNeill, W. (1977). *Plagues and Peoples*. New York: Doubleday.

Metspalu, M., Kivisild, T., Metspalu, E., *et al.* (2004). Most of the extant mtDNA boundaries in south and southwest Asia were likely shaped during the initial settlement of Eurasia by anatomically modern humans. *BMC Genetics*, **5**, 26.

Misra, A. and Khurana, L. (2008). Obesity and the metabolic syndrome in developing countries. *Journal of Clinical Endocrinology & Metabolism*, **93**(11 Suppl 1), S9–30.

Odling-Smee, F. J., Laland, K., and Feldman, M. W. (2003). *Niche Construction*. Princeton, NJ: Princeton University Press.

Perry, G. H., Dominy, N. J., Claw, K. G., *et al.* (2007). Diet and the evolution of human amylase gene copy number variation. *Nature Genetics*, **39**(10), 1256–60.

Pond, C. M. (1998). *The Fats of Life*. Cambridge, UK: Cambridge University Press.

Popkin, B. M. (2009). Global changes in diet and activity patterns as drivers of the nutrition transition. *Nestlé Nutrition Workshop Series Pediatric Program*, **63**, 1–10; discussion 10–14, 259–268.

Potts, R. (1996). *Humanity's Descent: The Consequences of Ecological Instability*. New York: William Morrow.

Quintana-Murci, L., Semino, O., Bandelt, H. J., *et al.* (1999). Genetic evidence of an early exit of *Homo sapiens sapiens* from Africa through eastern Africa. *Nature Genetics*, **23**(4), 437–41.

Reiches, M. W., Ellison, P. T., Lipson, S. F., *et al.* (2009). Pooled energy budget and human life history. *American Journal of Human Biology*, **21**(4), 421–9.

Richerson, P. J., Boyd, R., and Henrich, J. (2010). Colloquium paper: gene-culture coevolution in the age of genomics. *Proceedings of the National Academy of Sciences of the United States of America*, **107**(Suppl 2), 8985–92.

Roberts, D. F. (1953). Body weight, race and climate. *American Journal of Physical Anthropology*, **11**, 533–58.

Roseman, C. C. (2004). Detecting interregionally diversifying natural selection on modern human cranial form by using matched molecular and morphometric data. *Proceedings of the National Academy of Sciences of the United States of America*, **101**(35), 12 824–9.

Rudan, I., Carothers, A. D., Polasek, O., *et al.* (2008). Quantifying the increase in average human heterozygosity due to urbanisation. *European Journal of Human Genetics*, **16**(9), 1097–102.

Saastamoinen, M., van der Sterren, D., Vastenhout, N., Zwaan, B. J., and Brakefield, P. M. (2010). Predictive adaptive responses: condition-dependent impact of adult nutrition and flight in the tropical butterfly *Bicyclus anynana*. *American Naturalist*, **176**(6), 686–98.

Sabeti, P. C., Schaffner, S. F., Fry, B., *et al.* (2006). Positive natural selection in the human lineage. *Science*, **312**(5780), 1614–20.

Sear, R. and Mace, R. (2008). Who keeps children alive? A review of the effects of kin on child survival. *Evolution and Human Behavior*, **29**, 1–18.

Starling, A. P. and Stock, J T. (2007). Dental indicators of health and stress in early Egyptian and Nubian agriculturalists: a difficult transition and gradual recovery. *American Journal of Physical Anthropology*, **134**(4), 520–8.

Stearns, S. C. (1992). *The Evolution of Life Histories*. Oxford, UK: Oxford University Press.

Stock, J. T. (2008). Are humans still evolving?. *EMBO Reports*, **9**, S51–4.

Stock, J. T. (2012). Human evolution after the origin of our species: bridging the gap between palaeoanthropology and bioarchaeology. In *Proceedings of the 12th Annual Conference of the British Association for Biological Anthropology and Osteoarchaeology (BABAO)*, ed. P Mitchell and J Buckberry. Oxford, UK: Archaeopress.

Stock, J. T. and Migliano, A. B. (2009). Stature, mortality, and life history among indigenous populations of the Andaman Islands, 1871–1986. *Current Anthropology*, **50**, 713–25.

Stock, J. T. and Pinhasi, R. (2011). Changing paradigms in our understanding of the transition to agriculture: human bioarchaeology, behaviour and adaptation. In *Human Bioarchaeology of the Transition to Agriculture*, ed. J. Stock and R. Pinhasi, pp. 1–15. New York: Wiley-Liss.

Stock, J. T., O'Neill, M., Ruff, C. B., *et al.* (2011). Body size, skeletal biomechanics, mobility and habitual activity from the late Palaeolithic to mid-Dynastic Nile Valley. In *Human Bioarchaeology of the Transition to Agriculture*, ed. J. Stock and R. Pinhasi, pp. 347–70. New York: Wiley-Liss.

Thangaraj, K., Chaubey, G., Kivisild, T., *et al.* (2005). Reconstructing the origin of Andaman Islanders. *Science*, **308**(5724), 996.

Tishkoff, S. A., Dietzsch, E., Speed, W., *et al.* (1996). Global patterns of linkage disequilibrium at the CD4 locus and modern human origins. *Science*, **271**(5254), 1380–7.

Tishkoff, S. A., Reed, F. A., Ranciaro, A., *et al.* (2007). Convergent adaptation of human lactase persistence in Africa and Europe. *Nature Genetics*, **39**(1), 31–40.

Voight, B. F., Kudaravalli, S., Wen, X., and Pritchard, J. K. (2006). A map of recent positive selection in the human genome. *PLoS Biology*, **4**(3), e72.

Vrba, E. (1985). Ecological and adaptive changes associated with early hominid evolution. In *Ancestors: The Hard Evidence*, ed. E. Delson, pp. 63–71. New York: Alan Liss.

Walker, R., Gurven, M., Hill, K., *et al.* (2006). Growth rates and life histories in twenty-two small-scale societies. *American Journal of Human Biology*, **18**(3), 295–311.

Wells, J. C. (2003). The thrifty phenotype hypothesis: thrifty offspring or thrifty mother? *Journal of Theoretical Biology*, **221**(1), 143–61.

Wells, J. C. (2007a). Flaws in the theory of predictive adaptive responses. *Trends in Endocrinology and Metabolism*, **18**(9), 331–7.

Wells, J. C. (2007b). The thrifty phenotype as an adaptive maternal effect. *Biological Reviews of the Cambridge Philosophical Society*, **82**(1), 143–72.

Wells, J. C. (2009a). Ethnic variability in adiposity and cardiovascular risk: the variable disease selection hypothesis. *International Journal of Epidemiology*, **38**, 63–71.

Wells, J. C. (2009b). Thrift: a guide to thrifty genes, thrifty phenotypes and thrifty norms. *International Journal of Obesity (London)*, **33**(12), 1331–8.

Wells, J. C. (2010). Maternal capital and the metabolic ghetto: an evolutionary perspective on the transgenerational basis of health inequalities. *American Journal of Human Biology*, **22**(1), 1–17.

Wells, J. C. (2012). The capital economy in hominin evolution: redistributions across the life-course and between individuals. *Current Anthropology*, (in press).

Wells, J. C. and Stock, J. T. (2007). The biology of the colonizing ape. *American Journal of Physical Anthropology*, Suppl **45**, 191–222.

Wells, J. C. and Stock, J. T. (2011). Re-examining heritability: genetics, life history and plasticity. *Trends in Endocrinology and Metabolism*, **22**, 421–8.

Wells, J. C., Cole, T. J., Bruner, D., and Treleaven, P. (2008a). Body shape in American and British adults: between-country and inter-ethnic comparisons. *International Journal of Obesity (London)*, **32**(1), 152–9.

Wells, J. C., Griffin, L., and Treleaven, P. (2010). Independent changes in female body shape with parity and age: a life-history approach to female adiposity. *American Journal of Human Biology*, **22**(4), 456–62.

Wells, J. C., Ruto, A., and Treleaven, P. (2008b). Whole-body three-dimensional photonic scanning: a new technique for obesity research and clinical practice. *International Journal of Obesity (London)*, **32**(2), 232–8.

Wells, J. C., Treleaven, P., and Charoensiriwath, S. (2012). Body shape by 3-D photonic scanning in Thai and UK adults: comparison of National Sizing Surveys. *International Journal of Obesity (London)*, **36**, 148–54.

Wells, J. C. K. (2009c). *The Evolutionary Biology of Human Body Fat: Thrift and Control*. Cambridge, UK: Cambridge University Press.

Yang, J., Benyamin, B., McEvoy, B. P., *et al.* (2010). Common SNPs explain a large proportion of the heritability for human height. *Nature Genetics*, **42**(7), 565–9.

4

Evolutionary basis of human migration

INTRODUCTION

Human migration is not only a ubiquitous process in the modern world, but one with deep roots. The ease of travel today has greatly accelerated migration, leading not only to increased rates of migration, but to new forms such as transnational migration in which families move to a new country only long enough to move on to another. At the same time, recent finds in the fossil record make it clear that humans and their immediate ancestors have been migrating in one form or another since the origins of the genus *Homo*, almost 2 million years ago.

Such antiquity suggests that migration itself may be a context for natural selection, linking success in migration with successful reproduction (Wells and Stock, 2007; Wells and Stock, this volume). If so, we can expect that migration has left traces in the human genome that link ancient and modern human migration. These would include not only the neutral markers that have been used to trace movements of human populations (see this volume), but beneficial genes selected for by successful migration.

To date, attempts to link genetic variation with the causes of migration have focused primarily on the DRD4 dopamine receptor 7R+ allele (Chen *et al.*, 1999; Matthews and Butler, 2011; Tovo-Rodrigues *et al.*, 2010). Chen *et al.* (1999) found a simple association between variation in the frequency of DRD4 7R+ and the distance to which a population has moved from its original location, a finding that has been confirmed more recently by Matthews and Butler (2011) taking into account neutral gene structure. At the same time DRD4 has also

Causes and Consequences of Human Migration, ed. Michael H. Crawford and Benjamin C. Campbell. Published by Cambridge University Press. © Cambridge University Press 2012.

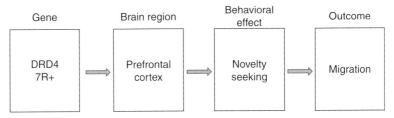

Gene	Brain region	Behavioral effect	Outcome
DRD4 7R+	Prefrontal cortex	Novelty seeking	Migration

Figure 4.1 Hypothesized relationship of DRD4 and migration. This figure provides an explicit outline of the potential intermediate steps linking DRD4 7R+ with migration. DRD4 is most prevalent in the prefrontal cortex where the 7R+ allele has been associated with differences in novelty-seeking behavior. Novelty seeking in turn is thought to be related to a preference for novel places, and thus may be involved in promoting movement to new places, i.e. migration.

been linked to novelty seeking (Benjamin *et al.*, 2000; Ebstein *et al.*, 1997; Roussos *et al.*, 2009). Thus on the assumption that novelty seeking motivates individuals to move to a new place of residence, it has been suggested that DRD4 7R+ may be associated with migration.

This hypothesis, which captures current thinking about migration and genetics, is shown diagrammatically in Figure 4.1. As should be clear from the diagram, the hypothesis represents a rather simple unicausal model of what we know are complexly interwoven processes underlying migration, an issue that has received tremendous attention from social scientists over the years. The presence of DRD4 7R+ leads to higher novelty seeking which in turn is related to the propensity to migrate in search of novelty.

At the worst such a simple model fundamentally misattributes the posited associations between genes, personality, and migration. If taken at face value, it may be seen as suggesting that DRD4 7R+ is the "migration gene," the sort of simplistic biological causality abandoned in the wake of sociobiology. A recent meta-analysis supports a relationship between DRD4 7R+ and novelty seeking, though the effect is small (Munafo *et al.*, 2008). But the neurological basis for novelty seeking is unclear and the idea that novelty seeking plays a role in migration lacks empirical support. More importantly, given that DRD4 is thought to have arisen at most 50 000 years ago, DRD4 and novelty seeking cannot account for migratory tendencies in any of the *Homo* species prior to that point. Yet, something drove humans to cover the globe.

At best the simplicity of the model represents each link in the chain by its single strongest thread, allowing us to focus on the most likely connections between the intermediate variables. For instance, dopaminergic genes other than DRD4, such as COMT, have been associated with novelty seeking (Salo *et al.*, 2010; Strobel *et al.*, 2003; Tsai *et al.*, 2004), but are their effects as important of those as DRD4? In addition, other dimensions of personality, such as achievement orientation (Boneva and Frieze, 2001) and openness to experience (Jokela, 2009) have been shown to play a role in aspects of migration. Is their impact on migration in place of novelty seeking or in concert with it?

Our exploration of the literature on migration and personality, brain imaging of personality, and possible genetic underpinning points to achievement and social dominance in addition to novelty seeking as key personality traits that are both related to migration and associated with various dopaminergic genes. Furthermore, brain imaging results suggest that these personality traits are associated with dopaminergic systems in the brain that not only monitor bodily status, but also form the basis of social decision-making. We summarize these considerations in a conceptual model of migration that distinguishes between the role of dopaminergic systems associated with motivation and drive and prefrontal dopamine in novelty seeking and risk taking.

PERSONALITY AND MIGRATION

Speculations about migration-related personality characteristics go back to at least 1970 when Jennings (1970) suggested that there might be a mobiocentric personality type, one who valued action and motion and was always on the move. Similarly, Morrison and Wheeler (1976) suggested that some individuals were more likely to migrate because they were pioneering personalities that favored novelty seeking.

More recent studies provide support for these pioneering speculations. Boneva and Frieze (2001) report a series of studies, based on close to 1000 students from three Eastern European countries, which find two important personality dimensions associated with migration intentions. Students who expressed a greater desire to live most of their adult life in another country, whom the authors refer to as "primary" migrants, also reported (1) higher achievement and power motivation; (2) reduced affiliation motivation. The authors link the higher achievement goals to greater willingness to take risks, such as those associated with migration.

Boneva and Frieze (2001) argue that their results reflect the hypothesis that increased motivation for achievement together with decreased affiliation motivation leads to values of increased work centrality and decreased family centrality. This combination increases the pull factor of relocating to another country while reducing the strength of push factors, increasing the overall propensity for migration. Importantly, Boneva and Frieze's findings are based on young adults who may see moving to another country as the best way of achieving their long-term goals. Whether they are able to act on such intentions is another matter.

Interestingly, in Boneva and Frieze's (2001) results women who expressed a desire to migrate showed increased achievement motivation relative to those not interested in leaving the country, similar to men. However, they did not exhibit a reduction in affiliation motivation. These findings not only suggest sex differences in the elements underlying an overall motivation to migrate, but suggest that they may be related to differences in kin ties, an important factor in the relationship of migration to family formation.

More recently, a handful of epidemiological-style studies have provided additional evidence of the link between personality and migratory behavior at middle age using standard personality measures. Based on 1534 middle-aged twins of both sexes, Silventoinen *et al.* (2008) found that migration from Finland to Sweden was associated with life dissatisfaction among both men and women. Among men, but not women, neuroticism and extraversion also predicted higher probability of migration. In another study based in Finland, Jokela *et al.* (2008) report that among 17 333 men and women aged 15 to 30 years, individuals who had moved from their original location ranked higher on sociability, activity levels, and emotionality than those who had not.

These results from Scandanavia are supported by a similar study in the United States (Jokela, 2009). Based on a representative sample of 3760 middle-aged men and women, Jokela reports that movement both within and between states was associated with high openness to experience and low agreeableness, while high extraversion was associated with movement within states.

Compared with the student-based results in which the desire to migrate differs by gender, the role of sex differences in migration among the middle-aged men and women is not clear. Silventoinen *et al.* (2008) ran separate models for men and women and were able to document the greater importance of neuroticism and extraversion for men as predictors of migration. However, whether these findings can be generalized is not clear. Both the Jokela *et al.* (2008) and Jokela (2009) studies included gender only as a control variable, so sex differences are not evident from the results.

Taken together, the existing studies, limited as they are in number, are suggestive in pointing toward a drive for achievement, dissatisfaction with one's life, neuroticism, extraversion, and openness to experience as personality characteristics underlying migration. The association of migration with life dissatisfaction is perhaps too obvious to need explanation. Those who are not happy where they are may well assume that they would be better off somewhere else. Similarly neuroticism reflects the tendency to experience negative moods, aligning it closely with life dissatisfaction as a motive for migration.

However, since drive for achievement, extraversion, and openness to experience do not appear central to decisions about moving locales, their association with migration warrants further amplification. One might think that drive for achievement would be associated with social success within the local context. After all, social success depends on learning the local social rules. However, the fact that drive for achievement is associated with migration suggests that it may represent drive more generally. Extraversion is associated with being energetic, experiencing positive moods, and enjoying the company of others, while openness to experience is defined as "the recurrent need to enlarge and examine experience" (Costa and McCrae, 1997). Both extraversion and openness to experience differ from agreeableness. Agreeableness is associated with knowledge of and comfort with familiar individuals, disincentivizing migration. Conversely, it would seem that drive, a positive attitude, the ability to absorb new experiences, and a sociable nature all increase the odds of migrating.

NEUROLOGICAL CORRELATES

Importantly for our purposes, some of the personality features associated with migration have been given a neurological foundation, in particular those associated with the so-called "big five" personality factors. Based on structural fMRI of 116 healthy men and women between the ages of 18 and 40 years, DeYoung *et al.* (2010) found that extraversion is related to the volume of the medial orbitofrontal cortex, a region associated with processing reward, while agreeableness is associated with neural activity in areas related to understanding the intentions and mental states of others, including the superior temporal sulcus, posterior cingulate, and fusiform gyrus. Neuroticism was associated with the volume of the medial temporal lobe and basal ganglia, medial frontal gyrus and mid-cingulate gyrus and caudate among others, all regions associated with punishment and negative effect.

DeYoung *et al.* (2010) do not report a specific neuroanatomical region associated with openness to experience. However, a recent fMRI study of brain activity does find a brain region associated with openness to experience (Sutin *et al.*, 2009), and reports differences between the sexes. Based on 100 men and women over 55 years of age, Sutin *et al.* (2009) found that openness to experience was related to the activity of the orbital frontal cortex (OFC) in both men and women, the dorsolateral prefrontal cortex (DLPFC) in women and the anterior cingulate cortex (ACC) in men.

Generally speaking, these neurological results are important in confirming a biological basis of the big five personality dimensions. Not surprisingly, neuroticism is associated with brain regions that process negative emotion, extraversion with areas that process positive reward, often associated with others, and agreeableness with brain regions processing close interpersonal understanding. For our purposes these results clarify the association of personality factors with migration. A tendency to experience negative emotion makes one's present circumstances less appealing, while more active processing of positive rewards leads to greater positive feedback from all circumstances including those that are unfamiliar, Furthermore, agreeableness represents greater brain activity committed to understanding the intentions and mental states of familiar individuals.

In addition, the neural correlates of personality may help to explain sex differences in personality and migration. The fact that openness to experience among men is associated with the OFC and ACC suggests that men's evaluation of rewards may be directly related to movement. In contrast, the association of openness to experience with the OFC and DLPC in women suggests that women may make an additional cognitive appraisal of a potentially rewarding experience, before acting on it. In other words, men act more directly on the basis of reward, while women reflect on reward and its consequences before acting (Figure 4.2).

DOPAMINERGIC GENE CORRELATES OF PERSONALITY

The association of migration with personality traits which can be mapped to particular regions of the brain raises obvious questions about genetic differences that might underlie such differences in brain activity. Notably, does the association between dopamine genes and migration patterns noted earlier reflect a sequence of gene $\rightarrow$ brain $\rightarrow$ personality $\rightarrow$ migration behavior? As noted previously, DRD4 7R+ is

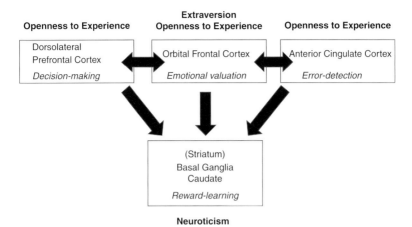

Figure 4.2 Areas of the dopaminergic reward pathway associated with personality. This schematic diagram shows the distinction between limbic and cortical structures of the dopaminergic reward system associated with migration-related personality dimensions. The basal ganglia and caudate, parts of the striatum associated with reward learning, have been related to neuroticism, or the tendency to experience things negatively. The anterior cingulate, orbital frontal, and dorsolateral prefrontal cortex have all been related to Openness to Experience. Together, these areas weigh the emotional value of rewards, decide a course of action, and detect deviations from the expected rewards. Taken as a whole, this diagram suggests that the striatum and the cortex play contrasting roles in decisions to migrate, with the striatum representing the current reward structure and the cortex assessing the likelihood of new circumstances changing that reward structure.

not the only dopamine-related gene that has been associated with normal variation in personality. It is necessary to consider other allelic variation in other dopaminergic genes as well.

Dopaminergic genes most prominently associated with personality include DRD2, COMT, and DAT1. DRD2 is a dopamine receptor primarily found in the striatum. The TaqA1+ allele has been associated with alcoholism (see Conner *et al.*, 2008 for a recent example) as well as pervasive childhood aggression (Zai *et al.*, 2012). Other DRD2 single nucleotide polymorphisms (SNPs) such as rs1076560 have also been associated with personality (Blasi *et al.*, 2009), but we focus on TaqA1+ here because of its association with functional changes in DRD2 binding (see section on "Functional implications of dopaminergic genes" below). Smillie *et al.* (2011) report an association of TaqA1+ with extraversion in a sample of 224 London college students, directly connecting

DRD2 and extraversion. At the same time, Wacker *et al.* (2005) report that TaqA1+ allele is associated with low neuroticism–anxiety among men, but not women, consistent with the existence of sex differences in personality and migration.

COMT (catechol-O-methyltransferase) metabolizes dopamine, thus removing it from the synaptic cleft, primarily with the prefrontal cortex. The VAL158MET polymorphism results in a reduced rate of dopamine degradation, and has been associated with cognitive capacity (see Dickinson and Elvevåg, 2009 for a recent review) as well as extra-version and novelty seeking (Reuter and Hennig, 2005). More recently, Reuter *et al.* (2011) report that the presence of one Val allele is associated with a doubling of altruistic giving in a sample of 101 German young adults. Reuter *et al.* (2006) report that the interaction between DRD2 TaqA1+ and COMT VAL158MET is positively related to drive among 295 healthy adult subjects. This is an important finding because it suggests that the release of dopamine and the number of receptors have inde-pendent effects on dopaminergic neurotransmission and its relation-ship to behavioral expression.

DAT1 (dopamine transporter1) has also been associated with per-sonality and behavior. DAT1 is a molecule that binds and removes dopamine from the synaptic cleft, predominantly with the striatum. Variation in DAT1, in particular the 10R VNTR, has been associated with increased number of sexual partners (Guo *et al.*, 2007) as well as anti-social behavior (Burt and Mikolajewski, 2008) among male adolescents and young adults. In addition, the interaction of the DAT1 9R VNTR and COMT VAL158MET has been related to event-related brain activity in the striatum and prefrontal cortex in the anticipation of reward (Dreher *et al.*, 2009) providing further evidence of the importance of multiple dopaminergic genes.

FUNCTIONAL IMPLICATIONS OF DOPAMINERGIC GENES

Interpretation of these genetic findings is facilitated by an understand-ing of dopaminergic function. Dopamine is fundamentally related to wanting/seeking/drive (Berridge and Robinson, 1998), and is expressed in the mesolimbic system with roots in the striatum and the ventral tegmental area and connections in the prefrontal cortex. Low DRD2 receptor binding in the striatum has been linked to a number of fundamental personality traits in humans, including social desirability (Reeves *et al.*, 2007), thought to be a measure of social submissiveness (Cervenka *et al.*, 2010) and trait impulsivity (Buckholtz *et al.*, 2010).

Table 4.1. *Proposed genetic components of novelty seeking*

Country	Sample	Number	Age	Sex	Gene effect?	Source
DRD4 7R+						
Israel	Non-related subjects	455	Adult	M/F	yes	Benjamin et al., 2000
Israel	Non-related subjects	124	Adult	M/F	yes	Ebstein et al., 1996
Israel	Medical students/staff	94	Adult	M/F	moderate	Ebstein et al., 1997
Sweden	Caucasians of European ancestry	256	Adult	M/F	no	Persson et al., 2000
Germany	University staff and students	136	Adult	M/F	yes	Strobel et al., 1999
U.S.A.	Asian-Americans	171	Adult	M/F	Korean: yes	Reist et al., 2007
U.S.A.	Baltimore Aging Study	188	Adult	M/F	no	Vandenbergh et al., 1997
Korea	Non-related subjects	243	Adolescent	M/F	F: yes, M: no	Lee et al., 2003a
Korea	Medical students	220	Adult	M/F	M: yes, F: no	Ham et al., 2006
Korea	Non-related subjects	214	Adult	M/F	no	Kim et al., 2006
China	Non-related subjects	120	Young adult	F	no	Tsai et al., 2004
Japan	Non-related subjects	69	Adult	M/F	yes	Tomitaka et al., 1999
2R and 5R						
Finland	Non-related subjects	150	Adult	M/F	yes	Keltikangas-Järvinen et al., 2003
Finland	Non-related subjects	190	Adult	M/F	yes	Ekelund et al., 1999
−521 C/T						
Hungary	Healthy volunteers	109	Adult	M/F	yes	Ronai et al., 2001
U.S.A.	African-Americans	71	Adult	M/F	F: yes	Bookman et al., 2002
Korea	Non-related subjects	101	Adolescent	F	yes	Lee et al., 2003b

Table 4.1. (cont.)

	Country	Sample	Number	Age	Sex	Gene effect?	Source
COMT							
	Germany	University students	363	Adult	M/F	yes	Reuter and Hennig, 2005
	Russia	Non-related subjects	130	Adult	M/F	yes	Golimbet et al., 2006
	China	Non-related subjects	120	Young adults	F	yes	Tsai et al., 2004
	U.S.A.	Right-handed subjects	27	Young adults	M/F	yes	Dreher et al., 2009
DAT1							
	New Zealand	Alcoholics/mentally ill	267	Adult	M/F	no	Sullivan et al., 1998
DRD2 TaqA1+							
	Sweden	Alcoholics	375	Adult	M/F	slight	Berggren et al., 2006
	United States	Alcoholics	44	Adult	M/F	no	Gelernter et al., 1991
	Germany	Healthy Caucasians	295	Adult	M/F	yes	Reuter et al., 2006

[a] Note: Most COMT/NS work has been done with drug users and/or individuals with psychological disorders.

The association of social submission and impulsivity in humans takes on a larger functional meaning in light of recent findings from non-human primates. Subordinate cynmolous monkeys demonstrate lower dopamine binding in the striatum (Morgan *et al.*, 2002), and reduced levels of dopamine metabolites in the CSF relative to dominant individuals (Kaplan *et al.*, 2002). Together these findings suggest that subordinates receive less of a dopamine reward signal; they both release less dopamine presynaptically and have fewer receptors to receive it post-synaptically.

Thus it appears that in both non-human primates and humans, subordinate individuals are less likely to experience habitual actions as rewarding. Hence they are more likely to seek novelty as a way of changing their social circumstances. Dominant individuals, conversely, find habitual activity more dopaminergically rewarding. Hence they are more likely to continue to do the same things that have made them successful socially.

Of particular interest to this chapter, DRD2 dopamine receptor binding in the insula has been inversely associated with novelty seeking in two disparate samples; 24 healthy young Japanese men (Suhara *et al.*, 2001) and 22 adult Finnish men and women with Parkinson's disease (Kaasinen *et al.*, 2004). The insula is thought to provide a representation of somatic status, experienced as well-being (Craig, 2002, 2009), suggesting that novelty seeking in humans may at times represent an attempt to seek new sources of well-being. More recent results have extended the inverse relationship of DRD2 receptor binding and novelty seeking to the striatum nigra/ventral tegmentum area (Zald *et al.*, 2008), suggesting that both the insula and striatum play a role in this basic neurological process of homeostasis.

Taken as a whole, the findings discussed above suggest that novelty seeking may represent a strategy to alleviate the detrimental somatic effects of subordinate social status. Dominant individuals are likely to have a clear sense of well-being which will tend to reinforce their current social behavior. In contrast, subordinates are more likely to have a reduced sense of well-being leading to a predisposition for novelty that might improve their condition.

Returning to allelic variation in DRD2, the presence of at least one DRD2 TaqA1+ allele has been associated with reduced dopamine binding in the striatum by one third (Pohjalainen *et al.*, 1998; Thompson *et al.*, 1997). Thus the association of alcoholism and violence with DRD2 TaqA1+ in humans may reflect a sort of self-medication for what is the equivalent of low social status in non-human primates. Interestingly, the rs1125394 SNP in DRD2 has also been associated with heterophily or the tendency of similar individuals to associate with each other (Fowler *et al.*, 2011), suggesting that variation in DRD2 may influence the social context in which novelty seeking takes place, as well as novelty seeking itself, thus potentially amplifying the effects of allelic variation.

IMPLICATIONS FOR MIGRATION PAST AND PRESENT

If the 7R allele of the DRD4 dopamine receptor did not arise until about 50 000 years ago (Wang *et al.*, 2004), it would not have played a role in human or hominid migration prior to that point. This does not rule out the possibility that variants in other genes such as COMT which affect prefrontal dopamine metabolism played a role in migration. However, it does suggest that the emergence of DRD4 7R+ represents only a single, and perhaps the most recent, change in the activity of a pre-existing dopaminergic reward system with multiple sources of genetic variation. In particular, genetic variation in DRD2 and DAT1 which has been linked to the activity of striatum may have been important.

Unfortunately, attempts to resolve the genetic history of the DRD2 TaqA1+ allele have not yielded a clear coalescence date (Jones and Peroutka, 1998; Kidd *et al.*, 1998), making it difficult to link the development of the DRD2 allele to a specific time period in human evolution. However, that does not mean we cannot speculate on the basis of more general information.

While the movement of *Homo erectus* out of Africa is often referred to as migration, colonization, and/or dispersal, in fact its exact nature is unclear. The speed with which *Homo erectus* appears in Asia (Swisher *et al.*, 1994; Zhu *et al.*, 2008) after its emergence in Africa may put us in mind of migration. However, given that the leading edge of the original movement out of Africa is by definition into unpopulated and novel areas, it can be more clearly described simply as range expansion. We lack (and will continue to lack) evidence for movement of individuals between already existing population groups, as in modern migration. We also lack evidence of continuing ties from dispersing individuals back to the original group, as in colonization; or even for exactly what classes of individuals would have left their natal group, as in dispersal.

It seems unlikely that we will ever be able to address these sorts of questions in sufficient detail to shed light on the dynamics of migration in *Homo erectus*. However, the association of DRD2 receptor density and social dominance outlined above may shed some light on the role of range expansion as a selective force in human evolution. Simply put, to the extent that novelty seeking associated with reduced DRD2 binding resulted in the movement of enough social subordinates, splitting from the natal group in novel territories would have become part of a potentially successful reproductive strategy.

Importantly, the impact of such a DRD2 allele would not be dependent on outcompeting other alleles in the old environment, but on the success of TaqA1+ carriers in a new environment. This would provide the opportunity for selection of other beneficial traits, such as increased fertility, or increased cognitive capacity, as hitchhikers. It might also increase the speed at which selection could operate, if individuals with similar DRD2 alleles tended to associate.

Returning to the discussion of sex differences in personality and migration above, we might presume that males would be most affected by the role of novelty seeking in alternative social and reproductive strategies. Testosterone has been shown to increase dopamine release in the striatum among rats (de Souza Silva *et al.*, 2009), and in human males, testosterone is at its highest level during young adulthood. Extraversion has been related to higher reproductive successes in a high fertility population (Alvergne *et al.*, 2010) and variation in extraversion, a trait associated with social dominance, has been positively related to the DRD2 TaqA1+ allele, as well as COMT. Finally extraversion is more strongly related to migration in males than females. Thus subordinate males may be more likely to leave their current group based on novelty seeking and in the process gain social status and greater reproductive success when they leave the old group behind.

However, similar forces associated with food might also have been at work for females. If the decision to leave one's existing group is associated with feeling endangered somatically, during a period of poor resource availability, females with DRD2 TaqA1+ alleles will be more likely to leave the group in search of better material conditions. If they did find conditions with better food availability, they would be more reproductively successful and the DRD2 TaqA1+ allele would be selected for. Essentially, the TaqA1+ allele would amount to a lower threshold for responding to variation in food availability by moving into new territory and seeking to change one's social status.

SUMMARY AND DIRECTIONS FOR FUTURE RESEARCH

Recent findings on the geographical distribution of the DRD4 7R+ allele and its relationship to novelty seeking have generated interest in this

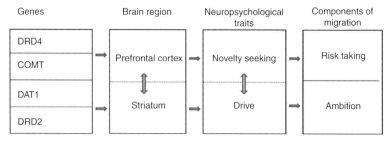

Figure 4.3 Hypothesized relationship of DRD2, DRD4, and migration. This diagram suggests the striatum and prefrontal cortex as separate but related pathways linking dopamine receptor and metabolism genes with migration based on evidence presented in the text. Both DRD4 receptors and COMT enzyme are more prevalent in the prefrontal cortex. Allelic variation in these genes as well as their interaction has been associated with novelty seeking. At the same time DRD2 receptors and the DAT1 dopamine transporter are more common in the striatum. Allelic variation DRD2 has been associated with drive and sociability. Allelic variation in DAT1 has also been associated with behavior. We include it here because of its potential interaction with DRD2. Finally, variation in novelty seeking and drive will lead to variation in risk taking and ambition, which interact to promote migration.

allele as the "migration" gene. Given the ubiquity of human migration over the past 50 000 years, more empirical work is needed to determine the role of DRD4 7R+ in migration among current populations and its implications for human history. However, estimates for emergence of DRD4 7R+ are too recent to provide insight into the deeper history of human migration and its role as a selective factor in human evolution. A broader perspective on the genetic underpinning of human migration is clearly called for.

Our review of the literature finds: (1) personality characteristics besides novelty seeking, including extraversion, neuroticism, and achievement motivation related to migration; (2) some of these personality characteristics have been shown by brain imaging to be related to dopaminergic neural system; (3) variation in dopaminergic genes other than DRD4, including COMT, DAT1, and DRD2, may have played a role in human migration right up to the present day (Previc, 2009). The TaqA1+ allele of the DRD2 dopamine receptor gene stands out as particularly important for its role in social drive and novelty seeking.

Figure 4.3 puts together these findings to present our best hypothesis about the genetic factors involved in migration. Given that migration is promoted both by ambition for economic successes and reproduction and by novelty seeking, it is necessary to take both striatal and prefrontal mechanisms into account. The role of the striatum is associated with allelic variation in DRD2 and DAT1. Individuals with DRD2 TaqA1+ will be more extraverted, and interested in social achievement. The 10R VNTR of DAT1 may also be associated with the social expression of drive in the form of sex and antisocial behavior either by itself or in interaction with DRD2 TaqA1+. The role of the prefrontal function in migration will be associated with the presence of DRD4 7R+ and COMT VAL158MET alleles. Again we might expect an interaction between these two alleles in predicting novelty seeking.

This model can be readily tested by considering the role of kin networks on push/pull factors for migration. Those migrants who are motivated to leave kin behind to move to a new location without kin, all other things being equal, may show an increased representation of TaqA1+ and 7R+ alleles. In contrast, for those immigrants who migrate to locations with pre-existing kin, we might expect pull factors to predominate over personal drive and novelty seeking. Hence we would expect an increased representation of TaqA1−, 7R− individuals. Finally, among individuals who are forced to migrate, such as refugees, we might expect that personality factors would be swamped by the environmental contingencies and migration would be random with respect to DRD4 and DRD2 polymorphisms.

Such a model could potentially be tested in any location where humans migrate, and especially where such migration is well established. In other words, almost anywhere on the globe. From a United States perspective, Mexican immigration would be of particular interest simply because it is of such current practical concern.

The results derived from testing the model would tell us much about the genetic influences on modern human migration. However, because of recent genetic changes, including the emergence of DRD4 7R+, they would be much less revealing about migration early in human evolution. There is one context that might shed some light on migration among *Homo erectus* – the peopling of the New World. This event involved rapid range expansion into novel territories (Meltzer, 1995), similar to the expansion of *Homo erectus* out of Africa. Whether we will ever be able to make more explicit parallels between the two events may well depend on empirical testing of the role of DRD4 and DRD2 allelic variation in modern human migration proposed here.

REFERENCES

Alvergne, A., Jokela, M., and Lummaa, V. (2010). Personality and reproductive success in a high fertility human population. *Proceedings of the National Academy of Sciences of the United States of America*, **107**, 11 745–50.

Benjamin, J., Osher, Y., Kotler, M., *et al.* (2000). Association between tridimensional personality questionnaire (TPQ) traits and three functional polymorphisms: dopamine receptor D4 (DRD4), serotonin transporter promoter region (5-HTTLPR) and catechol O-methyltransferase (COMT). *Molecular Psychiatry*, **5**, 96–100.

Berggren, U., Fahlke, C., Aronsson, E., *et al.* (2006). The TAQ1 DRD2 A1 allele is associated with alcohol-dependence although its effect size is small. *Alcohol*, **41**, 479–85.

Berridge, K. C. and Robinson, T. E. (1998). What is the role of dopamine in reward: hedonic impact, reward learning, or incentive salience? *Brain Research Reviews*, **28**, 309–69.

Blasi, G., Lo Bianco, L., Taurisano, P., *et al.* (2009). Functional variation of the dopamine D2 receptor gene is associated with emotional control as well as brain activity and connectivity during emotion processing in humans. *Journal of Neuroscience*, **29**, 14 812–9.

Boneva, B. S. and Frieze, I. H. (2001). Toward a concept of a migrant personality. *Journal of Social Issues*, **57**, 477–90.

Bookman, E. B., Taylor, R. E., Adams-Campbell, L., and Kittles, R. A. (2002). DRD4 promoter SNPs and gender effects on extraversion in African Americans. *Molecular Psychiatry*, **7**, 786–9.

Buckholtz, J. W., Treadway, M. T., Cowan, R. L., *et al.* (2010). Dopaminergic network differences in human impulsivity. *Science*, **329**, 532.

Burt, S. A. and Mikolajewski, A. J. (2008). Preliminary evidence that specific candidate genes are associated with adolescent-onset antisocial behavior. *Aggressive Behavior*, **34**,437–45.

Cervenka, S., Gustavsson, J. P., Halldin, C., and Farde, L. (2010). Association between striatal and extrastriatal dopamine D2-receptor binding and social desirability. *Neuroimage*, **50**, 323–8.

Chen, C. S., Burton, M., Greenberger, E., and Dmitrieva, J. (1999). Population migration and the variation of dopamine D4 receptor (DRD4) allele frequencies around the globe. *Evolution and Human Behavior*, **20**, 309–24.

Connor, J. P., Young, R. M., Saunders, J. B., *et al.* (2008). The A1 allele of the D2 dopamine receptor gene region, alcohol expectancies and drinking refusal self-efficacy are associated with alcohol dependence severity. *Psychiatry Research*, **160**, 94–105.

Costa, P. T., Jr. and McCrae, R. R. (1997). Stability and change in personality assessment: the revised NEO Personality Inventory in the year 2000. *Journal of Personality Assessment*, **68**, 86–94.

Craig, A. D. (2002). How do you feel? Interoception: the sense of the physiological condition of the body. *Nature Reviews Neuroscience*, **3**, 655–66.

Craig, A. D. (2009). How do you feel – now? The anterior insula and human awareness. *Nature Reviews Neuroscience*, **10**, 59–70.

de Souza Silva, M. A., Mattern, C., Topic, B., Buddenberg, T. E, and Huston, J. P. (2009). Dopaminergic and serotonergic activity in neostriatum and nucleus accumbens enhanced by intranasal administration of testosterone. *European Neuropsychopharmacology*, **19**, 53–63.

DeYoung, C. G., Hirsh, J. B., Shane, M. S., *et al.* (2010). Testing predictions from personality neuroscience. Brain structure and the big five. *Psychological Science*, **21**, 820–8.

Dickinson, D. and Elevåg, B. (2009). Genes, cognition and brain through a COMT lens. *Neuroscience*, **164**(1), 72–87.

Dreher, J. C., Kohn, P., Kolachana, B., Weinberger, D. R., and Berman, K. F. (2009). Variation in dopamine genes influences responsivity of the human reward system. *Proceedings of the National Academy of Sciences of the United States of America*, **106**, 617–22.

Ebstein, R. P., Novick, O., Umansky, R., *et al.* (1996). Dopamine D4 receptor (D4DR) exon III polymorphism associated with the human personality trait of novelty seeking. *Nature and Genetics*, **12**, 78–80.

Ebstein, R. P., Segman, R., Benjamin, J., *et al.* (1997). 5-HT2C (HTR2C) serotonin receptor gene polymorphism associated with the human personality trait of reward dependence: interaction with dopamine D4 receptor (D4DR) and dopamine D3 receptor (D3DR) polymorphisms. *American Journal of Medical Genetics*, **74**, 65–72.

Ekelund, J., Lichtermann, D., Järvelin, M. R., and Peltonen, L. (1999). Association between novelty seeking and the type 4 dopamine receptor gene in a large Finnish cohort sample. *American Journal of Psychiatry*, **156**, 1453–5.

Fowler, J. H., Settle, J. E., and Christakis, N. A. (2011). Correlated genotypes in friendship networks. *Proceedings of the National Academy of Sciences of the United States of America*, **108**, 1993–7.

Gelernter, J., O'Malley, S., Risch, N., *et al.* (1991). No association between an allele at the D2 dopamine receptor gene (DRD2) and alcoholism. *JAMA*, **266**, 1801–7.

Golimbet, V. E., Alfimova, M. V., Gritsenko, I. K., and Ebshtein, R P. (2006). Dopamine system genes and personality traits of extraversion and novelty seeking. *Zh Vyssh Nerv Deiat Im I P Pavlova*, **56**, 457–63.

Guo, G., Tong, Y., Xie, C. W., and Lange, L. A. (2007). Dopamine transporter, gender, and number of sexual partners among young adults. *European Journal of Human Genetics*, **15**, 279–87.

Ham, B. J., Lee, Y. M., Kim, M. K, *et al.* (2006). Personality, dopamine receptor D4 exon III polymorphisms, and academic achievement in medical students. *Neuropsychobiology*, **53**, 203–9.

Jennings E. E. (1970). Mobicentric man. *Pyschology Today*, **4**, 34–6, 70–2.

Jokela, M. (2009). Personality predicts migration within and between U.S. states. *Journal of Research in Personality*, **43**, 79–83.

Jokela, M., Elovainio, M., Kivimäki, M., and Keltikangas-Järvinen, L. (2008). Temperament and migration patterns in Finland. *Psychological Science*, **19**, 831–7.

Jones, K. W. and Peroutka, S. J. (1998). Step-wise analysis of polymorphisms in the human dopamine D2 receptor gene. *Neuropharmacology*, **37**, 803–14.

Kaasinen, V., Aalto, S., Någren, K., and Rinne, J. O. (2004). Insular dopamine D2 receptors and novelty seeking personality in Parkinson's disease. *Movement Disorders*, **19**,1348–51.

Kaplan, J. R., Manuck, S. B., Fontenot, M. B., and Mann, J. J. (2002). Central nervous system monoamine correlates of social dominance in cynomolgus monkeys (*Macaca fascicularis*). *Neuropsychopharmacology*, **26**, 431–43.

Keltikangas-Järvinen, L., Elovainio, M., Kivimäki, M., *et al.* (2003). Association between the type 4 dopamine receptor gene polymorphism and novelty seeking. *Psychosomatic Medicine*, **65**, 471–6.

Kidd, K. K., Morar, B., Castiglione, C. M., *et al.* (1998). A global survey of haplotype frequencies and linkage disequilibrium at the DRD2 locus. *Human Genetics*, **103**, 211–27.

Kim, S. J., Kim, Y. S., Kim, C. H., and Lee, H. S. (2006). Lack of association between polymorphisms of the dopamine receptor D4 and dopamine transporter genes and personality traits in a Korean population. *Yonsei Medical Journal*, **47**, 787–92.

Lee, H. J., Lee, H. S., Kim, Y. K., *et al.* (2003a). D2 and D4 dopamine receptor gene polymorphisms and personality traits in a young Korean population. *American Journal of Medical Genetics*, **121B**, 44–9.

Lee, H. J., Lee, H. S., Kim, Y. K., *et al.* (2003b). Allelic variants interaction of dopamine receptor D4 polymorphism correlate with personality traits in young Korean female population. *American Journal of Medical Genetics*, **118B**, 76–80.

Matthews, L. J. and Butler, P. M. (2011). Novelty-seeking DRD4 polymorphisms are associated with human migration distance out-of-Africa controlling for neutral population gene structure. *American Journal of Physical Anthropology*, **145**, 382–9.

Meltzer, D. J. (1995) Clocking the first Americans. *Annual Review of Anthropology*, **24**, 21–45.

Momozawa, Y., Takeuchi, Y., Kusunose, R., Kikusui, T., and Mori, Y. (2005). Association between equine temperament and polymorphisms in dopamine D4 receptor gene. *Mammalian Genome*, **16**, 538–44.

Morgan, D., Grant, K. A., Gage, H. D., *et al.* (2002). Social dominance in monkeys: dopamine D2 receptors and cocaine self-administration. *Nature Neuroscience*, **5**, 169–74.

Morrison, P. and Wheeler, J. (1976). *The Image of Elsewhere in the American Tradition of Migration.* Rand Paper No. P-5729. Santa Monica, CA: Rand.

Munafo, M. R., Yalcin, B., Willis-Owen, S. A., Flint, J. (2008). Association of the dopamine receptor (DRD4) gene and approach-related personality traits: meta-analysis and new data. *Biological Psychiatry*, **63**, 197–206.

Persson, M. L., Wassermann, D., Geiger, T., *et al.* (2000). Dopamine D4 receptor gene polymorphism and personality traits in healthy volunteers. *European Archives of Psychiatry and Clinical Neuroscience*, **250**, 203–6.

Pohjalainen, T., Rinne, J. O., Någren, K., *et al.* (1998). The A1 allele of the human D2 dopamine receptor gene predicts low D2 receptor availability in healthy volunteers. *Molecular Psychiatry*, **3**, 256–60.

Previc, F. H. (2009). *The Dopaminergic Mind in Human Evolution and History.* Cambridge, UK: Cambridge University Press.

Reeves, S. J., Mehta, M. A., Montgomery, A. J., *et al.* (2007). Striatal dopamine (D2) receptor availability predicts socially desirable responding. *Neuroimage*, **34**, 1782–9.

Reist, C., Ozdemir, V., Wang, E., *et al.* (2007). Novelty seeking and the dopamine D4 receptor gene (DRD4) revisited in Asians: haplotype characterization and relevance of the 2-repeat allele. *American Journal of Medical Genetics*, **144B**, 453–7.

Reuter, M. and Hennig, J. (2005). Association of the functional catechol-O-methyltransferase VAL158MET polymorphism with the personality trait of extraversion. *NeuroReport*, **16**, 1135–8.

Reuter, M., Frenzel, C., Walter, N. T., Markett, S., and Montag, C. (2011). Investigating the genetic basis of altruism: the role of the COMT Val158Met polymorphism. *Social Cognitive & Affective Neuroscience*, **6**, 662–8.

Reuter, M., Schmitz, A., Corr, P., and Hennig, J. (2006). Molecular genetics support Gray's personality theory: the interaction of COMT and DRD2 polymorphisms predicts the behavior approach system. *International Journal of Neuropsychopharmacology*, **9**, 155–66.

Ronai, Z., Barta, C., Guttman, A., *et al.* (2001). Genotyping the −521C/T functional polymorphism in the promoter region of dopamine D4 receptor (DRD4) gene. *Electrophoresis*, **22**, 1102–5.

Roussos, P., Giakoumaki, S. G., and Bitsios, P. (2009). Cognitive and emotional processing in high novelty seeking associated with the L-DRD4 genotype. *Neuropsychologia*, **47**, 1654–9.

Salo, J., Pulkki-Råback, L., Hintsanen, M., Lehtimäki, T., and Keltikangas-Järvinen, L. (2010). The interaction between serotonin receptor 2A and catechol-O-methyltransferase gene polymorphisms is associated with the novelty-seeking subscale impulsiveness. *Psychiatric Genetics*, **20**, 273–81.

Silventoinen, K., Hammar, N., Hedlund, E., *et al.* (2008). Selective international migration by social position, health behaviour and personality. *European Journal of Public Health*, **18**, 150–5.

Smillie, L. D., Cooper, A. J., and Pickering, A. D. (2011). Individual differences in reward-prediction-error: extraversion and feedback-related negativity. *Social Cognitive & Affective Neuroscience*, **6**, 646–52.

Strobel, A., Lesch, K. P., Jatzke, S., Paetzold, F., and Brocke, B. (2003). Further evidence for a modulation of novelty seeking by DRD4 exon III, 5-HTTLPR, and COMT val/met variants. *Molecular Psychiatry*, **8**, 371–2.

Strobel, A., Wehr, A., Michel, A., and Brocke, B. (1999). Association between the dopamine D4 receptor (DRD4) exon III polymorphism and measures of novelty seeking in a German population. *Molecular Psychiatry*, **4**, 378–84.

Suhara, T., Yasuno, F., Sudo, Y., *et al.* (2001). Dopamine D2 receptors in the insular cortex and the personality trait of novelty seeking. *NeuroImage*, **13**, 891–5.

Sullivan, P. F., Fifield, W. J., Kennedy, M. A., *et al.* (1998). No association between novelty seeking and the type 4 dopamine receptor gene (DRD4) in two New Zealand samples. *American Journal of Psychiatry*, **155**, 98–101.

Sutin, A. R., Beason-Held, L. L., Resnick, S. M., and Costa, P. T. (2009). Sex differences in resting-state neural correlates of openness to experience among older adults. *Cerebral Cortex*, **19**, 2797–802.

Swisher, C. C., 3rd, Curtis, G. H., Jacob, T., *et al.* (1994). Age of the earliest known hominids in Java, Indonesia. *Science*, **263**, 1118–21.

Thompson, J., Thomas, N., Singleton, A., *et al.* (1997). D2 dopamine receptor gene (DRD2) Taq1A polymorphism: reduced dopamine D2 receptor binding in the human striatum associated with the A1 allele. *Pharmacogenetics*, **7**, 479–84.

Tomitaka, M., Tomitaka, S. -I., Otuka, Y., *et al.* (1999). Association between novelty seeking and dopamine receptor D4 (DRD4) exon III polymorphism in Japanese subjects. *American Journal of Medical Genetics*, **88**, 469–71.

Tovo-Rodrigues, L., Callegari-Jacques, S. M., Petzl-Erler, M. L., *et al.* (2010). Dopamine receptor D4 allele distribution in Amerindians: a reflection of past behavior differences? *American Journal of Physical Anthropology*, **143**, 458–64.

Tsai, S. J., Hong, C. J., Yu, Y. W., and Chen, T. J. (2004). Association study of catechol-O-methyltransferase gene and dopamine D4 receptor gene polymorphisms and personality traits in healthy young Chinese females. *Neuropsychobiology*, **50**, 153–6.

Vandenbergh, D. J., Zonderman, A. B., Wang, J., Uhl, G. R., and Costa, P. T., Jr. (1997). No association between novelty seeking and dopamine D4 receptor (D4DR) exon III seven repeat alleles in Baltimore Logitudinal Study of Aging participants. *Molecular Psychiatry*, **2**, 417–19.

Wacker, J., Reuter, M., Hennig, J., and Stemmler, G. (2005). Sexually dimorphic link between dopamine DRD receptor gene and neuroticism-anxiety. *NeuroReport*, **16**, 611–14.

Wang, E., Ding, Y. C., Flodman, P., *et al.* (2004). The genetic architecture of selection at the human dopamine receptor D4 (DRD4) gene locus. *American Journal of Human Genetics*, **74**, 931–44.

Wells, J. C. and Stock, J. T. (2007). The biology of the colonizing ape. *American Journal of Physical Anthropology*, Suppl **45**, 191–222.

Zai, C. C., Ehtesham, S., Choi, E., *et al.* (2012). Dopaminergic system genes in childhood aggression: possible role for DRD2. *World Journal of Biological Psychiatry*, **13**, 65–74.

Zald, D. H., Cowan, R. L., Riccardi, P., *et al.* (2008). Midbrain dopamine receptor availability is inversely associated with novelty-seeking traits in humans. *Journal of Neuroscience*, **28**, 14 372–8.

Zhu, R. X., Potts, R., Pan, Y. X., *et al.* (2008). Early evidence of the genus *Homo* in East Asia. *Journal of Human Evolution*, **55**, 1075–85.

5

Evolutionary consequences of human migration: genetic, historic, and archaeological perspectives in the Caribbean and Aleutian Islands

INTRODUCTION

This chapter provides a broad overview of migration, its history and causes, as well as its geographic and genetic influences on two human groups living in radically different areas of the world – the Caribbean and Aleutian Islands. Prehistoric colonization and settlement by both Garifuna and Aleuts, severely disrupted by forced relocation from outside (British, Russian, or American) during the eighteenth and nineteenth centuries, resulted in substantial cultural and genetic transformations in both groups. The Garifuna forced migration stimulated a unique evolutionary success story along the coast of Central America, while the Aleut populations experienced highly asymmetric patterns of gene flow from Russian colonists and Scandinavian and British fishermen.

What is migration?

Migration is the relocation of people from one geographical region of the world to another region. Movements of culturally and/or linguistically homogeneous migrants were traditionally termed diasporas (Brubaker, 2005). For example, the dispersion of Jews from the Middle East into Babylonia in the sixth century BC, followed by further migrations into Europe and Asia, has been characterized as the Jewish diaspora. The terminology was further broadened to include other

Causes and Consequences of Human Migration, ed. Michael H. Crawford and Benjamin C. Campbell. Published by Cambridge University Press. © Cambridge University Press 2012.

forced movements and population relocations, such as the African diaspora (Alpers, 2001). These migrations result in the fission of the parental populations, founder effects, reproductive isolation, exposure of genomes to new environments, and gene flow – if the region was previously inhabited.

As documented by the fossil record and discussed in Chapter 2 by Stoneking, early hominin forms have been migrating out of Africa for at least 1.8 million years. These earliest demic expansions of *Homo erectus* resulted in the settlement of the more temperate climes of the Middle East, Asia, and Europe. In the second major diaspora, anatomically modern *Homo sapiens* (AMHS) expanded out of Africa more than 100 000 years ago and replaced the earlier hominin forms, such as Neandertals, but with gene flow of a low magnitude (Green *et al.*, 2010).

Human migrations can be categorized into two major types:

1. Demic expansions of populations into previously uninhabited regions of the world. This form of migration first occurred 1.8 million years ago when an early form of *Homo erectus* migrated out of Africa. Settlement of Oceania and the Americas were later manifestations of this form of migration.
2. Migration of humans into previously inhabited regions, such as AMHS moving into the Middle East, Europe and Asia, *c.*100 000 years ago.

The evolutionary consequences of these two forms of migration differ due to varying degrees of population fission, kin migration, and genetic drift – resulting in the loss of genetic variability. In contrast, populations migrating into previously occupied regions can be characterized by an increase in genetic variability, the introduction of new genetic materials into populations, and the "testing" of mutations (that arose in different environments) through natural selection.

Causes of migration

An assortment of social, climatic, demographic, economic, and biological factors have been implicated as potential causes of human migration. Push/pull factors have been used to explain massive human migrations. "Push" factors include relocation due to some environmental changes – such as greater aridity, social problems associated with famines, overpopulation, wars, disease, floods, absence of security, and religious persecution. "Pull" factors denote migration into regions that are more desirable, such as those having milder climates, more resources – for example, availability of food, land, grasslands for pastoral populations, economic opportunities such as employment, and freedom from religious or political persecution. Usually, migration is caused not by a single factor but by a multitude of interacting and synergistic effects. In this chapter we explore various "push/pull" scenarios for the colonization of the Aleutian Islands.

Migration may be involuntary as in the case of African slaves being forcibly brought to the New World for economic purposes and labor. The consequences of this form of migration is discussed by Lorena Madrigal in her chapter on the slave trade and East-Indian migrants to the Caribbean. In addition, we will discuss in this chapter the evolutionary consequences of the forced relocation by the British military of the Garifuna (Black Caribs) from St. Vincent Island to Roatan and Honduras, in contrast with Aleut transplantation by the Russian government for the purpose of harvesting sea mammal furs and sale in Europe.

Measurement of migration

Rates of migration are often difficult to measure in human populations. In the past, most human groups lacked written languages and thus did not record vital statistics – no birth, death, or evidence of relocation. Rough migration estimates can be generated using age–sex distributions based upon census data. Some migration data can be gleaned from non-literate populations, using standardized demographic pro formae that detail past residences, migrations of relatives, and places of birth of spouses.

Historically, church and municipal documentation of births, deaths, and marriage records are spotty and date back to only the fourteenth century in Europe. In England, relocation permissions were required for the movement of freemen and "villeins" (slaves of the feudal master) in the system imposed by the Norman invasion era (c. eleventh century). The quality of church records varies from parish to parish and from priest to priest. For example, the church records of one municipio of Valle Maira in northern Italy displayed lacunae in the records for about 20 years as revealed by time series analyses (Lin and Crawford, 1983). The cause of the fewer births, deaths, and marriages in that parish were due to an alcoholic priest who failed to record these vital events in the church books. Another source of migration information can be found on tombstone inscriptions that detail the birth places of the deceased. However, there is great variability in these inscription details from cemetery to cemetery and region to region.

The molecular revolution starting in the 1980s provided more reliable uniparental measures of sex-specific migration, such as mitochondrial DNA (mtDNA) sequences and haplogroups that reflect maternal migration. In contrast, the non-recombining Y-chromosome haplotypes reveal paternal movements. Prior to the application of these uniparental markers, recombining classical genetic markers were usually less informative in regards to migration. An exception, based on an albumin marker, turned out to be highly informative in assessing gene flow from highland Maya Indians into the coastal Black Carib (Garifuna) populations. The Native American genetic heritage of these highly admixed Black Caribs was Arawak and Carib from South America. Thus, these populations should not exhibit at polymorphic frequencies Albumin Mexico – a genetic variant that is polymorphic in Mexican Native Americans but absent in South America. However, the genetic marker Albumin Mexico was found at polymorphic frequencies in coastal Garifuna villages in Belize and Guatemala. By measuring the frequency of this albumin marker, it was possible to estimate gene flow from highland populations of the Yucatan into the coastal Garifuna settlements. It is likely that this gene flow occurred during market days when the Maya males visited the coastal settlements and possibly Garifuna brothels (Crawford *et al.*, 1984).

Evolutionary consequences of migration

Migration has shaped genetic variation in contemporary human populations as the early humans expanded throughout the world. In each region human populations had to adapt genetically to unique environments, such as heat, cold, high altitude, and an assortment of new disease vectors. This geographic expansion of human populations resulted in the loss of genetic variability. Prugnolle *et al.* (2005) demonstrated (based on 51 human populations and 377 autosomal microsatellite markers) that there is a linear decline in genetic diversity (Hs) the greater the distances of the location of these contemporary populations are from Africa. This loss of genetic variability is likely due to population fission, often along familial lines resulting in migrants who were not representative of the parental population (see Chapter 6 by Alan Fix). In small migrant offshoots, specific alleles are lost or fixed at high frequencies as a result of stochastic processes, such as genetic drift. Founder effect and small effective population sizes can result in rapid evolutionary change and the differentiation of subpopulations. If the region into which populations migrate was inhabited at an earlier time, gene flow introduces new genetic materials and increases genetic variability. Subsequent gene flow can restore genes that were lost through genetic drift or can introduce new alleles acquired through mutation in another population. Mutations that occurred in one environment are introduced into new populations and are tested under new environmental conditions.

In this chapter, the causes and evolutionary consequences of migration will be examined in two regions of the world (based on our field investigations) with vastly different patterns of gene flow and evolutionary consequences. These regions of migration include:

1. The Caribbean and Central America with triracially admixed populations that were forcibly transplanted from St. Vincent Island to Roatan (Bay Islands), followed by the successful colonization of the Atlantic coast of Central America. A more detailed migration history of the Garifuna is explored in Chapter 25 of this volume by Chris Phillips-Krawczak. The Phillips-Krawczak follow-up field investigations on St. Vincent Island and Belize utilized uniparental molecular markers instead of admixture based on standard recombining markers (such as immunoglobulins, blood groups, and polymorphic proteins) discussed in this chapter.

2. The causes and genetic/evolutionary consequences of the settlement of the Aleutian Islands (from 9000 to 3000 years ago), and the expansion of the Russian empire in the nineteenth century and its genetic and evolutionary sequelae.

GARIFUNA MIGRATIONS

Origins

St. Vincent Island of the Lesser Antilles contains an admixed population consisting of Island Carib, Arawak Indian and West Africans (see Figure 5.1). According to archaeological excavations, the island of St. Vincent was initially settled by Arawaks from South America in approximately AD 100 (see Chapter 25 by Phillips-Krawczak). Another Native American group, the Caribs, from Venezuela migrated into the Caribbean at *c.* AD 1200 and admixed with the Arawak (Rouse, 1949). From 1517 to 1646 an African component (through shipwrecked slaves and escapees from Barbados – a slave commercial center) was added to the St. Vincent Island gene pool. Some gene flow from French and English colonists added to the high genetic diversity on St. Vincent

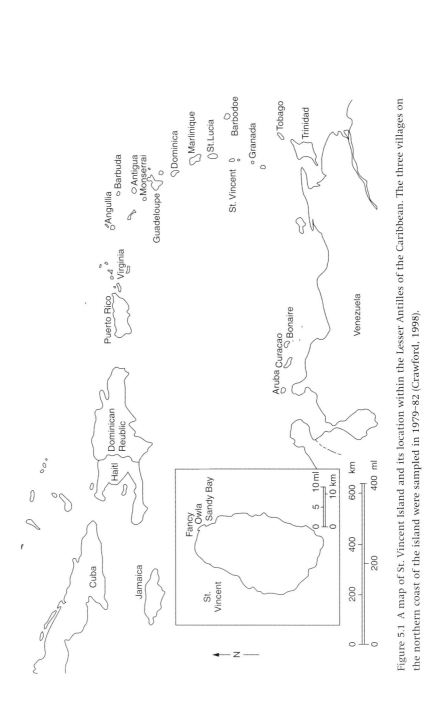

Figure 5.1 A map of St. Vincent Island and its location within the Lesser Antilles of the Caribbean. The three villages on the northern coast of the island were sampled in 1979–82 (Crawford, 1998).

Island (Crawford, 1983). This triracial population, the Black Caribs (or Garifuna), attempted to resist British colonial take-over of the most fertile land on the island and in 1796 the British military rounded up and deported 4200 Garifuna – initially to a concentration camp on an adjacent Baliseau Island. While the Garifuna were awaiting naval transport, epidemics (most likely typhus) swept through the camp and halved the captive population on Baliseau. As a result, in 1797 only 2026 Garifuna arrived in Roatan in the Bay Islands (Gonzalez, 1984). In 1797–8, a Spanish fleet was sent to the Bay Islands and relocated the fewer than 2000 Garifuna from Roatan to Honduras in Central America.

The transplanted Garifuna population rapidly colonized the coast of Central America, expanding from an initial village in 1798 (established in Honduras, proximal to the contemporary Trujillo) to 54 villages stretching from Dangriga in Belize to LaFe in Nicaragua. From fewer than 2000 Garifuna transplanted to the coast of Central America in 1798, the population numerically expanded to over 200 000 within a few generations (Crawford, 1983). What contributed to this rapid population expansion was an exceptionally high fertility rate, as shown for the oldest generation of Sambo Creek, Honduras (estimated as 10.9 live born per woman at 45 years or older; Brennan, 1983), and relatively low mortality due to Garifuna genetic resistance to falciparum malaria (Madrigal, 1988). There is no evidence for the presence of malaria in Central America until it was introduced by infected African slaves brought to work in the fruit plantations. The Native American coastal populations, having no genetic adaptations against malaria, experienced high mortality and populations were forced to relocate themselves to the Highlands of Belize and Guatemala to escape this new scourge (Crawford, 1998). This relocation of many Native American villages to the Highlands opened the coastal regions of Central America to the rapid colonization by the Garifuna.

According to Gullick (1984), a total of 45 Garifuna escaped into the mountain region of St. Vincent and avoided the round-up and deportation by the British troops in 1796. This small founding population gave rise to approximately 1100–2000 descendants currently residing in three villages on the slopes of the volcano of St. Vincent Island (see Figure 5.1).

GENETIC CONSEQUENCES OF FORCED MIGRATIONS

The consequences of the forced and push/pull migrations into St. Vincent Island and Central America include the formation of a series of highly admixed and genetically diverse settlements. Results from gamma globulin (GM) genetic markers (informative because of their population specificity for measuring admixture between continental populations), show that 42% of the gene pool of Sandy Bay on St. Vincent Island is of Native American (Arawak–Carib) ancestry and 41% is of African origin (Schanfield *et al.*, 1984). In contrast, the Garifuna on the coast of Central America display a much lower Native American component (22%–29%) and a much higher African ancestry (70%–75%) (Crawford *et al.*, 1981). Sandy Bay (see Figure 5.1 for location of Black Carib communities on St. Vincent Island) gene pool also exhibits a higher European component of 17%, greater than in any of the Garifuna populations on the coast of Central America (1%–5%).

The outcome of the migrations of the Garifuna to Central America is a unique evolutionary success story (Crawford, 1984). The Carib–Arawak genes, mostly lost in the Caribbean due to depopulation associated with slavery and disease, are preserved in the Garifuna and widely distributed in 54 villages from Stann Creek in Belize to La Fe in Nicaragua in Central America. Because of their sub-Saharan African ancestry, the Garifuna have genetic resistance against malaria. In addition to hemoglobin S and C, the newly repackaged Garifuna genome includes genes that affect the life cycle of the *Plasmodium* organism and add to the polygenic adaptation to the four species of malaria. The adaptive genes include: glucose-6-phosphate dehydrogenase (G-6-PD) deficiency, Duffy null allele, thalassemia major and minor, tumor necrosis factor (TNF), human leukocyte antigen (HLA), and gamma globulins (GM) variation (Crawford *et al.*, 1981; Schanfield *et al.*, 1984). Thus, mutations that arose in Africa and the Mediterranean regions have been "repackaged" by the gene flow resulting from the migration and natural selection to contribute to an evolutionary success story of the Garifuna. In addition, the Garifuna founding populations exhibited exceptionally high genetic diversity that was an evolutionary advantage to fissioning populations (Crawford, 1983). It is this combination of genes resistant to malaria brought to Central America by the Garifuna and the enormous genetic diversity of a triracially admixed founding population that could successfully experience consecutive population fissions and adapt to the diverse coastal environments of Central America.

MIGRATION ALONG THE ALEUTIAN ARCHIPELAGO

Migration and settlement patterns along the Aleutian Archipelago have been reconstructed on the basis of archaeological and molecular genetic evidence. In this chapter we examine the chronology and causes of the expansion from Siberia into the Aleutian Islands and consider the genetic, demographic, and evolutionary consequences. We also document the consequences of Aleut contact with Russian colonists in the western Islands and English and Scandinavian fishermen of the eastern Aleutian Islands.

Both genetic and radiocarbon evidence indicate that the earliest Aleuts crossed the exposed Bering Land Bridge before turning and migrating across the Aleutian chain from east to west (Crawford, 2007; West *et al.*, 2007). Radiocarbon dates indicate Aleuts were in the eastern Aleutians 9000 years ago (Davis and Knecht, 2010; Laughlin, 1963; McCartney, 1984), arrived in the central Aleutians by 6000 years ago (O'Leary, 2001; Savinetsky *et al.*, 2012), and colonized the far western Aleutians by 3200 years ago (Corbett *et al.*, 2010; West *et al.*, 1999). Glaciers had started to recede across the entire archipelago by 9000 years ago making the entire chain potentially habitable near the beginning of the Holocene (Savinetsky *et al.*, 2004, 2010).

Aleuts, among the world's best seafarers, used kayaks built of driftwood, whalebone, and sea mammal skins for quick travel and hunting. They constructed *umiaks*, skin-covered boats resembling tubs, for carrying families and larger loads. In the eastern Aleutians, where islands are within sight of each other, Aleuts easily explored and moved to adjacent islands (Figure 5.2). It was simple enough to kayak to the next island to the west to explore suitable habitation and foraging territories. Umiaks carrying families and household goods could safely make the journey to closely spaced islands when sea waves were comparatively calm.

Continued westward colonization across the Bering Sea must have constituted a truly dangerous enterprise. Western islands are located farther apart, and it is impossible to see adjacent islands from any given vantage point. A 221-km wide, and extremely rough, Aleutian interisland pass separates the Rat from the Near Islands except for one tiny island, Buldir (Figure 5.2). Historical and archaeological evidence indicates that Aleuts never prehistorically settled the Commander Islands, 330 km northwest of Attu Island (Hrdlička, 1945).

It is unclear why Aleuts entered the Aleutians and undertook long and dangerous voyages to ultimately settle the entire archipelago. Were Aleuts *drawn* by new, and richer, marine resources and new untapped hunting territories? Or were they sometimes *pushed*, either by (1) increasing human population with its associated competition, warfare, and decreasing resources, or (2) natural disasters including volcanic

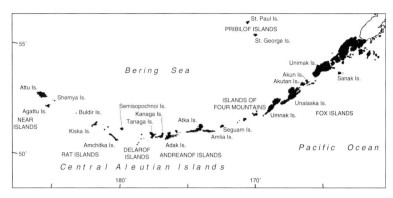

Figure 5.2 A map of the Aleutian Archipelago, eastern Siberia, and western Alaska.

eruptions, tsunamis, or earthquakes? It is likely that Aleuts were either pulled or pushed given particular circumstances.

The pull: climatic opportunities and natural resources

Current research indicates that climate apparently played an important, if not critical, role in Aleut migrations. Analyzing diatoms from a natural peat bog deposit on Adak Island, Savinetsky *et al.* (2012) determined that Aleuts first colonized the central Aleutians in approximately 6000 BP (years before present) during the coldest period of the Holocene in the Bering Sea region. In the North Pacific Rim, cooler to extremely cold climatic intervals coincide with high biodiversity and productivity (Savinetsky *et al.*, 2004, 2010, 2012). The recovery of bones of saffron cod, an extremely cold toler-ant fish recovered from the 6000-year-old Adak settlement, supports human migration to the central Aleutians during a particularly inhospit-able but highly bioproductive period (Savinetsky *et al.*, 2012).

Approximately 4000 years ago, another climatic fluctuation created a window of opportunity for Aleuts to migrate to the Near Islands. Archaeological research indicates that Aleuts first colonized Shemya Island in the extreme western Aleutians by 3200 years ago (Corbett *et al.*, 2010; West *et al.*, 1999). Peat bog analysis on Shemya Island reveals the climate was cooler but much drier than today and was accompanied by weakened cyclonic activity characterized by less wind (Savinetsky *et al.*, 2010). Reduced wind speeds and associated calmer seas (Sorkina, 1963 in Savinetsky *et al.*, 2010) likely enabled the first long-distance voyages and transportation of family units in umiaks through wide interisland passages to new islands in the far west.

The ecological model "optimal foraging theory" (Winterhalder and Smith, 1981) suggests organisms locate, capture, and consume resources containing the most calories while expending the least amount of energy to do it. Clearly Aleuts could maximize their net energy intake per unit time by colonizing a new landscape. Evidence of this tactic is inferred at the earliest recognized site (3200 BP) on Shemya Island. Orchard and Crockford (2010), measuring cod bones, determined that Aleuts preferred and caught extremely large cod 1300 mm long. One thousand years later, in Shemya archaeological sites, the most common fish were rockfish, sculpins, and flatfish; cod were present, but less abundant, and their maximum size was smaller (1043 mm). At the earliest Shemya site, Aleuts relied on easily accessible, colony-nesting birds, including puffins and murres. However, in later Shemya sites, harder to catch pelagic species – albatrosses, shearwaters, and fulmars – predominated (Lefèvre *et al.*, 2010) The Shemya evidence suggests that when Aleuts colonized a new territory, they selected the largest, most abundant, most easily accessible, and calorie dense resource. When Aleuts depleted these top-ranked resources, they could (1) rely on smaller, harder to obtain, or less calorie rich resources, (2) range further afield to acquire new resources, or (3) move to new, previously untapped foraging territories.

The push: population movement, expansion, and new technologies

The earliest Aleuts entered the archipelago from the Alaska Peninsula *c.* 9000 years ago equipped with a stone tool technology based on blades. This first technology, dating between 9000 to 7000 BP and associated with simple tent-like structures, depressions, and hearths, was never transported to the central or western Aleutians (Hatfield, 2010). Aleuts implemented bifacial technology around 7000 BP and apparently carried this technology westward across the archipelago to both the central and western Aleutians (Corbett *et al.*, 2010; Hatfield, 2010). Bifacial technology may have (1) developed *in situ*, or (2) arrived from the Alaskan mainland either through trade or a second human migration into the eastern Aleutians (Hatfield, 2010). At *c.* 4000 to 3000 BP, the Arctic Small Tool Tradition (Davis and Knecht, 2010; Hatfield, 2010) arrived in the eastern Aleutians from the Alaska Peninusula. Extending from Greenland to the Bering Strait, this technology never made its way to the central and western Aleutians.

Archaeological surveys suggest Aleutian population increased across the archipelago beginning 3000 years ago. Sea level stabilized by 4000 BP resulting in village sites occurring along or near current coastlines. It remains unclear if an abundance of coastal village sites represents an actual prehistoric population increase or a bias in current archaeological survey practices (Hatfield, 2010). Recent work by Hanson and Corbett (2010) on central Aleutian inland sites is providing new data on Aleut settlement patterns.

Osteological evidence supports a scenario for multiple migrations into the eastern Aleutians. Aleš Hrdlička (1945) explored the archipelago while collecting Aleut skeletons and artifacts for the Smithsonian Institution. Hrdlička discovered two types of distinct Aleut crania – a dolicocephalic type which he assigned to pre-Aleuts and a brachiocephalic type to which he assigned the name Aleut. Hrdlička proposed that pre-Aleuts first colonized the Aleutians and at some later time a second migration of Aleuts swept across the archipelago replacing the pre-Aleuts. Recent morphologic, genetic, radiometric, and stable isotope analyses of human remains collected by Hrdlička from Kagamil and Ship Rock burial caves and Chaluka midden in the eastern Aleutians have been conducted (Coltrain, 2010; Coltrain *et al.*, 2006). These new data suggest that pre-Aleuts apparently first settled the Aleutian Archipelago. At *c.* 1000 BP a new type of "Aleut" with a different-shaped head was coexisting with the pre-Aleut variety. These newcomers, apparently from the Alaskan Peninsula, ate a higher trophic diet, possessed a more complex technology including ground slate and jet artifacts, used refuge rocks for defense, and built large communal long houses to support relatively dense populations. This migration into the eastern Aleutians occurred 2200 years after the Near Islands in the west were colonized.

It remains unclear if increasing population size and influx of new populations into the eastern Aleutians was a possible motivation for human movement. Populations prior to Russian contact in 1741 are estimated to have numbered as low as 9000–12 000 (Liapunova, 1996), 12 000–15 000 (Lantis, 1970, 1984), or as high as 40 000 (Turner, 1967 in Frolich, 2002). However, the population number of prehistoric Aleuts remains unknown (Reedy-Maschner, 2010). The Bering Sea region is ecologically rich with ocean fisheries, large sea mammal populations, kelp forests, intertidal zones, spawning streams, and a highly diverse bird population. Currently, Dutch Harbor in the eastern Aleutians is the most productive commercial seafood processing port in the United States. It is probably safe to assume that prehistoric human populations were never large enough and technologically equipped to significantly impact natural resources in large hunting territories. Aleuts diminished resources in the immediate vicinity of villages, but the impact of hunter-gatherers on the greater Bering Sea ecosystem was largely insignificant. However, influxes of new humans into already occupied, and perhaps densely populated, eastern islands after 1000 BP apparently resulted in some type of conflict, if not all-out warfare, between Aleuts and certainly with Alutiiq peoples living on Kodiak Island (Knecht and Davis, 2003; Maschner and Reedy-Maschner, 1998).

Natural disasters

Volcanic in origin and situated on a subduction zone on the northern border of the Ring of Fire, the Aleutians boast considerable geologic instability. Volcanic eruptions, seismic events (including uplift and subsidence), and tsunamis could disrupt food sources by killing fish and ground-nesting bird colonies, clogging salmon streams, and impacting shellfish beds and sea mammal rookeries. Volcanic eruptions occurred throughout the Holocene and Aleuts responded to these natural occurrences through movement and changes in settlement pattern. From a geological point of view, volcanoes, earthquakes, and tsunamis are short-term events, but from the hunter-gatherer perspective such geological perturbations might have been sufficiently long-lived to cause serious impacts on local economics and the human psyche in a given region (Black, 1981:315, 317).

The August 2008 eruption of Kasatochi, a volcanic island in the central Aleutians, is a proxy for impacts of past volcanic activities on humans and the Bering Sea ecosystem. The Kasatochi explosion, with a plume that rose 14 000–15 000 meters (45 000–50 000 ft), killed several thousand bird chicks; destroyed the breeding colonies of over 100 000 ground-nesting birds, and blanketed the Kasatochi coast with meters of ash. The associated pyroclastic-flow deposits created a new coastline, now about 400 m further into the sea, meanwhile burying shellfish communities. The pyroclastic flows also initiated a small tsunami that was recorded by tide gauges at Atka, Adak, and Amchitka in the Andreanof and Rat Islands (AVO, 2011).

Such geological disasters are identified in the archaeological record. Davis and Knecht (2010:513) report that the Hog Island sites in Unalaska Bay were "capped by an overlying pyroclastic flow deposit. The fast-moving gas and ash came from a caldera-forming eruption by nearby Mt. Makushin. The pyroclastic flow was immediately on top of the occupation; if any inhabitants were present, they would have been overcome by the conflagration." On Adak Island, a well-documented

series of volcanic ash layers intercalate with prehistoric human habitation zones (Okuno *et al.*, 2007). On Buldir Island thick sand deposits
mixed with archaeological layers might indicate high wave events
(Arkady Savinetsky, 2011, pers. comm.). If geological events were significant enough, Aleuts would have relocated village sites for at least
several years, if not decades, until the local ecosystem had recovered.

Forced migration: the historic period

In 1741, Vitus Bering, accompanied by the naturalist George Stellar,
investigated and claimed the Aleutian chain for Peter the Great. The
Russian period marked the beginning of commercial hunting for otters,
fur seals, and sea lions along with the introduction of Arctic fox farming.
First contact had a drastic impact on Aleutian populations and their
hunter-gatherer culture, economy, and maritime environment. Murder,
diseases including smallpox and influenza, and the relocation of Aleut
males from their traditional villages and hunting territories to trap
valuable furs for the Chinese and European markets disrupted Aleut
social structure and religion, relocated traditional settlements, and significantly reduced the Aleut population (Black, 1984; Veltre, 1990). Adult
Aleut males were transported from their villages to the uninhabited
Pribilof Islands to the north and Commander Islands to the far west to
hunt otters and seals. This forced relocation allowed gene flow between
Aleut women and male Russians, Kamchadel, Itel'men, Koriak, Yakut,
and Tungus sailors and trappers (Reedy-Maschner, 2010). This genetic
amalgamation is exhibited in modern Aleut populations. When the
United States purchased Alaska in 1867, the Aleutian native population
numbered approximately 2000. During the nineteenth century, European males, particularly the Scandinavians, seeking natural resources
(seal pelts and fish) also mated with Aleut women, further adding European genes to the Aleut gene pool (Reedy-Maschner, 2010). Through two
centuries of historical contact with the outside world, it is probably safe
to say that no "unadmixed" Aleuts exist today.

GENETIC CONSEQUENCES OF MIGRATION IN THE ALEUTIAN ISLANDS

The settlement of the Aleutian Islands by Siberian populations resulted
in a reduction of the genetic diversity of the contemporary populations
with only two (A and D haplogroups) of the five Asian founding mtDNA
haplogroups (A, B, C, D, and X) observed (see Figure 5.3). The Aleuts

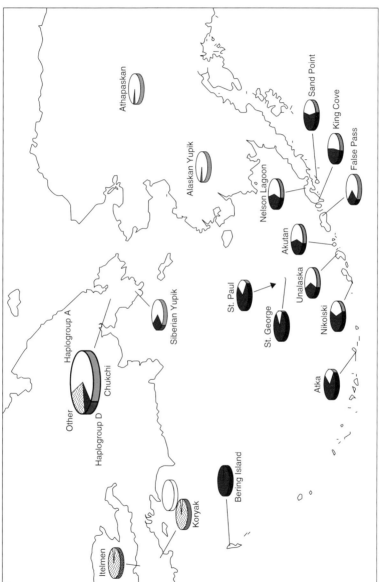

Figure 5.3 The Aleutian Islands showing the distribution of mtDNA haplogroup frequencies (Crawford, 2007).

share a D2a1 mtDNA subtype with the 4000 BP Saqqaq Paleo-Eskimo from eastern Greenland (Gilbert *et al.*, 2008). The genetic structure of the indigenous populations of the Aleutian Islands resulting from the earliest migration and settlement of the islands by Siberian migrants is preserved in the maternal lineage – characterized by mtDNA sequences. The subsequent forced relocation of the Aleuts by the Russians to the Commander Islands resulted, through founder effect, in further reduction of genetic variability by the fixation of the D2a1 haplogroup and the loss of A2a (Crawford, 2007; Rubicz *et al.*, 2010). European mtDNA haplogroups were not detected in the western and central islands among individuals who identified themselves culturally as Aleuts; however, a low frequency of western European mtDNA haplogroups were detected in the eastern islands from non-Aleut women marrying into the communities (Zlojutro *et al.*, 2009). In contrast, the Y-chromosome markers reveal a predominantly east European haplogroup (85%) and only 15% of Aleut males exhibited Native American Q or Q3 haplogroups (Zlojutro *et al.*, 2009). Thus, the gene flow from Russian colonialists was highly asymmetric: Russian males marrying Aleut females. Therefore, to accurately measure gene flow into the Aleutian Islands, both NRY and mtDNA markers are required to detect the asymmetry of the gene flow. Autosomal, recombining STRs provide an intermediate picture of the relationships between the population subdivisions.

How can we be certain that the genetic structure revealed by mtDNA sequences is indeed the result of the original settlement of the Aleutian Islands plus subsequent genetic microdifferentiation? Mantel tests indicate that an intimate and statistically significant relationship ($r = 0.7$; $p < 0.000$) still persists between the geography of the archipelago (as measured in kilometers as the crow flies between the islands) and the genetic distances (measured as inter-match distances using mtDNA sequences; Crawford, 2007). Spatial autocorrelation plot (using the method of Bertorelle and Barbujani, 1995) indicates a strong, linear relationship between geography (lag distances in kilometers) and genetics (product moment coefficient, analogous to Moran's I) with a P value of < 0.000 (see Figure 5.4). However, the highest correlation between populations is in the 500-km distance, followed by lower correlations in the 1000-km lag and negative correlations at greater distances. This pattern usually reflects kin migration – the most likely pattern of Aleut settlement of the archipelago (Crawford *et al.*, 2010). Figure 5.5 indicates the locations of genetic discontinuity based on HVSI mtDNA sequences. The triangulation plot indicates that a genetic barrier exists in the central Aleutian Islands, most likely the result of

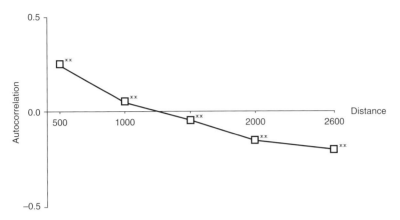

Figure 5.4 Spatial autocorrelation plot of the populations of the Aleutian Islands, based on mtDNA sequences and the methods of Bertorelle and Barbujani (1995). The double asterisk denotes a highly significant relationship between geography and genetics (Crawford, 2007).

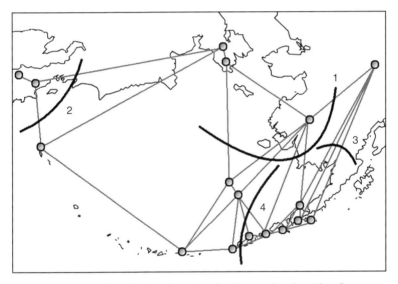

Figure 5.5 Triangulation plot using the Monmonier algorithm for identifying genetic discontinuity (Monmonier, 1973). The numbered arcs represent areas of genetic discontinuity: (1) a separation between Athabaskan and Eskimo populations from Aleut groups; (2) discontinuity between Kamchatkan native populations and Aleuts; (3) separation between Eskimo populations of the Alaskan Peninsula from Aleut groups; (4) genetic discontinuity among central Aleutian Island populations.

pauses in the population movements and genetic differentiation, followed by a later expansion after climatic change. After the initial expansion into the eastern Aleutian Islands, *c.* 9000 BP, the colonization of the Central Islands did not start until approximately 6000 years ago during the coldest period of the Holocene in the Bering Sea. Another climatic fluctuation, approximately 4000 years ago, resulted in a cooler, drier climate with weakened cyclonic activity and less wind. This climatic change enabled long-distance voyages through wide interisland passages to the Near Islands.

There is no indication of a statistically significant relationship between genetic distances measured by non-recombining Y-chromosome (NRY) markers and geographical distances. A comparison of matrices based on Y-haplotype distances and geographic distances between the island communities yields a correlation of $r = 0.379$; $p > 0.130$ ns (Crawford *et al.*, 2010). Migrations play prominent roles in explaining the distribution of genes throughout the Aleutian Archipelago. Russian Y-chromosomes and surnames occur in the western and central islands, while Scandinavian and English Y-chromosomes are distributed throughout the eastern islands (Graf *et al.*, 2010). The western European incursion into the eastern Aleutian Islands and the Alaska Peninsula reflect the purchase of Alaska in the nineteenth century from Russia by the United States, followed by settlement of west European fishermen on specific eastern islands.

CONCLUSION

The two geographically and historically diverse examples of the causes and evolutionary consequences of migration reveal some similarities and many differences. The forced migration of Africans through the slave trade resulted in a triracial hybrid Garifuna population that had a selective advantage in malarial environments. Thus, the Garifuna represent an evolutionary success story in their take-over of the coast of Central America. In addition, the Garifuna repackaged genomes contained a proportion of Arawak and Carib genes that have disappeared through most of the Caribbean Islands due to slavery, war, and disease. The Native American genomes have been preserved in the Garifuna and distributed along the coast of Central America.

The prehistoric Aleuts (a.k.a. Unangax) provide a rare glimpse into the role of climatic changes influencing push/pull human migrations and settlement. Environmental fluctuations, in part revealed by diatoms from peat bog analyses on Shemya and Adak Islands, provide insight into the colonization of the island chain. These migrations at 6000 and 4000 years ago, made possible by weakened cyclonic activity, have left indelible genetic discontinuities due to kin migration followed by genetic microdifferentiation of island populations.

REFERENCES

Alpers, E. A. (2001). *Defining the African Diaspora*. Los Angeles, CA: Center for Comparative Social Analysis Workshop, University of California.

AVO (Alaska Volcano Observatory) (2011). Kasatochi reported activity. Online: www.avo.alaska.edu/volcanoes/volcact.php?volcname=Kasatochi&eruptionid =605&page=basics

Bertorelle, G. and Barbujani, G. (1995). Analysis of DNA diversity by spatial autocorrelation. *Genetics*, **140**, 811–19.

Black, L. T. (1981). Volcanism as a factor in human ecology: the Aleutian case. *Ethnohistory*, **28**(4), 313–33.

Black, L. T. (1984). *Atka: An Ethnohistory of the Western Aleutians*. Kingston, Canada: Limestone Press.

Brennan, E. R. (1983). Factors underlying decreasing fertility among the Garifuna of Honduras. *American Journal of Physical Anthropology*, **60**, 177.

Brubaker, R. (2005). The "diaspora" diaspora. *Ethnic and Racial Studies*, **28**(1), 1–19.

Coltrain, J. (2010). Temporal and dietary reconstruction in past Aleut populations: stable-and radio-isotope evidence revisited. *Arctic*, **63**(4), 391–8.

Coltrain, J., Hayes, M. G., and O'Rourke, D. H. (2006). Hrdlicka's Aleutian population-replacement hypothesis: a radiometric evaluation. *Current Anthropology*, **47**, 537–48.

Corbett, D. G., West, D., and Lefèvre, C (2010). *The People at the End of the World: The Western Aleutians Project and the Archaeology of Shemya Island*. Aurora Monograph Series VIII. Anchorage, AK: Alaska Anthropological Association.

Crawford, M. H. (1983). The anthropological genetics of the Black Caribs (Garifuna) of Central America and the Caribbean. *Yearbook of Physical Anthropology*, **25**, 155–86.

Crawford, M. H. (1984). *Current Developments in Anthropological Genetics*, Vol. 3: *Black Caribs: A Case Study of Biocultural Adaptation*. New York: Plenum Press.

Crawford, M. H. (1998). *Origins of Native Americans. Anthropological Genetic Perspective*. Cambridge, UK: Cambridge University Press.

Crawford, M. H. (2007). Genetic structure of circumpolar populations: a synthesis. *American Journal of Human Biology*, **19**, 203–17.

Crawford, M. H., Dykes, D. D., Skradski, K., and Polesky, H. F. (1984). Blood group, serum protein, and red blood cell enzyme polymorphisms, and admixture among the Black Caribs and Creoles of Central America and the Caribbean. In *Current Developments in Anthropological Genetics*, Vol. 3: *Black Caribs. A Case Study in Biocultural Adaptation*, ed. M. H. Crawford, pp. 302–33. New York: Plenum Press.

Crawford, M. H., Gonzalez, N., Schanfield, M. S. *et al.* (1981). The Black Caribs (Garifuna) of Livingstone, Guatemala: genetic markers and admixture estimates. *Human Biology*, **53**, 87–104.

Crawford, M. H., Rubicz, R. C., and Zlojutro, M. (2010). Origin of Aleuts and the genetic structure of populations of the archipelago: molecular and archaeological perspectives. *Human Biology*, **82**(5–6), 695–717.

Davis, R. S. and Knecht, R. A. (2010). Continuity and change in the eastern Aleutian archaeological sequence. *Human Biology*, **82**(5–6), 507–24.

Frolich, B. (2002). Aleutian settlement distribution on Adak, Kagalaska, Buldir and Attu islands, Aleutian Islands, Alaska. In *To the Aleutians and Beyond: The Anthropology of William S Laughlin*, ed. B. Frohlich, A. Harper, and R. Gilberg, pp. 63–88. Publication of the National Museum Ethnographic Series 20. Copenhagen: National Museum of Denmark.

Gilbert, M. T., Kivsild, T., Gronnow, B., *et al.* (2008). Paleo-Eskimos mtDNA genome reveals matrilineal discontinuity in Greenland. *Science*, **320**(5884), 1787–9.

Gonzalez, N. L. (1984). Garifuna (Black Carib) social organization. In *Current Developments in Anthropological Genetics*, Vol. 3: *Black Caribs: A Case Study in Biocultural Adaptation*, ed. M. H. Crawford, pp. 51–66. New York: Plenum Press.

Graf, O. M., Zlojutro, M., Rubicz, R., and Crawford, M. H. (2010). Surname distributions and their associations with Y-chromosome markers in the Aleutian Islands. *Human Biology*, **2**(5–6), 745–57.

Green, R. E., Krause, J., Briggs, A., *et al.* (2010). A draft sequence of the Neandertal genome. *Science*, **328**, 710–22.

Gullick, C. J. M. R. (1984). The changing Vincentian Carib population. In *Current Developments in Anthropological Genetics*, Vol. 3: *Black Caribs: A Case Study in Biocultural Adaptation*, ed. M. H. Crawford, pp. 37–50. New York: Plenum Press.

Hanson, D. K. and Corbett, D. G. (2010). Shifting ground: archaeological surveys of upland Adak Island, the Aleutian Islands, Alaska and changing assumptions of Unangan land use patterns. *Polar Geography*, **33**, 165–78.

Hatfield, V. (2010). Material culture across the Aleutian archipelago. *Human Biology*, **82**(5–6), 525–56.

Hrdlička, A. (1945). *The Aleutian and Commander Islands and Their Inhabitants*. Philadelphia, PA: Wistar Institute of Anatomy and Biology.

Knecht, R. and Davis, R. (2003). *Archaeological Evaluation of Tanaxtaxak, the Amaknak Spit Site (UNL-055) Final Report*. On file at the Museum of the Aleutians, Unalaska, Alaska.

Lantis, M. (1970). The Aleut social system, 1750–1810, from early historical sources. In *Ethnohistory in Southwestern Alaska and the Southern Yukon*, ed. M. Lantis, pp. 139–295. Lexington, KY: University Press of Kentucky.

Lantis, M. (1984). Aleut. In *Handbook of North American Indians , Vol. 5: Arctic*, ed. D. Damas. Washington, DC: Smithsonian Institution Press.

Laughlin, W. S. (1963). The earliest Aleuts. *Anthropological Papers of the University of Alaska*, **10**(2), 73–91.

Lefèvre, C., Corbett, D., Crockford, S., *et al.* (2010). Faunal remains and intersite comparisons, In *The People at the End of the World: The Western Aleutians Project and the Archaeology of Shemya Island*, ed. D. Corbett, D. West, and C. Lefèvre, pp. 121–56. Aurora Monograph Series VIII. Anchorage, AK: Alaska Anthropological Association.

Liapunova, R. G. (1996). *Essays on the Ethnography of the Aleuts* (trans. J. Shelest). Rasmuson Library Historical Translation Series 9. Fairbanks, AK: University of Alaska Press.

Lin, P. M. and Crawford, M. H. (1983). A comparison of mortality patterns in human populations residing under diverse ecological conditions: a time series analysis. *Human Biology*, **55**, 35–62.

Madrigal, L. (1988). Hemoglobin genotype and fertility in a malarial environment: Limón, Costa Rica. Ph.D. dissertation, University of Kansas, Lawrence.

Maschner, H. and Reedy-Maschner, K. (1998). Raid, retreat, defend (repeat): the archaeology and ethnohistory of warfare on the North Pacific Rim. *Journal of Anthropological Archaeology*, **17**, 19–51.

McCartney, A. P. (1984). Prehistory of the Aleutian region. In *Handbook of North American Indians , Vol. 5: Arctic*, ed. D. Damas. Washington, DC: Smithsonian Institution Press.

Monmonier, M. (1973). Maximum-difference barriers: an alternative numerical regionalization method. *Geographical Analysis*, **3**, 245–61.

Okuno, M., Gualtieri, L., West, D., *et al.* (2007). Aleut shell mounds intercalated with tephra layers in Adak Island and adjacent volcanoes in the west-central Aleutians, Alaska, USA. *Journal of the Geological Society of Japan*, **113**(8), XI–XII.

O'Leary, M. (2001). Volcanic ash stratigraphy for Adak Island, central Aleutian archipelago. In *Archaeology in the Aleut Zone of Alaska, Some Recent Research*, ed. D. Dumond, pp. 215–34. University of Oregon Anthropological Papers 58. Eugene, OR: University of Oregon Press.

Orchard, T. and Crockford, S. (2010). Size estimation of Pacific cod (*Gadus macrocephalus*) remains from Shemya Island. In *The People at the End of the World: The Western Aleutians Project and the Archaeology of Shemya Island*, ed. D. Corbett, D. West, and C. Lefèvre, pp. 93–8. Aurora Monograph Series VIII. Anchorage, AK: Alaska Anthropological Association.

Prugnolle, F., Manica, A., and Balloux, F. (2005). Geography predicts neutral genetic diversity of human populations. *Current Biology*, **15**(5), R159–60.

Reedy-Maschner, K. (2010). Where did all the Aleut men go? Aleut male attrition and related patterns in the Aleutian historical demography and social organization. *Human Biology*, **82**(5–6), 583–611.

Rouse, L. (1949). The Caribs. In *Handbook of South American Indians , Vol. 4: The Circum-Caribbean Tribes* , pp. 547–65. Washington, DC: Smithsonian Institution Press.

Rubicz, R. C., Zlojutro, M., Sun, G., *et al.* (2010). Genetic architecture of a small, recently aggregated Aleut population: Bering Island, Russia. *Human Biology*, **82**(5–6), 719–36.

Savinetsky, A. B., Kiseleva, N. K., and Khassanov, B. F. (2004). Dynamics of sea mammal and bird populations of the Bering Sea region over the last several millennia. *Palaeogeography, Palaeoclimatology, Palaeoecology*, **209**, 335–52.

Savinetsky, A. B., Kiseleva, N. K., and Khassanov, B. F. (2010). Paleoenvironment – Holocene deposits from Shemya Island. In *The People at the End of the World: The Western Aleutians Project and the Archaeology of Shemya Island*, ed. D. Corbett, D. West, and C. Lefèvre, pp. 71–82. Aurora Monograph Series VIII. Anchorage, AK: Alaska Anthropological Association.

Savinetsky, A. B., West, D. L., Antipushina, Z., *et al.* (2012). The reconstruction of ecosystems history of Adak Island (Aleutian Islands) during the Holocene. In *The People Before: The Geology, Paleoecology and Archaeology of Adak Island, Alaska*, ed. D. West, V. Hatfield, E. Wilmerding, C. Lefèvre, and L. Gualtieri, Chapter 5. Alaska British Archaeological Reports International Series. Oxford, UK: British Archaeological Reports.

Schanfield, M. S., Brown, R., and Crawford, M. H. (1984). Immunoglobulin allotypes in the Black Caribs and Creoles of Belize. In *Current Developments in Anthropological Genetics*, Vol. 3: *Black Caribs: A Case Study of Biocultural Adaptation*, ed. M. H. Crawford, pp. 215–69. New York: Plenum Press.

Sorkina, A. (1963). *Tipy atmosfernoi tserkuliatsii I sviazannykh s nei vetrovykh polie nad severnoi chast'iu Tikhogo okeana (Atmospheric Circulation and the Related Wind Fields Over the North Pacific)*. Moscow: Gidro-meteorologicheskoe Izdatel'stvo.

Veltre, D. (1990). Perspectives on Aleut culture change during the Russian period. In *Russian America: The Forgotten Frontier*, ed. B. S. Smith and R. J. Barnett, pp. 175–83. Tacoma, WA: Washington State Historical Society.

West, D., Crawford, M., and Savinetsky, A. (2007). Genetics, prehistory and the colonisation of the Aleutian Islands. *Earth and Environmental Science Transactions of the Royal Society of Edinburgh*, **98**, 47–57.

West, D., Lefèvre, C., Corbett, D., and Savinetsky, A. (1999). Radiocarbon dates for the Near Islands, Aleutian Islands, Alaska. *Current Research in the Pleistocene*, **16**, 83–5.

Winterhalder, B. and Smith, E. A. (1981). *Hunter-gatherer Foraging Strategies: Ethnographic and Archaeological Analyses*. Chicago, IL: University of Chicago Press.

Zlojutro, M., Rubicz, R. C., and Crawford, M. H. (2009). Mitochondrial DNA and Y-chromosome variation in five Eastern Aleut communities: evidence for genetic substructure in the Aleut population. *Annals of Human Biology*, **36** (5), 511–26.

6

Kin-structured migration and colonization

INTRODUCTION

The process of Mendelian heredity whereby genes are passed from parents to offspring creates biological kinship; kin in this sense are individuals sharing alleles identical by descent from a common ancestor. This mechanism is the basis of inclusive fitness (Hamilton, 1964) and kin selection (Maynard Smith, 1964). Cooperation, even altruism, becomes rational from this shared gene perspective. In contrast, mating with close kin, inbreeding, may have negative fitness consequences. Thus genetic kinship motivates social behavior promoting association and cooperation among kin and regulating mating to avoid inbreeding.

Dispersal, the non-return migration of individuals, has associated costs and benefits (see Shields, 1987). Among other costs, dispersers lose the support of their biological kin in the natal population. On the positive side, finding unrelated mates in the new population avoids inbreeding depression.

Humans, as social animals, share this basic pattern of kin cooperation and the avoidance of inbreeding. However, in addition, human societies are characterized by elaborate systems of kin reckoning and relationships. These systems of consanguinity and affinity have formed the basis for social relations throughout most of our history. The diversity of forms of kinship has been a major focus of research by anthropologists over the history of the discipline.

Thus human migration and dispersal, while subject to the same costs and benefits as any other species, may be more complexly

Causes and Consequences of Human Migration, ed. Michael H. Crawford and Benjamin C. Campbell. Published by Cambridge University Press. © Cambridge University Press 2012.

structured by kinship rules and patterns. As James (2008:6) says, kin relationships "can in principle stretch out over distance and time, providing a framework for human mobility...". The cooperating group of local kin may become part of a network of related communities over space and time. Exchange of mates and groups of migrants occurs within this framework and, not surprisingly in a universe of kin relations, migrating and colonizing groups may comprise kin, a pattern termed "kin-structured migration" or KSM (Fix, 1978, 2004).

KSM will be the focus of this chapter: the causes of kin structuring, the sociocultural and techno-environmental conditions which promote kin structuring, and especially on its genetic consequences. Although migration is the focal topic, colonization, which is simply migration to a previously unoccupied habitat, will also be discussed.

The larger issue framing this discussion is the importance of population structure in understanding human variation and evolution. Lacking such an understanding of the factors affecting human mating, dispersal, and subdivision, "explanations" of global patterns of gene distributions are often just "good stories." Genes, like potsherds, do not travel by themselves: migrating/colonizing organisms are required. The environmental and/or cultural (including kinship) mechanisms promoting and structuring migration need to be taken into account to evaluate these stories.

KIN STRUCTURE

Biological kin share genes; therefore, a group of kin are more genetically similar than a random group of individuals. For example, full sibs share half their genes by inheritance from their two parents; half-sibs, sharing only one parent, possess one quarter of their genes identical by descent; first cousins possess one eighth, and so on. The gene pool of a group of full siblings, no matter how large, comprises only the four genes for any locus derived from their two parents as compared with twice the population number in an unrelated group. Just as relatedness reduces the effective population size (N_e) for genetic drift, kin structuring can be seen to reduce the effective number of migrants (m_e). Again as for genetic drift, the fewer independent genomes in a kin-structured group increases the likelihood of deviation from the parental gene frequency. Put another way, a migrant kin group may represent a biased sample of the population of origin.

CAUSES AND PREVALENCE OF KSM

Individuals and groups of individuals migrate for many reasons (see other chapters in this volume). Rates of migration depend on the ecology and economics of the sending and receiving populations. Local populations of some classic hunting-gathering societies such as the !Kung San seem in constant flux whereas other small-scale agricultural societies such as the Gainj of New Guinea are much more closed (see Fix, 1999 for these and other examples). The pattern of migration, whether individuals or groups, moving for economic or marital reasons, random or kin structured, is also variable among populations. A comprehensive theory of migration would encompass all these aspects.

One measure of the importance of KSM is its prevalence; is it widespread across the geographic range and/or throughout the evolutionary history of our species? This question, in turn, is dependent on the relative strength of the factors promoting kin structuring.

Although kinship plays some role in all human (and many animal) populations, its importance as an organizing principle for society varies. In many of the small-scale human societies familiar to anthropologists, kinship is *the* sociopolitical charter for group structure and behavior; in the contemporary United States, in contrast, kin other than the nuclear family often are not the central players in social life. However, kin-structured *migration* depends not only on the social importance of kin but also crucially on the rate and pattern of migration.

Not surprisingly, the societies in which KSM was first extensively documented, the Semai Senoi of Malaysia (Fix, 1978) and the Yanomamo of Venezuela (Neel and Salzano, 1967), are both village-level polities (*local group level* of Johnson and Earle, 1987) in which kinship is the primary factor in social life. Further, both have been characterized as "fission–fusion" type societies (Fix, 1975; Neel and Salzano, 1967; see also Salzano, 2009). Local settlement populations of both are generally small (less than 250 individuals) and comprise groups of kin. In the short term, settlements are relatively endogamous; however, periodically the local group splits or a group hives off and migrates to another established local group or founds a new settlement in an unoccupied area. Particularly among the Yanomamo, fission is the result of social tensions arising in the settlement. In the absence of authority to settle disputes, migration away from the local group removes the antagonists and resolves the problem. Because of the extensive nature of land use among the horticultural Yanomamo, much unoccupied territory is available for founding new settlements. Since splits occur between opposed kin groups, and in the Yanomamo case these are generally patrilineally organized, Neel and Salzano (1967) called the process "lineal effect," emphasizing the unilineal descent principle linking the kin groups.

The Semai Senoi also practiced swidden cultivation in a tropical forest environment (Dentan, 1968; Fix, 1982). They are similar to the Yanomamo in several respects including the fission–fusion dynamic and relatively small settlements comprising mainly kin groups (Fix, 1975). The Semai differ strikingly in other features, however. In contrast to the importance of feuding among the Yanomamo (Chagnon, 1968), the Semai are a completely non-violent people (Dentan, 1968). Further, Semai descent reckoning is bilateral rather than unilineal; kindreds rather than lineages are the social components of Semai society. Fission may result from unresolved disputes but also whenever any abnormal situation occurs in a settlement such as a severe disease outbreak causing "too many" deaths.

The consequences of Semai settlement fission is also similar to the Yanomamo: groups of kin, now linked by bilateral rather than lineal ties, migrate as a group. For this reason, kin-structured migration and kin-structured colonization are more generally applicable terms with which to replace "lineal effect."

Clearly KSM is not limited to societies practicing unilineal descent or, for that matter, swidden cultivators. Several studies of "Old Order" brethren such as the Amish and the Hutterites in the Americas have identified kin structuring as part of colony fission (Crawford et al., 1989; Hurd, 1983; Melton et al., 2010; Olsen, 1987). Gonzalez-Martin and Toja (2002) showed that migrant collectives in the small nation of Andorra comprised kin groups. Other examples include the families emigrating from Tristan da Cunha (Roberts, 1968) and the role of kinship in structuring migration in the French West Indies (Leslie et al., 1980).

Indeed, migration of groups of biological kin may not be uncommon among non-human populations. Storz (1999:564) states: "Because kinship appears to play an important role in maintaining behavioral cohesiveness of social groups (Armitage, 1984), fissioning of groups along kin lines may prove to be a common feature of the demography of social mammals." Cheverud et al. (1978), working from the excellent genealogical records kept for the rhesus macaques of Cayo Santiago, showed that social groups fissioned along kin lines. Even non-social mammals such as prosimian primates show evidence of kin-based spatial patterning suggesting non-random kin-structured dispersal (Kappeler *et al.*, 2002). Nor is kin-based fissioning confined to mammal species. For example, Whitlock (1994) demonstrated non-random familial-based fission groups among forked fungus beetles. At even greater remove from humans, Don Levin and I (Levin and Fix, 1989) argued that KSM might be especially effective in some plant species.

Despite its widespread occurrence, certainly not all migration is kin structured. Manderscheid *et al.* (1994) asked the question "Is migration kin structured?". After attempting to discover the effects of KSM on genetic variation among a small sample of populations, they concluded that they could find no evidence for it. This conclusion, of course, does not answer their question since it only applies to the populations they studied and further depends on the statistical power of their test of the genetic effects of KSM (see Fix, 1999 for further discussion of this point). In fact, five of the six human societies included in their sample are confined to a single culture area – Papua New Guinea. Many of these societies, including the Gainj (Wood, 1987), part of their sample, are densely populated agricultural communities with low rates of migration. Movements of groups of kin are unlikely to occur under these circumstances and migration is mostly movements of individual women to their husband's villages at marriage.

In a very different context, the founders of the Plymouth Colony in 1620–3 also failed to show kin linkages (McCullough and Barton, 1991). This group of migrants included many nuclear families but since recruitment was from a wide area of England and religion rather than kinship was the organizing principle for the community, kin ties among families were rare.

Thus the extent to which migration is kin structured will depend on societal and environmental conditions. Large, high-density, low-mobility populations where most migrants are individuals define one pole of a continuum; small-scale, kin-based, high-mobility, or expanding populations the other (see Fix, 1999 for more examples).

GENETIC CONSEQUENCES OF KSM

An important role of migration in evolutionary theory is to reduce genetic variation among exchanging populations. Indeed, for many of the classic population structure models, migration was the primary force stabilizing regional gene frequencies as well as the cause for genetic similarity among local populations of the region (Fix, 1999).

Clearly this result depends on migrants being a representative sample of the donor population gene pool. However, any sampling event may produce deviation from the mean frequency of the population, as Sewall Wright (1955) pointed out long ago.

KSM and kin-structured founder (lineal) effect can produce potentially highly deviant allele frequencies among a group of migrants since the sample is biased rather than random. A group of kin share genes through common descent; individual members of the group do not represent independent genomes. As a consequence, KSM not only may not retard local genetic differentiation, it may contribute to it. Alan Rogers (1988) for this reason has included KSM as another component of genetic drift. Founder effect has traditionally been seen as a differentiating force aligned with intergenerational random genetic drift. Neel and his associates (Neel and Salzano, 1967; Smouse *et al.*, 1981) demonstrated that kin structure significantly augments founder effect since the likelihood of a genetically biased sample of kin deviating from the population average is greatly increased.

A major evolutionary consequence of KSM and kin-structured colonization is genetic microdifferentiation (Fix, 1978; Neel and Salzano, 1967). The classic view of the causes of genetic variation among local populations is that small colonies undergo intergenerational random drift in isolation; that is, without the homogenizing effect of migration and gene flow. However, when migration and/or colonization is kin structured, large numbers of migrants may actually increase genetic variation among populations.

An example of KSM from the Semai Senoi (Fix, 1978) shows how even an adaptive allele such as hemoglobin E, protective against malaria, can become locally highly variable in frequency. Figure 6.1 presents the core of a migrant group that fissioned from one settlement and fused with another. As previously noted, Semai settlements are small ($N = 50$–250) and the large family represented in this pedigree can make an impact both on the population from which it split and the one with which it fused. Note that the numerous members of the family homo- or heterozygous for hemoglobin E represent a large subtraction from the donor group and a large addition to the Hb E frequency in the recipient. Table 6.1 shows the Hb E frequencies for seven Semai settlements. There is no apparent difference among these settlements in the prevalence of malaria. None are particularly isolated from the others; all show high rates of intermigration. The most likely explanation for this variation is the history of fission and fusion and founding of new settlements by kin-structured groups.

Table 6.1. *Hemoglobin E allele frequencies (Q_E) in seven Semai settlement populations*

Settlement	N	N_T	Q_E
SA	272	196	0.168
KE	69	34	0.206
RU	107	75	0.346
KL	54	31	0.242
BU	107	80	0.250
KA	50	32	0.187
CH	117	72	0.160
Total	776	520	0.215

Note: N refers to the total population of each settlement (in 1968) and N_T to the number of individuals tested.
Source: From Fix and Lie-Injo (1975).

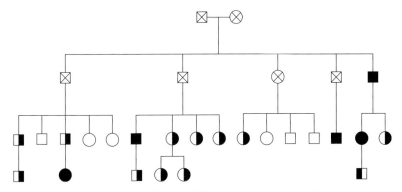

Figure 6.1 Genealogy of a Semai fission migrant group. Males are shown as squares; females as circles. Hemoglobin E homozygotes (EE) are darkened, heterozygotes (AE) half-darkened, and AA homozygotes are undarkened. Deceased individuals are crossed. (From Fix, 1978.)

On the basis of detailed reconstructed village histories, Smouse *et al.* (1981) and Hunley *et al.* (2008) provide strong evidence for the impact of kin-structured founder (lineal) effect in the Yanomamo.

Thus two societies for which we have excellent documentation for KSM and kin-structured founder effect, Semai and Yanomamo, are markedly genetically microdifferentiated. For both cases, the causal relationship has been clearly established.

Theoretical work has also verified the role of KSM in increasing genetic variation. Rogers (1987) has shown that the expectation of genetic variation among a set of local populations is a function of the size of the groups, the effective migration rate among groups, and the degree of kin structuring of the migrants. The latter parameter depends on both the size of the migrant group and the degree of relatedness of the migrants. This result fits well with the empirical findings from the Semai and Yanomamo where the fission–fusion dynamic produces relatively large migrant groups of close relatives. Rogers (1987) concludes that KSM might increase the ratio of among to within group variances by as much as threefold.

Bryan Epperson (1994, 2003) has also studied the role of stochastic and kin-structured migration in increasing variation among populations. An important conclusion of his work is the importance of *shared* effects among subpopulations. He (Epperson, 1994) found that when migrant groups originating in one local population move to different nearby populations, the genetic effects on the receiving populations may be correlated, thereby drastically changing the spatial pattern of variation.

Michael Wade and colleagues (Wade *et al.*, 1994) modeled the effects of kin-structured colonization on genetic variation, particularly the difference that might be expected between autosomal and mitochondrial genomes when dispersion is due to the movement of a few related females. They note that their model, although not focused on human populations, is relevant to situations of range expansion and invasion of new habitats, certainly a feature of early human history. They show that bottlenecks associated with kin-structured colonization sharply reduce cytoplasmic diversity while preserving much of the variation in the nuclear genome.

The fact that a kin structured migrant group represents fewer independent genomes than the actual number of individuals in the group means that the effective migration rate is reduced. Calculation of migration rates based on simply the number of migrants fails to correctly measure the true impact on donor and recipient gene pools. In comparison, since movement among local populations is often quite substantial in small-scale societies (Fix, 1999), in contrast to the "myth of the primitive isolate" (Terrell *et al.*, 1997), genetic microdifferentiation and genetic drift are quite compatible with demographically realistic migration rates and sizes of migrant groups.

For instance, Barbujani *et al.* (1995) found that several explanations were consistent with the observed pattern of gene frequency clines across Europe first attributed to demic diffusion of agriculturalists by Ammerman and Cavalli-Sforza (1984). One explanation that fit the data involved repetitive founder effects as expanding agricultural-ists completely replaced the indigenous European foragers. A problem (disregarding other objections to the argument) with the Barbujani *et al.* model was the extremely small size of the founding colonies (eight individuals) required to produce the founder effects generating the cline in gene frequencies. While conceivable, such tiny founding groups seem unlikely on sociocultural grounds. However, kin-structured groups of *effective* size eight could include a larger number of related individuals. I (Fix, 1997) showed via simulation that kin-structured migrant groups comprising 25 persons emulated the effective rate required by the Barbujani *et al.* model.

Another illustration of the effect of kin structure in reducing the effective size of migrant and founding groups is Eller's (2002) model of the population structure of Pleistocene human populations. Eller was concerned with the very small effective breeding size (N_e) inferred for the entire human species at some point in prehistory. Estimates using genetic data from contemporary populations were on the order of 10 000 persons (Harpending *et al.*, 1993), a very severe bottleneck.

Such a small breeding population seemed to validate the origins of modern humans from a single African population; a wider geo-graphic network of gene flow among prehistoric populations would have been unlikely to be maintained without a larger species popula-tion. However, as Eller (2002) pointed out, the *effective* size (N_e) may be sharply reduced from the breeding size (N_b) by several factors including unequal sex ratio and variation in male and female mating success (Nunney, 1999) as well as temporal fluctuations in population size (Vucetich *et al.*, 1997). The census size (N_c) will always be larger than either N_b or N_c since young and old persons are not members of the breeding population.

Eller (2002) focused on another source of lowered N_e: population extinction and recolonization. She argued that if local populations in the Pleistocene were subject to periodic extinction and their habitat was reinhabited by founders from a different local group, N_b would be much reduced.

We have no direct evidence as to whether such a population structure was common in prehistory. There are certainly well-documented cases of extreme population bottlenecks occurring in con-temporary small-scale societies, the island of Tristan da Cunha being the best example (Roberts, 1968). The complete population record kept by members of the island from its founding in the early nineteenth century allowed Roberts and his colleagues to follow the contributions of specific ancestors through the entire history of the population. Although never going extinct, the island population experienced dramatic bottlenecks. The genetic contributions of individuals waxed and waned as large groups emigrated from the island or died in accidents. Roberts (1968) also pointed out that the magnitude of gene frequency shifts was increased by the kin structuring of emigrant groups, which he called "booster effect."

In Eller's (2002) model, local population extinction was followed by recolonization, allowing for founder effects. A continuing series of such founder events would increase genetic variation (F_{ST}) and reduce the overall effective size of the total set of populations (or metapopulation; Hanski and Gilpin, 1997). Using a simplification for mathematical tractability, the classic island model of migration, along with assumptions regarding equal probability of extinction for all demes, she was able to show that both the extinction rate and the degree of population differentiation (F_{ST}) will affect the ratio of N_b to N_e. Higher extinction rates generate more founding events, increasing F_{ST} and lowering N_e in relation to N_b.

She did not include KSM in the formal model, but did note that if "the colonization process includes a small number of colonists or genetically related colonists due to inbreeding or kin-structured migration" (Eller, 2002:9), the disparity between census and effective sizes is more likely. Indeed, kin-structured founder effect, as Neel and Salzano (1967) established long ago, greatly augments random founder effect in producing genetic microdifferentiation. Under these circumstances, population bottlenecks of the sort experienced on Tristan da Cunha, with large in- and out-flows of kin-structured migrant groups, would produce outcomes similar to the extinction/recolonization process.

IMPORTANCE OF POPULATION STRUCTURE IN ANTHROPOLOGICAL GENETICS

Few if any species comprise a single panmictic population of randomly interbreeding individuals. Certainly the human species is hierarchically structured into large geographic groups, regional populations, and a myriad of somewhat endogamous local populations.

For much of its history, anthropological genetics has been concerned with studying population structure (Harpending, 2007); that is, the sizes of local demes and the amount and pattern of migration among them (Fix, 1999). These studies tended to focus on genetic variation among regional sets of local populations (e.g. Neel and

Salzano, 1967) and identified spatial, demographic, and sociocultural variables as determinants of genetic structure.

More recently, many human geneticists have shifted to a global level of analysis, examining the human genome in an attempt to recover the demographic and migrational history of the species based on presumably neutral molecular markers. As Harpending (2007) reminds us, such inference fails when natural selection affects the frequencies of genetic variants, an increasingly likely complication as new data implicating strong recent selection in the human genome come to light (Cochran and Harpending, 2009).

However, the failure to take into account natural selection is not the only shortcoming of global analysis. Based on genetic data, the large-scale geographic pattern of similarity is used to infer the biological historical relationships among populations. A salient example is the big book of Cavalli-Sforza and colleagues (Cavalli-Sforza *et al.*, 1994) which presents human history as a set of tree diagrams, an analysis that implicitly assumes the genetic divergence arises only from population splitting, migration, and isolation (see Fix, 2008 for a critique). There is no justification for this assumption. Empirical studies of human populations exhibit considerable diversity in patterns of migration and population structure (Fix, 1999).

If we are to understand human demographic history over the long span, it is important to understand the variety of population processes that are responsible for genetic patterns. As Cox (2006:390) states, "because demographic process in small groups are the currency of large-scale demographic events, a better appreciation of stochasticity in small human populations is a prerequisite to understanding major demographic events in human history."

Migration patterns are key elements defining population structure. Classical models of migration, including the island model and isolation by distance, failed to consider the inherent stochasticity to which Cox (2006) refers. Migrants from small groups always represent a sample of their parental gene pool and therefore their gene frequencies at many loci may differ by chance alone. KSM increases the probability of such deviations since the migrant sample is biased by shared ancestry.

When new colonies are formed by kin-structured groups, initial genetic divergence between the original and new populations may be great. Rather than reflecting a long period of isolation and divergence through intergenerational random genetic drift, genetic differentiation may be recent. Under these circumstances, reconstructing population history from contemporary genetic similarity or differences is not simply a matter of constructing dendrograms. Rather an understanding of the sociocultural characteristics of the populations and the amount and pattern of migration, great or small, individual or group, kin-structured or not, is a prerequisite. Similar contemporary allele distributions may be compatible with many migrational scenarios. Additional, complementary evidence is needed to decide among these alternatives. For those societies possessing attributes compatible with KSM, the added stochastic variability of migration and colony formation should be incorporated in genetic demographic models.

In so far as many ancestral human groups were dependent on extensive systems of land use, were small, with low population densities, and were highly mobile (Fix, 1999), KSM may have played an important role in human genetic history. Since the early history of our species involved an extreme range expansion, and if such colonization of new areas was accomplished by groups of related families (as would occur in societies such as the Yanomamo or Semai), the potential role of kin-structured founder effect is great.

Finally, the study of population structure and kinship helps justify the term "anthropology" in anthropological genetics. Anthropology has traditionally been concerned with human variation, cultural, linguistic, and biological, through time. For this reason, anthropology is best positioned to understand the multiple factors determining genetic variation. Migration, its patterns, causes, and consequences, is central to population structure analysis and thus to the broader understanding of human genetic structure and history.

REFERENCES

Ammerman, A. J. and Cavalli-Sforza, L. L. (1984). *The Neolithic Transition and the Genetics of Populations in Europe*. Princeton, NJ: Princeton University Press.

Armitage, K. B. (1984). Recruitment in yellow-bellied marmot populations: kinship, philopatry, and individual variability. In *The Biology of Ground-dwelling Squirrels*, ed. J. O. Murie and G. R. Michener, pp. 377–403. Lincoln, NE: University of Nebraska Press.

Barbujani, G., Sokal, R. R., and Oden, N. L. (1995). Indo-European origins: a computer-simulation test of five hypotheses. *American Journal of Physical Anthropology*, **96**, 109–32.

Cavalli-Sforza, L. L., Menozzi, P., and Piazza, A. (1994). *The History and Geography of Human Genes*. Princeton, NJ: Princeton University Press.

Chagnon, N. A. (1968). *Yanomamo: The Fierce People*. New York: Holt, Rinehart and Winston.

Cheverud, J., Buettner-Janusch, J., and Sade, D. (1978). Social group fission and the origin of intergroup genetic differentiation among the rhesus monkeys of Cyao Santiago. *American Journal of Physical Anthropology*, **49**, 449–56.

Cochran, G. and Harpending, H. (2009). *The 10,000 Year Explosion*. New York: Basic Books.

Cox, M. (2006). Extreme patterns of variance in small populations: placing limits on human Y-chromosome diversity through time in the Vanuatu Archipelago. *Annals of Human Genetics*, **71**, 390–406.

Crawford, M. H., Dykes, D. D., and Polesky, H. F. (1989). Genetic structure of Mennonite populations of Kansas and Nebraska. *Human Biology*, **61**, 493–514.

Dentan, R. K. (1968). *The Semai: A Nonviolent People of Malaya*. New York: Holt, Rinehart and Winston.

Eller, E. (2002). Population extinction and recolonization in human demographic history. *Mathematical Biosciences*, **177&178**, 1–10.

Epperson, B. K. (1994). Spatial and space-time correlations in systems of subpopulations with stochastic migration. *Theoretical Population Biology*, **46**, 160–97.

Epperson, B. K. (2003). *Geographical Genetics*. Monographs in Population Biology 38. Princeton, NJ: Princeton University Press.

Fix, A. G. (1975). Fission-fusion and lineal effect: aspects of the population structure of the Semai Senoi of Malaysia. *American Journal of Physical Anthropology*, **43**, 295–302.

Fix, A. G. (1978). The role of kin-structured migration in genetic microdifferentiation. *Annals of Human Genetics*, **41**, 329–39.

Fix, A. G. (1982). Genetic structure of the Semai. In *Current Developments in Anthropological Genetics: Ecology and Population Structure*, ed. M. H. Crawford and J. H. Mielke, pp. 179–204. New York: Plenum.

Fix, A. G. (1997). Gene frequency clines produced by kin-structured founder effects. *Human Biology*, **69**, 663–73.

Fix, A. G. (1999). *Migration and Colonization in Human Microevolution*. Cambridge, UK: Cambridge University Press.

Fix, A. G. (2004). Kin-structured migration: causes and consequences. *American Journal of Human Biology*, **16**, 387–94.

Fix, A. G. (2008). Genetic dendrograms and Malaysian population history. *Structure and Dynamics: eJournal of Anthropology and Related Sciences*, 3:2: article 7. (http://repositories.cdlib.org/imbs/socdyn/sdeas/vol3/iss2/art7)

Fix, A. G. and Lie-Injo, L. E. (1975). Genetic microdifferentiation in the Semai Senoi of Malaysia. *American Journal of Physical Anthropology*, **43**, 47–55.

Gonzalez-Martin, A. and Toja, D. I. (2002). Inbreeding, isonymy, and kin-structured migration in the principality of Andorra. *Human Biology*, **7**, 587–600.

Hamilton, W. D. (1964). The genetical evolution of social behavior, I and II. *Journal of Theoretical Biology*, **7**, 1–52.

Hanski, I. A. and Gilpin, M. E. (1997). *Metapopulation Biology: Ecology, Genetics, and Evolution*. San Diego, CA: Academic Press.

Harpending, H. (2007). Anthropological genetics: present and future. In *Anthropological Genetics: Theory, Methods and Applications*, ed. M. Crawford, pp. 456–66. Cambridge, UK: Cambridge University Press.

Harpending, H., Sherry, S., Rogers, A., and Stoneking, M. (1993). The genetic structure of ancient human populations. *Current Anthropology*, **34**, 483–96.

Hunley, K. L., Spence, J. E., and Merriwether, D. A. (2008). The impact of group fissions on genetic structure in Native South America and implications for human evolution. *American Journal of Physical Anthropology*, **135**, 195–205.

Hurd, J. P. (1983). Kin relatedness and church fissioning among the "Nebraska" Amish of Pennsylvania. *Social Biology*, **30**, 59–66.

James, W. (2008). Why "kinship"? New questions on an old topic. In *Early Human Kinship: From Sex to Social Reproduction*, ed. N. J. Allen, H. Callan, R. Dunbar, and W. James, pp. 3–20. Oxford, UK: Blackwell.

Johnson, A. W. and Earle, T. (1987). *The Evolution of Human Societies: From Foraging Group to Agrarian State*. Stanford, CA: Stanford University Press.

Kappeler, P. M., Wimmer, B., Zinner, D., and Tautz, D. (2002). The hidden matrilineal structure of a solitary lemur: implications for primate social evolution. *Proceedings of the Royal Society of London: B*, **269**, 1755–63.

Leslie, P. W., Dyke, B., and Morrill, W. T. (1980). Celibacy, emigration, and genetic structure in small populations. *Human Biology*, **52**, 115–30.

Levin, D. A. and Fix, A. G. (1989). A model of kin-migration in plants. *Theoretical and Applied Genetics*, **77**, 332–6.

Manderscheid, E., Brannan, J., and Rogers, A. R. (1994). Is migration kin structured? *Human Biology*, **66**, 49–58.

Maynard Smith, J. (1964). Group selection and kin selection. *Nature*, **201**, 1145–7.

McCullough, J. M. and Barton, E. Y. (1991). Relatedness and kin-structured migration in a founding population: Plymouth. *Human Biology*, **63**, 355–66.

Melton, P. E, Mosher, J. J., Rubicz, R., Slojutro, M., and Crawford, M. H. (2010). Mitochondrial DNA diversity in Mennonite communities from the midwestern United States. *Human Biology*, **82**, 267–89.

Neel, J. V. and Salzano, F. M. (1967). Further studies on the Xavante Indians. X: Some hypotheses-generalizations resulting from these studies. *American Journal of Human Genetics*, **19**, 554–74.

Nunney, L. (1999). The effective size of a hierarchically structured population. *Evolution*, **53**, 1–10.

Olsen, C. L. (1987). The demography of colony fission from 1878–1970 among the Hutterites of North America. *American Anthropologist*, **89**, 823–37.

Roberts, D. F. (1968). Genetic effects of population size reduction. *Nature*, **220**, 1084–8.

Rogers, A. R. (1987). A model of kin-structured migration. *Evolution*, **41**, 417–26.

Rogers, A. R. (1988). Three components of genetic drift in subdivided populations. *American Journal of Physical Anthropology*, **77**, 435–50.

Salzano, F. M (2009). The fission-fusion concept. *Current Anthropology*, **50**, 959.

Shields, W. M. (1987). Dispersal and mating systems: investigating their causal connections. In *Mammalian Dispersal Patterns*, ed. B. D. Chepko-Sade and Z. T. Halpin, pp. 3–24. Chicago, IL: University of Chicago Press.

Smouse, P. E., Vitzthum, V. J., and Neel, J. V. (1981). The impact of random and lineal fission on the genetic divergence of small human groups: a case study among the Yanomama. *Genetics*, **98**, 179–91.

Storz, J. F. (1999). Genetic consequences of mammalian social structure. *Journal of Mammology*, **80**, 553–69.

Terrell, J. E., Hunt, T. L., and Gosden, C. (1997). The dimensions of social life in the Pacific: human diversity and the myth of the primitive isolate. *Current Anthropology*, **38**, 155–96.

Vucetich, J. H., Waite, T. A., and Nunney, L. (1997). Fluctuating population size and the ratio of effective to census population size. *Evolution*, **51**, 2017–21.

Wade, M. J., McKnight, M. L., and Shaffer, H. B. (1994). The effects of kin-structured colonization on nuclear and cytoplasmic genetic diversity. *Evolution*, **48**, 1114–20.

Whitlock, M. C. (1994). Fission and the genetic variance among populations: the changing demography of forked fungus beetle populations. *American Naturalist*, **143**, 820–9.

Wood, J. W. (1987). The genetic demography of the Gainj of Papua New Guinea. 2: Determinants of effective population size. *American Naturalist,* **129**, 165–87.

Wright, S. (1955). Classification of the factors of evolution. *Cold Spring Harbor Symposium Quantitative Biology*, **20**, 16–24.

7

The role of diet and epigenetics in migration: molecular mechanisms underlying the consequences of change

INTRODUCTION

Genotypes establish the developmental parameters and constraints on human traits, but environmental factors interacting with genes ultimately shape many phenotypes. These resulting phenotypes must prove beneficial for both survival and reproduction to continue any species. During their evolutionary history, human beings have demonstrated great capacity for survival and reproductive success while adapting to a wide range of environments. By interacting with increasingly complex cultural strategies to manage environmental advantages, genetic variation found in the human genome supported the human ancestral migrations out of Africa and around the globe. However, the manner by which genes and environment communicate to affect phenotypes remains unclear. The plasticity seen in fetal development and neonatal growth patterns appears to reflect the presence of early physiological acclimatization to environmental signals (Cutfield *et al.*, 2007). Such signals leave lasting directives for gene expression, metabolic pathways and future adaptation capabilities without DNA mutation (Waterland and Garza, 1999). Additionally, these signals provide potentially reversible regulations of gene expression that more rapidly respond to environmental fluctuation than responses originating through changes in the DNA sequencing (Burdge *et al.*, 2007). These "epigenetic" regulatory signals are transgenerational (Haig, 2004), yet the patterns are less robust across generations given their responsiveness to the environment. The reversible nature of these signal mechanisms leaves many unanswered

Causes and Consequences of Human Migration, ed. Michael H. Crawford and Benjamin C. Campbell. Published by Cambridge University Press. © Cambridge University Press 2012.

questions regarding the mode of environmental influence on phenotypic development during human evolution. Today's migrating populations experiencing rapid and dramatic changes in climate, food chain,
social, and economic factors provide a unique model for testing the
epigenetic hypotheses in humans.

Dietary intake is the primary environmental determinant of
phenotypic development. The resulting nutritional effects are continuous, variable, and complex, since nutrients may alter human gene
expression and physiological variation, the capacity for survival,
and ultimately evolution. The nutritional phenotype at any given
moment in time is context dependent (i.e. age, sex, and health status),
representing the sum of many gene-by-gene (epistatic) and gene-by-
environmental (nutrient) interactions during the life course. Therefore,
identifying the nutritional effects underlying human evolution presents
a major challenge. Dietary intake primarily impacts evolution through
differential survivorship and fertility when macronutrients fail to provide adequate energy and components for growth, development, and
maintenance (Ellison, 2008). Micronutrients produce a more concentrated effect on gene expression. Their direct functions include acting
as ligands for transcription factor receptor and affecting signal transduction. Indirect effects occur with alteration of intermediate products
within metabolic pathways and energy production itself (Kaput and
Rodriguez, 2004). Dietary intake has additional far-reaching effects on
gene selection, and studies are now uncovering the evidence of nutrient
variation as evolutionary pressures on human populations. For instance,
variation in allelic frequencies is documented for enzymes of digestion,
metabolism, and utilization of nutrients, including lactose (Bersaglieri
et al., 2004), starches (Perry *et al.*, 2007), folate (Lucock and Yates, 2005;
Stover, 2006), alcohol (Eng *et al.*, 2007), and fructose (Ali *et al.*, 1998; Cox,
2002). Further studies identify genetic variation underlying nutrient
requirements (Stover, 2006), taste preferences (Kim and Drayna, 2005;
Tepper *et al.*, 2009), and lipid metabolism (Ordovas and Corella, 2005),
and illustrate the interwoven nature of human genes and diet. The
presence of genetic variation associated with dietary pressures noted
among populations strongly suggests that some variants conferred
advantages of survival that were instrumental during human migration
and expansion (Cochran and Harpending, 2009).

Illuminating the manner through which nutritional variation
affects gene expression, phenotypic variation and evolution is
increasingly possible today. Nutrients interact to create epigenetic
mechanisms, which function outside the DNA sequences and provide

another mode of communication between nutrition and genes (Scarino, 2008). This epigenome, operating through the mechanisms of DNA methylation, histone modification, and non-coding RNA, modulates the cross talk between genes and the nutritional environment. Its influence on developmental plasticity produces more rapid, flexible, and reversible phenotypic variation than altering of the DNA sequences (Burdge *et al.*, 2007; Delage and Dashwood, 2008; Mattick and Makunin, 2006; Ross and Milner, 2007). Moreover, this epigenome reflects recent history of generational nutritional exposure and may continue to serve as a more immediate source for communication of adaptation during an individual's interaction with the environment (Burdge *et al.*, 2007; Gluckman *et al.*, 2005; Ho and Burggren, 2010; Kuzawa, 2004). These epigenetic mechanisms are instrumental in the process of metabolic imprinting, which creates parent-specific patterns of gene expression during ontogeny (Hitchins and Moore, 2002; Waterland and Garza, 1999). The metabolic imprinting is considered to be transgenerational and permanent throughout an individual's lifetime. However, recent research has shown maternal dietary effects on the stability of fetal epigenetic patterns, thereby indicating a modifiable nature of metabolic imprinting (Heijmans *et al.*, 2008; Tobi *et al.*, 2009). Moreover, human studies now suggest dietary remodeling of epigenomes occurs throughout the life cycle (Choi and Friso, 2010; Gallou-Kabani *et al.*, 2007). This proposed transience of epigenetic signal mechanisms secondary to nutritional variation, however, makes consistency of their effects less robust and difficult to substantiate over many generations (Gluckman *et al.*, 2009; Ho and Burggren, 2010). While research documents dietary effects on epigenetic markers in animals, the process is far from clear in humans (Burdge *et al.*, 2007; Delage and Dashwood, 2008). Contemporary immigrants and their offspring, experiencing dramatic environmental and nutritional changes in a compressed time frame may, in fact, exhibit the effects of rapid and substantial alteration of the epigenome during the transition and these epigenetic markers may persist through several generations.

The consequences of migration may be seen as either beneficial and adaptive or detrimental, becoming the precursors of increased morbidity and mortality. The working premise of this chapter is that epigenetic mechanisms and metabolic fetal imprinting interact with varying diets to create nutritional epigenomes and phenotypes (Waterland and Garza, 1999), which are instrumental in human evolution. Despite their transmissibility, these epigenomes remain buffeted by environmental changes and are thus transient in nature, making their evolutionary significance difficult to interpret. The objectives of this chapter are to: (1) review the relationship of nutrients and human molecular mechanisms; (2) explore current literature documenting nutrition as a selective force in genetic and epigenetic evolution; (3) apply these concepts to examine health consequences encountered by contemporary migrating human populations; and (4) offer a strategy by which anthropological geneticists and nutritionists can utilize this information to test various hypotheses of nutrition and epigenetics in human populations.

RELATIONSHIP OF NUTRIENTS AND MOLECULAR MECHANISMS

Biocultural components of the nutritional phenotype

The nutritional phenotype is defined as the accumulation of the interactive processes between genotype, environmental factors, and nutritional behaviors. These interactions create individually unique patterns of metabolism, nutrient utilization, and gene expression. They are dynamic throughout the life course, dependent upon sex, age, stage of development, hormone balance, stress, health status, and timing of environmental exposures. Recent research suggests a consistent underlying nutritional phenotype originating in populations that historically experienced distinct dietary profiles over many generations (Hancock *et al.*, 2010; Holmes *et al.*, 2008). Such populations encounter greater health risks during transition to a widely disparate culture, especially during a fast-paced global transition.

Nutritional phenotypes represent the integrated patterns of chemical processes developed for survival. This complex network of pathways is challenged by: (1) the need to obtain, transport, and manage energy and nutrients; (2) maintenance of a constant internal environment within viable parameters of temperature, pH, cellular content, and energy for optimal function; (3) feedback mechanisms and communication between systems, tissues, and cells (Gropper *et al.*, 2005; Wardlaw and Insel, 1995). To meet these challenges, the individuals adapt to the nutrients available in the immediate environment, ultimately accentuating metabolic pathways advantageous in that environment and the individual's genetic programming. The resulting phenotype sets the stage for future metabolic adaptations. Interaction with diverse food chains, geographic-specific symbiotic gut flora, pathogens, and toxicological exposures further influence metabolism and continuously affect the metabolites available for an individual's use

(Balaresque *et al.*, 2007; Cobiac, 2007; Feil, 2006; Li *et al.*, 2008). Their dynamic biochemical profiles indicating an individual's nutrient exposure and metabolic outcome is tailored to a nutrient–environmental interaction and can be examined through biomarkers of nutrients, hormones, enzymes, and the cascade of intermediate and end products along the metabolic pathways (van Ommen *et al.*, 2010). This phenotype can be measured by allelic variation in the genome, transcriptome, and proteome to identify levels of gene expression. Biomarkers identifying patterns of dietary intake and diet-responsive metabolic pathways, and levels of physical exercise, body composition, and anthropometrics to indicate energy balance are also included (Goodacre, 2007; Zeisel *et al.*, 2005). Current advances in the study of epigenetics documenting maternal nutritional effects on fetal genetic imprinting *in utero* suggest that measures of imprinting, such as methylation patterns, be added to the list of quantified phenotype components. This epigenome should accompany familial dietary data and population history in order to profile nutritional influence from previous generations.

Causes of nutritional variation are both multifactorial and global, creating ongoing adaptive pressures during migration. Complex cultural behaviors affect nutrient variation and bioavailability, such as the choices of cooking utensils and food additives, both of which introduce novel elements into the system. Preparation and mixing of foods potentially enhance or impede nutrient bioavailability, taboos regulate intake, and dietary acculturation after migration alters nutritional status (Freimer *et al.*, 1983; Mintz and Du Bois, 2002). Agricultural practices, erosion, and leaching have depleted soils of nutrients in some areas (see review by Khoshgoftarmanesh *et al.*, 2010), while potential negative effects of genetic modification of foods coupled with lack of complete knowledge concerning bioactive elements and pesticides create pressures in others (Cellini *et al.*, 2004; Domingo, 2007; Kulper *et al.*, 2001; Magana-Gomez *et al.*, 2008; Walters, 2004). All of these factors carry the potential to become selective pressures when introduced to newly arrived individuals.

Changes in phenotypic profiles have become evident through the expression of a previously unidentified or silent gene whose functional relevance appears as a result of altered nutrient intake and metabolism (Kaput, 2004). Modern dietary patterns now impact physiological homeostasis through myriad disruptions. Alteration of the acid-base balance disrupts enzyme action, extreme imbalance of essential fatty acid ratios offset the balance of eicosanoid signaling in immune and inflammatory processes, a disrupted sodium–potassium ratio affects membrane dynamics, and altered glycemic loads impact related hormone signaling

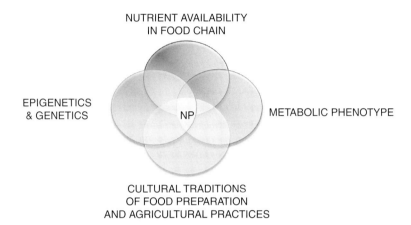

Nutritional Phenotypes

The sum influence of many gene-by-environmental interactions
over the life course

NUTRIENT AVAILABILITY
IN FOOD CHAIN

EPIGENETICS
& GENETICS

NP

METABOLIC PHENOTYPE

CULTURAL TRADITIONS
OF FOOD PREPARATION
AND AGRICULTURAL PRACTICES

Individuals have unique patterns of expression

Figure 7.1 Integrated model for the nutritional phenotype which illustrates the interwoven relationship of genetics, biology, culture, and environment.

and serum glucose levels (Cordain *et al.*, 2005). These alterations create an internal human environment that encourages the appearance of numerous and novel adaptive combinations in gene expression.

The nutritional phenotype (Figure 7.1) exists as a continuum of expression identified through the human genome, transcriptome, proteome, and metabolome (Go *et al.*, 2005). It is dependent upon ongoing interaction of cultural changes and the responsive epigenetic and genetic changes over time. The presence of any stable or consistent underlying nutritional phenotype existing throughout the life course remains unclear at this time.

NUTRITION AS A FORCE OF NATURAL SELECTION
AND EVOLUTION

Nutrition and gene expression

The complexity of the human organism presents multiple opportunities to demonstrate effects initiated by the interaction of genes and nutrients. The relationship is circular: nutrient variation in foods impacts the forces of evolution such as mutation and selection, and the genetic outcome in turn affects nutrient requirements. This cycle begins *in utero* with metabolic responsiveness to the maternal nutritional cues, thus creating the epigenome which also structures individual requirements, altering their capacity for biological access, metabolism, and utilization of nutrients (Molloy, 2004; Stover and Caudill, 2008). Additionally, the developmental trajectory of each individual is adjusted in response to the maternal nutritional cues in order to maximize survival (Gluckman *et al.*, 2009).

Adequate functioning of the genetic programming is primary to survival. Many nutrients impact a host of functions directly affecting DNA synthesis, structure, and integrity. Beyond the obvious sources of energy and necessary structural components found in diverse macronutrient fatty acids and amino acids, the importance of bioactive compounds and micronutrients to our genetic mechanisms is now being uncovered. B vitamins are crucial coenzymes in the synthesis and maintenance of DNA and for cell metabolism. Folate (B_9) is critical for one-carbon metabolism and synthesis of the epigenetic DNA methylation (Friso and Choi, 2002; Gropper *et al.*, 2005; Stover, 2009). Deficiencies of B vitamins result in chromosomal damage, including DNA damage mimicking that of radiation exposure and a range of problems including brain dysfunction and neuronal damage, immune function, and birth defects (Ames *et al.*, 2002). Nevertheless, excessive intake or supplementation of B vitamins to vulnerable individuals may actually prove deleterious to DNA structure (Mead, 2007; Ulrich and Potter, 2006).

Nutrients have significant effects on basic genetic expression and metabolic efficiency. Direct effects of nutrients on gene expression are documented in fatty acids, vitamin A and D metabolites, or soy's isoflavone genistein, which serve as ligands for transcription factor receptors. Receptors involved with vitamin A affect expression of the uncoupling protein (UCP) genes affecting thermogenesis (De Caterina and Madonna, 2004). Vitamin D receptors mediate the action of vitamin D in calcium homeostasis, bone density, and are thought to be involved in adipogenesis for energy storage (Wood, 2008). Zinc and green tea polyphenols are involved in signal transduction (Cousins *et al.*, 2010; Kaput and Rodriguez, 2004). Decreased intake of dietary nucleotides may result in the inhibition of a signal transduction pathway occurring as part of a feedback system seen in the down-regulation of necessary enzymes supporting cell growth, proliferation, and DNA synthesis (Cousins *et al.*, 2010; De Caterina and Madonna, 2004; Kaput and

Rodriguez, 2004). Variation in fatty acid intake affects the action of 5-LO (5-lipoxygenase), an enzyme which catalyzes polyunsaturated fatty acids into leukotrienes, eicosanoid hormones for mediating the inflammatory response. The omega-6 enhances while the omega-3 blunts inflammatory responses (Dwyer *et al.*, 2004).

Alteration in hormone function creates an additional form of epigenetic control over gene expression (Haig, 2004). Depending upon their construction, hormones affect transcription through an intricate cascade of protein membrane receptors, transduction, and cell signaling. Hormones binding with nuclear receptors alter transcription via the acetylation of histones which impacts the epigenetic mechanism of chromatin remodeling and ultimately gene expression. These tissue-specific nuclear receptors are sensitive to the developmental stage and serve as important mediators for the use of available nutrients during human development – in both fetal and neonatal development (Dauncey *et al.*, 2001). All of these nutrient–gene interactions affect human physiological function for adaptation and homeostatic balance. Disruptions of these functions result in disease.

The patterns of modern human migration provide the opportunity for nutritional phenotypes exhibiting a stable gene expression developed in one environment over generations to address novel forces found in new food chains (Schisler *et al.*, 2009). Such challenges place individuals at increased risk of disease during the transitions, and over prolonged exposure result in changes of allelic variation in populations. The epigenetic effects from such a challenge are unclear in humans at this time; however, microevolution during a compressed time frame is documented in recent dietary studies investigating exposures to changes in food processing and manufacture, as well as evaluation studies of dietary manipulation for disease prevention. Alteration in the food chain by a Western practice dramatically increased the intake of high fructose corn syrup resulting in increased prevalence of fructose intolerance. Research suggests that expression of previously silent alleles occurred with altered fructose intake (Ali and Cox, 1995; Coffee and Tolan, 2010). Dietary management reducing specific protein intake was established to prevent severe mental deficits resulting from phenylketonuria (PKU), a genetic inability to metabolize the amino acid phenylalanine. Supplementation of folic acid into foods was initiated to prevent birth defects. Both were effective preventive treatments; however, both dietary practices produced a selective environment for the survival of individuals, thus increasing vulnerable alleles in the populations (Lucock, 2007). Further research to determine the manner by which epigenetic mechanisms function in humans during these dietary shifts is greatly needed.

Nutrition and gene expression during expansion and evolution

Volumes have been written addressing the impact of diet and nutritional shifts during early human migrations and expansion (Crawford and Marsh, 1995; Harris and Ross, 1987; Ungar, 2007). Despite the surfeit of literature, nutritional effects on the relationship of human molecular biology, physiology, and evolution remain a matter of great debate, and nutrigenomics, the study of nutritional effects on gene expression, remains in its infancy. Although the increased intake of meat and fish is the focus of many studies, it appears that our capacity as omnivores is the key to modern human existence. The extensive metabolic pathways used to extract energy from a variety of macronutrient sources, coupled with the ability to modulate these pathways during physiological adaptation to substrate availability (Whitney and Rolfes, 2008) and environmental pressures, such as cold climates (Leonard *et al.*, 2005) and altitude (Flueck, 2009; Hochachka *et al.*, 1998), illustrate the role of human metabolic plasticity in survival. Increased intake of animal foods provided substantial nutrient density to support constructional changes in brain development and the subsequent energy requirements. Increased nutrient density allowed reduction in gut morphology, which was no longer needed to extract adequate nutrients (Aiello and Wheeler, 1995). It appears that this reduction in gut morphology increased physical flexibility and mobility to acquire greater variety of high-nutrient foods. Greater ability to obtain high-nutrient foods, coupled with reduced energy expenditure spent acquiring sufficient amounts of low-density foods, combine to encourage increased capacity to store energy in adipose tissue (Rotillo and Marchese, 2010). All these changes supported higher fertility, lower mortality, and increased human survivorship during fluctuations of food supplies associated with migration.

Dietary changes alone did not create the substantial evolutionary changes, but acted as a positive selective force interacting with genetic mutations. Comparative studies between humans and non-human primates point to variation of genetic effects between the two species in such genes as the MYH16 and its decrease of the masticatory muscle in humans (Perry *et al.*, 2005; Stedman *et al.*, 2004). The result was believed to reduce a morphological constraint on the brain case, thus allowing greater brain growth, cell differentiation, and greater expression of several genes affecting brain size (Zhang, 2003). This is further supported by increased fat intake – especially long-chain fatty acids and cholesterol from animal sources. The increased fat intake was coupled with the liver's efficient packaging and shipping of these lipids through the vascular system to meet cellular needs. Ultimately, the capacity to acquire nutrient-dense macronutrients and increase mitochondrial production of ATP supported energy demands of the increasingly complex nervous system and its intricate signaling (Allen, 2009).

Experimental work comparing gene expression in human–mouse orthologous diet-related genes identified those genes showing greater differences in promoter regions and amino acid sequences between human and chimpanzee than random genes. Implementing diets mimicking chimpanzee and human dietary profiles provoked differential genetic expression; greater gene expression was associated with diets profiling human intake. Moreover, genes expressed in the mouse liver were greater than those in the mouse brain (Somel *et al.*, 2008), thus adding plausibility to the hypothesis that increased capacity of liver to metabolize, package, and deliver fats for energy and construction played a major role in evolution. This increased capacity for cholesterol and triglyceride transport is also identified in a study by Haygood *et al.* (2007), who suggested that dietary pressures may be responsible for some of the phenotypic differences seen between humans and chimpanzees. Their study focused on positive selection of genetic promoter regions to account for differential gene expression between human and non-human primates. Many of the affected genes identified were related to metabolic processes. Specific areas which showed significant selection in genes and transcription factors were those regulating glucose metabolism, increased capacity for effective lipid transport, and adipocyte metabolism in response to dietary changes. While these genes are thought to have enhanced human evolution through increased metabolic capabilities, today in the face of dramatically different dietary patterns, many of them now play important roles in disease susceptibility (Haygood *et al.*, 2007).

Increased meat intake in humans, coupled with aquatic protein sources furnishing the essential fatty acids, expanded the repertoire of amino acids necessary to synthesize more functionally diverse proteins and fatty acids used extensively in brain and retinal synapses (Rotillo and Marchese, 2010). Finch and Stanford (2004) hypothesized that human selection favored genes supporting meat intake. Specifically they cited the example of three widely studied alleles of apolipoprotein E (*APOE e2*, *e3*, and *e4*), which program a major ligand involved in lipoprotein transport of fat and cholesterol through the blood to cells. The three APOE isoforms exhibit distinct functional variation. Although the *e3* allele is the most common in populations around the world, the ancestral allele *e4* is reported to produce the more efficient ligand for cell receptors of triglyceride-laden lipoproteins VLDL (very low density lipoprotein) (Kozlov *et al.*, 2009; Mahley and Rall, 1999) and shows greater responsiveness of serum cholesterol levels to dietary manipulation in humans (Ordovas *et al.*, 1995). Studies reporting higher frequencies of *e4* in northern European populations surmise that this allele supported increased survival under the stress of cold climate and seasonal starvation (Kozlov *et al.*, 2008; Lucotte *et al.*, 1997). Additionally, increased reproductive success of individuals carrying the *e4* has been reported in indigenous populations, but not European populations, again pointing to gene-by-environment involvement (Corbo *et al.*, 2004). The reproductive success and survival associated with *e4* explains the greater frequency of the *e4* polymorphism and lower or absent frequency of the *e2* polymorphism found in many indigenous populations, both in the circumpolar regions and South America (Crews *et al.*, 1993; Kamboh *et al.*, 1991, 1996; Mosher, 2002). Steroid hormones, vital for reproduction, organ development, and stress response are all synthesized from their common precursor cholesterol (Martinez-Arguelles and Papadopoulos, 2010), and thus are plausible explanations the Finch and Stanford theory due to *APOE* involvement with cholesterol as well as triglyceride transport to the cells. However, the presence of *e4* is also associated with higher serum cholesterol and major disease risks in Western populations (Jofre-Monseny *et al.*, 2008). This association of high cholesterol with *e4* is not found in circumpolar populations, as they have some of the lowest lipid profiles in the world despite their higher frequencies of *e4* (Kamboh *et al.*, 1996; Mosher, 2002).

An additional genetic adaptation to meat eating is suggested by changes associated with the polymorphisms of AGXT, which produce the enzyme alanine:glyoxylate amino transferase (AGT) responsible for detoxifying glyoxalate through transamination into the amino acid glycine (Birdsey *et al.*, 2004). Glycine is used as a major inhibitory neurotransmitter of the central nervous system, and in protein and nucleic acid synthesis. Without this detoxification process, excess levels of oxalate result in kidney and other organ damage (Coulter-Mackie and Rumsby, 2004; Nogueira *et al.*, 2000). AGT intracellular distribution is correlated with dietary profiles in mammals – higher in the mitochondria for carnivores, in the peroxisome for herbivores, and in both for omnivores. The evidence for specific dietary pressure on AGXT allelic frequency in human populations has been suggested; however, this remains controversial (Caldwell *et al.*, 2004; Ségurel *et al.*, 2010).

The benefits from animal protein intake are well documented. Meats are an excellent source of the vitamin B complex, which along with the essential amino acid tryptophan, support nicotinamide adenine dinucleotide (NAD) synthesis for oxidation/reduction reactions during ATP synthesis via glycolysis, the citric acid cycle, and the electron transport chain (Kaput and Rodriguez, 2004; Lucock, 2007). Meat also supplies zinc (Mann, 2000) which is thought to modulate the omega-3 plasma levels (Logan, 2004), affect gene expression (Mazzatti *et al.*, 2008), and mediate energy homeostasis via the hormone cell signal leptin synthesized in adipocytes (Mantzoros and Moschos, 1998). Zinc is also vital for proper functioning of the immune system, important for the survival of the organism (Gropper *et al.*, 2005). Increased meat intake is also associated with increased fat intake, thus supporting improved absorption of fat-soluble vitamins A, D, E, and K. As previously mentioned, both vitamins A and D are known ligands for nuclear receptors affecting gene expression, cell differentiation, visual acuity, and macronutrient metabolism (Kaput and Rodriguez, 2004; Lucock, 2007; Wood, 2008). Vitamin D binds with peroxisome proliferator-activated receptors (PPAR) affecting adipogenesis (Wood, 2008) and with the vitamin D receptor (VDR) regulates epidermal barrier formation (Oda *et al.*, 2009). Although we can only surmise the outcome of these specific nutrient effects during early evolution, nutrient–gene interactions appear vital to human survival.

Beyond the substantial evidence for selective pressures operating on meat intake, other dietary factors continue to influence genetic frequencies. Gene patterns associated with digestion, absorption, and metabolism also coincide with demographic and dietary trends. The advent of agriculture and increase in food production, storage, and processing brought new selective pressures. Population variation in allelic frequencies has been reported in the following: lactase gene (LCT) (Bersaglieri *et al.*, 2004), amylase (AMY 1) (Perry *et al.*, 2007), alcohol dehydrogenase 2 (ALDH2) (Oota *et al.*, 2004), and several genes for metabolizing sugars – MAN2A1 for mannose and S1 for sucrose (Voight *et al.*, 2006). Associated with fat intake, both peroxisome proliferator-activated receptor gamma (PPARγ), a nuclear receptor active in fat metabolism, and the SLC25A20 carnitine shuttle affecting fatty acid transport across the mitochondrial membrane were identified (Voight *et al.*, 2006; Wang *et al.*, 2003).

Recent programs of population supplementation appear to have long-reaching results. Research examining effects of folate supplementation during pregnancy now suggests that maternal supplementation produced offspring changes in allelic frequency of those genes creating the enzymes responsible for folate metabolism. Successful outcome of pregnancies which previously might have resulted in fetal loss has created increased frequencies of potentially detrimental homozygotes of vulnerable alleles associated with the relationship of folate and genetics of methyltransferase 5, 10-methylenetetrahydrofolate reductase (MTHFR) (Jennings *et al.*, 2010). These MTHFR genes are vital to the processes of folate metabolism, epigenetic methylation, and imprinting.

Nutrition, epigenetics, and consequences of migration

The relationship of folate and genetics of methyltransferase – this last example of dietary effects on genotypic variation – is of major importance in the study of human evolution. Folate is a cofactor in one-carbon metabolism and nucleic acid synthesis, and therefore vital to cell division in growth and development, tissue repair, and survival. Those mechanisms of folate metabolism and subsequent DNA methylation processes create epigenetic markers during fetal imprinting and subsequent methylation during fetal development, thus initiating patterned responses to environmental nutritional signals. The DNA methylation primarily silences gene expression (Horsthemke, 2010). The recent study by Hancock *et al.* (2010) examining genetic variation of adaptive phenotypes in a variety of historically distinct dietary environments, identified folate biosynthesis pathways as one of the genetic groups exhibiting allelic variation between populations. Populations with histories denoting high intake of roots and tubers as the major portion of their diets showed a significant reliance on pathways of folate synthesis. As roots and tubers are very low in folate, such findings suggest that enhancement of these pathways was important to human survival.

Additional specification of metabolic emphasis was noted in populations reliant on roots and tubers. Comparing these populations with other groups residing in circumpolar regions, pathways affecting metabolism for starch and sucrose were primary, while the significant pathways emphasized in the circumpolar populations were lipid transport and protein metabolism, but not folate biosynthesis (Hancock *et al.*, 2010). Studies suggest the explanation concerning folate synthesis may be associated with a V677 mutation in MTHFR, known to exacerbate physiological vulnerability to decreased folate intake. This mutation is not found in the circumpolar populations (Hegele *et al.*, 1997). Given their substantial reliance on animal and sea mammal diets, the increased emphasis on lipid and protein metabolic pathways, however, supports their increased basal metabolic rates for cold adaptation reported in the circumpolar groups (Leonard *et al.*, 2002). The profound dietary shift in circumpolar populations from traditional nutritional profiles to more westernized diets has been shown to be a complex matter. Established reliance on pathways for protein and fat metabolism operating over generations clashed with the increased carbohydrate intake. The dietary shift to increased carbohydrate resulted in obesity and all of its associated disease risks (Eilat-Adar *et al.*, 2009; Shephard and Rode, 1996). This example supports a hypothesis of an underlying and somewhat stable nutritional phenotype existing in populations experiencing consistent dietary environments. Moreover, it may present an example of epigenetic reprogramming when faced with a mismatch of generational history and sudden dietary shifts to nutritional patterns. Such shifts may require several generations being exposed to the new diet before observable epigenetic changes occur to cope with the new dietary environment. Similar patterns of adaptation may be noted in populations experiencing rapid and dramatic migrations, as illustrated by the generational effects of stress responses and fetal development in immigrants discussed in Kuzawa and Sweet, 2009.

What drives the physiological adaptation to dietary changes? Can any variation in methylation patterns, and thus epigenetic programming, be identified across generations? A schemata illustrating generational effects of epigenetic programming and dietary pressures is shown in Figure 7.2. This scenario depicts the potential difference in outcome when individuals face a nutrient landscape consistent with their programming versus the impact of a mismatch between their generational programming and the dietary environment in which they find themselves. Such a mismatch may become a significant selective force and produce patterns of microevolution.

CONSEQUENCES OF MIGRATION IN MODERN HUMAN POPULATIONS

Widespread evidence reporting the detrimental effects on first generations exposed to the increase of simple carbohydrates concentrated in the Western diet was documented globally in the mid twentieth century (Price, 2000). Generational effects are now being identified and associated with factors of glucose metabolism, obesity, and subsequent insulin resistance in both animal and human models (El-Osta *et al.*,

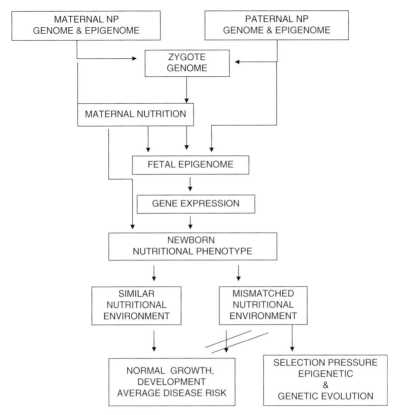

Figure 7.2 Scenario for generational nutritional effects. Epigenetic effects are passed down through generations, are transient, and are reversible, given the dynamic relationship of nutritional environment and DNA methylation.

2008; Remacle *et al.*, 2004; Van Assche *et al.*, 2001). Ultimately, the generational health effects created from severe nutritional insults during war and famine (Heijmans *et al.*, 2008) or rapid and dramatically nutritional transitions encountered during today's experience in migration and/or modernization (Popkin, 1998; Popkin and Gordon-Larsen, 2004) may be explained by adaptive nutritional phenotypes created in the epigenome and mismatched to the challenging new dietary environment (Gluckman and Hanson, 2006). Such mismatch or severe deficiencies in both folate intake and adequate energy to create healthy epigenomes during nutritional stress can be construed as setting the stage for fetal origins of disease (Kahn *et al.*, 2005). Given the recent evidence identifying molecular variation in metabolic pathways of populations with distinct dietary histories, research in human populations is needed to address the following questions:

1. Are there stable underlying nutritional phenotypes consistent throughout the life cycle?
2. What is the variation of these phenotypes among populations?
3. What is the genetic architecture of these phenotypes?
4. What variation of epigenetic methylation exists among nutritional phenotypes?
5. What are the effects of rapid nutritional shifts on the stability of nutritional phenotype and on the patterns of methylation?
6. What are the generational health effects of rapid change in nutritional profiles?
7. Does subsequent epigenetic adaptation and evolution confer reduction in disease risk?
8. What specific factors drive the adaptation and evolution of these phenotypes?

Epigenetic consequences of health in the migration and transitions of human populations

The health risks of migration are widely documented, and often tied to the concept of acculturation, which would include a component of dietary variation whether or not directly specified. Immigrants face dietary alteration of homeostatic balances (Cordain *et al.*, 2005) and a pre-primed nutritional phenotype foreign to the adopted food chain (Gluckman *et al.*, 2007). The health effects observed in those who have migrated may originate from altered metabolic fetal imprinting and mismatched fetal adaptation, as suggested by Barker's hypothesis of the fetal origin of adult diseases (Barker, 2004) and Gluckman's predictive adaptive response hypothesis (Gluckman *et al.*, 2005).

Is obesity a necessary consequence of migration? Dramatic increases are seen in dietary intake of both simple carbohydrates and foods which are macronutrient dense but micronutrient poor. This produces a paradoxical combination of malnutrition and obesity (Varela-Silva *et al.*, 2007). Effects of altered glycemic loads on the body are abundantly discussed in the literature today. Studies identifying a "metabolic memory" associated with exposure to hyperglycemic episodes illustrate continuing detrimental effects on the vascular system after a diabetic's glucose levels are returned to a normal range. Continued oxidative stress secondary to hyperglycemia increases advanced glycation end products which in turn up-regulate inflammatory cytokines (Siebel *et al.*, 2010; Singh *et al.*, 2001). Obesity, associated with both dietary and diabetic origins, is connected with malfunction of histone demethylase and epigenetic programming. The resulting impairment of proliferator-activated receptor alpha (PPAR-alpha) in skeletal muscle and effects on expression of the uncoupling protein 1 in brown adipose tissue, demonstrated in animal models, suggest underlying features of the obesity phenotype. Additional animal studies connect obesity and serum glucose levels to sirtuin function and histone modification, an epigenetic mechanism which affects metabolism, gene expression, and possibly longevity (Adams and Klaidman, 2007; Lombard *et al.*, 2008; Michan and Sinclair, 2007; Siebel *et al.*, 2010).

Variation in the effects of maternal nutritional insult on fetal outcome can be measured as change in neonatal birth weight with all of its implications, or through measures of known biomarkers that increase disease risk, such as plasma lipid levels. Effects of these biomarkers appear to be both ethnic specific (Scholl *et al.*, 2004) and sex specific (reviewed in Mosher and Crawford, 2010). Human generational studies indicate that nutritional deprivation during the fetal development and early infancy create a substrate preference for carbohydrate metabolism (Varela-Silva *et al.*, 2007), and this metabolic preference may coincide with reduction in fetal organ or skeletal muscle development (Kuzawa and Sweet, 2009). Subsequent dyslipidemias during adolescence and adulthood, and their resulting risks for cardiovascular diseases, may occur during disproportionate growth patterns resulting from a response to the deficits encountered *in utero*. Explanations documenting a greater vulnerability of males to this situation suggest that males have a greater demand for energy *in utero* to meet their growth demands (Kuzawa and Adair, 2003, 2004; Skidmore *et al.*, 2004; Lawlor *et al.*, 2006). However, epigenetics are believed to play a role, either through metabolic imprinting or hormonal regulation.

Lifelong effects of maternal nutritional deficits on the offspring epigenome in human populations are evidenced by studies on individuals whose mothers were pregnant with them during the Dutch Hunger Winter of 1944–5. These offspring showed variation of increased prevalence of metabolic dysfunctions and disease risk, with differences correlated to the timing during pregnancy of maternal famine exposure (Gluckman *et al.*, 2009; Heijmans *et al.*, 2008). Examining insulin-like growth factor II (IGF-2), strongly associated with human growth and development, Heijmans *et al.* (2008) reported that the DNA methylation status of this gene may be recognized through at least middle age. The Dutch study demonstrated that the IGF-2 methylation patterns differed between the offspring conceived during this stress from the methylation patterns of their siblings, conceived and born during a time their mothers were not exposed to trauma. Those exposed *in utero* to the stressors of this period exhibited a 5.2% lower methylation rate than did their siblings, and this pattern occurred in 72% of the sibships. The effects were predominant for those individuals exposed early in the pregnancy to the deficit as opposed to those only exposed to the nutritional deficits during the last trimester. Although additional stressors of the winter cold and severe emotional pressures accompanying the Dutch Hunger Winter may have played a role, the most consistent exposure across the population appears to be dietary. Reports of consistent dietary rations across the population at that time were assessed as higher in carbohydrate (69%) and low in protein and fats, most likely deficient in methyl donors needed for the epigenetic imprinting critical during the early stages of pregnancy. The timing of the insult during the pregnancy was important to epigenetic programming. The authors caution the use of birth weight as a marker of intrauterine distress and epigenetic alterations, as most fetal weight is acquired in the last trimester. Those Dutch conceived prior to the famine but born during the famine may have displayed lower birth weight, but did not exhibit epigenetic changes (Heijmans *et al.*, 2008; Tobi *et al.*, 2009).

Health effects on those conceived during the Dutch famine include impaired glucose tolerance and insulin secretion (de Rooij *et al.*, 2006) and a preference for high fat diet. While no difference in serum cholesterol levels was noted, survivors of the famine exposure did exhibit a higher prevalence of atherogenic lipid profile defined by the LDL/HDL ratio (low density lipoprotein to high density lipoprotein) (Lussana *et al.*, 2008). Levels of HDL were lower in both males and females exposed to the famine during early gestation (de Rooij *et al.*, 2007) and associated with a greater occurrence of coronary artery disease (Painter *et al.*, 2006). Increased obesity was also found in those exposed early in their gestation but there was no increase in the metabolic syndrome connected to the experience, leaving the authors to suggest that severe maternal deficit was not associated with the syndrome as a whole (de Rooij *et al.*, 2007).

Subsequent population research to identify effects of the Dutch famine on epigenetic programming and its long-term ramifications was completed by Tobi *et al.* (2009). Their study examined 15 candidate genes associated with growth, metabolism, and cardiovascular disease. Some of the candidates were imprinted genes, others were not imprinted. Comparing those exposed to same-sex siblings who were neither

conceived nor born between November and May of 1945, results indicated that both timing of exposure and sex differences play roles in
specific variation in DNA methylation. DNA methylation variation associated with gestational timing of exposure was noted in the following:
Interleukin 10, a cytokine with widespread effects inhibiting both
immune and inflammatory mechanisms (Moore *et al.*, 2001); insulin-
like growth factors which stimulate diverse cellular functions and
fetal development (Fowden and Forhead, 2009), both of which show
association with early gestational effects; and GNASAS, a paternally
imprinted locus modulating a complex system of promoters through
the cell signal G protein alpha-subunit pathway. This GNAS gene, which
affects calcium homeostasis and related disease sequelae (de Nanclares
et al., 2007), shows effects of maternal dietary stress both in early and
late gestation (Tobi *et al.*, 2009). Finally, increased methylation of the
MEG3 gene, a maternally imprinted gene suggested to function as an
imprinting control center (Kagami *et al.*, 2010), was also documented
among famine-exposed individuals (Tobi *et al.*, 2009).

Sex-specific differences of epigenetic methylation were identified
by Tobi *et al.* (2009) in the Dutch population. Higher DNA methylation in
INSIGF and lower methylation in leptin, the adipokine signal modulating energy homeostasis, was documented in males. Low rates of methylation in females were shown in apoprotein C1 which plays a role in
lipid metabolism (Jong *et al.*, 1999; Westerterp *et al.*, 2007). Animal
studies support sex-specific variation of maternal dietary effects on
DNA methylation of offspring in mice (Gallou-Kabani *et al.*, 2010). Evidence of sex-specific variation underlying metabolic adaptations in
circumpolar populations (Braun *et al.*, 2000; Leonard *et al.*, 2009) and
dimorphic patterns underlying lipid metabolism and adipokines beginning during fetal development (reviewed in Mosher and Crawford,
2010) make recent findings identifying sex-specific variation in DNA
methylation (Tobi *et al.*, 2009) all the more significant. A complete
understanding of these results is unavailable at this time; however,
they may be tied to specific sensitivities to insulin and leptin signals
in energy homeostasis (Woods *et al.*, 2003) or response to catecholamine
release (Horton *et al.*, 1998).

Several studies have linked dietary aspects of fathers and grand-
fathers with sex- specific transgenerational effects and health outcomes
in male but not female grandchildren (Whitelaw and Whitelaw, 2006).
This evidence of parent of origin effects appear the reverse along
the female line, as grandmothers' diets were associated with mortality
risk ratios in granddaughters, but not grandsons. The epigenetic

explanation is unknown; however one hypothesis suggested that sections of the genome may not be cleared of DNA methylation before subsequent imprinting. A second hypothesis pointed to social factors, emphasizing that these studies did not address the molecular aspects (Kaati *et al.*, 2002; Pembrey *et al.*, 2006; Whitelaw and Whitelaw, 2006).

Implications of rapid environmental changes during migration

The implications of these early epigenetic findings in gene expression, environmental connections, and sex-specific vulnerability are yet to be fully explained. Recent research of contemporary Dutch populations, unassociated with the famine history, did not replicate similar epigenetic patterning of these candidate genes when comparing infants born small for gestational age (SGA) to infants whose weight was appropriate for gestational age (AGA) (Tobi *et al.*, 2011). Therefore, replicating the epigenetic outcome of the famine studies may prove difficult when examining larger populations suffering some levels of continual malnutrition. Epigenetic alteration from sudden and dramatic nutritional changes and stressors during preconception and periconception stages is certainly suggested in the Dutch study, and unaffected by any maternal metabolic memory, should the mothers have been experiencing adequate nutrition prior to the famine. The epigenetic effects and resulting morbidity of the offspring generation appeared substantial in the Dutch cohort, however. Exacerbation of the physiological factors originating from emotional stress cannot be ignored in that specific situation and might well be applicable to immigrants who experience rapid and dramatic cultural and dietary changes.

Sex-specific differences are not unexpected, given the complex pattern of imprinting during the embryonic stages. Markers of lipid metabolism are notably higher in neonate females than males (Bansal *et al.*, 2005; Pac-Kozuchowska, 2007), with females exhibiting the more protective profile's lower ratio of total cholesterol levels/high density lipoproteins (HDL) and a higher leptin level than males (Nelson *et al.*, 2007). As previously mentioned, subsequent dyslipidemias developing in adolescence and adulthood may be tied to disproportionate growth patterns resulting from nutritional deficits encountered while *in utero* (Barker, 1995; Godfrey, 2002). Such early nutritional effects appeared to have a greater detrimental impact in males than females, with some theorizing that such an outcome is related to the greater energy demand during rapid fetal growth in males (Kuzawa and Adair, 2003; Lawlor *et al.*, 2006). The effects of a mismatch between fetal programming, given maternal nutritional signals coupled with exposure to improved nutrition after delivery, was also more evident in males. This mismatch is shown in second-generation Chinese immigrants whose parents had moved from rural to urban areas, where their children experienced greatly improved dietary intake. The males appeared to be more vulnerable to increased proportion of body fat and dyslipidemias when exposed to increased fat during adolescence, while females did not exhibit negative profiles (Schooling *et al.*, 2007, 2008). Whether these findings imply a metabolic memory from *in utero*-associated changes in epigenetic methylation is yet to be examined.

Adding to the complexity of migration studies is the "migration paradox" reported in some immigrant populations. This paradox suggests the possibility of a metabolic memory. Studies comparing first-generation immigrants to their ethnic counterparts born in the United States report that immigrants have better health initially after their move and this effect may in fact prove somewhat protective to the immigrants' health status in general. Additionally, immigrants have better reproductive outcome in the first generation of children born soon after immigration than U.S.-born counterparts (Kuzawa and Sweet, 2009), but these results – measured through birth weight and neonatal deaths – appear ethnic specific (Alexander *et al.*, 2003; Singh and Yu, 1996). The arbitrary parameters designating expected health effects to low birth weight may be misleading when comparing ethnicities (Juarez *et al.*, 2010) and much controversy regarding the reported paradox can be found in the literature. Studies do document the detrimental effects of acculturation, however, with increasing acculturation associated with diminishing protective effects (Fennelly, 2007). The literature points to factors including the strength of social and family support, along with strong group identity, as being protective. These factors may include maintenance of traditional dietary practices, but studies do not examine subtle nutritional differences arising from major geographical and agricultural changes. No reports of human population migration studies examining the epigenetic variation were found in a literature search of PubMed.

NATURAL EXPERIMENTS FOUND IN MIGRATING POPULATIONS

Modern migrating populations experiencing rapid and dramatic environmental changes provide a natural experiment by which to examine the consequences of substantial nutritional shifts on genetic and/or epigenetic factors in humans. Extrapolation from such research may illuminate the relationship of nutrition and adaptation in human evolution. Most research supporting diet-by-epigenetic interaction is completed in animals while research regarding epigenetic mechanisms in humans focuses primarily on their association with disease states and consequences of IVF (in vitro fertilization) (Cutfield *et al.*, 2007; Dolinoy *et al.*, 2007; Franklin and Mansuy, 2010; Gluckman *et al.*, 2011; Niemitz and Feinberg, 2004). Literature investigating baseline human epigenetic variation among populations is lacking. Migrating populations provide the unique natural experiment design for both familial and population based research to pose these questions addressing the effects of nutritional variation on epigenetic mechanisms in normal, albeit stressed, individuals with varying nutritional histories. Comparison of epigenetic markers between generations – one with a consistent dietary history of the original country of origin over several generations; the following generation who experience the transition; and the new generation conceived, born, and raised in the new environment – compared with families of similar geographical origin who did not immigrate, may expose novel patterns of epigenetic markers associated with dramatic changes in dietary nutrients. The epigenetic patterns may impose limits on phenotypic plasticity seen over several subsequent generations (Heijmans *et al.*, 2009). A research project – a multiple generation, multiple ethnicity study of migrating populations – to examine epigenetic variation is currently in process by this author and other members of this consortium on migration. Populations to be studied are Asian, African, and several of the Americas.

Conclusion

Human migration presents individuals with novel environmental challenges to adaptation and survival. Although dietary effects on human evolution are widely documented, the mosaic process has been gradual, and taking place over many generations. Modern migrations face greater stresses within a constrained time period. Therefore, a more thorough understanding of the relationship between specific nutrients, human development, and health outcomes is imperative. Elucidating effects of gene-by-nutrient or epigenome-by-nutrient interaction may provide a window through which to view the underlying physiological mechanisms which have long affected humans during migration, adaptation, and evolution. The manner in which nutrients affect gene expression, however, is a new and expanding field of exploration. The traditional nutrient studies profiling dietary intake and cooking practices are now mixed with assessments of their metabolic fate using biomarkers to identify and correlate actual nutrient status of an individual with dietary intake. The current direction integrating these accepted traditional approaches with population history, genetics, nutrigenomics, metabolomics, and epigenetic markers opens possibilities to examine the concepts of stable versus transient metabolic phenotypes, nutritional phenotypes, and the manner by which generational dietary mismatch impacts the outcome of successful migration.

This chapter serves as a brief overview of current literature addressing the role of diet in molecular evolution and epigenetic mechanisms as a manner of communication between the nutritional environment and the human genome. Research identifying the population variation in genes associated with both diet and metabolic pathways is just beginning, yet animal studies along with the recent documentation of human generational epigenetic effects in survivors of the Dutch famine and in twin studies lend credence to such a study direction. With the advancement of our global society and its increased opportunities for migration, anthropological geneticists may now take advantage of a natural experiment by examining gene-by-environmental interaction and the manner by which diet and epigenetics affect human evolution.

ACKNOWLEDGMENTS

With great appreciation for the editing and thoughtful suggestions and expert editing of Rebecca Ortega and Fiona Felker, biological anthropology students of Western Washington University.

REFERENCES

Adams, J. D. and Klaidman, L. K. (2007). Sirtuins, nicotinamide and aging: a critical review. *Letters in Drug Design & Discovery*, **4**, 44–8.
Aiello, L. C. and Wheeler, P. (1995). The expensive-tissue hypothesis: the brain and the digestive system in human and primate evolution. *Current Anthropology*, **36**(2), 199–221.
Alexander, G. R., Kogan, M., Bader, D., *et al.* (2003). US birth weight/gestational age-specific neonatal mortality: 1995–1997 rates for whites, Hispanics and blacks. *Pediatrics*, **111**(1), e61–6.
Ali, M. and Cox, T. M. (1995). Diverse mutations in the aldolase B gene that underlie the prevalence of hereditary fructose intolerance. *American Journal of Human Genetics*, **56**(4), 1002–5.
Ali, M., Rellos, P., and Cox, T. M. (1998). Hereditary fructose intolerance. *Journal of Medicine and Genetics*, **35**, 353–65.
Allen, J. S. (2009). *The Lives of the Brain*. Cambridge, UK: Belknap Press.

Ames, B. N., Elson-Schwab, I., and Silver, E. (2002). High-dose vitamins stimulate variant enzymes with decreased coenzyme-binding affinity (increased Km): relevance to genetic disease and polymorphisms. *American Journal of Clinical Nutrition*, **75**, 616–58.

Balaresque, P. L., Ballereau, S. H., and Jobling, M. A. (2007). Challenges in human genetic diversity: demographic history and adaptation. *Human Molecular Genetics*, **16**(Spec No. 2), R134–9.

Bansal, D., Cruickshank, J. K., McElduff, P., and Durrington, P. N. (2005). Cord blood lipoproteins and prenatal influences. *Current Opinion in Lipidology*, **16**(4), 400–8.

Barker, D. J. (1995). Fetal origins of coronary heart disease. *British Medical Journal*, **311**(6998), 171–4.

Barker, D. J. (2004). The developmental origins of adult disease. *Journal of American College of Nutrition*, **23**(6), 588S–595S.

Bersaglieri, T., Sabeti, P. C., Patterson, N., *et al.* (2004). Genetic signatures of strong recent positive selection at the lactase gene. *American Journal of Human Genetics*, **74**, 1111–20.

Birdsey, G. M., Dryden, N. H., Shah, A. V., *et al.* (2004). Differential enzyme targeting as an evolutionary adaptation to herbivory in carnivores. *Molecular Biology and Evolution*, **21**(4), 632–46.

Braun, B., Mawson, J. T., Muza, S. R., *et al.* (2000). Women at altitude: carbohydrate utilization during exercise at 4,300m. *Journal of Applied Physiology*, **88**(1), 246–56.

Burdge, G. C., Hanson, M. A., Slater-Jefferies, J. L., and Lillycrop, K. A. (2007). Epigenetic regulation of transcription: a mechanism for inducing variations in the phenotype:fetal programming by differences in nutrition during early life? *British Journal of Nutrition*, **97**(6), 1036–46.

Caldwell, E. F., Mayor, L. R., Thomas, M. G., and Danpure, C. J. (2004). Diet and the frequency of the alanine: gloxylate aminotransferase Pro11Leu polymorphism in different human populations. *Human Genetics*, **115**(6), 504–9.

Cellini, F., Chesson, A., Colquhoun, I., *et al.* (2004). Unintended effects and their detection in genetically modified crops. *Food and Chemical Toxicology (FTC)*, **42**, 1089–125.

Choi, S. W. and Friso, S. (2010). Epigenetics: a new bridge between nutrition and health. *Advances in Nutrition*, **1**, 8–16.

Cobiac, L. (2007). Epigenomics and nutrition. *Forum of Nutrition*, **60**, 31–41.

Cochran, G. and Harpending, H. (2009). *The 10,000 Year Explosion*. Philadelphia, PA: Basic Books.

Coffee, E. M. and Tolan, D. R. (2010). Mutations in the promoter region of the aldolase B gene that cause hereditary fructose intolerance. *Journal of Inheritable Metabolic Disorders*, **33**(6), 715–25.

Corbo, R. M., Ulizzi, L., Scacchi, R., *et al.* (2004). Apolipoprotein E polymorphism and fertility: a study in pre-industrial populations. *Molecular Human Reproduction*, **10**(8), 617–20.

Cordain, L., Eaton, S. B., Sebastian, A., *et al.* (2005). Origins and evolution of the Western diet: health implications for the 21st century. *American Journal of Clinical Nutrition*, **81**(2), 341–54.

Coulter-Mackie, M. B. and Rumsby, G. (2004). Genetic heterogeneity in primary hyperoxaluria type 1: impact on diagnosis. *Molecular Genetics and Metabolism*, **83**(1–2), 38–46.

Cousins, R. J., Aydemir, T. B., and Lichten, L. A. (2010). Plenary Lecture 2: Transcription factors, regulatory elements and nutrient-gene communication. *Proceedings for Nutritional Society*, **69**, 91–4.

Cox, T. M. (2002). The genetic consequences of our sweet tooth. *Nature Reviews Genetics*, **3**(6), 481–7.

Crawford, M. and Marsh, D. E. L. (1995). *Nutrition and Evolution*. New Canaan, CT:. Keats Publishing.

Crews, D. E., Kamboh, M. I., Mancilha-Carvalho, J. J., and Kottke, B. (1993). Population genetics of apolipoprotein A-4, E, and H polymorphisms in Yanomami Indians of northwestern Brazil: associations with lipids, lipoproteins, and carbohydrate metabolism. *Human Biology*, **65**(2), 211–24.

Cutfield, W. S., Hofman, P. L., Mitchell, M., and Morison, I. M. (2007). Could epigenetics play a role in the developmental origins of health and disease? *Pediatric Research*, **61**(5), 68R–75R.

Dauncey, M. J., White, P., Burton, K. A., and Katsumata, M. (2001). Nutrition-hormone receptor-gene interactions: implications for development and disease. *Proceedings of the Nutrition Society*, **60**, 63–72.

De Caterina, R. and Madonna, R. (2004). Nutrients and gene expression. *World Review of Nutrition and Dietetics*, **93**, 99–133.

Delage, B. and Dashwood, R. H. (2008). Dietary manipulation of histone structure and function. *Annual Review of Nutrition*, **28**, 347–66.

de Nanclares, G. P., Fernández-Rebollo, E., Santin, I., *et al.* (2007). Epigenetic defects of GNAS in patients with pseudohypoparathyroidism and mild features of Albright's hereditary. *Journal of Clinical Endocrinology & Metabolism*, **92**(6), 2370–3.

de Rooij, S. R., Painter, R. C., Holleman, F., *et al.* (2007). The metabolic syndrome in adults prenatally exposed to the Dutch famine. *American Journal of Clinical Nutrition*, **86**(4), 1219–24.

de Rooij, S. R., Painter, R. C., Phillips, D. I., *et al.* (2006). The effects of the Pro12Ala polymorphism of the peroxisome proliferator-activated receptor-gamma2gene on glucose/insulin metabolism interact with prenatal exposure to famine. *Diabetes Care*, **29**(5), 1052–7.

Dolinoy, D. C., Das, R., Weidman, J. R., and Jirtle, R. L. (2007). Metastable epialleles, imprinting and the fetal origins of adult diseases. *Pediatric Research*, **61**(5), 30R–37R.

Domingo, J. L. (2007). Toxicity studies of genetically modified plants: a review of the published literature. *Critical Reviews in Food Science and Nutrition*, **47**(8), 721–33.

Dwyer, J. H., Allayee, H., Dwyer, K. M., *et al.* (2004). Arachidonate 5-lipoxygenase promoter genotype, arachidonic acid, and atherosclerosis. *New England Journal of Medicine*, **350**, 29–37.

Eilat-Adar, S., Mete, M., Nobmann, E. D., *et al.* (2009). Dietary patterns are linked to cardiovascular risk factors but not to inflammatory markers in Alaska Eskimos. *Journal of Nutrition*, **139**(2), 2322–8.

Ellison, P. T. (2008). Energetics, reproductive ecology, and human evolution. *PaleoAnthropology*, **2008**, 172–200.

El-Osta, A., Brasacchio, D., Yao, D., *et al.* (2008). Transient high glucose causes persistent changes and altered gene expression during subsequent normoglycemia. *Journal of Experimental Medicine*, **205**(10), 2409–17.

Eng, M. Y., Luczak, S. E., and Wall, T. L. (2007). ALDH2, ADH1B, and ADH1C genotypes in Asians: a literature review. *Alcohol Research & Health*, **30**(1), 22–7.

Feil, R. (2006) Environmental and nutritional effects on the regulation of genes. *Mutation Research*, **600**(1–2), 46–57.

Fennelly, K. (2007). The "healthy migrant" effect. *Minnesota Medicine*, **90**(3), 51–3.

Finch, C. E. and Stanford, C. B. (2004). Meat-adaptive genes and the evolution of slower aging in humans. *Quarterly Review of Biology*, **79**(1), 3–50.

Flueck, M. (2009). Myocellular limitations of human performance and their modification through genome-dependent responses at altitude. *Experimental Physiology*, **95**, 451–62.

Fowden, A. L. and Forhead, A. J. (2009). Endocrine regulation of feto-placental growth. *Hormone Research*, **72**, 257–65.

Franklin, T. B. and Mansuy, I. M. (2010). Epigenetic inheritance in mammals: evidence for the impact of adverse environmental effects. *Neurobiology of Disease*, **39**(1), 61–5.

Freimer, N., Eichenberg, D., and Kretchmer, N. (1983). Cultural variation: nutritional and clinical implications. *Western Journal of Medicine*, **139**(6), 928–33.

Friso, S. and Choi, S. W. (2002). Gene-nutrient interactions and DNA methylation. *Journal of Nutrition*, **132**(8 Suppl), 2382S–2387S.

Gallou-Kabani, C., Gabory, A., Tost, J., *et al.* (2010). Sex- and diet-specific changes of imprinted gene expression and DNA methylation in mouse placenta under a high-fat diet. *PLoS ONE*, **5**(12), e14398.

Gallou-Kabani, C., Vigé, A., Gross, M. S., and Junien, C. (2007). Nutri-epigenomics: lifelong remodeling of our epigenomes by nutritional and metabolic factors and beyond. *Clinical Chemistry and Laboratory Medicine*, **45**(3), 321–327.

Gluckman, P. D. and Hanson, M. A. (2006) The consequences of being born small: an adaptive perspective. *Hormone Research*, **65**(Suppl 3), 5–14.

Gluckman, P. D., Beedle, A., and Hanson, M. (2009). *Principles of Evolutionary Medicine*. Oxford, UK: Oxford University Press.

Gluckman, P. D., Hanson, M. A., and Beedle, A. S. (2007). Early life events and their consequences for later disease: a life history and evolutionary perspective. *American Journal of Human Biology*, **19**, 1–19.

Gluckman, P. D., Hanson, M. A., Beedle, A. S., Buklijas, T., and Low, F. M. (2011) Epigenetics of human disease. In *Epigenetics: Linking Genotype and Phenotype in Development and Evolution*, ed. B. Hallgrimsson and B. K. Hall, pp. 398–423. Berkley, CA: University of California Press.

Gluckman, P. D., Hanson, M. A., and Spencer, H. G. (2005). Predictive adaptive responses and human evolution. *Trends in Ecology & Evolution*, **20**(10), 527–33.

Go, V. L., Nguyen, C. T., Harris, D. M., and Lee, W. N. (2005). Nutrient-gene interaction: metabolic genotype-phenotype relationship. *Journal of Nutrition*, **135**(12 Suppl), 3016S–3020S.

Godfrey, K. M. (2002). The role of the placenta in fetal programming: a review. *Placenta*, **23**(Suppl A), S20–7.

Goodacre, R. (2007). Metabolomics of a superorganism. *Journal of Nutrition*, **137**(1 Suppl), 259S–266S.

Gropper, S. S., Smith, J. L., and Groff, J. L. (2005). *Advanced Nutrition and Human Metabolism*. Belmont, CA: Wadsworth.

Haig, D. (2004). *The (Dual) Origin of Epigenetics*. Cold Spring Harbor Symposia on Quantitative Biology. Long Island, NY: Cold Spring Harbor Laboratory Press.

Hancock, A. M., Alkorta-Aranburu, G., Witonsky, D. B., and DiRienzo, A. (2010). Adaptations to new environments in humans: the role of subtle allele frequency shifts. *Philosophical Transactions of the Royal Society of London B: Biological Sciences*, **365**(1552), 2459–68.

Harris, M. and Ross, E. B. (eds.) (1987). *Food and Evolution: Toward a Theory of Human Food Habits*. Philadelphia, PA: Temple University Press.

Haygood, R., Fedrigo, O., Hanson, B., *et al.* (2007). Promoter regions of many neural-and nutrition related genes have experienced positive selection during human evolution. *Nature Genetics*, **39**(9), 1140–4.

Hegele, R. A., Tully, C., Young, T. K., and Connelly, P. W. (1997). V677 mutation of methylenetetrahydrofolate reductase and cardiovascular disease in Canadian Inuit. *The Lancet*, **349**(9060), 1221.

Heijmans, B. T., Tobi, W. E., Lumey, L. H., and Slagboom, P. E. (2009) The epigenome: archive of the prenatal environment. *Epigenetics*, **4**(8), 526–31.

Heijmans, B. T., Tobi, E. W., Stein, A. D., *et al.* (2008). Persistent epigenetic differences associated with prenatal exposure to famine in humans. *Proceedings of the National Academy of Sciences of the United States of America*, **105**(44), 17 046–9.

Hitchins, M. P. and Moore, G. E. (2002). Genomic imprinting in fetal growth and development. *Expert Reviews in Molecular Medicine*, **4**(11), 1–19.

Ho, D. H. and Burggren, W. W. (2010). Epigenetics and transgenerational transfer. *Journal of Experimental Biology*, **213**(1), 3–16.

Hochachka, P. W., Gunga, H. C., and Kirsch, K. (1998). Our ancestral physiological phenotype: an adaptation for hypoxia tolerance and for endurance performance. *Proceedings of the National Academy of Sciences of the United States of America*, **95**(4), 1915–20.

Holmes, E., Wilson, I. D., and Nicholson, J. K. (2008). Metabolic phenotyping in health and disease. *Cell*, **134**(5), 714–17.

Horsthemke, B. (2010). Mechanisms of imprint dysregulation. *American Journal of Medical Genetics*, **154C**(3), 321–8.

Horton, T. J., Pagliassotti, M. J., Hobbs, K., and Hill, J. O. (1998). Fuel metabolism in men and women during and after long-duration exercise. *Journal of Applied Physiology*, **85**(5), 1823–32.

Jennings, B. A., Willis, G. A., Skinner, J., and Relton, C. L. (2010). Genetic selection? A study of individual variation in the enzymes of folate metabolism. *BMC Medical Genetics*, **11**, 18–24.

Jofre-Monseny, L., Minihane, A. M., and Rimbach, G. (2008). Impact of apoE genotype on oxidative stress, inflammation and disease risk. *Molecular Nutrition & Food Research*, **52**(1), 131–45.

Jong, M. C., Hofker, M. H., and Havekes, L. M. (1999). Role of ApoCs in lipoprotein metabolism: function: differences between ApoC1, ApoC2 and Apo C3. *Arteriosclerosis, Thrombosis, and Vascular Biology*, **19**(3), 472–84.

Juarez, S., Ploubidis, G. B., and Clarke, L. (2010). Testing the epidemiological paradox through birthweight in the Spanish context: a true or an artificial effect? Paper presented at European Population Conference, Vienna. Extended Abstract. Princeton, NJ: Office of Population Research, Princeton University.

Kaati, G., Bygren, L. O., and Edvinsson, S. (2002). Cardiovascular and diabetes mortality determined by nutrition during parents' and grandparents' slow growth period. *European Journal of Human Genetics*, **10**(11), 682–8.

Kagami, M., O'Sullivan, M. J., Green, A. J., *et al.* (2010). The IG-DMR and the MEG3-DMR at chromosome 14q32.2: hierarchical interaction and distinct functional properties as imprinting control centers. *PLoS Genetics*, **6**(6), e1000992.

Kahn, O. A., Torrens, C., Noakes, D. E., *et al.* (2005). Effects of pre-natal and early post-natal undernutrition on adult internal thoracic artery function. *European Journal of Cardio-Thoracic Surgery*, **28**, 811–15.

Kamboh, M. I., Crawford, M. H., Aston, C. E., *et al.* (1996). Population distribution of APOE, APOH and APOA4 polymorphisms and their relationships with quantitative plasma lipid levels among the Evenki herders of Siberia. *Human Biology*, **68**, 231–43.

Kamboh, M. I., Weiss, K. M., and Ferrell, R. E. (1991). Genetic studies of human apolipoproteins. XVI: APOE polymorphism and cholesterol levels in the Mayans of the Yucatan Peninsula, Mexico. *Clinical Genetics*, **39**, 26–32.

Kaput, J. (2004). Diet-disease gene interactions. *Nutrition*, **20**(1), 26–31.

Kaput, J. and Rodriguez, R. L. (2004). Nutritional genomics: the next frontier in the postgenomic era. *Physiological Genomics*, **16**, 166–77.

Khoshgoftarmanesh, A. H., Schulin, R., Chaney, R. L., *et al.* (2010). Micronutrient-efficient genotypes for crop yield and nutritional quality in sustainable agriculture. A review. *Agronomy for Sustainable Development*, **30**, 83–107.

Kim, U. K. and Drayna, D. (2005). Genetics of individual differences in bitter taste perception: lessons from the PTC gene. *Clinical Genetics*, **67**(4), 275–80.

Kozlov, A., Borinskaya, S., Vershubsky, G., *et al.* (2008). Genes related to the metabolism of nutrients in Kola Sami population. *International Journal of Circumpolar Health*, **67**(1), 56–66.

Kozlov, A. I., Sanina, E. D., Vershubskaya, G. G., and Ateeva, Y. A. (2009). Energy demands and the mechanisms of lipid metabolism regulation in Easter Finns eating the traditional diet. *Human Physiology*, **35**(6), 765–9.

Kulper, H. A., Kleter, G. A., Noteborn, H. P., and Kok, E. J. (2001). Assessment of the food safety issues related to genetically modified foods. *Plant Journal*, **27**(6), 503–28.

Kuzawa, C. W. (2004). Modeling fetal adaptation to nutrient restrictions: testing the fetal origins hypothesis with a supply-demand model. *Journal of Nutrition*, **134**(1), 194–200.

Kuzawa, C. W. and Adair, L. S. (2003). Lipid profiles in adolescent Filipinos: relation to birth weight and maternal energy status during pregnancy. *American Journal of Clinical Nutrition*, **77**(4), 960–6.

Kuzawa, C. W. and Adair, L. S. (2004). A supply-demand model of fetal energy sufficiencypredicts lipid profiles in male but not female Filipino adolescents. *European Journal of Clinical Nutrition*, **58**, 438–48.

Kuzawa, C. W. and Sweet, E. (2009). Epigenetics and the embodiment of race: developmental origins of US racial disparities in cardiovascular health. *American Journal of Human Biology*, **21**(1), 2–15.

Lawlor, D. A., Clark, H., Smith, G. D., and Leon, D. A. (2006). Intrauterine growth and intelligence within sibling pairs: findings from the Aberdeen children of the 1950s cohort. *Pediatrics*, **117**(5), e894–902.

Leonard, W. R., Snodgrass, J. J., and Sorensen, M. V. (2005). Metabolic adaptation in indigenous Siberian populations. *Annual Review of Anthropology*, **34**, 451–71.

Leonard, W. R., Sorensen, M. V., Galloway, V. A., *et al.* (2002). Climatic influences on basal metabolic rates among circumpolar populations. *American Journal of Human Biology*, **14**(5), 609–20.

Leonard, W. R., Sorensen, M. V., and Mosher, M. J. (2009). Reduced fat oxidation and obesity risks among the Buryat of Southern Siberia. *American Journal of Human Biology*, **21**(5), 664–70.

Li, C. J., Elsasser, T. H., and Li, R. W. (2008). Epigenetic regulation of genomes: nutrient-specific modulation. *Developmental Biology Basel*, **132**, 391–8.

Logan, A. C. (2004). Omega-3 fatty acids and major depression: a primer for the mental health professional. *Lipids in Health and Disease*, **9**, 25–33.

Lombard, D. B., Schwer, B., Alt, F. W., and Mostoslavsky, R. (2008). SIRT6 in DNA repair, metabolism and ageing. *Journal of International Medicine*, **263**(2), 128–41.

Lucock, M. (2007). *Molecular Nutrition and Genomics: Nutrition and the Ascent of Humankind*. Hoboken, NJ: John Wiley and Sons.

Lucock, M. and Yates, Z. (2005). Folic acid – vitamin and panacea or genetic time bomb? *Nature Reviews Genetics*, **6**, 235–40.

Lucotte, G., Loirat, F., and Hazout, S. (1997). Pattern of gradient of apolipoprotein E*4 frequencies in western Europe. *Human Biology*, **69**(2), 253–62.

Lussana, F., Painter, R. C., Ocke, M. C., *et al.* (2008). Prenatal exposure to the Dutch famine is associated with a preference for fatty foods and a more athero-genic lipid profile. *American Journal of Clinical Nutrition*, **88**(6), 1648–52.

Magana-Gomez, J. A., Cervantes, G. L., Yepiz-Plascencia, G., and de la Barca, A. M. (2008). Pancreatic response of rats fed genetically modified soybean. *Journal of Applied Toxicology*, **28**(2), 217–26.

Mahley, R. W. and Rall, S. C. (1999). Is epsilon4 the ancestral human apoE allele? *Neurobiology of Aging*, **20**(4), 429–30.

Mann, N. (2000). Dietary lean red meat and human evolution. *European Journal of Nutrition*, **39**(2), 71–9.

Mantzoros, C. S. and Moschos, S. J. (1998). Leptin: in search of role(s) in human physiology and pathophysiology. *Clinical Endocrinology*, **49**, 551–67.

Martinez-Arguelles, D. B. and Papadopoulos, V. (2010). Epigenetic regulation of the expression involved in steroid hormone biosynthesis and action. *Steroids*, **75**(7), 467–76.

Mattick, J. S. and Makunin, I. V. (2006). Non-coding RNA. *Human Molecular Genetics*, **15** (Spec.1), R17–29.

Mazzatti, D. J., Mocchegiani, E., and Powell, J. R. (2008). Age-specific modulation of genes involved in lipid and cholesterol homeostasis by dietary zinc. *Rejuvenation Research*, **11**(2), 281–5.

McElroy, A. and Townsend, P. K. (2004). *Medical Anthropology in Ecological Perspective*, 4th edn. Boulder, CO: Westview Press.

Mead, M. N. (2007). Nutrigenomics: the genome-food interface. *Environmental Health Perspectives*, **115**(12), A582–9.

Michan, S. and Sinclair, D. (2007). Sirtuins in mammals: insights into their biological function. *Biochemical Journal*, **404**(1), 1–13.

Mintz, S. W. and Du Bois, C. M. (2002). The anthropology of food and eating. *Annual Review of Anthropology*, **31**, 99–119.

Molloy, A. M. (2004). Genetic variation and nutritional requirements. *World Review of Nutrition and Dietetics*, **93**, 153–63.

Moore, K. W., de Waal, M. R., Coffman, R. L., and O'Garra, A. (2001). Interleukin-10 and the interleukin-10 receptor. *Annual Review of Immunology*, **19**, 683–765.

Mosher, M. J. (2002). The genetic architecture of plasma lipids in Siberian Buryat: an ecogenetic approach. Ph.D. dissertation, University of Kansas, Lawrence.

Mosher, M. J. and Crawford, M. H. (2010). Human sexual dimorphism under-lying gene-by-nutrient interaction. In *Nutritional Education*, ed. I. R. Laidyth, pp. 91–118. Hauppauge, NY: Nova Science Pub.

Nelson, S. M., Freeman, D. J., Sattar, N., *et al.* (2007). IGF-1 and leptin associate with fetal HDL cholesterol at birth: examination in offspring of mothers with type 1 diabetes. *Diabetes*, **56**(11), 2705–9.

Niemitz, E. L. and Feinberg, A. P. (2004). Epigenetics and assisted reproductive tech-nology: a call for investigation. *American Journal of Human Genetics*, **74**, 599–609.

Nogueira, P. K., Vuong, T. S., Boutoon, O., *et al.* (2000). Partial deletion of the AXGT gene (EX1_EX7DEL): a new genotype in hyperoxaluria type 1. *Human Muta-tion*, **15**, 384–5.

Oda, Y., Uchida, Y., Moradian, S., *et al.* (2009) Vitamin D receptor and coactovators SRC2 and 3 regulate epidermis-specific sphingolipid production and permea-bility barrier formation. *Journal of Investigative Dermatology*, **129**(6), 1367–78.

Oota, H., Pakstis, A. J., Bonne-Tamir, B., *et al.* (2004). The evolution and population genetics of the ALDH2 locus: random genetic drift, selection, and low levels of recombination. *Annals of Human Genetics*, **68**(2), 93–109.

Ordovas, J. M. and Corella, D. (2005). Genetic variation and lipid metabolism: modulation by dietary factors. *Current Cardiology Reports*, **7**(6), 480–6.

Ordovas, J. M., Lopez-Miranda, J., Mata, P., *et al.* (1995). Gene-diet interaction in determining plasma lipid response to dietary intervention. *Atherosclerosis*, **118**(Suppl), S11–27.

Pac-Kozuchowska, E. (2007). Evaluation of lipids, lipoproteins and apolipoproteins concentration in cord blood serum of newborns from rural and urban environments. *Annals of Agricultural & Environmental Medicine*, **14**(1), 25–9.

Painter, R. C., de Rooij, S. R., and Bossuyt, P. M. (2006). Early onset of coronary artery disease after prenatal exposure to the Dutch famine. *American Journal of Clinical Nutrition*, **84**(2), 322–7.

Pembrey, M. E., Bygren, L. O., Kaati, G., *et al.* (2006). Sex-specific, male-line transgeneration responses in humans. *European Journal of Human Genetics*, **14**, 159–66.

Perry, G. H., Dominy, N. J., and Claw, K. G. (2007). Diet and the evolution of human amylase gene copy number variation. *Nature Genetics*, **39**(10), 1256–60.

Perry, G. H., Verrelli, B. C., and Stone, A. C. (2005). Comparative analyses reveal a complex history of molecular evolution for human MYH16. *Molecular Biology and Evolution*, **22**(3), 379–82.

Popkin, B. M. (1998). The nutritional transition and its health implications in lower-income countries. *Public Health Nutrition*, **1**(1), 5–21.

Popkin, B. M. and Gordon-Larsen, P. (2004). The nutrition transition: worldwide obesity dynamics and their determinents. *International Journal of Obesity Related Metabolic Disorders*, **28**(Suppl 3), S2–9.

Price, W. A. (2000). *Nutrition and Physical Degeneration*, 6th edn. La Mesa, CA: Price-Pottenger Nutrition Foundation.

Remacle, C., Bieswal, F., and Reusens, B. (2004). Programming of obesity and cardiovascular disease. *International Journal of Obesity Related Metabolic Disorders*, **28**(Suppl 3), S46–53.

Ross, S. A. and Milner, J. A. (2007). Epigenetic modulation and cancer: effect of metabolic syndrome? *American Journal of Clinical Nutrition*, **86**(3), S872–7.

Rotillo, G. and Marchese, E. (2010). Nutritional factors in human dispersals. *Annals of Human Biology*, **37**(3), 312–24.

Scarino, M. (2008). A sideways glance. Do you remember your grandmother's food? How epigenetic changes transmit consequences of nutritional exposure from one generation to the next. *Genes and Nutrition*, **3**(1), 1–3.

Schisler, J. C., Charles, P. C., Parker, J. S., *et al.* (2009). Stable patterns of gene expression regulating carbohydrate metabolism determined by geographic ancestry. *PLoS ONE*, **4**(12), e8183.

Scholl, T. O., Chen, X., Khoo, C. S., and Lenders, C. (2004). The dietary glycemic index during pregnancy: influence on infant birth weight, fetal growth, and biomarkers of carbohydrate metabolism. *American Journal of Epidemiology*, **159**(5), 467–74.

Schooling, C. M., Jiang, C. Q., Lam, T. H., *et al.* (2008). Life-course origins of social inequalities in metabolic risk in the population of a developing country. *American Journal of Epidemiology*, **167**(4), 419–28.

Schooling, C. M., Lam, T. H., Thomas, G. N., *et al.* (2007). Growth environment and sex differences in lipid, body shape and diabetes risk. *PLoS ONE*, **2**(10), e1070.

Ségurel, L., Lafosse, S., Heyer, E., and Vitalis, R. (2010). Frequency of the AGT Pro11Leu polymorphism in humans: Does diet matter? *Annals of Human Genetics*, **74**(1), 57–64.

Shephard, R. J. and Rode, A. (1996). *The Health Consequences of "Modernization"*. Cambridge, UK: Cambridge University Press.

Siebel, A. L., Fernandez, A. Z., and El-Osta, A. (2010). Glycemic memory associated with epigenetic changes. *Biochemical Pharmacology*, **80**(12), 1853–9.

Singh, G. K. and Yu, S. M. (1996). Adverse pregnancy outcomes: differences between US and foreign-born women in major US racial and ethnic groups. *American Journal of Public Health*, **86**(6), 837–43.

Singh, R., Barden, A., Mori, T., and Beilin, L. (2001). Advanced glycation end-products: a review. *Diabetologia*, **44**(2), 129–46.

Skidmore, P. M., Hardy, R. J., Kuh, D. J., *et al.* (2004). Birth weight and lipid in a national birth cohort study. *Arteriosclerosis, Thrombosis, and Vascular Biology*, **24**(3), 588–94.

Somel, M., Creely, H., Franz, H., *et al.* (2008). Human and chimpanzee gene expression differences replicated in mice fed different diets. *PLoS ONE*, 3(1), e1504.

Stedman, H. H., Kozyak, B. W., Nelson, A., *et al.* (2004). *Nature*, **428**(6981), 415–18.

Stover, P. J. (2006). Influence of human genetic variation on nutritional requirements. *American Journal of Clinical Nutrition*, **83**(Suppl), 436S–442S.

Stover, P. J. (2009). One-carbon metabolism-genome interactions in folate-associated pathologies. *Journal of Nutrition*, **139**(12), 2402–5.

Stover, P. J. and Caudill, M. A. (2008). Genetic and epigenetic contributions to human nutrition and health: managing genome-diet interactions. *Journal of the American Dietetic Association*, **108**(9), 1480–7.

Tepper, B. J., White, E. A., Koelliker, Y., *et al.* (2009). Genetic variation in taste sensitivity to 6-n-proplthiouracil and its relationship to taste perception and food selection. *Annals of the New York Academy of Science*, **1170**, 126–39.

Tobi, E. W., Heijmans, B. T., Kremer, D., *et al.* (2011). DNA methylation of IGF2, GNASAS, INSIGF and LEP and being born small for gestational age. *Epigenetics*, **3**(6), 2(epub).

Tobi, E. W., Lumey, L. H., Talens, R. P., *et al.* (2009). DNA methylation differences after exposure to prenatal famine are common and timing- and sex-specific. *Human Molecular Genetics*, **18**(21), 4046–53.

Ulrich, C. M. and Potter, J. D. (2006). Folate supplementation: too much of a good thing? *Cancer Epidemiology, Biomarkers & Prevention*, **15**, 189–93.

Ungar, P. S. (ed.) (2007). *Evolution of the Human Diet*. New York: Oxford University Press.

Van Assche, F. A., Holemans, K., and Aerts, L. (2001). Long-term consequences for offspring of diabetes during pregnancy. *British Medical Bulletin*, **60**(1), 173–82.

van Ommen, B., Bouwman, J., Dragsted, L. O., *et al.* (2010). Challenges of molecular nutrition research 6: the nutritional phenotype database to store, share and evaluate nutritional systems biology studies. *Genes & Nutrition*, **5**(3), 189–203.

Varela-Silva, M. I., Frisancho, A. R., Bogin, B., *et al.* (2007). Behavioral, environmental, metabolic and intergenerational components of early life undernutrition leading to later obesity in developing nations and in minority groups in the USA. *Collegium Antropologicum*, **31**(1), 39–46.

Voight, B. F., Kudaravalli, S., Wen, X., and Pritchard, J. K. (2006). A map of recent positive selection in the human genome. *PLoS Biology*, **4** (3), e72.

Walters, J. R. (2004). Cell and molecular biology of the small intestine: new insights into differentiation, growth and repair. *Current Opinion in Gastroenterology*, **20**(2), 70–6.

Wang, Y. X., Lee, C. H., Tiep, S., *et al.* (2003). Peroxisome-proliferator-activated receptor delta activates fat metabolism to prevent obesity. *Cell*, **113**(2), 159–70.

Wardlaw, G. M. and Insel, P. M. (1995). *Perspectives in Nutrition*, 3rd edn. St Louis, MO: Mosby.

Waterland, R. A. and Garza, C. (1999). Potential mechanisms of metabolic imprinting that lead to chronic disease. *American Journal of Clinical Nutrition*, **69**, 179–97.

Westerterp, M., Berbée, J. F., Pires, N. M., *et al.* (2007). Apolipoprotein C-1 is crucially involved in lipopolysaccharide-induced atherosclerosis development in apolipoprotein E-knockout mice. *Circulation*, **116**(19), 2173–81.

Whitelaw, N. C. and Whitelaw, E. (2006). How lifetimes shape epigenotype within and across generations. *Human Molecular Genetics*, **15**(Spec No. 2), 131–7.

Whitney, E. and Rolfes, S. R. (eds.) (2008). *Understanding Nutrition*, 11th edn. Belmont, CA: Thomson Wadsworth.

Wood, R. J. (2008). Vitamin D and adipogenesis: new molecular insights. *Nutrition Review*, **66**, 40–6.

Woods, S. C., Gotoh, K., and Clegg, D. J. (2003). Gender differences in the control of energy homeostasis. *Experimental Biology & Medicine (Maywood)*, **228**(10), 1175–80.

Zeisel, S. H., Freake, H. C., Bauman, D. E., *et al.* (2005). The nutritional phenotype in the age of metabolomics. *Journal of Nutrition*, **135**(7), 1613–16.

Zhang, J. (2003). Evolution of the human ASPM gene, a major determinant of brain size. *Genetics*, **165**, 2063–70.

Section 2 Geography and migration

8

Population structure and migration in Africa: correlations between archaeological, linguistic, and genetic data

INTRODUCTION

Modern humans emerged in Africa ~200 thousand years ago (kya), and expanded from an estimated census size of just over a million individuals (Hawks *et al.*, 2000) during the Middle Stone Age (MSA) to ~7 billion inhabitants today (www.census.gov/main/www/popclock.html). The long-term human effective population size (i.e. the number of breeding adults) is inferred to be ~10 000 individuals based on studies of variation in proteins (Haigh and Smith, 1972; Takahata, 1993), autosomal DNA (Erlich *et al.*, 1996; Takahata, 1993; Tenesa, 2007), X chromosome DNA (Cox *et al.*, 2008), Y-chromosome DNA (Takahata, 1993), and mitochondrial DNA (Takahata, 1993). After migrating from Africa within the past 50–100 kya, modern humans have successfully colonized most of the terrestrial parts of the globe. Genetic evidence indicates that human populations underwent several major population expansion and migration events over the last 100 kya (Atkinson *et al.*, 2009; Cox *et al.*, 2009; Excoffier and Schneider, 1999; Harpending *et al.*, 1993; Rogers and Harpending, 1992). Patterns of *mt*DNA and nuclear genetic diversity indicate that there was an initial major population expansion in Africa ~110–70 kya (Atkinson *et al.*, 2009; Excoffier and Schneider, 1999; Harpending *et al.*, 1993; Rogers and Harpending, 1992) and subsequent migration and expansion events around the globe at periods ~60–55 kya, ~40–25 kya, and ~12 kya (Atkinson *et al.*, 2009; Cox *et al.*, 2009; Harpending *et al.*, 1993; Liu *et al.*, 2006). Modern humans evolved

Causes and Consequences of Human Migration, ed. Michael H. Crawford and Benjamin C. Campbell. Published by Cambridge University Press. © Cambridge University Press 2012.

during a hyper arid period in Africa and might have been restricted to parts of Africa with favorable ecological conditions (Ambrose, 1998a; Hawks *et al.*, 2000). Population expansions and migrations during the Pleistocene, followed by exponential expansion during the Holocene, were correlated with shifts in climatic conditions and technological innovation (Pennington, 1996; Powell *et al.*, 2009). Migration has played an important role in shaping the pattern of genetic and cultural variation in African populations (Cox *et al.*, 2008), which currently consist of >2000 diverse ethnolinguistic groups, representing ~30% of the linguistic diversity in the world (Haspelmath *et al.*, 2008; Lewis, 2009). Here we summarize the paleoclimatic conditions, major cultural and linguistic shifts, and major migration events in Africa which have contributed to the current patterns of genetic variation in the continent.

EFFECT OF PALEOCLIMATIC CHANGE ON MIGRATION IN AFRICA

The pattern of genetic variation in modern human populations reflects our demographic history which has been influenced by large-scale climatic fluctuations (Clark *et al.*, 2003). Extreme climatic changes cause fluctuations in resource availability that impact human population densities and distributions (Morin, 2008). The climatic changes that have occurred during the Pleistocene are thought to have affected the global distribution of humans in different ecological regions through a series of demographic events (Ray and Excoffier, 2009) including range shifts, range contractions and expansions, isolation events, local extinctions, demographic bottlenecks, and demographic expansions (Ray and Excoffier, 2009). The areas conducive to human habitation shrank during cold periods and increased during warmer periods, with the range of ancestral hunting and gathering populations expanding and contracting in response to shifting resource opportunities as the climate changed (Klein, 1992; Ray and Excoffier, 2009) (Figure 8.1). The climatic conditions in tropical Africa are also sensitive to global climatic dynamics (reviewed in Chiang, 2009) and are dominated by variability in effective moisture (defined as precipitation minus evaporation), rather than temperature, caused by the circulation of the African monsoon and the seasonal migration of the Intertropical Convergence Zone (Scholz *et al.*, 2007). The glacial period was marked by colder temperatures coupled with dry conditions, resulting in temperatures in Africa as much as 7–10 °C lower than the current average

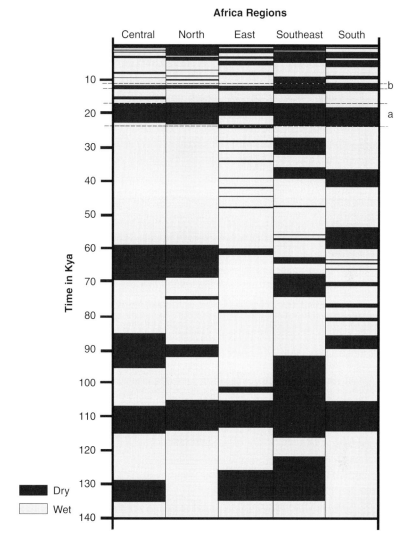

Figure 8.1 A rough guide to paleoclimatic conditions in Africa collated from the literature. Periods that are shown to be under dry conditions represent times when there was less relative humidity compared with modern conditions, but extreme drought occurred during portions of some of these times. There is a lack of detailed chronologies documenting continuous climatic changes, and records are still not very coherent because of disparate proxies used, lack of proper preservations in some regions, and problems in dating. Moreover, within the ad hoc regions represented here there might be regional pockets that have conflicting inferred paleoclimatic conditions (Kiage and Liu, 2006). Long periods of either dry or humid conditions have interruptions, with significant

annual temperature (Clark, 1988) (Figure 8.1). There is also evidence for contraction of the Central Africa equatorial forest due to the climatic changes during the Last Glacial Maximum (Cornelissen, 2002; Jolly *et al.*, 1997). This climatic shift resulted in expansion of savanna and

---

Figure 8.1 (cont.) subregional variations. The dashed lines represent boundaries of periods with extreme climatic fluctuations due to the Last Glacial Maximum (a), and the Younger Dryas (b), during which there were cold and dry climatic conditions. Conditions were generally cooler during the time that encompasses glacial periods when most regions were affected with overall reduction in temperature, precipitation, and increased aridity (Barham and Mitchell, 2008). However, it was generally warmer and wet after 12 kya. Considering that there is a general trend of decreasing species richness and vegetation density away from the tropics (Niklas *et al.*, 2003), vegetation zones increased or decreased in response to paleoclimatic conditions; that is, the tropical forest and two subsequent zones, savanna and grasslands, increased northwards and southwards away from the equator during the warm/wet conditions, while desert and semi-desert regions shrank. However, during cold/dry conditions the trend is reversed, with desert and semi-desert regions expanding and grassland, savanna, and tropical forest regions shrinking towards the equator (Jolly *et al.*, 1998). (*Sources:* Adamson *et al.*, 1980; Alin and Cohen, 2003; Alley *et al.*, 1997; Armitage *et al.*, 2007; Bar-Matthews *et al.*, 2010; Barker and Gasse, 2003; Bergner and Trauth, 2004; Bergner *et al.*, 2009; Beuning *et al.*, 2011; Blaauw *et al.*, 2011; Bonnefille and Riollet, 1988; Bouimetarhan *et al.*, 2009; Burnett *et al.*, 2011; Burrough and Thomas, 2008; Burrough *et al.*, 2007, 2009; Carto *et al.*, 2009; Castaneda *et al.*, 2007, 2009; Causse *et al.*, 2003; Cowling *et al.*, 1999; deMenocal, 2000; Dupont *et al.*, 2000; Finch and Hill, 2008; Garcin *et al.*, 2006, 2009; Gasse, 2000; Gasse *et al.*, 2008; Geyh and Thiedig, 2008; Giraudi, 2005; Giresse *et al.*, 1994; Haslett and Davies, 2006; Hassan, 1997; Huffman, 2008; Jahns, 1995, 1996; Johnson *et al.*, 2002; Kennedy, 2005; Kiage, 2006; Kim *et al.*, 2010; Kropelin *et al.*, 2008; Kuper and Kropelin, 2006; Lamb *et al.*, 2004, 2007; Lewis, 2008; Lyons *et al.*, 2011; Maley, 1977; Marchant *et al.*, 1997; Moeyersons *et al.*, 2002; Mohammed *et al.*, 1996; Ngomanda *et al.*, 2009; Nguetsop *et al.*, 2004; Norstrom *et al.*, 2009; Partridge *et al.*, 1993, 1997; Revel *et al.*, 2010; Russell and Johnson, 2005; Schefuss *et al.*, 2005; Scholz *et al.*, 2007, 2011a, 2011b; Scott and Woodborne, 2007; Shaw *et al.*, 2003; Sinninghe Damsté *et al.*, 2011; Smith *et al.*, 2004, 2007; Stager, 1988; Stager *et al.*, 2003, 2009; Stokes *et al.*, 1998; Stone *et al.*, 2011; Talbot and Johannessen, 1992; Tierney *et al.*, 2008, 2011; Tjallingii *et al.*, 2008; Trauth *et al.*, 2003; Vaks *et al.*, 2007; Van Zinderen Bakker and Coetzee, 1988; Verschuren *et al.*, 2009; Vincens *et al.*, 1999; Williams *et al.*, 2010.)

grassland vegetation which provided productive foraging opportunities for hunter-gatherer populations (Cornelissen, 2002).

Climates in Africa exhibit a broadly zonal pattern, with varying seasonal distributions of precipitation (Gasse, 2000). Human populations have migrated in order to reduce ecological stress that resulted from climatic change (Zhang *et al.*, 2007). Because human migrations usually take place along ecologically favorable corridors – through savanna environments and along water sources such as rivers, seas, or lakes (Amos and Manica, 2006; Clist, 1989; McIntosh and McIntosh, 1983; Mellars, 2006; Powell *et al.*, 2009) – regionally specific paleoclimatic conditions restricted the times and routes of movement. It is likely, therefore, that climatic conditions preceding the Holocene played a role in determining the extant pattern of genetic variation in Africa.

EFFECT OF CULTURAL CHANGE ON MIGRATION IN AFRICA

In addition to favorable paleoclimate conditions (Ambrose, 1998a; Lahr and Foley, 1998), migration of anatomically modern humans within Africa and across the globe was also facilitated by sociocultural and technological advancements (Mellars, 2006). The Middle Stone Age (MSA), which began ~300–200 kya and lasted until ~40 kya (Ambrose, 2001), corresponds to the period of the appearance of the first anatomically modern humans (AMH) in Africa (Clark, 1988; Stringer and Andrews, 1988). African MSA tools show inter- and intraregional stylistic variation reflecting the environment of the populations that created the tools (e.g. adapted for forest versus savanna environment) and the availability of raw materials (Clark, 1988; McBrearty and Brooks, 2000). Some of the regionally associated MSA traditions that occurred in large geographic areas and persisted for long periods include: Lupemban (Central Africa) (Clist, 1989; Cornelissen, 2002); Aterian, which is technologically related to the Lupemban technologies of Central/West Africa and might have originated in Central Africa (North and Northwest Africa) (Barham and Mitchell, 2008; Beyin, 2006; Castaneda *et al.*, 2009; Peer *et al.*, 1998); and Sangoan (part of East Africa and southern Africa up to Zimbabwe) (Clark, 1988; Cooke, 1962). Other common lithic traditions include the Nubian (southern Egypt, Sudan into western Ethiopia) and "Lower Nile Valley" (Egypt) traditions (Beyin, 2006; Brandt, 1986; Peer *et al.*, 1998) (Figure 8.2). In addition, there were diverse Middle Stone Age industries in eastern Africa and other less widespread industries such as Somaliland

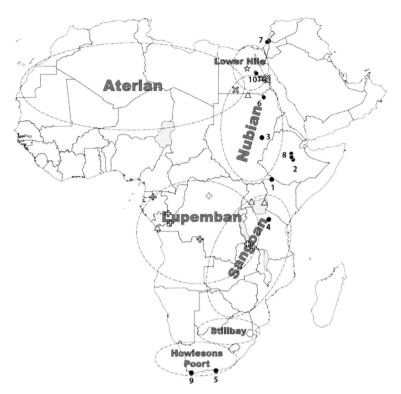

Figure 8.2 Regional distribution of Middle Stone Age cultural traditions mentioned in the text. This is a broad inference in distribution patterns in MSA lithic traditions that emerge based on limited archaeological data sites, with evidence of the cultures highlighted in the map that have been dated to ~40 kya, the time when the transition from MSA to LSA began. Because of lack of reliable dating techniques, materials from MSA do not yield firm dates, especially in areas with few excavated materials. There are younger sites from the tradition but they are mainly within the vicinity of the sites listed here. The geographical locations marked should not be considered as the limits of any of the cultural traditions but as an ad hoc guide based on available evidence. The earliest fossil evidence for anatomically modern humans is in southern Ethiopia and dated to ~190–165 kya (McDougall *et al.*, 2005), although other sites have been identified in eastern and southern Africa ranging from ~160 to 50 kya, chronologically listed in the figure beginning with the oldest evidence: **1**, 195–150 kya (McDougall *et al.*, 2005); **2**, 160–150 kya (Clark *et al.*, 2003); **3**, 140–150 kya (McDermott *et al.*, 1996); **4**, 130–110 kya (Brauer and Mehlman, 1988); **5**, 120–100 kya (Feathers, 2002); **6**, 110–90 kya (McDermott *et al.*, 1993; Mercier *et al.*, 1993; Vandermeersch, 1989); **7**, 100–90 kya (McDermott *et al.*, 1993; Schwarcz *et al.*, 1988); **8**, 105–80 kya (Haile-Selassie *et al.*, 2004); **9**, 67–90 kya (Feathers, 2002); **10**, 80–50 kya (Vermeersch *et al.*, 1998), with each point on the map corresponding to the geographic location of the fossil evidence site.

Stillbay (Horn of Africa) (Brandt, 1986; Clark, 1988), Howiesons Poort and South African Stillbay (South Africa) (Jacobs *et al.*, 2008). However, these industries were either restricted to a limited area (Brandt, 1986; Clark, 1988) and/or ended before 60 kya (Howiesons Poort and South African Stillbay) (Jacobs *et al.*, 2008) (Figure 8.2). These regional traditions have spatial correspondence with the proposed origin and distribution of the major language families in Africa (Figure 8.2), and makers of these industries might have had an influence on extant genetic patterns in Africa.

Before the advent of agriculture during the early Holocene, hunting-gathering populations are thought to have inhabited resource-rich forest margins and savanna grasslands (Ambrose, 1986). The area covered by such a habitat increased or decreased in size during the favorable and unfavorable climatic conditions, respectively. Therefore, while humans have continuously occupied Africa, evidence of this occupation is restricted to particular regions in Africa, perhaps due to differences in ecological conditions and suitability for survival of ancestral hunter-gatherer populations. Current patterns have also been affected by lack of preservation, and the difficulty of detection of sites in tropical forests and the distribution of archaeological field work. Nevertheless, East African sites have the most continuous sequences of Middle and Late Stone Age assemblages (Ambrose, 1998b, 2001; Willoughby and Sipe, 2002). In fact, there is limited archaeological evidence of human occupation in northern and southern Africa between ~40 kya and 20 kya. Specifically, in North Africa, there is a lack of archaeological evidence of human occupation after the end of the Aterian industries 30 kya until 18 kya (Close, 1988), when repopulation from the Sahel or the Nile valley occurred after environmental conditions improved. Improvement in climatic conditions after 15 kya (Barham and Mitchell, 2008) caused the Sahara and Sahel to become wet, resulting in extensive vegetation cover, lakes, and wetlands, and thriving animal communities. This environmental shift (Figure 8.1) allowed numerous human settlements from the late Pleistocene until the middle Holocene, 14.5–5.5 kya, after which a sudden transition to desert conditions occurred (deMenocal *et al.*, 2000; Foley *et al.*, 2003; Gabriel, 1987; Jousse, 2006, and references therein).

The earliest evidence for material culture commonly associated with modern humans occurred during the MSA in Africa (Clark, 1988). For example, personal ornaments such as shell beads and bone ornaments as well as use of ochre, often cited as evidence for early technological and behavioral developments, have been found in Africa and the

Levant as early as 100 kya (Bouzouggar *et al.*, 2007; d'Errico *et al.*, 2010; Henshilwood *et al.*, 2002, 2009, 2011; Hovers *et al.*, 2003). However, more widespread distribution of ornaments occurred during the MSA transition to LSA around 40 kya (Ambrose, 1998a, 1998b; McBrearty and Brooks, 2008; Thackeray, 1989). The MSA period is also marked by the appearance of materials obtained from distant sources through travel or down-the-line exchange (Ambrose, 1998a, 1998b; McBrearty and Brooks, 2008; Thackeray, 1989). The time period associated with cultural shifts ~40 kya is also characterized by shifts in social structure, whereby disparate hunter-gatherer populations (bands made up of related families and unrelated individuals) began to interact, forming larger groups (Ambrose, 1998a, 1998b; Hill *et al.*, 2011; McBrearty and Brooks, 2008; Sahlins, 1961). In fact, simulated models of the dynamics of cultural and demographic change predict that cultural innovations during that time period might have led to human demographic expansion, which in turn led to additional cultural innovation, and so on (Powell *et al.*, 2009; Shennan, 2001; Zilhão, 2007), the "cumulative cultural evolution" model (Boyd and Richerson, 1996; Hill *et al.*, 2011). Cultural innovation (symbolism and ornamentation) is related to fundamental aspects of human cultural and social behaviors like the formation of clusters of human kin groups (Bower, 2005). These clusters of gave rise to ethnic groups (or tribes) which generally share a common language and cultural norms (Sahlins, 1961). Over time, tribal populations become differentiated and intergroup competition ensues (Newcomer, 1972; Sahlins, 1961) due to population pressure, resulting in expansion into new ecological areas that yield necessary resources (Sahlins, 1961; Newcomer, 1972). Increased technological and stylistic variability is a hallmark of the African Middle Stone Age compared with the earlier Acheulian, and this trend towards increased diversity continued during the early portion of the Later Stone Age (Clark, 1988; McBrearty and Brooks, 2000).

THE ROLE OF LANGUAGE ON PATTERNS OF HUMAN POPULATION SUBSTRUCTURE

Linguists have classified all languages in Africa into four major language families: Khoesan (containing click consonants, spoken by hunter-gatherer San populations in southern Africa as well as the Hadza and Sandawe hunter-gatherers in Tanzania), Niger-Kordofanian (spoken primarily by agriculturalist populations spread contiguously across sub-Saharan Africa from West Africa to eastern and southern

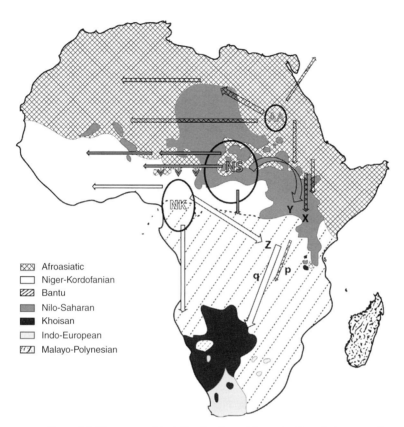

Figure 8.3 The geographical distribution of the major linguistic groups in Africa. The map was drawn using the information on geographical locations of ethnic speakers in Africa that are based on published sources (from Ehret, 1971, 1993, 1995, 2001; Greenberg, 1963, 1972; Haspelmath *et al.*, 2008; Lewis, 2009; Vansina, 1995). The geographical range occupied by the Bantu, the major linguistic subfamily within the Niger-Kordofanian phylum mentioned in the text, is also shown. Putative centers of origin and estimated time of initial expansion based on linguistic studies for three of the four language families are also listed: **AA**, Afroasiatic (14 kya) (Ehret, 1995); **NS**, Nilo-Saharan (18, 10–8 kya) (Blench, 1993, 2006; Ehret, 1993); **NK**, Niger-Kordofanian (5 kya) (Ehret, 2001; Nurse, 1997). Afroasiatic-speaking pastoralists were the first food-producing populations to migrate into East Africa ~5 kya (**X**) (Barthelme, 1977; Butzer *et al.*, 1969; Leakey, 1931; Robbins, 1972), followed by Nilo-Saharan-speaking pastoralists ~3 kya (**Y**) (Ambrose, 1982; Bower, 1973; Distefano, 1990; Leakey, 1931), and later Bantu-speaking agriculturalists after ~2.5 kya (**Z**) (Posnansky, 1961a, 1961b). **P** and **q** represent initial expansion of pastoralists (2.5 kya) and later Bantu-speaking agriculturalists (after 2 kya) to southern Africa from East Africa, respectively.

Africa), Nilo-Saharan (spoken predominantly by pastoralist populations in central and eastern Africa), and Afroasiatic (spoken predominantly by agropastoralists and pastoralist populations in northern and eastern Africa) (Figure 8.3). The putative origin of Niger-Kordofanian languages is in Central–West Africa (Ehret, 2001; Nurse, 1997), while Nilo-Saharan languages are thought to have originated in Chad/Sudan (Blench, 1993; Ehret, 1993), and Afroasiatic languages from a region that encompasses the Nile Valley to the Ethiopian highlands (Ehret, 1995, 1998) (Figure 8.3). Even though the limit of resolution of the time to most recent common ancestry (TMRCA) of all human language families is ~10–20 kya (Ambrose, 1982; Mehlman, 1979), d'Errico *et al.* (2003) speculate that modern language diversification might have occurred in tandem with behavioral changes associated with symbolism ~40 kya. They (d'Errico *et al.*, 2003) further speculate that the existence of regional lithic industries during the MSA (Clark, 1988; McBrearty and Brooks, 2000) may reflect linguistic borders between distinct language families. Thus, after differentiation into ancestral core language families, human language might have played a role in reinforcing human population structure.

Several population genetic studies exploring the relationships between genetic diversity, geography, and language on a global (Cavalli-Sforza *et al.*, 1988; Chen *et al.*, 1995), continental (Barbujani and Sokal, 1990; Rosser *et al.*, 2000; Wood *et al.*, 2005) and regional scale (Bryc *et al.*, 2010; Hunley *et al.*, 2008; Scheinfeldt *et al.*, 2010) have shown correlations between genetic variation, language, and geography among human populations. This correlation is expected since both linguistic and genetic diversity should reflect the same history of population migration, divergence, and admixture, although exceptions may occasionally occur (e.g. when there is language exchange without gene flow and vice versa (Smouse and Long, 1992). Therefore, some aspects of language can be used to trace back migration events. For example, a recent study (Atkinson, 2012a) that looked at phonemes, the smallest units of sound that distinguish one word from another, from 504 languages across the world showed that geographic variation in phonetic diversity is clinal in pattern and fits a model of expansion from an inferred origin in Africa, with highest levels of phonetic diversity observed in the Khoisan languages. These results are consistent with the extant global patterns of genetic (Degiorgio *et al.*, 2009; Hofer *et al.*, 2009) and phenotypic (Betti *et al.*, 2008; Manica *et al.*, 2007) diversity that fits a serial founder effect model with increasing genetic and phenotypic distance correlated with geographic distance from Africa.

However, recent reanalysis (Hunley *et al.*, 2012) and criticisms (Cysouw *et al.*, 2012; Hunley *et al.*, 2012; Van Tuyl and Pereltsvaig, 2012; Wang *et al.*, 2012) of Atkinson's (2012b) results have questioned the reported linguistic evidence for an expansion from Africa. First, in contrast to Atkinson (Atkinson, 2012b), Hunley *et al.* (Hunley *et al.*, 2012) find that the correlation between phoneme levels and distance from putative origins is strongest when the origin is located outside Africa (Eurasia), not Africa. Thus they (Hunley *et al.*, 2012) infer that phoneme inventories provide information about recent contacts between languages, and because phonemes change rapidly, they are not stable enough to provide information about more ancient evolutionary processes (Cysouw *et al.*, 2012; Hunley *et al.*, 2012). Moreover, the simplified normalized phoneme data as analyzed by Atkinson (2012a) ignore other important phonetic features (Cysouw *et al.*, 2012; Van Tuyl and Pereltsvaig, 2012; Wang *et al.*, 2012), and inferences made by Atkinson (2012a) are maybe an artifact of interactions in correlation techniques employed (Van Tuyl and Pereltsvaig, 2012), wrong methodology and biased interpretations (Cysouw *et al.*, 2012, Wang *et al.*, 2012). Atkinson (2012b) in response to criticisms from others concede that some aspects of language "complexity" may not conform to the serial founder effect, but argue that the results from reanalysis from both Wang *et al.* (2012) and Cysouw *et al.* (2012) are consistent with his observations (Atkinson, 2012a, 2012b).

Generally, populations speaking languages belonging to the four African language families also show differences in subsistence patterns – Khoisan (hunting-gathering), Nilo-Saharan (pastoralism and agropastoralism), Niger-Kordofanian (agriculture and agropastoralism), and Afroasiatic (pastoralism and agropastoralism) (Ambrose, 1982). The earliest form of food production that supplanted the foraging economy of LSA hunter-gatherers in East and North Africa, including the Sahel, was livestock husbandry (rearing cattle, sheep, and goats) beginning ~8–5 kya (Blench, 2006; Garcea, 2004, 2006) while farming occurred after 4 kya (reviewed in Marshall, 2002). However, in the West/Central African tropical forests, farming preceded pastoralism (Marshall and Hildebrand, 2002; Schoenbrun, 1993). According to linguistic evidence, the three language families associated with food production in Africa originated in Central/West Africa (Niger-Kordofanian) (Blench, 2006; Ehret, 2001; Nurse, 1997; Roland, 1966; Vansina, 1995) and northeast Africa (Nilo-Saharan and Afroasiatic) (Blench, 1993; Ehret, 1993) (Figure 8.3). The migration of Nilo-Saharan and Afroasiatic speaking pastoralists from northeast Africa to central and eastern Africa, and of Niger-Kordofanian speaking agriculturalists from Central/West Africa to the rest of Africa within the past 5000 years likely had major cultural and genetic impacts on many African populations, including indigenous hunting and gathering populations.

INFERRING AFRICAN DEMOGRAPHIC HISTORY USING GENETIC DATA

Genetic evidence for ancient substructure in Africa

Analyses of genetic data indicate that Africans have higher levels of genetic diversity relative to non-Africans (Cann *et al.*, 1987, 2002; Marth *et al.*, 2004; Tishkoff *et al.*, 1998). The extant patterns of genetic variation in global populations fit a serial founder effect model with increasing genetic distance correlated with geographic distance from East Africa, indicating the cumulative effect of genetic drift as humans expanded into the rest of the world (Hofer *et al.*, 2009; Prugnolle *et al.*, 2005; Ramachandran *et al.*, 2005). Additionally, studies of autosomal genetic variation show that genetic distance between populations increases with geographic distance within Africa (Hofer *et al.*, 2009; Prugnolle *et al.*, 2005; Ramachandran *et al.*, 2005). However, human populations may have already been structured into subpopulations prior to the out-of-Africa event (Satta and Takahata, 2004), as inferred from evolutionary genetic evidence (Labuda *et al.*, 2000; Plagnol and Wall, 2006; Satta and Takahata, 2004; Wall *et al.*, 2009). For example, analyses of genetic variation at a pseudogene (Garrigan *et al.*, 2005a, 2005b) and the DXS1238 microsatellite on the X-chromosome (Yotova *et al.*, 2007) suggest that ancestral modern humans might have arisen from a structured population in Africa, and that isolation and admixture events likely occurred among ancient African subpopulations. Moreover, on the basis of data from nucleotide polymorphisms in an 8-kb intronic segment flanking exon 44 (*dys44*) of the human dystrophin gene on Xp21, Labuda *et al.* (2000) argued that the gene pool of sub-Saharan Africans descends from two population lineages that had evolved separately for some time and eventually hybridized. They suggest that greater genetic diversity in sub-Saharan Africans as compared with other continental populations could be partially due to ancient admixture with archaic population(s) (Labuda *et al.*, 2000; Zietkiewicz *et al.*, 1998), analogous to the proposed admixture between Neanderthals and modern humans in Eurasia (Abi-Rached *et al.*, 2011; Green *et al.*, 2010; Reich *et al.*, 2011; Yotova *et al.*, 2011). Recent studies (Plagnol and Wall, 2006; Wall *et al.*, 2009) of the West

African Yoruba population also showed some evidence of ancestral admixture from an undetermined archaic source population (Plagnol and Wall, 2006), an observation supported by a recent sequencing study of nuclear genetic variation in other modern African populations (Hammer *et al.*, 2011).

Results from a recent analysis of human autosomal genetic variation in Africa using the program STRUCTURE (Pritchard *et al.*, 2000) indicate existence of large amounts of population substructure (i.e. high levels of genetic heterogeneity among populations). STRUCTURE (Pritchard *et al.*, 2000) uses a clustering algorithm which identifies subgroups that have distinctive allele frequencies by placing individuals into a specific number of K clusters using a Bayesian algorithm, where K is chosen in advance but can be varied across independent runs. K provides a rough guide for determining how many parental populations would be required to explain the variation in the data (Bamshad *et al.*, 2003). Analysis of genome-wide microsatellite and in/del polymorphism data from 121 African populations identified 14 ancestral population clusters in Africa (Tishkoff *et al.*, 2009). Analyses at lower K values may indicate older population structure in Africa. Interestingly, at $K = 5$, the Hadza hunting-gathering population from Tanzania is distinguished, the Pygmy and San populations cluster together, while the other three clusters broadly represent populations speaking Nilo-Saharan, Afroasiatic and Niger-Kordofanian languages (Tishkoff *et al.*, 2009). It is not possible to infer the age of these ancestral population clusters from STRUCTURE analysis. However, these results are consistent with substructure inferred from linguistic and archaeological data (Ehret, 1993, 1998; Sutton, 1974). Indeed, it is possible that some of the ancestral population clusters could have been geographically structured prior to 20 kya.

Genetic migration inferred from uniparentally inherited markers

The Y chromosome and *mt*DNA are particularly informative for reconstructing human evolution due to uniparental inheritance via males and females, respectively, and the absence of recombination. Human populations exhibit structure in both *mt*DNA and Y chromosome variation, and haplotype lineages defined by a set of single nucleotide polymorphisms (SNPs) in the non-recombining portion of the Y chromosomes (NRY) and whole *mt*DNA genome, respectively (Figure 8.4), have distinct distribution patterns across the globe. Data

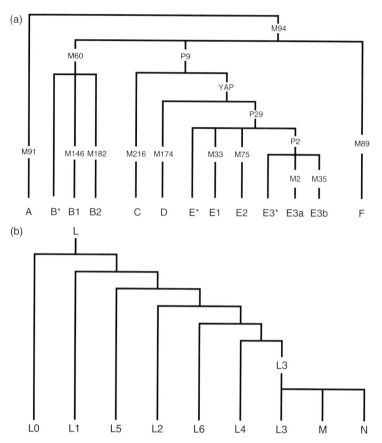

Figure 8.4 (a) Schematogram showing the classification of the major lineages of Y-chromosome haplogroups and their relationship to each other. The M#, P#, and YAP labels leading to haplogroup/s are SNPs and indels that are used to define these haplogroups. Subdivision within haplogroups is shown using numbers (from 1) followed by lower case letters (from a). Haplogroup F encompasses haplogroups F to T. Haplogroups A, B and E are found mainly in Africa while the rest are found mainly outside Africa. (b) Overview of *mt*DNA haplogroup phylogeny. In the *mt*DNA haplogroup nomenclature, the letter names of the haplogroups run from A to Z, with further subdivisions using numbers (from 0) and lower case letters (from a). The naming was done in the order of their discovery and does not reflect the actual genetic relationships. Haplogroups M and N encompass all the haplogroups lettered A to Z excluding haplogroup L. Haplogroups L (L0–L6) are mainly found in Africa while the rest are found mainly outside Africa (Behar *et al.*, 2008; Kivisild *et al.*, 2004; Macaulay *et al.*, 1999; Quintana-Murci *et al.*, 1999; Richards *et al.*, 1998; Salas *et al.*, 2002).

from patterns of variation in the Y chromosome are consistent with the patterns inferred from autosomal data that suggest ancient population structure in Africa. The oldest Y-chromosome lineages, haplogroup A, have a TMRCA older than 100 kya (Gronau *et al.*, 2011). There are several sublineages of haplogroup A that have a restricted geographical distribution (Batini *et al.*, 2011; Hammer and Zegura, 2002). Specifically, the A1 haplotype lineage is observed only in Central/West Africa (Batini *et al.*, 2011; Berniell-Lee *et al.*, 2009; King *et al.*, 2007; Wood *et al.*, 2005), the A3b2 lineage is observed commonly in East Africa, while the A3b1 lineage is observed only in southern African populations (Batini *et al.*, 2011; Wood *et al.*, 2005). Haplogroup A2 is observed mostly in southern African populations (Batini *et al.*, 2011; Wood *et al.*, 2005), but occurs at low frequency in Central African Pygmy populations (Batini *et al.*, 2011). Moreover, the slightly younger Y-chromosome B-haplogroup lineages that have a TMRCA of ~74 kya (Cruciani *et al.*, 2011) show a similar restricted geographic distribution as observed for the A haplogroup. Y-chromosome haplotype lineages B* and B1 are observed mostly in Central Africa, while B2a is observed mostly in East African populations. The ancestral haplotype from which B2b is derived, B2b*, is found in all three regions (Central/western, eastern and southern Africa) but is at highest frequency in East African hunter-gatherers. Recent refined analysis of the B haplogroup also shows that B2b1/B2b4a and B2b2 are geographically restricted to southern and eastern Africa, respectively, while B2b3 and B2b4b are specific to Central Africa. The B2b4* lineage is most common in Central African pygmy populations but is also present at low frequency in southern African Khoisan speakers (Batini *et al.*, 2011). Within Central Africa, B2b3, B2b4b, and B2b4* lineages are almost exclusively found among western Pygmies whereas B2b2 and B2b1–B2b4a lineages are found only in eastern Pygmies and South African Khoisan speakers (Batini *et al.*, 2011). This observation indicates a possible ancestral relationship between Pygmy and Khoisan speaking populations, a conclusion also inferred from population structure analysis of autosomal markers (Tishkoff *et al.*, 2009; Veeramah *et al.*, 2012), although a more recent admixture cannot be ruled out. The younger Y-chromosome lineages, those with TMRCAs of less than 50 kya (Cruciani *et al.*, 2011; Karafet *et al.*, 2008), also show clear differences in their geographic distributions, with E2a and E3b observed mostly in East African populations while E1 and E3a are observed mostly in Central/West African populations.

Analogous to variation observed on the Y chromosome, *mt*DNA haplotypes show geographic structuring. The oldest *mt*DNA lineages,

L0d and L0k, have a TMRCA of ~140–150 kya (Behar *et al.*, 2008; Soares *et al.*, 2009) and are observed mainly among Khoisan-speaking hunter-gatherer populations in southern Africa (Gonder *et al.*, 2007). The next oldest lineages (TMRCA estimates are shown in parentheses) include L1 (138 kya) and L2 (89 kya) (Behar *et al.*, 2008; Soares *et al.*, 2009) observed mainly in Central/West Africa, and L5 (150–160 kya), L0f (115 kya), L6 (110 kya), L4 (90 kya), and L0b (80 kya) (Behar *et al.*, 2008; Soares *et al.*, 2009) observed mainly in East Africa. This phylogeographic pattern mirrors what is observed for the distribution of Y-chromosome haplogroup A. Also echoing patterns observed for younger Y-chromosome lineages, the younger *mt*DNA L3 lineages (TMRCA < 70 kya) (Behar *et al.*, 2008; Soares *et al.*, 2009) are mostly observed in Central/West Africa (L3b, L3d, L3e) and in East Africa (L3a, L3h, L3iand, and L3x). Many of these latter lineages have more recently been introduced into other geographic regions in Africa, indicating the important role that migration from eastern and Central Africa has played in shaping human demography and genetic diversity in Africa during the LSA, especially during the Holocene.

Divergence times for mtDNA lineages L0d and L0k from other sub-Saharan African lineages L1–L6 is estimated at ~90–150 kya. On the basis of this ancient divergence time, Behar *et al.* (2008) suggested that the early human populations in Africa were split into two matrilineally structured population clusters. They argued that one ancestral population cluster was made up of populations ancestral to modern Khoisan-speaking populations, currently in southern Africa, while the other cluster represents populations ancestral to all other modern human global populations (Behar *et al.*, 2008). Consistent with the finding of Behar *et al.* (2008), coalescent-based Bayesian analysis of neutrally evolving loci across the genomes of six individuals, representative of diverse global human populations, also indicates that the San population of southern Africa diverged from other human populations ~157–108 kya, while the Eurasians diverged from an ancestral African population ~64–38 kya (Gronau *et al.*, 2011). Behar *et al.* (2008) further speculate that the L1–L5 *mt*DNA lineages observed among the Khoisan speakers in southern Africa are a result of recent introgression from Bantu speakers from Central Africa. The distribution pattern described above for *mt*DNA and Y-chromosome lineages suggests the possibility of at least three regionally structured ancestral populations in Africa, with descendants currently residing in Central/West Africa, northeastern Africa and southern Africa. However, one must be cautious about making inferences about ancient population structure based on genetic lineages since the time of coalescence of genetic lineages may precede the time of population divergence. Additionally, the location of lineages in modern populations may not reflect their distribution in the past. For example, linguistic and genetic data suggest that Khoisan-speaking populations in southern Africa may have originated in eastern Africa (Semino *et al.*, 2002; Smith, 1992). Overall, the distribution pattern of maternal and paternal lineages in extant African populations is a reflection of structured ancestral populations in Africa.

Results from studies of the evolutionary history of human parasites, such as the gut bacterium *Helicobacter pylori* (*Hp*) (Dominguez-Bello *et al.*, 2008; Falush *et al.*, 2003; Linz *et al.*, 2007; Schwarz *et al.*, 2008), are also consistent with the existence of ancestral structure in human populations. Linz *et al.* (2007) analyzed 716 isolates of *Hp* from 51 global human populations and identified five clusters representing *Hp*'s ancestral sources. Using STRUCTURE analysis, the study showed strong phylogeographic structure in *Hp* concordant with human phylogeography (Falush *et al.*, 2003; Linz *et al.*, 2007). Three of the five clusters identified are from Africa: hpAfrica1 (West Africa and South Africa), hpAfrica2 (South Africa), hpNEAfrica (East Africa) and the remaining two are from Europe and Asia, respectively (Falush *et al.*, 2003; Linz *et al.*, 2007; Schwarz *et al.*, 2008). The *hp*NEAfrica cluster was predominant among *Hp* isolated in populations from Ethiopia, Somalia, Sudan, and Nilo-Saharan speakers in northern Nigeria (Linz *et al.*, 2007). The three clusters in Africa may correspond to ancestral structured populations in Africa from which modern populations descend. It is possible that hpAfrica1, which is shared by West Africans and South Africans, might reflect Bantu expansions to southern Africa originating from Central/western Africa.

The precise location of origin of modern humans has been a contentious issue, with some arguing for a South African origin (Compton, 2011; Henn *et al.*, 2011; Tishkoff *et al.*, 2009), while others argue for an East African origin (Prugnolle *et al.*, 2005; Ray *et al.*, 2005). Studies of autosomal data (Henn *et al.*, 2011; Prugnolle *et al.*, 2005; Ray *et al.*, 2005) have resulted in conflicting inferences about the geographic origin of modern humans, with some indicating East Africa (Prugnolle *et al.*, 2005; Ray *et al.*, 2005), while others indicate South Africa (Henn *et al.*, 2011) as a site of origin. Uniparental markers also yield patterns that lead to conflicting inferences about the possible geographic origin of modern humans. Below is a summary of some of the evidence from different disciplines for the possible geographic site of origin of modern humans.

1. The oldest fossil evidence for modern human origins is in East Africa (Figure 8.2). However, the earliest evidence of ochre and shell bead making technologies associated with modern human behavior (which has been argued by some to indicate the source of modern human migration within Africa; Compton, 2011) is in South Africa (Henshilwood *et al.*, 2002, 2009, 2011).

2. Studies of autosomal genetic diversity support either an East African (Prugnolle *et al.*, 2005; Ray *et al.*, 2005) or South African origin (Henn *et al.*, 2011; Tishkoff *et al.*, 2009) for modern humans. The inferred South African origin is based on high levels of genetic variation in the San populations (Henn *et al.*, 2011; Tishkoff *et al.*, 2009). However, linguistic and archaeological data suggest a possible East African origin of Khoesan-speaking populations (Semino *et al.*, 2002; Smith, 1992).

3. The Y-chromosome lineages with the oldest TMRCA of 142 kya (A1b) are only observed in populations from Central/northwest Africa (Cruciani *et al.*, 2011). By contrast, the *mt*DNA lineages with the oldest TMRCA of 140–160 kya are most common in populations from other parts of sub-Saharan Africa: L0d and L0k (South Africa) (Behar *et al.*, 2008; Soares *et al.*, 2009), and L5 (East Africa) (Hirbo *et al.*, unpublished).

4. Based on autosomal (Veeramah *et al.*, 2012) and *mt*DNA data (Behar *et al.*, 2008), South African Khoesan populations diverged from other sub-Saharan African populations ~157–90 kya (Veeramah *et al.*, 2012). This split might have been related to the initial human dispersal from the center of origin of modern humans. If, indeed, modern humans originated in East Africa, it is interesting to note that this time period corresponds to a period in tropical Africa when it was inferred to have been a megadrought (Cohen *et al.*, 2007), which may have forced populations to migrate to northern or southern Africa where conditions were more favorable (Figure 8.1) (Ambrose, 1998b; Compton, 2011). However, there is a break in the fossil and archaeological record for modern human origins in southern Africa after ~60–70 kya, and it has been suggested that the hunter-gatherer populations that existed in the south might have migrated to wetter regions of Central and East Africa (Ambrose, 1998b; Compton, 2011). Thus, it is possible that there have been long-range migration events north and south across Africa over different time periods (Figure 8.5).

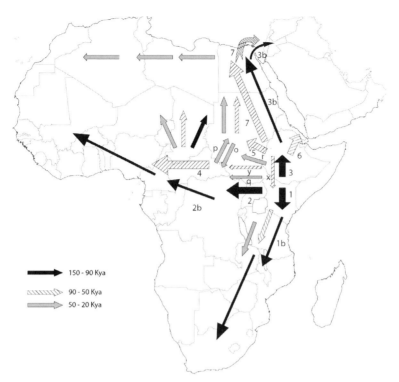

Figure 8.5 Possible ancestral migration events within Africa inferred from
*mt*DNA and Y-chromosome lineage data modified from Behar *et al.*, 2008
considering paleoclimatic conditions that prevailed within the continent.
Age estimates of *mt*DNA lineages are based on updated data of ~9000
published complete *mt*DNA genome sequences, adjusted based on new
mutation rate estimates by Soares *et al.* (2009). Y-chromosome lineage age
estimates are from two recent studies (Cruciani *et al.*, 2011; Karafet *et al.*,
2008). The general direction of human ancestral dispersal, which should
not be treated as firm migratory paths, with associated lineages (*mt*DNA
lineages are italicized) are shown: **A**, 150–90 kya – the initial divergence of
human populations that corresponds to a period of megadrought in East
Africa that might have resulted in a split into subpopulations located in the
north (**2** and **3**) and south (**1**) of the tropics: **1**, *L0d1/2*, *L0k*, A2; **2**, *L1*, *L2*, A1; **3**,
L0abf, *L3′L4*, *L5*, *L6*, A3, BT. This initial expansion also includes the failed out-
of-Africa expansion through the Levant; **3b**, large-scale climatic changes
during this period accentuated the isolation of regional populations. **B**,
90–50 kya expansion from northeast Africa that includes the out-of-Africa
event: **4**, *L1b*, *L2b′c′d*, A1b; **y**, *L3b′c′d*, B; **x**, *L4*, *L3a*, B2; **5**, *L5*, *L3h*, *L3f*; **6**, out-
of-Africa through the southern route *M* and some *N*, D, C and some F; **7**, out-
of-Africa through the northern route via Levant – some *N*, some F, **C**,
50–20 kya LSA expansion within Africa: **p**, *L2a*, *L3e*, *L3d*, *L3c*; **q**, *L0a*, *L3e′k*, E1a,
E1b1a; **o**, *L3f*, E2b. Migration during the Holocene is shown in Figure 8.3.

SUMMARY AND CONCLUSIONS

Integrated genetic, archaeological, and linguistic data indicate that genetic variation in modern African populations has been shaped by ancient population structure, shifts in demography that correspond with shifts in climate and technology, and both ancient and recent migration events. Information gleaned from paleoclimatic evidence indicates that climatic conditions in Africa have undergone periodic changes between warm/wet and cold/dry conditions with subsequent changes in vegetation cover. Since vegetation cover is correlated with resource availability, human populations have expanded or shrunk depending on prevailing climatic conditions. Considering that both climatic conditions and resulting vegetation cover are zonal in nature, they might potentially have pushed populations into regional clusters or refugia during unfavorable conditions. However, during favorable climatic conditions these populations might have expanded and developed unique traditions adapted to their environments. There have been distinct cultural traditions in Africa dating back to >50 kya. However, there are limited archaeological data from 20 to 40 kya, making it challenging to infer direct lines of descent. Populations that had major contributions to extant genetic patterns in Africa might represent those that arose from ancestors that survived in regional refugia during extreme paleoclimatic conditions. Interestingly, wet conditions favorable for population refugia during the Last Glacial Maximum (23–19 kya) are inferred to have occurred in areas (Gasse *et al.*, 2008; Kim *et al.*, 2008; Nichol, 1999) that roughly correspond to putative centers of origin for the three language families in Africa: Afroasiatic (fringes of the Ethiopian highlands), Nilo-Saharan (Sudan), and Niger-Kordofanian (Nigerian-Cameroonian border).

Overall, genetic data indicate high levels of substructure in Africa, and several studies suggest that this substructure may be quite ancient. Examination of correlations between archaeological, linguistic, and genetic data may be informative for reconstructing ancient population history (Scheinfeldt *et al.*, 2010). Of particular interest is the correlation between the geographic distribution of Middle Stone Age cultural traditions, the distribution of major language families, and the major ancestral clusters inferred from genetic data (Tishkoff *et al.*, 2009) (Figures 8.1, 8.2, 8.3). It is possible that genetically defined population clusters in Africa may be correlated with linguistic and culturally defined ancestral populations inferred from the archaeological and linguistic records.

Moreover, distribution patterns of paternal and maternal lineages across Africa in extant human populations may reflect substructure that existed on the continent. However, most *mt*DNA and Y-chromosome genetic lineages are much older than languages, making it difficult to associate a lineage with a specific language family. In fact, because of the limitations of the language-dating methods, all of the African languages other than Khoisan spoken by hunter-gatherer populations have been estimated to be younger than 20 kya (Blench, 2006; Ehret, 1976, 1995). By contrast, the oldest maternal and paternal genetic lineages date to more than 100 kya. These genetic lineages may have already been spatially structured among disparate hunter-gatherer populations prior to the time of cultural and behavioral modernity. Development of common culture and languages might have occurred after the merging of hunter-gatherer populations that lived in the same geographical vicinity to form larger groups. Subsequent linguistic differentiation between different groups might then have reinforced existing geographically demarcated differentiation. Pleistocene human migration may also have been culturally mediated (Premo and Hublin, 2009), since the movement of populations may initially have been "restricted" to cultures sharing attributes like language, rituals, and socioeconomic activities. The tendency to interact within a limited sphere might have maintained culturally defined population structure (Premo and Hublin, 2009). Subsequent population expansion during the Holocene, due to the development of agriculture and pastoralism, changed the range of areas occupied by populations from different language families. These migrations also resulted in gene flow between populations. Because of this, the two major events that occurred due to changes in subsistence patterns, namely the Bantu and pastoralist migration events, likely had major influences on extant genetic patterns in Africa, but did not erase signatures of ancestral structure.

In the future, more archaeological excavations are needed in Africa to fill in gaps in the fossil and cultural records. Future excavations from underexplored regions like Central Africa, parts of southern Africa and the Sahel will be particularly informative for reconstructing ancient human migration history. Improvement in ancient DNA analysis may also make it possible to directly study the genomes of ancient populations in Africa and to bridge data from genetic and archaeological data. Moreover, as there has been a recent decrease in the costs of generating whole-genome SNP data and next-generation sequencing data, it will be informative to study genome-wide variation across more ethnically and geographically diverse African populations. Future studies that could help clarify the demographic history of African populations include simulation and modeling approaches to analyze autosomal data from unlinked loci to test a number of hypotheses raised by the current review. For example, an Isolation and Migration (IM) method can be used to distinguish time of common ancestry and migration events between populations based on non-recombining regions of the genome (Hey and Nielsen, 2004; Nielsen and Wakeley, 2001). Another approach for inferring demographic parameters and testing evolutionary hypotheses is Approximate Bayesian Computation (ABC) (Beaumont *et al.*, 2002; Cornuet *et al.*, 2008), in which parameters such as population divergence, admixture (migration rate) and effective population size can be modeled by comparing summary statistics estimated from simulated and observed data. Archaeological, paleoclimatic, and linguistic data coupled with African genetic data will offer rich fodder for interdisciplinary integration and allow interpretations that will sharpen our picture of human population history in Africa.

REFERENCES

Abi-Rached, L., Jobin, M. J., Kulkarni, S., *et al.* (2011). The shaping of modern human immune systems by multiregional admixture with archaic humans. *Science*, **334**, 89–94.

Adamson, D. A., Gasse, F., Street, F. A., and Williams, M. A. J. (1980). Late Quaternary history of the Nile. *Nature*, 288, 50–5.

Alin, S. R. and Cohen, A. S. (2003). Lake-level history of Lake Tanganyika, East-Africa, for the past 2500 years based on ostracode-inferred water-depth reconstruction. *Palaeogeography, Palaeoclimatology, Palaeoecology*, **199**, 31–49.

Alley, R. B., Mayewski, P. A., Sowers, T., *et al.* (1997) Holocene climatic instability: a prominent, widespread event 8200 yr ago. *Geology*, **25**, 483–6.

Ambrose, S. (1986). Hunter-gatherer adaptations to non-marginal environments: an ecological and archaeological assessment of the Dorobo Model. *Sprache und Geschichte in Afrika (SUGIA)*, **7.2**, 11–42.

Ambrose, S. H. (1982). Archaeology and linguistic reconstructions of history in East Africa. In *The Archaeological and Linguistic Reconstruction of Africa History*, ed. C. Ehret and M. Posnansky, pp. 104–57. Berkeley, CA: University of Califonia Press.

Ambrose, S. H. (1998a). Late Pleistocene human population bottlenecks, volcanic winter, and differentiation of modern humans. *Journal of Human Evolution*, **34**(6), 623–51.

Ambrose, S. H. (1998b). Chronology of the later Stone Age and food production in East Africa. *Journal of Archaeological Science*, **25**, 377–92.

Ambrose, S. H. (2001). Paleolithic technology and human evolution. *Science*, **291** (5509), 1748–53.

Ambrose, S. H. (2003). East African Neolithic. In *Encyclopedia of Prehistory*, Vol. 1: *Africa*, ed. P. N. Peregrine and M. Ember, pp. 97–109. New York Kluwer Academic/Plenum Publishers.

Amos, W. and Manica, A. (2006). Global genetic positioning: evidence for early human population centers in coastal habitats. *Proceedings of the National Academy of Sciences of the United States of America*, **103**(3), 820–4.

Armitage, S. J., Drake, N. A., Stokes, S., *et al.* (2007). Multiple phases of North African humidity recorded in lacustrine sediments from the Fazzan Basin, Libyan Sahara. *Quaternary Geochronology*, **2**, 181–6.

Armitage, S. J., Drake, N. A., Stokes, S., *et al.* (2011). The southern route "out of Africa": evidence for an early expansion of modern humans into Arabia. *Science*, **331**(6016), 453–6.

Atkinson, Q. D. (2012a). Phonemic diversity supports a serial founder effect model of language expansion from Africa. *Science*, **332**(6027), 346–9.

Atkinson, Q. D. (2012b). Response to comments on "Phonemic diversity supports a serial founder effect model of language expansion from Africa". *Science*, **335**, 657.

Atkinson, Q. D., Gray, R. D., and Drummond, A. J. (2009). Bayesian coalescent inference of major human mitochondrial DNA haplogroup expansions in Africa. *Proceedings of the Royal Society B: Biological Sciences*, **276**(1655), 367–73.

Bamshad, M. J., Wooding, S., Watkins, W. S., *et al.* (2003). Human population genetic structure and inference of group membership. *American Journal of Human Genetics*, **72**(3), 578–89.

Barbujani, G. and Sokal, R. R. (1990). Zones of sharp genetic change in Europe are also linguistic boundaries. *Proceedings of the National Academy of Sciences of the United States of America*, **87**(5), 1816–9.

Barham, L. and Mitchell, P. (2008). *The First Africans: African Archaeology from the Earliest Tool Makers to Most Recent Foragers*. Cambridge World Archaeology. Cambridge, UK: Cambridge University Press.

Barker, P. and Gasse, F. O. (2003). New evidence for a reduced water balance in East Africa during the Last Glacial Maximum: implication for model-data comparison. *Quaternary Science Reviews*, **22**, 823–37.

Bar-Matthews, M., Marean, C. W., Jacobs, Z., *et al.* (2010). A high resolution and continuous isotopic speleothem record of paleoclimate and paleoenvironment from 90 to 53 ka from Pinnacle Point on the south coast of South Africa. *Quaternary Science Reviews*, **29**, 2131–45.

Barthelme, J. W. (1977). Holocene sites north-east of Lake Turkana: preliminary report. *Azania*, **12**, 33–41.

Batini, C., Ferri, G., Destro-Bisol, G., *et al.* (2011). Signatures of the pre-agricultural peopling processes in sub-Saharan Africa as revealed by the phylogeography of early Y chromosome lineages. *Molecular Biology and Evolution*, **28**(9), 2603–13.

Batzer, M. A. and Deininger, P. L. (2002). Alu repeats and human genomic diversity. *Nature Reviews Genetics*, **3**(5), 370–9.

Beaumont, M. A., Zhang, W., and Balding, D. J. (2002). Approximate Bayesian computation in population genetics. *Genetics*, **162**(4), 2025–35.

Behar, D. M., Villems, R., Soodyall, H., *et al.* (2008). The dawn of human matrilineal diversity. *American Journal of Human Genetics*, **82**(5), 1130–40.

Bergner, A. G. N. and Trauth, M. H. (2004). Comparison of the hydrological and hydrochemical evolution of Lake Naivasha (Kenya) during three highstands between 175 and 60 kyr BP. *Palaeogeography, Palaeoclimatology, Palaeoecology*, **215**, 17–36.

Bergner, A. G. N., Strecker, M. R., Trauth, M. H., *et al.* (2009). Tectonic and climatic control on evolution of rift lakes in the Central Kenya Rift, East Africa. *Quaternary Science Reviews*, **28**, 2804–16.

Berniell-Lee, G., Calafell, F., Bosch, E., *et al.* (2009). Genetic and demographic implications of the Bantu expansion: insights from human paternal lineages. *Molecular Biology and Evolution*, **26**(7), 1581–9.

Betti, L., Balloux, F., Amos, W., Hanihara, T., and Manica, A. (2008). Distance from Africa, not climate, explains within-population phenotypic diversity in humans. *Proceedings of the Royal Society B: Biological Sciences*, **276**, 809–14.

Beuning, K. R. M., Zimmerman, K. A., Ivory, S. J., and Cohen, A. S. (2011). Vegetation response to glacial-interglacial climate variability near Lake Malawi in the southern African tropics. *Palaeogeography, Palaeoclimatology, Palaeoecology*, **303**, 81–92.

Beyin, A. (2006). The Bab al Mandab vs the Nile-Levant: an appraisal of the two dispersal routes for early modern humans out of Africa. *African Archaeological Reviews*, **23**, 5–30.

Blaauw, M., Van Geel, B., Kristen, I., *et al.* (2011). High-resolution 14C dating of a 25,000-year lake-sediment record from equatorial East Africa. *Quaternary Science Reviews*, **30**, 3043–59.

Blench, R. (1993). Recent developments in African language classification and their implications for prehistory. In *The Archaeology of Africa: Food, Metals and Towns*, ed. P. S. T. Shaw, B. Andah, and A. Okpoko, pp. 71–103. London: Routledge Press.

Blench, R. (2006). *Archaeology, Language, and the African Past*. African Archaeology Series 10. Lanham, MD: AltaMira Press.

Bonnefille, R. and Riollet, G. (1988) The Kashiru pollen sequence (Burundi) palaeoclimatic implications for the last 40,000 yr B.P. in tropical Africa. *Quaternary Research*, **30**, 19–35.

Bouimetarhan, I., Dupont, L., Schefuß, E., *et al.* (2009). Palynological evidence for climatic and oceanic variability off NW Africa during the late Holocene. *Quaternary Research*, **72**, 188–97.

Bouzouggar, A., Barton, N., Vanhaeren, M., *et al.* (2007). 82,000-year-old shell beads from North Africa and implications for the origins of modern human behavior. *Proceedings of the National Academy of Sciences of the United States of America*, **104**(24), 9964–9.

Bower, J. R. F. (1973). Seronera: excavations at a stone bowl site in the Serengeti National Park, Tanzania. *Azania*, **8**, 71–104.

Bower, J. R. F. (2005). On "modern behavior" and the evolution of human intelligence. *Current Anthropology*, **46**(1), 121–2.

Boyd, R. and Richerson, P. (1996). Why culture is common, but cultural evolution is rare. In *Evolution of Social Behaviour Patterns in Primates and Man*, ed. W. G. Runciman, J. Maynard Smith, and R. I. M. Dunbar, pp. 77–83. Oxford, UK: Oxford University Press.

Brandt, S. A. (1986). The Upper Pleistocene and Early Holocene prehistory of the Horn of Africa. *African Archaeological Review*, **4**, 41–82.

Brauer, G. and Mehlman, M. J. (1988). Hominid molars from a Middle Stone Age level at the Mumba Rock Shelter, Tanzania. *American Journal of Physical Anthropology*, **75**(1), 69–76.

Bryc, K., Auton, A., Nelson, M. R., *et al.* (2010). Genome-wide patterns of population structure and admixture in West Africans and African Americans. *Proceedings of the National Academy of Sciences of the United States of America*, **107**(2), 786–91.

Burnett, A. P., Soreghan, M. J., Scholz, C. A., and Brown, E. T. (2011). Tropical East African climate change and its relation to global climate: a record from Lake Tanganyika, tropical East Africa, over the past 90+ kyr. *Palaeogeography, Palaeoclimatology, Palaeoecology*, **303**, 155–67.

Burrough, S. L. and Thomas, D. S. G. (2008). Late Quaternary lake-level fluctuations in the Mababe Depression: Middle Kalahari palaeolakes and the role of Zambezi inflows. *Quaternary Research*, **69**, 388–403.

Burrough, S. L., Thomas, D. S. G., and Bailey, R. M. (2009). Mega-lake in the Kalahari: a Late Pleistocene record of the Palaeolake Makgadikgadi system. *Quaternary Science Reviews*, **28**, 1392–411.

Burrough, S. L., Thomas, D. S. G., Shaw, P. A., and Bailey, R. M. (2007). Multiphase Quaternary highstands at Lake Ngami, Kalahari, northern Botswana. *Palaeogeography, Palaeoclimatology, Palaeoecology*, **253**, 280–99.

Butzer, K. W., Brown F. H., and Thurber, D. L. (1969). Horizontal sediments of the lower Omo Basin: the Kibish Formation. *Quarternaria*, **11**, 15–29.

Cann, H. M., De Toma, C., Cazes, L., *et al.* (2002). A human genome diversity cell line panel. *Science*, **296**, 261–2.

Cann, R. L., Stoneking, M., and Wilson, A. C. (1987). Mitochondrial DNA and human evolution. *Nature*, **325**(6099), 31–6.

Carto, S. L., Weaver, A. J., Hetherington, R. E., Lam, Y., and Wiebe, E. C. (2009). Out of Africa and into an ice age: on the role of global climate change in the late Pleistocene migration of early modern humans out of Africa. *Journal of Human Evolution*, **56**, 139–51.

Castaneda, I. S., Mulitzab, S., Schefuß, S., *et al.* (2009). Wet phases in the Sahara/Sahel region and human migration patterns in North Africa. *Proceedings of the National Academy of Sciences of the United States of America*, **106**(48), 20 159–63.

Castaneda, I. S., Werne, J., and Johnson, T. C. (2007). Wet and arid phases in the southeeast African tropics since the Last Glacial Maximum. *Geology*, **35**, 823–6.

Causse, C., Ghaleb, B., Chkir, N., *et al.* (2003). Humidity changes in southern Tunisia during the Late Pleistocene inferred from U-Th dating of mollusc shells. *Applied Geochemistry*, **18**(11), 1691–703.

Cavalli-Sforza, L. L., Piazzat, A., Menozzif, P., and Mountain, J. (1988). Reconstruction of human evolution: bringing together genetic, archaeological, and linguistic data. *Proceedings of the National Academy of Sciences of the United States of America*, **85**(16), 6002–6.

Chen, Y. S., Torroni, A., Excoffier, L., *et al.* (1995). Analysis of mtDNA variation in African populations reveals the most ancient of all human continent-specific haplogroups. *American Journal of Human Genetics*, **57**(1), 133–49.

Chiang, J. C. H. (2009). The tropics in paleoclimate. *Annual Review of Earth and Planetary Sciences*, **37**(1), 263–97.

Clark, J. D. (1988). The Middle Stone Age of East Africa and the beginnings of regional identity. *Journal of World Prehistory*, **2**(3), 235–305.

Clark, J. D., Beyene, Y., Woldegabriel, G., *et al.* (2003). Stratigraphic, chronological and behavioural contexts of Pleistocene *Homo sapiens* from Middle Awash, Ethiopia. *Nature*, **423**(6941), 747–52.

Clist, B. (1989). Archaeology in Gabon, 1886–1988. *African Archaeological Review*, **7**(1), 59–95.

Close, A. E. (1988). Current research and recent radiocarbon, dates from northern Africa, III. *Journal of African History*, **29**(2), 145–76.

Cohen, A. S., Stone, J. R., Beuning, K. R. M., *et al.* (2007). Ecological consequences of Early Late Pleistocene megadroughts in tropical Africa. *Proceedings of the National Academy of Sciences of the United States of America*, **104**, 16 422–7.

Compton, J. S. (2011). Pleistocene sea-level fluctuations and human evolution on the southern coastal plain of South Africa. *Quaternary Science Reviews*, **30**, 506–27.

Cooke, C. K. (1962). The Sangoan industries of Southern Rhodesia. *South African Archaeological Bulletin*, **17**(68), 212–30.

Cornelissen, E. (2002). Human responses to changing environments in Central Africa between 40,000 and 12,000 B.P. *Journal of World Prehistory*, **16**(3), 197–235.

Cornuet, J. M., Santos, F., Beaumont, M. A., *et al.* (2008). Inferring population history with DIY ABC: a user-friendly approach to approximate Bayesian computation. *Bioinformatics*, **24**(23), 2713–9.

Cowling, R. M., Cartwright, C. R., Parkington, J. E., and Allsopp, J. C. (1999). Fossil wood charcoal assemblages from Elands Bay Cave, South Africa: implications for Late Quaternary vegetation and climates in the winter-rainfall fynbos biome. *Journal of Biogeography*, **26**, 367–78.

Cox, M. P., Morales, D. A., Woerner, A. E., *et al.* (2009). Autosomal resequence data reveal Late Stone Age signals of population expansion in sub-Saharan African foraging and farming populations. *PLoS ONE*, **4**(7), e6366.

Cox, M. P., Woerner, A. E., Wall, J. D., and Hammer, M. F. (2008). Intergenic DNA sequences from the human X chromosome reveal high rates of global gene flow. *BMC Genetics*, **9**, 76.

Cruciani, F., Trombetta, B., Massaia, A., *et al.* (2011). A revised root for the human Y chromosomal phylogenetic tree: the origin of patrilineal diversity in Africa. *American Journal of Human Genetics*, **88**(6), 814–18.

Cysouw, M., Dediu, D., and Moran, S. (2012). Comment on "Phonemic diversity supports a serial founder effect model of language expansion from Africa". *Science*, **335**, 657.

d'Errico, F., Henshilwood, C., Lawson, G., *et al.* (2003). Archaeological evidence for the emergence of language, symbolism, and music: an alternative multidisciplinary perspective. *Journal of World Prehistory*, **17**(1), 1–70.

d'Errico, F., Salomon, H., Vignaud, C., and Stringer, C. (2010). Pigments from the Middle Palaeolithic levels of Es-Skhul (Mount Carmel, Israel). *Journal of Archaeological Science*, **37**, 3099–110.

Degiorgio, M., Jakobsson, M., and Rosenberg, N. A. (2009). Out of Africa: modern human origins special feature: explaining worldwide patterns of human genetic variation using a coalescent-based serial founder model of migration outward from Africa. *Proceedings of the National Academy of Sciences of the United States of America*,**106**(38), 16 057–62.

deMenocal, P., Ortiz, J., Guilderson, T., *et al.* (2000). Abrupt onset and termination of the African Humid Period: rapid climate responses to gradual insolation forcing. *Quaternary Science Reviews*, **19**, 347–61.

Distefano, J. A. (1990). Hunters or hunted? Towards a history of the Okiek of Kenya. *History in Africa*, **17**, 41–57.

Dominguez-Bello, M. G., Perez, M. E., Bortolini, M. C., *et al.* (2008). Amerindian *Helicobacter pylori* strains go extinct, as European strains expand their host range. *PLoS ONE*, **3**(10), e3307.

Dupont, L. M., Jahns, S., Marret, F., and Ning, S. (2000). Vegetation change in equatorial West Africa: time-slices for the last 150 ka. *Palaeogeography, Palaeoclimatology, Palaeoecology*, **155**, 95–122.

Ehret, C. (1971). *Southern Nilotic history: Linguistic Approaches to the Study of the Past.* Evanston, IL: Northwestern University Press.

Ehret, C. (1976). Linguistic evidence and its correlation with archaeology. *World Archaeology*, **8**(1), 5–18.

Ehret, C. (1993). Nilo-Saharans and the Saharo-Sudanese Neolithic. In *The Archaeology of Africa: Food, Metals and Towns*, ed. P. S. T. Shaw, B. Andah, and A. Okpoko, pp. 104–25. London: Routledge Press.

Ehret, C. (1995). *Reconstructing Proto-Afroasiatic (Proto-Afrasian): Vowels, Tone, Consonants, and Vocabulary*. University of California Publications in Linguistics 126. Berkeley, CA: University of California Press.

Ehret, C. (1998). *An African Classical Age: Eastern and Southern Africa in World History, 1000 B.C. to A.D. 400*. Charlottesville, VA: University Press of Virginia.

Ehret, C. (2001). Bantu expansions: re-envisioning a central problem of early African history. *International Journal of African Historical Studies*, **34**(1), 5–41.

Erlich, H. A., Bergstrom, T. F., Stoneking, M., and Gyllensten, U. (1996). HLA sequence polymorphism and the origin of humans. *Science*, **274**(5292), 1552b–4b.

Excoffier, L. and Schneider, S. (1999). Why hunter-gatherer populations do not show signs of Pleistocene demographic expansions. *Proceedings of the National Academy of Sciences of the United States of America*, **96**(19), 10 597–602.

Falush, D., Wirth, T., Linz, B., *et al.* (2003). Traces of human migrations in *Helicobacter pylori* populations. *Science*, **299**(5612), 1582–5.

Feathers, J. K. (2002). Luminescence dating in less than ideal conditions: case studies from Klasies River main site and Duinefontein, South Africa. *Journal of Archaeological Science*, **29**(2), 177–94.

Finch, J. M. and Hill, T. R. (2008). A late Quaternary pollen sequence from Mfabeni Peatland, South Africa: reconstructing forest history in Maputaland. *Quaternary Research*, **70**, 442–50.

Foley, J. A., Coe, M. T., Scheffer, M., and Wang, G. (2003). Regime shifts in the Sahara and Sahel: interactions between ecological and climatic systems in northern Africa. *Ecosystems*, **6**(6), 524–39.

Gabriel, B. (1987). Palaeoecological evidence from Neolithic fireplaces in the Sahara. *African Archaeological Review*, **5**, 93–103.

Garcea, E. A. A. (2004). An alternative way towards food production: the perspective from the Libyan Sahara. *Journal of World Prehistory*, **18**, 107–54.

Garcea, E. A. A. (2006). Semi-permanent foragers in semi-arid environments of North Africa. *World Archaeology*, **38**, 197–219.

Garcin, Y., Junginger, A., Melnick, D., *et al.* (2009). Late Pleistocene–Holocene rise and collapse of Lake Suguta, northern Kenya Rift. *Quaternary Science Reviews*, **28**, 911–25.

Garcin, Y., Williamson, D., Taieb, M., *et al.* (2006). Centennial to millennial changes in maar-lake deposition during the last 45,000 years in tropical Southern Africa (Lake Masoko, Tanzania). *Palaeogeography, Palaeoclimatology, Palaeoecology*, **239**, 334–54.

Garrigan, D., Mobasher, Z., Kingan, S. B., Wilder, J. A., and Hammer, M. F. (2005a). Deep haplotype divergence and long-range linkage disequilibrium at xp21.1 provide evidence that humans descend from a structured ancestral population. *Genetics*, **170**(4), 1849–56.

Garrigan, D., Mobasher, Z., Severson, T., *et al.* (2005b). Evidence for archaic Asian ancestry on the human X chromosome. *Molecular Biology and Evolution*, **22**(2), 189–92.

Gasse, F. (2000). Hydrological changes in the African tropics since the Last Glacial Maximum. *Quaternary Science Reviews*, **19**, 189–211.

Gasse, F., Chalie, F., Vincens, A., Williams, M. A. J., and Williamson, D. (2008). Climatic patterns in equatorial and southern Africa from 30,000 to 10,000 years ago reconstructed from terrestrial and near-shore proxy data. *Quaternary Science Reviews*, **27**, 2316–40.

Geyh, M. A. and Thiedig, F. (2008). The Middle Pleistocene Al Mahruqah Formation in the Murzuq Basin, northern Sahara, Libya evidence for orbitally-forced humid episodes during the last 500,000 years. *Palaeogeography, Palaeoclimatology, Palaeoecology*, **257**, 1–21.

Giraudi, C. (2005). Eolian sand in peridesert northwestern Libya and implications for Late Pleistocene and Holocene Sahara expansions. *Palaeogeography, Palaeoclimatology, Palaeoecology*, **218**, 161–73.

Giresse, P., Maley, J., and Brenac, P. (1994). Late Quaternary palaeoenvironments in the Lake Barombi Mbo (West Cameroon) deduced from pollen and carbon isotopes of organic matter. *Palaeogeography, Palaeoclimatology, Palaeoecology*, **107**, 65–78.

Gonder, M. K., Mortensen, H. M., Reed, F. A., *et al.* (2007). Whole-mtDNA genome sequence analysis of ancient African lineages. *Molecular Biology and Evolution*, **24**(3), 757–68.

Green, R. E., Krause, J., Briggs, A. W., *et al.* (2010). A draft sequence of the Neandertal genome. *Science*, **328**(5979), 710–22.

Greenberg, J. H. (1963). *The Languages of Africa*. Bloomington, IN: Indiana University Research Center in Anthropology, Folklore, and Linguistics.

Greenberg, J. H. (1972). Linguistic evidence regarding Bantu origins. *Journal of African History*, **13**(2), 189–216.

Gronau, I., Hubisz, M. J., Gulko, B., *et al.* (2011). Bayesian inference of ancient human demography from individual genome sequences. *Nature and Genetics*, **43**, 1031–4.

Haigh, J. and Smith, J. M. (1972). Population size and protein variation in man. *Genetic Research*, **19**(1), 73–89.

Haile-Selassie, Y., Asfaw, B., and White, T. D. (2004). Hominid cranial remains from upper Pleistocene deposits at Aduma, Middle Awash, Ethiopia. *American Journal of Physical Anthropology*, **123**(1), 1–10.

Hammer, M. F. and Zegura, S. L. (2002). The human Y chromosome haplogroup tree: nomenclature and phylogeography of its major divisions. *Annual Review of Anthropology*, **31**, 303–21.

Hammer, M. F., Woerner, A. E., Mendez, F. L., Watkins, J. C., and Wall, J. D. (2011). Genetic evidence for archaic admixture in Africa. *Proceedings of the National Academy of Sciences of the United States of America*, **108**(37), 15 123–8.

Harpending, H. C., Sherry, S. T., Rogers, A. R., and Stoneking, M. (1993). The genetic structure of ancient human populations. *Current Anthropology*, **34**(4), 483–96.

Haslett, S. K. and Davies, C. F. C. (2006). Late Quaternary climate–ocean changes in western North Africa: offshore geochemical evidence. *Transactions of the Institute of British Geographers*, **31**, 34–52.

Haspelmath, M., Dryer, M. S., Gil, D., and Comrie, B. (eds.) (2008). *The World Atlas of Language Structures Online*. Munich: Max Planck Digital Library (http://wals.info/).

Hassan, F. A. (1997). Holocene palaeoclimates of Africa. *African Archaeological Review*, **14**(4), 213–30.

Hawks, J., Hunley, K., Lee, S. H., and Wolpoff, M. (2000). Population bottlenecks and Pleistocene human evolution. *Molecular Biology and Evolution*, **17**(1), 2–22.

Henn, B. M., Gignoux, C. R., Jobin, M., *et al.* (2011). Hunter-gatherer genomic diversity suggests a southern African origin for modern humans. *Proceedings of the National Academy of Sciences of the United States of America*, **108**, 5154–62.

Henshilwood, C. S., D'Errico, F., Niekerk, V., *et al.* (2011). A 100,000-year-old ochre-processing workshop at Blombos Cave, South Africa. *Science*, **334**, 219–22.

Henshilwood, C. S., D'Errico, F., and Watts, I. (2009). Engraved ochres from the Middle Stone Age levels at Blombos Cave, South Africa. *Journal of Human Evolution*, **57**, 27–47.

Henshilwood, C. S., D'Errico, F., Yates, R., *et al.* (2002). Emergence of modern human behavior: Middle Stone Age engravings from South Africa. *Science*, **295**(5558), 1278–80.

Hey, J. and Nielsen, R. (2004). Multilocus methods for estimating population sizes, migration rates and divergence time, with applications to the divergence of *Drosophila pseudoobscura* and *D. persimilis*. *Genetics*, **167**(2), 747–60.

Hill, K. R., Walker, R. S., Božičević, M., *et al.* (2011). Co-residence patterns in hunter-gatherer societies show unique human social structure. *Science*, **331**(6022), 1286–9.

Hofer, T., Ray, N., Wegmann, D., and Excoffier, L. (2009). Large allele frequency differences between human continental groups are more likely to have occurred by drift during range expansions than by selection. *Annals of Human Genetics*, **73**(1), 95–108.

Hovers, E., Ilani, S, Bar-Yosef, O., and Vandermeersch, B. (2003). An early case of color symbolism: ochre use by modern humans in Qafzeh Cave. *Current Anthropology*, **44**(4), 491–522.

Huffman, T. N. (2008) Climate change during the Iron Age in the Shashe-Limpopo Basin, southern Africa. *Journal of Archaeological Science*, **35**, 2032–47.

Hunley, K., Bowern, C., and Healy, M. (2012). Rejection of a serial founder effects model of genetic and linguistic coevolution. *Proceedings of the Royal Society B: Biological Sciences*, **279**(1736), 2281–8.

Hunley, K., Dunn, M., Lindstrom, E., *et al.* (2008). Genetic and linguistic coevolution in Northern Island Melanesia. *PLoS Genetics*, **4**(10), e1000239.

Jacobs, Z., Roberts, R. G., Galbraith, R. F., *et al.* (2008). Ages for the Middle Stone Age of Southern Africa: implications for human behavior and dispersal. *Science*, **322**(5902), 733–5.

Jahns, S. (1995). A Holocene pollen diagram from El Atrun, northern Sudan. *Vegetation History and Archaeobotany*, **4**, 23–30.

Jahns, S. (1996). Vegetation history and climate changes in West Equatorial Africa during the Late Pleistocene and Holocene, based on a marine pollen diagram from the Congo fan. *Vegetation History and Archaeobotany*, **5**, 207–13.

Johnson, T. C., Brown, E. T., McManus, J., *et al.* (2002). A high-resolution Paleoclimate record spanning the past 25,000 years in southern East Africa. *Science*, **296**, 113–32.

Jolly, D., Harrison, S. P., Damnati, B., and Bonnefille, R. (1998). Simulated climate and biomes of Africa during the Late Quaternary: comparison with pollen and lake status data. *Quaternary Science Reviews*, **17**, 629–57.

Jolly, D., Taylor, D., Marchant, R., *et al.* (1997). Vegetation dynamics in Central Africa since 18,000 yr BP: pollen records from the interlacustrine highlands of Burundi, Rwanda and Western Uganda. *Journal of Biogeography*, **24**(4), 495–512.

Jousse, H. (2006). What is the impact of Holocene climatic changes on human societies? Analysis of West African Neolithic populations dietary customs. *Quaternary International*, **151**, 63–73.

Karafet, T. M., Mendez, F. L., Meilerman, M. B., *et al.* (2008). New binary poly-morphisms reshape and increase resolution of the human Y chromosomal haplogroup tree. *Genome Research*, **18**(5), 830–8.

Kennedy, M. (2005). Synchrony of Southern Hemisphere Late Pleistocene arid episodes: a review of luminescence chronologies from arid aeolian land-scapes south of the Equator. *Quaternary Science Reviews*, **24**, 2555–83.

Kiage, L. M. and Liu, K. B. (2006). Late Quaternary paleoenvironmental changes in East Africa: a review of multiproxy evidence from palynology, lake sedi-ments, and associated records. *Progress in Physical Geography*, **30**, 633.

Kim, S.-J., Crowley, T., Erickson, D., *et al.* (2008). High-resolution climate simula-tion of the last glacial maximum. *Climate Dynamics*, **31**, 1–16.

Kim, S.-Y., Scourse, J., Marret, F., and Lim, D. -I. (2010). A 26,000-year integrate-d record of marine and terrestrial environmental change off Gabon, west equatorial Africa. *Palaeogeography, Palaeoclimatology, Palaeoecology*, **297**, 428–38.

King, T. E., Parkin, E. J., Swinfield, G., *et al.* (2007). Africans in Yorkshire? The deepest-rooting clade of the Y phylogeny within an English genealogy. *European Journal of Human Genetics*, **15**(3), 288–93.

Kivisild, T., Reidla, M., Metspalu, E., *et al.* (2004). Ethiopian mitochondrial DNA heritage: tracking gene flow across and around the gate of tears. *American Journal of Human Genetics*, **75**(5), 752–70.

Klein, R. G. (1992). The archeology of modern human origins. *Evolutionary Anthro-pology: Issues, News, and Reviews*, **1**(1), 5–14.

Kropelin, S., Verschuren, D., Lezine, A.-M., *et al.* (2008). Climate-driven ecosystem succession in the Sahara: the past 6000 years. *Science*, **320**, 765–8.

Kuper, R. and Kropelin, S. (2006). Climate-controlled Holocene occupation in the Sahara: motor of Africa's evolution. *Science*, **313**(5788), 803–7.

Labuda, D., Zietkiewicz, E., and Yotova, V. (2000). Archaic lineages in the history of modern humans. *Genetics*, **156**(2), 799–808.

Lahr, M. M. and Foley, R. A. (1998). Towards a theory of modern human origins: geography, demography, and diversity in recent human evolution. *American Journal of Physical Anthropology*, **Suppl 27**, 137–76.

Lamb, A. L., Leng, M. J., Umer. M. M., and Lamb, H. F. (2004). Holocene climate and vegetation change in the Main Ethiopian Rift Valley, inferred from the composition (C/N and δ13C) of lacustrine organic matter. *Quaternary Science Reviews*, **23**, 881–91.

Lamb, H. F., Bates, C. R., Coombes, P. V., *et al.* (2007). Late Pleistocene desiccation of Lake Tana, source of the Blue Nile. *Quaternary Science Reviews*, **26**, 287–99.

Leakey, L. S. B. (1931). *The Stone Age Cultures of Kenya Colony*. Cambridge, UK: Cambridge University Press.

Lewis, C. A. (2008). Late Quaternary climatic changes, and associated human responses, during the last ~45000 yr in the Eastern and adjoining Western Cape, South Africa. *Earth-Science Reviews*, **88** , 167–87.

Lewis, M. P. (2009). *Ethnologue: Languages of the World*, 16th edn. Dallas, TX: SIL International. Online version: www.ethnologue.com/.

Linz, B., Balloux, F., Moodley, Y., *et al.* (2007). An African origin for the intimate association between humans and *Helicobacter pylori*. *Nature*, **445**(7130), 915–18.

Liu, H., Prugnolle, F., Manica, A., and Balloux, F. (2006). A geographically explicit genetic model of worldwide human-settlement history. *American Journal of Human Genetics*, **79**(2), 230–7.

Lyons, R. P., Scholz, C. A., Buoniconti, M. R., and Martin, M. R. (2011). Late Quaternary stratigraphic analysis of the Lake Malawi Rift, East Africa: an integration of drill-core and seismic-reflection data. *Palaeogeography, Palaeoclimatology, Palaeoecology*, **303**, 20–37.

Macaulay, V., Richards, M., Hickey, E., *et al.* (1999). The emerging tree of West Eurasian mtDNAs: a synthesis of control-region sequences and RFLPs. *American Journal of Human Genetics*, **64**(1), 232–49.

Maley, J. (1977). Palaeoclimates of Central Sahara during the early Holocene. *Nature*, **269**, 573–7.

Manica, A., Amos, W., Balloux, F., and Hanihara, T. (2007). The effect of ancient population bottlenecks on human phenotypic variation. *Nature*, **448**(7151), 346–8.

Marchant, R., Taylor, D., and Hamilton, A. (1997). Late Pleistocene and Holocene history at Mubwindi Swamp, southwest Uganda. *Quaternary Research*, **47**, 316–28.

Marshall, F. and Hildebrand, E. (2002). Cattle before crops: the beginnings of food production in Africa. *Journal of World Prehistory*, **16**, 99–143.

Marth, G. T., Czabarka, E., Murvai, J., and Sherry, S. T. (2004). The allele frequency spectrum in genome-wide human variation data reveals signals of differential demographic history in three large world populations. *Genetics*, **166**, 351–72.

McBrearty, S. and Brooks, A. S. (2000). The revolution that wasn't: a new interpretation of the origin of modern human behavior. *Journal of Human Evolution*, **39**(5), 453–563.

McDermott, F., Grün, R., Stringer, C. B., and Hawkesworth, C. J. (1993). Massspectrometric U-series dates for Israeli Neanderthal/early modern hominid sites. *Nature*, **363**(6426), 252–5.

McDermott, F., Stringer, C., Grün, R., *et al.* (1996). New Late-Pleistocene uranium-thorium and ESR dates for the Singa hominid (Sudan). *Journal of Human Evolution*, **31**(6), 507–16.

McDougall, I., Brown, F. H., and Fleagle, J. G. (2005). Stratigraphic placement and age of modern humans from Kibish, Ethiopia. *Nature*, **433**(7027), 733–6.

McIntosh, S. K. and McIntosh, R. J. (1983). Current directions in West African prehistory. *Annual Review of Anthropology*, **12**, 215–58.

Mehlman, M. J. (1979). Mumba-Hohle revisited: the relevance of a forgotten excavation to some current issues in East African prehistory. *World Archaeology*, **11**(1), 80–94.

Mellars, P. (2006). Why did modern human populations disperse from Africa *c.* 60,000 years ago? A new model. *Proceedings of the National Academy of Sciences of the United States of America*, **103**(25), 9381–6.

Mendez, F. L., Watkins, J. C., and Hammer, M. F. (2012). Global genetic variation at OAS1 provides evidence of archaic admixture in Melanesian populations. *Molecular Biology and Evolution*, in press.

Mercier, N., Valladas, H., Bar-Yosef, O., *et al.* (1993). Thermoluminescence date for the Mousterian burial site of Es-Skhul, Mt. Carmel. *Journal of Archaeological Science*, **20**(2), 169–74.

Moeyersons, J., Vermeersch, P. M., and Van Peer, P. (2002). Dry cave deposits and their palaeoenvironmental significance during the last 115 ka, Sodmein Cave, Red Sea Mountains, Egypt. *Quaternary Science Reviews*, **21**, 837–51.

Mohammed, M. U., Bonnefille, R., and Johnson, T. C. (1996). Pollen and isotopic records in Late Holocene sediments from Lake Turkana, Kenya. *Palaeogeography, Palaeoclimatology, Palaeoecology*, **119**, 371–83.

Morin, E. (2008). Evidence for declines in human population densities during the early Upper Paleolithic in western Europe. *Proceedings of the National Academy of Sciences of the United States of America*, **105**(1), 48–53.

Newcomer, P. J. (1972). The Nuer are Dinka: an essay on origins and environmental determinism. *Man*, **7**(1), 5–11.

Ngomanda, A., Neumann, K., Schweizer, A., and Maley, J. (2009). Seasonality change and the third millennium BP rainforest crisis in southern Cameroon (Central Africa). *Quaternary Research*, **71**, 307–18.

Nguetsop, V. F. O., Servant-Vildary, S., and Servant, M. (2004). Late Holocene climatic changes in west Africa, a high resolution diatom record from equatorial Cameroon. *Quaternary Science Reviews*, **23**, 591–609.

Nichol, J. E. (1999). Geomorphological evidence and Pleistocene refugia in Africa. *Geographical Journal*, **165**, 79–89.

Nielsen, R. and Wakeley, J. (2001). Distinguishing migration from isolation: a Markov chain Monte Carlo approach. *Genetics*, **158**(2), 885–96.

Niklas, K. J., Midgley, J. J., and Rand, R. H. (2003). Size-dependent species richness: trends within plant communities and across latitude. *Ecology Letters*, **6**, 631–6.

Norstrom, E., Scott, L., Partridge, T. C., Risberg, J., and Holmgren, K. (2009). Reconstruction of environmental and climate changes at Braamhoek wetland, eastern escarpment South Africa, during the last 16,000 years with emphasis on the Pleistocene-Holocene transition. *Palaeogeography, Palaeoclimatology, Palaeoecology*, **271**, 240–58.

Nurse, D. (1997). The contributions of linguistics to the study of history in Africa. *Journal of African History*, **38**(3), 359–91.

Partridge, T. C., Demenocal, P. B., Lorentz, S. A., Paiker, M. J., and Vogel, J. C. (1997). Orbital forcing of climate over South Africa: a 200,000-year rainfall record from the Pretoria Saltpan. *Quaternary Science Reviews*, **16**, 1125–33.

Partridge, T. C., Kerr, S. J., Metcalfe, S. E., *et al.* (1993). The Pretoria Saltpan: a 200,000 year Southern African lacustrine sequence. *Palaeogeography, Palaeoclimatology, Palaeoecology*, **101**, 317–37.

Peer, P. V., Demidenko, Y. E., Garcea, E. A. A., *et al.* (1998). The Nile Corridor and the Out-of-Africa model: an examination of the archaeological record [and Comments and Reply]. *Current Anthropology*, **39**(2), S115–S140.

Pennington, R. L. (1996). Causes of early human population growth. *American Journal of Physical Anthropology*, **99**(2), 259–74.

Plagnol, V. and Wall, J. D. (2006). Possible ancestral structure in human populations. *PLoS Genetics*, **2**(7), e105.

Posnansky, M. (1961a). Pottery types from archaeological sites in East Africa. *Journal of African History*, **2**(2), 177–98.

Posnansky, M. (1961b). Dimple-based pottery from Uganda. *Man*, **61**, 141–2.

Powell, A., Shennan, S., and Thomas, M. G. (2009). Late Pleistocene demography and the appearance of modern human behavior. *Science*, **324**(5932), 1298–301.

Premo, L. S. and Hublin, J. J. (2009). Culture, population structure, and low genetic diversity in Pleistocene hominins. *Proceedings of the National Academy of Sciences of the United States of America*, **106**(1), 33–7.

Pritchard, J. K., Stephens, M., and Donnelly, P. (2000). Inference of population structure using multilocus genotype data. *Genetics*, **155**(2), 945–59.

Prugnolle, F., Manica, A., and Balloux, F. (2005). Geography predicts neutral genetic diversity of human populations. *Current Biology*, **15**(5), R159–60.

Quintana-Murci, L., Semino, O., Bandelt, H. J., *et al.* (1999). Genetic evidence of an early exit of *Homo sapiens sapiens* from Africa through eastern Africa. *Nature Genetics*, **23**(4), 437–41.

Ramachandran, S., Deshpande, O., Roseman, C. C., *et al.* (2005). Support from the relationship of genetic and geographic distance in human populations for a serial founder effect originating in Africa. *Proceedings of the National Academy of Sciences of the United States of America*, **102**(44), 15 942–7.

Ray, N. and Excoffier, L. (2009). Inferring past demography using spatially explicit population genetic models. *Human Biology*, **81**(2–3), 141–57.

Ray, N., Currat, M., Berthier, P., and Excoffier, L. (2005). Recovering the geographic origin of early modern humans by realistic and spatially explicit simulations. *Genome Research*, **15**(8), 1161–17.

Reich, D., Green, R. E., Kircher, M., *et al.* (2011). Genetic history of an archaic hominin group from Denisova Cave in Siberia. *Nature*, **468**(7327), 1053–60.

Revel, M., Ducassou, E., Grousset, F. E., *et al.* (2010). 100,000 years of African monsoon variability recorded in sediments of the Nile margin. *Quaternary Science Reviews*, **29**, 1342–62.

Richards, M. B., Macaulay, V. A., Bandelt, H. J., and Sykes, B. C. (1998). Phylogeography of mitochondrial DNA in western Europe. *Annals of Human Genetics*, **62**(3), 241–60.

Robbins, L. H. (1972). Archeology in the Turkana District, Kenya. *Science*, **176**(4033), 359–66.

Rogers, A. R. and Harpending, H. (1992). Population growth makes waves in the distribution of pairwise genetic differences. *Molecular Biology and Evolution*, **9**(3), 552–69.

Roland, O. (1966). Bantu genesis: an inquiry into some problems of early Bantu history. *African Affairs*, **65**(260), 245–58.

Rosser, Z. H., Zerjal, T., Hurles, M. E., *et al.* (2000). Y-chromosomal diversity in Europe is clinal and influenced primarily by geography, rather than by language. *American Journal of Human Genetics*, **67**(6), 1526–43.

Russell, J. M. and Johnson, T. C. (2005). A high-resolution geochemical record from Lake Edward, Uganda, Congo and the timing and causes of tropical African drought during the late Holocene. *Quaternary Science Reviews*, **24**, 1375–89.

Sahlins, M. D. (1961). The segmentary lineage: an organization of predatory expansion. *American Anthropologist*, **63**(2), 322–45.

Salas, A., Richards, M., De La Fe, T., *et al.* (2002). The making of the African mtDNA landscape. *American Journal of Human Genetics*, **71**(5), 1082–111.

Satta, Y. and Takahata, N. (2004). The distribution of the ancestral haplotype in finite stepping-stone models with population expansion. *Molecular Ecology*, **13**(4), 877–86.

Schefuss, E., Schouten, S., and Schneider, R. R. (2005). Climatic controls on central African hydrology during the past 20,000 years. *Nature*, **437**(7061), 1003–6.

Scheinfeldt, L. B., Soi, S., and Tishkoff, S. A. (2010). Colloquium paper: working toward a synthesis of archaeological, linguistic, and genetic data for inferring African population history. *Proceedings of the National Academy of Sciences of the United States of America*, **107**(Suppl 2), 8931–8.

Schoenbrun, D. L. (1993). Cattle herds and banana gardens: the historical geography of the western Great Lakes region, ca AD 800–1500. *African Archaeological Review*, **11**, 39–72.

Scholz, C. A., Cohen, A. S., Johnson, T. C., *et al.* (2011a). Scientific drilling in the Great Rift Valley: the 2005 Lake Malawi scientific drilling project –

an overview of the past 145,000 years of climate variability in Southern Hemisphere East Africa. *Palaeogeography, Palaeoclimatology, Palaeoecology*, **303**, 3–19.

Scholz, C. A., Johnson, T. C., Cohen, A. S., *et al.* (2007). East African megadroughts between 135 and 75 thousand years ago and bearing on early-modern human origins. *Proceedings of the National Academy of Sciences of the United States of America*, **104**(42), 16 416–21.

Scholz, C. A., Talbot, M. R., Brown, E. T., and Lyons, R. P. (2011b). Lithostratigraphy, physical properties and organic matter variability in Lake Malawi drillcore sediments over the past 145,000 years. *Palaeogeography, Palaeoclimatology, Palaeoecology*, **303**, 38–50.

Schwarcz, H. P., Grün, R., Vandermeersch, B., *et al.* (1988). ESR dates for the hominid burial site of Qafzeh in Israel. *Journal of Human Evolution*, **17**(8), 733–7.

Schwarz, S., Morelli, G., Kusecek, B., *et al.* (2008). Horizontal versus familial transmission of *Helicobacter pylori*. *PLoS Pathology*, **4**(10), e1000180.

Scott, L. and Woodborne, S. (2007). Vegetation history inferred from pollen in Late Quaternary faecal deposits (hyraceum) in the Cape winter-rain region and its bearing on past climates in South Africa. *Quaternary Science Reviews*, **26**, 941–53.

Semino, O., Santachiara-Benerecetti, A. S., Falaschi, F., Cavalli-Sforza, L. L., and Underhill, P. A. (2002). Ethiopians and Khoisan share the deepest clades of the human Y-chromosome phylogeny. *American Journal of Human Genetics*, **70**(1), 265–8.

Shaw, P. A., Bateman, M. D., Thomas, D. S. G., and Davies, F. (2003). Holocene fluctuations of Lake Ngami, Middle Kalahari: chronology and responses to climatic change. *Quaternary International*, **111**, 23–35.

Shennan, S. (2001). Demography and cultural innovation: a model and its implications for the emergence of modern human culture. *Cambridge Archaeological Journal*, **11**(01), 5–16.

Sinninghe Damsté, J. S., Verschuren, D., Ossebaar, J., *et al.* (2011). A 25,000-year record of climate-induced changes in lowland vegetation of eastern equatorial Africa revealed by the stable carbon-isotopic composition of fossil plant leaf waxes. *Earth and Planetary Science Letters*, **302**, 236–46.

Smith, A. B. (1992). Origins and spread of pastoralism in Africa. *Annual Review of Anthropology*, **21**, 125–41.

Smith, J. R., Giegengack, R., and Schwarcz, H. P. (2004). Constraints on Pleistocene pluvial climates through stable-isotope analysis of fossil-spring tufas and associated gastropods, Kharga Oasis, Egypt. *Palaeogeography, Palaeoclimatology, Palaeoecology*, **206**, 157–75.

Smith, J. R., Hawkins, A. L., Asmerom, Y., *et al.* (2007). New age constraints on the Middle Stone Age occupations of Kharga Oasis, Western Desert, Egypt. *Journal of Human Evolution*, **52**(6), 690–701.

Smouse, P. E. and Long, J. C. (1992). Matrix correlation analysis in anthropology and genetics. *American Journal of Physical Anthropology*, **35**(S15), 187–213.

Soares, P., Ermini, L., Thomson, N., *et al.* (2009). Correcting for purifying selection: an improved human mitochondrial molecular clock. *American Journal of Human Genetics*, **84**(6), 740–59.

Stager, J. C. (1988). Environmental changes at Lake Cheshi, Zambia since 40,000 years B.P. *Quaternary Research*, **29**, 54–65.

Stager, J. C., Cocquyt, C., Bonnefille, R., Weyhenmeyer, C., and Bowerman, N. (2009). A late Holocene paleoclimatic history of Lake Tanganyika, East Africa. *Quaternary Research*, **72**, 47–56.

Stager, J. C., Cumming, B. F., and Meeker, L. D. (2003). A 10,000-year high-resolution diatom record from Pilkington Bay, Lake Victoria, East Africa. *Quaternary Research*, **59**, 172–81.

Stokes, S., Haynes, G., Thomas, D. S. G., *et al.* (1998). Punctuated aridity in southern Africa during the last glacial cycle: the chronology of linear dune construction in the northeastern Kalahari. *Palaeogeography, Palaeoclimatology, Palaeoecology*, **137**, 305–22.

Stone, J. R., Westover, K. S., and Cohen, A. S. (2011). Late Pleistocene paleohydro-graphy and diatom paleoecology of the central basin of Lake Malawi, Africa. *Palaeogeography, Palaeoclimatology, Palaeoecology*, **303**, 51–70.

Stringer, C. B. and Andrews, P. (1988). Genetic and fossil evidence for the origin of modern humans. *Science*, **239**(4845), 1263–8.

Sutton, J. E. G. (1974). The aquatic civilization of Middle Africa. *Journal of African History*, **15**(4), 527–46.

Takahata, N. (1993). Allelic genealogy and human evolution. *Molecular Biology and Evolution*, **10**(1), 2–22.

Talbot, M. R. and Johannessen, T. (1992). A high resolution palaeoclimatic record for the last 27,500 years in tropical West Africa from the carbon and nitro-gen isotopic composition of lacustrine organic matter. *Earth and Planetary Science Letters*, **110**, 23–37.

Tenesa, A., Navarro, P., Hayes, B. J., *et al.* (2007). Recent human effective popu-lation size estimated from linkage disequilibrium. *Genome Research*, **17**(4), 520–6.

Thackeray, A. I. (1989). Changing fashions in the Middle Stone age: the stone artefact sequence from Klasies River Main Site, South Africa. *African Archaeo-logical Review*, **7**, 33–57.

Tierney, J. E., Russell, J. M., Huang, Y., *et al.* (2008). Northern Hemisphere controls on tropical Southeast African climate during the past 60,000 years. *Science*, **322**, 252–5.

Tierney, J. E., Russell, J. M., Sinninghe Damsté, J. S., Huang, Y., and Verschuren, D. (2011). Late Quaternary behavior of the East African monsoon and the importance of the Congo Air Boundary. *Quaternary Science Reviews*, **30**, 798–807.

Tishkoff, S. A., Goldman, A., Calafell, F., *et al.* (1998). A global haplotype analysis of the myotonic dystrophy locus: implications for the evolution of modern humans and for the origin of myotonic dystrophy mutations. *American Journal of Human Genetics*, **62**(6), 1389–402.

Tishkoff, S. A., Reed, F. A., Friedlaender, F. R., *et al.* (2009). The genetic structure and history of Africans and African Americans. *Science*, **324**(5930), 1035–44.

Tjallingii, R., Claussen, M., Stuut, J.-B. W., *et al.* (2008). Coherent high- and low-latitude control of the northwest African hydrological balance. *Nature Geo-science*, **1**(10), 670–5.

Trauth, M. H., Deino, A. L., Bergner, A. G. N., and Strecker, M. R. (2003). East African climate change and orbital forcing during the last 175 kyr BP. *Earth and Planetary Science Letters*, **206**, 297–313.

Umer, M. M., Bonnefille, R., and Johnson, T. C. (1996). Pollen and isotopic records in Late Holocene sediments from Lake Turkana, Kenya. *Palaeogeography, Palaeoclimatology, Palaeoecology*, **119**, 371–83.

Vaks, A., Bar-Matthews, M., Ayalon, A., *et al.* (2007). Desert speleothems reveal climatic window for African exodus of early modern humans. *Geology*, **35**(9), 831–4.

Vandermeersch, B. (1989). The evolution of modern humans: recent evidence from Southwest Asia. In *The Human Revolution: Behavioural and Biological Perspectives on the Origins of Modern Humans*, ed. P. Mellars and C. B. Stringer, pp. 155–64. Princeton, NJ: Princeton University Press.

Vansina, J. (1995). New linguistic evidence and "the Bantu Expansion". *Journal of African History*, **36**(2), 173–95.

Van Tuyl, R. and Pereltsvaig, A. (2012). Comment on "Phonemic diversity supports a serial founder effect model of language expansion from Africa". *Science*, 335, 657.

Van Zinderen Bakker, E. M. and Coetzee, J. A. (1988). A review of Late Quaternary pollen studies in East, Central and Southern Africa. *Review of Palaeobotany and Palynology*, **55**, 155–74.

Veeramah, K. R., Wegmann, D., Woerner, A., *et al.* (2012). An early divergence of KhoeSan ancestors from those of other modern humans is supported by an ABC-based analysis of autosomal resequencing data. *Molecular Biology and Evolution*, **29**, 617–30; doi:10.1093/molbev/msr212.

Vermeersch, P. M., Paulissen, E., Stokes, S., *et al.* (1998). A middle Palaeolithic burial of a modern human at Taramsa Hill, Egypt. *Antiquity*, **72** 475–82.

Verschuren, D., Sinninghe Damsté, J. S., Moernaut, J., *et al.* (2009). Half-precessional dynamics of monsoon rainfall near the East African Equator. *Nature*, **462**, 637–41.

Vincens, A., Schwartz, D., Elenga, H., *et al.* (1999). Forest response to climate changes in Atlantic Equatorial Africa during the last 4000 years BP and inheritance on the modern landscapes. *Journal of Biogeography*, **26**, 879–85.

Wall, J. D., Lohmueller, K. E., and Plagnol, V. (2009). Detecting ancient admixture and estimating demographic parameters in multiple human populations. *Molecular Biology and Evolution*, **26**, 1823–7.

Wang, C.-C., Ding, Q.-L., Tao, H., and Li, H. (2012). Comment on "Phonemic diversity supports a serial founder effect model of language expansion from Africa". *Science*, **335**, 657.

Williams, M. A. J., Williams, F. M., Duller, G. A. T., *et al.* (2010). Late Quaternary floods and droughts in the Nile valley, Sudan: new evidence from optically stimulated luminescence and AMS radiocarbon dating. *Quaternary Science Reviews*, **29**, 1116–37.

Willoughby, P. R. and Sipe, C. G. (2002). Stone Age prehistory of the Songwe River Valley, Lake Rukwa Basin, southwestern Tanzania. *African Archaeological Review*, **19**(4), 203–21.

Wood, E. T., Stover, D. A., Ehret, C., *et al.* (2005). Contrasting patterns of Y chromosome and mtDNA variation in Africa: evidence for sex-biased demographic processes. *European Journal of Human Genetics*, **13**(7), 867–76.

Yotova, V., Lefebvre, J. F., Kohany, O., *et al.* (2007). Tracing genetic history of modern humans using X-chromosome lineages. *Human Genetics*, **122**(5), 431–43.

Yotova, V., Lefebvre, J.-F., Moreau, C., *et al.* (2011). An X-linked haplotype of Neandertal origin is present among all non-African populations. *Molecular Biology and Evolution*, **28**(7), 1957–62.

Zhang, D. D., Brecke, P., Lee, H. F., He, Y. Q., and Zhang, J. (2007). Global climate change, war, and population decline in recent human history. *Proceedings of the National Academy of Sciences of the United States of America*, **104**(49), 19 214–9.

Zietkiewicz, E., Yotova, V., Jarnik, M., *et al.* (1998). Genetic structure of the ancestral population of modern humans. *Journal of Molecular Evolution*, **47**(2), 146–55.

Zilhão, J. (2007). The emergence of ornaments and art: an archaeological perspective on the origins of "Behavioral Modernity". *Journal of Archaeological Research*, **15**(1), 1–54.

PHILIPPE LEFÈVRE-WITIER

9

Human migrations in North Africa

INTRODUCTION

It may be said of human migrations that they have simple and sometimes unique causes, but in reality these causes are multiple with varied consequences. North Africa is no exception to this formula. Here, I describe a few examples of migrations in the region. The territorial occupation by Iwellemeden "Saharan walkers" are followed by "Mediterranean sailor" invaders whose needs will be far more limited: ports, trading ports, and urban habitats were therefore limited to coasts. They are the Near Eastern Phoenicians of the twelfth century BC. Then others, coveting more farmland, food, and therefore territorial expansions, are the Romans, settlers of the Eastern Maghreb or "Ifriqiya" (present-day Tunisia).

The Magreb is a land of great immensity and infinite space, welcoming human activity. But it is also a land of great severity where the wind, this master of aridity, has established the largest desert in the world, the Sahara desert. One consequence is that since the Neolithic Era, the Maghreb has received far more successive civilizations than urban masses were able to erase and replace the prehistoric bases of its population (Bousquet, 1961). Despite the difficult conditions, humans have learned to master this space using mobility, especially in the Sahara, a key region of this "desert culture" born there tens of thousands years ago.

Causes and Consequences of Human Migration, ed. Michael H. Crawford and Benjamin C. Campbell. Published by Cambridge University Press. © Cambridge University Press 2012.

Among the numerous causes of human population mobility, one of the most significant is nutrition and the need it creates for land likely to produce food: agriculture, fishing, hunting, livestock farming. The favorable climatic conditions in the Sahara desert during the Neolithic Era in about the seventh century allowed the settlement of a large Berber population in which agropastoral farming was an important source of subsistence.

The relative stability of this Neolithic population, demonstrated by the archaeological excavations of many inhabited sites, was disrupted by drought around 3000 BC which imposed dramatic changes in the inhabitants' way of life. Increased aridity favored market gardening in the oasis zones, where gardeners learned how to manage the smallest drop of water through local or imported techniques (*foggara*). However, thousands of acres of pasture were rendered unsuitable for wild or domestic animal consumption.

As a consequence of this aridity, tribes and flocks had to move long distances to assure adequate forage for the animals. The tribes and their herds moved over great distances for long periods of time. As an example, I recently described the migration of Iwellemeden Tuaregs over 2500 kilometers, from the Atlas piedmont to the Nigerian Azaouak; that is, from the Maghreb to sub-Saharan Sahel (Lefèvre-Witier, 2010). In this study, I described many other long-distance migrations such as the Fula people – leaving Tassili n'Ajjer (Algerian Sahara) with their cattle to migrate to Burkina-Faso (former Upper Volta.)

Success of the Phoenician and Roman settlements in the ancient Maghreb

The Phoenicians dispersed their trading ports from Tripolitania to Morocco. It was a considerable enterprise of storage, transport (nowadays we would call this an import–export business), and fishing. Their main settlement, Carthage, was founded in 814 BC, on the eastern boundary coast of the Maghreb. Even in this city of cultural, economic, and demographic importance, the contribution of stable Phoenician settlers was relatively low. Their early arrival by at least 12 centuries BC is an important historical milestone for the presence of a foreign people in Africa. However it is the Punic wars among Berbers, Phoenicians, and Romans that mark the change in civilization, religion, and power represented by the fall of Carthage in 146 BC.

The Maghreb and the Sahara desert had been without domination or control for a millennium, but following the fall of Carthage, they would be Romano-Christian for 800 years. Like that of the Phoenicians, the Roman influx was essentially urban. The number of settlers was limited to the eastern part of the "Ifriqiya" Maghreb. It was there that agricultural production was assured by Berber peasants, great producers of wheat, oil, and wines. Here the great names of the Romano-Christian and Jewish Africa, such as Tertullian, Apuleus, Fronto, Saint Cyprian, and Saint Augustine, were born.

The first decades of the Roman seizure of power in Barbary were nevertheless marked by numerous conflicts with local Berber potentates such as Jugurtha, chief of the Eastern Numids, until tribal chiefs accepted "Romanization." These included Juba II in Cherchell near Tipaza, Bocchus in Mauretania and the Severe Dynasty of which Septimus even became Imperator in Roma around the year 200 BC. It was a heyday for Roman Africa which then reached a peak that lasted until the beginning of the third century AD. Expansion took place under Caesar in Cherchell, Ptolemy (AD 24–40) and Caligula to the west in Agadir (Morocco), then Septimus Severe in the east towards Tripoli.

From AD 238 onwards a certain decadence started that lasted until the arrival of the Vandals at the beginning of the fifth century (AD 430) then of the Byzantines (AD 532) (Bousquet, 1961). With these two sets of invaders, the notion of "migration" seemed irrelevant. Their demographic and genetic contribution appears limited to cultural enrichment of the Maghreb.

Roman decadence and Vandal and Byzantine invasions of the Maghreb coasts

The effect of the Punic wars on the evolution of the human population of the Maghreb leads to consideration of the local Berber groups faced with the many invaders who settled or were in the process of settling, from the second century BC to the sixth century AD.

In the second century BC, three Berber kingdoms can be identified, without knowing exactly how they were constituted. In the east, on the borders of the Punic territory are the Gaetuli and the Musulamii, a federation of Mauretanian tribes coming from Morocco as well as from the Aurès Mountains. This is a federation of tribes composed of nomadic shepherds from the Saharan borders to the Mediterranean coast. In the east were the tribes of Constantine (Cirta). Approximately 200 BC a powerful chief, Masinissa, emerged. His political action to some extent created an autonomous and rich Barbary, through the multiplication of geographically stable wheat producers (so coveted by the Romans) urbanized in fortified villages. With Masinissa, the opposition between nomads and peasants was confirmed and organized under the wing of tribal chiefs, who guaranteed land rights as well as fiscal benefits from their production!

The Romans achieved Masinissa's goal of conquering Carthage, considered as the capital city of the whole of Barbary, by razing the city to the ground in AD 146. This was the termination of the third Punic war and the death of Masinissa, in AD 148. The Romans annexed all Phoenician territories around the city and around the ports for themselves.

After numerous conflicts between the Romans and the Numid and Mauretanian Berbers, led by renowned chiefs such as Jugurtha, Juba I, Juba II, and Ptolomy, "Rome controlled the Barbary for nearly four centuries (40–429) until the Vandal invasions" (Julien, 1994.)

The European Vandals (430) and Near East Byzantine entries (532), had little impact on the way of life of the native populations of the Maghreb. At the same time the Vandals do represent a major migration since their leader Genseric arrived from Spain with a large number of people, including 15 000 soldiers and 65 000 tribesman. The transplantation of such a large population dependent on agriculture for subsistence provoked the expropriations of much land at the expense of the Berbers and Romans who were already settled in the rural areas. In fact, the Vandals took over the entire Maghreb region (Mauretania and Numidia).

Genseric created a powerful state with more Germanic than Roman structures, maintaining a strict parity among Vandals and Romans, but forbidding interracial marriages. Yet the Roman way of life and Latin as the official language were rapidly adopted. Almost nothing of the Vandal culture and language survived in spite of a century of an authoritarian presence lasting until 447, when Genseric died. During the next 50 years, the history of Vandal Barbary can be characterized by peasant revolts with rural Berbers and wars of succession at the level of royal power. In 530 a strong opposition appeared between Gelimer, a Vandal king, Genseric's great-grandson, and Justinian, emperor of Constantinople who, despite long centuries of peace, decided to invade Africa. As a result the Byzantines recaptured power in North Africa from 533 to 698. It is a century without many significant events in spite of Justinian's ambition to "restore" Africa. The Byzantines swept away the whole Vandal organization and enslaved all

Vandal soldiers. They promoted the Romanization and Christianity of the preceding centuries, still very much alive in the Maghreb. Yet the Justinian administration plundered and exerted fiscal pressures on the populations with the result of a general impoverishment, a ruinous exhaustion of the seven provinces in the Byzantine Maghreb. The fortifications that formed the bases of the Byzantine defense system quickly disintegrated. Practically nothing remains today of the administrative organization that persisted for one century. The fifth century also experienced the migration to Ifriqiya of trained dromedaries, led by nomadic camel drivers from the Egyptian Sahara.

THE FIRST ARABIC CONQUEST

Some of these camel drivers were Near Eastern Arabs who, as a result of their penetration into northwestern Egypt, discovered Barbary, a subcontinent with beautiful landscapes, an original civilization, and a totally unknown language. After the death of the Prophet Muhammad in 632 in Mecca, there was a wave of "Arabizing" and "Islamizing" of holy places. By the end of the seventh century there was a numerical explosion of tribes leading migrants to build a territorial empire from Gibraltar to the Indus river. This monotheistic civilization, abounding in cultural and intellectual qualities, promoted by a single language, was rapidly assimilated and encouraged by millions of believers. When he passed through Ifriqiya in 670, Oqba ibn Nafi, a military chief, had founded the town of Kairouan in 698. Despite strong Berber opposition from female military chiefs Kusaila and Kahina, the whole of Ifriqiya, after the storming of Carthage and the founding of Tunis, rallied to the Arabs. Within a century, the Western sphere of influence of what Isabelle Duchemin calls "the Arabic-Muslim epic" (Duchemin, 2008–2009) conquered Barbary and Spain but its expansion was stopped in France, in Poitiers, by Charles Martel (732). Thus, from 698 onwards, the fate of Barbary was sealed. Until the time of French colonization it was strongly linked to the eastern countries.

Tarik's invasion of Spain was accelerated thanks to the presence of many Berbers among his troops, who rushed by the thousands to the Iberian Peninsula. In Poitiers, 80 000 soldiers were of Berber origin; many of whom remained after the invasion in France and Spain. This Arabic–Berber migration left its striking mark on the populations of Spain. The Berber founders of this civilization in Spain can be traced back to Barbary in 1492 only, under the name of "Andalus," since their mothers were Iberian (reverse migration).

While Tarik was crossing Barbary, a Berber resistance against him had been organized. Curiously, as early as the eighth century, Berbers rallied to an Arabic heretical sect, the Kharedjites, making peace with the Arabs by adopting their language for all religious or scholarly affairs. It is interesting to follow the fate of these Kharedjite groups because this period of conflict provoked, for more than a century, a form of "endomigration." The descendants of this peaceful endomigration are none other than the Mozabite shopkeepers, or even grocers, present in almost all the towns of Algeria and Tunisia. The origins of the forebears of the 10 000 Kharedjites (or Ibadites), extant today, is the result of the creation of a kingdom by a Persian migrant. Tiaret, the capital city, situated in the central Maghreb, dominated the entire Maghreb region and Libyan east, populated by Zenata nomads and farmers from the Aurès Mountains and Tripolitania. The kingdom of Tiaret, with a history of victorious conflicts, came to a tragic end, being defeated first in Ifriqiya between 772 and 787 by the Fatimids, then in 911 by the storming of Tiaret.

The conquest of the city drove all of its inhabitants into the Sahara desert in Sedra (near Ouargla) where they were initiated into the cultivation of date palm trees. From there they moved to a more severe environment, on the same latitude, the M'zab, where they developed large palm groves and build five cities with remarkable architecture and urbanism. Even today, the M'zab are considered a jewel of the northern Sahara. Two additional cities were built later. Other groups of Kharedjite migrants settled further east, in Djerba and in the Nafusa Mountains, while others settled west of the Tafilalt (in the south of Morocco).

These "shopkeepers" maintained their migratory spirit throughout. Today the Ibadite communities continue to send men into North Africa, and provide funds to initiate new businesses. The story of the Ibadite population in the M'zab is a good example of medium-range mobility in the African framework that we are exploring (endomigration).

At the same time (late eighth, early ninth century) other kingdoms and dynasties blossomed in the Barbary. The Idrisids are found west of Morocco; while in the east were the Aghlabids. The Fatimid and Zirid dynasties came next, with a capital city of Madyia (near today's Monastir, in Tunisia). The latter dynasties are responsible for the capital and one of the most important migrations in the history of North Africa. This migration corresponds to the second Arabic invasion, by the Banu Hilal and Banu Soleim from 1050 onwards. In 1047, the

Fatimid El Moez conquered Egypt, thus expanding his kingdom to Cairo. His lieutenant, Ziri, assumed control of the tribe in the Maghreb. After El Moez's death, the Zirids refused to be taxed by the new Fatimid caliph El Moustansir and declared their independence. The anti-tax policy of the Zirids cost them an exemplary punishment in 1050 with the dispatch of the Banu Hilal and Banu Soleil to Ifriqiya. These two Arabic tribes had already been deported in 978 from Arabia to Egypt for banditry, plundering, and repeated slaughtering around the holy cities of Mecca and Medina.

In the case of the Hilal and Soleim, is it appropriate to call it a migration? In spite of the caliph's distant control, the groups' movement was rather like a "tsunami" sweeping over Ifriqiya. Ibn Khaldoun characterized it as a "cloud of grasshoppers" to evoke the raid and destructive aspect of these hordes from the Said in Upper Egypt. They entered the Maghreb through the Tripolatania where El Moez's Zirid Zenatas stopped them in Haydaran in 1052; but the Banu Hilal marched on Kairouan, where they plundered and slaughtered the population.

The Banu Hilal's stay in the eastern region of the Maghreb gave large advantages to nomadic camel drivers constantly seeking pasturelands but not power. They were men from the steppe and the desert and some authors consider their coming as a major contribution to the birth of the "desert civilization" of which the Saharan Tuaregs are now the clearest representatives. Because of their violent behaviors, the tribes of Banu Hilal and Soleim generated a permanent anarchy in the center of the Maghreb's two rival principalities. They were responsible for a great economic decline that impacted trade and navigation throughout North Africa. Two centuries were required to re-establish order in that region. During the same time, the great number of Arabs that came to the Maghred led to Arabization and Islamization in the rural areas. At that time stable Berber-speaking people took refuge in coastal and mountainous areas. They gave up large areas of arable land to the Banu Hilal and Soleim and later to the Maqil Arabs, except in the west where the breeding of livestock prevailed due to the presence of the Almoravids – whose religious, pastoral, and political movements will be dealt with in the next section.

ALMORAVIDS AND ALMOHADS

In 1052, while the epic of the Banu Hilal started in Tripolitania, the story of west of the Maghreb is the powerful saga of the Sanhaja nomads, desert Berbers, of the Djuddalas and then of the Lemtunas led by Yahya ibn Umar and his brother Abu Bakr. This religious movement did not at first lead to any kind of migration. Its mission was to unite the tribes in order to convert to Islam through jihad (fighting.) We will see later how military movements were organized for specific conflicts. This mythical idea of a mission is the "rabita" which gave its name to the movement: al mourabitun. In 1059, the "Almoravids" became a "kingdom of the veiled," under the leadership of Abu Bakr. These Sanhaja desert Berbers founded their capital city, Marrakech. Led by Yusif ibn Tashfin, they moved to the north of Morocco and to Spain. In 1094 he annexed the entire Muslim Spain and completed the Berber migration initiated by the earlier eighth century invasion.

In this late eleventh century, it is relevant to discuss a religious migration populating the region. An empire was born, stretching from the Ebro to Senegal, along the Atlantic coast. This was an empire enriched by the gold of the African Sahel and marked by the architectural luxury of its capital city Marrakech and an urban lifestyle.

The Almohads, from the neighboring Moroccan Upper Atlas Mountains, were a new unorthodox religious movement born in the early twelfth century. They arose in the Masmuda tribes of Ibn Tumart, then of Abd al-Mu'min, an audacious chief who conquered Almoravid Spain and the entire Maghreb region. This religious movement is not considered as a migration but rather the first seizure of power in the Barbary by a native dynasty. The Almohads were later crushed by the armies of the Christians and of the Marinids.

In spite of their final failure, the Almohads must be considered as the greatest representatives in the history of the Berbers, not only from a military and administrative point of view, but from a religious one as well (Bousquet, 1961). After the passing of two Berber empires, there are few major population movements in North Africa. The thirteenth and fourteenth centuries saw great population stability thanks to an important degree of tribal anarchy but without much mobility.

In the late thirteenth century, the North African structure of power was organized into three kingdoms according to a logic established during the previous centuries. In 1236, the Hafcid dynasty settled in Tunis on the territory of East Ifriqiya. In the center, the Abdalwadids founded yet another kingdom, with Tlemcen as capital city, while in the same year the Merinids seized power in Fez. None of these three kingdoms were as prestigious as the Almohad Empire. They lived a sedentary existence until the mid-fifteenth century. From the fifteenth to the sixteenth century, conflicts between the Wattasids from Fez and the Saadi from the south of Morocco, as well as between Portuguese and

Spaniards, periodically caused conflict in the western Maghreb. The political–religious events of this period include: Granada was recaptured from the Muslims (1492) and the Portuguese established Santa Cruz de Aguer (Agadir; Atlantic coast of Morocco) in 1505.

TURKISH DOMINATION OF THE MAGHREB

Migratory activities in North Africa resumed in the early sixteenth century with the Turkish domination of Algeria and Tunisia until the arrival of the French (1516–1830).

After a few successful acts of piracy, including the storming of Algiers by his brother Oruç (settled in Djidjelli, and his death in 1518), Barbarossa Hayreddin returned to Algiers and founded the Regency. He also established close relations with the Ottomans of Constantinople who appointed him Pasha and Beylerbey (emir among the emirs) of the new state of Algiers. By the storming of Tunis and the abolition of the Hafcid kingdom in 1534, Barbarossa Hayreddin Pasha took control of the Mitidja plain and the entire region of the central and eastern Maghreb. Invited to Constantinople as an admiral in the Ottoman fleet in 1538, he died there in 1546 leaving Hasan Agha as a Pasha of Algiers (1536–43).

In Algiers and other towns in Algeria and Tunisia, the Turkish government tried to draw as much economic benefit as possible, while keeping aloof from the country and its inhabitants (Julien, 1994, pp. 677–86). Thus, for more than a century (sixteenth century) Algiers appeared to seafarers not as the capital city of a new Ottoman province, but as the seat of a pirate state in which the conversion of the captives (renegades) to Islam stood as a certificate of citizenship (Boyer, 1985).

The Beylerbeys governed the Regency directly or through their lieutenants (Khalifa), acting as the "Kings of Algiers," faithful to the Sublime Porte. Their actions took the form of:

- enriching Algiers through the piracy of vessels
- enriching Algeria by pressuring natives through taxes and intensive production
- fearing the Janissaries, the powerful military police
- favoring borders and the distinction between Algeria, Tunisia, and Morocco
- fighting against the Moroccan Sharifs and the Spaniards of the "Presides."

Hasan Agha fought against Charles V in 1541 in a failed attempt by the King of Spain to capture Algiers. He was replaced by a succession of Beylerbeys who maintained a strict war against Christians until Euldj Ali, the last but prestigious "king of Algiers" who, in collaboration with Dragur Raïs, put an end to the Hafcid dynasty in Tunisia by capturing Tunis and La Goulette. When Euldj Ali died in 1587, the Sultan created three areas: Tripolitania, Tunisia, and Algeria, thus anticipating the future structure of the Maghreb. He eliminated the Beys from Algiers; their power went to the Aghas, to the militia, and the Deys. In Tunisia, the same process gave the power to Deys then to Beys. But the two Pashas of these Regencies were independent from Constantinople and their "races" were made much easier during the whole of the seventeenth century, "the golden age of corsairs." Inhabitants from the Maghreb grew rich thanks to plunder. They decked their homes with the most precious objects and delicacies from the European and Eastern worlds. Slaves also ran into thousands, with 25 000 Christian captives in Algiers during the sixteenth century! The economic conditions were different from the previous century when destitution was everywhere in the streets of Algiers. Thousands died of plague and starvation, 5600 people in 1580, and 25 000 from 1472 to 1574! But the race was sufficient to conceal the voids because a powerful and continuous immigration movement was necessary to make up the deficits (Julien, 1994).

The last few pages of this chapter are dedicated to Algeria, which, in recent times (since 1830), has proven its ability to withstand "populating migration," contemptuously called "colonization" until 1962, when it became politically independent. The times we discuss now preceded the arrival of the French in Africa. They correspond to the seventeenth and eighteenth century; that is, from the death of Bey Euldj Ali to 1798 when Napoleonic armies bought wheat from Algerians, thus creating a debt leading first to the 1830 Algerian–French conflict and to major out-migration.

The seventeenth century, the so-called golden age of Algiers, was followed by a century of economic deterioration. Indeed, the race largely slowed down and living conditions were such that Algiers lost its beautiful prosperity. Half of its population disappeared when 500 people a day perished from unknown causes. In spite of the clear recession of the international and domestic trades in the eighteenth century (only the French and the English still maintained important exchanges), the Deys, who reigned over a sixth of Algeria, watched their own interests and accumulated huge fortunes. This greed was probably an important factor of the Deys' asking for the reimbursement of the Napoleonic debt in 1827. This demand led to the famous "fan affair," in which the Dey struck the French consul with a fan, as a response to the consul's insolence.

This feather fan provoked a three-year blockade of the Algiers port, then an attack on Algiers in 1830 and the permanent migration of thousands of European "settlers" over the course of 132 years. As in many other circumstances, a political upheaval was born in a mere blink of an eye.

MIGRATIONS OF EUROPEAN SETTLERS TO THE MAGHREB

I chose to focus, in our study on migrations, on the recent history of Algeria because of the contrast between the trivial incident of the feathered fan affair and the upheaval it provoked through French colonization. The first French settlers traveled in the holds of military ships. In 57 years (1887) they had already taken over 400 000 hectares of farmlands. By the end of World War I, they had multiplied the size of the farmland fifteenfold. Most, 98%, of the land was in the Tell, the coastal part of the Maghreb most favorable to agriculture. By the late eighteenth century, it is fair to say that Algeria had become an extension of France. It had its own civil personality, its colonial assembly, as well as a budget of a "populating colony" unlike the protectorates of Tunisia (1881) or Morocco (1912). In a populating colony, migrants become the owners of rural estates, of which they also represent the workforce, whereas in the protectorates, property was brought under state control in the name of France and the local people remained the active producers.

All these colonial transfers were made essentially through plunder – that is, in the most abusive way. The Algerians were doomed throughout the nineteenth century to a Mediterranean and south European migration. From this hybrid migration, a territory, "Algerian France," was born, presented to schoolboys as a new French department. An original population also appears, the Pieds-Noirs, "passionate lovers and devoted sons" of this northern part of Africa (Stora, 2004).

Within a century, a total of 833 000 European Pieds-Noirs, among whom 657 000 were French, had already settled. In 1954, those born in Algeria combined with those leaving reached a million migrants to Algeria. But how did we reach this impressive number, according to French political leaders?

In the beginning of the Algerian colonization, living and health conditions played major roles in driving the migration. The forced development and profitability of farms, harsh or warm climate (according to the migrants' origins), malaria, and infections led to a disheartening negative outcome for many. For example, between 1842 and 1846 there were 198 000 arrivals and 118 000 departures.

The impatience of the French government led them to choose an emergency solution: deportation. From 1848 on, Paris was "cleansed" of social and political movements such as people involved in the 1848 revolution and later, in 1871, "Communards." In addition, people from Alsace and Lorraine, fleeing from the Prussian occupation, and peasants, victims of the Industrial Revolution, were helped to emigrate, as well as poor or very poor peasants from the south of France (Hautes and Basses Alpes, Drôme, Gard, Pyrénées orientales, Corsica).

In addition to transportation, about which we do not have precise details, there was a foreign complement of migrants termed "the wave of emigrants from the Mediterranean shores," otherwise referred to as "emigrants from southern Europe." Because of their common history with the Maghreb (see above), the Spaniards were the first to come to this new Algeria, no longer to be conquered but colonized and above all cultivated. In 1849, 35 000 Spaniards were already there; this number increased fivefold in 1886, only 50 years later. In 1911, just a few years before World War I, a census in and around Oran reports 95 000 French settlers, 92 000 Spaniards with French nationality, and 93 000 without, showing how efficient was this Spanish migration. The Italian migration has been much more limited. In 1886, when Spaniards numbered 160 000, there were only 15 000 Italians, who primarily developed farmlands from Constantine to Annaba (Bône). At the same time as migrants came from Italy, just as many Maltese settled around Annaba.

By the late nineteenth century, the population of settlers reached half a million, French and foreigners of various ethnicity equally. The young people born in Algeria began to outnumber their migrant parents. It is a new European–African population, full of initiative and energy. Most of their parents came to cultivate the land for profit, peace, and love. After 1954, they found civil war and hate. This turn of events led native Muslims to a total independence and French migrants to an incredible "reverse-migration." This reverse migration by ships and planes was rapid and well organized, given the number of migrants.

TRANSFER OF THE HARKIS

In 1962, the influx of European migrants came to an end. A new country was built within the huge African jigsaw. While the "Pieds-Noirs" came back to France with limited social and financial advantages, so did the

Muslims who had become "allies" of the French army during the war (Harkis). Their countrymen hated them and they could stay in Algeria but only by risking their lives. Illegally or legally repatriated, 120 000 to 150 000 crossed the Mediterranean with or without their families. They received a lukewarm, in some cases unfriendly, reception. Prefects housed the newly arrived: in the barracks of military camps that had already been used for other migrants; in uncomfortable transit camps supposed to be only temporary; in forest hamlets far from neighboring villages; in 17 urban large housing projects in the east of France.

Associations were created to help these "Harkis." In addition, new "shelters" were built, which were better equipped and adapted to family life.

DAILY MIGRATION

Yet, all these efforts to welcome and integrate (recently on a professional basis) the Harkis were only developed in four areas of the east of France, which meant they felt total relegation. In 1968, one half of Harkis were still receiving daily economic assistance. Nowadays, the Harkis and their descendants, most of them rather well integrated, can be compared to the type of migration I will call "daily migration," which every year attracts 40 000 to 50 000 people from Maghreb to France. Our developed countries need this importation of temporary workers. For these migrants we should certainly plan a specific social assistance. And because the Muslim community rose to close to 3.7 million in 2011, we have to plan to build mosques in many towns as well.

PRESENT AND FUTURE

This "daily migration" probably will not keep the same regular but discreet rhythm it had adopted in 1920. Indeed, in 1958, Europe had favored a clear growth of the Muslim (and particularly Maghreb) communities. Recently, political events in Arab Muslim (Mediterranean or not) countries proved that these sudden migratory rises could appear on our coasts, like the arrival of Tunisians in Italy via the island of Lampedusa. We must prepare to welcome our close cousins in the large "Mediterranean" partly "Euro" and partly "Afro" family despite the long past history of greed and aversion, of hate and love, of fights and migrations.

REFERENCES

Bousquet, G. H. (1961). *Les Berbères*. Paris: P.U.F.

Boyer, P. (1985). Les renégats et la marine de la Régence d'Alger [Renegades and navy of the Algiers Regency]. *Revue de l'Occident Musulman et de la Méditerranée*, **39**, 93–106.

Duchemin, I. (2008–2009). La grande épopée arabo-musulmane. In Blandin, C. (ed.) *L'Atlas des Migrations: Les Routes de l'Humanité*, pp. 24–5. Paris: Le Monde Hors-Série, Monde SA, Malesherbes Publications SA and Sciences-Po.

Julien, C. A. (1994). *Histoire de l'Afrique du Nord: Des Origines à 1830*. Paris: Grande Bibliothèque Payot.

Lefè vre-Witier, P. (2010). Iwellemeden Neolithic migration. Presentation at the conference on "Human migration," Kansas University, Lawrence, KS.

Stora, B. (2004). *Histoire de l'Algérie Coloniale: 1830–1954*. Collection Repères. Paris: La Découverte.

JOHN M. JANZEN

10

Identity, voice, community: new African immigrants to Kansas

INTRODUCTION

The story of recent African migration to the American heartland is a very small vignette of migration throughout human history, of post-colonial global labor and opportunity migration; and, of the historic migrations that in earlier centuries and decades populated the country-sides and cities of the expanding American frontier. This chapter reports on a project conducted by the African Studies Center at the University of Kansas from 2005 to 2007 about recent African migration into the urban centers of northeast and southcentral Kansas – Kansas City, Lawrence, Topeka, Emporia, Wichita. The project was conceived in a fall 2004 seminar organized by Center assistant, and later Associate Director, Khalid Elhassan, in which representatives of the region's African immigrant communities came to share their stories of migration, their visions for their communities, and how they might work with the Center in topics of mutual interest.[1] Their strong endorsement led the Center to join the Kansas Humanities Council's "We the People" initiative, an extension of the national program by the same name. Core features of the project included interviews of community members about their immigrant experience; several community meetings with speakers from the communities for discussion, and interpretations of these experiences by project humanists Omofolabo Ajayi and David Katzman of the University of Kansas faculty; and the preparation of a videofilm. The project's public education thrust sought to explain to Kansans and Americans who the new immigrants are, the circumstances of their leaving home, why they had come here, and what

Causes and Consequences of Human Migration, ed. Michael H. Crawford and Benjamin C. Campbell. Published by Cambridge University Press. © Cambridge University Press 2012.

distinctive human perspectives and practices they contribute to American society. The project thus combined solid scholarly research (Lohrentz, 2004) and analysis with public awareness raising.[2]

PERSPECTIVES ON MIGRATION, RESEARCH, AND PUBLIC PROGRAMMING

Migration is an old American phenomenon. Most Americans have a history of immigration in their background. Although this project focused on a regional representation of over a million African-born immigrants and their offspring who live in the United States, this group fits within a larger picture (Apraku, 1991; Djamba, 1999; Takougang, 2003). Immigrants and immigration policy have captured much attention and aroused political debate in recent years, in the United States as well as in other countries. While most Americans think of Mexican or Hispanic immigrants when they think "immigrants," in fact there are many other groups who have come to the United States in the past decade or two.

David Katzman, Professor of History and American Studies at the University of Kansas, notes the significance of migrants in American history.

> . . . the United States is made up of, and is dependent on, immigrants coming here, taking risks. The question is: Why do people come? Why do people move [permanently . . .] not just some people doing politics and then going back. People come from point to point for economic or political or religious reasons . . . they move constantly for a lot of reasons other than the myths that our streets are paved with gold.

Yet today migration scholarship frames this phenomenon in *global* perspective, as much as a local, state, or national perspective (Foner, 2003; Okome, 2002a, 2002b). Even the term *"transnational migration"* reflects an effort to transcend the boundaries of territories, societies, states, and nations to grasp the dynamic characteristics of migration and the unfolding identities of those who move from one nation-state to another, or continue shuttling back and forth. Scholarship focuses on transnational flows of people and capital, on the "push" of war, poverty, and persecution, and "pull" factors of economic opportunity, education, and religious freedom (Finkelstein and Zeiderman, 2006:23–4).

The Identity, Voice, and Community project explored in interviews and public meetings such themes and questions as: How does "who we are?" and "who others say we are?" shape the immigrant experience in a new place? How is the experience of leaving, arriving, and getting settled told? By whom? How is memory – individual, collective, societal – established? Do these stories become part of an American story? What ways emerge in relating to new neighbors and the larger American society? Do job and work offer significant connections? How do the new immigrants keep in touch with their relatives, friends, neighbors, and home communities? What is the role of electronic media? Are these experiences of building community and maintaining networks enhanced or destroyed by migration?[3]

Because of the makeup of the team, perspectives from a number of disciplines were involved and shaped the overall interpretations. John Janzen, project director and principal investigator, a sociocultural anthropologist, working with Melissa Filippi-Franz, a graduate student in anthropology, developed interview protocols. Janzen, Filippi-Franz, and Khalid Elhassan, Ph.D., Center Program Coordinator, and Project co-principal investigator, conducted related interviews. Garth Myers, Associate Professor of Geography and Associate Director of the Center, used methods from his discipline, together with a Ph.D. former student of his Mohamed Dosi Mohamed, Zanzibari-American, and Assistant Professor of Swahili, Leonce Rushubirwa. These individuals conducted intensive research and group interviews with this community in Wichita and Kansas City (Dosi *et al.*, 2007). Khalid Elhassan, a Sudanese-American, with a Ph.D. in Education and African Studies, was involved with the Sudanese community in particular and also provided his disciplinary perspective in the public programming. Later in the project, political science student and Center intern Abdulrahme Gitale worked closely with the Somali community. The multidisciplinary representation of the team gave the project both depth and breadth in its coverage. Humanists David Katzman added perspectives of history and American Studies, and Omofolabo Ajayi added the perspective of performance studies and Women's Studies.

From the start this project was run in the manner that anthropologists would call *Collaborative Ethnography* (Lassiter, 2005). The scholarly participants were involved in many of the decisions along the way. Some were the very individuals who had participated as community members in the African Studies Seminar in fall 2004. The project in fact grew out of participants' suggestions of what they would like to see the Center do with and for them. We circulated the proposal and word of its funding to all of our partners so that they would understand what we were planning, and that they could expect us to be in contact with them. We next tested our questionnaire on three interviewees, and made some adjustments, before the larger number were conducted.

Two public meetings were held in spring, 2006. Our two guest humanists, Omofolabo Ajayi and David Katzman, had access to the interview texts to prepare for their comments. Prior to both public meetings the project director invited participants, humanists, and a few guests to a reception-meal at the Alladin Café in Lawrence, before moving on to the Public Library. In Kansas City participants met at the African Market on Main Street for a reception-meal, before continuing on to the public meeting at the Jewish Vocational Services.

INITIAL FINDINGS

Brief conclusions and some generalized findings are possible about the approximately 10 000 African-born immigrants who have come to the mostly urban belt from Kansas City to Lawrence, Topeka, Emporia, and Wichita in the past 20 years, as shown in Table 10.1.[4] These are a small cross-section of the nearly 900 000 foreign-born Africans in the 2000 census, and over a million if counted from the 1990 census (www.census.gov; Arthur, 2000:154). However, further analysis is needed of the material collected, as well as comparisons with similar regional concentrations of immigrants. Further, it should be possible to explore the transnational dynamics that are unique to the African experience and those that are similar to the global phenomenon of migration.

WHY THEY CAME

African migrants to the United States in general, just as those in the urban belt of Kansas, are extremely diverse in their social composition, and the circumstances of their migration. Professor Omofolabo Ajayi, in the first community meeting, suggested that 1986 was a watershed for African students and other Africans who had occasion to come to the United States. Before that date they tended to return home following their initial visit or original reason for coming. They had hope for a good life at home. After 1986, they began to stay. Increasingly, this sense of hope for a good life at home faded, replaced by the image of a better life in the United States, of fantastic incomes – a land where streets were paved with gold. "Globalization" was also mentioned as an underlying reason, particularly as expressed in structural adjustment in

Table 10.1. *Table of immigrants to Kansas by country of origin, approximate numbers based on census figures and community leaders' estimates; Elhassan's individual survey of African immigrants in Lawrence, Kansas, in 2006*

Country of origin	Wichita, Topeka, Kansas City corridor	Lawrence only, Khalid Elhassan's 2006 survey
Somalia	4–5000	2
Nigeria	2–3000	20
Kenya	1–2000	36
Sudan	750–1000	14
Tanzania (incl. Zanzibar)	500	7
Ethiopia	500	2
Sierra Leone	200	0
Ten other countries	500	30
Total	**9450–12 700**	**112**

home country economies (see also Okome, 2002a, 2002b) that deflated national currencies and introduced difficult living conditions on many.

But Ajayi contrasted this seductive image of America with the actual experience of life in America that requires very hard work, often followed by disappointment. She noted that countrymen and relatives at home often did not believe these stories of hard work, accusing their relatives of lying to legitimately avoid having to share their wealth. A kind of disjuncture emerged between the new immigrants and their kin back home, one that falsely reinforced the lure of further migration.

In the interviews it became clear that Kansas African immigrants have come for a wide range of reasons, related to war, political oppression and religious persecution, economic and professional opportunity, and the desire to join kin and countrymen (KASC, 2006). These varied reasons are to a degree generalizable by country because of particular national circumstances. Thus, Somalis came mainly as refugees having fled unending civil war and collapse of government at home (Filippi-Franz, 2009; Ghazali, 2010); they live mostly in the Kansas City region, employed as service workers. Kenyans in Kansas are for the most part successful business people, or professionals. Nigerians have come over the years as political asylees, students, and professionals. Tanzanians reflect a very similar picture, with the prominent Zanzibari group having its national organization headquartered in Wichita. Ethiopians have resided in

Kansas City and Wichita for a decade or more, the result of civil war, repression, and drought/famine at home. Sudanese have come from all regions, either as refugees and political asylees. They have in some cases, such as Akot Arec in Olathe, achieved successful community-building initiatives. Sierra Leonians have come as refugees following that country's civil war. These reasons for migrating among the African immigrants to Kansas are similar to those among African immigrants elsewhere in the United States.

MAKING A LIVING

The occupations and income-generating labors of the new African immigrants are as diverse as the circumstances of their coming. Despite the high educational level they represent, many are disappointed not to find work in their area of training, especially if trained in Africa: for example professionals, doctors, teachers, researchers. They often find work in the service sector, as taxi drivers, low-level healthcare workers, construction workers, night watchmen, janitors, etc. Many have found work in the healthcare field, although often at a level far below their training, for example as orderlies or nursing assistants. The urban corridor of Kansas also saw some of the raw labor migration of semi-skilled workers. At least a thousand Somali immigrants from elsewhere converged on Emporia, Kansas, to work in the slaughter houses and packing plants. Yet in 2009 the plant was closed by a consolidation brought on by the financial crisis of that year. Somali housing locales, a restaurant, and their unfamiliar new faces caused a moderately hysterical outcry in the town despite city planners' efforts to incorporate this new community. Then they were gone before these issues could even be dealt with (Shields, 2008).

Those who have received their education in the United States are much more able to achieve the certification required to be medical and educational professionals, researchers, engineers, and other skilled occupations. Typical for most immigrants, children's education is seen as a cherished goal of access to the American Dream.

IMMIGRANT ORGANIZATIONS

Faced with many perplexing challenges and issues, the new African immigrants do what immigrants have done historically: they create self-help organizations to negotiate the bureaucratic maze with which they are confronted, and to make connections to work, residence, and educational opportunities. The interviews, publications,

Table 10.2. *Organizations or associations among African immigrants to Kansas, based on observations, visits with organization leaders and representatives, and reference to named entities in interviews*

The Somali Foundation
Association of Somali Community of Kansas City
Somali Bantu Foundation
East African Association
United Sudanese Association
Southern Sudanese Association of Greater Kansas City
Jump Start Sudan Inc.
Nigerian Association, Kansas City
Tanzanian Association, Wichita
Zanzibari-International Association
Zanzibari-American Association, Wichita
Sierra Leone United Descendants Association
Kenyan Association of Kansas City
African Association, Kansas City
Senegalese Association, Kansas City

and videofilm brought to light 15 formal or semi-formal organizations among the Kansas African immigrants (Table 10.2).

The associations – or rather the connections that they represent – are of immeasurable help for some immigrants who have difficulty with passage out of their home countries, with asylum situations in the United States. Mohamed Dosi dealt at length with this situation in his interview, describing both his own case and how he had helped create the Zanzibari America Association to help others.

> *... I was instrumental in establishing the Zanzibar-American Association.*
> *This community was established to help people settle and especially to help them to settle in the U.S. From the beginning when I came to the U.S., once you're here you may stay and go out, but do the best to be legal, and most likely you will get opportunity to move on from where you are. Without the legal status you don't have much chance for improvement, for moving up. Nobody will take you up. Even yourself, if you are employed, and someone offers you to be boss, you won't take it, because you're afraid. The more they know you, they will offer you opportunity. . . . The organization helps, immediately they find someone to . . . help, even a small reason to solve some problem, you have somebody say yes I'll help, offer asylum, or help, these are the people who help. I have been even asked to help write the application for asylum, that way my contribution is huge, I make sure such a person can get a job.*

Mohamed Dosi suggested that one well-placed individual like himself who knows immigration officials can provide invaluable advice and connections to his countrymen seeking solutions to their migration and bureaucratic dilemmas. This helping person who is in touch with officials may become a beacon-light for those seeking escape from difficult situations back home. Dosi describes the course trajectory of a fellow countryman that resembles his own situation.

> [For example, a] . . . Zanzibar member of the electoral commission was arrested, the police came to take the ballot boxes, the police followed them, my role was to give the boxes to the electoral commission, not the police. He refused to give the ballots to the police. . . . He had a lot of trouble. He escaped from Z to Pemba, from there to Dar.; [He] knew an American lady, [she] helped with visa to U.S. They had trouble at home, they were attacked, mobs, here he was.

Dosi is convinced from his experience that the immigrant associations play a very important role not only in helping those who have particular problems, but in inspiring those who are afraid to share their failures to make contact with others and to overcome their fear of speaking out about their home situations that leads them to seek emigration.

The immigration organizations play a significant role as well once immigrants have arrived. The Somali Foundation hosts many meetings to teach its immigrant members – most of whom are technically refugees – practical matters such as such as health programs, English language classes, driving classes, women's programs including classes on nutrition, financial management, and childcare; youth recreation, cultural celebrations, translation and advocacy work. Farah Abdi, the Foundation president, explains:

> . . . over the town there are not many facilities that we can use or if even some facilities we don't have the access to.
>   . . . most of our children need housing and family housing and where are we going to move? . . . and we have to make a housing . . . And a basketball court and . . . they cannot because . . . our culture because . . . national holidays . . . or Muslim feasts.
>   . . . second point that is community and other African communities and . . .
>   . . . new need to investigate . . . the way that we can provide [services . . .]

Mohamed Aburass, former member of parliament in Sudan from the Nuba Hills region, and now a taxi driver in Kansas City, describes the beginnings of the United Sudanese Association.

> The Sudanese refugees who came over here, and me one of them – I came as a refugee in 1999 – and as we came over here we thought about how to gather ourselves, without saying "who is a refugee?" "who is a lottery," and who is someone else in

Sudan. When we go out of Sudan, everyone is a brother. So we gathered ourselves over here and we have an organization called the United Sudanese Association . . . we are doing our work from our homes . . . we are at the beginning we don't have a letter, we meet in our homes, and now we are trying to find out where to go.

. . . This association which we are having, we have activities. . . . how to teach our kids our culture. So we have a class right now and they are doing their activities they used to do it by the weekend for two hours . . . The second activity is to keep our community together that if anybody has any kind of celebration where anyone has deceased or passed away, we come together, as is our culture . . . we come to sit together. We hold celebrations like national celebrations, in Sudan we used to do it like religious celebrations like Ramadan, we also do it amicably over here. We have also another activity, sport, we have a Sudanese team, sport activity weekend, to gather these people together . . .

Jane Irungu commented at some length in her interview on the centrality of Kenyan associations in Kansas City, Lawrence, and Topeka, and how she had at first upon coming to the United States to join her husband, depended on these ties for many services and her social contacts. But in recent years she suggested she was no longer involved, because she was too busy at work, parenting children. Church ties also took the place of the immigrant association.

Several of the project interviewees indicated that their immigrant associations that had offered invaluable help and connections were, however, not in touch with other associations. In other words, these associations were either national or subnational, perhaps ethnic, or even village or kin related. Such focused networks may provide great help when confidence and trust are of great importance. One interviewee stated that his association was like an opposition party and thus had little connection to the other one that was closer to the national embassy and the government. But they also suggest that the African immigrant association may not be as helpful later on with "making it" in American society as contacts with others outside of one's national or ethnic group.

Still, the immigrant associations provide an indispensable bridging network between the immigrant's earlier situation and the new society. American historian David Katzman, in a community meeting, offered that the African immigrant organizations were an altogether typical and characteristic feature of the immigrant experience that has shaped American society.

Immigrants build their own communities . . ., that's why immigrants form organizations in that process they change American culture and society a very old process a lot of similarities of previous generations and now . . . and I hear the project's voices with a lot of similarities to previous generations.

Immigrant organizations and networks often reflect the political alliances and fractures of the home country or situation, for example the fractures of a civil war, the religious divide, class divisions. But this situation then also calls forth the desire to break with the fractures of the home country and to strive for unity in the United States. Seeking unity amongst groups where there has been civil war and division was emphasized in a project-sponsored community meeting in Kansas City in comments by Mohamed Aburass, president of the United Sudanese Association, together with Mohamed Omer of the North Sudan Association.

> . . . when the war took place it was just like Northern Sudan and Southern Sudan. And after a while they said "Muslims against Christians." After a while it was "Arabs against Africans." It got very bad. When we came here all these sides were affecting us. So those people who came straight from the field the camps in Kenya, they came here and didn't want to speak with those who came from Khartoum. And that is a problem for us. This is a kind of deterrent for how we come together. . . . you try to get rid of me, you try to destroy my house, what can I do with you? What am I going to do with you? When I find you this is a good time for me to get rid of you. But I'm not going to do like that now. We are doing our best, and giving ourselves the time, for us to come together.

For many of the African immigrants, however, the conflicts that divided people at home pale before the need to, and advantages of, cooperation and collaboration. Farah Abdi, president of the Kansas City Somali Association, stressed the need to build positive lives and communities in America. Perhaps because of the agony of flight, and the continuing chaos of Somalia, Abdi urges his contrymen and other African immigrants to concentrate on building strong American communities, training the children to succeed in America, and generally to make a positive contribution to "this multinational country." This general philosophy appears to guide Farah Abdi as the Somali Foundation offers all kinds of services and training to its people.

IDENTITY: "AFRICAN" OR "AMERICAN"

New African immigrants arrive in the United States and discover that they are suddenly generic "black" or "African-American." They are uncomfortable with these new identities that American society thrusts upon them, as these answers to interview questions about identity reveal.

ABDI: *Well, it depends. . . . So if I am with other people and people wanted to know, someone will ask you, what is your nationality? Or where are you originally from? I say Somali. But one thing that I never say, is that I'm African-American.*

AKOT: *I'm a Sudanese American. And actually, you know, when I'm in Sudan, I will tell the people that I'm American because I'm proud to be American. And if I'm here I'll tell the people I'm a Sudanese, because I'm proud to be Sudanese. So that's my identity.*

FARAH: *I can say that my identity is Somalian and even if I become a U.S. citizen I will no longer lose my Somali being and Somali national and even this United States government or the immigration and naturalization services will write my passport and my identity as a Somalian always, it will never disappear. I will always be a Somalian. And now I'm a Somalian. And I think if I become a United States citizen I'm still a Somalian.*

This same interviewee, Farah Abdi, president of the Somali Foundation, went on to discuss the relationship of Somalis in the United States to African-Americans.

FARAH: *You know, there is usually a belief that most Somalians or other Africans who came to the United States there is a belief that they are not African-American and when we heard that African-American we think that it is not ours, or that it is something else or other people, but really if we consider the history of these people, we are the same, we are the same African origin, for example our children who are born here and the African-American who came, maybe their ancestor 7 or 8 centuries [generations] ago came as slaves, they are same origin, same ethnic, and even we don't know if they came from Somalia or other countries, but I think the main answer to that question I think we are the same, same people.*

Jane Irungu's eloquent account in the Lawrence public meeting of her encounters with United States census categories was both humorous and revealing.

I ask myself who I am, especially in America, I'm an African, but also a Kenyan, also a Kikuyu, and very specifically, I am from central province, so somebody from Kenya will know who that sequence means . . .

  When I'm in America, they call me what they want to call me, I construct my own identity, because it means who I am . . . Some call me an African, some call me an African American . . . but what I am trying to say is that I am the only one who can identify myself. Because when others identify me here, mostly they identify me wrongly, they give me the wrong definition. . . . I'll give you an example when we went to the hall to travel abroad, we filled out the forms, with a lot of check boxes. When I came to America, there were seven check boxes for identity.

African America, black, Hispanic, etc., are you alien, resident alien, are you other? I was so not checking these, none of those are who I am . . . I am not African American. OK, who are you? If I am in Kenya, I am white, but if I'm here I . . . am I black? Possibly. But I am not call myself black I am still trying to process the idea of being black, I never thought of myself as such. But it is still a process to identify myself. . . . I was used to identifying myself as Kikuyu from a part of the country yes I'm black, black, but you are putting us into one category . . .

So who am I what is my identity? It's a depending on the environment I construct my identity, as I want to define it. Depending on the environment. The core of who I am that has never changed. African Kikuyu doesn't change. But the other one who helps me meet with people, that one shifts. The same with the language. I can shift the language depending on who I'm relating to. American friends, English. Kikuyu or Swahili for my African friends. The language can shift depending on who I'm talking to. I shift what I eat, depending on what is available. . . So who I am has not changed . . .

The many ways that identity is negotiated and recreated are a fruitful area of story and further research.

WHY KANSAS?

Reasons for settling in Kansas in the interviews varied from "by accident," to "being a student at a Kansas university or college and settling," to "having family in the area whom they wished to join." Others cited the relatively easier time of making a living and of living conditions in general than in America's big cities. This related to the accessibility of schools and raising a family. "Friendly people" and "affordable housing" were also mentioned. Many immigrants' stories addressed this question, often spontaneously. The theme of distance from big cities echoed also in the case of the Zanzibari-American Association, whose national headquarters are in Wichita, far enough removed from Washington D.C. and other East African embassies and organizations that would overwhelm them. In a few cases like that of Okot Arec, Southern Sudanese refugee turned American citizen, Kansas afforded the opportunity to invite relatives and fellow Southern Sudanese to move from elsewhere to build a community.

CONCLUSION

The New African Immigrants to Kansas participants hoped that their involvement in this project would give them solutions to their problems, and help them gain positive visibility in American society. The interviews and the public discussions revealed a series of contradictions and transformations that shaped their experiences and gave their lives recognizable shape.

Generally they did not initially think of themselves as Africans but as Sudanese, Kenyans, Ethiopians, Somalis, and Nigerians. American society however saw them as more or less homogeneous "African" and thus, because of the racialist categories of American culture, "African-American." As many became U.S. citizens, or dual citizens of the United States and their original countries of origin, this challenge to their identity found various types of accommodation, usually in their seeking out a hyphenated self-representation such as Sudan-American, Somali-American, and the like.

Many of the African immigrants to Kansas came as professionals who had received their higher training at home, often with professional experience as physicians, nurses, teachers, administrators, legislators, business people. Yet because of licensing and certification protocols, and the specificity of professional standards, these immigrants often were barred from practicing the work for which they had been trained. Many of the African taxi drivers at Kansas City airport were trained professionals. This difficulty in finding work that suited their training represented a significant frustration for the immigrants.

The allure of migration to America, the "land of opportunity," was thus in the thinking of these immigrants, fraught with disillusionment, or at least disappointment and the realization that "making it" in America is hard work. This realization came with the discovery that their relatives back in Africa refused to believe them when they said they did not earn or save lots of money. Saying "life is hard" was held to be a pretext for not sending home large remittances to family who had perhaps sent their kin to America to study.

Against all these stark realities of life in a new land, the immigrants found that social ties to their fellow immigrants, sometimes more cohesively organized into associations, social service agencies, work-related connections, church and mosque support groups and networks, all provided significant assistance for the challenges of accommodation, adaptation, while remaining true to themselves.

None of these issues facing the new African immigrants were particularly unusual, suggested American historian David Katzman. Hearing the stories, reading the interviews, and listening to the discussions in the public meetings, led him to assure the immigrants that they were the latest of wave of migrants who have come to America and go on to become an integral part of its diverse society and unique history.

NOTES

1 Individuals who participated in the 2005 seminar on African migration at the University of Kansas, and became key figures in the interviews and other aspects of the project, are: **Martin Okpareke**, of Nigeria, works with Jewish Vocational Services, a major organization that has assisted immigrants since World War II; **Akot Arec** is a prominent figure in the Southern Sudanese community of Olathe, KS, numbering dozens of individuals. He worked for Catholic Charities in Kansas City, and founded and directed Jump Start Sudan, an initiative that sent relief supplies to Southern Sudan – he returned to South Sudan to contribute in its development and independence; **Stephen P. Weitkamp** is the Director of Refugee and Migrant Services of Catholic Charities, Kansas City; **Jessie Kwatamdia**, an immigrant from Nigeria, works with the Douglas County Senior Services. She came as a student, married an American, and now holds a significant role with a public agency that cares for the elderly; **Mohamed Badri** represents the Northern Sudanese Organization in Kansas City; **Farah Abdi** directs the Kansas City Somali Foundation that works with one of the largest groups of Africans in the region; **Mohamed Adam** was a part of the Zanzibari community of Lawrence and a partner of the national Zanzibari-American Association (ZANAMA), which has its headquarters in Wichita, KS. He is now Assistant Professor of Geography at the University of Memphis in Memphis, TN; **Hassan Kamara** represents the Sierra Leone group of Kansas City; **Albert Rwukwaro**, part of a sizeable group of Kenyans in Kansas, launched *African Voice*, the first African newspaper in the northeast Kansas region; **Jane Irungu**, lecturer in Swahili at Kansas University, and coordinator of the College's Global Awareness Program (GAP) represented the Kenyans of Topeka, KS, of whom many are in business and the professions; she is now Assistant Professor of Education at the University of Oregon, Eugene, OR.

2 The interview narratives, transcripts of public meetings, photographs, films, and the materials that went into the DVD "Identity, Voice, and Community: The New African Immigrants to Kansas" and all other project materials, are on deposit in the Spencer Research Library's Kansas Collection.

3 Questionnaires, open-ended conversations, and participant observation covered 1. Basic Personal Identification, 2. Circumstances of Migration, 3. Work Experience, 4. Immigrant Status, 5. Identity, 6. Story-telling and remembering, 7. Socialization, celebrations, festivities, 8. Relationships with Americans and others in new situation, 9. Family matters, 10.Relationship with kin living near and far, 11. Community Organizations, 12. Most difficult aspects of migration, and 13. Religious affiliation. This material is available at the Kansas African Studies Center and the Kansas Collections of the Spencer Research Library at the University of Kansas.

4 Table 10.1 numbers are gleaned from interviews with community leaders, extrapolations from census figures, and personal surveys.

REFERENCES

Apraku, K. K. (1991). *African Emigrés in the United States*. New York: Praeger Publishers.

Arthur, J. A. (2000). *Invisible Sojourners: African Immigrant Diaspora in the United States*. Westport, CT: Praeger Publishers.

Djamba, Y. K. (1999). African immigrants to the United States: a socio-demographic profile in comparison to Native Blacks. *Journal of Asian and African Studies*, **34**, 2.

Dosi, M., Rushubirwa, L., and Myers, G. (2007).Tanzanians in the Land of Oz: diaspora and transnationality in Wichita, Kansas. *Social and Cultural Geography*, **8**(5), 657–71.

Filippi-Franz, M. K. (2009). Reconstituted lives: Somali women's efforts to reformulate household and community values in Kansas City, Missouri. Ph.D. dissertation, University of Kansas Department of Anthropology,Lawrence.

Finkelstein, M. and Zeiderman, A. (2006). The practice and politics of global fieldwork: keynotes from James Ferguson and Anna Tsing. *Anthropology News*, September.

Foner, N. (ed.) (2003). *American Arrivals: Anthropology Engages the New Immigration*. Santa Fe, CA: School of American Research Press.

Ghazali, M. (2010). When the heart grows sad: loss, absence, and the embodiment of traumatic memory amongst Somali Bantu refugees in Kansas City. M.A. thesis, University of Kansas Department of Anthropology, Lawrence.

Kansas African Studies Center (KASC) (2006). *Identity, Voice, Community: New African Immigrants to Kansas: Interviews and Essays*. www.kasc.ku.edu/projects/immigrantproject/interviews/interviews.pdf

Lassiter, L. E. (2005). *The Chicago Guide to Collaborative Ethnography*. Chicago, IL: University of Chicago Press,

Lohrentz, K. (2004). Peoples of the Horn in the New African Diaspora: Eritrean, Ethiopian, Somali, and Sudanese émigrés in the United States and Canada, a bibliographic survey. Presented to the Kansas African Studies Center seminar series, September 14, 2004.

Okome, M. O. (2002a). The antinomies of globalization: some consequences of contemporary African immigration to the United States of America. *Irinkerindo: A Journal of African Migration*, 1 September.

Okome, M. O. (2002b). The antinomies of globalization: causes of contemporary African immigration to the United States of America. *Irinkerindo: A Journal of African Migration*, 1 September. http://www.africamigration.com/

Shields, A. (2008). Who else hires a Somali? The challenges of incorporating newcomers in new immigration destinations: the case of Emporia, Kansas. M.A. thesis, University of Kansas Department of Sociology, Lawrence.

Takougang, J. (2003). Contemporary African immigrants to the United States. *Irinkerindo: A Journal of African Migration*. http://www.africamigration.com/

11
_____

The African colonial migration into Mexico: history and biological consequences

INTRODUCTION

This study focuses on the magnitude of the contribution of the African component to the biological diversity of Mexican populations. We analyzed patterns of African migration arising from the slave trade during the colonial expansion, the ethnic composition of colonial populations, and their mating patterns, complemented by bioanthropological evidence of African presence in current Mexican populations (mainly genetic and morphological data).

There are some facts that need to be considered when working on the African contribution to American populations, in general, and those of African-Mexican descent, particularly: (1) African migrations into Mexico, unlike other human group movements, were not voluntary; (2) slave introduction varied across regions and times; (3) neither places of origin nor ethnic affiliations of slaves were a constant during the colonial time; (4) transatlantic shipping of slaves diminished when *Mestizo* and indigenous populations increased numerically, and it stopped – at least legally – when the British Crown outlawed the slave trade by the mid nineteenth century.

Quantitative data on the ethnic composition of the colonial society of Mexico are conserved in censuses, as well as in marriage and birth certificates in which racial categories were used (*Español*, *Mulato*, *Mestizo*, and so on). However, the register of ethnic categories of demographic events stopped after the end of the colonial regime. Archaeological and genetic evidence need to be taken into account for a better

Causes and Consequences of Human Migration, ed. Michael H. Crawford and Benjamin C. Campbell. Published by Cambridge University Press. © Cambridge University Press 2012.

understanding of the way Africa contributed to the biological features of the population of Mexico today.

Almost 500 years after the first Africans were brought into Mexico, their presence, although phenotypically diluted, still remains as part of our genome and culture, and the effect of having that genetic component within our genetic pool is still visible, not only because of the clinical features to which it is commonly associated, but as phenotypic characteristics displayed by Mexicans all over the country, yet not always noticed.

The genetic contribution of African groups to a sample of Mexican *Mestizos* from Mexico City has been estimated to range from 1% to 6%, and from 1% to 40% around the country, according to several authors (Barquera *et al.*, 2008; Cao *et al.*, 2004; Ellis *et al.*, 2000; González-Galarza *et al.*, 2011; Saldanha *et al.*, 2009; Spínola *et al.*, 2005; Tang *et al.*, 2000); some HLA haplotypes regarded as African are present in admixed populations with an expectedly high African contribution – such as Veracruz – but also in populations of the north of Mexico, traditionally regarded as having a low African genetic contribution. Hemoglobin and glucose-6-phosphate dehydrogenase African variants have also been reported in several Mexican populations. Other kinds of data, such as $^{87}Sr/^{86}Sr$ isotopic ratio and dental mutilations – both typical of sub-Saharan human groups – found on teeth in sixteenth-century burial sites in Campeche and Mexico City, are reviewed as evidence of the first migrants from Africa to Mexico (Tiesler, 2002). Demographic and historic data point up that most African slaves were of West Africa or West-Central Africa descent and were shipped down to coastal regions of Mexico, where they were further transported to areas where a great part of the indigenous population had died because of epidemics or during the European conquest.

A 500-YEAR OLD STORY . . .

By 1492, the year in which Christopher Columbus landed in the Americas, there were several different human groups that inhabited the territory of Mexico (Marr and Kiracofe, 2000). The Spanish colonization of Mexico (which began with the arrival of the Spaniards to the southeast region of Mexico by 1519; Díaz del Castillo, 1575) led to the beginning of a process of admixture between the indigenous populations and Europeans that came to the Americas to colonize their lands, but Spaniards and other European groups also brought African slaves to America from several parts of Africa. Tribes such as Tukolor,

Serer, Diola, Bifada, Malinke, Twi, Ashanta, Hausa, Kanuri, and Bantu served as sources of slaves from Zafi (Morocco), Elmina castle in São Jorge da Mina, Gold Coast (Côte d'Ivoire and Ghana), Cape Verde (Senegal), Senegambia (nowadays Senegal and the Gambia), Dahomey (Benin), Biafra (Nigeria), and the southeast, west and center of Africa –mainly from Angola and Namibia (Lisker *et al.*, 1965; Lovejoy, 1982).

Contrary to what is generally believed, slavery as a trade had only recently begun by that time. Despite that, this practice was not uncommon within the Iberian Peninsula. The commercial value of the slaves increased at the historic moment when the West Indies were (re)discovered. However, before the beginning of seventeenth century, African migration, although higher than European immigration according to Grunberg (2004), was low, and African slaves worked as domestic servants, artisans, and soldiers. When the first European settlements were established after the conquest, the slave trade surged with incommensurable strength. By the end of the transatlantic slave trade, after the British Crown outlawed the Atlantic trade by the decade of 1860, 10.6 to 19.4 million Africans were extracted from their homelands, although slaves that actually entered the Americas numbered 9.6 to 15.5 million, which means that 2–4 million Africans died during the period from their capture to their final destination within America (Manning, 1993). By this time, African slaves were used as a primary force in plantations, mines, and other activities involving a human mechanical workforce.

In the Viceroyalty of New Spain, approximately 130 000 to 150 000 Africans had been imported by 1779, the year when slave importation into Mexico stopped (Aguirre-Beltrán, 1972; Lisker *et al.*, 1965), with the most intense slave trade being carried out from 1600 to 1640. In just those 40 years, approximately 70 000 slaves were introduced into New Spain (Manning, 1993). This sudden demand for slaves was due to the pronounced shortage of a native working force resulting from conflicts during the conquest and diseases – such as the *Huey Cocoliztli* (a Nahuatl term for the "great disease," allegedly a hemorrhagic fever), and smallpox – that devastated the indigenous population of Mexico (Marr and Kiracofe, 2000). About 90% of the original population died and was substituted by Europeans and Creoles (Wang *et al.*, 2008), or Africans, Mulattos, and other human groups of African descent (Aguirre-Beltrán, 1972) (Table 11.1).

These situations added up to the *Leyes Nuevas* ("New Laws") of 1542, which banned indigenous slavery in the Viceroyalty of New Spain (Zavala, 1967). Nevertheless, by the end of colonial time in Mexico, only about 10 000 slaves remained, and of them, only 6000 were Africans, the

Table 11.1. *Ethnic composition of the population of the Viceroyalty of New Spain*

Year		Natives	Indomestizos[a]	Europeans	Euromestizos[a]	Africans	Afromestizos[a]	Total
1570	n	3 336 860	2 435	6 644	11 067	20 569	2 437	3 380 012
	%	98.70	0.07	0.20	0.03	0.60	0.07	
1646	n	1 279 607	109 042	13 780	168 568	35 089	116 529	1 712 615
	%	74.60	6.00	0.80	9.80	2.00	6.80	
1742	n	1 540 256	249 368	9 814	391 512	20 131	266 196	2 477 277
	%	62.20	10.00	0.40	15.80	0.80	10.80	
1793	n	2 319 741	418 568	7 904	677 458	6 100	369 790	3 799 561
	%	61.00	11.20	0.20	17.80	0.10	9.60	
1810	n	3 676 281	704 245	15 000	1 092 367	10 000	624 461	6 122 354
	%	60.00	11.50	0.20	17.90	0.10	10.10	

[a] Classifications according to Aguirre-Beltrán (1946); n, number of inhabitants.

Source: Information based on the censuses carried out during the colonial period. Modified from Aguirre-Beltrán (1946).

rest being Mulattos (Aguirre-Beltrán, 1972). This indicates the extent of dilution of the African component within the Mexican population, a two-edged sword: it brought down racism against the black component of the population, in detriment to acknowledging the greatness of its contribution to the currently observed cultural and biological diversity in Mexico.

EVIDENCE FROM THE FIRST MIGRATIONS

The first slaves that arrived in the Americas were domestic servants of Moorish, Berber people and *Negros* descent (mainly from western Sudan), who accompanied their owners, the first conquerors. However, soon after, slave importation from these origins was interrupted because of the fear of the propagation of Islam (Acuña-Alonzo, 2005). When the economical and political needs of the nascent New Spain required great amounts of human physical input to exploit the ground and underground of an unexpectedly rich land, slavery was reborn within the first colonies of the so-called New World. The first African slaves were brought to Mexico from Cuba and disembarked at the coasts of Veracruz and Campeche in the company of the conquistadores and colonizers (Acuña-Alonzo 2005; Aguirre-Beltrán, 1972). Evidence was acquired from remains of these first African immigrants in some multiethnic burials such as that found in 2000 in the center of the city of Campeche, on the coast of the Gulf of Mexico (Tiesler, 2002). This burial was discovered associated with a building used as a church by the mid sixteenth century, confirmed by maps of the colonial town and a medallion. At least 10 out of 180 individuals could be assigned to a presumable African ancestry by dental mutilation patterns not attributable to Native American groups present in the region previous to colonial times, and frequent among African slaves throughout the Caribbean. However, as dental mutilation is a widespread cultural expression, it cannot be categorically concluded that those human remains belonged to true African immigrants or their offspring born in America. Since strontium (Sr) enters the human organism through the food chain, Sr isotope intake may be of interest in determining the place of origin of an individual when the isotopical signature of the geographic region is analyzed. The ratio $^{87}Sr/^{86}Sr$ was informative in this case and four remains –all of them carrying distinctive dental decoration – were regarded as "non-local" and, given the high isotopical ratio, they were assigned as probable Africans (Price *et al.*, 2006).

UNIQUE FEATURES OF ADMIXTURE PROCESSES IN MEXICO

An erroneous conviction that the genetic pool of Mexican populations reflects its origins in the union of several indigenous human groups with Spaniards at the time of European conquest and colonialism still prevails (Jiménez-Sánchez, 2003). In fact, the genetic mix exhibited by this nation's human groups is very complex, as is demonstrated by their demographic history. Instead, a tri-hybrid model of admixture, considering African, Native American, and European ancestries, is essential to understand the present cultural and biological diversity shared among various populations across Latin America.

Despite the enormous cultural and biological diversity of the African slaves that were captured in Africa, the total variety of those human groups from which slaves were extracted was not fully represented by the time slaves reached American coasts. Besides a sex ratio disproportion (approximately 65% of males versus 35% of females), age, and health status (characteristics filtered in the slave "factories" before shipping and in the ports of entry, before the slave workforce was traded), somatic and psychological features were of interest of buyers, namely "tameness or rebelliousness, roughness or cleverness, incontinence or sobriety," among others (Aguirre-Beltrán, 1943), thus biasing the diversity that came into the Americas.

By the beginning of the nineteenth century, after the Independence movement of Mexico, in the ideological construction of the Latin American state nations, the *Mestizo* (defined as the fruit of the union of "Hispanic and Indigenous bloods") was celebrated as a new, vigorous race, identifying its new biological condition as a new social status, even going as far as proposing the superiority of the *Mestizo* race (Acuña-Alonzo, 2005); however, only two components were taken into account by then: the Spaniard and the Indigenous roots. It was only after the publication of Aguirre-Beltrán's *La población negra en México: estudio etnohistórico* (The Black Population in Mexico: Ethnohistoric study) in the mid twentieth century (Aguirre-Beltrán, 1946) that the biological contribution started to be of interest in the study of the admixed populations of Mexico. Even then, only ethnohistorical issues were analyzed, such as cultural prevalence, cultural patrimony and identity of Afromexican groups, and their contributions to the culture of the nation. Evidence of the importance of the African contribution to the current admixed populations of Mexico lay in two reliable sources: historic-demographic and anthropological-genetic data.

Quantitative data on the ethnic composition of the colonial society of Mexico are conserved in censuses and accounts in which, generally, the following ethnic categories were used: *Español* (Spaniard), *Castizo* (from *Mestizo* and Spaniard descent), *Mestizo* (from Indigenous and Spaniard descent), *Indio* (Native American), *Mulato* (Mulatto, of Spaniard and African descent), and *Pardo* or *Negro* (of African descent). This order reflects the contemporary social hierarchy and other sources like marriage and birth certificates allow inferences about the inter-action between these ethnic groups in social and biological reproduc-tion. Generally speaking, the most endogamous ethnic group was that of Spaniards, explained partly because they were the hierarchically dominant group and as such, they held social privileges that had to be maintained inside their ethnic unit. The Mulattos and *Negros* were the most exogamous groups, in an effort to give chances to their offspring to achieve better social positions. Nonetheless, the registry of ethnic categories ceased gradually after the colonial regime ended by the first half of the nineteenth century, so an important part of the sociodemo-graphic history of the populations of Mexico, and their socioethnic composition after the War of Independence is not very well known (Table 11.1).

The reasons that led to the dilution of the phenotypic characteristics – even when some of them (e.g. the establishment of racial hierarchy after skin color) are socially constructed, subjective categories – of the African component in many populations of Mexico remain unclear. However, several scholars conclude that a "cultural daltonism" may have influenced the process of assimilation, both culturally and biologically (refer to Nina de Friedemann, in Cunin, 2003, for a wider perspective on the subject), eventually leading to the "invisibility" of a human group which is, essentially, distinguished by its physical appearance; this capability of the individual to escape from the sight of other people and avoiding being classified as *black* may confer a way of getting away from cultural and social discrimination (de la Serna y Herrera *et al.*, 2009) and, thus, contribute to the impossibility of society accepting a "third root" in the construction of the nation.

Also, fecundity itself could be diminished within African immi-grants by several factors affecting the slaves once they were taken away from their homelands, namely (1) high mortality rates during the transatlantic voyage, (2) provisional imprisonment on their arrival in the Americas, (3) further journeys within the Americas to their final destination, (4) once under the owner's control, paternity or maternity were subject to the interests of the landlord, (5) ethnic heterogeneity and social disintegration, along with an uneven sex ratio, would be an obstacle, at least at the beginning of the transatlantic trade and the initial settlements during the colony (Acuña-Alonzo, 2005; Manning, 1993). It is clear that, in order to favor reproductive functions, marriage patterns, especially outside the *castas*,[1] played a key role, as is highlighted by the fact that only 20% of marriages took place among Africans (Aguirre-Beltrán, 1972), possibly because *Negros* constituted the lowest hierarchical group during the colony. Eventually, all these factors led to the dilution of the pure African component within colonial communities, going from its zenith in 1646, when Africans represented 2.00% of the population, to constituting only 0.10% by the end of the colonial period in 1810. In other human groups, African admixed ancestry arose from 0.07% at the beginning of the colonial era to 10.10% by the first years of the nineteenth century (Table 11.1).

Further migratory events occurred in the context of breakouts and immigrations into regions of specific labors (known as *encomiendas*), such as livestock raising and exploitation of sugarcane and cotton crops. Two of the most popular cultural expressions of the colonial and contemporary Mexico, *vaquería* and *charrería*,[2] as well as bullfighting, owe their origins to African immigrants and their descendants – mostly *Mulatos* – settled in the region known as Costa Chica, between the states of Oaxaca and Guerrero at the western coast of Mexico, where immigrants first arrived as part of the development of *encomiendas* in the region (Motta-Sánchez, 2006). Whereas most of the population of African descent settled across the coastline of the Gulf of Mexico and the Pacific coast – where they accounted for as much as 85% of the "non-Indian" population by the end of the eighteenth century – the African component is also present in the northern part of the country (Cook and Borah, 1974), traditionally regarded as descendants of European settlers with little or no admixture with autochthonous groups.

CONSEQUENCES OF THE ADMIXTURE PROCESSES

When the term "of African descent" is used, there are some considerations in applying it to different populations. According to Antón and Del Popolo (2008), an individual of African descent living in Latin America or the Caribbean is referred to as a person living within a "black" or "Afro-American" community, whose ancestors once lived in Africa and survived the Atlantic slave trade (between the sixteenth and nineteenth centuries). However, from a genetic and demographic point of view, "of African descent" may apply to all persons carrying genetic variants specific to African human groups within their genomes.

Recently, a descriptive study of the genetic composition of the Mexican population was published (Silva-Zolezzi *et al.*, 2009), in which almost 100 000 markers were analyzed in admixed individuals of different regions of Mexico. Although data are not representative of each state, because samples represented only urban areas, interesting results were shown at a genomic level. Guerrero and Veracruz states were regarded as the places with the most African component of the six states sampled. For Guerrero state, the African contribution was estimated at 4%. These results show congruency with the demographic history of the regions analyzed and demonstrate that admixed populations have greater genetic diversity when compared with parental populations.

Studies based on HLA and other genetic markers (such as STRs and AIMs) estimate that the African autosomal genetic contribution ranges from 0.0% to 40.5% across the country (Table 11.2). According to these data, the African presence can be detected in several regions of Mexico by admixture estimates, specific markers (like mtDNA haplogroups) or associations (HLA system), and specific variants of genes. Nevertheless, important geographic variation and differences in frequencies may be observed depending on factors such as whether it is a rural or an urban community, and the region where the population studied is settled: the African contribution reaches its maximum in central coasts and its minimum in urban northern areas. This means that genetic variants under selective pressure at Africa's ecological panorama were transplanted to this collection of new environments, as did the phenotypes they were associated with.

HIGHER PREVALENCE OF DIABETES, HYPERTENSION, AND HYPERCHOLESTEROLEMIA

African human groups and their physiology have long existed in the context of scarcity of food and physically demanding daily activity. However, when transplanted to the Americas, Africans and African descendants were exposed to a new environment and the surge of a new cuisine, with the best elements that each culture put, literally, on the table. But the best elements in cuisine are not necessarily optimal for every organism. Saturated fats and excess of carbohydrates in the meals constituted a metabolic impairment and thus organisms biologically adapted to succeed during famine by storage of calories were stuffed with animal products and processed sugars. Thus, obesity, along with non-insulin-dependent or type 2 diabetes mellitus, hypertension,

Table 11.2. *Admixture estimates through genetic analysis in Mexican populations*

Region			Parental population contribution (%)			Specific features	
Population	State		African	Native American	European	N	Authors
Monterrey[a]	Nuevo León		0	13.5	86.3	45	Cerda-Flores and Garza-Chapa (1989)
Monterrey[a]	Nuevo León		0	22.5	77.5	34	Cerda-Flores and Garza-Chapa (1989)
Monterrey[a]	Nuevo León		0	48.5	51.5	145	Cerda-Flores and Garza-Chapa (1989)
Monterrey[a]	Nuevo León		0	61	39	128	Cerda-Flores and Garza-Chapa (1989)
Cuanalán[a]	Edo. México		0	95.7	4.3	143	Crawford et al. (1974)
–[b]	Nuevo León		0	100	0	143	Cerda-Flores et al. (2003)
Mexico City[c]	DF		0.39	43.26	56.35	51	Lisker et al. (1995)
La Mesa[a]	Nayarit		0.8	79.2	20	96	Lisker and Babinsky (1986)
Tlapa[b,cd]	Guerrero		1	98	1	156	Bonilla et al. (2005)
Mexico City[a,c]	DF		1.4	27.6	70.8	474	Tiburcio et al. (1978)
Oaxaca City[a,c]	Oaxaca		1.8	67.6	30.6	220	Lisker et al. (1990)
Mexico City[a,c]	DF		2.5	57.4	40.1	1212	Grunbaum et al. (1980)
Cuanalán[a]	Edo. México		2.7	83.4	13.9	205	Crawford et al. (1974)
Chamizal[a]	Coahuila		2.8	52.5	44.7	121	Crawford et al. (1974)
Mexico City[a,c]	DF		2.93	56.22	40.85	510	Lisker et al. (1986)
–[c]	Nuevo León		3.02	36.99	59.99	143	Cerda-Flores et al. (2002b)
Mexico City	DF		4	45[e]	52	37	Price et al. (2007)
–[b]	Guerrero/Oaxaca		4	92.1	–	114	Sandoval et al. (2003)
Ciudad Juárez[b]	Chihuahua		4.1	87.7	9	123	Green et al. (2000)
Cuanalán[a]	Edo. México		4.6	66.5	28.9	129	Crawford et al. (1974)

Pochutla[a]	Oaxaca	4.9	–	19	749	Lisker (1981)
Mérida[a,c]	Yucatán	5	51.2	42.9	228	Lisker et al. (1990)
Mexico City[c]	DF	5	65	30	561	Martínez-Marignac et al. (2007)
Mexico City[c]	DF	5	69	26	378	Juárez-Cedillo et al. (2008)
Jalpa de Méndez[a]	Tabasco	5	78.3	16.7	101	Lisker and Babinsky (1986)
Ojinaga[b]	Chihuahua	5	91	3	100	Green et al. (2000)
–[c]	Nuevo León	5.02	39.99	54.99	143	Cerda-Flores et al. (2002a)
La Minita[a]	Coahuila	6.1	57.8	36.1	121	Crawford et al. (1974)
Saltillo[a,c]	Coahuila	7.3	54.7	38.0	257	Lisker et al. (1990)
Mexico City[c]	DF	7.82	55.24	36.94	50	Lisker et al. (1995)
Tlaxcala[a]	Tlaxcala	8	70	22	138	Crawford and Devor (1980)
León[a,c]	Guanajuato	8.4	51.3	40.3	202	Lisker et al. (1990)
–[c]	Central Region[e]	9.4	38.3	52.3	211	Hernández-Gutiérrez et al. (2005)
Metztitlán[c]	Hidalgo	10.5	64.4	25.1	180	Gorostiza et al. (2007)
Puebla[a,c]	Puebla	10.7	56.3	33	393	Lisker et al. (1988)
Mexico City[c]	DF	10.9	50.61	38.49	50	Lisker et al. (1995)
–[c]	Puebla	11	71.7	17.3	313	Rubi-Castellanos et al. (2009a)
–[c]	Yucatán	11.3	69.8	18.9	262	Rubi-Castellanos et al. (2009a)
–[c]	Chihuahua	11.7	38	50.3	162	Martínez-González et al. (2005)
Puebla[c]	Puebla	13.3	56.9	29.6	99	Barquera et al. (2008)
Mexico City[c]	DF	13.8	50.2	35.9	121	Barquera et al. (2008)
Culiacán[c]	Sinaloa	14.5	25.6	59.6	56	Barquera et al. (2008)
–[c]	Valley of Mexico	15.4	63.9	20.7	242	Luna-Vázquez et al. (2005)
–[c]	Jalisco	15.9	53.2	30.8	309	Rubi-Castellanos et al. (2009a)

Table 11.2. (cont.)

Region		Parental population contribution (%)			Specific features	
Population	State	African	Native American	European	N	Authors
–[c]	Campeche	15.9	75.7	8.5	106	Sánchez et al. (2005)
Veracruz[c]	Veracruz	17.2	73.5	9.4	130	Rubi-Castellanos et al. (2009b)
–[c]	Nuevo León	18.5	43.3	50.3	143	Cerda-Flores et al. (2002b)
Juquila[a]	Oaxaca	18.6	–	–	335	Lisker (1981)
Cuajinalapa[a]	Guerrero	19–55.9	–	–	592	Lisker (1981)
Paraíso[a]	Tabasco	21.7	47.4	30.9	161	Lisker (1981)
Yanga[c]	Veracruz	25.01	49.76	25.23	71	Acuña-Alonzo (2005)
Veracruz[a]	Veracruz	25.6	39.4	35	148	Lisker and Babinsky (1986)
El Carmen[a]	Campeche	28.4	43.2	28.4	109	Lisker and Babinsky (1986)
Saladero[a]	Veracruz	30.2	38.6	31.2	119	Lisker and Babinsky (1986)
Ometepec[a]	Guerrero	33.7	–	–	408	Lisker (1981)
Tamiahua[a]	Veracruz	40.5	30.7	28.8	109	Lisker and Babinsky (1986)

Notes: Data are ordered increasingly according to reported African ancestral contribution. Populations with same estimated African ancestry were ordered by Native American contribution. For studies in which no population or community information is available, only the state is indicated and a dash is placed in the population column. N refers to the sample size.

[a] Classical markers.

[b] mtDNA.

[c] Other autosomal markers (STRs, HLA, enzyme polymorphism, etc.).

[d] Y chromosome.

[e] Estado de México, Morelos, Puebla, Querétaro, and DF.

coronary and heart disease, and hypercholesterolemia became prevalent in the descendant population of Africans brought to the Americas (Luke *et al.*, 2001).

GLUCOSE-6-PHOSPHATE DEHYDROGENASE DEFICIENCY ('G6PD', xq28)

G6PD is involved in the hexose monophosphate pathway, the unique NADPH-generation process – and thus the supply of reducing energy – in mature erythrocytes, and its insufficiency is the most common human enzyme deficiency, affecting more than 400 million persons worldwide (Cappellini and Fiorelli, 2008), and has a geographic distribution which resembles that of *Plasmodium falciparum* malaria and sickle cell anemia, supporting the malaria protection hypothesis (see "Sickle cell anemia" below). First identified in African American population as a primaquine sensitivity-related hemolytic disorder, *G6PD* deficiency may cause a spectrum of clinically adverse events, such as favism, drug-sensitive hemolytic anemia, and jaundice in the newborn (Beutler *et al.*, 1968). *G6PD* deficiency was found in frequencies ranging from 0.28% to 6.22% at the Costa Chica region (Lisker *et al.*, 1965), but also at 1.79% at Guadalajara city (Vaca *et al.*, 1981) near the western coast of Mexico, and 0.66% in newborn males of Monterrey at the north part of the country (González-Quiroga *et al.*, 1990); in both places, the general assumption is that the African component is virtually absent.

HEMOGLOBIN S AND SICKLE CELL ANEMIA ('HBB', 11p15.4)

Sickle cell anemia is a multisystem disease in which mutations on the hemoglobin (*HBB*) gene lead to its polymerization, thus causing erythrocyte rigidity, sickling, and eventually chronic anemia, hemolysis, and vasculopathy. The S variant of *HBB*, often called HbS, is the most prevalent cause of the abovementioned clinical manifestations. When *Plasmodium falciparum*, the parasite that causes falciparum malaria, infects erythrocytes carrying abnormal HbS which then circulate through anatomic places of low oxygen concentration, such as small blood vessels, sickling takes place and physical injuries to the parasite membrane occur, thus conferring resistance to the infection by *P. falciparum*. Five haplotypes of HbS have been described in sub-Saharan African human groups according to restriction fragment length polymorphisms (RFLP) around the *HBB* gene: (1) Senegal (present in Senegal, Gambia, Guinea, Guinea-Bissau, Sierra Leone, Liberia and Côte d'Ivoire), (2) Benin (Côte d'Ivoire, Togo, Benin, Burkina Faso, and west Nigeria), (3) Bantu or CAR (Gabon, Central African Republic, Congo, Zaire, and Angola), (4) Cameroon (originally from the valley nearby Sanaga River in central Cameroon), and (5) Arab (from Arabia) (Hanchard *et al.*, 2007; Rodríguez-Romeroand *et al.*, 1998). Studies carried out in zones with a presumed high genetic African contribution and high prevalence of *Plasmodium* parasitism have found that HbS can be found in phenotypic frequencies as high as 6% at the Gulf of Mexico, 10.04–10.57% in Costa Chica region (Lisker *et al.*, 1965; Magaña *et al.*, 2002; Ruiz-Reyes, 1998), and 2.2–14.7% at the coastal towns of Veracruz (Peñaloza-Espinosa *et al.*, 2008).

However, other zones in the country also present small proportions of HbS. Northwest Mexico has 0.5% (Ibarra *et al.*, 1980). For the Costa Chica region, Lisker *et al.* (1965) attributed a Bantu constituent as the main contribution for African genetic composition of these communities when they found no HbS of West African origin (Kreuels *et al.*, 2010; Rucknagel and Neel, 1961) in their surveys throughout the region. Magaña *et al.* (2002) confirmed this assumption by finding that 78.8% of the total African contribution to the genetic pool of Costa Chica exhibited the Bantu HbS haplotype.

A less discussed, though no less relevant, matter is the question of whether malaria was not present in the Americas before the European conquest. Even though evidence points to a colonial introduction of the malarial parasites into the Americas, further multidisciplinary approaches need to be established to resolve the controversy over pre-conquest malaria (Caldas-de Castro and Singer, 2005). For instance, falciparum malaria is generally regarded as African and its introduction to the Americas was a result of the transatlantic slave trade.

SYSTEMIC LUPUS ERYTHEMATOSUS (VARIOUS 'LOCI' AT CHROMOSOMES 1, 3, 4, 6, 11, AND 16)

Systemic lupus erythematosus (SLE) is a multisystemic inflammatory disorder involving the skin, joints, kidneys, and serosal membranes due to a failure of the regulatory mechanisms that prevent autoimmunity, affecting women ten times as frequently as men. By the 1970s it was stated that SLE was linked to genetic factors, since it occurs three to four times more often in the black population than in the white (Fessel, 1974; Siegel *et al.*, 1970) and subsequent studies confirmed the previous data: a risk ratio of 32.5 for SLE was associated with West African ancestry (Molokhia *et al.*, 2003). Individuals of West African descent living outside their homelands have a higher risk of developing SLE than African descendants with two or more generations living in the same place; however, lupus itself is infrequent in West Africa (Greenwood, 1968), so an environmental contribution cannot be excluded. *Hispanic Americans* show a three to five times higher prevalence of SLE than European-derived human groups (Alarcón *et al.*, 2002; McKeigue, 2005).

The *C4A* gene, encoding complement C4A protein (at chromosome position 6p21.33, within the Major Histocompatibility Complex) has been linked to SLE when carrying the null (*C4A*0) allele (Christiansen *et al.*, 1983; Fielder *et al.*, 1983). This null allele has been reported in linkage disequilibrium with other genes and especially within the ancestral haplotype 8.1 (HLA-A*01/-C*07/-B*08/TNFAB*a2b3/TNFN*S/C2*C/Bf*s/C4A*Q0/HLA-DRB1*03:01/-DRB3*01:01/-DQA1*05:01/DQB1*02:01). This haplotype is mainly reported in Europeans, but is also found in frequencies over 1% in Kenya Lou and Nandi as well as within Kampala from Uganda (González-Galarza *et al.*, 2011), and has been identified consistently in patients with SLE in the United States and Mexico (Bekker-Mendez *et al.*, 1998; Granados *et al.*, 1996; Kumar *et al.*, 1991). In addition, the DRB1*15 allele (which can be found in as many as 26.60% in Cameroon Yaounde and also highly frequently in Equatorial Guinea and Pygmy from Central Africa; González-Galarza *et al.*, 2011) is also associated with SLE (Cortés *et al.*, 2004, Granados *et al.*, 2006), as well as diminished frequencies of native HLA alleles found in the SLE population (Bekker-Mendez *et al.*, 1998; Granados *et al.*, 1996). These studies support the explanation that admixture between imported human groups and Native American populations in the past accounts for the risk of developing SLE in Mexicans today (Vargas-Alarcón *et al.*, 2001).

HUMAN LEUKOCYTE ANTIGEN SYSTEM ('HLA', 6P21.1−21.3)

The HLA system spans 4 cM throughout the short arm of chromosome 6 within the Major Histocompatibility Complex (MHC), and consists of three classes: class II (centromeric, includes genes *-DPA, -DPB, -DQA, -DQB, -DMA, -DMB, -DRA*, and *-DRB*); class III (encoding genes for the complement, *TNF-α, TAP-1* and *TAP-2, PSMB8, PSMB9*, and related); and class I (telomeric, includes genes *-A, -B, -C, -E, -F, -G* and pseudogenes). The main function of HLA genes is antigen presentation to T cells to elicit an immune response, either cytotoxic (class I/CD8[+] T cell) or helper (classII/CD4[+] T cell). Given its function, diversity is one of the most notable characteristics of this system, and global distribution of HLA alleles is driven mainly by natural selection, but also by genetic drift, migration, and even sexual selection as some authors hypothesize because of the proximity of the HLA region to a cluster of olfactory receptors (OR) located ~ 560 Kb telomeric of the *GSABBR1* locus, directly adjacent to HLA-F (Chaix *et al.*, 2008; Ehlers *et al.*, 2000; Wedekind and Füri, 1997; Wedekind *et al.*, 1995).

HLA diversity, shaped this way, may overcome at least as a group almost every immune challenge the environment can offer. When human groups move towards a new territory, new pathogens, and thus new peptides, challenge immune systems and the HLA repertoire of those individuals. If biological diversity is sufficient to surmount the adverse panorama, then two things are expected to happen: (1) this group may coexist with the pathogen in the new environment and eventually, the pathogen may not represent a severe threat to the population – at least until a new advantageous mutation appears in the pathogen; and (2) coming generations may carry the allele or alleles responsible for such resistance in a higher frequency than the parental generation. However, sudden massive migration – such as the African migration into the Americas – does not allow that panorama to be completed, as confrontation with new pathogens and environments is abrupt. Moreover, stress derived from captivity, physically demanding work, and a rapid shift in diet – both biologically and culturally – could worsen the scenario.

However, the African genetic signature within the HLA system is still visible in the genetic pool of the Mexican population, mainly in admixed populations and especially in those regions traditionally regarded of high African contribution. Several haplotypes and associations have prevailed since colonization and are still present. Original haplotypes or their fractions mixed together with European or Native American alleles can be readily found in admixed populations throughout the country (Table 11.3 and Figure 11.1). Besides social hierarchy pressure on mating patterns and assuming that sexual selection through MHC/OR is feasible in humans, the question of whether or not HLA affects mating patterns remains to be solved, inasmuch as its apparent trend is towards dissimilarity within the HLA system and other genomic regions as well (Chaix *et al.*, 2008).

CONCLUSION

The African contribution to the Mexican population today is key to understanding the diversity exhibited by different populations within

Table 11.3. *African HLA haplotypes and associations imported by African slave trade into Mexico during the colonization*

Haplotype or association	Place of origin	HF in place of origin (%)	Found in:
A*01/B*15:16	A	1.00	1
A*01/B*49/DRB1*04/DQB1*03:02	C	1.60	2, 3
A*01/B*49/DRB1*13/DQB1*06	D	3.2	3, 4, 5
A*02/B*07/DRB1*13	E	1.50	1, 5, 6
A*02/B*35/DRB1*11	C, E	1.60 – 3.10	3, 5, 7
A*02/B*35/DRB1*13	E	2.30	3, 5, 8, 9
A*02/B*15:03	A, B, F, G	1.10 – 3.40	1, 3, 4, 5
A*23/B*15:03	A, B, E, H	1.10 – 2.40	1, 3, 9
A*23/B*35	H, I	1.60 – 6.00	1, 3, 5
A*23/B*58	B, C, E, I, J	1.00 – 2.50	1, 3, 4, 10
A*23/B*81	I, J	1.50 – 1.70	1, 11
A*30/B*42 (/DRB1*03:02/DQB1*04)	A, B, H, I, J, K	1.70 – 11.60	1, 3, 7
A*34/B*58	J	1.50	1, 3, 5
A*36/B*53	A, B, G, I, K	1.30 – 3.10	1, 3
A*68/B*53	A, B, G, H	1.00 – 4.70	1, 3, 4, 5
A*74/B*15:03	B, F, H, K	1.30 – 2.80	1, 3, 4

HF: Haplotypic frequence; A. Nandi from Kenya; B. Luo from Kenya; C. Cape Verde SE Islands; D. Rwanda; E. Guinea Bissau; F. Kampala from Uganda; G. São Tome Island; H. Mali; I. Yaoundé from Cameroon; J. Natal Zulu from South Africa; K. Zambia; 1. Veracruz; 2. Tamaulipas; 3. Mexico City; 4. Guadalajara City; 5. Puebla; 6. Morelos; 7. Michoacán; 8. Monterrey City; 9. Yucatán; 10. Oaxaca; 11. Tabasco.
Sources: Data from Barquera *et al.* (2008); Cao *et al.* (2004); Ellis *et al.* (2000); González-Galarza *et al.* (2011); Saldanha *et al.* (2009); Spínola *et al.* (2005); Tang *et al.* (2000); and unpublished data from Molecular Genetics Laboratory, ENAH, Mexico City.

the nation, both culturally and biologically. From the beginning of colonial times, the African component was present, from the companionship of conquerors to the human workforce, with consequences in their biology and social interactions and thus affecting fertility among transplanted Africans. In such a complex social environment, African slaves and their descendants tried to provide a better position for their children by promoting exogamous marriages with other hierarchically superior groups (mainly with indigenous people). This pattern of socially forced admixture led to the eventual dilution of the phenotypic component of the African contribution within Mexican populations. Nevertheless, genetic evidence of African colonial immigrants may be seen in diverse aspects of biological relevance, for example clinical

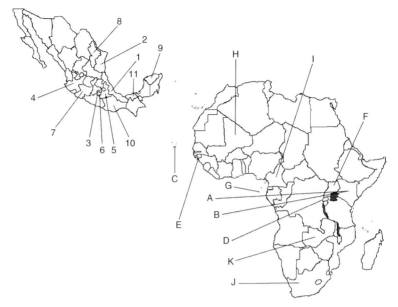

Figure 11.1 Geographical situation of the countries of origin of African slaves where genetic data are available (letters) and the states of Mexico with African contribution (numbers). Correspondence of letters and numbers is shown in Table 11.3.

features, allelic variants that may influence the response to parasitic, bacterial, and viral infections, as well as adaptation to the nascent *Mestizo* cuisine, the postmodern lifestyle with fast food and processed sugars, and even drug therapy.

To deny this hybrid origin of Native American, African, and European ancestry is to deny the complexity of unique social, biological, cultural, and ecological events which have been taking place in the Americas for the last five hundred years, which modeled the variety of *Mestizo* Mexicans and defined us as one of the most diverse human groups in every aspect. Further research on the magnitude of the African contribution in other Mexican human groups and other genetic systems has to be made in order to accomplish the goal of achieving a better understanding of how this component is shaping the biology of Mexican populations and how it influences issues of anthropological and biomedical interest, such as transplantation, differential responses to drug therapy, mating patterns, performance at sports, and metabolic response and adaptation to different lifestyles, including their associated food choices.

1 *Casta* (caste) refers to a complex system for hierarchical classification based on phenotypic, economic, and/or hereditary transmission of status. In the case of New Spain, the caste was designed on the basis of the origin of the ancestors of a person.
2 Both *vaquería* and *charrería* are rodeo-related competitions (often regarded as art-sports), which include interaction of vaqueros and herdsmen with animal husbandry, such as horses and cattle.

REFERENCES

Acuña-Alonzo, V. (2005). *La contribución genética africana a las poblaciones mexicanas contemporáneas*. Mexico City: Escuela Nacional de Antropología e Historia.
Aguirre-Beltrán, G. (1943). The slave trade in Mexico. *Hispanic American Historical Review*, **24**, 412–31.
Aguirre-Beltrán, G. (1946). *La población negra de México: Estudio etnohistórico*. Mexico City: Fondo de Cultura Económica.
Aguirre-Beltrán, G. (1972). *La población negra de México: Estudio etnohistórico*, 2nd edn. Mexico City: Fondo de Cultura Económica.
Alarcón, G. S., McGin, G., Jr., Petri, M., *et al.* (2002). Baseline characteristics of a multiethnic lupus cohort: profile. *Lupus*, **11**, 95–101.
Antón, J. and Del Popolo, F. (2008). *Visibilidad estadística de la población afrodescendiente de América Latina: aspectos conceptuales y metodológicos*. Santiago de Chile: United Nations, CEPAL, CELADE, European Union.
Barquera, R., Zúñiga, J., Hernández-Díaz, R., *et al.* (2008). HLA class I and class II haplotypes in admixed families from several regions of Mexico. *Molecular Immunology*, **45**, 1171–8.
Bekker-Mendez, C., Yamamoto-Furusho, J. K., Vargas-Alarcón, G., *et al.* (1998). Haplotype distribution of class II MHC genes in Mexican patients with systemic lupus erythematosus. *Scandinavian Journal of Rheumatology*, **27**, 373–6.
Beutler, E., Mathai, C. K., and Smith, J. E. (1968). Biochemical variants of glucose-6-phosphate dehydrogenase giving rise to congenital nonspherocytic hemolytic disease. *Blood*, **31**, 131–50.
Bonilla, C., Gutiérrez, G., Parra, E. J., Kline, C., and Shriver, M. D. (2005). Admixture analysis of a rural population of the state of Guerrero, Mexico. *American Journal of Physical Anthropology*, **128**, 861–9.
Caldas-de Castro, M. and Singer, B. H. (2005). Was malaria present in the Amazon before the European conquest? Available evidence and future research agenda. *Journal of Archaeological Science*, **32**, 337–40.
Cao, K., Moormann, A. M., Lyke, K. E., *et al.* (2004). Differentiation between African populations is evidenced by the diversity of alleles and haplotypes of HLA class I loci. *Tissue Antigens*, **63**, 293–325.
Cappellini, M. D. and Fiorelli, G. (2008). Glucose-6-phosphate dehydrogenase deficiency. *The Lancet*, **371**, 64–74.
Cerda-Flores, R. and Garza-Chapa, R. (1989). Variation in the gene frequencies of three generations of humans from Monterrey, Nuevo León, México. *Human Biology*, **61**, 249–61.
Cerda-Flores, R., Budowle, B., Jin, L., *et al.* (2002b). Maximum likelihood estimates of admixture in Northeastern Mexico using 13 short tandem repeat loci. *American Journal of Human Biology*, **14**, 429–39.

Cerda-Flores, R., Jin, L., Barton, S., and Chakraborty, R. (2003). Characterization of mtDNA in Northeastern Mexico. Paper presented to the Human Genome Meeting, Cancún, 27–30 April.

Cerda-Flores, R., Villalobos-Torres, M. C., Barrera-Salda, H. A., *et al.* (2002a). Genetic admixture in three Mexican Mestizo populations based on D1S80 and HLA-DQA1 loci. *American Journal of Human Biology*, **14**, 257–63.

Chaix, R., Cao, C., and Donnelly, P. (2008). Is mate choice in humans MHC-dependent? *PLoS Genetics*, **4**, e1000184.

Christiansen, F. T., Dawkins, R. L., Uko, G., *et al.* (1983). Complement allotyping in SLE: association with C4A null. *Australian and New Zealand Journal of Medicine*, **13**, 483–8.

Cook, F. S. and Borah, W. (1974). Racial groups in the Mexican Population since 1519. In *Essays in population history*, Vol. 2: *Mexico and the Caribbean*. Berkeley, CA: University of California.

Cortes, L. M., Baltazar, L. M., López-Cardona, M. G., *et al.* (2004). HLA class II haplotypes in Mexican systemic lupus erythematosus patients. *Human Immunology*, **65**, 1469–76.

Crawford, M. H. and Devor, E. J. (1980). Population structure and admixture in transplanted Tlaxcaltecan populations. *American Journal of Physical Anthropology*, **52**, 485–90.

Crawford, M. H., Leyson, W. C., Brown, K., Lees, F., and Taylor, L. (1974). Human biology in Mexico. II: A comparison of blood group, serum and red cell enzyme frequencies, and genetic distances of the Indian populations of Mexico. *American Journal of Physical Anthropology*, **41**, 251–268.

Cunin, E. (2003). *Identidades a flor de piel. Lo "negro" entre apariencias y pertenencias: categorías raciales y mestizajes en Cartagena*. Bogotá, Colombia: Instituto Colombiano de Antropología e Historia.

de la Serna y Herrera, M., Chacón-Fragoso, G., and Ebergenyi-Salinas, I. (2009). *Exploración antropológica para la formulación de la pregunta sobre las personas afromexicanas en el censo nacional de población y vivienda y en encuestas relacionadas*. Mexico City: Dirección General Adjunta de Estudios, Legislación y Políticas Públicas, Consejo Nacional para Prevenir la Discriminación.

Díaz del Castillo, B. (1575). *Historia verdadera de la conquista de la Nueva España*. Madrid: Emprenta del Reyno.

Ehlers, A., Beck, S., Forbes, S. A., *et al.* (2000). MHC-linked olfactory receptor loci exhibit polymorphism and contribute to extend HLA/OR haplotypes. *Genome Research*, **10**, 1968–78.

Ellis, J. M., Mack, S. J., Leke, R. F., *et al.* (2000). Diversity is demonstrated in class I HLA-A and HLA-B alleles in Cameroon, Africa: description of HLA-A*03012, *2612, *3006 and HLA-B*1403, *4016, *4703. *Tissue Antigens*, **56**, 291–302.

Fessel, W. J. (1974). Systemic lupus erythematosus in the community: incidence, prevalence, outcome, and first symptoms: the high prevalence in black women. *Archives of Internal Medicine*, **134**, 1027–35.

Fielder, A. H. L., Walport, M. J., Batchelor, J. R., *et al.* (1983). Family study of the major histocompatibility complex in patients with systemic lupus erythematosus: importance of null alleles of C4A and C4B in determining disease susceptibility. *British Medical Journal (Clinical research edn.)*, **286**, 425–8.

González-Galarza, F. F., Christmas, S., Middleton, D., and Jones, A. R. (2011). Allele frequency net: a database and online repository for immune gene frequencies in worldwide populations. *Nucleic Acid Research*, **39**, D913–D919.

González-Quiroga, G., Ramírez-del Río, J. L., Ortíz-Jalomo, R., *et al.* (1990) Relative frequency of glucose-6-phosphate dehydrogenase deficiency in jaundiced newborn infants in the metropolitan area of Monterrey, Nuevo León. *Archivos de Investigación Médica*, **21**, 223–7.

Gorostiza, A., González-Martín, A., Ramírez, C. L., *et al.* (2007). Allele frequencies of the 15 AmpFlStr Identifiler loci in the population of Metztitlán (Estado de Hidalgo), México. *Forensic Science International*, **166**, 230–2.

Granados, J., Vargas-Alarcón, G., Andrade, F., *et al.* (1996). The role of HLA-DR alleles and complotypes through the ethnic barrier in systemic lupus erythematosus in Mexicans. *Lupus*, **5**, 184–9.

Granados, J., Zúñiga, J., Acuña-Alonzo, V., Rosetti, F., and Vargas-Alarcón, G. (2006). Influence of alleles and haplotypes of the main histocompatibility complex on the susceptibility to systemic lupus erythematosus in the Mexican population. *Gaceta Médica de México*, **142**, 195–9.

Green, L. D., Derr, J. N., and Knight, A. (2000). mtDNA affinities of the peoples of North-Central Mexico. *American Journal of Human Genetics*, **66**, 989–98.

Greenwood, B. M. (1968). Autoimmune disease and parasitic infections in Nigerians. *Lancet*, **2**, 380–2.

Grunbaum, B. W., Selvin, S., Myhre, B. A., and Pace, N. (1980). Distribution of gene frequencies and discrimination probabilities for 22 human blood genetic systems in four racial groups. *Journal of Forensic Sciences*, **25**, 428–44.

Grunberg, B. (2004). El universo de los conquistadores: resultado de una investigación prosopográfica. *Signos Históricos*, **12**, 94–118.

Hanchard, N., Elzein, A., Trafford, C., *et al.* (2007). Classical sickle beta-globin haplotypes exhibit a high degree of long-range haplotype similarity in African and Afro-Caribbean populations. *BMC Genetics*, **8**, 52.

Hernández-Gutiérrez, S., Hernández-Franco, P., Martínez-Tripp, S., Ramos-Kuri, M. and Rangel-Villalobos, H. (2005). STR data for 15 loci in a population sample from the central region of Mexico. *Forensic Science International*, **151**, 97–100.

Ibarra, B., Zúñiga, P., Ramírez, M. L., Martínez-Orozco, L. C., and Cantú, J. M. (1980). Detection of hemoglobin alterations in a sample population in northwestern Mexico. Preliminary report. *Archivos de Investigación Médica*, **11**, 491–6.

Jiménez-Sánchez, G. (2003). Developing a platform for genomic medicine in Mexico. *Science*, **300**, 295–6.

Juárez-Cedillo, T., Zúñiga, J., Acuña-Alonzo, V., *et al.* (2008). Genetic admixture and diversity estimations in the Mexican Mestizo population from Mexico City using 15 STR polymorphic markers. *Forensic Science International Genetics*, **2**, e37–e39.

Kreuels, B., Kreuzberg, C., Kobbe, R., *et al.* (2010). Differing effects of HbS and HbC traits on uncomplicated falciparum malaria, anemia, and child growth. *Blood*, **115**, 4551–8.

Kumar, A., Kumar, P., and Schur, P. H. (1991). DR3 and nonDR3 associated complement component C4A deficiency in systemic lupus erythematosus. *Clinical Immunology and Immunopathology*, **60**, 55–64

Lisker, R. (1981). *La estructura genética de la población mexicana. Aspectos médicos y antropológicos.* Mexico City: Salvat Mexicana.

Lisker, R. and Babinsky, V. (1986). Admixture estimates in nine Mexican Indian groups and five East Coast localities. *Revista de Investigación Clínica*, **38**, 145–9.

Lisker, R., Loria, A., and Córdova, M. S. (1965). Studies on several genetic hematological traits of the Mexican population. 8: Hemoglobin S, Glucose-6-phosphate dehydrogenase deficiency, and other characteristics in a malarial region. *American Journal of Human Genetics*, **17**, 179–87.

Lisker, R., Pérez, R. B., Granados, J., *et al.* (1986). Gene frequencies and admixture estimates in a Mexico City population. *American Journal of Physical Anthropology*, **71**, 203–7.

Lisker, R., Pérez-Briseño, R., Granados, J., and Babinsky, V. (1988). Gene frequencies and admixture estimates in the State of Puebla, Mexico. *American Journal of Physical Anthropology*, **76**, 331–5.

Lisker, R., Ramírez, E., Pérez, R. B., Granados, J., and Babinsky, V. (1990). Gene frequencies and admixture estimates in four Mexican urban centers. *Human Biology*, **62**, 791–801.

Lisker, R., Ramírez, E., Pérez, G., *et al.* (1995). Genotypes of alcohol-metabolizing enzymes in Mexicans with alcoholic liver cirrhosis. *Archives of Medical Research (Mexico)*, **26**(Suppl.), S63–S67.

Lovejoy, P. E. (1982). The volume of the Atlantic slave trade: a synthesis. *Journal of African History*, **23**, 473–501.

Luke, A., Cooper, R. S., Prewitt, T. E., Adeyemo, A. A., and Forrester, T. E. (2001). Nutritional consequences of the African diaspora. *Annual Review of Nutrition*, **21**, 47–71.

Luna-Vázquez, A., Vilchis-Dorantes, G., Aguilar-Ruiz, M. O., *et al.* (2005). Population data for 15 loci (Identifiler kit) in a sample from the Valley of Mexico. *Legal Medicine (Tokyo, Japan)*, **7**, 331–3.

Magaña, M. T., Ongay, Z., Tagle, J., *et al.* (2002). Analysis of betaS and betaA genes in a Mexican population with African roots. *Blood Cells, Molecules and Diseases*, **28**, 121–6.

Manning, P. (1993). Migrations of Africans to the Americas: the impact on Africans, Africa and the New World. *History Teacher*, **26**, 279–96.

Marr, J. S. and Kiracofe, J. B. (2000). Was the Huey Cocoliztli a haemorrhagic fever? *Medical History*, **44**, 341–62.

Martínez-González, L. J., Martínez-Espín, E. M., Fernández-Rosado, F., *et al.* (2005). Mexican population data on fifteen STR loci (Identifiler set) in a Chihuahua (north central Mexico) sample. *Journal of Forensic Sciences*, **50**, 236–8.

Martínez-Marignac, V. L., Valladares, A., Cameron, E., *et al.* (2007). Admixture in Mexico City: implications for admixture mapping of type 2 diabetes genetic risk factors. *Human Genetics*, **120**, 807–19.

McKeigue, P. M. (2005). Prospects for admixture mapping of complex traits. *American Journal of Human Genetics*, **76**, 1–7.

Molokhia, M., Hoggart, C., Patrick, A. L., *et al.* (2003). Relation of risk of systemic lupus erythematosus to west African admixture in a Caribbean population. *Human Genetics*, **112**, 1–9.

Motta-Sánchez, J. A. (2006). Tras la heteroidentificación. El "movimiento negro" costachiquense y la selección de marbetes étnicos. *Dimensión Antropológica*, **38**, 115–50.

Peñaloza-Espinosa, R. I., Buentello-Malo, L., Hernández-Maya, M. A., *et al.* (2008). Frecuencia de la hemoglobina S en cinco poblaciones mexicanas y su importancia en la salud pública. *Salud Pública de México*, **50**, 325–9.

Price, A. L., Patterson, N., Yu, F., *et al.* (2007). A genomewide admixture map for Latino populations. *American Journal of Human Genetics*, **80**, 1024–36.

Price, T. D., Tiesler, V., and Burton, J. H. (2006). Early African diaspora in colonial Campeche, Mexico: strontium isotopic evidence. *American Journal of Physical Anthropology*, **130**, 485–90.

Rodríguez-Romero, W. E., Sáenz-Renauld, G. F., and Chaves-Villalobos, M. A. (1998). Haplotipos de la hemoglobina S: importancia epidemiológica, antropológica y clínica. *Revista Panamericana de Salud Pública*, **3**, 1–8.

Rubi-Castellanos, R., Anaya-Palafox, M., Mena-Rojas, E., *et al.* (2009a). Genetic data of 15 autosomal STRs (Identifiler kit) of three Mexican Mestizo population samples from the States of Jalisco (West), Puebla (center), and Yucatan (Southeast). *Forensic Science International Genetics*, **3**, e71–e76.

Rubi-Castellanos, R., Martínez-Cortés, G., Muñoz-Valle, J. F., *et al.* (2009b). Pre-Hispanic Mesoamerican demography approximates the present-day ancestry of Mestizos throughout the territory of Mexico. *American Journal of Physical Anthropology*, **139**, 284–94.

Rucknagel, D. L. and Neel, J. V. (1961). The hemoglobinopathies. *Progress in Medical Genetics*, **1**, 158–260.

Ruiz-Reyes, G. (1998). Abnormal hemoglobins and thalassemias in Mexico. *Revista de Investigación Clínica*, **50**, 163–70.

Saldanha, N., Spínola, C., Santos, M. R., *et al.* (2009). HLA polymorphism in Forros and Angolares from Sao Tome Island (west Africa): Evidence for the population origin. *Journal of Genetic Genealogy*, **5**, 76–85.

Sánchez, C., Barrot, C., Ortega, M., *et al.* (2005). Genetic diversity of 15 STRs in Choles from northeast of Chiapas (Mexico). *Journal of Forensic Sciences*, **50**, 1499–501.

Sandoval, L., Robles, C. A., Magaña, M. T., *et al.* (2003). Mitochondrial DNA variation in a Mestizo population from the Southwest Pacific Mexican coasts. Paper presented to the Human Genome Meeting, Cancún, 27–30 April.

Siegel, M., Holley, H. L., and Lee, S. L. (1970). Epidemiologic studies on systemic lupus erythematosus: comparative data for New York City and Jefferson County, Alabama, 1956–1965. *Arthritis and Rheumatism*, **13**, 802–11.

Silva-Zolezzi, I., Hidalgo-Miranda, A., Estrada-Gil, J., *et al.* (2009). Analysis of genomic diversity in Mexican Mestizo population to develop genomic medicine in Mexico. *Proceedings of the National Academy of Sciences of the United States of America*, **106**, 8611–16.

Spínola, H., Bruges-Armas, J., Middleton, D., and Brehm, A. (2005). HLA polymorphism in Cabo Verde and Guiné-Bissau inferred from sequence-based typing. *Human Immunology*, **66**, 1082–92.

Tang, J., Naik, E., Costello, C., *et al.* (2000). Characteristics of HLA class I and class II polymorphism in Rwandan women. *Experimental and Clinical Immunogenetics*, **17**, 185–98.

Tiburcio, V., Romero, A., and De Garay, A. L. (1978). Gene frequencies and racial intermixture in a Mestizo population from Mexico City. *Annals of Human Biology*, **5**, 131–8.

Tiesler, V. (2002). New cases of an African tooth decoration from colonial Campeche, México. *HOMO*, **52**, 277–82.

Vaca, G., Hernández, A., Ibarra, B., *et al.* (1981). Detection of inborn errors of metabolism in 1,117 patients studied because of suspected inherited disease. *Archivos de Investigación Médica*, **12**, 341–8.

Vargas-Alarcón, G., Salgado, N., Granados, J., *et al.* (2001). Class II allele and haplotype frequencies in Mexican systemic lupus erythematosus patients: the relevance of considering homologous chromosomes in determining susceptibility. *Human Immunology*, **62**, 814–20.

Wang, S., Ray, N., Rojas, W., *et al.* (2008). Geographic patterns of genome admixture in Latin American Mestizos. *PLoS Genetics*, **4**, e1000037.

Wedekind, C. and Füri, S. (1997). Body odour preferences in men and women: do they aim for specific MHC combinations or simply heterozygosity? *Proceedings of the Royal Society B: Biological Sciences*, **264**, 1471–9.

Wedekind, C., Seebeck, T., Bettens, F., and Paepke, A. J. (1995). MHC-dependent mate preferences in humans. *Proceedings of the Royal Society B: Biological Sciences*, **260**, 245–9.

Zavala, S. (1967). *Los esclavos indios en Nueva España*. Mexico City: El Colegio de México.

KRISTIN L. YOUNG, ERIC J. DEVOR, AND
MICHAEL H. CRAWFORD

12

Demic expansion or cultural diffusion: migration and Basque origins

INTRODUCTION

This chapter examines the possible ramifications of migration (Paleolithic versus Neolithic) on the mitochondrial gene pool of Europe. In the
anthropological literature, there has been much debate on the relative
contributions of Paleolithic and Neolithic populations to modern Europeans; a debate which continues to center around two competing
models (Balaresque *et al.*, 2010; Battaglia *et al.*, 2009; Sjodin and Francois, 2011). The Neolithic demic diffusion model (DDM) holds that the
majority of genetic variation found in modern Europeans is the result
of bands of migrating farmers spreading their technology (and genes)
into Europe with the advent of agriculture (Ammerman and Cavalli-
Sforza, 1984). Alternatively, the cultural diffusion model (CDM) asserts
that agricultural knowledge spread into Europe 10 000 years ago but
people did not, so the transfer of technology occurred without migration and the gene pool of modern Europeans is primarily of non-
Neolithic origin (Novelletto, 2007).

Genetic evidence has been used to support both models.
A southeast to northwest cline in the distribution of classical markers
across Europe has been interpreted as a genetic signature of the DDM
model (Cavalli-Sforza *et al.*, 1994). Similar clines have been noted for
other molecular systems and interpreted as evidence of "directional
population expansion" (Casalotti *et al.*, 1999; Chikhi *et al.*, 1998:9055).
Advocates of the cultural diffusion model maintain that the Paleolithic
expansion into Europe occurred from the same region as the Neolithic
expansion, so that the cline in genetic variation might reflect a

Causes and Consequences of Human Migration, ed. Michael H. Crawford and
Benjamin C. Campbell. Published by Cambridge University Press. © Cambridge
University Press 2012.

Paleolithic signal (Barbujani *et al.*, 1998). Y-chromosome analyses reveal that haplotype R1*M173 appears to indicate an expansion event after the Last Glacial Maximum (Wells *et al.*, 2001), and a "high degree of non-Neolithic ancestry" in populations of Iberia (Flores *et al.*, 2004). Examination of Y-chromosome diversity in southeastern Europe suggests that the spread of agriculture overlaps with the expansion of indigenous European haplogroup I*M423 (Battaglia *et al.*, 2009).

When examining European maternal lineages, analysis of mitochondrial HVS-I sequences shows little clinal variation and divergence dates suggest that many of the mitochondrial haplotypes in Europe have a pre-Neolithic origin (Richards *et al.*, 1996). While haplogroup V has been proposed as a signal of population expansion after the Last Glacial Maximum, the lack of this haplogroup in an ancient sample has raised doubts about this hypothesis (Izagirre and de la Rua, 1999; Torroni *et al.*, 1998). The presence of haplogroup J, which has been linked to the expansion of Neolithic groups into Europe, in the same ancient sample also suggests some level of admixture.

The Basque population, due to their linguistic and genetic distinctiveness (Izagirre *et al.*, 2001) and their relative isolation and distance from the epicenter of agricultural development during the Neolithic (beginning about 8500 BC) (Cavalli-Sforza and Piazza, 1993), seem an ideal population in which to examine the effects of Neolithic migration and gene flow into Europe. The Basque language, *Euskara*, is unrelated to any other extant European language. From a genetic perspective, early work on human blood types distinguished the Basques from other European populations by a low frequency of the ABO* B allele (1.1%) (Boyd and Boyd, 1937) and a high level of the Rh negative (RH*cde) allele (30.5–35.6%) (Chalmers *et al.*, 1948, 1949; Etcheverry, 1945), leading Mourant to state that "the Basques are a relict population which at least in Spain has suffered no significant admixture of elements akin to the general western European population" (Mourant, 1947:505).

This investigation examines the potential impact of the Neolithic expansion on the maternal lineage of the Basque population. Mitochondrial DNA (mtDNA) is a circular, double-stranded extranuclear genome that is inherited through the maternal line, from the mitochondria present in the ovum at fertilization. Genetic analysis of mtDNA involves restriction fragment length polymorphisms (RFLPs), as well as DNA sequences. RFLPs are used to define haplogroups, based on the presence/absence of enzyme-specific diagnostic cut sites. Such mtDNA haplogroups have been found to be generally continent specific, and in Europe, nine mtDNA haplogroups are common: H, I, J, K, T, U, V, W, X.

Sequencing of hypervariable segments (HVS-I and II) of the control region can further refine the haplogroup designations into haplotypes. For example, RFLP analysis can classify a sample as haplogroup H by the absence of an AluI cut site at position 7025 (Izagirre and de la Rua, 1999), while characteristic mutations within the hypervariable region can assist in refining the classification to a particular haplotype (i.e. an A–G transition at position 16162 defines haplotype H1a) (Loogvali *et al.*, 2004). Analysis of mitochondrial DNA, both haplogroup frequencies and control region sequences, has become a standard and widely used technique for inferring population history and evolution. The advantages of mtDNA are that it exhibits uniparental inheritance and no recombination, allowing for the analysis of maternal lineages and gene flow (migration).

Among the Basques, both contemporary and ancient populations have been examined using this system (Achilli *et al.*, 2004; Alzualde *et al.*, 2005, 2006; Bertranpetit *et al.*, 1995; Corte-Real *et al.*, 1996; Gonzalez *et al.*, 2003, 2006; Izagirre and de la Rua, 1999; Torroni *et al.*, 1998). One of the earliest studies analyzed 45 HVS-I sequences was from Guipuzcoa (Bertranpetit *et al.*, 1995). At the time, relatively little comparative data were available, and the authors were able to contrast the Basques with only one other European population, the Sardinians. Of the 27 different sequences present in the Basque sample, one third were identical to the Cambridge reference sequence (CRS), which belongs to haplogroup H. Sixty-one HVS-I sequences from Alava and Vizcaya, included as part of a larger analysis of genetic diversity on the Iberian Peninsula, also showed a preponderance of sequences belonging to haplogroup H (Corte-Real *et al.*, 1996). Thirty-four unrelated control region sequences were also analyzed from the sixth–seventh century site in Alava discussed previously (Alzualde *et al.*, 2006). Three different J haplotypes were reported, as well as one designated M1c. Haplogroup J has been described as a signature of the Neolithic expansion into Europe from the Middle East, while M1c is common in North Africa, suggesting that, historically, this particular population did not experience the genetic isolation often proposed to account for the distinctiveness of contemporary Basques. To date, mtDNA analyses among Basque populations have presented conflicting results. Studies of contemporary populations suggest that the Basques are a relatively isolated population with deep European roots, while ancient DNA demonstrates contact (but not necessarily gene flow) with possible non-European populations, at least in historical times.

Figure 12.1 Map of sample locations. Provincial capitals indicated by ball-and-stick.

MATERIALS AND METHODS

During summer field sessions (2000–2002), buccal DNA samples were collected from 652 autochthonous (those who claimed four Basque grandparents) participants of both sexes, in 35 mountain villages throughout the four Basque provinces of northern Spain (Figure 12.1). This study was approved by the University of Kansas Human Subjects Committee (HSCL #11955), and all participants provided written informed consent.

DNA extraction was performed using a standard phenol:chloroform protocol. Analysis of mitochondrial DNA included haplogroup assignment using restriction fragment length polymorphisms (RFLPs) and haplotype determination through sequencing of the first hypervariable segment of the control region (HVS-I). Mitochondrial haplogroups were established using a hierarchical approach (Santos *et al.*, 2004), so that the most frequent European haplogroup (H) was tested for all samples first. Those samples that gave a negative result for H were then further tested for the other European haplogroups (U, K, V, I, J, T, W, and X).

Sequencing the HVS-I region allows for the characterization of mtDNA haplotypes within each haplogroup, and was generally performed in the forward direction only, with the exception of those samples which have a T–C transition at position 16189. This transition creates a long run of cytosines, which can result in sequencing failure. Sequencing these samples in the reverse direction, from position 16400–16189, and then splicing the sequences together using sequence alignment editing software, generates a complete sequence which can be used in further analyses.

Haplogroup diagnostic restriction sites were amplified using PCR reagents obtained from Promega (Madison, Wisconsin), and primers synthesized by Integrated DNA Technologies (IDT, Coralville, Iowa) (Table 12.1). The amplified DNA was then digested with the corresponding restriction enzymes (Table 12.1) to determine haplogroup assignment. A random subset of samples was sequenced for the HVS-I region using Big Dye Sequencing kits and either an ABI 310 (Alava and Vizcaya samples) or an ABI 3130 Sequencer (Guipuzcoa and Vizcaya samples) (Applied Biosystems, Foster City, California). Mitochondrial sequences were edited using BioEdit software (Hall, 2007) and aligned to the published human mtDNA reference sequence (Anderson *et al.*, 1981). Nucleotides which differed from the reference sequence were recorded as mutations. Sequence data on 38 additional populations were collected from the literature for comparative purposes.

To measure mtDNA genetic variation and test for the effects of evolution on the Basques and comparative populations, several standard population genetic parameters were calculated using Arlequin 3.11 (Excoffier *et al.*, 2005), including nucleotide diversity, genetic distance, Tajima's D, and Fu's F_S. Nucleotide diversity measures the average number of nucleotide differences between two sequences. Genetic distances between populations were measured using the Kimura-2-parameter distance, which controls for differential mutation rates between transversions and transitions (Kimura, 1980). Relationships between populations were visualized using multidimensional scaling (MDS) plots of the genetic distance matrix (Kruskal, 1964), with stress values evaluated following the criteria of Sturrock and Rocha (2000). For Tajima's D, negative values indicate a population that has undergone an expansion event, while positive values of D suggest a genetic bottleneck (Tajima, 1989). Significant values of D could also result from selection or variations in mutation rate. Fu's F_S tests specifically for population expansion and the effects of selection on surrounding neutral alleles through genetic hitchhiking (when

Table 12.1. *Primers used in mtDNA RFLP and sequence analyses*

Haplogroup (Restriction site)	Primers	Sequence (5′ ⇒ 3′)	Annealing temperature
H	FOR 6958	5′ – CCTGACTGGCATTGTATT – 3′	58 °C
(−7025 AluI)	REV 7049	5′ – TGTAAAACGACGGCCAGTTGATAGGACATAGTGGAAGT – 3′	
U/K	FOR 12216	5′ – CACAAGAACTGCTAACTCATGC – 3′	55 °C
(+12308 Hinfl)	REV 12338	5′ – ATTACTTTTATTTGGAGTTGCACCAAGATT – 3′	
K	FOR 9003	5′ – CCTAACCGCTAACATTAC – 3′	51 °C
(−9052 HaeII)	REV 9105	5′ – TGTAAAACGACGGCCAGTGAAGATGATAAGTGTAGAGG – 3′	
V	FOR 4519	5′ – CACTCATCACAGCGCTAAGC – 3′	55 °C
(−4577 NlaIII)	REV 4620	5′ – TGGCAGCTTCTGTGGAAC – 3′	
J	FOR 13626	5′ – CCTAACAGGTCAACCTCGCT – 3′	64 °C
(−13704 BstNI)	REV 13729	5′ – TGTAAAACGACGGCCAGTCTGCGAATAGGCTTCCGGCT – 3′	
T	FOR 13001	5′ – GCAATTCAGCCCATTTAGGT – 3′	47 °C
(+13366 BamHI)	REV 13403	5′ – ATATCTTGTTCATTGTTAAG – 3′	
W	FOR 8908	5′ – TTCTTACCACAAGGCACACC – 3′	65 °C
(−8994 HaeIII)	REV 9033	5′ – AGGTGGCCTGCAGTAATGT – 3′	
X/I	FOR 1616	5′ – ACACAAAGCACCCAACTTACACTTAGGA – 3′	59 °C
(−1715 DdeI)	REV 1899	5′ – CTTAGCTTTGGGCTCTCCTTGC – 3′	
X/I	FOR 10235	5′ – TATTACCTTCTTATTATTTG – 3′	48.2 °C
(± 10394 DdeI)	REV 10569	5′ – CTAGGCATAGTAGGGAGGAT – 3′	
I	FOR 8191	5′ – ACCCACAGTTTCATGCCCAT – 3′	59 °C
(AvaII)	REV 8312	5′ – TAAGTTAGCTTTACAGTGGGCT – 3′	
HVS-I	15976 FOR	5′ – CCACCATTAGCACCCAAAGCTAAG – 3′	55 °C
	16401 REV	5′ – TGATTTCACGGAGGATGGTG – 3′	

selection is positive) or background selection (when deleterious alleles are being eliminated). Large negative values of F_S indicate an excess of mutations from what would be expected under the neutral mutation theory, and suggest that either selection or expansion has occurred in the population (Fu, 1997).

Spatial analysis of molecular variance (SAMOVA) was performed to identify genetic barriers between populations using SAMOVA 1.0 (Dupanloup *et al.*, 2002). In the SAMOVA procedure, group hierarchies are not determined a priori. Instead, the number of groups in the hierarchy (K) is chosen, and the SAMOVA algorithm identifies which grouping of populations maximizes F_{CT} by identifying genetic barriers between groups (Dupanloup *et al.*, 2002). This procedure is repeated until the maximum value of F_{CT} for the designated number of groups is indentified.

Mismatch/intermatch distributions were generated to further examine population histories and estimate dates of expansion (Rogers and Harpending, 1992). Mismatch analysis produces distributions of pairwise differences within populations which, according to coalescent theory, maintain a record of past population events including demographic and spatial expansions, which leave unimodal waves in the distribution, or long periods of population stability, which result in multimodal distributions (Excoffier, 2004; Hudson, 1990; Rogers and Harpending, 1992). Intermatch analysis was used to examine pairwise differences between populations, and to estimate divergence times between them (Sherry *et al.*, 1994). Under the neutral mutation model with no recombination, the mean number of mutations is constant, and mutations accrue along lines of descent independent of population size or substructure. For the present analysis, expansion time (τ) was estimated in two ways: method of moments (Rogers, 1995), and a generalized non-linear least-squares approach (Schneider and Excoffier, 1999). In the second case, 95% confidence intervals for τ were also generated and converted into date ranges of the time estimate for population expansion. The least-squares mismatch analysis was conducted to examine potential differences in population history between the Basques and other European groups using Arlequin 3.11 (Excoffier *et al.*, 2005). Intermatch distributions between the Basques and other European groups, along with estimated divergence times, were generated using iWave (Sherry *et al.*, 1994).

RESULTS

Mitochondrial DNA haplogroups found among the Basques, determined from analysis of restriction fragment length polymorphisms, are presented

Table 12.2. *Mitochondrial DNA haplogroups present among the Basques of Spain*

Province	H	I/X	J	N1b	T	V	W	U/K	U	K	Not determined[a]	Total
Alava	71	0	3	0	2	5	3	1	21	4	8	118
Vizcaya	111	2	20	0	3	15	1	4	31	10	36	233
Guipuzcoa	102	1	6	1	1	14	1	10	27	10	52	225
Total[b]	314	3	29	1	6	34	5	15	80	24	104	615

[a] Individuals which did not amplify for one or more haplogroups.

[b] Total includes samples from Navarre.

in Table 12.2. The sample size for Navarre included only 30 individuals, and so was not used in province level analyses (and thus is not listed separately in Table 12.2), but was included in the total haplogroup calculations. One hundred and four individuals did not amplify for one or more haplogroups, and are thus listed as not determined. Eighty-five percent of the total sample belongs either to haplogroup H or U/K, the most frequent European haplogroups. Fifteen samples tested positive for 12308 *HinfI*, the determining RFLP site for haplogroups U and K, but then did not amplify for 9052 *HaeII*, the restriction site which distinguishes between those two haplogroups. As a result, they are coded as U/K. Haplogroup V comprises 6.6% of the total sample, while 5.6% of the sample is haplogroup J. Haplogroups I/X, T, W and N1b make up the remaining 2.8%.

Control region (HVS-I) sequences determined for a random sample of 129 Basque are presented in Table 12.3, with HVS-I positions given minus 16 000. The majority of sequences (55.8%) belong to haplogroup H, with 32% matching the Cambridge Reference Sequence (CRS). Other frequent haplogroups include U (14.7%), defined in part by a transition at 16270, and V (10.9%), defined by a transition at position 16298. Eight haplotypes display transversions: B164 has a T–G transversion at position 16235, B203 A–T at 16235, B602 C–A at 16328, B148 A–C at 16220, B633 C–G at 16176, B133 G–T at 16390, B141 C–A at 16114, and B441 G–C at 16129. All other mutations listed in Table 12.3 are transitions. Of the ten common European mtDNA haplogroups, neither X nor I was detected in the sequence analysis, and only one sample each of haplogroups W and N1b was found.

The mismatch distribution of pairwise differences displayed in the bottom panel of Figure 12.2 shows that both Alava and Vizcaya have unimodal distributions, with a peak at three pairwise differences. A unimodal distribution is expected in populations that have undergone an expansion event, in agreement with the neutrality statistics. The distribution for Guipuzcoa, however, appears bimodal, with peaks

Table 12.3. *Basque HVS-I sequences (HVS-I positions shown −16 000)*

CRS	69 c	93 t	114 c	126 t	129 g	145 g	150 c	153 g	162 a	167 c	168 c	172 t	174 c	176 c	185 c	188 c	189 c	192 t	193 c	218 c	220 c	221 a	223 c	224 c	234 t	235 c	239 a	240 c	241 a	242 c	249 t	256 c	259 c	266 c	270 c	278 c	286 c	290 c	291 c	292 c	293 a	294 c	295 c	296 c	298 t	300 a	302 a	304 t	311 t	319 g	320 c	323 t	325 t	328 c	343 a	356 t	362 t	366 c	390 g	Hap	N
B120	.	.	.	.	.	.	.	.	.	.	.	.	.	.	.	.	.	.	.	.	.	.	.	.	.	.	.	.	.	.	.	.	.	.	.	.	.	.	.	.	.	.	.	.	.	.	.	.	.	.	.	.	.	.	.	.	.	.	.	H	23
B125	.	.	.	.	A	.	.	.	.	.	.	.	.	.	.	.	.	.	.	.	.	.	.	.	.	.	.	.	.	.	.	.	.	.	.	.	.	.	.	.	.	.	.	.	.	.	.	.	.	.	.	.	.	.	.	.	.	.	.	H	10
B123	.	.	.	.	.	.	.	.	.	.	.	.	.	.	.	.	.	.	.	.	.	.	.	.	.	.	.	.	.	.	.	.	.	.	.	.	.	.	.	.	.	.	.	.	.	.	.	.	C	.	.	.	.	.	.	.	.	.	.	H	3
B136	.	.	.	.	.	.	.	.	.	.	.	.	.	.	.	.	.	.	.	.	.	.	.	.	.	.	.	.	.	.	.	.	.	.	.	.	.	.	.	.	G	.	.	.	.	.	.	C	.	.	.	.	.	.	.	.	.	.	.	H	3
B478	.	.	.	.	.	.	.	.	.	.	.	.	.	.	.	.	.	.	.	.	.	.	.	.	.	.	.	.	.	.	.	.	.	.	.	.	.	.	.	.	.	.	.	.	.	.	.	C	.	.	.	.	.	.	.	.	.	.	.	H	3
B151	.	C	.	.	.	.	.	.	.	.	.	.	.	.	.	.	.	.	.	.	.	.	.	.	.	.	.	.	.	.	.	.	.	.	.	.	.	.	.	.	.	.	.	.	.	.	.	.	.	.	.	.	.	.	.	.	.	.	.	H	2
B198	.	.	.	.	.	.	.	.	.	.	.	.	.	.	.	.	.	T	.	.	.	.	.	.	.	.	.	.	.	.	.	.	.	.	.	.	.	.	.	.	.	.	.	.	.	.	.	.	.	.	.	.	.	.	.	.	.	.	.	H	2
B385	.	.	.	.	.	.	.	.	.	.	.	.	.	.	.	.	.	.	.	.	.	.	.	.	.	.	.	.	.	.	.	.	.	.	.	T	.	.	.	.	.	.	.	.	.	.	.	.	.	.	.	.	.	.	.	.	.	.	.	H	2
B104	.	.	.	.	.	.	.	.	.	.	.	.	.	.	.	.	.	.	.	.	.	.	.	.	.	.	T	.	.	.	.	.	.	.	.	.	.	.	.	.	.	.	.	.	.	.	.	C	G	.	.	.	.	.	.	.	.	.	.	H	2
B164	.	.	.	.	.	.	.	.	.	.	.	.	.	.	.	.	.	.	.	.	.	.	.	.	T	.	.	.	.	.	.	.	.	.	.	.	.	.	.	.	.	.	.	.	.	.	.	.	.	.	.	.	.	.	.	.	.	.	.	H	2
B186	.	.	.	.	.	.	.	.	.	.	.	.	.	.	.	C	C	.	.	.	.	.	.	.	.	.	.	.	.	.	.	.	.	.	.	.	.	.	.	.	.	.	.	.	.	.	.	.	.	.	.	.	.	.	.	.	.	.	.	H	2
B122	.	.	.	.	.	.	.	.	.	.	.	.	.	.	.	.	C	.	.	.	.	.	.	.	.	.	.	.	.	.	.	.	.	.	.	.	.	.	.	.	.	.	.	.	.	.	.	.	.	.	.	.	.	.	.	.	.	.	.	H	1
B132	.	.	.	.	.	.	.	.	.	.	.	.	.	.	.	.	.	.	.	.	.	.	.	.	.	.	.	.	.	.	.	.	.	.	.	.	.	.	.	.	.	.	.	.	.	.	.	.	.	.	.	.	.	.	.	.	C	.	.	H	1
B161	.	.	.	.	.	.	.	.	.	.	.	.	.	.	.	.	.	.	.	.	.	.	.	.	.	.	.	.	.	.	.	.	.	.	.	.	.	T	.	.	.	.	.	.	.	.	.	.	.	.	.	.	.	.	.	.	.	.	.	H	1
B175	.	.	.	.	.	.	.	.	.	.	.	.	.	.	.	.	.	.	.	.	.	.	.	.	.	.	.	.	.	.	.	.	.	.	.	.	.	.	T	.	.	.	.	.	.	.	.	.	.	.	.	.	.	.	.	.	.	.	.	H	1
B203	.	.	.	.	.	.	.	.	.	.	.	.	.	.	.	.	.	.	.	.	.	.	.	.	.	T	.	.	.	.	.	.	.	.	.	.	T	.	.	.	.	.	.	.	.	.	.	.	.	.	.	.	.	.	.	.	.	.	.	H	1
B304	.	.	.	.	.	.	.	.	.	.	.	.	.	.	.	.	.	.	.	.	.	.	.	.	.	.	.	.	.	.	.	.	.	.	.	T	.	.	.	.	.	.	.	.	.	.	.	.	.	.	.	.	.	.	.	.	.	.	.	H	1
B463	.	.	.	.	.	.	.	.	.	.	.	.	.	.	.	T	.	.	.	.	.	.	.	.	.	.	.	.	.	.	.	.	.	.	.	.	.	.	.	.	.	.	.	.	.	.	.	.	.	.	.	.	.	.	.	.	.	.	.	H	1
B543	.	.	.	.	.	.	.	.	.	.	.	.	.	.	.	C	.	.	.	.	.	.	.	.	.	.	.	.	.	.	.	.	.	.	.	.	.	.	.	.	.	.	.	.	.	.	.	.	.	.	.	.	.	.	.	.	.	.	.	H	1
B119	.	.	.	.	A	.	.	G	.	.	.	.	.	.	.	.	C	.	.	.	.	.	.	.	.	.	.	.	.	.	.	.	.	.	.	.	.	.	.	.	.	.	.	.	.	.	.	.	.	.	.	.	.	.	.	.	.	.	.	H	1
B155	.	.	.	.	.	.	.	.	.	.	.	.	.	.	.	.	.	.	.	.	.	.	.	.	.	.	.	.	.	.	.	.	T	.	.	.	.	.	.	.	.	.	.	.	.	.	.	.	.	.	.	.	.	.	.	.	.	.	.	H	1
B190	.	.	.	.	.	.	.	.	.	.	.	T	.	.	.	.	.	.	.	.	.	.	.	.	.	.	.	.	.	.	.	.	.	.	.	.	.	.	.	.	.	.	.	.	.	.	.	C	A	.	.	.	.	.	.	.	.	.	.	H	1
B297	.	.	.	.	.	.	.	.	.	.	.	T	.	.	.	.	.	.	.	.	.	.	.	.	.	.	.	.	.	.	.	.	.	.	.	.	.	.	.	.	.	.	.	.	.	.	.	.	.	.	.	.	C	.	.	.	.	.	.	H	1
B299	.	.	.	.	.	.	.	.	.	.	.	.	.	.	.	.	.	.	.	.	.	.	.	.	.	G	.	.	.	.	.	.	.	.	.	.	.	.	T	.	.	.	.	.	.	.	.	.	.	.	.	.	.	.	.	.	.	.	.	H	1
B318	.	.	.	.	.	.	.	.	.	.	C	.	.	.	.	.	.	.	.	.	.	.	.	.	.	.	.	.	.	.	.	.	.	.	.	.	.	.	.	.	.	.	.	.	.	.	.	.	C	.	.	.	.	.	.	.	.	.	.	H	1
B420	.	.	.	.	.	.	.	.	.	.	.	.	.	.	.	.	.	.	.	.	.	T	.	.	.	.	.	.	.	.	.	.	.	T	.	.	.	.	.	.	.	.	.	.	.	.	.	.	C	.	.	.	.	.	.	.	.	.	.	H	1
B134	.	.	.	.	.	.	.	.	.	.	.	.	.	.	.	.	.	.	.	T	.	.	.	.	.	.	.	.	.	.	.	.	.	.	.	.	.	.	.	.	.	.	.	.	.	.	.	C	C	T	C	C	.	.	.	.	.	.	.	H	1
B315	.	.	.	.	.	.	.	.	.	.	.	.	.	.	.	.	.	.	.	.	.	.	.	.	.	.	.	.	.	.	.	.	.	.	.	.	.	.	.	.	.	.	.	.	C	.	.	.	.	.	.	.	.	C	.	A	.	.	.	H	1
B602	.	.	.	.	.	.	.	.	.	.	.	.	.	.	.	.	.	.	.	T	.	.	.	.	.	.	.	.	.	.	.	.	.	.	.	.	.	.	.	.	.	.	.	.	.	C	.	.	.	.	.	.	.	.	A	C	.	.	.	H	1

Sample	69	93	114	126	129	145	150	153	162	167	168	172	174	176	185	188	189	192	193	218	220	221	223	224	234	235	239	240	241	242	249	256	259	266	270	278	286	290	291	292	293	294	295	296	298	300	302	304	311	319	320	323	325	328	343	356	362	366	390	Hap	N
CRS	c	t	c	t	g	g	c	g	a	c	c	t	c	c	c	c	c	c	c	c	c	c	a	a	c	t	c	c	c	c	a	c	a	a	c	t	c	c	c	c	a	a	c	c	c	t	c	a	t	t	c	t	c	a	t	t	c	g	H	—	—
B464	.	.	T	.	.	.	.	.	.	.	.	.	.	.	.	.	.	.	.	.	.	.	.	.	.	.	.	.	.	.	.	.	.	.	.	.	.	.	.	.	.	.	.	.	.	.	.	.	.	.	.	.	.	.	.	.	.	.	.	J	2
B145	.	.	T	.	.	.	.	.	.	.	.	.	.	.	.	.	.	.	.	.	.	.	.	.	.	.	.	.	.	.	.	.	.	.	.	.	.	.	.	.	.	.	.	.	.	.	.	.	.	.	.	.	.	.	.	.	.	T	.	J	2
B130	.	.	.	C	.	.	.	.	.	.	.	.	.	.	.	.	.	.	.	.	.	.	.	.	.	.	.	.	.	.	.	.	.	.	.	.	.	.	.	.	.	.	.	.	.	G	.	.	.	.	.	.	.	.	.	.	.	.	.	J	1
B140	.	.	T	C	.	.	.	.	.	.	.	.	.	.	.	.	.	.	.	.	.	.	.	.	.	.	.	.	.	.	.	.	.	.	.	.	.	.	.	.	.	.	.	.	.	G	.	.	.	.	.	.	.	.	.	.	.	.	.	J	1
B153	.	.	.	C	.	.	.	.	.	.	.	.	.	.	T	.	C	.	.	.	.	.	.	.	.	.	.	.	.	.	.	.	.	.	.	.	.	.	.	.	.	.	.	.	.	.	.	.	.	.	.	.	.	.	.	.	.	.	.	J	1
B169	.	.	.	C	.	.	.	.	.	.	.	.	.	.	.	.	.	.	.	.	.	.	.	.	.	.	.	.	.	.	.	.	.	.	.	T	.	.	.	.	.	.	.	.	.	.	.	.	.	.	.	.	.	.	.	.	.	T	.	J	1
B202	.	.	T	C	.	.	.	.	.	.	.	.	.	.	.	.	.	.	.	.	.	.	.	.	.	.	.	.	.	.	.	.	.	.	.	T	.	.	.	.	.	.	.	.	.	.	.	.	.	.	.	.	.	.	.	.	.	.	.	J	1
B182	.	.	T	C	.	.	.	.	.	.	.	.	.	.	.	.	.	.	T	.	.	.	.	.	G	.	.	.	.	.	.	.	.	.	.	T	.	.	.	.	.	.	.	.	.	.	.	.	.	.	.	.	.	.	.	.	.	.	.	J	1
B137	.	.	.	.	.	.	.	.	.	.	.	.	.	.	.	.	.	.	.	.	.	.	.	.	.	.	.	.	.	.	.	.	.	.	.	T	.	.	.	.	.	.	.	.	.	.	.	.	C	.	.	.	.	.	.	.	.	.	.	K	2
B148	.	.	.	.	.	.	.	.	.	.	.	.	.	.	.	.	.	.	.	.	C	.	C	.	.	.	.	.	.	.	.	.	.	.	.	.	.	.	.	.	.	.	.	.	.	.	.	.	C	.	.	.	.	.	.	.	.	.	.	K	1
B149	.	.	.	.	.	.	.	.	.	.	.	.	.	.	.	.	C	.	.	.	.	.	C	.	C	.	.	.	.	.	.	.	.	.	.	.	.	.	.	.	.	.	.	.	.	.	.	.	C	A	.	.	.	.	.	.	.	.	.	K	1
B519	.	.	.	.	.	.	.	.	.	.	.	.	.	.	.	.	C	.	.	.	.	.	C	T	.	.	.	.	.	.	.	.	.	.	.	.	.	.	.	.	.	.	.	.	.	.	.	.	C	.	.	.	.	.	.	.	.	.	.	K	1
B643	.	.	.	.	.	.	T	.	.	.	.	.	.	.	.	.	.	.	.	.	.	.	C	.	.	.	.	.	.	.	.	.	.	.	.	.	.	.	.	.	.	.	.	.	.	.	.	.	C	.	.	.	.	.	.	.	.	.	.	K	1
B195	.	.	.	.	.	.	.	.	.	.	.	.	.	G	.	.	.	.	T	.	.	.	T	.	C	.	.	.	.	.	.	.	.	.	.	.	.	.	.	.	.	.	.	.	.	.	.	.	C	T	.	.	.	.	.	.	.	.	.	K	1
B633	.	.	.	.	.	.	A	.	.	.	.	.	.	G	.	.	.	.	.	.	.	.	T	.	.	.	.	.	.	.	.	.	.	.	.	.	.	.	T	.	.	.	.	.	.	.	.	.	.	.	.	.	.	.	.	.	.	.	A	A NIb	1
B172	.	.	.	C	.	.	.	.	.	.	.	.	.	.	.	.	.	.	.	.	.	.	.	.	.	.	.	.	.	.	.	.	.	.	.	.	.	.	.	.	T	T	.	.	.	G	.	.	.	.	.	.	.	.	.	.	.	T	.	T	2
B199	.	.	.	C	.	.	A	.	.	.	.	.	.	.	.	.	.	.	.	.	.	.	.	.	.	.	.	.	.	.	.	.	.	.	.	.	.	.	.	.	.	T	.	.	.	.	.	.	.	.	.	.	.	.	.	.	.	T	.	T	1
B144	C	.	C	C	.	.	.	.	.	.	.	.	.	.	.	.	.	.	.	.	.	.	.	.	.	.	.	.	.	.	.	.	.	.	.	.	.	.	.	.	.	T	.	.	C	C	.	.	.	.	.	.	.	.	.	.	.	T	.	T	1
B133	.	.	.	C	.	.	.	.	.	.	.	.	.	.	.	.	.	.	.	.	.	.	.	.	.	.	.	.	.	.	.	.	.	.	.	.	.	.	.	.	T	T	.	T	C	C	.	.	.	.	.	.	.	.	.	.	.	T T	.	T	1
B116	.	.	.	.	.	.	.	.	.	.	.	.	.	.	.	.	T	.	.	.	.	.	.	.	.	.	.	.	.	.	.	.	.	T	.	.	.	.	.	.	.	.	.	.	.	.	.	.	A	.	.	.	.	.	.	.	.	.	.	U	7
B191	.	.	.	.	.	.	.	.	.	.	.	.	.	.	T	.	.	.	.	.	.	.	.	.	.	.	.	.	.	.	.	T	.	T	.	T	.	.	.	.	.	.	.	.	.	.	.	.	.	.	.	.	.	.	.	.	.	.	.	U	2
B185	.	.	.	.	.	.	.	.	.	.	.	.	.	.	.	.	.	.	.	.	.	.	.	.	.	.	.	.	.	.	.	.	T	T	.	T	.	.	.	.	.	.	.	.	.	.	.	.	.	.	.	.	.	.	.	.	.	.	.	U	1
B204	.	.	.	.	.	.	.	.	.	.	.	.	.	.	.	.	.	.	.	.	.	.	.	.	.	.	.	.	.	.	.	.	.	.	.	.	.	.	.	.	.	.	.	.	.	.	.	.	C	.	.	.	.	.	.	.	.	.	.	U	1
B205	.	.	.	.	.	.	.	.	.	.	.	.	.	.	.	.	.	.	.	.	.	.	.	.	.	.	.	G	.	.	.	.	.	.	.	.	.	.	.	.	.	.	.	.	.	.	C	.	.	.	.	.	.	.	.	.	.	.	.	U	1
B207	.	.	.	.	.	.	.	.	.	.	.	.	T	.	.	.	.	T	.	.	.	.	.	.	.	.	.	.	.	.	.	.	.	.	.	.	.	.	.	.	.	.	.	.	.	.	.	.	C	.	.	.	.	.	.	.	.	.	.	U	1
B141	.	.	A	.	.	.	.	.	.	.	.	.	.	.	.	.	.	T	.	.	.	.	.	.	.	.	.	.	.	.	.	.	.	.	.	.	.	.	.	.	.	T	.	.	.	.	.	.	.	.	.	.	.	.	.	.	.	.	.	U	1
B441	.	.	.	C	.	.	.	.	.	.	.	.	.	.	.	.	C	.	.	.	.	.	.	.	.	.	.	.	G	.	.	.	.	.	.	.	.	.	.	.	.	.	.	.	.	.	.	.	A	.	.	.	.	.	.	.	C	.	.	U	1
B296	T	C	.	.	.	.	.	.	.	.	.	.	.	.	.	.	.	.	.	.	.	.	.	.	.	.	.	.	.	.	.	.	.	.	.	T	.	.	.	.	.	.	.	.	.	.	.	.	.	.	.	.	.	.	G	.	.	.	.	U	1
B154	.	.	.	.	.	.	.	.	.	.	T	.	.	.	.	.	.	.	.	.	.	.	.	.	.	.	.	.	.	.	.	.	.	.	.	.	.	.	.	.	.	.	.	.	.	.	.	.	.	.	.	.	.	.	G	.	.	.	.	U	1
B526	.	.	.	.	.	.	.	.	.	.	.	.	.	.	.	.	.	.	.	.	.	.	.	.	.	.	.	.	.	.	.	.	.	T	.	.	.	.	.	.	.	.	.	.	.	.	.	.	A	.	.	.	.	.	.	.	C	.	.	U	1

Table 12.3. (cont.)

CRS	69	93	114	126	129	145	150	153	162	167	168	172	174	176	185	188	189	192	193	218	220	221	223	224	234	235	239	240	241	242	249	256	259	266	270	278	286	290	291	292	293	294	295	296	298	300	302	304	311	319	320	323	325	328	343	356	362	366	390	Hap	N
CRS	c	t	c	t	g	g	c	g	a	c	c	t	c	c	c	c	c	c	t	c	c	c	a	c	c	t	c	a	c	a	a	c	t	c	c	c	c	c	c	c	c	a	c	c	c	t	a	a	t	t	g	c	t	t	c	a	t	t	c	H	–
B614	.	.	.	.	.	.	.	.	.	T	.	.	.	.	.	.	.	.	T	.	.	.	.	.	.	.	.	.	.	.	.	.	.	.	.	.	.	.	.	.	.	.	.	.	.	.	.	.	C	.	.	.	.	.	.	C	.	.	.	U	1
B152	.	C	.	.	.	.	.	.	.	.	.	.	.	.	.	.	.	.	.	.	.	.	.	.	.	.	.	.	.	.	.	.	.	.	T	.	.	.	.	.	.	.	.	.	C	.	.	.	.	.	.	.	.	.	.	.	.	.	.	V	8
B167	.	.	.	.	A	.	.	.	.	.	.	.	.	.	.	.	.	.	.	.	.	.	.	.	.	.	.	.	.	.	.	.	.	.	.	.	.	.	.	.	.	.	.	.	C	.	.	.	.	.	.	.	.	.	.	.	.	.	.	V	2
B101	.	.	.	.	.	.	.	.	.	.	.	.	.	.	.	.	.	.	.	.	.	.	.	.	.	.	.	.	.	.	.	.	.	.	.	.	.	.	.	.	.	.	.	.	C	.	.	.	.	.	.	.	.	.	.	.	.	.	.	V	1
B163	.	.	.	.	.	.	.	.	.	.	.	.	.	.	.	.	.	.	.	.	.	.	.	.	.	.	.	.	.	.	C	.	.	.	.	.	.	.	.	.	.	.	.	.	C	.	.	.	.	.	.	.	.	.	.	.	.	.	.	V	1
B179	.	.	.	.	.	.	.	.	.	.	.	.	.	.	.	.	C	.	.	.	.	.	.	.	.	.	.	.	.	.	.	.	.	.	.	.	.	.	.	.	.	.	.	.	C	.	.	.	.	.	.	.	.	.	.	.	.	.	.	V	1
B381	.	.	.	.	.	.	.	.	.	.	.	.	.	.	.	.	.	.	.	.	.	.	.	.	.	.	.	G	.	.	.	.	.	.	.	.	.	.	T	.	.	.	T	.	C	.	.	.	.	.	.	.	.	.	.	.	.	.	.	V	1
B382	.	.	.	.	.	.	.	.	.	.	.	.	.	.	.	.	.	.	.	.	.	.	T	.	.	.	.	.	.	.	.	.	.	.	.	.	.	.	T	.	.	.	.	.	.	.	.	.	.	.	.	.	.	.	.	.	.	.	.	W	1

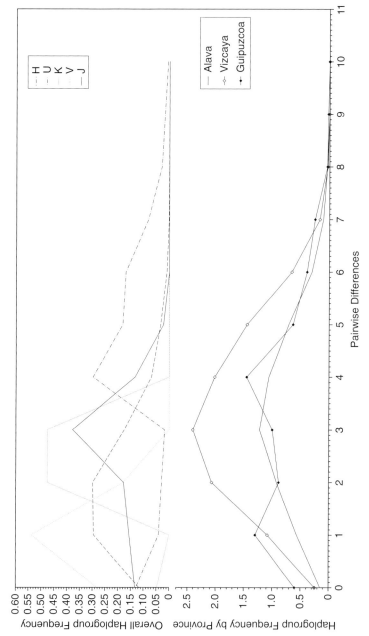

Figure 12.2 Mismatch distributions for mtDNA HVSI sequence data for total sample (top) and by province (bottom).

at one and four pairwise differences. The raggedness index for this distribution is non-significant, however (0.038, $p = 0.473$), and the sum of squared deviations goodness-of-fit test does not reject the null hypothesis of a population expansion (SSD $= 0.01$, $p = 0.423$). Examination of mismatch distributions for individual haplogroups (top panel, Figure 12.2) demonstrates that J, K, and T each have unimodal peaks at three, while V has a unimodal peak at one difference, and haplogroup U has a unimodal peak at four differences. This suggests that haplogroup V has experienced a more recent expansion event, while the expansion of haplogroup U is more ancient. It is possible that the mismatch distribution for Guipuzcoa reflects these distinct expansion events, rather than representing a population that has had a relatively constant size. Table 12.4 presents nucleotide diversity values for HVS-I sequences, as well as two measures of selective neutrality (Tajima's D and Fu's F_S) for 39 populations. Nucleotide diversity ranges from a low of 0.0102 among Basque sequences collected from the literature, to a high of 0.166 in the Spanish province of Andalusia. The Basque samples in the present study have the second lowest nucleotide diversity (0.0114), along with another Atlantic Fringe population, the Welsh. Values of Tajima's D are uniformly negative and significant for the European groups, suggesting that, from a mitochondrial perspective, these populations have experienced an expansion. This is confirmed by the highly significant negative values of Fu's F_S, which also indicate an expansion process acting on these populations, including the Basques.

Relationships between populations are shown in the MDS plot with SAMOVA genetic barriers (Figure 12.3), which accounts for 74% of the total variation. The STRESS (0.15897, $p = 0.01$) and Mantel correlation ($r = 0.89094$) indicate a good fit between the MDS with the original distance matrix. In this plot, the Basques are distinct in Europe, and this placement is confirmed by SAMOVA where the European populations show the highest F_{CT} (0.01016410) when divided into just two groups: (1) the Basques, and (2) all other European populations.

HVS-I sequence data were also used to perform mismatch analyses for all 39 European populations, and intermatch comparisons were made between the study population and other comparative groups, in order to estimate the time of population expansion within groups, and coalescent times between groups (Table 12.5). In all populations, low raggedness values (r) indicate expansion (0.0083–0.0367). For the least squares method, tau values (τ_l) range from 1.50 in Wales to 4.90 in Italy, while the two Basque populations have τ_l estimates of 2.90 and 3.20 (present study). These estimates translate into expansion times between

Table 12.4. *Diversity and neutrality measures in 39 populations*

Population	N	Nucleotide diversity	Tajima's D	p	Fu's F_S	p
Basque (present study)	131	0.0114	−2.2347	0.0000	−26.3302	0.0000
Austria	99	0.0150	−2.1892	0.0000	−25.8355	0.0000
Basque	156	0.0102	−2.1623	0.0020	−26.4817	0.0000
Belgium	33	0.0133	−2.1837	0.0010	−26.2654	0.0000
Bosnia	144	0.0134	−2.1644	0.0000	−25.9169	0.0000
Brittany	62	0.0139	−1.9638	0.0070	−25.9929	0.0000
Bulgaria	141	0.0149	−2.1201	0.0000	−25.7191	0.0000
Central Portugal	162	0.0157	−2.2912	0.0000	−25.5705	0.0000
Cornwall	92	0.0128	−2.1523	0.0000	−26.1625	0.0000
Czech Republic	83	0.0150	−1.8405	0.0120	−25.8537	0.0000
Denmark	38	0.0127	−1.8313	0.0130	−14.0898	0.0000
England	242	0.0144	−2.2435	0.0000	−25.5208	0.0000
Estonia	149	0.0151	−1.8498	0.0080	−25.6779	0.0000
Finland	153	0.0134	−2.1087	0.0020	−25.9171	0.0000
France	379	0.0140	−2.2524	0.0000	−25.3638	0.0000
Germany	582	0.0136	−2.2316	0.0000	−25.1813	0.0000
Greece	179	0.0140	−2.1798	0.0010	−25.7464	0.0000
Hungary	78	0.0155	−2.1801	0.0000	−25.8040	0.0000
Ireland	300	0.0131	−2.2031	0.0000	−25.6119	0.0000
Italy	248	0.0165	−2.1600	0.0010	−25.2345	0.0000
Karelia	83	0.0134	−1.6779	0.0180	−26.0622	0.0000

Table 12.4. (cont.)

Population	N	Nucleotide diversity	Tajima's D	p	Fu's F_S	p
North Portugal	183	0.0155	-2.1155	0.0000	-25.5225	0.0000
Norway	629	0.0138	-2.2561	0.0000	-25.1448	0.0000
Poland	473	0.0150	-2.1753	0.0000	-25.1370	0.0000
Romania	92	0.0152	-1.9705	0.0060	-25.8165	0.0000
Russia	379	0.0151	-2.0862	0.0000	-25.2211	0.0000
Sardinia	115	0.0142	-2.0650	0.0030	-25.8827	0.0000
Scotland	895	0.0145	-2.0769	0.0000	-24.8724	0.0000
Sicily	196	0.0126	-2.1140	0.0000	-25.8978	0.0000
Slovenia	104	0.0134	-2.0924	0.0000	-26.0431	0.0000
South Portugal	195	0.0155	-2.0802	0.0010	-25.4956	0.0000
Spain Andalusia	114	0.0166	-2.1079	0.0030	-25.6010	0.0000
Spain Castile	38	0.0136	-1.9700	0.0080	-25.8585	0.0000
Spain Catalonia	61	0.0135	-1.8250	0.0120	-26.0352	0.0000
Spain Galicia	135	0.0128	-2.2315	0.0000	-26.0502	0.0000
Spain Leon	61	0.0127	-2.1492	0.0010	-26.1400	0.0000
Sweden	32	0.0159	-1.8895	0.0090	-24.8519	0.0000
Switzerland	224	0.0140	-2.2030	0.0010	-25.6315	0.0000
Wales	92	0.0114	-2.1053	0.0020	-26.4037	0.0000

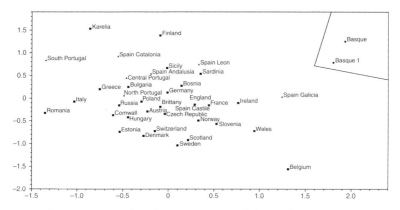

Figure 12.3 MDS plot of 39 European populations using mtDNA HVS-I data. Basques (black circles), Iberian populations (triangles), other Europeans (squares). STRESS = 0.15879 (p = 0.01), r = 0.89094. Genetic barriers detected by SAMOVA indicated as black lines.

16 469 and 53 799 years for Europe, and 31 840 and 35 134 years among the Basques. For the method of moments, tau values (τ_m) range from 1.21 in central Portugal to 5.36 in Scotland, with τ_m estimates among the Basques between 2.64 and 3.15 (present study). These estimates give expansion times between 13 326 and 58 847 years in Europe, and 28 958 and 34 599 years for the Basques. While the two methods of determining expansion times provide somewhat different values, all time estimates based on the method of moments fall within the date ranges based on the least squares approach. Divergence times between the Basques and other European populations suggest a common maternal ancestor between 16 967 and 47 377 years ago.

DISCUSSION

Previous haplogroup analysis of Basque populations reported a preponderance of haplogroup H/HV (74%), with the addition of haplogroups U (11%), T (6%), K (5%), J (3%), and I/W/X (2%) (Achilli *et al.*, 2004; Bertranpetit *et al.*, 1995; Corte-Real *et al.*, 1996). Historical populations (sixth and seventh centuries AD) in the Basque region had lower frequencies of H (42%), but higher frequencies of U (16%), K (17%), T/X (12%), and J (12%) (Alzualde *et al.*, 2005). Haplogroup V had a frequency of 0.68% in the historic population, much lower than the frequencies reported in modern Basque groups (3–20%) (Torroni *et al.*, 2001). Prehistoric populations in the region, dating between the Neolithic and the Bronze Age,

Table 12.5. *Tau values and time estimates based on mismatch distributions in 39 European populations*

Population	N	τ_l	95% CI	r	Time estimate	Date range	τ_m	Time estimate	Divergence time
Basque (present study)	131	3.20	2.166–3.750	0.0246	35 134	23 781–41 173	3.15	34 559	–
Austria	99	4.00	2.072–7.330	0.0084	43 917	22 749–80 479	3.04	33 376	33 114
Basque	156	2.90	1.551–3.777	0.0278	31 840	17 029–41 469	2.64	28 958	32 635
Belgium	33	3.00	1.994–4.008	0.0367	32 938	21 893–44 005	3.60	39 509	37 751
Bosnia	144	3.00	1.562–6.467	0.0173	32 938	17 150–71 003	2.77	30 447	32 276
Brittany	62	3.30	1.189–8.375	0.0126	36 232	13 055–91 952	3.16	34 656	35 040
Bulgaria	141	3.30	2.766–3.754	0.0137	36 232	30 369–41 217	3.38	37 110	37 844
Central Portugal	162	2.20	0.758–8.320	0.0101	24 155	8 322–91 348	1.21	13 263	16 967
Cornwall	92	2.20	1.697–2.777	0.0188	24 155	18 632–30 490	2.54	27 921	31 270
Czech Republic	83	3.80	3.076–5.311	0.0195	41 722	33 773–58 311	4.15	45 511	40 407
Denmark	38	3.20	1.209–7.609	0.0145	35 134	13 274–83 542	2.34	25 672	28 629
England	242	3.00	1.449–7.500	0.0118	32 938	15 909–82 345	2.90	31 835	32 210
Estonia	149	3.10	1.869–6.789	0.0125	34 036	20 520–74 539	3.25	35 654	36 474
Finland	153	3.90	1.723–5.744	0.0171	42 819	18 917–63 065	3.25	35 704	38 130
France	379	2.80	1.809–6.111	0.0146	30 742	19 862–67 095	3.01	33 047	32 604
Germany	582	3.30	2.428–4.951	0.0171	36 232	27 251–54 359	3.10	34 002	36 398
Greece	179	3.00	2.539–3.438	0.0169	32 938	27 877–37 747	3.26	35 753	37 386
Hungary	78	2.90	2.186–3.539	0.0186	31 840	24 001–38 856	3.19	34 983	33 055
Ireland	300	3.40	1.975–5.271	0.0155	37 330	21 684–57 872	4.74	51 999	43 654
Italy	248	4.90	2.746–6.059	0.0113	53 799	30 149–66 524	3.70	40 624	36 840
Karelia	83	2.70	1.365–5.773	0.0157	29 644	14 987–63 384	2.88	31 599	34 111

Table 12.5. (cont.)

Population	N	τ_l	95% CI	r	Time estimate	Date range	τ_m	Time estimate	Divergence time
North Portugal	183	3.90	1.787–8.381	0.0083	42 819	19 620–92 018	2.98	32 743	31 374
Norway	629	3.20	1.863–6.439	0.0115	35 134	20 455–70 696	3.47	38 060	35 891
Poland	473	3.30	1.279–10.848	0.0101	36 232	14 043–119 104	2.62	28 813	34 365
Romania	92	3.10	2.508–3.756	0.0174	34 036	27 536–41 238	3.55	38 959	36 653
Russia	379	3.50	2.215–6.023	0.0128	38 428	24 319–66 129	3.79	41 656	37 939
Sardinia	115	3.90	1.879–6.027	0.0125	42 819	20 630–66 173	2.67	29 294	29 914
Scotland	895	3.50	2.338–6.072	0.0123	38 428	25 669–66 667	5.36	58 847	47 377
Sicily	196	3.40	1.318–6.863	0.0093	37 330	14 471–75 351	2.36	25 896	28 740
Slovenia	104	2.40	1.873–2.920	0.0200	26 350	20 564–32 060	2.59	28 428	31 210
South Portugal	195	2.70	0.900–8.486	0.0077	29 644	9 881–93 170	2.58	28 305	27 592
Spain Andalusia	114	3.90	1.900–7.652	0.0091	42 819	20 861–84 014	3.41	37 419	33 390
Spain Castile	38	3.90	2.111–5.113	0.0202	42 819	23 177–56 137	3.77	41 410	38 258
Spain Catalonia	61	3.90	1.541–7.033	0.0163	42 819	16 919–77 218	2.48	27 192	29 719
Spain Galicia	135	1.70	1.309–2.195	0.0145	18 665	14 372–24 100	1.86	20 406	24 332
Spain Leon	61	2.40	0.967–7.842	0.0137	26 350	10 617–86 100	2.19	24 099	26 923
Sweden	32	3.80	2.740–5.865	0.0163	41 722	30 083–64 394	4.40	48 300	41 930
Switzerland	224	3.80	2.312–5.109	0.0164	41 722	25 384–56 094	3.87	42 526	41 149
Wales	92	1.50	0.541–6.420	0.0170	16 469	5 940–70 487	1.94	21 268	26 789

N, number of mtDNA sequences in the sample; τ_l, expansion time in mutational units (least squares method); r, raggedness index; CI, confidence intervals for τ_l; τ_m, expansion time in mutational units (method of moments).

also have lower frequencies of H (33%), but higher frequencies of K (23%), U (19%), J (14%), and T/X (10%), and an absence of V (Izagirre and de la Rua, 1999). In the present study, the most frequent haplogroup was H (63%), followed by U (16%). Haplogroups V (7%), J (6%), and K (5%) were present at moderate frequencies, while haplogroups T (1%), W (1%), I/X (0.6%) and N1b (0.2%) were found at low frequencies.

Analysis of European mtDNA HVS-I sequences demonstrated little clinal variation, and divergence dates suggested that many of the mitochondrial haplotypes in Europe had a pre-Neolithic origin (Richards *et al.*, 1996). After correction of divergence times by removing variation present before the migration in the form of shared haplotypes (Sykes, 1999), only one major haplogroup – J – could be placed in the Neolithic. However, it has been suggested that this haplogroup has been under the influence of selection, which could potentially interfere with attempts to accurately date its emergence (Pierron *et al.*, 2011).

Haplogroup U (in particular U5) is the one of the oldest mitochondrial haplogroups in Europe, dating to around 50 000 BP in the Early Upper Paleolithic, and is considered to have developed *in situ* in Europe and reflects the migration of anatomically modern humans into the continent (Richards *et al.*, 2002; Salas *et al.*, 1998; Sykes, 1999). Of the 19 U mtDNA sequences identified in the current sample, 11 (58%) are U5. By contrast, haplogroup U8a, dating to around 28 000 BP and reported at a frequency of 1.1% in other modern Basques, was not detected in the present sample (Gonzalez *et al.*, 2006).

H – the most frequent haplogroup in many extant European populations – is comparatively young, dating to 18 000 BP during the Middle/Late Upper Paleolithic (Pereira *et al.*, 2005). The other haplogroups (T, I, V, W) have been dated to between 14 000 and 11 000 BP (Francalacci *et al.*, 1996). Haplogroup V was once believed, due to its relatively high frequency and heterogeneity, to have arisen in the Basque region during the Late Upper Paleolithic (Torroni *et al.*, 2001). However, analysis in prehistoric and historic populations revealed low to no frequency of V in these groups, and recent work has suggested that the homeland for this haplogroup, while still European, be moved to Cantabria just west of the Basque country (Alzualde *et al.*, 2006; Izagirre and de la Rua, 1999; Lell and Wallace, 2000; Richards *et al.*, 2002). It should be noted, however, that the separation times for these lineages reflect the age of the particular genetic system, not the age of the population in which it occurs (Casalotti *et al.*, 1999; Sampietro *et al.*, 2007).

Haplogroup N1b has not been reported previously in the Basque country. This haplogroup is found at low frequencies elsewhere in

Europe, and is present at high frequencies (10%) in Ashkenazi Jewish populations (Behar *et al.*, 2004, 2006). However, the majority of Ashkenazi N1b sequences harbor a C–A transversion at position 16176, while the N1b identified in the Basque sample has the more common C–G transversion. This mutation has been reported in one Ashkenazim from Germany, but is more commonly found in non-Jewish groups, including populations in France (1.4%), Italy (4.6%) Bosnia (0.69%), Poland (0.23%), Croatia (2.8%) and the Czech Republic (1.1%) (Babalini *et al.*, 2005; Dubut *et al.*, 2004; Malyarchuk *et al.*, 2002, 2003, 2006). It has also been found at low frequencies in the Middle East (1–5%), the Caucasus (1–3%) as well as in Egypt (2.5–5%) (Gonzalez *et al.*, 2008; Rowold *et al.*, 2007). Haplogroup N1b is rare but not unusual in Europe, and is generally considered a Western Eurasian haplogroup, so the presence N1b among the Basques is not entirely unexpected. However, since autochthony was determined by Basque surnames and residence of four grandparents, it is possible that gene flow which occurred prior to the last three generations was unaccounted for. In agreement with the analysis of biparental markers and Y chromosomes (Young *et al.*, 2011a, 2011b), the mitochondrial DNA evidence demonstrates that the Basques are European, with high frequencies of the most common European haplogroup, H.

The present analysis also demonstrated the genetic distinctiveness of the Basques, with SAMOVA detecting a genetic barrier between the Basques and all other European populations. Other studies have attributed the Basque distinction to little gene flow with surrounding groups and a long period of genetic isolation (Aguirre *et al.*, 1991; Manzano *et al.*, 1996). Haplogroups dating to the Neolithic, both mtDNA (haplogroup J) and Y chromosome (haplogroups J2a, G2a, and E1b1b) (Young *et al.*, 2011b) have been detected in the present sample. Overall, the Basques have 10.9% Neolithic haplotypes in the paternal lineage (Young *et al.*, 2011b), and about half that (5.68%) in the maternal line. The presence of 15 individuals in an ancient Basque sample (5000–3400 BP) belonging to mitochondrial haplogroup J suggests that this admixture has not been recent (Izagirre and de la Rua, 1999). This result does not imply that ancient Basque populations experienced gene flow directly from Neolithic farmers, as an analysis of skeletal remains from the Neolithic Transition in Iberia found little evidence of population replacement (i.e. major dietary changes reflected in skeletal morphology or trace mineral composition) (Jackes *et al.*, 1997). In addition, expansion times calculated from mitochondrial HVS-I sequences for European populations date overwhelmingly to the Paleolithic, meaning population expansions occurred well before the advent of agriculture.

The percentage of non-Neolithic ancestry found in European populations increases with increasing geographic distance from the Fertile Crescent, arguing strongly against the demic diffusion model of complete replacement of Paleolithic foragers by a wave of advancing Neolithic farmers.

In regards to the Neolithic demic diffusion versus cultural diffusion debate, neither seems to be strictly true, particularly in Iberia. The genetic evidence presents a more complex picture of European origins, with a southeast to northwest cline in frequencies for certain loci and haplotypes (mitochondrial haplogroups J, T1, and U3; Y-chromosome haplogroups J2a, G2a, and E1b1b), and a deeper time depth in Europe for others (mitochondrial haplogroups U8a, U5, H1, and H3; Y-chromosome haplogroups R1b and I2a2) (McEvoy *et al.*, 2004; Richards *et al.*, 2002; Sykes, 2003).

A survey of human occupation of Europe during the Paleolithic/Neolithic transition explains how this result could occur (Pinhasi *et al.*, 2000). Beginning in 14 000 BP, Europe was lightly populated, with a concentration of Late Paleolithic sites in present-day France and Germany. Over the next 3000 years, evidence of human occupation spread north and east, reaching Italy, the British Isles, and Scandinavia, with sites more sparsely distributed and little evidence of human activity in Greece or most of Eastern Europe. From 10 000 to 7000 BP, evidence of Neolithic sites first appears in Anatolia, and spreads rapidly into those areas that were sparsely populated by Mesolithic hunter-gatherers. Admixture models based on these archaeological data suggest regional variation across Europe (Lahr *et al.*, 2000), with areas close to the epicenter of agricultural innovation and/or sparsely populated by Mesolithic groups showing little evidence of admixture and an almost exclusively Neolithic gene pool. Those areas which were densely populated during the Mesolithic and received few Neolithic migrants would show low admixture values and a high percentage of non-Neolithic genes, while those which were more densely populated by Mesolithic groups followed by a moderate level of immigration by Neolithic farmers would have gene pools comprised approximately equally of non-Neolithic and Neolithic genes. During the Mesolithic, the Iberian Peninsula was also sparsely populated. Sites were primarily coastal, reflecting the relative wealth of resources (Straus, 1991b; Zilhao, 2000). During the Last Glacial Maximum, the northern coast of Iberia was one of two refuge areas, and the archaeological record shows increased occupation in this region between 21 000 and 16 000 BP (47 sites compared with only 26 for the entire Early Upper Paleolithic) (Housley *et al.*, 1997; Straus, 1991a). Rather than showing a "wave of advance," Neolithic settlement in Iberia demonstrates a leapfrog pattern along the coasts (Zilhao, 2000). Mesolithic populations would have been well established in these areas, and would likely have assimilated groups of Neolithic "maritime pioneers" (Lahr *et al.*, 2000; Zilhao, 1998, 2003).

Given the archaeological evidence, the cline described by Ammerman and Cavalli-Sforza (1984) minimizes the dynamic population movements during the Late Paleolithic and Mesolithic in Europe, as well as the impact of regional admixture. The authors now suggest that the first principal component (and the southeast–northwest cline observed for classical markers) be seen as a proxy for the *amount* of Neolithic admixture present in Europe, rather than as evidence of a complete replacement (Cavalli-Sforza, 2003).

NOTE

Data available from the first author upon request.

ACKNOWLEDGMENTS

The authors would like to thank the Basque participants, Dr. Arantza Apraiz for sample collection, Dr. Rohina Rubicz for her assistance with DNA extraction, and Michael Grose of the University of Kansas Biodiversity Institute for sequencing samples from Guipuzcoa and Vizcaya. This work was supported in part by a National Geographic Society Grant (Project 6935–00) to the University of Kansas Laboratory of Biological Anthropology.

REFERENCES

Achilli, A., Rengo, C., Magri, C., *et al.* (2004). The molecular dissection of mtDNA haplogroup H confirms that the Franco-Cantabrian glacial refuge was a major source for the European gene pool. *American Journal of Human Genetics*, **75**, 910–8.

Aguirre, A., Vicario, A., Mazon, L. I., *et al.* (1991). Are the Basques a single and a unique population? *American Journal of Human Genetics*, **49**, 450–8.

Alzualde, A., Izagirre, N., Alonso, S., *et al.* (2006). Insights into the "isolation" of the Basques: mtDNA lineages from the historical site of Aldaieta (6th–7th centuries AD). *American Journal of Physical Anthropology*, **130**, 394–404.

Alzualde, A., Izagirre, N., Alonso, S., Alonso, A., and de la Rua, C. (2005). Temporal mitochondrial DNA variation in the Basque Country: influence of postneolithic events. *Annals of Human Genetics*, **69**, 665–79.

Ammerman, A. J. and Cavalli-Sforza, L. L. (1984). *The Neolithic Transition and the Genetics of Populations in Europe*. Princeton, NJ: Princeton University Press.

Anderson, S., Bankier, A. T., Barrell, B. G., *et al.* (1981). Sequence and organization of the human mitochondrial genome. *Nature*, **290**, 457–65.

Babalini, C., Martinez-Labarga, C., Tolk, H. V., *et al.* (2005). The population history of the Croatian linguistic minority of Molise (southern Italy): a maternal view. *European Journal of Human Genetics*, **13**, 902–12.

Balaresque, P., Bowden, G. R., Adams, S. M., *et al.* (2010). A predominantly neolithic origin for European paternal lineages. *PLoS Biology*, **8**, e1000285.

Barbujani, G., Bertorelle, G., and Chikhi, L. (1998). Evidence for Paleolithic and Neolithic gene flow in Europe. *American Journal of Human Genetics*, **62**, 488–92.

Battaglia, V., Fornarino, S., Al-Zahery, N., *et al.* (2009). Y-chromosomal evidence of the cultural diffusion of agriculture in Southeast Europe. *European Journal of Human Genetics*, **17**, 820–30.

Behar, D. M., Hammer, M. F., Garrigan, D., *et al.* (2004). MtDNA evidence for a genetic bottleneck in the early history of the Ashkenazi Jewish population. *European Journal of Human Genetics*, **12**, 355–64.

Behar, D. M., Metspalu, E., Kivisild, T., *et al.* (2006). The matrilineal ancestry of Ashkenazi Jewry: portrait of a recent founder event. *American Journal of Human Genetics*, **78**, 487–97.

Bertranpetit, J., Sala, J., Calafell, F., *et al.* (1995). Human mitochondrial DNA variation and the origin of Basques. *Annals of Human Genetics*, **59**, 63–81.

Boyd, W. C. and Boyd, L. G. (1937). New data on blood groups and other inherited factors in Europe and Egypt. *American Journal of Physical Anthropology*, **23**, 49–70.

Casalotti, R., Simoni, L., Belledi, M., and Barbujani, G. (1999). Y-chromosome polymorphisms and the origins of the European gene pool. *Proceedings of the Royal Society B: Biological Sciences*, **266**, 1959–65.

Cavalli-Sforza, L. L. (2003). Returning to the Neolithic transition in Europe. In *The Widening Harvest: The Neolithic Transition in Europe*, ed. A. J. Ammerman and P. Biagi. Boston, MA: Archaeological Institute of America.

Cavalli-Sforza, L. L. and Piazza, A. (1993). Human genomic diversity in Europe: a summary of recent research and prospects for the future. *European Journal of Human Genetics*, **1**, 3–18.

Cavalli-Sforza, L. L., Menozzi, P., and Piazza, A. (1994). *The History and Geography of Human Genes*. Princeton, NJ: Princeton University Press.

Chalmers, J. N., Ikin, E. W., and Mourant, A. E. (1948). Basque blood groups. *Nature*, **27**.

Chalmers, J. N., Ikin, E. W., and Mourant, A. E. (1949). The ABO, MN and Rh blood groups of the Basque people. *American Journal of Physical Anthropology*, **7**, 529–44.

Chikhi, L., Destro-Bisol, G., Bertorelle, G., Pascali, V., and Barbujani, G. (1998). Clines of nuclear DNA markers suggest a largely Neolithic ancestry of the European gene pool. *Proceedings of the National Academy of Sciences of the United States of America*, **95**, 9053–8.

Corte-Real, H. B., Macaulay, V. A., Richards, M. B., *et al.* (1996). Genetic diversity in the Iberian Peninsula determined from mitochondrial sequence analysis. *Annals of Human Genetics*, **60**, 331–50.

Dubut, V., Chollet, L., Murail, P., *et al.* (2004). mtDNA polymorphisms in five French groups: importance of regional sampling. *European Journal of Human Genetics*, **12**, 293–300.

Dupanloup, I., Schneider, S., and Excoffier, L. (2002). A simulated annealing approach to define the genetic structure of populations. *Molecular Ecology*, **11**, 2571–81.

Etcheverry, M. A. (1945). El factor rhesus, su genética e importancia clínica. *El Dia Medico*, **17**, 1237–59.

Excoffier, L. (2004). Patterns of DNA sequence diversity and genetic structure after a range expansion: lessons from the infinite-island model. *Molecular Ecology*, **13**, 853–64.

Excoffier, L., Laval, G., and Schneider, J. A. (2005). Arlequin ver. 3.0: an integrated software package for population genetics data analysis. *Evolutionary Bioinformatics Online*, **1**, 47–50.

Flores, C., Maca-Meyer, N., Gonzalez, A. M., *et al.* (2004). Reduced genetic structure of the Iberian peninsula revealed by Y-chromosome analysis: implications for population demography. *European Journal of Human Genetics*, **12**, 855–63.

Francalacci, P., Bertranpetit, J., Calafell, F., and Underhill, P. A. (1996). Sequence diversity of the control region of mitochondrial DNA in Tuscany and its implications for the peopling of Europe. *American Journal of Physical Anthropology*, **100**, 443–60.

Fu, Y. X. (1997). Statistical tests of neutrality of mutations against population growth, hitchhiking and background selection. *Genetics*, **147**, 915–25.

Gonzalez, A. M., Brehm, A., Perez, J. A., *et al.* (2003). Mitochondrial DNA affinities at the Atlantic fringe of Europe. *American Journal of Physical Anthropology*, **120**, 391–404.

Gonzalez, A. M., Garcia, O., Larruga, J. M., and Cabrera, V. M. (2006). The mitochondrial lineage U8a reveals a Paleolithic settlement in the Basque country. *BMC Genomics*, **7**, 124.

Gonzalez, A. M., Karadsheh, N., Maca-Meyer, N., *et al.* (2008). Mitochondrial DNA variation in Jordanians and their genetic relationship to other Middle East populations. *Annals of Human Biology*, **35**, 212–231.

Hall, T. (2007). *BioEdit. 7.0.8 edn.* Carlsbad, CA: Ibis Biosciences.

Housley, R. A., Gamble, C. S., Street, M., and Pettitt, P. (1997). Radiocarbon evidence for the lateglacial human recolonisation of Northern Europe. *Proceedings of the Prehistoric Society*, **63**, 25–54.

Hudson, R. R. (1990). Gene genealogies and the coalescent process. *Oxford Surveys in Evolutionary Biology*, **7**, 1–44.

Izagirre, N. and De La Rua, C. (1999). An mtDNA analysis in ancient Basque populations: implications for haplogroup V as a marker for a major Paleolithic expansion from southwestern Europe. *American Journal of Human Genetics*, **65**, 199–207.

Izagirre, N., Alonso, S., and De La Rua, C. (2001). DNA analysis and the evolutionary history of the Basque population: a review. *Journal of Anthropological Research*, **57**, 325–44.

Jackes, M., Lubell, D., and Meiklejohn, C. (1997). On physical anthropological aspects of the Mesolithic-Neolithic transition in the Iberian Peninsula. *Current Anthropology*, **38**, 839–46.

Kimura, M. (1980). A simple method for estimating evolutionary rates of base substitutions through comparative studies of nucleotide sequences. *Journal of Molecular Evolution*, **16**, 111–20.

Kruskal, J. B. (1964). Nonmetric multidimensional scaling: a numerical method. *Psychometrika*, **29**, 28–42.

Lahr, M. M., Foley, R. A., and Pinhasi, R. (2000). Expected regional patterns of Mesolithic-Neolithic human population admixture in Europe based on archaeological evidence. In *Archaeogenetics: DNA and the Population Prehistory of Europe*, ed. C. Renfrew and K. Boyle, K. Cambridge, UK: McDonald Institute for Archaeological Research.

Lell, J. T. and Wallace, D. C. (2000). The peopling of Europe from the maternal and paternal perspectives. *American Journal of Human Genetics*, **67**, 1376–81.

Loogvali, E. L., Roostalu, U., Malyarchuk, B. A., *et al.* (2004). Disuniting uniformity: a pied cladistic canvas of mtDNA haplogroup H in Eurasia. *Molecular Biology and Evolution*, **21**, 2012–21.

Malyarchuk, B. A., Grzybowski, T., Derenko, M. V., *et al.* (2002). Mitochondrial DNA variability in Poles and Russians. *Annals of Human Genetics*, **66**, 261–83.

Malyarchuk, B. A., Grzybowski, T., Derenko, M. V., *et al.* (2003). Mitochondrial DNA variability in Bosnians and Slovenians. *Annals of Human Genetics*, **67**, 412–25.

Malyarchuk, B. A., Vanecek, T., Perkova, M. A., Derenko, M. V., and Sip, M. (2006). Mitochondrial DNA variability in the Czech population, with application to the ethnic history of Slavs. *Human Biology*, **78**, 681–96.

Manzano, C., Aguirre, A. I., Iriondo, M., *et al.* (1996). Genetic polymorphisms of the Basques from Gipuzkoa: genetic heterogeneity of the Basque population. *Annals of Human Biology*, **23**, 285–96.

McEvoy, B., Richards, M., Forster, P., and Bradley, D. G. (2004). The Longue Duree of genetic ancestry: multiple genetic marker systems and Celtic origins on the Atlantic facade of Europe. *American Journal of Human Genetics*, **75**, 693–702.

Mourant, A. E. (1947). The blood groups of the basques. *Nature*, **160**, 505–6.

Novelletto, A. (2007). Y chromosome variation in Europe: continental and local processes in the formation of the extant gene pool. *Annals of Human Biology*, **34**, 139–72.

Pereira, L., Richards, M., Goios, A., *et al.* (2005). High-resolution mtDNA evidence for the late-glacial resettlement of Europe from an Iberian refugium. *Genome Research*, **15**, 19–24.

Pierron, D., Chang, I., Arachiche, A., *et al.* (2011). Mutation rate switch inside Eurasian mitochondrial haplogroups: impact of selection and consequences for dating settlement in Europe. *PLoS ONE*, **6**, e21543.

Pinhasi, R., Foley, R. A., and Lahr, M. M. (2000). Spatial and temporal patterns in the Mesolithic-Neolithic archaeological record of Europe. In *Archaeogenetics: DNA and the Population Prehistory of Europe*, ed. C. Renfrew and K. Boyle. Cambridge, UK: McDonald Institute for Archaeological Research.

Richards, M., Corte-Real, H., Forster, P., *et al.* (1996). Paleolithic and neolithic lineages in the European mitochondrial gene pool. *American Journal of Human Genetics*, **59**, 185–203.

Richards, M., Macaulay, V., Torroni, A., and Bandelt, H. J. (2002). In search of geographical patterns in European mitochondrial DNA. *American Journal of Human Genetics*, **71**, 1168–74.

Rogers, A. R. (1995). Genetic evidence for a Pleistocene population explosion. *Evolution*, **49**, 608–15.

Rogers, A. R. and Harpending, H. (1992). Population growth makes waves in the distribution of pairwise genetic differences. *Molecular Biology and Evolution*, **9**, 552–69.

Rowold, D. J., Luis, J. R., Terreros, M. C., and Herrera, R. J. (2007). Mitochondrial DNA geneflow indicates preferred usage of the Levant Corridor over the Horn of Africa passageway. *Journal of Human Genetics*, **52**, 436–47.

Salas, A., Comas, D., Lareu, M. V., Bertranpetit, J., and Carracedo, A. (1998). mtDNA analysis of the Galician population: a genetic edge of European variation. *European Journal of Human Genetics*, **6**, 365–75.

Sampietro, M. L., Lao, O., Caramelli, D., *et al.* (2007). Palaeogenetic evidence supports a dual model of Neolithic spreading into Europe. *Proceedings of the Royal Society B: Biological Sciences*, **274**, 2161–7.

Santos, C., Montiel, R., Anglés, N., *et al.* (2004). Determination of human Caucasian mitochondrial DNA haplogroups by means of a hierarchical approach. *Human Biology*, **76**, 431–53.

Schneider, S. and Excoffier, L. (1999). Estimation of past demographic parameters from the distribution of pairwise differences when the mutation rates vary among sites: application to human mitochondrial DNA. *Genetics*, **152**, 1079–89.

Sherry, S. T., Rogers, A. R., Harpending, H., *et al.* (1994). Mismatch distributions of mtDNA reveal recent human population expansions. *Human Biology*, **66**, 761–75.

Sjodin, P. and Francois, O. (2011). Wave-of-advance models of the diffusion of the Y chromosome haplogroup R1b1b2 in Europe. *PLoS ONE*, **6**, e21592.

Straus, L. G. (1991a). Human geography of the Late Upper Paleolithic in Western Europe: present state of the question. *Journal of Anthropological Research*, **47**, 259–78.

Straus, L. G. (1991b). Southwestern Europe at the Last Glacial Maximum. *Current Anthropology*, **32**, 189–99.

Sturrock, K. and Rocha, J. (2000). A multidimensional scaling stress evaluation table. *Field Methods*, **12**, 49–60.

Sykes, B. (1999). The molecular genetics of European ancestry. *Philosophical Transactions of the Royal Society of London B: Biological Sciences*, **354**, 131–9.

Sykes, B. (2003). European ancestry: the mitochondrial landscape. In *The Widening Harvest: The Neolithic Transition in Europe*, ed. A. J. Ammerman and P. Biagi. Boston, MA: Archaeological Institute of America.

Tajima, F. (1989). Statistical method for testing the neutral mutation hypothesis by DNA polymorphism. *Genetics*, **123**, 585–95.

Torroni, A., Bandelt, H. J., D'urbano, L., *et al.* (1998). mtDNA analysis reveals a major late Paleolithic population expansion from southwestern to northeastern Europe. *American Journal of Human Genetics*, **62**, 1137–52.

Torroni, A., Bandelt, H. J., Macaulay, V., *et al.* (2001). A signal, from human mtDNA, of postglacial recolonization in Europe. *American Journal of Human Genetics*, **69**, 844–52.

Wells, R. S., Yuldasheva, N., Ruzibakiev, R., *et al.* (2001). The Eurasian heartland: a continental perspective on Y-chromosome diversity. *Proceedings of the National Academy of Sciences of the United States of America*, **98**, 10 244–9.

Young, K. L., Sun, G., Deka, R., and Crawford, M. H. (2011a). Autosomal short tandem repeat genetic variation of the Basques in Spain. *Croatian Medical Journal*, **52**, 372–83.

Young, K. L., Sun, G., Deka, R., and Crawford, M. H. (2011b). Paternal genetic history of the Basque population of Spain. *Human Biology*, **83**, Article 1.

Zilhao, J. (1998). On logical and empirical aspects of the Mesolithic-Neolithic transition in the Iberian Peninsula. *Current Anthropology*, **39**, 690–8.

Zilhao, J. (2000). From the Mesolithic to the Neolithic in the Iberian Peninsula. In *Europe's First Farmers*, ed. T. D. Price. Cambridge, UK: Cambridge University Press.

Zilhao, J. (2003). The Neolithic transition in Portugal and the role of demic diffusion in the spread of agriculture across West Mediterranean Europe. In *The Widening Harvest: The Neolithic Transition in Europe*, ed. A. J. Ammerman, and P. Biagi. Boston, MA: Archaeological Institute of America.

MOSES S. SCHANFIELD, RAQUEL A. LAZARIN,
AND ERIC SUNDERLAND

13

Consequences of migration among the Roma: immunoglobulin markers as a tool in investigating population relationships

INTRODUCTION

This volume is aimed at looking at the causes and consequences of human migration. Our chapter concentrates on the Roma of Europe. Although, as we will see, the causes of the migration of the Roma populations from their homeland in India is lost in time, there is a great deal of evidence of the consequences of their migration over time. Most studies of the Roma look at single systems. The following review includes linguistic and genetic data on the Roma. The genetic data are divided among single nucleotide polymorphism (SNP) disease markers, mitochondrial DNA (mtDNA) and non-recombinant Y-chromosome SNP (NRY SNP) markers, and autosomal STR data with a synthesis of the data on the immunoglobulin allotype ancestry informative SNP markers. Though some markers are less useful than others, the general genetic pattern traces the Roma to the northern India–Pakistan region.

The Roma (Gypsies) currently live in endogamous communities scattered throughout Europe and elsewhere, which have been described as a "conglomerate of genetically isolated found populations" (Kalaydjieva et al., 2001). According to the review by Kalaydjieva et al. (2001) the largest Roma populations live in Bulgaria, Hungary, Romania, Slovakia, and Spain, followed by significant populations in the Czech Republic, France, Germany, Greece, Italy, Macedonia, Montenegro, Russia. Serbia, and Turkey, with smaller populations in Albania, Austria, Belarus, the Benelux countries, Bosnia, Croatia, Poland, Portugal, Switzerland, Ukraine, and the

Causes and Consequences of Human Migration, ed. Michael H. Crawford and
Benjamin C. Campbell. Published by Cambridge University Press. © Cambridge
University Press 2012.

United Kingdom, while the smallest groups live in the peripheral Baltic States, Denmark, Finland, and Sweden. The term "Gypsy" comes from the concept that the population originated in Egypt and often refers to highly mobile populations. The Roma or Rom consider the term derogatory and most of the European Roma populations are sedentary. External terms for the Roma usually considered derogatory include Gypsy, Gitane, Gitano, Ijito, Jifti, Cingene, Sigane, Zigeuner, Sigojner, Tattare, and Tatere, while internal terms include Rom, Sinti, Mafia, and Calo or Kaalo. They are also named based on where they live – Vlah (Romania), Serbica (Serbia), Rom-ungro (Hungary) – and occupational classes – Lovari (horse), Kalderash (kettle), or Kalayde (tin smith) (Bakker, 2007).

For some time it has been speculated that the Roma originated in northwest India. Sometime prior to the eleventh century, these tribal people left India, traveled west through Persia and, likely, Armenia, and Turkey, reaching the Balkans by the eleventh century, spreading through Europe by the fifteenth century (Kalaydjieva *et al.*, 2001). There is little or no documentation for most of these journeys until Roma started appearing in records in the fifteenth and sixteenth centuries. Further, there is little agreement on how many migrations there were, or where they came from. There is some consensus that they came from northwestern India, and speculation that they were Rajputs, Punjabis, and/or a warrior class. There is a story with some documentation that the Persian monarch Behram Gour requested 12 000 musicians from an Indian king (Romani.org home page; www.rroma.org/). Other stories suggest they left India to escape from Muslim invaders. Other than anecdotal stories, there are no well-documented explanations for why the Roma left India.

The first indication that the Roma originated in India was linguistic. The connection of the Roma language to Indic was established in the eighteenth century with simultaneous discoveries in Britain, Germany, Hungary, and Russia (reviewed in Bakker, 2007), based on historical linguistics. According to Bakker (2007) the core vocabulary, almost all grammatical endings, and many sound correspondences are Indic, leading to the conclusion that Romani is an Indic language. Based on general consensus there are four major dialect groups: Vlax (Romania, and from there all over Europe); Balkan (found in Bulgaria, Croatia, Iran, Kosovo, Macedonia, Serbia, and Turkey); Central (Hungary and neighboring countries); and North conglomerate divided into Northeast and Northwest (all other peripheral areas of Western Europe from Italy to Finland). The approximate boundaries of these dialects are shown in Figure 13.1. Note: some isolates, especially those in Spain, do not fit into these four groups (Bakker, 2007).

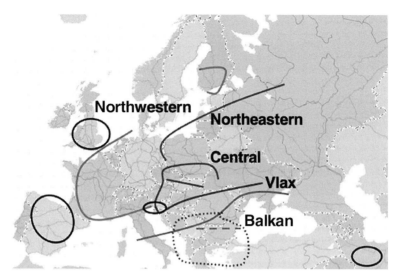

Figure 13.1 Consensus Romani dialects shown on European map. Approximate boundaries are indicated by the solid lines. The black circles represent isolated Romany dialects. (Taken from Bakker, 2007, with permission of the author.)

The inclusion of loan words from Dardic (northern India/Pakistan mountains), Persian and Kurdish, Armenian, Greek, and southern Slavic could indicate migration, or simply reflect words picked up. Interestingly there are no Arabic loan words (Bakker, 2007). Bakker (2007) has created a grammatical construction of Romani over time to coincide with possible migrations and concludes that the Roma arrived in Europe around 1200, and the dialects began when the Roma groups spread throughout Europe, with most groups settling by the middle of the sixteenth century when they started appearing in documents and census roles. Bakker, however, also believes there are several problems including: when did the ancestors of the Roma leave India, why did they leave, did they come from India, where did the Greek loan words come from and why are there no Arabic loan words in Romani (Bakker, 2007)? To this we can add: was there more than one migration, and did they come from more than one area? Bakker (2007) suggests that cultural evidence supports an Indian origin, as do genetic data.

It is difficult to delineate the Roma population in question for numerous reasons. Given the disparate groups of Roma found in any area it appears likely that there was not a single population of origin, though this is debated. Additionally, within a given area the population is subdivided into endogamous groups, often based on occupations or other criteria, which have undergone further drift, leading to additional microdifferentiation. Additionally, other nomadic people may be lumped together with the Roma by the host nation, which usually doesn't recognize distinct groups. This has resulted in historical references to Roma that could apply to various traveling peoples such as the "Tinkers" of Ireland or other "traveler" groups.

The Banjara of India are a nomadic people who share many cultural traits with the Roma. To date, the Banjara roam India along with other tribal travelers and are active in Roma politics (Kenrick, 2004). The Banjara are thought to be related to the Roma population in that they originated from the same progenitors. It is proposed that this early shared ancestry – located around Rajasthan – gave rise not only to the Roma, but also to the Kshatriya and the Sikhs (Mroz, 1991). However, at this point in time there have been no genetic studies looking at the relationships of the Banjara and Roma.

This link between the Roma and the upper castes of India has led to a belief that they originated in northwest India. The Aryan invasion of the Dravidian populations of India led to a strong caste division with the darker Dravidians being forced into subjugation and thus becoming the lower castes. The lighter skinned Aryans, by contrast, populated the upper castes, from which it is hypothesized that the Roma are descended (Mroz, 1991), though this is not universally held (Kalaydjieva *et al.*, 2001).

The Roma have faced rejection in many places they have attempted to make their home. Their attempts to keep their own laws within the tribe are often countermanded by the host nation (Kenrick, 2004). The Banjara have faced similar problems in India, with many attempts at forced sedentarization and close observation (Satya, 1997).

Populations of Roma have been studied in several European locations, including Bulgaria, Croatia, Czech Republic, France, Hungary, Romania, Slovakia, Spain, and Wales. Other populations exist throughout the world, including North America, and even Australia. Though Roma populations were persecuted along with Jews during World War II there are currently about 8–10 million Roma in Europe (Kalaydjieva *et al.*, 2001).

Since there is not a clearly documented history of the Roma, many have endeavored to investigate their genetic identity. Genetic studies on the Roma tend to fall into two groups, those looking at Mendelian genetic diseases in one or more populations of Roma to see if they have a common origin, or genetic studies to look at the anthropological genetic history of the Roma. The latter studies are often limited to a single lineage specific marker such as mtDNA or NRY markers.

Questions of interest include: How closely related are subgroups of Roma? How similar are their genetic profiles to the people of India? How similar are their genetic profiles to the people of the host nation? Gresham *et al.* (2001) found that there is significant substructuring and evidence of separate admixture events leading to the currently recognized groups of Roma in Bulgaria using Y and mtDNA; however, no comparisons were made with Indian populations. Kalaydjieva *et al.* in a review of genetic studies on the Roma looked at the relationship between Roma, northwest Indian, and European populations using ABO, RH, MN, and Haptoglobin data (Kalaydjieva *et al.*, 2001). The tree generated did not show consistent associations, in that Hungarian, Welsh, Slovenian, and Swedish Roma were closest to northwest Indian Punjabi and Rajputs, while British Roma and Slovakian Roma were further from northwest India than Europeans. Other studies of Roma have repeatedly shown them to be more closely related to the people of India than to their local neighbors (Harper *et al.*, 1977; van Loghem *et al.*, 1985). More recent studies have used the lineage specific mtDNA (Malyarchuk *et al.*, 2005; Martinović-Klarić *et al.*, 2009; Mendizabal *et al.*, 2011) and NRY (Pamjav *et al.*, 2011; Zalán *et al.*, 2011) markers and some single gene diseases to trace Roma origins to India (Kalaydjieva *et al.*, 2005). These studies have indicated that Roma populations share mtDNA haplotype M5a1, and the NRY haplotypes H1a-M82 with Indian populations. In addition, a single gene disease causing autosomal recessive myasthenia (CHRNE 1267delG) maps back to a common ancestor in India or Pakistan (Kalaydjieva *et al.*, 2005), again supporting a common genetic origin in India.

However, with the exception of genetic disease SNPs, there has been limited use of nuclear markers. With the exception of the immunoglobulin allotype SNPS (see below), only STR loci have been used. Unfortunately, STR loci are of limited use in doing ancestry studies (Gusmão *et al.*, 2010; Novokmet and Pavčec, 2007). Novokmet and Pavčec (2007), using the 15 STR loci in Identifiler (Applied Biosystems, Foster City, CA), found that Romani and European Roma had lower F_{ST} values among each other than their European non-Roma populations. In contrast, Gusmão *et al.* (2010) again using Identifiler (Applied Biosystems, Foster City, CA), using different numbers of available loci, starting with Portuguese Roma, and comparing them with both Europeans and Indian populations, found that Croatian, Macedonian, Portuguese, and Slovakian Roma were in the top half of a PCA plot with the Indian populations while the host non-Roma populations were in the bottom half, again suggesting a closer relationship to Indian populations than to Europeans. These data clearly are in conflict with data from mtDNA and NRY markers.

Unfortunately, Gusmão *et al.* (2010) attempted to estimate admixture in the Roma populations using STR data and generated admixture estimates indicating that the Roma are largely European; as this contradicts marriage patterns and other data, it can be attributed to the choice of model used (see below).

The apparent maintenance of Indian genetic identity is likely due to the endogamous nature of most Roma marriages. Harper *et al.* (1977) studies of blood group phenotypes for European Roma show differences between Roma groups. However, there was greater similarity between Roma groups and Indian populations than between the Roma populations and the host communities; much of this is the same data that Kalaydjieva *et al.* (2001) used. Nevertheless, almost all studies indicate that there is extreme microdifferentiation/drift among Roma populations in the same area. Data from Klarić *et al.* (2009) on NRY SNPS from two Croatian Roma populations indicate that there are marked differences in allele frequencies for E1b1b1a (a Middle eastern haplogroup), I1 and R1a (European), but little variation in H1a with a frequency of approximately 50% and a direct link to India. Using European NRY haplogroups there is significantly less European admixture detected than that suggested by Gusmão *et al.*, 2010.

Studies of endogamy and inbreeding in Roma populations are quite limited with only two studies at the marriage/population level of inbreeding in Roma (Ferák *et al.*, 1987; Martin and Gamella, 2005). Ferák *et al.* (1987) looked at 444 individuals from 101 families in four villages and found an inbreeding coefficient of 0.017, the highest reported in Europe. Martin and Gamella (2005) looked at 1267 marriages in 23 Andalusian towns and found an $F = 0.0074$, which they reported to be significantly higher than Spanish and European data. Several studies have reported inbreeding from autosomal recessive disease pedigrees (Ferák *et al.*, 1982; Harper and Roberts, 1988), with the F values between those found in the two studies listed above. The authors could find no specific studies of exogamy rates within the Roma communities; however, both Cohn (1973) and Martin and Gamella (2005) suggest that it is infrequent, and that the children of these matings may or may not be welcome in the Roma community depending on the residence of the individuals.

The results of studies of specific genetic diseases among Roma populations support the concept of multiple founding populations with marked genetic drift among them. Examples include the variation in the cystic fibrosis Δ508 mutation between groups of Hungarian Roma (Endreffy *et al.*, 2002); a new mutation causing Gitelman syndrome (Coto *et al.*, 2004); a high frequency of the uncommon W24X mutation in deaf Roma which is shared with Indian and Pakistani populations but uncommon in Europeans (Minárik *et al.*, 2003); Galacktokinase mutations supporting drift (Kalaydjieva *et al.*, 1999); and mutant PKU alleles in Wales, UK (Tyfield *et al.*, 1989). An extensive review of genetic studies of the Roma can be found in Kalaydjieva *et al.* (2001) and in the extensive study of within and between group mutations in Roma groups by Morar *et al.* (2004).

IMMUNOGLOBULIN ALLOTYPES

Immunoglobulin allotypes have been used extensively in the latter half of the twentieth century as serological identifiers of populations prior to the development of mtDNA and Y-chromosome markers. Like the mtDNA and NRY markers, the heavy chain markers (GM) are SNPs inherited in haplotypes; however, there is a low level of recombination of these autosomal markers. The KM markers are much simpler auto-somal SNPs. Population studies indicate that GM and KM polymorphism can be used to differentiate populations (Schanfield, 1980). The presence, absence, and variation in frequencies of haplotypes in a sample can indicate ethnic ancestry, specially the GM heavy chain allotypes. This makes the immunoglobulin allotypes a useful system for analyzing the relationships between various Roma groups, host populations, and possible Indian ancestors. Previous studies of Roma for immunoglobulin allotypes consist of limited data published by Gyódi *et al.* (1981) on G1M A, X and F, and KM 1; a study by van Loghem *et al.* (1985) looked at the relationship of Hungarian Roma to populations from India; and a study of mixed Roma collected in France (Daveau *et al.*, 1975). This chapter represents the first attempt to use immunoglobulin allotypes on Slovakian and Welsh Roma and to integrate all of the data into a single synthesis.

Immunoglobulin allotyping was performed on Roma samples collected in Slovakia (primarily eastern Slovakia) provided by Professor Vladimir Ferák, Department of Molecular Biology, Comensius University, Bratislava, Slovakia, and in Wales (Harper *et al.*, 1977) ("Gypsies" of non-Roma ancestry were excluded), as well as samples from neighboring Welsh populations (Caucasian) generated as previously described (Schanfield *et al.*, 2008). These data were compared with published data for European Roma and from northern India based on location of the

Rom samples and speculation on the origin of the Roma. Data from northern India include Koli, a scheduled caste from Himachal Pradesh (Papiha *et al.*, 1996), Punjabis and Sikhs from the Punjab (Daveau *et al.*, 1980; Field *et al.*, 1988), and samples from Delhi consisting of individuals from Punjab, Haryana, Delhi, and western Uttar Pradesh and divided into caste groups (Schanfield and Kirk, 1981). Though articles on Roma (cited above) stated the origin of Roma to be in northwestern India, no consistent definition could be found, although there appears to be some consensus of northern India – thus that area was chosen, but as we shall see it is not uniform. In addition, samples from southern India including Maharashtra living in Mumbai and Tamil Nadu (Schanfield and Kirk, 1981) and a mixed sample from the Andhra Pradesh (van Loghem *et al.*, 1985) were also used. Nomeclature follows Ropartz *et al.* (1976) and Shows *et al.* (1987).

Our initial analysis was to consider regional variation using the European Roma, European control populations, and northwest Indian population samples to represent regions. Expected heterozygosity for the GM haplotypes were calculated using $1 - \Sigma p_i^2$, while $2p(1 - p)$ was used for KM. Within region variation (F_R), reduction in heterozygosity within regions (F_{WR}), reduction in heterozygosity between regions (F_{RT}), and total reduction in heterozygosity (F_{ST}) were calculated as described in Nei (1987) and Nei and Kumar (2000). The significance of F statistics was calculated using $2NF$, where N is the harmonic mean of the sample sizes as suggested by Nei (1987). Due to the limitation of F analysis, cluster analysis was performed on the principal components analysis reduced GM and KM frequencies.

Extraction of data using principal components analysis, hierarchical cluster analysis, and K-means analysis was performed using the Statistica (release 7 and 8; Statsoft, Inc). Hierarchical cluster analysis was performed on a Squared Euclidian distance matrix in which the factor scores from the PCA analysis were used as independent variables, using Ward's method, which assumes no genetic relationship and is based on analysis of variance. The significance of the clusters could be evaluated using K-means.

The GM haplotype and KM allotype frequencies for the Slovak Roma, Welsh Roma, and Welsh Caucasians are presented in Table 13.1. Data from the French and Hungarian Roma and the other reference populations are also presented in Table 13.1. A few generalizations comparing the data in Table 13.1 can be made. The frequency of the Indo-European marker haplotype $GM^*F\ B$ is significantly higher in the European reference populations (mean 0.724, range 0.639–0.777) than

Table 13.1. *Comparative data for immunoglobulin allotypes in Roma samples, host country samples, and northwestern Indian and other Indian samples*

	N	*A G	*X G	*F B	*A T	*AF B	*A B	Other	KM*1	Source
Roma										
Slovakia (RO SL)	116	0.211	0.000	0.422	0.013	0.293	0.060	0.000	0.031	1
Hungary (RO HU)	177	0.079	0.006	0.605	0.045	0.251	0.014	0.000	0.017	2
Wales (RO WA)	74	0.188	0.137	0.527	0.048	0.095	0.000	0.006	0.140	1
France (RO FR)	226	0.169	0.041	0.522	0.067	0.177	0.022	0.000	0.118	3
Country of residence controls										
Slovakia (SLOV)	71	0.120	0.049	0.831	0.000	0.000	0.000	0.000	0.043	4
Hungary (HUNG)	184	0.147	0.049	0.777	0.014	0.005	0.003	0.005	0.073	5
Wales (WALE)	144	0.228	0.112	0.639	0.000	0.007	0.010	0.003	0.110	1
France (FREN)	47	0.202	0.096	0.702	0.000	0.000	0.000	0.000	0.077	4
Northern India										
Koli (KOLI), (Himachal Pradesh)	52	0.335	0.049	0.515	0.067	0.023	0.000	0.010	0.059	6
Punjabis (PUNJ), (Punjab)	101	0.279	0.142	0.396	0.000	0.149	0.010	0.022	0.056	7
Sikhs (SIKH), (Punjab)	103	0.252	0.149	0.459	0.094	0.021	0.025	0.000	0.061	8
Brahmin (BRAH), Delhi	26	0.135	0.096	0.596	0.019	0.000	0.154	0.000	0.080	9
Kshatriya (KSHA), Delhi	72	0.211	0.044	0.547	0.000	0.039	0.159	0.000	0.078	9
Vaishya (VAIS), Delhi	21	0.325	0.050	0.550	0.000	0.000	0.075	0.000	0.100	9
Shudra (SHUD), Delhi	32	0.329	0.078	0.500	0.000	0.000	0.093	0.000	0.079	9
Southern India										
Maharashtra (MAHA)	124	0.348	0.144	0.425	0.004	0.019	0.061	0.000	0.062	9
Andhra Pradesh (ANDR)	629	0.220	0.103	0.331	0.046	0.279	0.011	0.010	0.081	2
Tamil Nadu (TAMI)	170	0.426	0.198	0.296	0.014	0.012	0.052	0.000	0.079	9

Capitalized acronym in parenthesis is the designator for the populations in Figure 13.2.

Sources: 1. Present study; 2. van Loghem *et al.*, 1985; 3. Daveau *et al.*, 1975; 4. Stevenson and Schanfield, 1981; 5. Schanfield *et al.*, 1975; 6. Papiha *et al.*, 1996;
7. Daveau *et al.*, 1980; 8. Field *et al.*, 1988; 9. Schanfield and Kirk, 1981.

in the Roma populations (mean 0.519, range 0.422–0.605) or in the Northern Indian populations (omitting Delhi, see below) (mean 0.457, range 0.396–0.515). The frequency in south India is even lower (mean 0.351, range 0.296–0.425). The northern Asian marker haplotype $GM^*A\ T$ is found in higher frequencies in the Northern Indian (0.054) and Roma populations (0.043) while it is only present in a very low frequency (0.004) in the European non-Roma populations and other Indian populations, with the exception of the Andhra Pradesh, which is a mixed sample including Asian tribals (van Loghem $et\ al.$, 1985). Similarly, the Southeast Asian marker haplotype $GM^*A,F\ B$ is also higher in Roma (mean 0.204) and Northwest Indian populations (mean 0.064), than in other Indian populations, with the exception of the Andhra Pradesh. The archaic $GM^*A\ B$ haplotype is highly variable across populations and in India, though Schanfield and Kirk (1981) suggested it might be a central Asian marker.

The average KM^*1 frequencies are similar in all of the populations. However, as can be seen in Table 13.2. there is a great deal of heterogeneity among the Roma populations for all of the GM haplotypes and KM^*1. This type of variation makes it difficult to directly compare populations.

The results of the F analysis are found in Table 13.2. Northern India was limited to Koli, Punjabi, and Sikhs after PCA and cluster analysis clearly indicated that the Delhi population was different (see Figure 13.2). It should be noted that there is a marked interaction between sample size and F, such that if the sample size is large, highly significant χ^2 can be generated by F values well below Wright's 0.05 threshold for modest genetic differentiation (Wright, 1965). The internal variation (F_R) among the four Roma samples ($F_R = 0.025$) is approximately 30% greater than that of the European host countries ($F_R = 0.019$), and approaches significance. The Roma value is also greater than that seen among the three northern Indian populations listed above ($F_R = 0.016$). When the European host populations and northern Indians are compared with the Roma samples, two very different patterns emerge. In the Europeans versus Roma comparison there is a much higher between-group variation ($F_{RT} = 0.041$) that reaches significance at $p = 0.002$, when compared with the within-group variation ($F_{WR} = 0.023$), while the combined $F_{ST} = 0.062$ is highly significant ($p = 0.0001$). In contrast, in Roma versus Northern India the within-group variation ($F_{WR} = 0.021$) is greater than the between-group variation ($F_{RT} = 0.016$) with neither significant, such that the combined $F_{ST} = 0.036$ is also not significant. For the KM locus the only significant deviation occurs among the KM^*1 frequencies in the Roma ($F_R = 0.040$, $p = 0.0015$) (see discussion).

Table 13.2. F analysis of variance comparing European Roma, European host, and Indian reference populations

GM	N*	*A G	*X G	*F B	*A T	*AF B	*AZ B	Other	He	F_R	p
Among Europeans	84	0.174	0.077	0.737	0.004	0.003	0.004	0.002	0.420	0.019	0.074
Among European Roma	124	0.162	0.046	0.519	0.043	0.204	0.024	0.002	0.658	0.025	0.013
Among northern Indians	77	0.289	0.113	0.457	0.054	0.064	0.012	0.011	0.688	0.016	0.117
GM	N*	F_{WR}	p	F_{RT}	p	F_{ST}	p				
Europeans vs. Roma	118	0.023	0.021	**0.041**	0.002*	**0.062**	0.0001*				
Northern India vs. Roma	99	0.021	0.043	0.016	0.077	0.036	0.0075				
KM	N*	KM*1	He	F_R	p						
Among European	84	0.076	0.140	0.008	0.245						
Among European Roma	124	0.076	0.141	**0.040**	0.0015*						
Among NW India	77	0.059	0.110	0.000	0.913						
KM	N*	F_{WR}	p	F_{RT}	p	F_{ST}	p				
Europeans vs. Roma	118	0.024	0.017	0.000	0.916	0.0242	0.017				
NW India vs. Roma	99	0.025	0.026	0.001	0.628	0.027	0.022				

European Roma and Europeans include data from France, Hungary, Slovakia, and Wales; Northern India includes Koli, Punjabi, and Sikhs.
N* indicates harmonic mean of sample sizes. Bonferroni corrected $\alpha' = 0.0028$ (0.05/18). Only P values less than 0.003 are considered significant and have an asterisk and are in bold print.

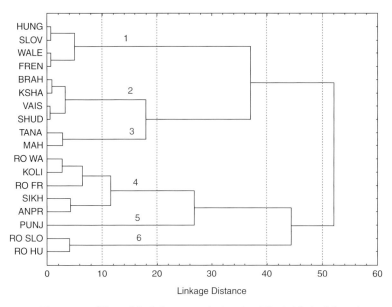

Figure 13.2 Hierarchical cluster analysis using Wards Method (based on analysis of variance and making no genetic assumptions of the populations) using a Squared Euclidian distance matrix of orthogonal factor scores. The numbers (1–6) in the figure represent the highest F value for major splits. The figure is divided into two distinct clusters, each of which has two components. The upper main cluster includes the European host countries and a cluster that includes the Indian samples from Delhi (Northwest India), Maharastra, and the Tamil Nadu (see Table 13.1). The lower cluster also has two components consisting of the Roma populations from Wales and France and the Sikh together, with the Koli and Punjabi of Northern India and Andhra Pradesh separated out and the Slovak and Hungarian Roma as a separate group among the Northwest Indians and Roma.

Using principal components analysis (PCA) it is possible to reduce a large number of alleles into uncorrelated synthetic variables which can be used in hierarchical cluster analysis to see relationships among populations. The results of this analysis are presented in Figure 13.2. PCA reduced the seven GM haplotypes and KM to four significant factors which accounted for 81.3% of the total variation in the genetic matrix. Factor 1 accounts for 27.2% of the variance and is positively loaded on the Eurasian haplotypes $GM^*A\ G$ and $GM^*X\ G$ and negatively loaded on the Indo-European marker haplotype $GM^*F\ B$. Factor 2 accounts for 24.3% of the variance and is strongly negatively loaded on the Southeast Asian marker haplotype $GM^*A,F\ B$. Factor 3 accounts for 17.3% of the variance and is positively loaded on the archaic haplotype $GM^*A\ B$ and negatively loaded on KM^*1. Factor 4 accounts for 12.5% of the variance and is positively loaded on the Northeast Asian marker haplotype $GM^*A\ T$.

Figure 13.2. is the graphic representation of the hierarchical cluster analysis using Ward's method on a Squared Euclidian distance matrix of factor scores. K-means analysis indicates that the maximum F was at six groups. In Figure 13.2 these branches are numbered 1–6. The major division between branches "3" and "4" with a deep root places the three Northern Indian populations with the Roma samples, and separates this group from the branch which contains the European populations on one branch and the other Indian populations on the other. It should be noted that the split labeled "6" has the Slovakian and Hungarian Roma separated from the other Roma and Northern Indian population, suggesting a deep separation of these two populations from the French and Welsh Roma. Similarly, the separation of the Europeans from other Indian populations appears deeply rooted. The overall topology of the tree appears to be geographically related, as the physically closest populations cluster together, even if significantly different. The clustering of the Andra Pradesh sample with the Koli of Himachal Pradesh is the only grouping error in the clusters and is best explained by the high frequency of $GM^*A\ T$ and $GM^*A,F\ B$ in Andra Pradesh (see Table 13.1), which makes it similar to the Roma and Northern Indian populations based on "factor 2" scores. This may be due to non-Hindu East Asian tribal populations in the Andhra Pradesh (van Loghem *et al*., 1985).

DISCUSSION

The divergence seen in the Roma populations presented here could be the result of several factors including admixture, multiple migrations from India, or differentiation due to secondary migration once in Europe. If admixture with host populations is the cause of differentiations, as suggested by Gresham *et al.* (2001) there would be an expectation that the local Roma populations would look more like their host populations. This is not seen in Figure 13.2; in contrast the European host populations cluster together, while the Roma populations cluster with the Northern Indian samples. Another possible source of differentiation could be that the groups represented originated from different seminal tribes that left India at different times, or that when the Roma left the Balkans to go to different areas of Europe there was significant sampling error in the founding populations. Certainly, the Y haplotype data on the Croatian Bayash indicate the marked heterogeneity that

can be seen at a local level, though that study provides little information on the broader question (Klaric *et al.*, 2009). The clustering of
geographically proximal populations suggests that there were significant differences in the founding populations. However, it cannot be
determined whether these differences represent different source Indian
populations that due to temporal differences in arrival time in Europe
went to different places or whether they represent sampling variation
that occurred in the Balkans in the populations that went north rather
than west.

Interestingly, the genetic association seen in Figure 13.2 correlates
fairly well with the linguistic differentiation, with the Hungarian and
Slovak Roma speaking the "Central" dialect while the French and Welsh
Roma appear to be more or less associated with the "Northwestern"
dialect. The differentiation of the Roma and Northern Indian populations (Koli, Punjabi, and Sikhs) from the other Indian populations is
characterized by both Northeast Asian gene flow (probably from Tibet
or Moguls) and Southeast Asian gene flow, but little of the archaic *GM*A B*
haplotype. The variation in gene flow in these samples can reflect sampling variation, as well as sample size variation. Some haplotypes are
consistent with the anthropological evidence of dispersion, but others
vary. These factors in combination with the millennia that the Roma
have been separated make genetic relationships difficult to identify.

A more recent study of Bulgarian Roma populations of the Vlax
linguistic group looked at mtDNA, the Y chromosome, and eight autosomal loci (Chaix *et al.*, 2004). Coalescent-based methods show that these
groups underwent two divergence events – one in the seventeenth
century and one in the nineteenth century. Another study looking at
Hungarian Roma found that although STR loci allele frequencies were
different between Roma and other Hungarian populations, the Roma
could not be differentiated by their phenotype frequencies (Furedi *et al.*,
1997) pointing up the weakness of STR loci in this type of study.
Although these microsatellite markers have not been shown to be as
robust as immunoglobulins at differentiating populations by ethnicity,
they are widely available and may begin to shed more light on the trail
of the Roma as more studies are done. In contrast, the study by Klaric
et al. (2009) though demonstrating marked local variation among male
lineages in Croatian Bayash Roma, and indications of gene flow from
Balkan males, found the majority of Y haplogroups to be of Indian
origin, supporting the Indian origin hypothesis.

Data generated by the immunoglobulin allotypes and the literature
allow us to test theories of Roma origins. From the immunoglobulin

allotypes several conclusions can be reached: There is more heterogeneity among Roma ($F_R = 0.025$, $p = 0.013$) than among the resident European populations ($F_R = 0.019$, $p = 0.074$) or the Northern Indians ($F_R = 0.016$, $p = 0.117$); there is significant heterogeneity between European Roma and their country of residence ($F_{ST} = 0.062$, $p = 0.0001$); however there is only a slight increase in heterogeneity when comparing European Roma ($F_R = 0.025$, $p = 0.013$) to Northwest India plus the Roma ($F_{ST} = 0.036$, $p = 0.0075$). Kalaydjieva *et al.* (2001) found an F_{ST} of 3.47% among a large series of Roma tested for ABO, RH, MN, and Haptoglobin, but a lower F_{ST} between Roma and Europeans (1.81%). The European Roma F_{ST} of 1.81% for blood groups and Haptoglobin is much smaller than the F_{ST} of 5.7% for the GM haplotypes, suggesting that the blood group markers used may not be as useful in this type of study. Note: the F_{ST} values are of more interest than the probabilities as the probabilities are totally driven by the sample sizes or harmonic mean sample sizes. Values of F_{ST} above 0.05 are starting to represent increased microdifferentiantion.

The *F* analysis (Table 13.2) and Figure 13.2 clearly address the question of how much variation there is among the Roma of Europe. Other studies have looked at intra-country variation and have found significant microdifferentiation (Chaix *et al.*, 2004). At the macro level, there appears to be significant variation among the Roma populations of Europe at multiple levels. The differentiation of the central European (Slovak and Hungarian) Roma from the Western European Roma (French and Welsh) certainly supports genetic differentiation between regions; however, there is also variation within each region, as can be seen in Figure 13.2 and Table 13.2. Though not significant in the *F* analysis, these differences are highly significant in the *K*-means analysis, indicating that the regional populations were founded by distinct groups followed by further microdifferentiantion due to local drift. The significant heterogeneity at the KM locus in Roma parallels the regional differences in frequencies between the central European Roma and Western European Roma ($F_{RT} = 0.039$, $p = 0.0018$, $F_{ST} = 0.040$, $p = 0.0015$) (see Tables 13.1, 13.2).

Note: the samples tested for immunoglobulin allotypes were not subdivided by band or region within countries and therefore represent a country average, while many of the mtDNA and NRY studies are subdivided within countries, providing a different picture. A differentiation based on differences in blood group B was proposed by Clarke (1973), in which on linguistic grounds Roma were divided into a high frequency of blood group B or a low frequency. However, Clarke

(1973) had access to limited data. In the more extensive tabulation of ABO data presented by Harper *et al.* (1977), the association does not hold, though there is some association: Hungary and Czechoslovakia have high frequencies of blood type B, while Wales and Britain have low frequencies. However Roma from France can have high or low frequencies of blood type B, with a within France $F_{ST} = 0.047$, $p = 0.016$ (data not presented). Because of variation within France it is not clear whether the blood group B frequencies totally parallel GM and KM.

The Roma are not closely related to their European host populations. As seen in Table 13.2 and in Figure 13.2, genetic differences between the Roma populations and their host European populations exceed $F = 0.05$, Wright's threshold for the beginning of significant microdifferentiation ($F_{ST} = 0.062$, $p = 0.0001$). Based on Figure 13.2 the Welsh and French Roma are closest to the Sikh population, while Slovakian and Hungarian Roma are quite disparate from the Indian and other Roma populations, but still within the northern Indian/Roma cluster.

These data support a multiple origin model of either multiple Roma populations originating in northern India with genetic drift among populations following arrival in their current place of residence or significant sampling variation between the founders going to central Europe versus Western Europe from a central source in the Balkans. Additional allotype data from different European Roma populations are needed to test the two hypotheses. The suggestion that the Roma are related to upper caste Aryans is not really testable based on the samples available. Though Schanfield and Kirk (1981) found that upper caste Brahmin and Kshatriya in various areas of India had some similarities to each other, the regional differences were more profound. The closest high caste samples studied are a mixed group from Delhi, where high caste (Brahmin and Kshatriya) individuals clustered together and were significantly different from the low caste (Vaish and Shudra). However, all of these samples cluster more closely with the other Indian samples and do not cluster with the northern Indian and Roma samples. Thus, if the Roma represent Aryan invaders, they represent Aryan invaders that have had little or no gene flow from Dravidian populations but have had gene flow from Northeast and Southeast Asian populations, genetically differentiating them from current Indian caste populations. Unfortunately, in the absence of data on the Banjara it is not possible to look at the relationship between them and the Roma.

CONCLUSION

In conclusion we have been able to shed almost no light on the causes of the migration of the ancestors of the Roma, or how many migrations there were. Nevertheless, we can say that the consequences have been microdifferentiation and drift leading to variable frequencies and variation in the occurrence of uncommon Mendelian diseases in the various endogamous Roma populations in Europe. This probably originated in the cultural isolation by host populations and internal endogamy of the Roma. Though it has been suggested that the Roma are highly inbred, the study of marriage or genetic disease provides little supporting evidence. Thus, the Roma of Europe appear to be a good model for the study of a highly differentiated, large population that has undergone subdivision and drift over at least the last 500 years.

ACKNOWLEDGMENTS

The authors would like to express their gratitude to Professor Vladimir Ferák, Department of Molecular Biology, Comensius University, Bratislava, Slovakia, for the serum specimens from the Slovak Roma, his valuable comments on the manuscript, and the English translation of his study on inbreeding in the Slovakian Roma. The authors would like to thank Post Doctoral Fellow Rebecca Brown, and summer intern Daren Valentine for assistance in allotyping samples and the anonymous reviewer for the useful comments.

REFERENCES

Bakker, P. (2007). Roma: reconstruction migrations with linguistic and genetic data. Presented at Workshop on Migration, Ile de Porquerolles, France, Sept. 5–7, 2007 http://lacito.vjf.cnrs.fr/colloque/diaporamas/bakker.pdf

Chaix, R., Austerlitz, F., Kalaydjieva, L., and Heyer, E. (2004). Vlax Roma history: what do coalescent-based methods tell us? *European Journal of Human Genetics*, **12**, 285–92.

Clarke, V. (1973). Genetic factors in some British gypsies. In *Genetic Variation in Britain*, ed. D. F. Roberts and E. Sunderland, pp. 181–195. London: Taylor and Francis.

Cohn, W. (1973). *The Gypsies*. Menlo Park, CA: Addison-Wesley.

Coto, E., Rodriguez, J., Jeck, N., *et al.* (2004). A new mutation (intron 9+1G>T) in the SLC12A3 gene is linked to Gitelmen syndrome in Roms. *Kidney International*, **65**, 25–9.

Daveau, M., Rivat, L., Lalouel, J. M., *et al.* (1980). Frequencies of Gm and Km allotypes in the population of Singapore, Sri Lanka and Punjabis in North India. *Human Heredity*, **30**, 237–44.

Daveau, M., L. Rivat, Langaney, A., Feingold, N., and Ropartz, C. (1975). Gm and Inv allotypes in a Gypsy sample. *Human Heredity*, **25**, 135–43.

Endreffy, E., Nemeth, K., Fekete, G., Gyurkovits, K., and Stankovics, J. (2002). Molecular genetic diagnostic difficulties in two Hungarian Gypsy samples with cystic fibrosis. *International Journal of Human Genetics*, **2**, 41–4.

Ferák, V., Genčik, A., and Genčikova, A. (1982). Population genetic aspects of primary congenital glaucoma. II: Fitness, parental consanguinity, founder effect. *Human Genetics*, **61**, 198–200.

Ferák, V., D. Siváková, D., and Sieglová, Z. (1987). The Slovak gypsies (Romany) – a population with the highest coefficient of inbreeding in Europe (Slovakian). *Braisl Lek Listy*, **87**, 168–75.

Field, S. L., Surje, S., and Ray, A. (1988). Immunoglobulin (GM and KM) allotypes in the Sikh population of India. *American Journal of Physical Anthropology*, **75**, 31–5.

Furedi, S., Angyal M., Kozma, Z., *et al.* (1997). Semi-automatic DNA profiling in a Hungarian Romany population using the STR loci HumVWFA31, HumTH01, HumTPOX, and HumCSF1PO. *International Journal of Legal Medicine*, **110**, 184–7.

Gresham, D., Morar, B., Underhill, P. A., *et al.* (2001). Origins and divergence of the Roma (Gypsies). *American Journal of Human Genetics*, **69**, 1314–31.

Gusmão, A., Valente, C., Gomes, V., *et al.* (2010) A genetic historical sketch of European Gypsies: the perspective from autosomal markers. *American Journal of Physical Anthropology*, **141**, 507–14.

Gyódi, E., Tauszik, T., Petranyi, G., *et al.* (1981). The HLA antigen distribution in the gypsy population of Hungary. *Tissue Antigens*, **18**, 1–12.

Harper, P. and Roberts, D. F. (1988). Mating patterns and genetic disease. In *Human Mating Patterns*, ed. C. G. N. Mascie-Taylor and A. J. Boyce, pp. 169–182. Cambridge, UK, Cambridge University Press.

Harper, P. S., Williams, E. M., and Sunderland, E. (1977). Genetic markers in Welsh Gypsies. *Journal of Medical Genetics*, **14**, 177–82.

Kalaydjieva, L., Gresham, D., and Calafell, F. (2001). Genetic studies of the Roma (Gypsies): a review. *BMC Medical Genetics*, **2**, 5.

Kalaydjieva, L., Morar, B., Chaix, R., and Tang, H. (2005) A newly discovered founder population: the Roma/Gypsies. *BioEssays*, **27**, 1084–94.

Kalaydjieva, L., Perez-Lezuan, D., Angelicheva, D., *et al.* (1999). A founder mutation in the GK1 gene is responsible for galactokinase deficiency in Roma (Gypsies). *American Journal of Human Genetics*, **65**, 1299–307.

Kenrick, D. (2004). *Gypsies: From the Ganges to the Thames*. Hatfield, UK: University of Hertfordshire Press.

Klaric, I. M., Salihovic, M. P, Lauc, L., *et al.* (2009). Dissecting the molecular architecture and origin of Bayash Romani patrilineages: genetic influences from South-Asia and the Balkans. *American Journal of Physical Anthropology*, **138**, 333–42.

Malyarchuk, B. A., Grzybowski, T., Derenko, M. V., Czarny, J., and Miścicka-Śliwka, D. (2005). Mitochondrial DNA diversity in the Polish Roma. *American Journal of Human Genetics*, **70**, 195–206.

Martin, E. and Gamella, J. F. (2005). Marriage practices and ethnic differentiation: the case of Spanish Gypsies (1870–2000). *History of the Family*, **10**, 45–63.

Martinović-Klarić, I., Peričić-Salihović, M., Barać-Lauc, L., *et al.* (2009). Dissecting the molecular architecture and origin of Bayash Romani patrilineages: genetic influences from South-Asia and Balkans. *American Journal of Physical Anthropology*, **138**, 333–42.

Mendizabal, I., Valente, C., Gusmão, A., *et al.* (2011). Reconstructing the Indian origin and dispersal of European Roma: a maternal genetic perspective. *PLoS One*, **6**, e15988; doi:10.1371/journal.pone.0015988.

Minárik, G., Ferák, V., Ferákova, E., *et al.* (2003). High frequency of GJB2 mutation W24X among Slovak Romany (Gypsy) patients with non-syndromic hearing loss (NSHL). *General Physiology and Biophysics*, **22**, 549–56.

Morar, B., Gresham, D., Angelicheva, D., *et al.* (2004). Mutation history of the Roma/Gypsies. *American Journal of Human Genetics*, **75**, 596–609.

Mroz, L. (1991). Problems of the origin of gypsies: the Banjara and the Gadulia Lohar peoples of Rajasthan, India. *Ethnologia Polona*, **15/16**, 81–103.

Nei, M. (1987). *Molecular Evolutionary Genetics*. New York: Columbia University Press

Nei, M. and Kumar, S. (2000). *Molecular Evolution and Phylogenetics*. New York: Oxford University Press.

Novokmet, N. and Pavčec, Z. (2007). Genetic polymorphism of 15 AmpFlSTR identifiler loci in Romani populations from Northwestern Croatia. *Forensic Science International*, **168**, e43–e46 (online publication).

Pamjav, H., Zalán, A., Béres, J., Nagy, M., and Chang, Y. M. (2011). Genetics structure of the paternal lineage of the Roma people. *American Journal of Physical Anthropology*, **145**, 21–9.

Papiha, S. S., Schanfield, M. S., and Chakraborty, R. (1996). Immunoglobulin allotypes and estimation of genetic admixture among populations of Kinnaur District, Himachal Pradesh, India. *Human Biology*, **68** 777–94.

Ropartz, C., Schanfield, M. S., and Steinberg, A. G. (1976). Review of the notation for the allotypic and related markers of human immunoglobulins: WHO meeting on human immunoglobulin allotypic markers held 16–19 July 1974, Rouen, France. *European Journal of Immunology*, **6**, 599–601.

Satya, L. (1997). Colonial sedentarisation and subjugation: the case of the Banjaras of Berar 1850–1900. *Journal of Peasant Studies*, **24**, 314–36.

Schanfield, M. S. (1980). The anthropological usefulness of highly polymorphic systems: HLA and immunoglobulin allotypes. In *Current Developments in Anthropological Genetics*. Vol. 1: *Theory and Methods*, ed. M. H. Crawford and J. Mielke, pp. 65–86. New York: Plenum Press.

Schanfield, M. S. and Kirk, R. L. (1981). Further studies on the immunoglobulin allotypes (Gm and Km) in India. *Acta Anthropogenetica*, **5**, 1–21.

Schanfield, M. S, Ferrell, R. E, Hossaini, A. A., Sandler, S. G., and Stevenson, J. C. (2008). Immunoglobulin allotypes in Southwest Asia: populations at the crossroads. *American Journal of Human Biology*, **20**, 671–82.

Schanfield, M. S., Gergely, J., and Fudenberg, H. H. (1975). Immunoglobulin allotypes of European populations. I: Gm and Km (Inv) allotypic markers in Hungarians. *Human Heredity*, **25**, 370–7.

Shows, T. B., McAlpine, P. J., Boucheix, C., *et al.* (1987). Guidelines for human gene nomenclature: an international system for human gene nomenclature (ISGN, 1987). *Cytogenetics and Cell Genetics*, **46**, 11–28.

Stevenson, J. C. and Schanfield, M. S. (1981). Immunoglobulin allotypes in European populations. III: Gm, Am and Km allotypes in people of European ancestry in the United States. *Human Biology*, **53**, 521–42.

Tyfield, L., Meredith, A. L., Osborn, M. J., and Harper, P. S. (1989). Identification of the haplotype pattern associated with the mutant PKU allele in the Gypsy population of Wales. *Journal of Medical Genetics*, **26**, 499–503.

van Loghem, E., Tauszik, T., Hollan, S., and Nijenhuis, L. E. (1985). Immunoglobulin allotypes in Hungarian Gypsies. *Journal of Immunogenetics*, **12**, 131–7.

Wright, S. (1965). The interpretation of population structure using F-statistics with special regards to systems of mating. *Evolution*, **19**, 395–420.

Zalán, A., Béres, J., and Pamjav, H. (2011). Paternal genetic history of the Vlax Roma. *Forensic Science International: Genetics*, **5**, 109–13.

14

Migration, assimilation, and admixture: genes of a Scot?

INTRODUCTION

During the last four centuries, millions of Scots have left the British Isles as a result of push factors including overpopulation, religious persecution, and political and economic upheaval. Many of these individuals found their way to the Americas, where the promise of land and opportunities in trades such as tobacco, sugar, and textiles offered a better way of life and outweighed the costs and dangers of a transAtlantic journey (Landsman, 1999). Scots began to arrive in the American colonies during the 1600s, and have contributed much to the American culture that exists today. In the 2006 American Community Survey, the United States Census Bureau reported over 6 million Americans (1.7% of the total population) claimed Scottish ancestry. Another 5.3 million (1.5% of the U.S. population) claimed a Scotch–Irish ancestry, a term usually indicating descent from the estimated 100 000 Scots that left the Scottish lowlands for the Irish Province of Ulster during the 1600s, and migrated to North America some five generations later (Houston, 1996). There are an estimated 24 million (estimated from D.A. Bruce, 1998) or so individuals around the world who claim Scottish ancestry despite having never seen Scotland itself. How and why an individual identifies with a particular ethnic group after being removed from their "homeland" for several generations has long been a perplexing question. This chapter describes the movement of Scots to the Americas, the genetic structure and diversity seen within Scotland, and presents the maternal and paternal genetic markers of a group of

Causes and Consequences of Human Migration, ed. Michael H. Crawford and Benjamin C. Campbell. Published by Cambridge University Press. © Cambridge University Press 2012.

Americans who claim Scottish ancestry, to show how molecular markers can be used to illustrate the migratory behaviors of humans.

Immigration to the New World colonies began in the 1600s and by 1700 some 6000 Scots had arrived (Fogleman, 1992; Houston, 1996).

This would change in the 1700s, when a shift in the economic structure of Scotland led to a breakdown in the traditional clan system, a system in which a group of people were historically tied to a chief (Magnusson, 2000; Scottish Government, 2004). The word clan comes from the Gaelic term *clann*, meaning children or descendants, and the clan system provided protection for the people who pledged their loyalties to a particular chief. This system had defined the Scottish political system for centuries, and a shift away from a clan-based economy led to a slow increase in migration both within and outside of Scotland, as Scots looked for work, land, and resources. Following the Union of Parliaments in 1707, when the Scottish and English parliaments joined to form Great Britain, the government stepped in and provided Scots more opportunities for migration to the New World (Magnusson, 2000). Between 1735 and 1754, small groups of Scottish Highlanders were being recruited as laborers for settlement in the new American colonies. In many cases, groups of Scots, particularly from the Highlands and the Scottish Isles, were actively recruited to work as laborers in Pennsylvania, North Carolina, New York, Florida, and Georgia (McDonald and McDonald, 1980; Murdoch, 1998). Further migration followed the Jacobite uprising of 1745−6, when many Highlander refugees travelled directly to North Carolina (McDonald and McDonald, 1980).

Small groups from the Lowlands of Scotland were also leaving for the American colonies up until the 1760s. While families did travel to the Americas, the emigrants were largely made up of young men who tended to move directly to commercial centers after arriving in Philadelphia (Landsman, 1999; McDonald and McDonald, 1980). Between 1763 and 1776, an increase of Scottish families from both the Lowlands and the Highlands began to emigrate (Landsman, 1999; Murdoch, 1998). Records from this time period show that Scottish Highlanders began to form settlements in the state of New York, and continued to occupy the interior portions of the North Carolina colony (Landsman, 1999; Murdoch, 1998). The movement into North Carolina was marked by the arrival of over 1600 immigrants nearly all of which were from Argyll. By 1771, individuals from other regions of the Highlands, including the Isle of Skye, began to head to the American colonies as a part of organized efforts (Murdoch, 1998).

Immigration halted during the American Revolutionary War despite poor harvests and increasing rent on tenant farms. But, when the war ended, emigration from Scotland and Ireland resumed at an increased rate. By 1790, individuals of Scottish ancestry were making up a significant portion of the American population with about 24% of all European immigrants claiming Scottish ancestry (Fogleman, 1992). The census of 1790 shows that there were particular areas where Scots tended to settle. In New England, where approximately one eighth of the populations were of Scottish ancestry, Scots preferred the upper portions of the region over lower New England. From Pennsylvania southward, some estimates indicate that up to a fourth of the population was made of Scots (McDonald and McDonald, 1980). By 1801, nearly 9700 individuals from the Isle of Skye had left Scotland for the United States (Murdoch, 1998).

The peak of Scottish migration to the United States came during the time of the Highland Clearances, which occurred between 1790 and 1855. The Highland Clearances were the result of a shift in the political and economic structure of Scotland. The nobility of the eastern and southern portions of the Highlands were acting under the guise of improvement and were altering their lands from small tenant farms to large-scale sheep pastures. This transition meant the permanent removal, or forced seasonal labor movements, of the families who had run these small farms for generations (Landsman, 1999; Symonds, 1999; Withers, 1988). The transition to large-scale sheep pastures was also accompanied by an increased reliance on staple crops. By the early 1800s, the potato had become a major component of the Scottish diet, particularly in the heavily populated northwestern portions of Scotland where over half of the land was used for potato cultivation, in some locations accounting for up to 80% of all nourishment (Gray, 1955; Withers, 1988). The reliance on a staple crop led to an increase in population size, despite earlier depopulation through permanent out-migration (Devine, 1979; Gray, 1955; Withers, 1988). Between 1801 and 1841, the total population of Scotland had increased by 7%, with some regions increasing in population size by 53% (Gray, 1955).

Migration due to this population growth and worsening economic conditions would be exacerbated by the Potato Famine that struck Scotland between 1839 and 1856, destroying potato crops in some of the poorest regions of the country (Devine, 1988). In 1846,

76% of crofting districts and 59% of the farming districts reported total crop failures (Devine, 1988). Nearly a third of the Highland's entire population left for opportunities in industrial areas of Scotland, England, and the United States (Devine, 1979; Landsman, 1999). This push encouraged nearly half of these migrants to look towards the United States (Landsman, 1999). As with earlier migrations, the majority of these migrants were men. Records from U.S. Passenger Lists from 1836 to 1853 showed that young, single males made up a large component, some 55–70%, of all males leaving English ports, though records do not differentiate between Welsh, English, or Scottish passengers (Cohn, 1995). In the aftermath of the Clearances, between 1870 and 1910, male migrants outnumbered female migrants at an approximate 3:2 ratio (Greenwood, 2008). These and other historical documents indicate that roughly 2.33 million Scots left the British Isles between 1825 and 1938 (Symonds, 1999; Szasz, 2000). The tremendous decline in the Scottish population can still be seen today, as the Highlands remain one of the least densely populated areas in Europe (Basu, 2007).

Two major trends can be detected in the historical records. The first is that Highlander migration was dominated by single males, although families and single females also participated in this movement. The second trend is that a majority of the New World immigrants came from the Western Islands of Scotland, from the mainland region of Argyll on the west coast of Scotland, and from the Central Highlands of Inverness. If an individual identifies with an ethnic identity that is handed down from a maternal or paternal line, then the individual should have "Scottish" maternal or paternal markers. However, assimilation and admixture into a larger American culture may have erased some of the genetic markers that would be expected in a group that identified with their Scottish ancestry. This chapter examines identity through mitochondrial DNA (mtDNA) and Y-chromosome markers, and addresses the question: do individuals who claim Scottish identity have maternal or paternal genes associated with Scotland?

MOLECULAR EVIDENCE FOR PEOPLING OF SCOTLAND

Two portions of the human genome have been used extensively to understand the movement of humans throughout history. Mitochondrial DNA (mtDNA) is passed on through a maternal mode of inheritance so that every daughter will carry a copy of her mother's genome, and in turn will pass it on to her offspring. This molecule can be characterized by a combination of mutations in the coding region, such as single nucleotide polymorphisms (SNPs) or restriction fragment length polymorphisms (RFLPs), and faster mutating sites within the control region of the chromosome (Giles *et al.*, 1980). To complement the information given in mtDNA, a large portion of the non-recombining Y chromosome (NRY) is inherited in a paternal mode (Novelletto, 2007). A combination of slow mutating SNPs and faster mutating segments of DNA, called short tandem repeats (STRs) are found in the NRY, and have been used to classify the worldwide Y-chromosomal variation into major haplogroups and subclades (Karafet *et al.*, 2008; YCC, 2002). Studies of both mtDNA and the Y chromosome have allowed the exploration of both a male and female side to human history.

In Europe, mitochondrial studies have identified ten major haplogroups using slow mutating regions within the coding region of the chromosome. These haplogroups characterize nearly all European genomes and include haplogroups H, U, T, K, J, X, I, V, W, and M (Finnila *et al.*, 2000). The diversity in mtDNA decreases with latitude in Europe, and the farther northwest the population, the higher the frequency of haplogroups associated with the expansion out of the Iberian refuge following the Last Glacial Maximum (LGM) (Gonzalez *et al.*, 2003). This expansion, which reached Scotland by 10 000 years ago (10 kya), brought some of the oldest and most common haplogroups to Scotland, haplogroups V, H, and U5 (Oppenheimer, 2006; Torroni *et al.*, 1998). Haplogroup V is found mostly within Europe at a frequency of about 7%, and to 10–15 000 years old (Izagirre and de la Rua, 1999). A subhaplogroup, U5, dates to around 50 kya in Europe, and is present in Scotland with a frequency of around 8% (Richards *et al.*, 2000; Sykes, 2006). The most common haplogroup in Europe, haplogroup H, arose around 30–25 kya, and characterizes between 40% and 50% of all European population's mtDNA (Richards *et al.*, 2000). The major subhaplogroups of H that are thought to have spread out of the Iberian refugia belong to haplogroups H1 and H3 (Achilli *et al.*, 2004). Haplogroup V dates to around 16 kya and was dispersed from the Iberian Peninsula throughout western Europe following the LGM (Torroni *et al.*, 2001). Foraging groups that made their way to Scottish lands would have found an environment abundant in resources, particularly along the coasts, but the carrying capacity of the land would have not been able to sustain large numbers of people. Estimates of population size of foraging groups indicate that the region could sustain a population of some 2750–5500 inhabitants (Hunter and Ralston, 1999).

The oldest evidence for agriculture in Scotland dates to about 6 kya (Weale *et al.*, 2002). For Scotland, the transition to agriculture is thought to have been a gradual one, with the majority of the descendants of the orginal foraging populations making up the majority of the gene pool and a small number of individuals whose ancestors originated in the Near East with agriculture bringing in new genetic material (Oppenheimer, 2006). Mitochondrial DNA haplogroups associated with the Neolithic expansion include J, T, U3, and U5a1, which are found in low frequencies in Scotland (Gonzalez *et al.*, 2003; Richards *et al.*, 2000). This shift allowed for a a growth in population, as the transition from hunting and gathering to agriculture can lead to a 5–50-fold growth in population density within the first thousand years. The total European population would expand sharply after this cultural transition occured (Novelletto, 2007).

The initial settlement of Scotland, and the later admixture of these people with individuals carrying markers associated with the spread of agriculture, form the base of the Scottish genetic landscape. However, many other interactions may have contributed to the Scottish gene pool. For example, Scotland and Ireland have had a long history of genetic and cultural interaction. In the beginning of the first millennium, between AD 500 and 1000, the Irish king, known as Dal Riata, set up three colonies in present-day Scotland (Magnusson, 2000). No written records exist about the genetic interaction and possible fusion of the original inhabitants with the incoming Irish settlers (Oppenheimer, 2006). However, as both groups originate from early settlers in the Mesolithicwith later Neolithic influences, they would have had similar genetic backgrounds (Sykes, 2006). Because of these similarities, maternal contributions from Ireland are hard to identify as Ireland and Scotland share many of their mtDNA lineages (Helgason *et al.*, 2000).

The Viking age in Scotland lasted for 400 years and had different effects on the mainland than in the various islands through which the Vikings made contact. Several mtDNA haplotypes of haplogroup H and K appear to be of Scandinavian origin (Helgason *et al.*, 2001). In the northern isles of Scotland, where the Vikings had their greatest influence, there was a maternal Scandinavian imput of up to 38% (Helgason *et al.*, 2001). This influence weakens on the coastal mainland where Scandinavian mtDNA input drops to around 14% (Helgason *et al.*, 2001).

Other groups would influence the cultural and genetic makeup of Scotland and the British Isles over the next few thousand years. In an attempt to rule the whole of Britain, Julius Agricola, the Roman Governor of the Province of Britannia, launched a full-scale invasion of

Scotland in AD 83 (Magnusson, 2000). This attempt failed, and after more than a century of unsuccessful attempts, and with military expenses greater than any other province within the empire, the Romans finally withdrew from Scotland in AD 214 (Kearney, 2006). Angles from northern Germany began to arrive in southeastern England during the fourth century to assist the Romans in their attempts to conquer the island (Magnusson, 2000). By the fifth century, Angles were in England for their own conquests, and would eventually conquer most of eastern Scotland. While Roman and Anglo invasion can be seen through cultural, economic, and political influences, there were no large-scale movements of people, particularly women, into Scotland (Weale *et al.*, 2002). As such, the mtDNA markers associated with these groups are rare in Scotland, and are probably the result of recent admixture. These movements of maternal markers can be seen in Figure 14.1.

In Europe, differerentiation of the Y chromosome has been found to be strongly correlated with geography (Roewer *et al.*, 2005; Rosser *et al.*, 2000). Roewer *et al.* (2005) found that Y-STR diversity in Europe differs more with longitude than with latitude. There have been several studies of European Y-chromosomal variation that have indicated that members of the R1b haplogroups are associated with the earliest movements of people into the British Isles, including the expansion out of the Iberian Peninsula following the LGM and the movement of people into Europe during the Neolithic. These haplogroups are found at a higher frequency at the northwestern corners of the European continent and islands (Roewer *et al.*, 2005). The most common haplogroup, R1b, characterizes 77% of the Scottish population (Oppenheimer, 2006). Due to a low effective population size of one fourth of the total population, the Y chromosome is more subject to the effects of genetic drift, and may explain the high frequencies of particular R1b haplotypes found in northwestern Europe (Myres *et al.*, 2010; Rosser *et al.*, 2000). Scandinavia also shares several Y-chromosome haplotypes with Scotland due to Viking men mating with local women during Viking occupation of the Northern Isles and the northwest coast of Scotland (Helgason *et al.*, 2000; Sykes, 2006). The most prevalent Viking Y haplotypes are those which belong to haplogroups I1a and R1a, although haplotypes belonging to R1b are represented as well. In Scotland, as well as the rest of Europe, the Y chromosome is largely described by the five major haplogroups: R, I, J, G, and E (Jobling *et al.*, 2004).

A few Y-chromosome haplotypes may have spread into the English population through a Roman presence, including haplotypes from

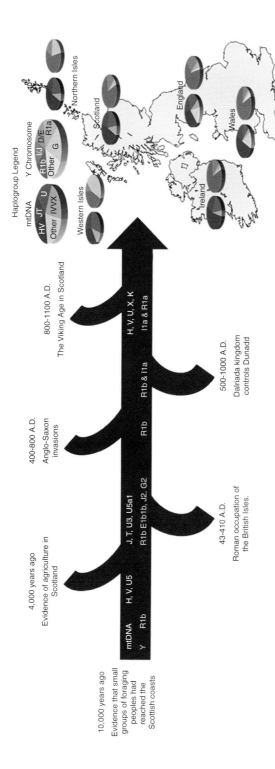

Figure 14.1 Arrival of major mtDNA (top white) and Y-chromosome (bottom gray) haplogroups to Scotland and the British Isles, and the distribution of these haplogroups throughout the region.

haplogroups J, G, and possibly E. These haplotypes probably made their way into Scottish populations through later migrations from Britain (Bird, 2007). All of these haplogroups are present in low frequencies in Scottish populations. Y-chromosome signatures of Anglo-Saxon genetic contributions can be seen in the pfrequency of haplogroups Ia and R1b, particularly R1b1c9, in Scotland, but due to genetic similarities and shared haplotypes between the two areas, the amount of influence is difficult to determine (Faux, 2008).

Disease and famine has also played a role in shaping the cultural and genetic structure of human populations (Hatcher, 1996). For Scotland, these two factors played a role in decreasing the mtDNA and Y-chromosome diversity both before massive out-migration began, and before the sampling of individuals that represent the Scottish comparative population were obtained. Before the large-scale migrations to the New World began in the 1700s, several waves of disease would affect the genetic diversity of Scotland. The "Black Death" of 1348–9 was one of the most devastating epidemics in recorded history. While records of mortality during this time period are scarce, a rough estimate of 30–45% of the English (including Scottish) population fell to the first wave of plague epidemics. Several other waves would appear in 1361–2, 1369, and 1375 (Hatcher, 1996). Famines in the 1690s may have led to the deaths of 10% of Scots, and the Potato Famine of the 1840s played a role in increasing rates of Scot emigration to the New World and Irish emigration to areas of Scotland (Anderson, 1996). The influenza pandemic of 1918–19 had the highest mortality of any infectious disease in Scotland's history, with over 17 500 deaths attributed to influenza or complications arising as a result of influenza (General Register Office for Scotland, 2005). World War I would also decrease the genetic diversity of Scotland, particularly that found in the Y chromosome. Some 690 000 Scots, 41% of Scottish men between the ages of 15–49, participated in the war. At least 12% of these men died in service (Winter, 1977). Another 265 000 men died in service in World War II (Anderson, 1996). These are just a few examples of historical events that have shaped the genetic landscape of Scotland.

The movements of people into Scotland would largely be seen following the LGM up until the mid 1800s when Irish migrants came following the Potato Famine. These movements would bring new genes to the region, increasing the diversity of genetic markers, while forces such as massive out-migration, war, and disease over the last few centuries decreased the genetic variability in mtDNA and the Y chromosome that may have been present in the Scottish population.

Not only did Scots move to other regions of the United Kingdom and the United States, but they would also emigrate to Canada, Australia, New Zealand, South Africa, and other regions of Europe (Basu, 2007). The current genetic variability is the result of the movements of these peoples.

MATERIALS AND METHODS

To illustrate the utility of molecular markers in identifying migratory movements, participants for this study were recruited from the Kansas City Highland Games in June of 2006. Each participant gave his or her signed consent that met the University of Kansas Internal Review Board's requirements. Participants gave a mouth rinse for DNA analysis and completed a brief questionnaire, which included their name, date of birth, sex, place of birth, first language, clan affiliation, as well as genealogical information consisting of both parents and maternal and paternal grandparents. A total of 57 males and 35 females volunteered for this study.

Comparative European populations which contained data for mtDNA HVS-I sequences and for Y-STRs were compiled from the literature. Populations were chosen to represent those groups which contributed the most reported European ethnicities to the United States of America and include groups representing Scotland, England, Germany, Ireland, Italy, France, Poland, Netherlands, Belgium, Norway, Sweden, and Denmark. MtDNA sequences from Scotland were obtained from Helgason *et al.* (2001) and other European sequences were obtained from McEvoy *et al.* (2004). Y-STR data were obtained from Capelli *et al.* (2003) and Goodacre *et al.* (2005) for Scotland, and Roewer *et al.* (2005) for comparative European populations.

DNA was extracted from the samples using a Chelex extraction method following Zlojutro *et al.* (2008). Problematic samples were extracted using QIAamp Minikit (Qiagen, Valencia, CA) following the manufacturer's protocol. The non-coding portion of mtDNA HVS-I was amplified between positions 15976 and 16401. Polymerase chain reaction (PCR) of the HVS-I and RFLP sites was performed and the fragments were visualized through electrophoresis on a 1.5% Seakem Agarose gel, and photodocumented under a UV fluorescent light. Following amplification, the samples were purified using Qiagen's QIAquick PCR purification kit following the manufacturer's protocol (Qiagen, Valencia, CA). Purified samples of HVS-I were sent to the University of Kansas DNA Sequencing Laboratory, where they were sequenced by Dr. Mike Grose using an ABI 3700 sequencer.

Sequence data of mtDNA HVS-I were aligned to the revised Cambridge Reference Sequence (Andrews *et al.*, 1999) using the program CLUSTALW (Thompson *et al.*, 1994) in MEGA version 4 (www. megasoftware.net/) (Tamura *et al.*, 2007). The sequences included up to 354 base pairs at positions 16045–16399, and mutational positions were identified. Mutational sites along the HVS-I were used in combination with RFLP data to confirm haplogroup assignments. PCR was performed on all male samples to amplify regions of the NRY chromosome. These reactions were performed in three multiplexes following Zlojutro (2008). Multiplex I (DYS385a/b, DYS390, DYS391, and DYS393), multiplex II (DYS19, DYS392, DYS438, and DYS439), and a single reaction mix for DYS389 I/II underwent PCR. The samples were visualized under a UV illuminator in a 1.5% Seakem LE Agarose gel and sent to the DNA Sequencing Lab (University of Kansas) for analyses by Dr. Mike Grose, where they were loaded onto the ABI3130xI. The alleles were scored and probable haplogroup assignments were inferred using Whit Athey's Haplogroup Predictor (www.hprg.com/hapest5/hapest5a/hapest5.htm? order=num), a program which is particularly well suited for populations of northwestern Europe (Athey, 2006).

Diversity measures of MtDNA HVS-I and Y-STRs were computed using Arlequin version 3.1 (http://cmpg.unibe.ch/software/ arlequin3/), and included: Nei's gene diversity (H) (Nei, 1987), the mean number of pairwise differences between all pairs of haplotypes within a sample (π), and two estimates of the expected diversity in a population (θ) (Excoffier and Schneider, 2005). Estimations of θ for mtDNA sequence diversity included θ_k, an estimate based on the expected number of alleles (k), and θ_S, an estimate of diversity based on the number of segregating sites in a sample. Measurements of mtDNA sequence diversity are based on the infinite sites model proposed by Kimura (1969), under the assumption that when the mutation rate at each site is small and the number of sites in a DNA segment is large the probability that a mutation will occur more than once at the same site is negligible. For Y-STR data, the stepwise mutation model was assumed following Ohta and Kimura (1973), which suggests that mutations increase or decrease an allele's length (or a single repeat) with equal probability (Jobling *et al.*, 2004).

Diversity measures for Y-STR data were calculated for the Kansas City Group and comparative populations. The first calculations included the available five loci (DYS19, DYS390, DYS391, DYS392, and DYS393) for Scottish populations found in the literature and included in Goodacre *et al.* (2005) and Capelli *et al.* (2003). The next combination compared European populations, including a combined set of all Scottish regions labeled as

Scotland and the KC Games group, using the same five loci listed above. Two tests of neutrality were also computed on mtDNA HVS-I sequence data, Tajima's D and Fu's F_S (Excoffier and Schneider, 2005; Fu, 1997).

A traditional Multidimensional Scaling (MDS) analysis was performed on Tamura and Nei's (1993) distances for mtDNA sequence data (Excoffier and Schneider, 2005). Slatkin's (1995) corrected linearized R_{ST} distances were used for MDS plots of Y-STR data as described in Manly (1994). A test of goodness-of-fit of the data to the graph can be assessed by the stress value defined by Kruskal (1964). MDS plots for this study included the use of 5, 6, 12, and 13 populations with the suggested two-dimensional maximum stress values for goodness-of-fit to the data as 0.000, 0.019, 0.183, and 0.199 respectively (Sturrock and Rocha, 2000).

RESULTS

A total of 80 individuals of Scottish ancestry were sequenced for HVS-I and underwent RFLP analyses. In all, the sample revealed 61 unique haplotypes belonging to haplogroups H, V, U, K, J, T, and W. Three individuals matched the CRS for HVS-I haplotypes but did not belong to haplogroup H, U, or V based on RFLP analysis. These three samples were classified as unknown. The most common haplogroup represented in the sample was haplogroup H, making up 51% of the sample with haplogroups U, J, V, T, K, and W making up between 14% and 1%. The most common haplotype in this study belonged to nine individuals who were in haplogroup H and matched the HVS-I Cambridge Reference Sequence. Table 14.1 lists the frequencies of haplogroups in the Kansas City Games group and regions of Scotland.

The summary statistics for the Kansas City Highland Games group and four regions of Scotland, and the 13 European comparative populations are given in Table 14.2. Compared with Scottish HVS-I sequences, the Kansas City Games group displays a slightly higher level of genetic and nucleotide diversity, despite having a smaller sample size than every region except Orkney. When levels of expected diversity are tested for neutrality, both Tajima's D and Fu's F_S give significant values. These results are consistent with other studies of European populations, and are usually indicative of population expansion or selection. Based on the historical data, these numbers are most likely due to a population expansion following the adaptation of an agricultural subsistence.

When the Kansas City Games group was compared with Scottish populations, 58% ($n = 46$) of the group had a haplotype that is frequent in Scotland. Of these, 56% ($n = 45$) matched with the Scottish mainland and

Table 14.1. *Haplogroup frequencies of Orkney, the Scottish Mainland, the Western Isles and Skye, and the Kansas City Scottish sample. European haplogroups H, J, K, T, U, V, and W are represented*

Hg	Orkney	Scottish mainland	W Isles and Skye	Kansas City
H	50.66	45.67	34.56	51.25
J	9.86	14.36	14.64	12.50
K	6.58	6.62	13.42	5.00
T	5.92	10.09	12.60	5.00
U	12.50	11.78	13.42	13.75
V	1.32	4.26	2.03	7.50
W	1.97	0.90	0.41	1.25
Other	11.00	6.00	9.00	3.75

other Scottish populations, one sample only matched with the Scotland mainland, one matched a haplotype found in the northwest coast of Scotland, and another sample matched with a haplotype found only in the Western Isles and the Isle of Skye. Figure 14.2 shows the percentage of the Kansas City Games group that share a haplotype with each Scottish region and the percentage of each region that shares a haplotype with the Kansas City Highland Games sample. Maternal lines are more commonly found on the Scottish mainland and the northwest of coast of Scotland, whereas the Scottish Isles share the least maternal lines.

A MDS plot was also constructed from Tamura and Nei's (1993) distances, and can be viewed in Figure 14.2a. Orkney and the Western Isles and Skye are separated from the other populations, and pulled to the upper half of the plot by their high frequency of haplotypes not found in the Kansas City Games group, and a relatively low frequency of haplotypes belonging to haplogroup V. This plot reflects the influence of Scandinavian maternal lines. Orkney is pulled to the right of the plot due to a high frequency of haplogroup X, which reaches 7–8% in Orkney. This high frequency of a relatively rare haplogroup has been explained as the result of genetic drift following either post-glacial expansion or movement of the haplogroup into the area following Scandinavian settlement (Helgason *et al.*, 2001; Reidla *et al.*, 2003). Haplogroup X is absent in the Kansas City group and present at small frequencies in the other Scottish regions. Haplogroup V is found at a low frequency of 4% in Orkney versus 8% in the Kansas City Games group. The presence or absence of haplotypes belonging to these two haplogroups is the major influence of the first axis of the plot. The second axis of the plot is largely influenced by the presence or absence

Table 14.2. Summary statistics for the Kansas City Games group, four Scottish populations, and comparative European populations based on mtDNA HVSI sequence data, including the number of samples (n), gene diversity (H), the number of pairwise differences between haplotypes (π), and the expected diversity based on k and S

Sample	n	H	s.d. (H)	π	s.d. (π)	θ_k	95% C.I. (θ_k)	θ_S	s.d (θ_S)	Tajima's D	Fu's F_S
KC Games	80	0.9677	0.0125	3.7943	1.931	71.7110	(45.6858–114.3927)	11.5082	3.2313	−2.2004	−26.0207
Scotland	895	0.966	0.0037	4.00695	2.21688	130.1041	(111.3963–151.6475)	15.18957	2.96154	−2.07693	−24.93809
Scotland ML	609	0.9675	0.0042	4.1734	2.0776	125.3302	(104.9506–149.3764)	15.0253	3.0708	−2.1057	−24.7506
NW Coast	197	0.9693	0.0073	4.3890	2.1769	69.8621	(52.1969–93.3399)	12.4619	3.0188	−2.0052	−25.3309
WIsles & Skye	160	0.9799	0.0040	4.4841	2.2202	57.7230	(41.8383–79.4799)	10.7979	2.7409	−1.8330	−25.4626
Orkney	77	0.9498	0.0145	4.0626	2.0489	27.3594	(17.3423–42.9931)	7.5287	2.2411	−1.5134	−25.7409
Germany	582	0.971	0.0043	3.75357	2.09696	n/a	n/a	16.41982	3.3429	−2.23165	−25.16511
England	242	0.9651	0.0078	3.97171	2.20672	140.4169	(108.0302–182.7598)	15.17129	3.4966	−2.24347	−25.52079
Cornwall	92	0.9603	0.0128	3.52007	2.00354	51.2470	(33.8323–77.8340)	10.60162	2.93554	−2.15228	−26.16246
Wales	92	0.9259	0.0208	3.14238	1.8204	34.1656	(22.4883–51.7604)	9.22734	2.59788	−2.1053	−26.40368

Table 14.2. (cont.)

Sample	n	H	s.d. (H)	π	s.d. (π)	θ_k	95% C.I. (θ_k)	θ_S	s.d (θ_S)	Tajima's D	Fu's F_S
Ireland	300	0.9567	0.008	3.6212	2.03685	113.3193	(89.3976–143.5096)	13.8549	3.12902	−2.20313	−25.61186
Italy	248	0.9717	0.007	4.56197	2.48906	175.8613	(135.3743–229.0425)	15.7671	3.60795	−2.16002	−25.23447
France	379	0.9713	0.0053	3.85871	2.14928	164.6082	(133.3325–203.1740)	16.12053	3.47385	−2.25248	−25.36002
Poland	473	0.9644	0.0058	4.14403	2.28465	164.1568	(135.6427–198.4943)	16.1835	3.38705	−2.17528	−25.13697
Denmark	38	0.9346	0.0289	3.49502	2.02361	20.9510	(11.2143–39.3554)	7.37817	2.48592	−1.83126	−14.08976
Norway	629	0.9528	0.0064	3.80351	2.12061	162.9112	(137.4551–192.8251)	17.37755	3.4841	−2.25614	−25.14476
Sweden	32	0.9879	0.0115	4.39919	2.48035	78.7792	(34.9157–190.9116)	9.18742	3.11626	−1.8895	−24.85186
Belgium	33	0.9924	0.0094	3.51326	2.04117	110.7921	(46.6067–287.6055)	9.116688	3.07634	−2.21682	−25.95553
Mean	287	0.96412	0.00968	3.927498	2.13470	99.958728	(80.4132–158.7163)	12.717636	3.077652	−2.0806617	−24.826729

Note: Tajima's D are significant at $p < 0.05$, Fu's F_S are significant at $p < 0.005$.

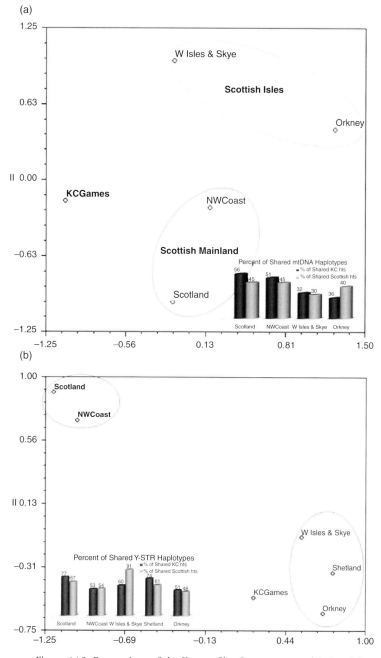

Figure 14.2 Comparison of the Kansas City Games group with Scottish samples through MDS plots and frequency of shared haplotypes. MtDNA comparisons are shown on the left, while Y-chromosome information is given on the right.

of haplotypes belonging to haplogroups K and U. Haplogroup K has the highest frequency in the Western Isles at 13% and the lowest frequencies are found in the Scottish mainland at 6.2% and the Kansas City Games group at 5%. Two subclades, haplogroup K2b found at 2.4% and haplogroup U1 found at 2%, are found in the Western Isles and the Isles of Skye and are present at less than 0.6% in all other Scottish populations (Helgason *et al.*, 2001).

Of the Kansas City Games group 61% shared a mtDNA haplotype with Scotland (Figure 14.2). However, of these shared haplotypes, only three are found only in Scotland, while the others are shared and dispersed throughout Europe. Wales shared the largest percentage of its haplotypes with the Kansas City Games group at 50%, although this may be a reflection of the small sample size of 92 individuals. Ireland, with a total sample size of 300, is second to Wales and shares 51% of its lineages with the Kansas City Games group. Unlike the Scottish populations, Irish females equaled or outnumbered males in their migration to the United States (Greenwood, 2008). As many of the maternal lineages in Ireland and Scotland are shared, it may be hard to differentiate between the two populations using this marker. There is also a large amount of haplotype sharing seen when the sample size of a population is small, as can be seen with the amount of sharing with Belgium, Sweden, Denmark, and Wales.

Summary statistics for 13 European populations and the Kansas City Games group's mtDNA HVS-I sequences (np 16090–16397) are listed in Table 14.2. Despite the small sample size, the Kansas City Games group displays Nei's genetic diversity ($H = 0.9677$) and number of pairwise differences between haplotypes ($\pi = 3.7943$) figures similar to the rest of Europe. Compared with the rest of Europe, the Kansas City Games group has lower expected levels of diversity when compared with the mean. These measures are sensitive to sample size, so they must be taken with some caution. When compared with populations in the North Atlantic (Scotland, England, Cornwall, Wales, and Ireland), they display a high level of expected diversity based on S, and a lower level of expected diversity based on estimates using k.

When Tamura and Nei's (1993) distances are used to compute a MDS plot (not shown) of the Kansas City group with other European populations, the Kansas City Games group is near the center of all European populations, and surrounded by Norway, Denmark, England, and France. Scotland, Germany, Ireland and Sweden are further from the Kansas City group but still form a cluster that includes all European populations except for Italy and Belgium. This tight clustering of several European populations is due to the amount of shared lineages between populations as a result of historic female migration. In sum, the Kansas City Games group seems to be a mix of European maternal genes, an indication that their Scottish identity might be the result of some other association. The stress value for the plot was given as 0.14439, lower than the suggested goodness-of-fit maximum value of 0.217 for 14 populations suggested by Sturrock and Rocha (2000).

A total of 47 males provide information for the paternal side of this study, with Y haplogroup G2a, I1, R1a and R1b found in the Kansas City Games group. Summary statistics of Y-STR diversity of 43 Kansas City Games males and five Scottish populations were computed and shown in Table 14.3. Although the sample size of the Kansas City Games group is small ($n = 43$), the H is higher here at 0.9812 than in any Scottish population. This indicates that some of the samples may have a paternal ancestry outside of Scotland. The population with the second highest H is Shetland. The lowest diversity is seen in the Scottish mainland where H equals 0.9059. The number of pairwise differences between haplotypes (π) in the Kansas City Games group is low compared with the Scottish populations.

The frequency of shared Y-STR haplotypes with Scottish populations (Figure 14.2b) is higher than the frequency of shared mtDNA haplotypes in the Kansas City Games group. Of the Kansas City Games haplotypes 77% are shared with the Scotland mainland, 74% are shared with Shetland, and 60%, 53%, and 51% are shared with the Western Isles and the Isle of Skye, the northwest coast, and Orkney respectively. The Western Isles and the Isle of Skye share the largest number of haplotypes with the Kansas City Games group, with over 90% matching a Kansas City Games haplotype. This may reflect the heavy historical migrations from these islands, noted by Murdoch (1998), and the absence of economic opportunities for Highland men following the Highland Clearances. At 48%, Orkney shares the least number of haplotypes with the Kansas City Games group.

A MDS plot showing the relationship between the Kansas City Games Group Y-STR distances and the Y diversity of Scottish regions was constructed and given in Figure 14.2b. In this plot, the Kansas City Games group clusters with the northern islands of Scotland including Orkney, Shetland, and the Western Isles and the Isle of Skye. The Scottish mainland and the northwest coast form a cluster in the upper left corner, and both of these groups show the greatest diversity of alleles at the five loci examined. Dispersal along the first axis is influenced by variation at the

Table 14.3. *Summary statistics for the Kansas City Games group, five Scottish populations, and comparative European populations based on Y-STR data, including the number of samples (n), number of haplotypes (hts), number of haplotypes (hts), gene diversity (H), and the number of pairwise differences between haplotypes (π). All statistics were run twice*

Population	n	#hts	#hts	H	s.d. (H)	H	s.d. (H)	π	s.d. (π)	π	sd (π)
Kansas City Games	42	30	36	0.9812	0.0089	0.9919	0.0074	2.1872	1.2344	4.0592	2.0662
Scotland	1186	199	n/a	0.9222	0.0041	n/a	n/a	2.4143	1.3117	n/a	n/a
Scottish mainland	495	99	n/a	0.9059	0.0082	n/a	n/a	2.1683	1.2046	n/a	n/a
Orkney	121	48	n/a	0.9507	0.0089	n/a	n/a	2.6208	1.4111	n/a	n/a
W Isles and Skye	160	47	n/a	0.9285	0.0120	n/a	n/a	2.4722	1.3431	n/a	n/a
Shetland	256	58	n/a	0.9544	0.0053	n/a	n/a	2.6605	1.4232	n/a	n/a
Northwest Coast	154	50	n/a	0.9339	0.0095	n/a	n/a	2.3401	1.2851	n/a	n/a
Germany	3442	534	1064	0.978	0.0008	0.9915	0.0005	2.9364	1.5394	4.2012	2.0873
Netherlands	275	92	136	0.9495	0.0062	0.9767	0.0038	2.6599	1.4226	3.8293	1.9364
Sweden	708	185	304	0.9655	0.0032	0.9818	0.0023	2.8146	1.4876	4.1884	2.0837
Belgium	125	57	87	0.9525	0.0106	0.9855	0.0047	2.7241	1.4560	3.9391	1.9867
Poland	1313	305	464	0.9661	0.0022	0.9878	0.0010	2.6591	1.4044	3.7299	1.8845
Norway	300	107	164	0.9654	0.0049	0.9859	0.0028	2.7157	1.4467	4.0831	2.0414
Italy	1340	351	692	0.9804	0.0016	0.9933	0.0008	3.1012	1.6117	4.3326	2.1448
Denmark	63	30	43	0.9493	0.0138	0.9811	0.0076	2.5422	1.3850	3.7921	1.9355
England	247	82	143	0.9468	0.008	0.9824	0.0040	2.5753	1.3860	3.7942	1.9174
France	208	102	138	0.9696	0.0061	0.9897	0.0025	2.9734	1.5613	4.1993	2.0943
Ireland	107	39	61	0.9178	0.018	0.9601	0.0122	2.2892	1.2655	3.3312	1.7238
Mean	585.7	134.2	277.7	0.95098	0.00735	0.98398	0.00413	2.60302	1.3988	3.9566	1.9918358

Note: White columns are for values calculated using five loci. Gray columns indicate values calculated for seven loci.

DYS392 locus, where the Scottish mainland has the highest frequencies of alleles 13 and 14, and the lowest frequencies of alleles 11 and 12. In contrast, Shetland exhibits the opposite with the lowest frequencies of 13 and 14 and the highest frequencies of alleles 11 and 12. DYS19 also contributes to this axis, with allele 14 having a relatively high frequency in Scotland compared with the other populations. The second axis is separated by allele variation at the DYS391 locus. Orkney displays the highest frequency of allele 10 and the lowest combined frequency of alleles 11 and 12 when compared with all other groups represented in the plot. The final stress for the MDS plot was 0.01652, below the suggested maximum stress value (Sturrock and Rocha, 2000).

For a broader view of the relationship of males in the Kansas City Games sample with Europe, further analyses were computed to compare the male Kansas City Games group with 13 European populations. The summary statistics of all European populations are displayed in Table 14.3, and show that the Kansas City Games group has a high level of genetic diversity (H) despite its relatively small sample size. Based on five loci, the diversity of the Kansas City Games group is 0.9812, higher than any other population analyzed. When this measure is expanded to include seven loci, H increases to 0.9919, a number higher than all other populations compared in this study, except Italy. However, when five or seven loci are used, the number of pairwise differences between haplotypes (π) is low for the Kansas City Games group when compared with the rest of Europe. This result is expected if some of these males who claim Scottish identity are not Scottish through paternal ancestry. If this is the case, then you would expect to see a high level of diversity in the small sample because the group would represent a variety of European populations instead of a group with a single geographical origin.

The percentage of shared Kansas City haplotypes with European populations, and shared European haplotypes with the Kansas City Games group, were examined. The Kansas City group shares over 70% of its seven allele haplotypes with Germany. The population that shares the most of its seven allele haplotypes with Kansas City Games group is Ireland with 41%. All of these haplotypes belong to haplogroup R1b, which has frequencies of over 90% in some parts of Ireland (Sykes, 2006). When the Kansas City group is compared with Scotland using the five available STRs, they shared 81% of the Scottish-American haplotypes, and the Scottish samples included in this analysis shared 79% of its haplotypes with the Kansas City group. However, matches of Y-STR haplotypes alone are not necessarily an indication of Scottish paternal

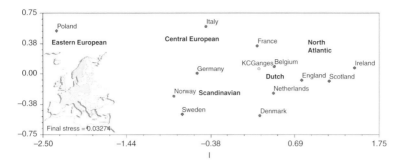

Figure 14.3 MDS plot of the Kansas City Games group and 13 European comparative populations based on Slatkin's RST distances of Y-STR data.

ancestry. Six of the individuals belonging to haplogroup R1b shared a haplotype with all five regions of Scotland and all of the European populations examined in this study. These individuals carry some of the most common Y-STR haplotypes found in Europe. There are also two individuals, with Scottish surnames and a given clan affiliation, who do not share a haplotype with any population examined.

Multidimensional scaling was also used to examine the relationship between the Kansas City Games group and European populations, and is shown in Figure 14.3. Unlike the plot of mitochondrial distances between populations, the plot based on distances between Y-STR haplotypes follows a general geographical cline of eastern to western Europe. There are also groupings of major European regions, and these are labeled in Figure 14.3 as Eastern European, Central European, Scandinavian, Dutch, and North Atlantic Islands. The Kansas City Games group clusters with the Dutch populations of Belgium and the Netherlands. The Kansas City group is also centered among the Dutch, Central European, North Atlantic, and Scandinavian groups, all of which share 40% or more of these region's haplotypes. Poland is separated from the Scandinavian and Central European clusters along the first axis of the plot as a result of its high frequencies of haplogroup R1a. The axes and groupings on the plot may further be explained by unique allelic frequencies at specific loci. For example, the first axis is a gradient of DYS19 alleles 14 and 16. In the Polish sample, allele 14 has a low frequency (0.19512) compared with the other samples, and allele 16 is found at the highest frequency (0.33003). The reverse is true of Ireland which has the highest frequency of allele 14 (0.83178) and a low frequency of allele 16 (0.02804). A similar distribution is seen for alleles at the DYS391 locus where Poland has a high frequency of allele 10 when compared with other populations.

DISCUSSION

The historical record indicates that individuals with a maternal ancestry from Scotland should largely be from the Irish settlement of Ulster, Scots of the Border Clans, or have ancestry from the Western Isles or Central Highlands of Scotland (Landsman, 1999; McDonald and McDonald, 1980; Murdoch, 1998). Female migration from Scotland was largely in the form of family immigration, as single females tended to seek work in local economic activities such as domestic labor or textile manufacturing in Scotland's industrial centers or seasonal agricultural or fishery work in the Lowlands or coastal areas. In contrast to Scottish female movement, the number of single women from Ireland that came to the colonies outnumbered the number of Irish men (Gordon, 2002). While exact numbers of how many of these women were from the Ulster plantations are not available, there were probably many single females involved in the large movement from Ulster to the New World.

Examination of HVS-I sequence information and RFLP data indicate that 60% of individuals in this study have HVS-I haplotypes that are found throughout Scotland, in particular the Scottish mainland and the northwest coast of Scotland. As with the rest of Europe, the Kansas City Games group has a high frequency of haplogroup H, which was dispersed through Europe following the repopulation of Europe out of the Iberian refugia. The haplotypes that are found in Scotland mainland are from the mtDNA haplogroups H, V, J, K, and U. However, there are only three haplotypes that are found exclusively in Scotland. The rest of these haplotypes are shared throughout Europe and, if the Kansas City Games group is an admixed European sample, explains the high level of expected diversity when compared with the mean expected diversity of all of the populations in this study.

Maternal Scottish ancestry is not expected to be as common as paternal ancestry in this study, as the historical record of female migration to the New World indicates fewer female than male immigrants. Those who did migrate directly from Scotland, particularly with their families, are expected to largely represent lineages found in the central Scottish Highlands and the Western Isles. Scotch-Irish females should resemble individuals from the Lowlands of Scotland. Analyses showed that the Kansas City Games group shares 60% of its haplotypes with Scottish populations. Of these haplotypes 30% are found in the Western Isles and the Isle of Skye, lower than any other Scottish population except Orkney. The Scottish mainland shares 56% of its lineages with the sample. If these haplotypes are the result of Scottish ancestry, then it appears the Kansas City Games group most closely resembles Scotland's central Highlands and Lowland regions. The expected heterozygosity ($H = 0.9734$) of the Kansas City Games group, and the number of pairwise differences between haplotypes ($\pi = 4.9555$) were high compared with regions of Scotland. These diversity measures indicate that there are maternal lines found in the Kansas City group that are not represented in the Scottish sample, suggesting that there are other populations contributing to the maternal diversity. MDS plots and NJ-trees based on HVS-I sequences support this, as the Kansas City Games group shares lineages with all European comparative populations, and cluster with other populations besides Scotland in both analyses. Due to the high levels of haplotype sharing amongst European populations, mtDNA data cannot identify lineages that are particularly "Scottish."

These results lead to one conclusion; the Kansas City group appears to be maternally European. Single male immigrants from Scotland outnumbered female immigrants to the New World, and it is likely that they had to find mates from other immigrating groups. Many of the mitochondrial lineages that are found in Scotland are shared with several European populations, and this sharing would only partially be resolved through further RFLP or SNP analyses that would more fully characterize each haplotype. Not only are the lineages shared throughout Europe, but the diversity of all mtDNA lineages in Europe, particularly haplogroups H and U5, make it difficult to determine if the Scottish comparative samples are an accurate representation of the diversity of Scotland. Helgason *et al.* (2001) noted that several studies have indicated that there are a large number of mtDNA lineages throughout Europe. This variation makes it difficult for any study to capture the true diversity within a population, regardless of a large sample size. The importance of this finding in relationship to this study is that there may be several mtDNA lineages within Scotland that have not yet been identified, especially in areas of the British Isles that have not been as heavily sampled as the mainland. Furthermore, recent gene flow, and a possible loss of diversity due to migration, has left Scotland with few private mtDNA lineages. Obtaining more complete genealogical information from each of the participants would have helped to distinguish between a haplotype match that is due to its high frequency in Europe or a haplotype that originated within Scotland.

Similar to female emigrants of Scotland, a large portion of males from the Central Highlands and the Western Isles moved to the colonies. Many Scotch-Irish males, descendants of Lowlanders brought to Ireland in the 1600s, emigrated to the New World from Ulster (McDonald and

McDonald, 1980). From the historical record one would expect to find males of paternal descent from Scotland most similar to these regions of Scotland, with some bias towards the Highland since the samples were obtained from the Kansas City Highland Games.

As expected, all of the major haplogroups found in Scotland, R1b, R1a, I, J, E1b1b, were detected in the Kansas City Games group. Haplogroup R1b is the most common haplogroup found in the Kansas City Games group at 70%, a high frequency typical of Western European populations due to its spread by male foragers following the LGM. These groups are less genetically influenced by the later movements of people during the Neolithic and the spread of agriculture. The most surprising results are the three individuals who belong to haplogroup G2a, a haplogroup that is not seen in the comparative Scottish populations in this study, but has been found in Scotland at very low frequencies. It has been suggested that this haplogroup was the result of Roman interactions in Britain, and later migrations from the descendants of the Romans to Scotland. Two of these three individuals have common Scottish surnames and Scottish clan affiliations. These results suggest that the genetic signatures are probably a mark of today's Scottish population, influenced by many different movements of people and shaped by disease, war, and out-migration, instead of a Scottish ancestral claim based on a non maternal/paternal relationship or one that is strictly cultural in nature. The other individual belonging to the G2a haplogroup has a surname that is found in Scotland, but more commonly seen throughout England.

As a whole, analysis of Y markers showed a greater resemblance to Scottish populations than did mtDNA markers. Haplotype matching of five loci DYS19, DYS390, DYS391, DYS392, and DYS393, show that the Kansas City Games group shares the largest% of its haplotypes with the Scottish mainland. However, of the Scottish groups, the Western Isles and the Isles of Skye share 91% of its haplotypes with the Kansas City group. These results alone are insufficient to support a paternal line through Scotland, since many of these haplotypes are found in populations throughout Europe. However, this strong resemblance to groups that have historically contributed to the American gene pool and clan affiliations that are distributed throughout these same islands are indications that many male individuals from the Kansas City sample are of direct Scottish paternal descent.

Some of the haplotypes found in this study do not appear to be of Scottish origin. However, not finding a match in the Scottish population does not exclude a sample originating from Scotland. Instead, this could be a result of sampling in the comparative data or a result of kin-structured migration. MtDNA diversity is high in Europe and there is some chance that lineages found in this study were brought to the United States by individuals from Scotland, yet their particular haplotypes are not represented in the comparative samples due to a small sample size. For Y-chromosome diversity, inclusion of SNPs would have added more conclusive evidence for Scottish paternal ancestry, especially in distinguishing between subclades of haplogroup R1b. Kin-structured migration is a form of migration in which migrating groups are related individuals and thus carry similar genes (Mielke and Fix, 2006). While early movements of Scottish immigrants were typical of single males, family-based movements from areas of the Potato Famine and the Highlands became typical in the 1800s. As a result of these events, it is possible that much genetic diversity, including that found in the Y chromosome and mtDNA, left Scotland and the Scottish Isles and can now only be found in emigrants from Scotland, who left for better opportunities overseas.

Paternal ancestry is expected to be higher for males of Scottish descent as male immigrants outnumbered female immigrants in the historical records. These males are expected to represent lineages in the Scottish central Highlands and the Scottish Isles. Results show that the genetic diversity of the Kansas City Games group is high when compared with Scotland, an indication that there are some other European paternal lineages represented by the sample. However, in contrast to the maternal line, the Kansas City group shares a larger number of haplotypes with Scotland (77%). These haplotypes are most common in the Western Isles and Isle of Skye, and the Scottish mainland (which includes the central Highlands). Analyses based on Slatkin's R_{ST} distances, including MDS plots and NJ-trees, indicate that the Kansas City group most closely resembles regions of Scotland where out-migration has been documented. These regions are also the areas of Scotland that had the strongest Viking genetic influence (Helgason *et al.*, 2000). This would explain the clustering of Shetland and Orkney with the Kansas City Games group, despite lower levels of emigration to the New World.

This study also utilized surname and clan distributions in support of a larger paternal versus maternal Scottish ancestry. Individuals with the same surname are more likely to be related genetically than individuals who do not share surnames (King *et al.*, 2006). The same can be said of clan affiliations which are often recognized through a paternal line. Distributions of male participants' surnames and clan affiliations, particularly those that have haplotypes found in Scotland, are most frequent in the Western Isles and the central Highlands. Many of these surnames are a result of Scandinavian influence and are found throughout Shetland, Orkney, and other Scottish Isles. Over one half of the male participants had a Scottish surname, clan affiliation, and a Y-STR haplotype found in Scotland. This suggests a strong Scottish paternal component to the Kansas City Games group.

This study provided a method for investigating cultural identity through molecular markers. In this example, maternal and paternal relationships can be examined using genetic data in support of the historical record. However, Y-chromosome data, typically less diverse and more locally distributed within Europe, seems better suited than mtDNA data for an investigation of Scottish ancestry. More refinement in genetic analyses, including the inclusion of more RFLP or sequencing in the mitochondrial genome and the inclusion of SNPs in Y-chromosome analyses, may provide more informative in future studies. Despite European admixture before and after settlement in the New World, and the use of limited markers, Scottish maternal and paternal genetic influences can still be detected in participants of this study.

ACKNOWLEDGMENTS

I would like to thank all of the participants who volunteered for this project. Without their enthusiasm and patience, this study would not have been possible. I would also like to thank Marion L. Mealy, who recruited volunteers, collected demographic information, and helped perform some of the lab work. Without her interest and dedication, this project would have not have begun.

This research was funded in part by a Clan Donald, USA Academic Scholarship and a Carroll D. Clark award from the University of Kansas, Department of Anthropology.

REFERENCES

Achilli, A., Rengo, C., Magri, C., *et al.* (2004). The molecular dissection of mtDNA haplogroup H confirms that the Franco-Canabrian glacial refuge was a major source for the European gene pool. *American Journal of Human Genetics*, **75**, 910–18.

Anderson, M. (1996). Population change in north-western Europe, 1750–1850. In *British Population History: From the Black Death to the Present Day*, ed. M. Anderson, pp. 191–279. Cambridge, UK: Cambridge University Press.

Andrews, R., Kubacka, I., Chinnery, P., *et al.* (1999). Reanalysis and revision of the Cambridge Reference Sequence for human mitochondrial DNA. *Nature Genetics*, **23**(2), 147.

Athey, T. W. (2005). Haplogroup prediction from Y-STR values using an allele-frequency approach. *Journal of Genetic Genealogy*, **1**, 1–7.

Athey, T. W. (2006). Haplogroup prediction from Y-STR values using a Bayesian-allele-frequency approach. *Journal of Genetic Genealogy*, **2**, 34–9.

Basu, P. (2007). *Highland Homecomings: Genealogy and Heritage Tourism in the Scottish Diaspora*. New York: Routledge Taylor & Francis Group.

Bird, S. C. (2007). Haplogroup E3b1a2 as a possible indicator of settlement in Roman Britain by soldiers of Balkan origin. *Journal of Genetic Genealogy*, **3**(2), 26–46.

Bruce, D. A. (1998). *The Mark of the Scots: Their Astonishing Contributions to History, Science, Democracy, Literature and the Arts*. New York: Citadel Press.

Capelli, C., Redhead, N., Abernethy, J. K., *et al.* (2003). A Y chromosome census of the British Isles. *Current Biology*, **13**, 979–84.

Cohn, R. L. (1995). Occupational evidence on the causes of immigration to the United States, 1836–1853. *Explorations in Economic History*, **32**, 383–408.

Devine, T. (1979). Temporary migration and the Scottish Highlands in the nineteenth century. *Economic History Review, New Series*, **32**(3), 344–59.

Devine, T. (1988). *The Great Highland Famine: Hunger, Emigration, and the Scottish Highlands in the Nineteenth Century*. Edinburgh, UK: John Donald Publishers.

Excoffier, L. L. and Schneider, S. (2005). Arlequin ver. 3.0: an integrated software package for population genetics data analysis. *Evolutionary Bioinformatics Online*, **1**, 47–50.

Faux, D. (2008). *Shetland Islands Haplogroup R1b*. Retrieved April 2009, from Shetland Islands: DNA–Genealogy Project: www.davidkfaux.org/shetlandhaplogroupR1b.html

Finnila, S., Hassinen, I. E., Ala-Kokko, L., and Majamaa, K. (2000). Phylogenetic network of mtDNA haplogroup U in northern Finland based on sequence analysis of the complete coding region by conformation-sensitive gel electrophoresis. *American Journal of Human Genetics*, **66**, 1017–26.

Fogleman, A. (1992). Migration to the thirteen British North American colonies, 1700–1775: new estimates. *Journal of Interdisciplinary History*, **22**(4), 691–709.

Fu, Y. (1997). Statistical tests of neutrality of mutations against population growth, hitchhiking and background selection. *Genetics*, **147**, 915–25.

General Register Office for Scotland (2005). *Scotland's Population 2004: The Registrar General's Annual Review of Demographic Trends*,150th edn. Edinburgh, UK: General Register Office for Scotland.

Giles, R., Blanc, H., Cann, H., and Wallace, D. (1980). Maternal inheritance of human mitochondrial DNA. *Proceedings of the National Academy of Science*, **77**(11), 6715–19.

Gonzalez, A. M., Brehm, A., Perez, J. A., *et al.* (2003). Mitochondrial DNA affinities at the Atlantic fringe of Europe. *American Journal of Physical Anthropology*, **120**, 391–404.

Goodacre, S., Helgason, A., Nicholson, J., *et al.* (2005). Genetic evidence for a family-based Scandinavian settlement of Shetland and Orkney during the Viking periods. *Heredity*, **95**, 129–35.

Gordon, W. M. (2002). *Mill Girls and Strangers: Single Women's Independent Migration in England, Scotland and the United States, 1850–1881*. Albany, NY: State University of New York Press.

Gray, M. (1955). The Highland Potato Famine of the 1840's. *Economic History Review*, **7**(3), 357–68.

Greenwood, M. J. (2008). Family and sex-specific U.S. immigration from Europe 1870–1910: a panel data study of rates and composition. *Explorations in Economic History*, **45**, 356–82.

Hatcher, J. (1996). Plague, population and the English Economy, 1348–1530. In *British Population History: From the Black Death to the Present Day*, ed. M. Anderson, pp. 9–93. Cambridge, UK: Cambridge University Press.

Helgason, A., Hickey, E., Goodacre, S., *et al.* (2001). mtDNA and the islands of the North Atlantic: estimating the proportions of Norse and Gaelic ancestry. *American Journal of Human Genetics*, **68**, 723–37.

Helgason, A., Siguroardottir, S., Nicholson, J., *et al.* (2000). Estimating Scandinavian and Gaelic ancestry in the male settlers of Iceland. *American Journal of Human Genetics*, **67**, 697–717.

Houston, R. (1996). The population history of Britain and Ireland 1500–1750. In *British Population History: From the Black Death to the Present Day*, ed. M. Anderson, pp. 95–190. Cambridge, UK: Cambridge University Press.

Hunter, J. and Ralston, I. (1999). *The Archaeology of Britain: An Introduction from the Upper Paleolithic to the Industrial Revolution*. London: Routledge.

Izagirre, N. and de la Rua, C. (1999) An mtDNA analysis in ancient Basque populations: implications for haplogroup V as a marker for a major Paleolithic expansion from southwestern Europe. *American Journal of Human Genetics*, **65**, 199–207.

Jobling, M., Hurles, M., and Tyler-Smith, C. (2004). *Human Evolutionary Genetics: Origins, Peoples and Disease*. New York: Garland Science.

Karafet, T. M., Mendez, F. L., Meilerman, M. B., *et al.* (2008). New binary polymorphisms reshape and increase resolution of the human Y chromosomal haplogroup tree. *Genome Research*, **18**, 830–8.

Kearney, H. (2006). *The British Isles: A History of Four Nations*. New York: Cambridge University Press.

Kimura, M. (1969). The number of heterozygous nucleotide sites maintained in a finite population due to a steady flux of mutations. *Genetics*, **61**, 893–903.

King, T. E., Ballereau, S. J., Schurer, K. E., and Jobling, M. A. (2006). Genetic signatures of coancestry within surnames. *Current Biology*, **16**, 384–8.

Kruskal, J. (1964). Multidimensional scaling by optimizing goodness of fit to a nonmetric hypothesis. *Psychometrika*, **29**, 1–27.

Landsman, N. C. (1999). Nation, migration, and the Province in the First British Empire: Scotland and the Americas, 1600–1800. *American Historical Review*, **104**(2), 463–75.

Magnusson, M. (2000). *Scotland: The Story of a Nation*. London: Harper Collins.

Manly, B. F. (1994). *Multivariate Statistical Methods*. New York: Chapman and Hall/CRC.

McDonald, F. and McDonald, E. S. (1980). The ethnic origins of the American people, 1790. *The William and Mary Quarterly*, **37**(2), 181–99.

McEvoy, B., Richards, M., Forster, P., and Bradley, D. G. (2004). The Longue Duree of genetic ancestry: multiple genetic marker systems and Celtic Origins on the Atlantic facade of Europe. *American Journal of Human Genetics*, **75**, 693–702.

Mielke, J. H. and Fix, A. G. (2006). The confluence of anthropological genetics and anthropological demography. In *Anthropological Genetics: Theory, Methods and Applications*, ed. M. H. Crawford, pp. 112–40. Cambridge, UK: Cambridge University Press.

Murdoch, A. (1998). Emigration from the Scottish Highlands to America in the eighteenth century. *British Journal for Eighteenth-Century Studies*, **21**, 161–74.

Myres, N. M., Rootsi, S., Lin, A. A., *et al.* (2010). A major Y-chromosome haplogroup R1b Holocene era founder efect in Central and Western Europe. *European Journal of Human Genetics*, **19**(1), 95–101.

Nei, M. (1987). *Molecular Evolutionary Genetics*. New York: Columbia University Press.

Novelletto, A. (2007). Y chromosome variation in Europe: continental and local processes in the formation of extant gene pool. *Annals of Human Biology*, **34**(2), 139–72.

Ohta, T. and Kimura, M. (1973). A model of mutation appropriate to estimate the number of electrophoretically detectable molecules in a finite population. *Genetic Research*, **22**, 201–4.

Oppenheimer, S. (2006). *The Origins of the British: A Genetic Detective Story*. London: Constable.

Reidla, M., Kivisild, T., Metspalu, E., *et al*. (2003). Origin and diffusion of mtDNA haplogroup X. *American Journal of Human Genetics*, **73**(5), 1178–90.

Richards, M., Macaulay, V., Hickey, E., *et al*. (2000). Tracing European founder lineages in the Near Eastern mtDNA pool. *American Journal of Human Genetics*, **67**, 1251–76.

Roewer, L., Croucher, P. J., Willuweit, S., *et al*. (2005). Signature of recent historical events in the European Y-chromosomal STR haplotype distribution. *Human Genetics*, **116**, 279–91.

Rosser, Z. H., Zerjal, T., Hurles, M. E., *et al*. (2000). Y-chromosomal diversity in Europe is clinal and influenced primarily by geography, rather than by language. *American Journal of Human Genetics*, **67**, 1526–43.

Scottish Government (2004). Networking? It runs in the blood of the Celts. Retrieved November 17, 2009, from Scotland: the Official Online Gateway: www.scotland.org/about/history-tradition-and-roots/features/culture/clan.html

Slatkin, M. (1995). A measure of population subdivision based on microsatellite allele frequencies. *Genetics*, **139**, 457–62.

Sturrock, K. and Rocha, J. (2000). Multidimensional scaling stress evaluation table. *Field Methods*, **12**(1), 49–60.

Sykes, B. (2006). *Blood of the Isles*. Toronto, Canada: Bantam Press.

Symonds, J. (1999). Toiling in the vale of tears: everyday life and resistance in South Uist, Outer Hebrides, 1760–1860. *International Journal of Historical Archaeology*, **3**, 101–22.

Szasz, F. M. (2000). *Scots in the North American West, 1790–1917*. Norman, OK: University of Oklahoma Press.

Tamura, K. and Nei, M. (1993). Estimation of the number of nucleotide substitutions in the control region of mitochondrial DNA in humans and chimpanzees. *Molecular Biology and Evolution*, **10**, 512–26.

Tamura, K., Dudley, J., Nei, M., and S, K. (2007). MEGA 4: Molecular Evolutionary Genetics Analysis (MEGA) Software Version 4.0. *Molecular Biology and Evolution*, **24**, 1596–99.

Thompson, J., Higgins, D. G., and Gibson, T. J. (1994). CLUSTAL W: improving the sensitivity of progressive multiple sequence alignment through sequence weighting, position-specific gap penalties and weight matrix choice. *Nucleic Acids Research*, **22**, 4673–80.

Torroni, A., Bandelt, H.-J., D'Urbano, L., *et al*. (1998). mtDNA analysis reveals a major Late Paleolithic population expansion from southwestern to northeastern Europe. *American Journal of Human Genetics*, **62**, 1137–52.

Torroni, A., Bandelt, H.-J., Macaulay, V., *et al*. (2001). A signal, from human mtDNA, of postglacial recolonization in Europe. *American Journal of Human Genetics*, **69**, 844–52.

Weale, M. E., Weiss, D. A., Jager, R. F., Bradman, N., and Thomas, M. G. (2002). Y chromosome evidence for Anglo-Saxon mass migration. *Molecular Biology and Evolution*, **19**, 1008–21.

Winter, J. (1977). Britain's "Lost Generation" of the First World War. *Population Studies*, **31**, 449–66.

Withers, C. W. (1988). Destitution and migration: labour mobility and relief from famine in Highland Scotland 1836–1850. *Journal of Historical Geography*, **14**, 128–50.

Y Chromosome Consortium (YCC) (2002). A nomenclature system for the tree of human y-chromosomal binary haplogroups. *Genome Research*, **12**, 339–48.

Zlojutro, M. (2008). Mitochondrial DNA and Y-chromosome variation of Eastern Aleut populations: implications for the genetic structure and peopling of the Aleutian Archipelago. Ph.D. dissertation, University of Kansas, Lawrence.

15

Mennonite migrations: genetic and demographic consequences

INTRODUCTION

In recent years, advances in molecular genetics have increased the understanding of past prehistoric demographic events. Yet, few molecular genetic studies have investigated more recent human migration, such as those from religious persecution (Behar *et al.*, 2008, 2010; Melton *et al.*, 2010; Non *et al.*, 2011; Pichler *et al.*, 2010). Throughout history, religious persecution has often led to human migration; which in turn has led to unique cultural and biological factors impacting human populations. The most classic example of religious migration in the scientific literature has focused on Jewish diasporas and movement of Ashkenazi and Sephardic populations in Europe (Behar *et al.*, 2008, 2010; Non *et al.*, 2011). Another example is the Reformation that occurred in sixteenth-century Europe. This in turn led to the migration of several groups throughout Europe and to the Americas. This chapter provides a brief summary of the Reformation and Anabaptist movement, and then compares existing knowledge of classical genetic polymorphism and molecular genetic markers to demonstrate that molecular genetic data provide a more accurate reflection of Mennonite demographic history.

The Reformation began in 1517 when Martin Luther hammered his 95 Theses to the door of the Catholic Church in present-day Wittenburg, Germany (MacCulloch, 2003). This movement began as an attempt to reform corruption within the Catholic Church. Western European Catholics were involved with false doctrines and practices, which included selling of indulgences, forgiveness of sins, and the buying and selling of church positions. Arguments regarding the explanation

Causes and Consequences of Human Migration, ed. Michael H. Crawford and Benjamin C. Campbell. Published by Cambridge University Press. © Cambridge University Press 2012.

of doctrine and spiritual differences among Reformation leaders led to the formation of different Protestant denominations. The most important of these denominations were the Lutherans, Calvinists, Presbyterians, and Anabaptists (MacCulloch, 2003).

The Anabaptist movement began shortly after the Reformation with shared religious beliefs in adult baptism, separation of church and state, and pacifism. These groups represented the far left of the Reformation movement and arose in Switzerland, Germany, and the Netherlands around 1525 (Rogers and Rogers, 2000). Anabaptist groups in these three regions were each associated with a charismatic leader and include: (1) Mennonites, followers of Menno Simons, originated in northern Europe and the Netherlands; (2) Amish, followers of Jacob Amman, formed in Switzerland and southern Germany; and (3) Hutterites, followers of Jacob Hutter, formed in Austria. After these groups formed, a number of small-scale rebellions broke out. Subsequently, local authorities began to view Anabaptists as a threat to social order and severely persecuted them. These Anabaptist groups were forced to migrate either to underdeveloped rural areas of Eastern Europe or the Americas. Anabaptist groups that emigrated to the United States belong primarily to three distinct groups: (1) Swiss–south German groups, including the Amish; (2) Prussian Mennonites; and (3) Austrian Hutterites.

The Amish immigrated into Pennsylvania in two waves: 1727–70 and 1815–60 (Smith and Krahn, 1981). The Hutterites first migrated to Moravia in 1529 after being expelled from the South Tyrol region in present-day Italy. In 1622, 10 000 individuals were expelled from Moravia to Transylvania, with the remaining community members forced to convert to Catholicism (Hostetler, 1985). In 1770, the Hutterites were forced to again relocate to the Ukraine and then, in 1874, approximately 1200 individuals migrated to South Dakota in the United States, where they are currently divided into three subdivisions: the Schmiedeleut; the Lehrerleut; and the Dariusleut (Eaton and Mayer, 1953).

Modern-day Mennonite congregations also underwent several migrations before settling in the Midwestern region of the United States. Therefore, these American Midwestern Mennonites (Figure 15.1) provide an excellent opportunity for using molecular genetics to study Anabaptist demographic events. Over the last 250 years, these Mennonite congregations have lived in three distinct geographic regions (Western Europe, Ukraine, and the United States). Their experiences at these three settings helped establish a unique cultural identity and a strong sense of shared community, particularly in the Ukraine, where they lived isolated from neighboring Russian and non-Mennonite

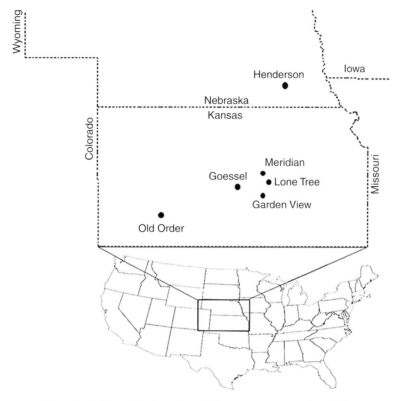

Figure 15.1 Geographic locations of Mennonite communities in Kansas and Nebraska (Melton *et al.*, 2010).

German settlers (Stevenson and Everson, 2000; Urry, 1989). The splintering and relocation of Mennonites was also enhanced by schisms resulting from differences in religious ideology. Mennonite congregations inhabiting the Midwestern United States can be divided into three different groups: (1) Alexanderwhol; (2) Holdeman; and (3) Old Colony. All three of these congregations have distinct demographic histories and a number of them have been previously investigated using both classical and molecular markers.

MENNONITE DEMOGRAPHIC HISTORY

Alexanderwohl congregation

Mennonite refugees from the Netherlands migrated to Prussia between 1527 and 1539 where they were joined by other German-speaking Anabaptist refugees (Rogers and Rogers, 2000). In 1699, 18 families of

Dutch and German refugees emigrated to Polish-controlled areas around Danzig (Gdansk) and formed the Przechówka congregation. This population increased in size and maintained meticulous genealogical records. In 1821, all but seven families moved to Russia and settled in the Ukraine, near the Molotcshna River. This congregation then adopted the name Alexanderwohl, in honor of the Russian czar at the time. Subsequent changes in economic conditions and Russian governmental policies concerning the military, along with internal subdivisions in these groups, resulted in the Alexanderwohl Mennonites migrating to the United States in 1874 (Rogers and Rogers, 2000). Upon arrival in the United States the group split into two separate divisions. One group settled west of Lincoln, Nebraska, near the present-day town of Henderson. The second group settled in Kansas, 40 miles north of Wichita.

Holdeman congregation

Another community of Mennonites in Kansas belongs to the Church of God in Christ Mennonites. This congregation was founded in 1858 by John Holdeman in Ohio and is a heterogeneous group of Pennsylvania Dutch and Germans (Ostroger Mennonites who migrated in 1875 from Volhynia in central Poland) mixed with Kleine Gemeinde Mennonites who migrated from southern Russia in 1874 (Crawford *et al.*, 1989). The Holdeman community in Kansas is split into churches in the communities of Meridian, Garden View, and Lone Tree.

Old Colony (Cuahtemoc)

The most recent Mennonite migrants to Kansas are the Old Colony (Chortiza) Mennonites who reside near Garden City in the southwestern corner of the state. Similar to members of Alexanderwohl congregation, Old Colony parishioners migrated from the Netherlands to the Vistula delta in Prussia seeking land and religious asylum around 1534. In 1788, due to limitations placed on their religion and land ownership they migrated to the Ukraine under conditions that they not proselytize and not intermarry with the surrounding Russian populace (Jaworski *et al.*, 1989). About 400 families founded a religious colony on the Dneipr river at Chortiza and the settlement prospered for approximately 100 years but shifts in religious tolerance by the Russian government led to this population migrating to western Canada in the 1870s (Jaworski *et al.*, 1989).

Increasing pressure from Canadian authorities and religious schisms with other groups led one community to migrate from western

Canada to Mexico. In the 1920s approximately 6000 individuals migrated to the region around Cuahtemoc, Chihuahua, in northern Mexico where they formed 15 colonies (Allen, 1988; Allen and Redekop, 1967, 1987). In the late 1990s, a small number of these individuals migrated to southwest Kansas around Garden City.

MENNONITE GENETICS

Data used for these genetic studies from Kansas and Nebraska Mennonite communities were originally collected in 1980 and 1981 for a multidisciplinary research project on biological aging. This research project compiled a unique data set from approximately 1200 individuals of Goessel and Meridian in Kansas and Henderson in Nebraska. These data included census questionnaires, hearing assessments, sleep patterns, 24-hour recall nutrition assessment, medical examinations, medical histories, blood chemistries, anthropometrics, neuromuscular measures, and family histories (Crawford, 2000a). In 2004, further research began to investigate the biological relationship between nutrition and genetics in Kansas Mennonite communities of Garden View, Lone Tree, Goessel, Meridian, and Garden City (Demarchi et al., 2005). Participants provided three-day nutritional profiles, anthropometrics, and whole blood samples. In both studies more than 50% of all adults from each congregation participated in the respective research and informed consent was acquired prior to collection.

The genetic history of the Mennonites and their relationship to other Anabaptist groups is indelibly stamped in their DNA. Prior to the 1980s genetic relationships among populations were reconstructed using frequencies of primary and secondary gene products contained in blood serum. These markers, now classified as classical genetic polymorphisms, are represented by blood group systems, serum protein markers, and immunoglobulins (*GM* and *KM*) as well as other genetic markers (Crawford, 2000b). The advent of high throughput sequencing in the late 1990s has resulted in the rapid characterization of the human genome and has led to increased insight into human genetic history. These molecular markers include mitochondrial DNA (mtDNA), Y chromosome, and autosomal genetic variants (Rubicz et al., 2006).

STATISTICAL GENETIC METHODS

Genetic relationships among populations are established through multivariate statistics to summarize allele or variant frequencies in genetic distance matrices. Due to the difficulty in interpreting large distance matrices a number of statistical methods have been developed to graphically display these data in two or three dimensions. These methods involve construction of phylogenetic dendograms, principal component analysis (PCA) using either multidimensional scaling (MDS) or a relationship matrix (R-matrix). A brief review of both molecular and classical genetic markers and statistical methods used to infer past genetic history of Midwestern Mennonite groups is herein summarized in order to determine the validity.

Classical genetic polymorphisms

Blood groups

A number of studies have investigated the genetic history of Mennonites using classical genetic polymorphisms (Comuzzie and Crawford, 1990; Crawford and Rogers, 1982; Crawford *et al.*, 1989; Martin *et al.*, 1996; Rogers, 1984). These have included blood group systems, serum proteins, and immunoglobulins (Crawford *et al.*, 1989; Martin *et al.*, 1996). To determine the degree of genetic variability contained within the Mennonite gene pool, a measure of specific gene frequencies is necessary. From 1979 to 1982, 1251 blood specimens were collected from volunteers in three Mennonite (Goessel, Meridian, and Henderson) communities from Kansas and Nebraska. Of the 31 blood markers tested, 19 genetic loci were polymorphic and are summarized in Table 15.1. The 12 monomorphic loci included Luthern, Gregory, Froese, Scianna2, Lw, Vel, Wright, and Miltenberger systems (Crawford *et al.*, 1989). A number of these loci are familial in Midwestern Mennonite communities, although genetic variation in them has been detected for other Anabaptist groups (Crawford, 2000b).

These allele frequencies clearly reflect the history of the Alexanderwhol congregation showing genetic correspondence between Goessel and Henderson as a result of their common origin. However, when 44 allele frequencies and 15 classical genetic polymorphisms from the three major Mennonite communities of Kansas and Nebraska were analyzed, a different picture regarding biological relationships emerged (Figure 15.2). The first axis separates Kansas communities from the Nebraskan congregation. Congregations that underwent fission from the Alexanderwohl parental population a relatively short time ago differ significantly from groups that split much earlier. Goessel separated from the Alexanderwohl church in 1909 and 1920 respectively. The basis for this separation of these two communities comes

Table 15.1. *Allele frequencies of 19 classical genetic blood groups, protein and serum polymorphisms in three Mennonite congregations from Kansas and Nebraska*

System and alleles	Mennonite congregation		
	Goessel	Meridian	Henderson
ABO			
ABO^{A1}	0.207	0.170	0.215
ABO^{A2}	0.089	0.022	0.064
ABO^{B}	0.104	0.061	0.096
ABO^{O}	0.600	0.747	0.625
MNSs			
MNS^{MS}	0.209	0.351	0.236
MNS^{Ms}	0.316	0.230	0.270
MNS^{NS}	0.031	0.032	0.068
MNS^{Ns}	0.444	0.404	0.426
Rhesus			
RH^{R1} (CDe)	0.403	0.372	0.428
RH^{R2} (cDE)	0.151	0.238	0.145
RH^{R0} (cDe)	0.019	0.000	0.054
RH^{R2} (cdE)	0.002	0.000	0.002
RH^{r} (cde)	0.423	0.390	0.359
Duffy			
FY^{A}	0.456	0.500	0.499
FY^{B}	0.544	0.500	0.501
Kidd			
JK^{A}	0.521	0.477	0.433
JK^{B}	0.479	0.523	0.567
P			
P^{P1}	0.495	0.555	0.554
P^{P2}	0.505	0.445	0.446
K			
K^{K}	0.066	0.076	0.093
K^{k}	0.934	0.924	0.907
KP			
KP^{A}	0.042	0.020	0.065
KP^{B}	0.958	0.980	0.935
Haptoglobin			
HP^{1}	0.353	0.235	0.345
HP^{2}	0.642	0.765	0.650
HP^{Carl}	0.005	0.000	0.005
Ceruloplasmin			
CP^{A}	0.003	0.001	0.009
CP^{B}	0.997	1.000	0.990

Table 15.1. (cont.)

System and alleles	Mennonite congregation		
	Goessel	Meridian	Henderson
CP^C	0.000	0.000	0.001
Properdin factor			
BF^F	0.167	0.224	0.247
BF^S	0.813	0.724	0.705
BF$^{S0.7}$	0.006	0.019	0.024
BF^{F1}	0.014	0.019	0.024
Group specific component			
GC^1	0.678	0.698	0.665
GC^2	0.322	0.032	0.334
GC^{Ab}	0.000	0.000	0.001
Group specific component (IEF)			
GC^{1S}	0.565	0.572	0.535
GC^{1F}	0.116	0.121	0.130
GC^2	0.319	0.307	0.334
GC^{1A1}	0.000	0.000	0.001
Adenosine deaminase			
ADA^1	0.968	0.895	0.958
ADA^2	0.032	0.105	0.042
Adekylate kinase			
AK^1	0.954	1.000	0.971
AK^2	0.046	0.000	0.029
6-phospogluconate dehydrogenase			
PGD^A	0.993	1.000	0.995
PGD^B	0.000	0.000	0.001
PGD^C	0.007	0.000	0.004
Acid phosphatase			
ACP^A	0.377	0.401	0.291
ACP^B	0.594	0.593	0.639
ACP^C	0.029	0.006	0.070
Esterase D			
ESD^1	0.911	0.808	0.901
ESD^2	0.089	0.192	0.099
Phosphoglucomutase (IEF)			
PGMI^{1+}	0.764	0.807	0.815
PGMI^{1-}	0.085	0.026	0.112
PGMI^{2+}	0.141	0.146	0.173
PGMI^{2-}	0.010	0.021	0.010
PGMI^R	0.001	0.000	0.002

Source: Crawford (2000b).

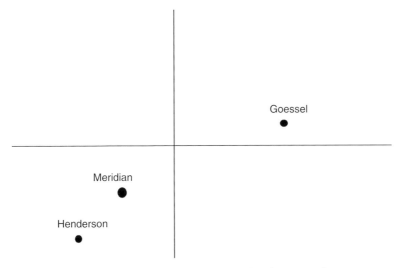

Figure 15.2 R-matrix of three Kansas and Nebraska Mennonite congregations using 44 alleles from 15 genetic loci (Crawford, 2000b).

from the allele frequencies for blood group P and serum protein esterase D (Table 15.1). The Nebraska Mennonite community of Henderson has a unique RH^R haplotype that distinguishes it from Goessel (Crawford, 2000b). A contributing factor to these results may be that these two communities fissioned along familial lines through kin-structured migration (i.e. a non-random subdivision of the gene pool). Thus founder effect contributed to the differences in gene frequencies between contemporary Mennonite populations (Crawford, 2000b).

Immunoglobulins

Martin and colleagues (1996) investigated immunoglobulin variation in Mennonites from 586 individuals in six Kansas and Nebraska Mennonite communities (Table 15.2). GM allotypes are structural variants of the heavy gamma chains of the IgG immunoglobulins. These allotypes are encoded by a group of tightly linked genes on the long arm of chromosome 14 (14q32.33) and are termed haplotypes. Unlike other classical genetic polymorphisms, these GM haplotypes tend to be population specific and have been previously used to characterize population affinities and measure genetic admixture (Crawford *et al.*, 1976; Schanfield *et al.*, 1984). These differences in haplotype frequencies among Mennonite populations are relatively small with GM*FB being the most common

Table 15.2. *Frequencies of immunolobulin haplotypes in three Mennonite congregations from Kansas and Nebraska*

Haplotype frequency	Mennonite congregation		
	Goessel	Meridian	Henderson
GM * A G	0.123	0.290	0.254
GM * X G	0.092	0.151	0.075
GM * FB	0.765	0.542	0.671
GM *ZAB	0.020	0.009	0.000
GM * A T	0.000	0.009	0.000
IGK * 1	0.054	0.027	0.037

Source: Martin *et al.* (1996)

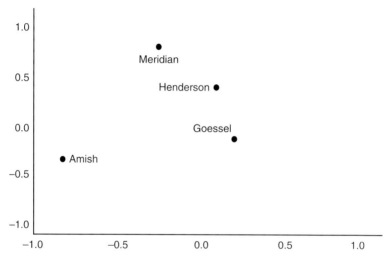

Figure 15.3 R-matrix of three Kansas and Nebraska Mennonite congregations along with Amish using eight alleles from five immunglobulin genetic loci (Martin *et al.*, 1996).

haplotype, ranging from 0.542 in Meridian to 0.765 in Goessel. Similarly, GM*A F varies from 0.123 in Goessel to 0.290 in Meridian.

Figure 15.3 shows a R-matrix plot of three Kansas and Nebraska Mennonite congregations along with Amish, using eight alleles from five classic genetic loci (ABO, MN, Rh, GM, and KM) Similar to its findings for blood marker polymorphisms, this study found a close relationship between Tabor and Goessel and the Amish and Meridian samples having the least affinity with the other Mennonite congregations. They also found a close biological relationship between Meridian

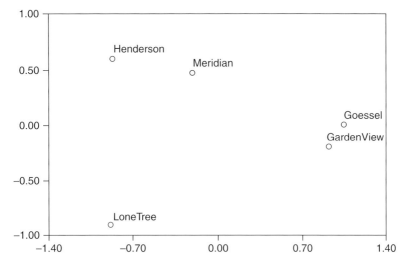

Figure 15.4 Bidimensional scaling representation of co-ancestry distances of Reynold *et al.* (1983), displaying biological relationships among five Mennonite communities from Kansas and Nebraska (Demarchi *et al.*, 2005).

and Henderson, which is not indicative of the historical records for these populations, with Meridian belonging to the Holdeman congregation and Henderson belonging to Alexanderwohl.

Molecular genetic polymorphisms

Apolipoproteins

Demarchi and colleagues (2005) studied seven apolipoprotein (APOA1 -75bp, APOA1 +83bp, APOB Ins/Del, APO *Xba*I, APOC3 *Sst*I, and APOE) and lipoprotein lipase (LPL) loci in five Mennonite communities from Kansas and Nebraska. Apoliproteins are known to have significant influence on interindividual variation of plasma lipid levels and increase cardiovascular risk in some populations (Kamboh *et al.* 1999; Tall *et al.*, 1997). Of these seven apolipoprotein loci investigated in Midwestern Mennonites, only one locus, APOB *Xba*I, departed significantly from Hardy–Weinberg equilibrium. Analyzing a MDS plot (Figure 15.4) they detected a closer biological relationship between Henderson and Meridian than between Henderson and Goessel. However, they did find a high mean r_{ii} (R_{ST}, an estimate equivalent to F_{ST}; Harpending and Jenkins, 1973) value of 0.02, which is unexpectedly elevated considering the close relationship

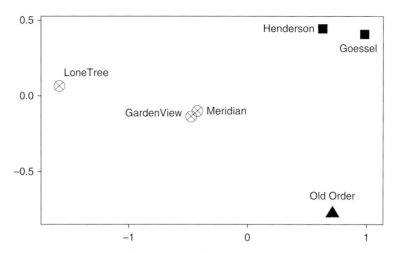

Figure 15.5 Multidimensional-scaling plot of six Mennonite communities aggregated by their associated congregation (Melton *et al.*, 2010).

between these Mennonite communities. A plausible explanation for this would be that this is representative of kin-structured migrations, which increase genetic variation among groups, and its effect being magnified in small populations (Fix, 2004).

Mitochondrial DNA

Melton *et al.* (2010) investigated mtDNA haplogroup and haplotype variation in 118 individuals from six Mennonite communities from Kansas and Nebraska. These Mennonites exhibited eight Western European mtDNA haplogroups: H, HV0, I, J, K, T, U, and X. Comparable to other Western European populations, haplogroup H was the most frequent in all six communities and ranged from 35% in Lone Tree to 75% in Old Colony Mennonites from Garden City. Fifty-eight mtDNA haplotypes were detected in these groups with only one shared between groups. Unlike both immunoglobulins and apolipoproteins, the MDS plot of these six communities demonstrated a relationship between Goessel and Henderson as well as Garden View and Meridian clustering (Figure 15.5). These mtDNA data also illustrated that these congregations split along familial lines. This is indicative of patterns of fission–fusion in these communities. These authors concluded that these haploid molecular genetic markers provided a more accurate reflection of biological relationships between Mennonite communities than evidence based on classical genetic polymorphisms or autosomal molecular markers.

DISCUSSION

Religious isolates have long been studied to understand the complex etiology of rare genetic disorders. Recently studies have begun to apply modern molecular genetic data to further understand the population structure and recent genetic history of Anabaptist religious populations. This chapter has focused on the comparison of molecular and classical genetic polymorphism in order to further elucidate the migration history of Mennonites inhabiting the Midwestern United States. These data reveal that the Mennonites have a typical Western European genetic makeup, despite having previously inhabited areas of Eastern Europe for an extended length of time. In addition, we find mtDNA variation in these communities provides a higher resolution and a more accurate reflection of the historical connections between Mennonite communities. The resulting population subdivision of these communities into congregations supports previously published reports regarding known patterns of kin-structured fission–fusion and founder effect (Crawford, 2000b; Crawford *et al.*, 1989; Martin *et al.*, 1996) and offers clarification of the biological relationship between genetic characteristics and demographic movement for these Mennonite groups.

The high genetic diversity demonstrated in some Mennonite communities by both classical and molecular genetic markers is not the result of high levels of inbreeding. Since the 1930s, reproductive isolation in Mennonites congregations has noticeably declined and marital migration from other Mennonite communities has been the primary source of gene flow into the Midwestern Mennonite population (Crawford *et al.*, 1989). The Mennonites from the Alexanderwohl colony experienced high inbreeding ($F = 0.0162$) in the nineteenth century while residing in Przechówko, Prussia (Rogers, 1984). Melton *et al.* (2010) found that on the basis of mtDNA diversity the closest maternal biological relationship that Mennonites had among European populations was with the Dutch. This suggests that as they moved throughout Europe there was little admixture with outside populations. After relocation to the United States, the inbreeding coefficient dropped from 0.02 to 0.0062. Over the last two generations the effects of inbreeding among Mennonites have been reduced as the majority of young Mennonites attending colleges in Tabor and Goessel have found marriage partners from outside Mennonite communities. Thus, the genetic history of Mennonites has been affected by the evolutionary process of fission and fusion.

The study of genetic variation in Kansas and Nebraska Mennonite populations is a useful tool for reconstructing the recent genetic

history of these religious congregations. The two communities representing the Alexanderwohl congregation, Goessel and Henderson,
are the descendants of 191 immigrant families from the Molotschna
Mennonite colony in the Ukraine. After arrival in Kansas, these
families underwent further fission, splitting into the two present-day
congregations. An important question is why the Alexanderwohl
community split into different groups after having survived for over
200 years in Europe as a single unit and why they chose not to
continue as a single collective colony. Historical accounts suggest that
the primary fission was due to pressure from competing railroad land
agents and differences in land preferences. Other accounts include
different leadership partiality and the infeasibility of a large group
settling in a single geographic location. Later on, further fissions
among groups were attributed to increased population size and difficulty in traveling long distances to a single church location (Rogers
and Rogers, 2000).

Rogers (1984) compared church records covering membership,
birth, deaths, United States residence, Russian residence, ships passenger lists, and genealogical data to determine if there was a detectable
pattern in the fissioning of these Mennonite communities. These data
indicated that communities in Kansas and Nebraska in 1874 were not
unilinearly related and the division of the 1874 immigrant party was
non-random. Between 1874 and 1921 local fissioning between settlements appears to have been due to a mixture of different ancestral
congregational membership and distinctive factors related to doctrinal
differences between individuals. However, in all cases based on these
data, fission occurred along kinship lines, leading to an unequal distribution of surnames among congregations (Rogers and Rogers, 2000).
This unequal distribution of surnames can be found in the more recent
Mennonite research as well. In the five communities that included
males, there were 87 surnames, of which only 17 were shared between
communities (P. E. Melton, unpublished data).

Evidence from mtDNA diversity in these communities appears to
explain this differentiation quite well with a clear biological relationship being demonstrated between Henderson and Goessel, which are
the two descendant congregations from Alexanderwohl. As previously
discussed, Crawford (2000b) used classical genetic polymorphisms from
25 loci, Martin *et al.* (1996) used immunoglobulins, and Demarchi *et al.*
(2005) used apolipoproteins but all found a closer biological relationship between the Meridian (Holdeman) and Henderson Mennonite communities, which is not reflective of known historical accounts. Classical

molecular polymorphisms and apolipoproteins are likely under selection pressure making them less useful for reconstruction of genetic history than haploid mtDNA genetic variants. However, since mtDNA is only reflective of the maternal side of genetic history, it is possible that these data reflect a cultural practice where females remained with their traditional congregations, whiles males moved between them. In order for this assumption to be confirmed, genetic data from the Y chromosome would be needed for these communities.

Those Mennonite communities belonging to the Holdeman congregation demonstrate considerable genetic variation, despite their recent history. This high diversity may be reflective of kin-based fission within this group. Historically, Garden View and Lone Tree split from Meridian recently and are considered to be more religiously conservative than those communities belonging to the Alexanderwohl congregation. As previously demonstrated, apolipoprotein genetic variation suggested a closer relationship between Goessel and Garden View and between Meridian and Henderson with Lone Tree as an outlier (Demarchi *et al.*, 2005). This differs from mtDNA where Lone Tree is once again an outlier but closer to Meridian and Garden View, suggesting that this population is distinct from these other two Holdeman communities. However, based on mtDNA haplotypes (Melton *et al.*, 2010), there is a closer maternal relationship between these Holdeman communities and this relationship is best explained through kinship-structured migrations. In this type of migration, when closely related individuals disperse among groups, the evolutionary effect of this can mimic genetic drift and lead to higher genetic differentiation between groups (Fix, 2004; Rogers, 1987). In a similar way to genetic drift, kin-structured migration demonstrates its greatest impact on smaller populations and is easily identified in low-density fission–fusion societies, such as the Yanamamō from South America or the Semai of Malaysia (Fix, 2004). On the basis of genetic data from Mennonites, Anabaptist populations appear to follow this fission–fusion model of human migration.

The most distinct and least studied of the Mennonite communities belong to the Old Colony congregation. Their unique genetic structure is reflective of their migration patterns from Europe to the Americas. Members of the Old Colony congregation first emigrated from Alberta in Canada to Chihuahua in Mexico in the 1920s. Then beginning in the late 1990s, parishioners from this congregation began to migrate to southwestern Kansas to escape ongoing violence from narcotics traffickers along the United States–Mexican border. On the basis of mtDNA genetic data, members of this congregation appear to have remained isolated from outside admixture with either the local Mestizo of Chihuahua or the autochonous Tarahumara populations. Old Colony Mennonites appear similar to Hutterites in their distinctive maternal genetic makeup. Pichler *et al.* (2010) found that Hutterites were distinct from other European populations. Hutterites were also found to be distinct from Mennonite communities based on mtDNA evidence (Melton *et al.*, 2010).

CONCLUSIONS

Genetic variation within these Mennonite communities is consistent with a founding population that originated in Europe and migrated to North America. Research on classical genetic polymorphisms (Crawford *et al.*, 1989), immunoglobulins (Martin *et al.*, 1996) and molecular markers (Demarchi *et al.*, 2005) under selective pressure have shown a biological relationship between disparate Mennonite groups with different evolutionary histories but close geographic affinity. Neutral or uniparental molecular markers, such as mtDNA, demonstrate a more accurate reflection regarding the migratory history of Mennonite populations. This better fit between neutral genetic markers and historical events is due to the higher resolution that molecular sequence data provides. Despite the short time frame (< 500 years) involved in the origin and differentiation of Mennonite populations, molecular genetic data clearly illustrate the effects of microevolution on small human populations. To date, only one study has investigated sequence data in these Anabaptist Mennonite congregations (Melton *et al.*, 2010) and mtDNA is only representative of maternal genetic history, therefore molecular genetic data from autosomal ancestry informative markers and the non-combining region of the Y chromosome should also be explored in order to further investigate the evolutionary and migratory history of Anabaptist populations.

REFERENCES

Allen, G. (1988). Random genetic drift inferred from surnames in Old Colony Mennonites. *Human Genetics*, **60**, 639–53.

Allen, G. and Redekop, C. W. (1967). Individual differences in survival and reproduction among Old Colony Mennonites in Mexico: Progress to October 1966. *Eugen Q*, **14**, 103–11.

Allen, G. and Redekop, C. W. (1987). Old Colony Mennonites in Mexico: migration and inbreeding. *Social Biology*, **34**, 166–79.

Behar, D. M., Metspalu, E., Kivisild, T., *et al.* (2008). Counting the founders: the matrilineal genetic ancestry of the Jewish Diaspora. *PLoS ONE*, 3(4), e2062.

Behar, D. M., Yunusbayev, B., Metspalu, M., *et al.* (2010). The genome-wide structure of the Jewish people. *Nature*, **466**(7303), 238–42.

Comuzzie, A. G. and Crawford, M. H. (1990). Genetic heterozygosity and morphological variation in Mennonites. *Human Biology*, **62**, 101–12.

Crawford, M. H. (ed.) (2000a). *Different Seasons: Biological Aging among the Mennonites of the Midwestern United States*. Publications in Anthropology. Lawrence, KS: University of Kansas.

Crawford, M. H. (2000b). Genetic structure of Mennonite populations. In *Different Seasons: Biological Aging among the Mennonites of the Midwestern United States*, ed. M. H. Crawford, pp. 31–40. Lawrence, KS: University of Kansas Press.

Crawford, M. H. and Rogers, L. (1982). Population genetics models in the study of aging and longevity in a Mennonite community. *Social Science and Medicine*, **16**, 149–53.

Crawford, M. H., Dykes, D. D., and Polesky, H. F. (1989). Genetic structure of Mennonite populations of Kansas and Nebraska. *Human Biology*, **61**, 493–514.

Crawford, M. H., Workman, P. L., McLean, C., and Lees, F. C. (1976). Admixture estimates and selection in Tlaxcala. In *The Tlaxcaltecans: Prehistory, Demography, Morphology, and Genetics* ed. M. H. Crawford, pp. 161–8. Lawrence KS: University of Kansas Press.

Demarchi, D., Mosher, M. J., and Crawford, M. H. (2005). Apolipoproteins (apoproteins) and LPL variation in Mennonite populations of Kansas and Nebraska. *American Journal of Human Biology*, **17**, 593–600.

Eaton, J. W. and Mayer, A. J. (1953). The social biology of very high fertility among the Hutterites: the demography of a unique population. *Human Biology*, **25**, 206–64.

Fix, A. G. (2004). Kin-structured migration: causes and consequences. *American Journal of Human Biology*, **16**, 387–94.

Harpending, H. and Jenkins, T. (1973). Genetic distance among southern African populations. In *Methods and Theories of Anthropological Genetics*, ed. M. H. Crawford and P. Workman, pp. 177–99. Albuquerque, NM: University of New Mexico Press.

Hostetler, J. A. (1985). History and relevance of the Hutterite population for genetic studies. *American Journal of Medical Genetics*, **22**, 453–62.

Jaworski, M. A., Severini, A., Mansour, G., *et al.* (1989). Inherited diseases in North American Mennonites: focus on Old Colony (Chortitza) Mennonites. *American Journal of Medical Genetics*, **32**, 158–68.

Kamboh, M. I., Bunker, C. H., Aston, C. E., *et al.* (1999). Genetic association of five apolipoprotein polymorphisms with serum lipoprotein- lipid levels in African blacks. *Genetic Epidemiology*, **16**, 205–22.

MacCulloch, D. (2003). *The Reformation: A History*. London: Viking Penguin.

Martin, K., Stevenson, J. C., Crawford, M. H., Everson, P. M., and Schanfield, M. S. (1996). Immunoglobin haplotype frequencies in Anabaptist population samples: Kansas and Nebraska Mennonites and Indiana Amish. *Human Biology*, **68**, 45–62.

Melton, P. E., Mosher, M. J., Rubicz, R., Zlojutro, M., and Crawford, M. H. (2010). Mitochondrial DNA diversity in Mennonites from the Midwestern United States. *Human Biology*, **82**, 267–89.

Non, A. L., Al-Meeri, A., Raaum, R. L., Sanchez, L. F., and Mulligan, C. J. (2011). Mitochondrial DNA reveals distinct evolutionary histories for Jewish populations in Yemen and Ethiopia. *American Journal of Physical Anthropology*, **144**, 1–10.

Pichler, I., Fuchsberger, C., Platzer, C., *et al.* (2010). Drawing the history of the Hutterite population on a genetic landscape: inference from Y-chromosome and mtDNA genotypes. *European Journal of Human Genetics*, **18**, 463–70.

Reynold, J., Weir, B. S., and Cockerham, C. C. (1983). Estimation of the coancestry coefficient: basis for a short-term genetic distance. *Genetics*, **105**, 767–79.

Rogers, A. R. (1987). A model of kin-structured migration. *Evolution*, **41**, 417–26.

Rogers, L. A. (1984). Phylogenetic identification of a religious isolate and the measurement of inbreeding. Ph.D. dissertation, University of Kansas, Lawrence.

Rogers, L. and Rogers, R. A. (2000). Mennonite history with special reference to Alexanderwhol and related congregations in Kansas and Nebraska. In *Different Seasons: Biological Aging among the Mennonites of the Midwestern United States*, ed. M. H. Crawford, pp. 7–18. Lawrence, KS: University of Kansas Press.

Rubicz, R., Melton, P., and Crawford, M. H. (2006). Molecular markers in anthropological genetic studies. In *Anthropological Genetics: Theory Methods and Applications*, ed. M. H. Crawford, pp. 141–86. Cambridge, UK: Cambridge University Press.

Schanfield, M. S., Brown, R., and Crawford, M. H. (1984) Immunoglobulin allotypes in the Black Caribs and Creoles of Belize and St. Vincent. In *Black Caribs: A Case Study of Biocultural Adaptation*, ed. M. H. Crawford, pp. 345–63. Lawrence KS: University of Kansas Press.

Smith, C. H. and Krahn, C. (1981). *Smith's Story of the Mennonites*, 5th edn. Newton, KS: Faith and Life Press.

Stevenson, J. and Everson, P. (2000). Historical demography of Mennonite populations. in *Different Seasons: Biological Aging among the Mennonites of the Midwestern United States*, ed. M. H. Crawford, pp. 19–30. Lawrence, KS: University of Kansas Press.

Tall, A., Welch, C., Applebaum-Bowden, D., and Wassef, M. (1997). Interaction of diet and genes in atherogenesis: report of an NHLBI working group. *Arteriosclerosis, Thrombosis, and Vascular Biology*, **17**, 3326–31.

Urry, J. (1989). *None But Saints: The Transformation of Mennonite Life in Russia 1789–1989*. Winnipeg, Canada: Hyperion Press.

16

Human migratory history: through the looking-glass of genetic geography of *Mycobacterium tuberculosis*

INTRODUCTION

Tuberculosis that is caused by *Mycobacterium tuberculosis* is an ancient disease that plagued humankind throughout its history and prehistory (Daniel, 2006). The oldest examples of spinal TB, in the form of fossil bones, date back to about 8000 BC (reviewed in Herzog, 1998). Findings in Egyptian mummies indicate that spinal caries existed around 2400 BC (Zink *et al.*, 2003). The legal text formulated by the Babylonian king Hammurabi 3900 years ago mentions a chronic lung disease, which could be TB. The famous "plague of Justinian" could be at least partly due to invasion of the Mediterranean urban cultures by young people from northern and eastern Europe who had never before come into contact with TB (Herzog, 1998). The first mention of TB in Chinese literature appears in a medical text written by Emperor Shennong of China (2700 BCE) describing *xulao bing* (weak consumption), which is believed to be TB (Yang, 1998). In East Asia/Far East (including China, Korea, and Japan), the earliest case of paleo-pathologically confirmed TB so far reported is from Hunan province in China in a female wet cadaver dated to about 200 BC, in the Western Han dynasty in the Kingdom of Changsha (Suzuki and Inoue, 2007 and references therein). TB has been endemic in Europe for a much longer period and reached epidemic proportions during the eighteenth and nineteenth centuries (TB mortality in the early 1800s in England was $> 500/100\ 000$) due to especially adverse social conditions until it began to decline from about 1870 onwards (Murray, 2004).

Causes and Consequences of Human Migration, ed. Michael H. Crawford and Benjamin C. Campbell. Published by Cambridge University Press. © Cambridge University Press 2012.

Therefore, the East Asian long-term endemic coexistence with *M. tuberculosis* is apparently independent of the relatively recent medieval European TB epidemics. Finally, most recently, modern TB reached the coastal people of Africa only in about 1910; it has been noticed that black populations have higher rates of TB and are also more likely to develop the more fulminant forms of the disease (reviewed in Bellamy, 1998; Stead, 1997).

Mycobacterium tuberculosis sensu stricto (*M. tuberculosis*) is a strictly human pathogen. The tubercle bacillus has the remarkable ability to persist in the human host in the form of a long-term asymptomatic infection referred to as latent TB. One third of the world population is estimated to have a latent TB infection. The latent or dormant TB was perhaps the predominant mode of coexistence of *M. tuberculosis* with its human host in a pre-industrialized time when transmission of the pathogen was historically vertical; that is, mainly family/household linked.

The main markers of *M. tuberculosis* genetic diversity are sequence polymorphisms (large deletions and SNPs), insertion sequences, as well as various repeats (one CRISPR and multiple minisatellite VNTR loci). Large unidirectional deletions and SNPs are good markers but they are not sufficiently studied in different *M. tuberculosis* populations yet to be used for global analysis. The Direct Repeat (DR) locus belongs to the large CRISPR family found in a half of eubacterial and most of archaeal genomes; it consists of minisatellite alternating exact direct repeats and variable spacers (Kamerbeek *et al.*, 1997) (Figure 16.1). The evolution of the DR locus in *M. tuberculosis* currently occurs via neutral consecutive deletions of either single units or contiguous blocks (van Embden *et al.*, 2000) which makes it suitable for phylogenetic inferences.

Mycobacterial interspersed repetitive units (MIRU) are polymorphic VNTR (variable number of tandem repeats) loci scattered throughout the bacterial chromosome (Figure 16.1) (Supply *et al.*, 2001). The number of repeat copies per locus may vary among strains, and the use of several such loci allows sufficient interstrain differentiation (Supply *et al.*, 2001). The MIRU-VNTR profiles are presented as multidigit numerical codes ("complex haplotypes"), each digit representing the copy number in a locus. The evolution of VNTR loci appears as a whole neutral, and these loci are independent from each other and apparently from the human host genome.

Evolution of the 12 MIRU-VNTR loci in *M. tuberculosis* was estimated by mathematical modeling to occur at a slow mutation rate for their repeats (Grant *et al.*, 2008); consequently, this property makes them suitable for inferring long-term evolutionary histories of *M. tuberculosis*

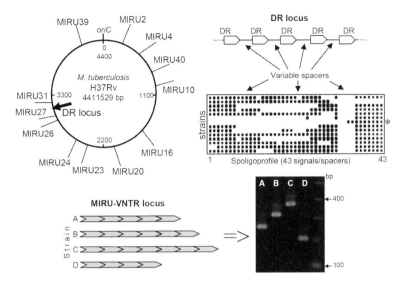

Figure 16.1 Position of the MIRU-VNTR and Direct Repeat loci on the Circle map of *Mycobacterium tuberculosis* genome (strain H37Rv), their structure and PCR or macroarray-based analysis. Hybridization profile of the Beijing genotype is shown by an asterisk.

genotypes. Even though the utility of VNTR loci as a whole (and when used alone) for inferring global phylogeny for *M. tuberculosis* species is uncertain (Yokoyama *et al.*, 2010), they are good markers for dealing with particular clonal lineages within the species (Mokrousov, 2008; Supply *et al.*, 2001).

Due to the virtual lack of horizontal genetic exchange between its strains, *M. tuberculosis* has a clonal population structure represented by separate lineages (also named families or genotypes). Those most known include Haarlem, Beijing, East-African Indian, Central-Asian, and Latin-American-Mediterranean (Gagneux and Small, 2007). Most likely, these families could have initially been endemic within specific geographical areas. Some remain circumscribed to the particular regions, whereas others have become omnipresent. Local specificity of clones may be explained by recent importation and fast dissemination due to specific pathogenic properties or outbreak conditions, or, somewhat alternatively, due to long-term historical presence in an area.

Among several genetic families identified within *M. tuberculosis*, the Beijing genotype is probably the most characterized *M. tuberculosis* lineage. For the first time, it was identified in the *M. tuberculosis* strains isolated in the Beijing area in China which coined the name (van Soolingen *et al.*, 1995). The characteristic structure of the DR locus is a marker that defines the Beijing genotype and distinguishes it from other families within *M. tuberculosis* (Figure 16.1). These strains are endemically prevalent in Southeast Asia, the area of origin and primary dispersal, as well as in northern Eurasia and South Africa, areas of their secondary dispersal (Bifani *et al.*, 2002; Mokrousov, 2008). They have been found in countries as distant as Argentina, Malawi, and Australia and new unexpected routes of their apparently recent transmission are being uncovered (reviewed in Mokrousov, 2008). The Beijing strains demonstrate some important pathogenic features, rapidly being disseminated worldwide, and, in a great part, are responsible for a current global epidemic of the drug-resistant TB.

The traditional genetic markers for inferring human genealogy, population genetic structure, and historic and recent migrations include Y chromosome, mitochondrial DNA, and microsatellite sequences. Their use for direct reconstruction of human evolution is sometimes limited because of relatively low genetic variability owing to recent strong bottlenecks. However, during the long course of its evolution the species *Homo sapiens* has acquired the "second genome"; that is, the total indigenous biota of humans, which coevolved with their hosts. During the processes of human dispersal around the world over the past 50 000–100 000 years, there have been several major transitions in the relationships of *H. sapiens* with the environment, resulting in the emergence of new infectious diseases (McMichael, 2004; Rinaldi, 2007). According to McMichael (2004), the three great historical transitions in the last 10 000 years occurred when: (1) early agrarian-based settlements enabled a human contact with sylvatic enzootic microbes; (2) early Eurasian civilizations came into direct military and commercial contact/conflict, 3000–2000 years ago, thereby exchanging their prevalent infection agents; and, more recently (3) European expansion since the seventeenth century caused the transoceanic spread of often lethal infectious diseases, for example measles, smallpox, and influenza.

Thus an alternative source of data for deciphering human migrations and origins can be provided by some of the microbes if their genetic variation is sufficiently high and their evolutionary histories correlate closely with that of the host. Horizontally/epidemically transmitted pathogens (e.g. influenza or HIV) are unlikely to mirror the population genetic structure of the human host; instead their population structures reflect the emergence and rapid outburst spreading of certain specific genotypes. Accordingly, microbe-based tracing of human history relies on use of non-epidemically or mainly latently manifested agents with a family/household mode of transmission.

It should also be kept in mind that some microbial "markers" have notable drawbacks with regard to tracing human migrations. Hepatitis G has a low infection rate from 1–4% in industrialized countries to 10–13% in developing countries which means it is difficult to collect a representative sample. In contrast, the possibility of recombination between genetically different strains (e.g. *H. pylori*) can obscure inference of phylogenetic relationships between geographically distant isolates (Pavesi, 2005; Wirth *et al.*, 2005). Hence remarkably useful features of *M. tuberculosis* for tracing human migrations are (1) its high prevalence as latent TB in humans (~1/3) and (2) lack of recombination.

The clonality of *M. tuberculosis* as a whole justifies a use of one of its lineages as a special model of the whole species. Therefore the objective of this study was to evaluate a global phylogeography of the worldwide disseminated and medically important *M. tuberculosis* Beijing family in the light of historical and recent human migrations.

STUDY: RESULTS AND HYPOTHESES

The M. tuberculosis Beijing family isolates were defined based on spoligotyping: isolates showing hybridization to at least three of the spacers 35 to 43 and absence of hybridization to spacers 1 to 34 were defined as the Beijing genotype (Kremer *et al.*, 2004) (Figure 16.1). Subsequent analysis of the genetic diversity was based on the 11 MIRU-VNTR loci of the classical MIRU-VNTR typing scheme (Supply *et al.*, 2001), namely, loci ##2, 4, 10, 16, 23, 24, 26, 27, 31, 39, 40 (Figure 16.1); locus MIRU-20 was excluded as it was not amplified in some studies.

The Hunter–Gaston Index (HGI) was used as an estimate of the allelic diversity for specific areas, for all loci taken together (Hunter and Gaston, 1988). Observed Distance (OD) between the geographical populations of the Beijing strains was calculated as described previously based on the difference in the frequencies of the VNTR subtypes (Mokrousov, 2008). The resulting matrix of interpopulation distances was used for multidimensional scaling (MDS) with PROXSCAL algorithm implemented in the SPSS 11.5 for Windows package (SPSS, Chicago, IL). The most parsimonious network (minimum spanning tree) of the Beijing MIRU types was built using the PARS routine of PHYLIP 3.6 package (Felsenstein, 2004).

VNTR database and its phylogenetic exploitation

Collecting VNTR data from different published sources yielded ~2400 strains (Affolabi *et al.*, 2009; Dou *et al.*, 2008; Lasunskaia *et al.*, 2010;

Mokrousov, 2008 and references therein; Mokrousov *et al.*, 2009a, 2009b; Nikolayevskyy *et al.*, 2007; Taype, 2007; Taype *et al.*, 2012; Wada *et al.*, 2009). The MIRU data were entered into an Excel spreadsheet and the strains were subdivided into MIRU types with unique 11-loci profiles. Populations and subpopulations included in the analysis were: Russia (Northwest; $n = 47$; Central-Volga region, $n = 129$; Middle Ural, $n = 50$; East Siberia, $n = 113$), China (Beijing, $n = 72$; Shanghai, $n = 74$; Hong Kong, $n = 243$; Wuhan, $n = 83$; Henan, $n = 32$; Taiwan, $n = 187$), Singapore ($n = 160$), Vietnam ($n = 53$), South Africa ($n = 329$), Japan (Kobe-Osaka, $n = 350$), Australia (Queensland, $n = 33$), Peru ($n = 33$). A minimal sample size equal to 30 individuals per population is usually applied to these sorts of studies to reliably quantify the genetic diversity within and among genetic variants (Khanlou *et al.*, 2011; Pruett and Winker, 2008; Watanabe and Omur, 2007). For this reason, other countries or territories (Bangladesh, Mongolia, South Korea, Malaysia, Thailand, United States, French Guiana, Central African Republic, Papua New Guinea, Ukraine, Benin) represented by only a few isolates or types were not included in the interpopulation comparison.

A comparison of the available 11-loci VNTR data of the ~2400 *M. tuberculosis* Beijing genotype strains identified a total of 258 different types; each included strains with identical 11-digit profiles. Evaluated with HGI, the most homogeneous were Russian populations with HGI below 0.7 in all cases. The most heterogeneous were East Asian populations and Australia (Figure 16.2). The highest HGI (> 0.9) was observed for Japan, Singapore, Henan, and Wuhan populations. Some world areas (Laos, Mongolia, Bangladesh) were represented by a small number of isolates and require caution in interpreting their level of diversity. A special case may be a high HGI of the *M. tuberculosis* Beijing population in Singapore as it may represent repeated introductions of *M. tuberculosis* genotypes from diverse geographical regions over a relatively short time span. Given the nature of Singapore as a major trade hub, this seems likely.

It may be noted that the four largest types – M2, M11, M28, and M33 – accounted for the majority (54%) of strains. Figure 16.2 shows a geographical distribution of the 10 major types, also taking into account a proportion of the Beijing genotype strains in the local populations of *M. tuberculosis*.

Figure 16.3 presents the MIRU-based most parsimonious network (minimum spanning tree) of the 50 globally or locally prevalent shared types. The largest type M11 is located in the core of the network; furthermore, it contains so-called ancient and modern strains

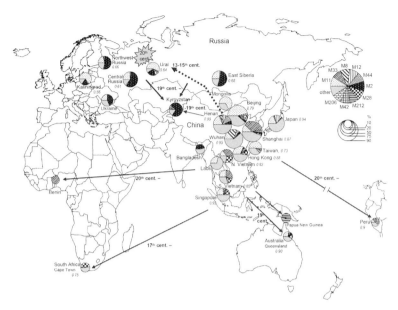

Figure 16.2 Geographical distribution and hypothesized routes of dissemination of the main MIRU types of the *Mycobacterium tuberculosis* Beijing genotype. Circle size is roughly proportional to the percentage of the Beijing genotype strains in a local population of *M. tuberculosis*. HGI diversity values for particular areas are based on 12 MIRU loci taken together.

(Mokrousov *et al.*, 2005). I interpret this situation as a reflection of its phylogenetically ancestral/primordial position.

A closer look at the distribution of types/populations across the minimum spanning tree revealed that the Chinese strains are located all over the network, at both inner and multiple terminal nodes (Figure 16.3). Together with highest diversity, this suggests the Chinese sample to be the most ancient. Japan and Vietnam make an intermediate case: strains from both areas are present in the core type M11 but found somewhat less frequently in other types than Chinese strains. In contrast, the South African strains are found only in the terminal positions due to their comparatively recent introduction and/or accompanying bottleneck events. Most of the strains from Peru and Australia are found in the major types, including core type M11, perhaps reflecting their relatively recent importation from East Asia not yet followed by extensive *in situ* evolution. Still, one should note the existence of some terminal types specific for Peru (M42, M206) and Papua New Guinea (M212). Finally, a majority

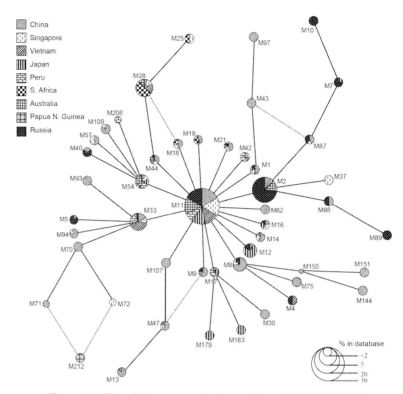

Figure 16.3 The minimum spanning tree of the major MIRU-VNTR types identified within *Mycobacterium. tuberculosis* Beijing genotype strains from different geographic areas. Each edge represents one change per locus. Circle size is roughly proportional to the number of strains. Dotted branches depict possible alternatives.

of Russian strains is located in both major inner nodes M11 and M2 but the Russian population shows the least diversity, a pattern that may reflect the relatively ancient introduction but only recent dissemination.

Patterns of genetic diversity are the result of locus-specific forces (natural selection) and population-level forces (e.g. demographic growth and range expansion). When multiple independent loci correlate with geography, population level forces are likely responsible. Conversely, when patterns diverge, natural selection is implicated in modulating observed diversity (Bereir *et al.*, 2007). Human within-population genetic diversity of native human populations decreases smoothly with geographic distance measured through landmasses from a sub-Saharan African origin, and genetic differentiation between populations also increases steadily with physical distance along landmasses (reviewed in Tanabe *et al.*, 2010). The same situation is observed for *M. tuberculosis*, whose general diversity pattern generally resembles that of its human host. A closer look at the types' distribution revealed several geographical gradients (Figure 16.2) discussed below.

Principal Components Analysis and its variant, multidimensional scaling (MDS), are widely used in human population genetics to visualize interpopulation relationships (Cavalli-Sforza *et al.*, 1996). Previously, I proposed a simple measure of genetic distance between geographic populations of clonal microbial species and applied it to the phylogeographic analysis of *M. tuberculosis* (Mokrousov, 2008). The first application of the MDS approach to *M. tuberculosis* VNTR data highlighted strong geographic specificities of the local clonal variants of *M. tuberculosis* Beijing genotype (Figure 16.4). In particular, a significant proximity of the geographically distant Russian *M. tuberculosis* populations may reflect a recent dissemination of the Beijing strains fueled by mass human migrations in twentieth-century Russia (Figure 16.4) which is also highlighted in an interesting, albeit somewhat speculative, paper of Sinkov *et al.* (2010).

Conversely, some weak and less expected affinities of the distant *M. tuberculosis* Beijing populations (northern Vietnam and South Africa; northwest Russia and east Siberia; Beijing and Hong Kong) are intriguing and warrant further detailed investigation. It is not unlikely that less expected affinities observed between distant *M. tuberculosis* populations may reflect hidden patterns of human migrations or yet unknown epidemiological links between distant regions. In Figure 16.4 one can distinguish a subcluster of the Russian populations, a more dispersed situation with Chinese populations, and, finally, a slightly apart position of Japan. Samples of Australia (not shown on Figure 16.4) and Peru are influenced by small size; they make special cases of the more recent importation of the Beijing strains. Notably, the largest genetic distance for South Africa correlates with the largest water distance. In my opinion, these observations support a general robustness of the analysis. In its turn, this indirectly supports a reliability of the less expected affinities, likely representing hidden patterns of human migrations reflected in the patterns of *M. tuberculosis* geographic diversity.

Beijing genotype in China

All Chinese governments since the Yin dynasty (~1600–1000 BC) up to the present encouraged migration. These massive movements resulted in major shifts in the overall demographics and language distribution

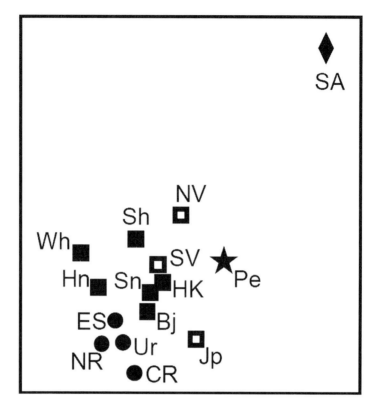

Figure 16.4 Relationships of the geographic populations of the *M. tuberculosis* Beijing family strains (*n* > 30), estimated as MDS graph based on the VNTR distance matrix. Abbreviations: Bj, Beijing; CR, central Russia; ES, East Siberia; Hn, Henan; HK, Hong Kong; Jp, Japan; NR, northwest Russia; NV, northern Vietnam; Pe, Peru; SA, South Africa; Sh, Shanghai; Sin, Singapore; SV, southern Vietnam; Ur, Ural; Wu, Wuhan. Closed squares depict Chinese; open squares, other East Asian; black circles, Russian populations.

over the entire country (LaPolla, 1999 and references therein). For example, the Jin government virtually emptied the city of Beijing in 1123, moving the people to the northeast. Later, in 1368, the Ming government moved large numbers of people mainly from Shanxi and Shandong into Beijing to populate the city. Interprovincial migration almost tripled between the 1990 and 2000 censuses: the friction of distance declined over time while unequal economic development has become crucial. This latter notion is supported by the drastic increase of

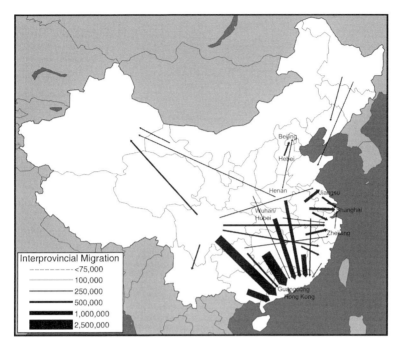

Figure 16.5 The 30 largest interprovincial migration flows in China, 1995–2000. (Reproduced with modification by permission of Bellwether Publishing, Ltd. from Fan, 2005.)

migration to Guangdong in the 1995–2000 period (11.5 million) accounting for 36% of all interprovincial migration in China (Fan, 2005) (Figure 16.5).

Here, I compared the *M. tuberculosis* diversity pattern and human demographic and linguistic history of China. The MDS analysis of the intra-Chinese diversity (six populations) is shown in the MDS graph (Figure 16.6). Interestingly, it revealed that relationships between mainland populations (Beijing, Shanghai, Henan, Wuhan) followed geographic relationships of these areas whereas an unexpected position of the island populations (Hong Kong and Taiwan) may be due to the bottleneck events. Thus, recent intra-Chinese migrations (Figure 16.5) were not sufficient to change the overall pattern of the *M. tuberculosis* diversity in mainland China.

Although this was somewhat beyond the scope of this study, it is interesting to show an example of the positive correlation between geographic and genetic (human surname-based) distances (Figure 16.7). The MDS graph (Figure 16.7) is based on the Chinese surname frequency data of Yuan *et al.* (2000) who showed historical inheritance of Chinese

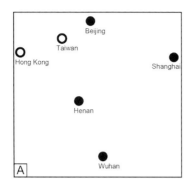 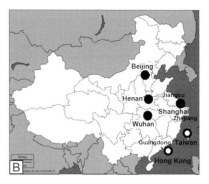

Figure 16.6 (A) Relationships of the six Chinese populations of the
Mycobacterium tuberculosis Beijing family strains, estimated as MDS graph
based on the VNTR distance matrix. (B) Map of China showing locations of
the studied populations. Black circles, mainland; open circles, island
populations. (Outline map of China (http://histgeo.ac-aix-marseille.fr/
carto/chine.htm): courtesy of the Académie d'Aix-Marseille Histoire-
Géographie.)

surnames to be continuous and stable through Song and Ming dynasties
and the present. The surname-based graph for six Chinese populations
showed that surname distribution followed the geography (Figure 16.7) in
spite of massive movements across China mentioned above. Figure 16.7 is
based on the Ming dynasty surname data (Yuan *et al.*, 2000) and clearly
resembles a geographic map (shown in Figure 16.6b).

It may be noted that Singapore and Hong Kong *M. tuberculosis*
Beijing genotype populations exhibit some affinity (Figure 16.4) that is
reasonably explained by their co-shared Chinese descent (Conference on
Chinese Population, 2002). Still, in other coordinates (not shown) they
clearly differ, as indeed they had essentially different sources of their
respective Chinese human populations. In Hong Kong, most of the 96%
Chinese population are Cantonese dialect speakers (Harrison and So,
1996) – that is, linguistically originating from the Guangdong province
in southern China – whereas the origins of the Chinese population were
much more diversified for Singapore with only 6% accounting for
Cantonese Chinese speakers (Singapore Department of Statistics, 2001).

It has previously been shown with some other microbial species
(polyomavirus JC, *Helicobacter pylori*) that a geographically unexpected
distribution of their genotypes may reflect hidden or less apparent
migrations of their human carriers (Falush *et al.*, 2003; Pavesi, 2005).
Likewise, enigmatic relatedness of the Beijing and Taiwan and Hong
Kong populations of *M. tuberculosis* (Figure 16.6) might mirror a yet

Figure 16.7 MDS graph of selected Chinese populations calculated from Han surname-based distances (raw data were extracted from Yuan *et al.*, 2000). Map of China: see Figure 16.6b.

unknown epidemiological link between these distant Chinese regions. Alternatively, it may reflect bottleneck event(s) during peopling of the Taiwan and Hong Kong insular areas.

Beijing genotype in Japan

A specific feature of *M. tuberculosis* Beijing population in Japan is a very high rate (up to 70–80%) of the so-called "ancient" sublineage. For example, this sublineage is detected in 20–25% in China and Vietnam and in 5% in Russia (Kremer *et al.*, 2009; Mokrousov *et al.*, 2005). Assuming the area of origin of the Beijing genotype to be the north of China (Mokrousov, 2008; van Soolingen *et al.*, 1995), this is remarkable: one would expect to see the highest rate of the primordial ancient strains in the area of origin but not elsewhere. One speculative explanation is that (1) ancient population Beijing genotype had a high rate of ancient sublineage, and (2) the Beijing strains were brought to Japan in ancient times, thus resulting in high rates of the ancient sublineage in Japan, fixed via a bottleneck event. The data on TB history in Japan appear to corroborate with this hypothesis, which ideally should be tested by direct analysis of the ancient mycobacterial DNA.

The comprehensive paleopathological paper of Suzuki and Inoue (2007) provided a detailed account of the early history and likely sources of TB in Japan. In spite of intensive studies of the skeletal samples, no case of spinal tuberculosis has been found in the Jomon period (Neolithic; *c*. 10 000 BC to 300 BC) but was described in the Aneolithic Yayoi period *c*. 300 BC to AD 300. The Yayoi culture first appeared in northern Kyushu and quickly spread throughout Japan, notably, through population expansion, fueled by immigration from the Asian continent. The total number of migrants from the Asian continent was estimated to be more than a million within the third to seventh centuries, at least four times outnumbering the Jomon population (Hanihara, 1987). These immigrants from Korea and North China not only introduced various cultural characteristics (including new agricultural practice), but they also brought some new infectious diseases, among them tuberculosis. Tuberculosis was usually fatal to the "virgin" prehistoric Jomon people who lived in a TB-free environment. Consequent host–pathogen coevolution should have changed the population immunity resulting in a change of infection from an acute to a chronic form, which is more commonly described in archaeological skeletal remains in the Kofun period that followed the Yayoi era (Suzuki and Inoue, 2007).

Beijing genotype in Russia/northern Eurasia

The exact timing of the first entry and primary dispersals of the Beijing strains in northern Eurasia (modern Russia) is elusive in spite of different hypotheses put forward in the recent years. The Russian Beijing genotype population is the least diverse of all local Beijing populations (Figure 16.2). As more diversity results from longer clonal expansion, this suggests that dissemination of the currently circulating and locally predominant Beijing strains in Russia started relatively recently. This may be readily explained by the cold climate and, until very recently, the extremely low population density in a vast area of Russia and Siberia (Christian, 1998; Klimanov *et al.*, 1995) compared with the warmer conditions and the fast growing and denser population in East Asia and South Africa (Cape Town area). Both network (Figure 16.3) and MDS (Figure 16.4) analyses suggest that Russia and South Africa were infected with distinct sub-pools of Beijing strains. However, a strong founder effect may have played a crucial role in the evolution of the Beijing genotype's population structure in South Africa and would consequently result in its outlying positions in the MDS graph (Figure 16.4). At the same time, two major Russian Beijing subtypes M11 (primordial) and M2 are located in the central part of the network (Figure 16.3), which implies that the Russian pool of the Beijing strains is relatively ancient: that is, introduced here since historically distant time.

My further reasoning about timing of the first entry of the Beijing genotype to Russia is as follows. The Beijing genotype is currently spreading in Europe due to immigration from the former Soviet Union and East Asia but its circulation is still limited to the immigrants' communities. One reason may be a long-term co-adaptation of local European *M. tuberculosis* subvariants to local human populations (latent infection) thereby outcompeting newly brought and hypervirulent Beijing strains killing their hosts prior to further transmission. In any case, the Beijing genotype is by no means a specifically endemic *M. tuberculosis* variant in Europe. Consequently, it seems reasonable to assume that the migrations that equally targeted both Russia and Europe are not likely to be the source of importation of the Beijing genotype into Russia. On the basis of the published principal components analysis and known history of European human populations, I ruled out those migrations that equally concerned both Russia and Europe. These are defined by Finno-Ugric, Scythe, and Hun expansions (Cavalli-Sforza *et al.*, 1996; Christian, 1998). Further, I speculate that trade contacts as such, even longlasting ones, are not sufficient for an effective dissemination of the *M. tuberculosis* strains if they are not supported by a kind of demic diffusion of the strains' carriers, manifested as population growth and migration. The Silk Road connected China with Europe for almost two millennia, 2 BC to AD 1600, and this route may have been opened much earlier, based on the transfer of the first ceramics technology from Japan to the Middle East and Europe at the beginning of agricultural practice (Cavalli-Sforza *et al.*, 1996). IS6110 sequence specific for *M. tuberculosis* was identified by PCR in 5 out of 15 skeletal remains found in tombs near old Jiaoche city, along the northern Silk Road (notably, a possible road of transmission) in Turfan, in Xinjiang-Uigur province. These tombs were dated back to the Cheshiquianguo period (*c.* 200 BC to AD 200), suggesting an outbreak of tuberculosis due to its high incidence in the area (Fusegawa *et al.*, 2003). Nevertheless, the Silk Road did not disseminate the Beijing genotype towards its westernmost terminus since Beijing strains are not identified as a European endemic variant.

Finally, I suggest the TB spread related to the Genghis (or Chinggiz) Khan invasion to be a more plausible solution of the puzzle. The Mongol empire of the thirteenth century brought the different parts of Eurasia closer than they had ever been before and created an economic and cultural system embracing much of the Eurasian landmass (Christian, 1998). It was also a period of remarkable ethnic mixing since the Mongol army grew by incorporating the armies of many different nations that it had defeated, including Han Chinese (Christian, 1998). McNeill (1976) suggested that Mongol invasions also unified Eurasia epidemiologically, allowing the exchange of the disease vectors throughout Eurasia. Genghis Khan did eventually come into the center of Europe, but only for a short time. This was sufficient for the well-documented dissemination of *Yersinia pestis* to occur, but not for that of the far less contagious *M. tuberculosis*. Even if some *M. tuberculosis* Beijing genotype strains had been brought to Europe in this way, this may not have manifested rapidly. Subsequently, the Black Death that devastated European peoples could have easily eliminated hypothetical rare carriers of the *M. tuberculosis* Beijing genotype. By contrast, further close interaction and human exchange between Ancient Rus' and Orda (Golden Horde) lasted for three centuries (no matter here whether it was disastrous or beneficial for Russia (Gumilev, 1993). Therefore it may be possible that the Mongol invasion and the subsequent yoke/cohabitation were indeed the vehicle that brought *M. tuberculosis* Beijing genotype strains to Russia. Archaeopathological and molecular studies similar to those carried out with mummies in Egypt and some European medieval cemeteries would hopefully shed light on this issue. Attempts to use statistical approaches including Bayesian algorithms to infer the time of the most recent common ancestor of different Beijing subtypes circulating in an area largely depend on the changing estimations of mutation rate of molecular markers, for example VNTR (Grant *et al.*, 2008; Reyes and Tanaka, 2010; Wirth *et al.*, 2008), and, in my opinion, should be interpreted with great caution.

According to another recent hypothesis, an importation of the Beijing genotype to Russia started from the 1920s through interaction of Chinese and Russian employees of the Chinese Eastern Railway and was further disseminated across Russia via the labor camp system GULAG (Sinkov *et al.*, 2010); its molecular proof is yet to be presented.

Interestingly, type M2, highly prevalent in Russia, is also found in very high rates in Kyrgyzstan (Figure 16.2), a highland Central Asian country of the former Soviet Union. Since early medieval times Kyrgyz people closely interacted with other Central/East Asian peoples (Uigurs, Mongols, Kalmyks, Manchu, Uzbeks). More recently, Kyrgyzstan was a part of the Russian Empire/Soviet Union in 1876–1991. Both Russia and East Asia are marked with high and endemic prevalence of the *M. tuberculosis* Beijing genotype. Consequently, a high prevalence of the Beijing genotype in Kyrgyzstan (60% in the general population) is not surprising. The fine subtyping based on MIRU-VNTR loci permitted us to trace more precisely the origins of the Beijing strains in Kyrgyzstan (Mokrousov *et al.*, 2009b). The largest MIRU type (75% of Beijing strains) corresponded to the M2 type that is highly prevalent in different Russian settings (Mokrousov, 2008). As a whole, comparison of both Beijing and non-Beijing types found in Kyrgyzstan with international databases revealed that they were mainly Russia specific, or, more generally speaking, specific for the vast Eurasian areas to the northwest and west of Kyrgyzstan. This finding strongly suggests this northern, Russian direction as a major route of importation of *M. tuberculosis* strains currently circulating in Kyrgyzstan, while medieval influence of the southern/eastern route (e.g. from China or India) apparently waned within the course of the twentieth century (Figure 16.2).

Beijing genotype in Africa

As mentioned above, the *M. tuberculosis* Beijing genotype is neither a frequent nor endemic variant in Africa as a whole. The exception is South Africa, namely the Cape Town area. The introduction of the Beijing genotype to South Africa appears to have occurred relatively recently. Strictly speaking, migrations from China itself are unlikely to be responsible for the importation of the Beijing genotype. Currently, the Chinese human population constitutes only 30 000 individuals in South Africa. Significant, but extremely transient, Chinese gene flow to South Africa occurred only 100 years ago, when around 50 000 Chinese workers were imported for the Rand gold mines in 1903–7. However, by 1910 they were all repatriated and their impact on the health situation in South Africa was likely to be negligible (reviewed in Mokrousov *et al.*, 2005). A study by van Helden *et al.* (2002) suggested that Beijing strains might have been introduced to South Africa following the sea trade route from East Asia to Europe that started 400 years ago. Indeed, in the seventeenth and eighteenth centuries, Dutch colonists at the Cape of Good Hope largely imported slaves from Indonesia, Madagascar, Mozambique, and India. Descendants of these slaves, who often married with Dutch settlers, later became known as "Cape Coloureds" or "Cape Malays," and presently form the majority of the 4.7 million population of the Western Cape Province (www.nationmaster.com/encyclopedia/South-Africa). Therefore, it is likely that the Beijing strains were historically recently brought to South Africa, and not directly from its primary focus of origin (China), but from the secondary one (Indonesia).

Further accumulation of the large body of new data from other world areas permitted a revisit of this hypothesis. The largest type in South African population of the Beijing genotype is M28 (Figure 16.2, Figure 16.3). At the same time, this type is also observed in Hong Kong, Singapore, and Vietnam and, to a lesser extent, Shanghai: notably all of them are coastal areas in East Asia (Figure 16.2). Consequently, the observed gradient in the distribution of type M28 suggests another and somewhat more recent route of introduction of the Beijing genotype to South Africa, namely the sea route from the southern sea-ports, Hong Kong, Singapore, and Vietnam but not Shanghai. This latter exception may be readily explained by the fact that Shanghai was closed until the mid nineteenth century from foreign contact (Liu, 2005). In any case, a distal position of South Africa in the MDS graph (Figure 16.4) reasonably reflects a founder effect of the initially small *M. tuberculosis* Beijing genotype population brought here from East Asia and adapted to the local human population during the course of the past few centuries, as recently suggested by Hanekom *et al.* (2007). Finally, it did not escape our notion that this type M28 is also found in another coastal area, Queensland, Australia; a meaning of this coastal "affinity" is yet to be seen.

To complete the African theme, the Beijing genotype is increasingly being described albeit in small percentages in the countries of sub-Saharan Africa (Affolabi *et al.*, 2009). The routes of their importation may be speculatively either (1) northwards from the Cape Town area as a part of intra-African exchange, or (2) from East Asia, in particular from China, in view of the active human and trade contacts intensified in recent years. Unfortunately few data on the VNTR diversity of the African Beijing strains have been published. One exception is Benin in

West Africa (Figure 16.2) with 10% of the Beijing genotype and all these Beijing strains belonging to type M33. This type is specific for China and Vietnam and found in very low rates in Cape Town. Hence it is reasonable to speculate that these strains in Benin may have been brought here through direct recent exchange with Asia rather than from South Africa.

Beijing genotype in other locations

The information on *M. tuberculosis* Beijing genotype VNTR diversity in South America, albeit limited, mirrors both external and internal migration as sources of Beijing strains in South America. Peru is considered to be a focus of the Beijing genotype in South America (Taype *et al.*, 2012). Remarkably, the MDS graph shows an outlying position for South Africa but not for Peru (Figure 16.4). Peru strains do not form special subgraphs in the phylogenetic network (Figure 16.3), and it seems that most of the Beijing pool in Peru is recently imported. Interestingly, the basal type M11 is also found in Peru while other major Peruvian types (co-shared with strains from East Asia) are linked by a single change to M11. This reflects their direct and recent importation from East Asia. At the same time, type M206 is the most prevalent in Peru and includes only Peruvian strains: this highlights a local emergence of this type.

Finally, in the MDS graph, Peru reveals some affinity to Hong Kong, Japan and Vietnam (Figure 16.4). While no information about Vietnam immigration to Peru is available, it is well known that the Japanese community in Peru, dating to 1899, is the largest in Latin America (Takenaka, 2004). At the same time, 2% of the Peru population has Chinese roots; notably, not just Chinese but Sino-Cantonese immigration to Peru started in the nineteenth century. The Hong Kong (~Guangdong/Cantonese) and Peru populations were similar (Figure 16.4).

In Brazil, few available profiles of the Beijing strains (Lasunskaia *et al.*, 2010) belong to either the East Asia or South America specific types. Type 42 includes single strains from Beijing, Vietnam, Singapore, 1 of 3 strains from Brazil, and, notably, the largest (7 of 30 strains) subsample from Peru. This type 42 was likely brought to Brazil from Peru rather than from East Asia. Finally, type 205 includes two strains: one from Peru and the other from Brazil, and likely reflects *in situ* evolution of the Beijing strains in South Africa.

The Beijing genotype in Albania presents an interesting case. In the 1960s until 1990, this country somewhat resembled the continuing autarchy of North Korea. Albania cut its links with the Warsaw Treaty in

1960 but retained them and even enhanced links with China (until 1978). Both Soviet–Albanian human links in 1945–1960 and Sino-Albanian links until 1978 were close. Therefore this dual vector of human relations is intriguingly reflected in the affinities of three available Beijing genotype strains from Albania. Two strains belong to type M7 that also includes three strains from Japan and six strains from Russia. At first glance, a Japan route appears unlikely; it seems rather that these M7 strains in Albania may trace their origin in Russia. Regarding the third strain from Albania, it belongs to type M12, which mostly includes a large percentage of strains from Japan (24/188), and also single isolates from various Russian and Chinese locations. This persisting affinity of Albanian and Japanese Beijing genotype strains is puzzling and requires further studies based on more strains and more molecular markers.

The data on Oceania are available for the adjacent areas in Australia (Queensland, Torres Strait) and Papua New Guinea (PNG) (Western Province, Torres Strait) (Gilpin *et al.*, 2004, 2008). The Australian sample included strains of both M11 and other "Asian" types; as we hypothesized previously, the penetration of Beijing strains to Australia may have started since the end of the nineteenth century following the discovery of gold (Mokrousov, 2008). Only two types are available for PNG: M212 (15 strains) and derived M213 (one strain). Interestingly, M212 is located most distally in the minimum spanning tree and differs from M71 (Shanghai) and M72 (Singapore) only by a single locus variation (Figure 16.3). This observation hints at a Chinese/Southeast Asian rather than Australian route of importation of Beijing strains to PNG (Figure 16.2).

CONCLUDING REMARKS AND PERSPECTIVES

Evolutionary histories of *H. sapiens* and human pathogens are, at least partly, co-mirrored and co-shaped. The main benefit of using microbes as proxies for human variability is that they show more genetic variation than human genes. This means that the microorganisms, with their rapid generation time (even slowly growing mycobacterial species), can accurately reconstruct ancient or recent human migratory events.

Over 35 years ago, W. H. McNeill (1976) reviewed the impact of the various local and global epidemics over the human history – the Black Death and the *conquistadores*' introduction of the European infections into the New World being the most notorious examples. More recently, comparative studies attempted timing of specific events in the genome evolution of *M. tuberculosis* (Mokrousov *et al.*, 2005) and tracing hidden patterns of human migrations through the study of genetic geography of various human pathogens such as *Plasmodium falciparum* tropical parasite (Tanabe *et al.*, 2010), *Coccidioides immitis* fungus (Fisher *et al.*, 2001), bacteria *Helicobacter pylori* (Covacci *et al.*, 1999; Falush *et al.*, 2003), *Mycobacterium leprae* (Monot *et al.*, 2005), *Streptococcus mutans* (Caufield, 2009), as well as DNA viruses (JC polyomavirus and human papillomavirus) and RNA viruses (hepatitis G virus and the human T-cell lymphotropic virus) (reviewed in Holmes, 2008; Pavesi, 2005).

A novel concept of "Big History" places human history within an overview of all known history, from the beginning of the Universe up until life on Earth today (Christian, 2003; Spier, 2005). Consequently, understanding of human–microbial interactions and coevolution may and should be placed in a broad historical perspective as a part of global natural, including human, history. One should note that these sorts of comparative studies correlating microbial phylogeography and human history are based on the general knowledge of global and local history and migrations and still lack robust quantitative measures.

The performed comparative analysis shows that genetic distances of *M. tuberculosis* Beijing genotype populations correlate with geography over uninterrupted landmasses. In contrast, large water distances and a long time frame can generate a remarkable outlier as exemplified by the case of South Africa. At the same time, some weak and less expected affinities of the distant *M. tuberculosis* Beijing populations are intriguing: they may reflect hidden epidemiological links due to unknown migrations.

The particular feature regarding the current dissemination of tuberculosis is that ordinary human exchange per se is not enough to expose and introduce new strains into an indigenous population, even in the present time of urbanization and overcrowding. The Beijing genotype is present in a high rate in the Baltic states, maybe due to the large influx of Russian migrants following World War II. In contrast, the Beijing genotype is not found in autochthonous populations of East Europe in spite of close links with Russia/Soviet Union in the recent and historical past. It appears that there is a kind of human resistance developed in the local population through its coexistence with historically established clones, acting against newly imported clones.

One should keep in mind that most if not all studies on other pathogens used gene sequences, a feature not yet available for *M. tuberculosis*. New large-scale SNP or genome-wide population-based studies targeting Beijing strains from indigenous populations in Central Asia, Siberia, and North America and, eventually, the analysis of fossil (including mummy) DNA samples will better test our hypothesis about the evolutionary history of this bacterial lineage. A comparison of phylogenies between *M. tuberculosis* strains and the Y-chromosome and mtDNA haplotypes directly sampled from TB patients from non-urban isolated areas less influenced by recent human migrations could also give clues to better understanding of our coevolution. The human microbiome is defined as a sum of all our resident microbes, our "other" genome. It is not unlikely that some of them will come to the scene as new yet unknown markers of human migrations.

REFERENCES

Affolabi, D., Anyo, G., Faïhun, F., *et al.* (2009). First molecular epidemiological study of tuberculosis in Benin. *International Journal of Tuberculosis and Lung Diseases*, **13**, 317–22.

Bellamy, R. (1998). Genetic susceptibility and pulmonary medicine. 3: Genetic susceptibility to tuberculosis in human populations. *Thorax*, **53**, 588–93.

Bereir, R. E., Hassan, H. Y., Salih, N. A., *et al.* (2007). Co-introgression of Y-chromosome haplogroups and the sickle cell gene across Africa's Sahel. *European Journal of Human Genetics*, **15**, 1183–5.

Bifani, J., Mathema, B., Kurepina, N. E., and Kreiswirth, B. N. (2002). Global dissemination of the *Mycobacterium tuberculosis* W-Beijing family strains. *Trends in Microbiology*, **10**, 45–52.

Caufield, P. W. (2009) Tracking human migration patterns through the oral bacterial flora. *Clinical Microbiolology and Infection*, **15**(Suppl 1), 37–9.

Cavalli-Sforza, L. L., Menozzi, P., and Piazza, A. (1996). *The History and Geography of Human Genes*. Princeton, NJ: Princeton University Press.

Christian, D. (1998). *A History of Russia, Central Asia and Mongolia*, Vol. 1: *Inner Eurasia from Prehistory to the Mongol Empire*. Oxford, UK: Blackwell.

Christian, D. (2003). World history in context. *Journal of World History*, **14**, 437–58.

Conference on Chinese Population and Socioeconomic Studies: Utilizing the 2000/2001 Round Census Data (2002). Hong Kong, SAR: Hong Kong University of Science and Technology.

Covacci, A., Telford, J. L., Del Giudice, G., Parsonnet, J., and Rappuoli, R. (1999). *Helicobacter pylori* virulence and genetic geography. *Science*, **284**, 1328–33.

Daniel, T. M. (2006). The history of tuberculosis. *Respiratory Medicine*, **100**, 1862–70.

Dou, H. Y., Tseng, F. C., Lin, C. W., *et al.* (2008). Molecular epidemiology and evolutionary genetics of *Mycobacterium tuberculosis* in Taipei. *BMC Infectious Diseases*, **8**, 170.

Falush, D., Wirth, T., Linz, B., *et al.* (2003). Traces of human migrations in *Helicobacter pylori* populations. *Science*, **299**, 1582–5.

Fan, C. C. (2005). Modeling interprovincial migration in China, 1985–2000. *Eurasian Geography Economics*, **46**, 165–84.

Felsenstein, J. (2004). *PHYLIP (Phylogeny Inference Package) version 3.6b*. Seattle, WA: Department of Genome Sciences, University of Washington.

Fisher, M. C., Koenig, G. L., White, T. J., *et al.* (2001). Biogeographic range expansion into South America by *Coccidioides immitis* mirrors New World patterns of human migration. *Proceedings of the National Academy of Sciences of the United States of America*, **98**, 4558–62.

Fusegawa, H., Wang, B. H., Sakurai, K. *et al.* (2003). Outbreak of tuberculosis in a 2000-year-old Chinese population. *Kansenshogaku Zasshi*, **77**, 146–9.

Gagneux, S. and Small, P. M. (2007). Global phylogeography of *Mycobacterium tuberculosis* and implications for tuberculosis product development. *Lancet Infectious Diseases*, **7**, 328–37.

Gilpin, C. M., Simpson, G., Vincent, S., *et al.* (2008). Evidence of primary transmission of multidrug-resistant tuberculosis in the Western Province of Papua New Guinea. *Medical Journal of Australia*, **188**, 148–52.

Gilpin, C. M., Songhurst, C., and Coulter, C. (2004). MIRU: the national tuberculosis genotyping strategy in Australia. Paper presented at 25th Congress of the European Society of Mycobacteriology, Alghero, Italy.

Grant, A., Arnold, C., Thorne, N., Gharbia, S., and Underwood, A. (2008). Mathematical modelling of *Mycobacterium tuberculosis* VNTR loci estimates a very slow mutation rate for the repeats. *Journal of Molecular Evolution*, **66**, 565–74.

Gumilev, L. N. (1993). *Ancient Rus and the Great Steppe*. Moscow: Mysl. (in Russian)

Hanekom, M., van der Spuy, G. D., Gey van Pittius, N. C., *et al.* (2007). Evidence that the spread of *Mycobacterium tuberculosis* strains with the Beijing genotype is human population dependent. *Journal of Clinical Microbiology*, **45**, 2263–56.

Hanihara, K. (1987). Estimation of the number of early migrants to Japan: a simulative study. *Journal of Anthropological Society of Nippon*, **95**, 391–403.

Harrison, G. and So, L. K. H. (1996). The background to language change in Hong Kong. *Current Issues in Language and Society*, **3**, 114–23.

Herzog, H. (1998). History of tuberculosis. *Respiration*, **65**, 5–15.

Holmes, E. C. (2008). Evolutionary history and phylogeography of human viruses. *Annual Reviews in Microbiology*, **62**, 307–28.

Hunter, P. R. and Gaston, M. A. (1988). Numerical index of the discriminatory ability of typing systems: an application of Simpsons's index of diversity. *Journal of Clinical Microbiology*, **26**, 2465–6.

Kamerbeek, J., Schouls, L., Kolk, A., *et al.* (1997). Simultaneous detection and strain differentiation of *Mycobacterium tuberculosis* for diagnosis and epidemiology. *Journal of Clinical Microbiology*, **35**, 907–14.

Khanlou, K. M., Vandepitte, K., Asl, L. K., and Van Bockstaele, E. (2011). Towards an optimal sampling strategy for assessing genetic variation within and among white clover (*Trifolium repens* L.) cultivars using AFLP. *Genetics and Molecular Biology*, **34**, 252–8.

Klimanov, V., Hotinsky, N., and Blagoschenskaya, N. (1995). Climate changes during historical period in the center of Russian plain. *Izvestia Akademii Nauk SSSR, Seria Geograficheskaya*, **1**, 89–96. (in Russian)

Kremer, K., Glynn, J. R., Lillebaek, T., *et al.* (2004). Definition of the Beijing/W lineage of *Mycobacterium tuberculosis* on the basis of genetic markers. *Journal of Clinical Microbiology*, **42**, 4040–9.

Kremer, K., van-der-Werf, M. J., Au, B. K., *et al.* (2009). Vaccine-induced immunity circumvented by typical *Mycobacterium tuberculosis* Beijing strains. *Emerging Infectious Diseases*, **15**, 335–9.

LaPolla, R. J. (1999). The role of migration and language contact in the development of the Sino-Tibetan language family. In *Areal Diffusion and Genetic Inheritance: Case Studies in Language Change*, ed. R. M. W. Dixon and A. Y. Aikhenvald. Oxford, UK: Oxford University Press.

Lasunskaia, E., Ribeiro, S., Manicheva, O., *et al.* (2010). Emerging multidrug resistant *M. tuberculosis* strains of the Beijing genotype circulating in Russia express a pattern of biological properties associated with enhanced virulence. *Microbes and Infection*, **12**, 467–75.

Liu, W. (2005). *History of Ningbo*. San Francisco, CA: Wildflowers Institute.

McMichael, A. J. (2004). Environmental and social influences on emerging infectious diseases: past, present and future. *Philosophical Transactions of the Royal Society B: Biological Sciences*, **359**, 1049–58.

McNeill, W. H. (1976). *Plagues and Peoples*. New York: Anchor Press.

Mokrousov, I. (2008). Genetic geography of *Mycobacterium tuberculosis* Beijing genotype: a multifacet mirror of human history? *Infection Genetics and Evolution*, **8**, 777–85.

Mokrousov, I., Ly, H. M., Otten, T., *et al.* (2005). Origin and primary dispersal of the *Mycobacterium tuberculosis* Beijing genotype: clues from human phylogeography. *Genome Research*, **15**, 1357–64.

Mokrousov, I., Otten, T., Zozio, T., *et al.* (2009a). At Baltic crossroads: a molecular snapshot of *Mycobacterium tuberculosis* population diversity in Kaliningrad, Russia. *FEMS Immunology and Medical Microbiology*, **55**, 13–22.

Mokrousov, I., Valcheva, V., Sovhozova, N., *et al.* (2009b). Penitentiary population of *Mycobacterium tuberculosis* in Kyrgyzstan: exceptionally high prevalence of the Beijing genotype and its Russia-specific subtype. *Infection Genetics and Evolution*, **9**, 1400–5.

Monot, M., Honore, N. Garnier, T., *et al.* (2005). On the origin of leprosy. *Science*, **308**, 1040–2.

Murray, J. F. (2004) A century of tuberculosis. *American Journal of Respiratory and Critical Care Medicine*, **169**, 1181–6.

Nikolayevskyy, V. V., Brown, T. J., Bazhora, Y. I., *et al.* (2007). Molecular epidemiology and prevalence of mutations conferring rifampicin and isoniazid resistance in *Mycobacterium tuberculosis* strains from the southern Ukraine. *Clinical Microbiology and Infection*, **13**, 129–38.

Pavesi, A. (2005). Utility of JC polyomavirus in tracing the pattern of human migrations dating to prehistoric times. *Journal of General Virology*, **86**, 1315–26.

Pruett, C. L. and Winker, K. (2008). The effects of sample size on population genetic diversity estimates in song sparrows *Melospiza melodia*. *Journal of Avian Biology*, **39**, 252–6.

Reyes, J. F. and Tanaka, M. M. (2010). Mutation rates of spoligotypes and variable numbers of tandem repeat loci in *Mycobacterium tuberculosis*. *Infection Genetics and Evolution*, **10**, 1046–51.

Rinaldi, A. (2007). Tiny travel companions. *EMBO Reports*, **8**, 121–5.

Singapore Department of Statistics (2001). *Census of Population 2000*.

Sinkov, V. V., Savilov, E. D., and Ogarkov, O. B. (2010). Epidemiology of tuberculosis in Russia: epidemiological and historical evidence in support of dissemination of the Beijing genotype in the 20th century. *Epidemiologiya i infekcionnie bolezni*, **6**, 23–58. (in Russian)

Spier, F. (2005). The small history of the Big History course at the University of Amsterdam. *World History Connected*, **2**, 2.

Stead, W. W. (1997). The origin and erratic global spread of tuberculosis: how the past explains the present and is the key to the future. *Clinics in Chest Medicine*, **18**, 65–77.

Supply, P., Lesjean, S., Savine, E., *et al.* (2001). Automated high-throughput genotyping for study of global epidemiology of *Mycobacterium tuberculosis* based on mycobacterial interspersed repetitive units. *Journal of Clinical Microbiology*, **39**, 3563–71.

Suzuki, T. and Inoue, T. (2007). Earliest evidence of spinal tuberculosis from the Aneolithic Yayoi period in Japan. *International Journal of Osteoarchaeology*, **17**, 392–402.

Takenaka, A. (2004). The Japanese in Peru: history of immigration, settlement and racialization. *Latin American Perspectives*, **31**, 77–98.

Tanabe, K., Mita, T., Jombart, T., *et al.* (2010). *Plasmodium falciparum* accompanied the human expansion out of Africa. *Current Biology*, **20**, 1283–9.

Taype, C. A. (2007). Host and pathogen genetics in tuberculosis and leishmaniasis. Ph.D. thesis, University of Leeds, UK.

Taype, C. A., Agapito, J. C., Accinelli, R. A., *et al.* (2012). Genetic diversity, population structure and drug resistance of *Mycobacterium tuberculosis* in Peru. *Infection Genetics and Evolution*, **12**, 577–85.

van Embden, J. D. A., Van Gorkom, T., Kremer, K., *et al.* (2000). Genetic variation and evolutionary origin of the direct repeat locus of *Mycobacterium tuberculosis* complex bacteria. *Journal of Bacteriology*, **182**, 2393–401.

van Helden, P. D., Warren, R. M., Victor, T. C., *et al.* (2002) Strain families of *M. tuberculosis*. *Trends in Microbiology*, **10**, 167–8.

van Soolingen, D., Qian, L., de Haas, P. E. W., *et al.* (1995). Predominance of a single genotype of *M. tuberculosis* in countries of East Asia. *Journal of Clinical Microbiology*, **33**, 3234–8.

Wada, T., Iwamoto, T., and Maeda, S. (2009) Genetic diversity of the *Mycobacterium tuberculosis* Beijing family in East Asia revealed through refined population structure analysis. *FEMS Microbiology Letters*, **291**, 35–43.

Watanabe, K. and Omur, T. (2007). Relationship between reservoir size and genetic differentiation of the stream caddisfly *Stenopsyche marmorata*. *Biological Conservation*, **136**, 203–11.

Wirth, T., Hildebrand, F., Allix-Béguec, C., *et al.* (2008). Origin, spread and demography of the *Mycobacterium tuberculosis* complex. *PLoS Pathogens*, **4**, e1000160.

Wirth, T., Meyer, A., and Achtman, M. (2005). Deciphering host migrations and origins by means of their microbes. *Molecular Ecology*, **14**, 3289–306.

Yang, S. Z. (1998). *The Divine Farmer's Materia Medica: A Translation of the Shen Nong Ben Cao Jing*. Boulder, CO: Blue Poppy Press.

Yokoyama, E, Hachisu, Y., Hashimoto, R., and Kishida, K. (2010). Concordance of variable-number tandem repeat (VNTR) and large sequence polymorphism (LSP) analyses of *Mycobacterium tuberculosis* strains. *Infection Genetics and Evolution*, **10**, 913–18.

Yuan, Y. D., Zhang, C., and Yang, H. M. (2000). Population genetics of Chinese surnames. II: Inheritance stability of surnames and regional consanguinity of population. *Yi Chuan Xue Bao*, **27**, 565–72. (in Chinese)

Zink, A. R., Sola, C., Reischl, U., *et al.* (2003). Characterization of *Mycobacterium tuberculosis* complex DNAs from Egyptian mummies by spoligotyping. *Journal of Clinical Microbiology*, **41**, 359–67.

17

Peopling the Tibetan plateau: migrants, genes, and genetic adaptations

INTRODUCTION

The Tibetan plateau offers an interesting case study of human migration and subsequent adaptation, both cultural and biological, to a challenging environment. The Tibetan plateau, the highest in the world, presented to any early migrant two distinct challenges: the short- and long-term physiological effects of life at high elevation and the constraints of a relatively resource-poor and patchy environment. Moreover, there are relatively few easy routes onto the plateau – most have passes in excess of 5000 m, are blocked by snowfall for at least part of the year, or are associated with cold periglacial environments in even the most benign of times (Figure 17.1). Taken together, these are formidable obstacles, and one often hears the following question when describing the early prehistory of the plateau: "Why bother?" Yet at some point, most probably at multiple points in time, people did bother to move onto the plateau, and once established with permanence, created complex polities that vied for political power in the ancient world.

In this chapter, I will explore the following basic questions. What are the primary constraints on human biology at high elevation? What does archaeology say about the timing of migrations, their sources, and their frequency? What do data from the analysis of both ancient and modern DNA contribute to this discussion? I will then review what is known of the genetics of adaptation to high elevation in native Tibetans and conclude with an examination of the consonance (or lack thereof) of the archaeological, biological, and genetic data and

Causes and Consequences of Human Migration, ed. Michael H. Crawford and Benjamin C. Campbell. Published by Cambridge University Press. © Cambridge University Press 2012.

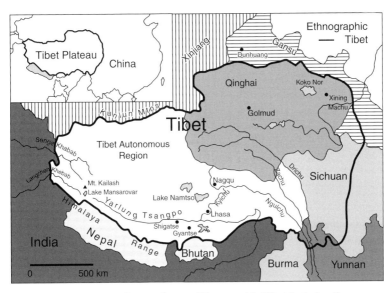

Figure 17.1 The Tibetan plateau. Ethnographic Tibet includes those areas in which the Tibetan language is spoken today. Languages related to Tibetan are also spoken in Bhutan, Sikkim, Nepal, and in the western Himalayas of India.

their implications for furthering our understanding of human migration to the plateau. Because of the relative scarcity of archaeological and genetic data, I will necessarily approach these questions at a macro level, and focus upon broad regional and extra-regional processes that reflect the movement of people from the surrounding lowlands to the plateau. Snow (2010:10) describes such movement as "peopling events." However, there may well have been hundreds, perhaps thousands, of dispersals or movements of individuals or families onto the plateau throughout prehistory. Many, if not most, of these likely left no presently observable traces in either the archaeological record or the genetic profile of modern peoples living on the plateau.

No matter what the scale of movement, however, every individual moving to the plateau was confronted by a suite of constraints upon their physiology that limited, among other things, their work capacity and their reproductive potential. These constraints operate at both short- and long-term temporal scales, and are exacerbated by cold, patchy, and low primary productivity habitats that challenged migrants to the plateau. The story of human migration to and the development of permanent populations on the Tibetan plateau are thus closely tied to the evolution of biological and cultural adaptations of individuals to these constraints. In turn, successful individual adaptation to life at high elevation had population-level consequences.

SHORT-TERM AND LONGER-TERM CONSTRAINTS
ON HUMAN BIOLOGY AT HIGH ELEVATION

High elevation environments are hard on unacclimatized lowlanders. The most obvious and severe constraint is hypoxia, which is simply the reduced partial pressure of oxygen at elevation. At sea level, for example, arterial blood is 97% saturated with oxygen; at 3000 m, it is at 90%, and at elevations of 4000–5000m, saturation decreases by almost 30% when compared with sea level (Beall, 2001:426–8; Frisancho, 1979:103). Hypoxia begins to affect lowlanders at *c.* 2500 m above sea level, and has both direct and indirect effects on health status, reproduction and growth, nutritional status, and work capacity. However, these effects on human biology are differentially expressed across time and can be characterized as being of either short- or long-term consequence. Importantly, hypoxia is the stressor that is least amenable to intervention and amelioration via cultural adaptations. Over the long run, then, the establishment of permanent habitation at elevations above 2500 m depended upon the appearance of acclimatizations (phenotypic plasticity), true adaptation (the appearance of genes capable of overcoming the selective pressures of hypoxia), or some combination of the two.

Short-term constraints

Almost all visitors to high elevations experience acute mountain sickness (AMS), the effects of which include headache, nausea, hyperventilation, and fatigue. For most people, these symptoms disappear within 48 hours, although a very small number of individuals may experience two more severe forms of AMS – high elevation pulmonary edema (HAPE) and high elevation cerebral edema (HACE). The former is a buildup of fluid in the lungs while the latter is a swelling of the brain. Both are potentially fatal and can only be resolved by rapid descent to lower elevation. Although the causes of these syndromes are unclear, a rapid ascent to high elevation appears to increase the probability of their onset. For foot-mobile peoples in the past, these severe forms of AMS would likely have been comparatively rare.

All migrants to high elevation experience a reduction in work capacity at high elevation. The degree of reduction in any individual is contingent upon multiple factors, such as nutritional status, health status, and age, but numerous studies have demonstrated that maximal work capacity (as measured by $V_{O2\ peak}$) declines rapidly by as much as 25–30% of sea level conditions (Marconi *et al.*, 2004, 2006:107). Over time, lowlanders acclimatize and begin to recover some of their sea level aerobic capacity. Debate is presently focused upon just how much time it takes to recover something approaching sea level capacity. Over a period of 60 days, fit lowlanders were able to recover 85% of their aerobic capacity. Over a span of years, however, fully acclimatized lowlanders are able to recapture as much as 90% of their capacity (Lundby *et al.*, 2004; Marconi *et al.*, 2006:107). However, native highlanders are shown to use oxygen more efficiently – that is, to expend less energy in common tasks – than are acclimatized lowlanders. Thus while lowlanders may recover a substantial portion of their low elevation aerobic work capacity, they are still, when compared with native highlanders, unable to work as hard or as long (Marconi *et al.*, 2006:113).

The short-term consequences of this are obvious. Reduced work capacity would affect resource procurement patterns of foraging peoples as they encountered the effects of life at high elevation. In effect, people would have to work longer (at least over a period of months, working harder would not be a viable option) to obtain the same number of calories as they did at lower elevations. In turn, low aerobic capacity may have led to changes in settlement patterns, frequency of mobility, and selection of resources to gather or pursue.

Longer-term constraints

Chronic mountain sickness (CMS) and problems with pregnancy and completed fertility are the two most significant constraints on life at high elevation. The latter is especially important, since it has a direct effect on population growth and survival. Indeed, a careful examination of pregnancy at high elevation has been seen as one way to get insight into possible selective factors that have promoted genetic adaptation to life at high elevation (Julian *et al.*, 2009; Moore *et al.*, 2004).

CMS (also known as Monge's Disease) affects both natives and long-time residents at high elevation and is characterized by the production of excessive numbers of red blood cells (known as polycythemia or erythrocytosis) and severe hypoxemia, which is the reduced partial pressure of oxygen in the blood (León-Velarde and Mejía, 2008:130). Polycythemia is a common short-term response of native lowlanders to exposure to hypoxia, and this has led some authors to argue that CMS is a "loss of adaptation" to it. Although once believed to affect only Andean natives, CMS has been observed in native Tibetans, although at low frequencies (Wu, 2005). Severe cases of CMS can worsen existing respiratory disorders and can lead to circulatory problems due to red cell mass in the blood. Other symptoms include breathlessness, fatigue, mental confusion, and sleep disruption. In the Andes, CMS tends to occur in older males, and is less common in females and the young. There is no clear relationship of gender and age in the small number of Tibetans known to have the disease. The only long-term and effective cure for CMS is descent to low elevation, where the symptoms disappear. However, a return to high elevation leads to the recurrence of the disease.

Associated with CMS is a potentially more serious condition – high altitude pulmonary hypertension, or HAPH (León-Velarde and Mejía, 2008:131). This clinical condition, which affects both children and adults, is created by pulmonary vasoconstriction, and is seen as an immediate response to exposure to hypoxia in unacclimatized lowlanders (Beall, 2001:428). For lowlanders, it is believed to more effectively distribute oxygen in the lungs, which in turn improves oxygen diffusion in the blood. Serious cases of HAPH can lead susceptible individuals toward HAPE or heart failure, and in unacclimatized lowlanders, HAPH can cause serious complications in pregnancy, which can lead to the increased risk of maternal and infant mortality and morbidity (Beall, 2001:442). Interestingly, Andean natives maintain pulmonary vasoconstriction whereas native Tibetans do not (Beall, 2001:438; Moore et al., 1998). These differences between native Tibetans and Andean peoples have led some authors to conclude that the patterns observed in native Tibetans are the result of natural selection (MacInnes et al., 2011).

The most serious long-term effects of moving to high elevation appear to be related to pregnancy. Pregnancy is stressful at low elevation, but at high elevation it is even more so, especially for unacclimatized lowlanders but even for long-term residents, whether they are acclimatized migrants or native peoples. At low elevation, pregnant women require more calories, cardiac output rises as much as 40%, maternal ventilation increases dramatically, and blood volume (primarily of blood plasma, not red blood cells) increases significantly (Moore, 2003:145–7). Although only one of many factors, the flow of oxygen to the growing fetus is of critical importance, because it has been observed repeatedly that a restricted fetal oxygenation leads to a condition of intrauterine growth restriction (IUGR), which in turn leads to low birth weights of neonates (Moore et al., 2004). Low birth weight neonates exhibit higher mortality than infants of normal weight. Interestingly, some have argued that the low birth weights of infants born to native highlanders is an adaptation to hypoxia, or at least compensatory to it because it reduces the oxygen requirements of the fetus (Krampl *et al.*, 2001); this claim will be examined below.

Two other medical conditions affect pregnancy at high elevation: pregnancy-induced hypertension (pre-eclampsia) and a higher incidence of extreme neonatal jaundice. Although these conditions can affect all women at all elevations, they are particularly severe at high elevation. Pre-eclampsia is a set of symptoms, the most prominent of which are high blood pressure and an abnormal amount of protein in the blood (Redman and Sargent, 2005). Causes of pre-eclampsia are multiple, and include insufficient blood flow to the uterus, poor diet, and immune system problems. Severe cases of pre-eclampsia restrict blood flow to the placenta, which can result in slower fetal growth due to a lack of nutrients or oxygen, and may also cause the placenta to separate from the walls of the uterus, thus leading to spontaneous abortion of the fetus and significant loss of blood in the mother. Another complication is the HELLP syndrome, which is the destruction of red blood cells, elevated liver enzymes, and low platelet count. Finally, pre-eclampsia can become full-blown eclampsia, which can lead to seizures and be fatal to both mother and fetus. Over the long term, pre-eclampsia may also increase the risk of cardiac disease in the mother. There is no cure for this condition aside from delivery. However, a premature birth risks a higher incidence of infant mortality.

Neonatal jaundice is a common condition for many newborns, but at high elevation, there is an increased incidence of hyperbilirubinemia (Beall, 2001:442; Moore *et al.*, 1984). One form of bilirubin is neurotoxic, and if left untreated, this condition can lead to infant death or significant developmental problems over time. Importantly, polycythemia is a known cause of pathologic neonatal jaundice. Before the modern era, no effective treatment for this condition existed.

A number of factors, then, combine to make pregnancy at high elevation risky for both mother and child. One conclusion to be drawn from this is that until women became acclimatized to hypoxia, there would have been excess female mortality and an increased incidence of infant mortality as well. Together, these combined to slow the rate of population growth. It is only after women became genetically adapted to high elevation that population could have grown at rates comparable to lower elevations.

The effects of cold at elevation

Cold stress is a constant problem for life at high elevation. In continental plateaus like Tibet, seasonal cold stress can be extreme, and even in the summer wind chill and shade can drop ambient air temperature substantially. The problem for the body when confronted by cold is to maintain core temperature by minimizing heat loss at all costs, and to do so humans have two physiological responses – peripheral vasoconstriction and metabolic heat production. Vasoconstriction simply reduces blood flow to the extremities. While this has the effect of maintaining core temperature, it also risks cold-induced damage to fingers, toes, and other exposed body parts. Increased metabolic heat is created by the shivering response. Shivering, however, induces more rapid respiration, which in turn leads to rapid dehydration, and in general, cold air contains less water vapor, thus exacerbating this problem. Shivering increases the heart rate, and thus places greater demands on the cardiovascular system in general. Finally, shivering expends energy, and thus individuals exposed to chronic cold will have an elevated basal metabolic rate, which of course demands more calories as well. Fire and, especially, adequate clothing, can blunt the effects of cold stress (Aldenderfer, 1998:10). Exercise can also increase body temperature, but is dependent upon sufficient calories so as to maintain a constant rate of exertion.

For newcomers to high elevation, these responses to cold are particularly costly. Hyperventilation is a common response to hypoxia, but is only effective for a short time. Increased respiration leads to significant heat loss and rapid dehydration, and, like shivering, burns energy. More rapid respiration also increases the heart rate. Overall, cold and hypoxia combine to increase caloric requirements when compared with low elevation peoples. But recall that newcomers to high elevation have clear limits on work capacity at least until they become acclimatized. These combined stressors make the initial stages of life at high elevation risky, and help to explain why high plateaus and mountain systems were occupied relatively late in human history (Aldenderfer, 2006b; Gamble, 1994:192–7).

ARCHAEOLOGICAL EVIDENCE FOR HUMAN MIGRATION ONTO THE TIBETAN PLATEAU

Archaeological research on the Tibetan plateau is still in a developmental stage (Aldenderfer and Zhang, 2004:2–11). Relatively few Chinese and Tibetan archaeologists and even fewer scholars from other nations

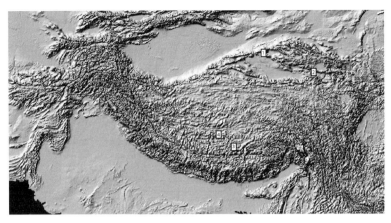

Figure 17.2 Location of Paleolithic sites on the Tibetan Plateau. (1) Xiao Qaidam, *c.* 33 000 years ago; (2) Heimahe 1, Jiangxigou 1, and Locality 93-13, 15 000-13 000 years ago; (3) Chusang, 32 000-28 000 years ago; and (4) Siling Tso, *c.* 30 000 years ago.

have had the opportunity to conduct research on the plateau. Consequently, there are major gaps in our knowledge of its prehistory as well as significant biases in the locations of research that must be considered as we assess the evidence for migrations onto the plateau and the eventual establishment of a permanent occupation there.

The earliest occupations of the Tibetan plateau

Presently, there are no securely dated archaeological sites older than 15 000 years ago on the Tibetan plateau. Although there has been speculation that the initial occupation of the Tibetan plateau was as early as 50 000 years ago, more recent research suggests that the earliest occupation of the plateau is no earlier than 30 000 years ago, and could even be much later in time (Aldenderfer, 2011; Figure 17.2). With a few exceptions, most sites of reputed Paleolithic age are surface exposures, and the estimation of their age is based upon the typological comparison of the stone tools and other artifacts found at them to dated sites often located hundreds, if not thousands, of kilometers away (see, for example, An, 1982). This cross-dating of sites is standard practice in archaeology, but it is often unreliable and thus must be used with caution (Aldenderfer and Zhang, 2004).

Xiao Qaidam (3100 m asl) is found on the extreme northern fringe of the plateau and the original dating of the geological context at Qaidam indicated that the site dated between 33 000 and 35 000 years ago (Huang, 1994). A more recent examination of the geological context of the site places it in time between 3000 and 11 000 years ago, with the latter the most probable date given the reassessment of the cross-dating of the stone tool assemblage by Brantingham and his colleagues (2011) and Sun *et al.* (2010).

Another problematic site of a reputed early date is Siling Tso, which is located some 300 km northwest of Lhasa at an elevation of 4600 m asl (Yuan *et al.*, 2007). Assemblages of stone tools are found on a series of terraces surrounding a large lake. Using cross-dating of tool forms, the authors argue that these tools are likely to date to the Late Pleistocene. The terraces upon which these tools date from 40 000–30 000 years ago, but it is unclear if the age of the terraces significantly constrains the age of the tools. Indeed, Brantingham *et al.* (2011) argue that these tool forms may in fact date to after 10 000 years ago based upon their work in Qinghai.

Chusang (4200 m asl), located in central Tibet near Lhasa, presents a similarly confused picture. First discovered in 1995, the site consists of 19 human hand and foot prints impressed into a now-calcified travertine deposit (Aldenderfer, 2006a, 2006b; Zhang and Li, 2002). All the prints were pressed into the same layer of the travertine, and because they had rough, unsmoothed edges, were not likely to have been cut or carved out of the rock. Size differences in the prints suggest that both adults and children were present when they were made. The travertine deposit began as a soft calcitic mud precipitated as dissolved CO_2 degassed and the hot spring water became supersaturated with calcium carbonate. The exact depositional environment of this mud is unclear from the recorded observations. The prints were formed sometime after this deposition, and the mud was subsequently lithified, presumably by the addition of calcium carbonate cement, forming the present hard calcareous travertine deposit. An initial dating of the geological context of the prints indicated that they were formed around 21 000 years ago (Zhang and Li, 2002). Re-examination and new dating of the context using the uranium-thorium isochron method suggests a date of occupation between 28 000 and 32 000 years ago (Aldenderfer, 2006a; 2007:159). Stone tools found immediately downslope from the site appear to be of considerable antiquity. If this dating holds up, Chusang is currently the oldest known site on the Tibetan plateau.

All other dated sites of pre-Holocene age are found in Qinghai on the northeastern margins of the plateau. Madsen *et al.* (2006) report the discovery of three archaeological sites – Heimahe 1, Jiangxigou 1, and Locality 93–13 – that contain a total of five distinct occupations dating between 15 000 and 13 000 years ago. They are found at elevations of 3200–3300 m asl, and although the excavations at them were of limited scale, sufficient data were recovered to indicate that the sites were short-term occupations and were thus part of a larger-scale settlement system that involved seasonal mobility.

Although the full extent of the system remains unknown, the authors speculate that the more permanent residences of these foraging peoples were likely located at significantly lower elevations (*c.* 2400 m asl) some 74 km distant (Madsen *et al.*, 2006:1440). One other site, Xiadawu (4000 m asl) is found along the Yellow River (Tib.: Machu) in the Kunlun range. It has a reported date of *c.* 11 000 years ago (Van der Woerd *et al.*, 2002), but little is known of how this site relates to others found in Qinghai.

Because of the limited amount of research done at these sites, it is difficult to argue with certainty about the permanence of their occupation. However, the Qinghai sites all appear to be short-term occupations, and given their location on the rim of the plateau, it seems reasonable to assume that more permanent base camps associated with them are to be found at lower elevations off the plateau. This is a key feature of the Brantingham *et al.* (2003; see also Madsen *et al.* 2006) three-step model of the peopling of the plateau. Although foragers visited sites at higher elevations, up to at least 4000 m, they did not live there permanently. Therefore, it is unlikely that these peoples had either genetic or acclimatizational adaptations to high elevation life, although the science supporting this assertion remains to be performed.

A similar step model has been proposed for the Andes (Aldenderfer, 1998); in far southern Peru, foraging peoples first used an elevation step between *c.* 3000 m and 3800 m, moving into sites in this range from lower elevation base camps. However, unlike the model proposed by Brantingham and colleagues, these Andean foragers quickly (within a 500-year period) became permanent residents at high elevation, presumably initiating the process of genetic adaptation to life at high elevation.

Chusang, and possibly Siling Tso, may well offer a different model for the peopling of the plateau. Given their location, it seems unlikely that they were a part of a settlement system that included a lower elevation component. One would have to move at least one thousand kilometers to the north, east, or west, or cross the Himalayan arc to the south to get to a lower elevation environment. Instead, it seems reasonable to postulate that the peoples of these sites represent an earlier occupation of the plateau that may well have persisted, albeit in small numbers, into the Holocene. This scenario is bolstered by the findings of Zhao *et al.* (2009), who, using mtDNA evidence from modern Tibetan peoples, argue that they observe traces of an earlier migration of people onto the plateau, one that dates before 21 000 years ago.

The period from 45 000 to 24 000 years ago was marked by a significant climatic amelioration in the region, especially along the northern margins of the plateau which saw the expansion of vast grasslands that attracted large numbers of herbivores, thus creating new and attractive niches for hunters to exploit. This resource "pull" likely attracted foragers to the plateau in small numbers (Aldenderfer, 2006b). These foragers survived the Last Glacial Maximum (*c.* 24 000–16 000 years ago), a period of intense cold and reduced resource density, and they most likely moved into the lower elevation zones of the central plateau, such as the Yarlung Tsangpo valley and its tributaries. Sites like Chusang, with its permanent hot spring, may have been particularly attractive.

Recent archaeological work in far western Tibet suggests an alternative pathway onto the plateau. Settlement pattern surveys have discovered a number of sites along the Sutlej drainage in Ngari Prefecture that have strong similarities to flake/blade assemblages found to the east on the plateau and China. Of considerable importance is the discovery of a Levallois-like flake on one of the high (oldest in geological terms) terraces of the river (Aldenderfer and Olsen, 2008:5). This technology is well represented in South Asia, and typically seen as "Middle Paleolithic" in age (James and Petraglia, 2006). In India, such assemblages can be as early as 150 000 years ago, although the nearest such assemblage to the study area, in the Dang-Deokhuri valley of central Nepal, is dated to *c.* 30 000 years ago (Corvinus, 2002). Another site with Levallois-like technology was located further in the interior in the upper reaches of the Sutlej near the modern village of Kyunglung and just below the headwaters of that river (Aldenderfer and Olsen, 2008:6).

The earliest certain permanent occupations of the Tibetan plateau

In contrast to the confusion surrounding the nature of the Paleolithic occupation of the plateau, our understanding of its use during the Holocene is clearer but far from ideal. It is during the period 6000–9000 years ago that the first permanent settlements appear (Aldenderfer, 2007; Brantingham *et al.*, 2007; Rhode *et al.*, 2007; see Figure 17.3).

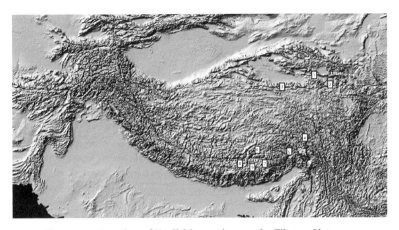

Figure 17.3 Location of Neolithic-era sites on the Tibetan Plateau.
(1) Qinghai sites, including Heimahe 3 (8400 years ago) and Jiangxigou
2 (6500–4950 years ago; (2) Zongri complex sites, c. 6500 years ago;
(3) Xidatan, c. 8200–6400 years ago; (4) Kha rub, 5900–4145 years ago and
Rngul mdv, c. 4160 years ago (Karou and Xioenda); (5) sites at the great
bend of the Yarlung Tsangpo; (6) Chugong, 3750–3150 years ago (Qugong);
(7) Bannga, (8) Phrang mgo (Changuogou); and (9) Qinba.

Climate across East and Central Asia improves significantly in the postglacial period, although this amelioration is punctuated by a series of
short intervals of cold and dry events. A wide range of archaeological
cultures based upon the use of domesticated plants and animals (usually referred to as the Neolithic) are known from the low elevation
zones on the eastern margins of the plateau. Although there has been
a substantial amount of archaeological research done on these cultures,
their relationships remain obscure (Liu, 2004). The earliest Neolithic
culture along the northeastern margin of plateau in Qinghai is know as
Yangshao, which is dated to 7000–5400 years ago (Aldenderfer,
2007:153; Chayet, 1994:51). This is followed by the Majiayao culture
(5400–4800 years ago) that is found in Gansu and eastern Qinghai.
A local variant of this culture is Zongri (c. 5600–4000 years ago) found
just below the edge of the plateau in Qinghai (Chen, 2002). In Sichuan,
Neolithic cultures are known from at least 7000 years ago (Bureau of
Cultural Relics, 1985:178). Although Neolithic-era cultures are known to
exist to the south along the Himalayan arc, the only one studied to any
extent is that found at Burzahom along the far western margins of the
plateau in Kashmir and which is dated to c. 4500 years ago (Sharma,
2000). Each of these archaeological cultures has been identified as a
potential source of migrants to the plateau, but there remains

controversy as to which, if any, can be considered an ancestral population to the Tibetan people found on the plateau today.

On the plateau itself only a small number of sites of this time
period have been identified and then excavated. In Qinghai, Jiangxigou
2 is found near the southern margin of Ngonpo Tso at an elevation of
3312 m asl. The site has three distinct uses with the earliest from
c. 9100–8170 years ago, a second from *c.* 6500–4950 years ago, and a
final one at *c.* 2000 years ago. The second occupation is said to contain
thick undecorated and thin cord-marked ceramics thought to date
around 6500 years ago, and the investigators suggest that the ceramics
are very similar to those of the low-elevation Zongri culture (Rhode
et al., 2007:604). Faunal remains include ovids (most likely the Himalayan Blue Sheep *Pseudois nayaur*) and artiodactyls. No evidence of structural remains was found, but the researchers speculate that given the
presence of ceramics, it is possible that the site may reflect a longer-
term occupation. Unfortunately, no plant evidence has been recovered
from the site. Heimahe 3, also on the south side of the lake at an
elevation of 3202 m asl, dates to *c.* 8400 years ago, and is seen as a
short-term occupation. Finally, Xidatan 2 (4300 m asl) and located some
550 km southwest of the lake, dates between 8200–6400 years ago. It
appears to be a short-term occupation, but one that has connections to
a source of obsidian (volcanic glass), located some 951 km further to the
west on the Chang Tang.

Aside from these sites, there are two others that give us insight
into the earliest permanent occupations on the plateau – Kha rub
(Chin.: Karou) and Chugong (Chin.: Qugong). Kha rub is located at
3100 m asl on a high terrace above the Mekong (Tib.: Zachu) River. The
occupation at the site ranges in date from 5900 to 4145 years ago.
Substantial semi-subterranean structures, copious amounts of ceramics, one cultivar (foxtail millet *Setaria italica*), and the remains of two
animals thought to be domesticated species – an unidentified bovid and
pigs (*Sus scrofa*) – have been discovered (Bureau of Cultural Relics
1985:168; Flad *et al.*, 2007). The site is clearly a permanent habitation.
At least ten other sites said to be of Neolithic age are found near Kha
rub along the Zachu and in the vicinity of Chamdo (Chayet, 1994:46) but
of these, only Rngul mdv (Chin.: Xiaoenda) has been chronometrically
dated. The site is contemporaneous with the latest occupation of Kha
rub (*c.* 4160 years ago; Aldenderfer, 2007: table 1).

Chugong is located 5 km north of Lhasa at an elevation of 3680 m
asl (Institute of Archaeology, 1999). It has two primary occupations that
range in time from *c.* 3750 to 3150 years ago. According to the

investigators, domesticated species recovered included yak (*Bos grunniens*), domesticated sheep (*Ovis aries shangi*), and pig (*Sus scrofa*). No structures were encountered. The ceramic assemblage, however, is large and impressive. Unfortunately, there is no indication of the plant remains present at the site. Other sites associated with Chugong and which have had some systematic work include Phrang mgo (Chin.: Changuogou), located south of Lhasa on the north bank of the Yarlung Tsangpo at an elevation of 3570 m asl (He, 1994; Li and Zhao, 1999) and Bangga in the Yarlung Valley (Zhao, 2002). Although not radiocarbon dated, the archaeological assemblage, especially the ceramics, at Phrang mgo is very similar to that found at Chugong. Remains of so-called "naked" barley (*Hordeum vulgare* L. var *nudum*; Fu *et al.*, 2000) have been recovered.

Excavations at Bangga have uncovered at least one rectangular semi-subterranean house, stone-lined interior storage pits (one of which was used for a secondary burial), and ceramics similar to those at Chugong. Sites thought to be part of the Chugong tradition but which have seen limited work are those in the great bend area (Nying-khri/Nyingchi) of the Yarlung Tsangpo, such as Jumu, Beibeng, and Maniweng, among others (Chayet, 1994:46–7). These sites also indicate the presence of a permanent population of agriculturalists on the plateau.

In summary, three regions of the plateau have evidence for relatively early permanent settlements: extreme northeastern Qinghai at 6500–5600 years ago, extreme eastern Tibet at 5900 years ago, and the Yarlung Tsangpo valley in central Tibet at 3750 years ago. While the data from the Paleolithic are admittedly fragmentary, taken together, the evidence from these sites argues for a long-term presence of people on the plateau throughout the Holocene, and quite probably, from Late Paleolithic times.

POPULATION AFFINITIES AND INFERRED POPULATION MOVEMENTS BASED UPON THE ANALYSIS OF DNA

As has been noted by many commentators, the analysis of DNA, both modern and ancient, has revolutionized the study of world prehistory. While the fossil and archaeological records continue to provide their own unique insights into the past, evidence from DNA both complements and challenges long-held beliefs on the movement of our ancestors across the globe. Such studies are now beginning to make an impact on our understanding of the movement of people to the Tibetan plateau.

Studies of modern DNA

In general, analyses of modern DNA postulate two primary migration routes onto the plateau: a northerly route via Qinghai in the northeastern Tibetan plateau, and a southerly route from the Hengduan basin in southwestern China. This latter route includes three major river drainages of the region: the Yangtze (which flows into eastern China, the Mekong, and the Salween (both of which flow into Southeast Asia). The study by Torroni *et al.* (1994:189) was one of the first to examine DNA evidence to make a claim about the origin of Tibetans. Although constrained by the techniques of the times, as well as small samples of somewhat uncertain provenance, his team identified a set of mtDNA lineages that in their opinion showed that Tibetans shared common ancestral origins with what they defined as "northern Mongoloid populations," which included various Siberian groups. In turn, these data were compared to a variety of Southeast Asian peoples, like the Vietnamese, Malays, and Taiwanese Han. No mainland Han samples were included. These data were used to support a model of migration onto the plateau from the north at an unspecified time.

Kang *et al.* (2010) provided support for this model using 15 autosomal STRs (short tandem repeats) in the analysis of more than 300 individuals from three populations: Tibetans near Lhasa, Tibetans living near Chamdo on the eastern fringe of the plateau, and the third from an ethnic group, the Deng, currently living in the extreme southeastern Tibetan plateau in the Himalayas of that area. They determined that both sets of Tibetans were distinct from the Deng, and that the Deng have clear similarities to other peoples of the eastern Himalayas. Further, these Himalayan groups are distinct from other East Asian populations, and that both groups of Tibetans are similar to North Asians, specifically from peoples in the Altaic region (Kang *et al.*, 2010:273). Wen *et al.* (2004) offer a more detailed insight into this presumed northerly migration process. They have identified a Y-chromosome bias in extant southern Tibeto-Burmese populations (especially those residing in Yunnan) that indicates to them the migration of males from the north that interbred with women native to the south.

Zhao *et al.* (2009) have identified what they describe as a very ancient Tibetan haplogroup – M16 – in their analyses of modern Tibetan DNA. They argue that this represents the remnants of a very early occupation of the plateau dating before the Last Glacial Maximum, more than 21 000 years ago, and which has persisted to the modern era. Another haplogroup, M9a, has dates between 15 000 and 20 000 ago. They also note, however, that most other Tibetan mtDNA hap-logroups are likely of Neolithic origin, and date these to between 2000 and 10 000 years (Zhao *et al.*, 2009: fig. 4). All of these haplogroups, however, have strong affinities to northern East Asian populations.

Su *et al.* (1999, 2000) developed two models asserting that deep in prehistory, a Southeast Asian population moved into southern China, specifically into Yunnan and Guangxi. Using a specific dominant Y-chromosome haplotype (M122C), they argue that this south-China-based population moved northward into the central and western Yellow River basin sometime between 20 000 and 40 000 years BP and label this group "Proto-Chinese," which over time genetically and linguistically diverges into what they call "Proto-Sino-Tibetan." Around 10 000 years BP, this population began to grow substantially, and budding daughter populations were forced into new niches, with some of these popula-tions moving further to the west along the Yellow River. Around 6000 years BP, another linguistic shift occurs, with what are now called "Proto-Tibeto-Burmans," which move from their western Yellow River and eastern Qinghai focus across the Tibetan plateau. With yet another linguistic split, one group (Baric speakers) moves to the south, crossing the Himalaya, and moves back into northern Yunnan, Bhutan, and northeastern India. Still another group (Bodhic speakers), after having received a significant genetic admixture of an unspecified central Asian or southwestern Siberian population, moves across the entire Tibetan plateau.

This model shares points of contact with Torroni *et al.* (1994). In effect, Su's "Proto-Chinese" group can be seen as the "northern Mongol-oid" population, although it stems from a very different source with deep roots in southeastern Asia. Qian *et al.* (2000), examining an analysis of three modern populations (two from the central plateau and one from Yunnan, but speaking the Khamic dialect of Tibetan), identified two dominant paternal lineages in the three populations: one likely from central Asia and exhibiting the YAP+ mutation, and the other from East Asia, which exhibits the M122C haplogroup. This latter result is consistent with the Su *et al.* (2000) model.

Wang *et al.* (2011) genotyped a very small population of Tibetans ($n = 30$) with over one million SNPs (single nucleotide polymorphisms) and used these data to posit an early migration to the Tibetan plateau via the Hengduan Mountains of southwestern China of what they call "Proto-Tibeto-Burmese" peoples. Like the "Baric" speakers of the Su model, this group moved from the middle and upper Yellow River basin to the north to Hengduan region, and from there moved onto the plateau. Wang *et al.* (2011) also argue that the modern Yi, an ethnic group living in Yunnan, are the population most similar (in terms of genetics) to modern Tibetans.

Finally, Shi *et al.* (2008) make a strong claim, based on an extensive analysis of Y-chromosome distributions across 73 East Asian populations, that the D-M174 lineage is extremely old in East Asia, dating perhaps as early as 60 000 years ago, represents a northerly migration from the southern East Asia, and is likely to be ancestral lineage to modern Tibetans: "Taken together, the current Tibetan and Japanese populations are probably the admixture of two ancient populations represented by D-M174 and O3-M122 respectively" (Shi *et al.* 2008:9). This model has points of contact with Su's, especially regards the East Asian origins of the M122 lineage, but appears to discount entirely a significant northerly input into the modern Tibetan genome.

And to add a bit more confusion to the mix of studies, a recent analysis of the Y-chromosome genomes of more than 3000 individuals from 116 populations within the modern boundaries of China of by Zhong *et al.* (2011), while generally supporting models of a northerly movement of peoples in to East Asia from Southeast Asia at a very early date, also detects a significant contribution of northern East Asian haplogroups, more specifically of peoples they label of Central–South Asian and/or West Eurasian origin. They date these northerly migrations after *c.* 18 000 years ago (following the Last Glacial Maximum, or LGM) and suggest that the majority of observed haplotypes in East Asia are of Neolithic (or later) origin.

Analyses of ancient DNA

The analysis of ancient DNA (aDNA) has much to contribute to our understanding of the peopling of the Tibetan plateau, but unfortunately, these contributions have yet to be realized because of a stunning paucity of samples of human remains from the plateau and the High Himalaya (Aldenderfer, 2011:142). Although Chinese and other archaeologists of the region have excavated hundreds, if not thousands, of tombs, it is the case that most of these remains have not been curated effectively and are thus lost to further research.

Aldenderfer (2006c) reports on an analysis of human remains from a series of tombs in far western Tibet that date between 500 BC and AD 100. Two samples of human remains were tested, and the mtDNA haplogroups identified from them are G2a and interestingly, M9a, one of the early haplogroups from the plateau. Two recent studies of Neolithic-era sites found below the northeastern rim of the plateau in Qinghai at Taojiazhai (1700 to 1900 years ago; 2330 m; Zhao *et al.*, 2011) and Lajia (3800 to 4000 years ago; *c.* 1800 m; Gao *et al.*, 2007) have also recovered aDNA. These studies offer the hope that more samples will be recovered and that aDNA will be well preserved in other areas of the plateau and its margins.

Ancient mtDNA has been recovered from a series of mortuary sites in Upper Mustang, Nepal, which lies just to the south of that country's border with Tibet (Aldenderfer, 2010a, 2010b). The sites (all of which are found at elevations exceeding 4000 m and thus would have required the suite of high elevation adaptations for successful perman-ent habitation) which have had remains examined date to three periods: *c.* 1200−400 BC, AD 400−500, and AD 1500−1600. MtDNA hap-logroups identified in the first period include M*, M3, M4, and M10, M*, F1, and M10 in the second period, and D4 and D4j1 in the third period. The individual with the F1 haplogroup found in the second period has an mtDNA profile that is an exact match to that of an individual recovered from one of the tombs at the Laija site in north-eastern Qinghai.

M* is a widespread macro-haplogroup across much of Central and Southeast Asia; M3 has a northwest Indian or Himalayan origin, while M4 is common in South Asia, as is M10. M25 is also common in north-west India. F1 is not common in South Asia, but is found in low frequencies in Tibet, and is widespread in East Asia. Finally, the D4 and D4j1 haplogroups are commonly encountered on the plateau and in Central Asia in general. The picture presented by the aDNA data from Upper Mustang is something of a melting pot, with people from a number of regions of the Himalayas and South Asia represented. These data suggest that the margins of the plateau to the east, west, and north will be similarly complex.

Dates and directions of migrations

The genetic data from both ancient and modern populations offer a complex mosaic of possibilities for ascertaining the range and timing of likely migrations to the Tibetan plateau. At least two studies of modern DNA suggest a Paleolithic era migration to the plateau that was appar-ently successful in that it left low frequencies of these haplogroups in modern Tibetan peoples. One of these studies − Zhao *et al.* (2009) − argues for a pre-LGM date for this migration, while the other − Wang *et al.* (2011) − suggests it took place just after the end of the LGM. Both, however, are consistent in identifying the likely direction of that migration as coming from northern East Asia.

The remaining studies of modern DNA propose that most of the genetic diversity found in modern Tibetans is of "Neolithic" age, with dates ranging from 6000 years ago to no more than roughly 3000 years ago. Two directions are postulated: a series of migrations from the Yellow River drainage that move to the south around 6000 years ago, and a migration from southwestern China and the Hengduan basin that could be as early as 6000 years ago or somewhat later. Note that a late date – around 3000 years ago – is consistent with Yi *et al.*'s (2010) assertion, based on the identification of the genes in Tibetans that appear to promote adaptation to life at high elevation, that Han and ethic Tibetans diverged genetically no more than 2750 years ago.

Despite these points of agreement, it remains the case that the picture presented by genetic analyses is far from settled. In part, this situation can be attributed to small sample sizes, biases in the selection of samples, poor control over the necessarily self-referential identification of ethnic relationship ("yes, of course I am a Tibetan!"), and a reliance upon inaccurate or inappropriate historical attributions of ethnic identity by investigators. Ethnonyms like "the Yi people" or the "Di-Qiang" are taken as givens, but in each instance there are significant questions about the composition of these groups and their relationships to others. Nevertheless, these studies do provide fertile ground for the development of new hypotheses about the peopling of the plateau, and as I will show, some of these analyses are more likely to have research value than others.

THE GENETICS OF HIGH-ALTITUDE ADAPTATION

Although it has long been suspected that there is a genetic basis for successful life at high elevation, it is only within the past ten years that significant and substantial evidence has been accumulated to support that hypothesis. Advances in our ability to sequence the human genome and study gene expression in detail have revolutionized the study of high-elevation adaptation (Beall, 2011), but in some ways, it has complicated it as well. One of the most interesting observations from this recent work is the verification of something long understood from previous studies: native Tibetans and native Andean peoples (Aymara and Quechua speakers of the Andean altiplano) have very different phenotypic responses to hypoxia, and that Andean peoples do not fully share the same suite of suspected genetic adaptations with their

Tibetan counterparts (Bingham *et al.*, 2009, 2010). And importantly, even in the three most compelling studies of native Tibetans and their possible genetic responses to hypoxia – Beall *et al.* (2010), Simonson *et al.* (2010) and Yi *et al.* (2010) – it has yet to be demonstrated that these genes actually provide a selective advantage to those who possess them. In other words, certain genes associated with physiological responses to hypoxia have been shown to be overrepresented in native Tibetans when compared with native lowlanders. But just how these genes actually work to promote fitness has yet to be determined. Given the subtleties of human physiology, the complexity of factors that influence gene expression, and the real possibility that epigenetic factors, especially those that influence the prenatal maternal environment, may have significant roles to play in genetic responses to life at high elevation, it is unsurprising that a single and relatively simple response to chronic hypoxia has yet to be identified.

Genes and cold stress

Although not a focus of recent studies of the genetics of high elevation life, no evidence has been discovered that suggests native Tibetans have developed unique adaptations to cold stress. As noted above, cultural adaptations in place for at least the past 50 000 years, most prominently the habitual use of fire, the ability to make complex clothing, and the cognitive capacity to successfully adapt to strongly seasonal environments, are sufficient to ameliorate in great part all but the most extreme stresses of cold environments (Aldenderfer, 2006b:364–6). Any migrants moving onto the plateau during this time frame, especially from a putative northern route, would have possessed the full range of cultural adaptations necessary to cope with the rigors of cold on the plateau. Further, there is no indication in native Tibetans of genetic components that would promote the conservation of calories, more efficient use of those calories consumed (although see below for a possible exception to this), or enhanced abilities to process fats and proteins.

Genes and hypoxia

Not surprisingly, most recent research on native Tibetans has been to seek the genetic components of their obviously successful adaptation to hypoxia. Beall (2011), MacInnis and Rupert (2011), and Rupert (2010) provide useful summaries of the key studies and their findings. Native

Tibetans, when compared with Han or European lowlanders, have high allele frequencies in genes involved with oxygen homeostasis: the oxygen sensor *EGLN* and the transcription factor *EPAS1* (also known as HIF-2A, or hypoxia inducible factor 2A). Phenotypically, these variants are associated with lower hemoglobin concentrations in the blood.

Recall that native lowlanders respond quickly to acute hypoxia by dramatically spiking the production of red blood cells. That native Tibetans have successfully adapted to high elevation with low hematocrits is thus of considerable significance. This discovery has created some consternation. One question that has been raised is why selection is apparently operating upon a transcription gene rather than a structural gene, such as one related to the blood hormone erythropoietin (EPO) or a transcription gene like hypoxia-inducible transcription factor 1A (HIF-1A) that regulates more than 100 hypoxia-inducible genes (Tissot van Patot and Gassmann, 2011:157). These genes are primarily concerned with promoting efficiency in oxygen transport at the molecular level, so it was assumed that these genes would have been the most likely to witness positive selection. Indeed, EPO is commonly used by athletes to increase their hematocrit (blood doping), thereby increasing their aerobic capacity (V_{O2} max) and thus their endurance.

However, it appears that *EPAS1* and *EGLN* offer a number of other potential adaptive benefits that are at present poorly understood. Among the most significant of these are related to iron homeostasis, mitochrondrial stress, and lipid metabolism, and fetal, neonatal, and placental development (Tissot van Patot and Gassmann, 2011: table 1). Iron homeostasis refers to the body's ability to absorb dietary iron. Under conditions of hypoxia, this is an important concern, since hypoxia stimulates red blood cell production, thus the consumption of bodily stores of iron. At present, there is no compelling evidence that suggests that native highlanders are better able to absorb dietary iron more efficiently than native lowlanders, but the hypothesis remains intriguing. It should be obvious that any ability to extract nutrients from consumed food at high elevation would be of signal importance given the relative paucity of calories in these environments.

EPAS1 appears to play a major role in the reduction of mitochondrial stress, which is a simply the reduced ability of the mitochondria to produce energy effectively. Hypoxia forces mitochrondria to respire more rapidly, and the *EPAS1* gene regulates the transcription of various anti-oxidants and proteins that promote mitochondrial homeostasis. Working with HIF-1A, which increases glycolysis in response to hypoxia, *EPAS1* appears to have a key role in the creation an efficient bodily response to energy consumption at high elevation. Since high elevation life demands more calories due to, among other things, an increased basal metabolic rate, this gene may well confer a distinct selective advantage. And while it remains to be fully established, *EPAS1* is known to improve the body's ability to store lipids, which are poorly digested and more rapidly consumed or passed through the body at high elevation. Lipids are in generally short supply in high-elevation environments; most large mammal species thicken their coats rather than create large stores of bodily fat packets, and most plant species are lipid poor (Schaller, 1998). Finally, if these metabolic adaptations are confirmed, these may have been crucial in overcoming the reduction of work capacity seen in newcomers to high elevation. Through its effects on glycolysis, *EPAS1* may have promoted better energy production and conservation.

Among the most important potential effects of *EPAS1* on genetic adaptation to high elevation is its role in promoting healthy fetal, neonatal, and placental growth. Since pregnancy at high elevation is constantly at risk due to hypoxia, especially for lowlanders or unacclimatized newcomers, any gene or set of genes that create a more effective maternal environment would exhibit strong evidence of positive selection. Just how *EPAS1* promotes this is still under analysis, but it is known that it promotes the growth of new blood vessels from existing ones.

Recall that restricted fetal oxygenation leads to a condition of intrauterine growth restriction (IUGR), which in turn leads to low birth weights of neonates (Moore *et al.*, 2004). Low birth weight neonates exhibit higher mortality than infants of normal weight. Also, poor oxygenation of the placenta often leads to its separation from the uterine wall, thus increasing the probability of spontaneous abortion and the loss of the fetus. If restricted blood flow to the placenta increases maternal risk of pre-eclampsia, the fixing of this gene in a population of emerging highlanders would increase completed fertility, and would set the stage for population growth. This, perhaps more than any other effect on human physiology, is the most important potential contribution of *EPAS1* to a genetic adaptation to high elevation.

The importance of *EPAS1* in fetal development presents a new perspective on the debate about low birth weights commonly observed in native highlanders and whether this is an adaptation to hypoxia. Early debate focused on the potential advantages of low birth weights at high elevation – mothers would require fewer calories, as would the fetus, the maternal environment would be subject to less potential

developmental stress, and the maternal circulatory system would benefit from the reduced volume of blood flow to the placenta. As Moore
(2003:144–5) notes, however, it appears that reduced birth weights seen
in high elevation contexts are "compensatory" rather than adaptive
since there appears to be no survival advantage for low birth weight
neonates when compared with those of similar size found in low elevation contexts. If *EPAS1* promotes improved fetal and placental oxygenation as has been hypothesized, defining at what point in pregnancy its
influence is most crucial would help to better understand how quickly
lowland females adapt to hypoxia. This in turn would help to define
how quickly sustained population growth could take place – that is,
how many generations would be required to see a clear positive selection for this gene. Ultimately, such an analysis might help, at least in
part, in the evaluation of claims by Yi *et al.* (2010) that given the
postulated divergence of Tibetans and Han at no more than 2750 years
ago, it is the most rapid demonstration of natural selection acting on a
human population.

Genes and high elevation illness

The evidence for genetic bases for high elevation illnesses is somewhat
murky. Since disease can be expressed at an individual, family, or
population level, it is challenging to identify a set of candidate genes
that might promote resistance or susceptibility to high elevation illnesses. Further, mutations in these genes may be the cause rather than
a direct positive or negative selection on them. In a review of recent
studies of high elevations illnesses, MacInnis *et al.* (2011) have identified
two population-level relationships between genes and illness: those
associated with resistance to the various types of acute mountain
sickness (HAPE and HACE), and those related to CMS and HAPH.
A suite of genes responsible for promoting blood flow or hormones
involved in the production of nitric oxide (important for vasodilation)
have been implicated as potential contributors to susceptibility to both
HACPE and HACE, but to date no population level differences between
highlanders and lowlanders have been convincingly identified. It is
quite likely that individual resistance to the effects of MAS may have
been important for the first migrants to high elevation, but no studies
have examined this hypothesis in detail.

Our understanding of CMS and HAPH is somewhat better. Native
Tibetans, in general, tend to suffer less from both of these conditions
than do natives of the Andean altiplano. Indeed, until recently, it was

believed that Tibetans did not suffer from CMS. Recall that CMS is characterized by an elevated hematocrit that tends to appear late in life, and was thought initially to represent a "loss" of adaptation in those in which the syndrome appeared. The identification of *EPAS1* and *EGLN* in native Tibetans is strong evidence of genetic resistance to CMS since they act to reduce hematocrit levels. That it occurs at low frequency in Tibet is most likely explained by the observation that the gene, while very common in modern Tibetans, is not fully fixed in the Tibetan genome. An important caveat to the role *EPAS1* may play in resistance to CMS and HAPH is noted by MacInnis *et al.* (2011:351), who suggest that since CMS has a typical onset late in adult life, it is not likely to have been a driver of positive selection, and it may well be of secondary consequence as a promoter of genetic adaptation to life at high elevation.

CONSONANCE AND CONFLICT: MIGRATION TO AND ADAPTATION ON THE TIBETAN PLATEAU

How does the evidence from these distinct data sources reflect the population dynamics and the history of migration onto the Tibetan plateau? Not surprisingly, these data show points of agreement as well as significant differences.

Both the archaeological and genetic evidence are in agreement that the primary routes for getting people on the plateau have been from the north via Qinghai and from the south via a corridor in the Hengduan Mountains on the extreme margins of eastern Tibet. Although there is evidence for the movement of people onto the plateau from the southwest, possibly from the Indian subcontinent, too few sites have been identified to strongly support this claim. And while it is well known in historical times that there were strong connections of plateau peoples with the polities to the west of the plateau in what is now Afghanistan and beyond, both sites and genetic signatures of these probable contacts are lacking.

Although there is some agreement between these data types about routes, there is less agreement about the timing of population movements. This should not be surprising, as it is important to remember that migrations are not events but processes, and that they happen at multiple temporal and spatial scales. Further, each of these data types has clear limitations on their ability to define short-term events. Archaeological phases, for example, may well have durations of thousands of years, and even during the better-studied Neolithic, the temporal span of even the most well-defined archaeological cultures ranges into the hundreds of years, thus including many human generations. Time estimates of population movements based upon divergence of haplogroups and mutation rates are little better.

Nevertheless, the data from genetics appear to support a Paleolithic-era movement of people onto the plateau. The date range varies, but at least one movement is likely to have dated before the LGM, and is at least 21 000 years ago. Further, there are genetic signatures of haplogroups that are likely to date to just after the end of the LGM, or around 18 000 years ago. But the archaeological data supporting this hypothesis are quite weak. A series of sites of pre-LGM age have been identified but have yet to be widely accepted. And while the archaeological data for a post-LGM movement are stronger, especially in the Qinghai region, there are currently no pre-Holocene (*c.* 10 000 years ago) found on the central plateau. Thus while genetics support a model of an early, persistent, and successful human occupation of the plateau, the corresponding archaeological evidence for it is quite limited. There is consensus, however, that no matter when these early migrations may have taken place, they with certainty came from a northerly direction, and thus the founding populations were of Central Asian, or more likely, northern East Asian ancestry.

The assertion that there was a successful early occupation of the plateau raises a number of interesting questions. If these peoples were indeed permanent dwellers at high elevation, they would have had to develop physiological responses to chronic hypoxia to live successfully at high elevation. Whether (or if) these genetic adaptations were similar to those proposed for modern native Tibetans is a question that cannot be answered directly given the absence of human remains with intact aDNA that date to this period. And while certain haplogroups observed today in native Tibetans have an early date, it is far from clear if these early migrants have had a significant contribution to the adaptive capacity of modern peoples. Indirect evidence from archaeology, however, suggests that their possible contribution was greater than currently imagined (see below).

Tracking possible migrations to the plateau after 10 000 years ago becomes somewhat easier in that there are more archaeological and genetic data that can be used to identify routes of entry, and thus their source populations, as well as the timing of these movements. Recall that the earliest securely dated permanent populations known from the plateau are found in three places: in northeastern Qinghai at 6500–5500 years ago, in extreme eastern Tibet at 5900 years ago, and in the central

Yarlung Tsangpo valley at 3750 years ago. The data from genetics assert that migrations onto the plateau from the north began around 6000 years ago, and from the south 6000–3000 years ago. Are these people migrants to the plateau, the descendants of a small, but permanent, population of foragers, or some combination of both possibilities?

For the Qinghai sites, Rhode *et al.* (2007:609), following Chen (2002), argue that Jiangxigou 2 may reflect the movement of Majiayao peoples into the region and the "assimilation of agricultural and ceramic traditions by local Tibetan groups, followed by settled agricultural communities peopled by these local groups." This is trait diffusion, which reflects the movement of ideas, objects, and technologies into new cultural contexts. While there may have been intermarriage between the local inhabitants and migrants, the genetic signature of this is not clear, although Wen *et al.*'s (2004) model of a northern Y-chromosome bias in southern Tibeto-Burman peoples may be applicable here. This would imply not wholesale demic diffusion (movement of groups of people) but instead men moving into the highlands and marrying local women. In this instance, local women would have had the full suite of genetic adaptations to chronic hypoxia seen in modern Tibetans. An alternative to this hypothesis is that low-elevation populations replaced the highlanders. While possible, it is not plausible in that women would have to adapt to chronic hypoxia at a rate even faster than that postulated by Yi *et al.* (2010). Moreover, the archaeological data from the Qinghai sites do not correspond to a large-scale replacement of people and their material culture.

A similar situation appears to be the case at Kha rub (Karou). Although the site has at least two low-elevation species present that were necessarily first domesticated at lower elevation – foxtail millet and pigs – most researchers believe that the material culture at the site reflects an indigenous origin – that is, a population already present on the plateau margins that adopted these domesticates into their subsistence practice (Aldenderfer, 2007:154). Note that the date of occupation of this site, as early as 6000 years ago, is consistent with the dating of the postulated movement of people from the Hengduan basin to the north. However, since the site is found at 3100 m, it would have been difficult for low-elevation women to reproduce successfully until they either acclimatized or obtained the set of genetic adaptations known to cope effectively with chronic hypoxia. If we are looking at demic diffusion here, the rate of movement of people onto the plateau from this direction, then, would have been relatively slow until these adaptations were in place. Further, note that Wen *et al.*'s model is not applicable here because there is no Y-chromosome bias seen in modern Tibetan populations that had its origins in the south. This observation supports a slower, later demic diffusion onto the plateau, or alternatively, one that began earlier and has yet be verified archaeologically on the plateau.

Finally, the material culture at Chugong, along with domesti-cated yak and barley, suggests an *in situ* cultural development from indigenous (i.e. high plateau) origins. We can offer the hypothesis that these people are the likely descendants of Zhao *et al.*'s (2009) early permanent settlers on the plateau.

Taken together, these data, admittedly thin, are nevertheless provocative, and permit a number of additional hypotheses and observations. These data offer little empirical support to Yi *et al.*'s (2010) assertion that Tibetans and Han diverged both genetically and culturally no more than 2750 years ago. Based on archaeological data as well as the existence of persistent and ancient haplogroups on the plateau, genetic adaptations to chronic hypoxia appeared at least 6000–10 000 years ago if not earlier. Although one of the authors of the reports concedes that the date of divergence could in fact be 6000 years ago (Aldenderfer, 2011:146), there are few data that support this assertion. A consequence of this argument is the rejection of Yi *et al.*'s claim that the appearance of genetic adapta-tions to chronic hypoxia represents the most rapid effect on natural selection in humans.

Given that there have been multiple migration events onto the plateau, this also raises the question of how the uniformity of genetic adaptive response seen in modern Tibetans has arisen. Although con-vergent evolution may be invoked to explain this uniformity, I think a more parsimonious explanation is to argue that the contribution of the small, but permanent, pre-Holocene population of foragers to the modern gene pool of Tibetans is far larger and of greater consequence than has been previously considered.

This chapter has raised more questions that it has answered about migration and adaptation to a life of chronic hypoxia on the Tibetan plateau. Critical next steps will be to determine if those genes impli-cated in adaptation actually provide a selective advantage to those who possess them. The focus of this research should be on women, because it is clear from this review that long-term population growth on the plateau could only occur after women were able to bring pregnancies to term with regularity.

REFERENCES

Aldenderfer, M. (1998). *Montane Foragers: Asana and the South-Central Andean Archaic*. Iowa City, IA: University of Iowa Press.

Aldenderfer, M. (2006a). High risk exploratory research: confirming an Upper Paleolithic occupation of the central Tibetan plateau. Final report submitted to the National Science Foundation for grant BCS-0244327.

Aldenderfer, M. (2006b). Modeling plateau peoples: the early human use of the world's high plateau. *World Archaeology*, **38**, 357–70.

Aldenderfer, M. (2006c). Defining Zhang zhung ethnicity: an archaeological perspective from far western Tibet. In *Western Tibet and the Western Himalayas: Essays on History, Literature, Art, and Archaeology*, Proceedings of the Tenth IATS, ed. A. Heller and G. Orofino, pp. 1–21. Leiden, Netherlands: Brill.

Aldenderfer, M. (2007). Modeling the Neolithic on the Tibetan Plateau. In *Late Quaternary Climate Change and Human Adaptation in Arid China*, ed. D. Madsen, F -H. Chen, and G. Xing, pp. 151–65. Developments in Quaternary Science 9. Amsterdam, Netherlands: Elsevier.

Aldenderfer, M. (2010a). Archaeological reconnaissance and exploration of pre-Buddhist and Buddhist cave and terrace systems of Upper Mustang, Nepal. Report submitted to the Committee for Research and Exploration, National Geographic Society.

Aldenderfer, M. (2010b). Archaeological research at Choedzom, Upper Mustang, Nepal. Report submitted to the Committee for Research and Exploration, National Geographic Society.

Aldenderfer, M. (2011). Peopling the Tibetan Plateau: insights from archaeology. *High Altitude Medicine and Biology*, **12**, 141–7.

Aldenderfer, M. and Olsen, J. (2008). Archaeological research conducted in Ngari Prefecture, Tibet Autonomous Region and in the Amdo region, Qinghai in 2007. Report submitted to the Henry Luce Foundation.

Aldenderfer, M. and Zhang, Y. (2004). The prehistory of the Tibetan Plateau to the seventh century A.D.: perspectives from China and the West. *Journal of World Prehistory*, **18**, 1–55.

An, Z., *et al.* (1982). Paleoliths and microliths from Shenja and Shuanghu, northern Tibet. *Current Anthropology*, **23**, 493–9.

Beall, C. (2001). Adaptations to altitude: a current assessment. *Annual Review of Anthropology*, **30**, 423–56.

Beall, C. (2011). Genetic changes in Tibet. *High Elevation Medicine and Biology*, **12**, 101–2.

Beall, C., Cavalleri, G., Deng, L., *et al.* (2010). Natural selection on EPAS1 (HIF2alpha) associated with low hemoglobin concentration in Tibetan highlanders. *Proceedings of the National Academy of Sciences*, **107**, 11 459–64.

Bingham, A., Bauchet, M., Pinto, D., *et al.* (2010). Identifying signatures of natural selection in Tibetan and Andean populations using dense genome scan data. *PLoS Genetics*, **6**(9), e1001116; doi:10.1371/journal.pgen.1001116.

Bingham, A., Mao, X., Brutsaert, T., *et al.* (2009). Identifying positive selection candidate loci for high altitude adaptation. *Human Genomics*, **4**, 79–90.

Brantingham, J., Ma, H., Olsen, J., *et al.* (2003). Speculation on the timing and nature of Late Pleistocene hunter-gatherer colonization of the Tibetan Plateau. *Chinese Science Bulletin*, **48**, 1510–16.

Brantingham, P. J., Xing, G., Madsen, D., *et al.* (2011). Late occupation of the high-elevation northern Tibetan Plateau. *Geoarchaeology*, **12**, 141–7.

Brantingham, P. J., Xing, G., Olsen, J., *et al.* (2007). A short chronology for the peopling of the Tibetan plateau. In *Late Quaternary Climate Change and Human*

Adaptation in Arid China, ed. D. Madsen, F-H. Chen, and G. Xing, pp. 129–50. Developments in Quaternary Science 9. Amsterdam, Netherlands: Elsevier.

Bureau of Cultural Relics, Tibet Autonomous Region, Department of History, Sichuan University (1985). *Karou: A Neolithic Site in Tibet*. Beijing: Cultural Relics Publishing House. (in Chinese)

Chayet, A. (1994). *Art et Archéologie du Tibet*. Paris: Picard.

Chen, H. (2002). A study of the Zongri remains. Ph.D. dissertation, Peking University, School of Archaeology and Museology, Beijing.

Corvinus, G. (2002). Arjun 3: a Middle Paleolithic site in the Deokuri Valley, Nepal. *Man and Environment*, **27**, 31–44.

Flad, R., Yuan, J., and Li, S. (2007). Zooarchaeological evidence for animal domestication in northwest China. In *Late Quaternary Climate Change and Human Adaptation in Arid China*, ed. D. Madsen, F -H. Chen, and G. Xing, pp. 167–204. Developments in Quaternary Science 9. Amsterdam, Netherlands: Elsevier.

Frisancho, R. (1979). *Human Adaptation: A Functional Interpretation*. St. Louis, MO: Mosby.

Fu, D., Xu, T., and Feng, Z. (2000). The ancient carbonized barley (*Hordeum vulgare* L. var. *nudum*) kernel discovered in the middle Yalu Tsanypo river basin in Tibet. *Southwest China Journal of Agricultural Sciences*, **13**, 38–41.

Gamble, C. (1994). *Timewalkers: The Prehistory of Global Colonization*. Cambridge, MA: Harvard University Press.

Gao, S -Z., Yang, Y-D., Xu, Y., *et al.* (2007). Tracing the genetic history of the Chinese people: mitochondrial DNA analysis of a Neolithic population from the Lajia site. *American Journal of Physical Anthropology*, **133**, 1128–36.

He, Q. (1994). A report on the investigation of the Neolithic sites in Changougou, Gongga County, Tibet. *Xizang Kaogu*, **1**, 28. (in Chinese)

Huang, W. (1994). The prehistoric human occupation of the Qinghai-Xizang plateau. *Götinger Geographische Abhandlungen*, **95**, 201–19.

Institute of Archaeology, Chinese Academy of Social Science, Bureau of Cultural Relics, Tibet Autonomous Region (1999). *Qugong in Lhasa: Excavations of an Ancient Site and Tombs*. Beijing: Encyclopedia of China Publishing House. (in Chinese)

James, H. and Petraglia, M. (2006). Modern human origins and the evolution of behavior in the later Pleistocene record of South Asia. *Current Anthropology*, **46**, S3–S27.

Julian, C., Wilson, M., and Moore, L. (2009). Evolutionary adaptation to high altitude: a view from in utero. *American Journal of Human Biology*, **21**, 614–22.

Kang, L., Li, S., Gupta, S., *et al.* (2010). Genetic structures of the Tibetans and the Deng people in the Himalayas viewed from autosomal STRs. *Journal of Human Genetics*, **55**, 270–7.

Krampl, E., Espinoza-Dorado, J., Lees, C., Moscoso, G., and Bland, J. (2001). Maternal uterine artery Doppler studies at high altitiude and sea level. *Ultrasound Obstetrics and Gynecology*, **18**, 578–82.

León-Velarde, F. and Mejía, O. (2008). Gene expression in chronic high altitude diseases. *High Altitude Medicine and Biology*, **9**, 130–9.

Li, J. and Zhao, H. (1999). The Changuoguo Neolithic site in Gongga, Tibet. *Kaogu*, **4**, 1-10. (in Chinese)

Liu, L. (2004). *The Chinese Neolithic: Trajectories Toward Early States*. Cambridge, UK: Cambridge University Press.

Lundby, C., Calbet, J. A. L., Van Hall, G., Saltin, B., and Sander, M. (2004). Pulmonary gas exchange at maximal exercise in Danish lowlanders during 8 wk of acclimatization to 4,100 m and in high-altitude Aymara natives. *American Journal of Physiology: Regulatory, Integrative and Comparative Physiology*, **287**, R1202–8.

MacInnis, M. and Rupert, J. (2011). 'ome on the range: altitude adaptations, positive selection, and Himalayan genomics. *High Elevation Medicine and Biology*, **12**, 133–9.

MacInnis, M., Koehle, M., and Rupert, J. (2011). Evidence for a genetic basis for altitude illness: 2010 update. *High Elevation Medicine and Biology*, **12**, 349–68.

Madsen, D. B., Haizhou, M., Brantingham, P. J., *et al.* (2006). The Late Upper Paleolithic occupation of the northern Tibetan Plateau margin. *Journal of Archaeological Science*, **33**, 1433–44.

Marconi, C., Marzorati, M., and Cerratelli, P. (2006). Work capacity of permanent residents of high elevation. *High Altitude Medicine and Biology*, **7**, 105–15.

Marconi, C., Marzorati, M., Grassi, B., *et al.* (2004). Second-generation Tibetan lowlanders acclimatize to high altitude more quickly than Caucasians. *Journal of Physiology*, **556**, 661–71.

Moore, L. (2003). Fetal growth restriction and material oxygen transport during high altitude pregnancy. *High Altitude Medicine and Biology*, **4**(2), 141–56.

Moore L., Newberry, M., Freeby, G., and Crnic, L. (1984). Increased incidence of neonatal hyperbilirubinemia at 3,100 m in Colorado. *American Journal of Diseases in Children*, **138**, 157–61.

Moore, L., Niermeyer, S., and Zamudio, S. (1998). Human adaptation to high altitude: regional and life-cycle perspectives. *American Journal of Physical Anthropology*, **27**, 25–64.

Moore, L., Shriver, M., Bemis, L., *et al.* (2004). Maternal adaptation to high-altitude pregnancy: an experiment of nature – a review. *Trophoblast Research: Placenta*, **25**, Supplement, S60–S71.

Qian, Y., Qian, B. Su B., *et al.* (2000). Multiple origins of Tibetan Y chromosomes. *Human Genetics*, **106**, 453–4.

Redman, C. and Sargent, I. (2005). Latest advances in understanding preeclampsia. *Science*, **308**, 1592–4.

Rhode, D., Zhang, H., Madsen, D., *et al.* (2007). Epipaleolithic/early Neolithic settlements at Qinghai Lake, western China. *Journal of Archaeological Science*, **34**, 600–12.

Rupert, J. (2010). Will blood tell? Three recent articles demonstrate genetic selection in Tibetans. *High Elevation Medicine and Biology*, **11**, 307–8.

Schaller, G. (1998). *Wildlife of the Tibetan Steppe*. Chicago, IL: University of Chicago Press.

Sharma, A. K. (2000). *Early Man in Jammu, Kashmir, and Ladakh*. Delhi: Agam Kala Prakashan.

Shi, H., Zhong, H., Peng, Y., *et al.* (2008). Y chromosome evidence of earliest modern human settlement in East Asia and multiple origins of Tibetan and Japanese populations. *BMC Biology*, **6**, 45; doi: 10.I 186/1741–7007–6–45.

Simonson, T., Yang, Y., Huff, C., *et al.* (2010). Genetic evidence for high-altitude adaptation in Tibet. *Science*, **329**, 72–5.

Snow, D. (2010). The multidisciplinary study of human migrations: Problems and principles. In *Ancient Human Migrations: A Multidisciplinary Approach*, ed. P. Peregrine, I. Peiros, and M. Feldman, pp. 6–20. Salt Lake City, UT: University of Utah Press.

Su, B., Xiao, J., Deka, R., *et al.* (2000). Y chromosome haplotypes reveal prehistorical migrations to the Himalayas. *Human Genetics*, **107**, 582–90.

Su, B., Xiao, J., Underhill, P., *et al.* (1999). Y-chromosome data evidence for a northward migration of modern humans into eastern Asia during the last Ice Age. *American Journal of Human Genetics*, **65**, 1718–24.

Sun, Y., Lai, Z., Long, H., Jun, X., and Fan, Q. (2010). Quartz OSL dating of archaeological sites in Xiao Qaidam Lake of the NE Qinghai-Tibetan plateau and its implications for paleoenvironmental changes. *Quaternary Geochronology*, **5**, 360–4.

Tissot van Patot, M. and Gassmann, M. (2011). Hypoxia: adapting to high altitude by mutating EPAS-1, the gene encoding HIF-2A. *High Elevation Medicine and Biology*, **12**, 157–67.

Torroni, A., Miller, J., Moore., L., *et al.* (1994). Mitochondrial DNA analysis in Tibet: implications for the origin of the Tibetan population and its adaptation to high altitude. *American Journal of Physical Anthropology*, **92**, 189–99.

Van der Woerd, J., Tapponnier, P., Ryerson, F., *et al.* (2002). Uniform postglacial slip-rate along the central 600 km of the Kunlun Fault (Tibet) from ^{26}Al, ^{10}Be, and ^{14}C dating of riser offsets, and climatic origin of the regional morphology. *Geophysical Letters International*, **148**, 356–88.

Wang, B., Zhang, Y -B., Zhang, F., *et al.* (2011). On the origins of Tibetans and their genetic basis in adapting high-altitude environments. *PLoS ONE*, **6**, e17002; doi:10.1371/journal.pone.0017002.

Wen, B., Xie, X. Gao, S., *et al.* (2004). Analyses of genetic structure of Tibet-Burman populations reveals sex-biased admixture in southern Tibeto-Burmans. *American Journal of Human Genetics*, **74**, 856–65.

Wu, T. (2005). Chronic mountain sickness on the Qinghia-Tibetan plateau. *Chinese Medical Journal*, **118**, 161–8.

Yi, X., Liang, Y., Huerta-Sanchez, E., *et al.* (2010). Sequencing of 50 human exomes reveals adaptation to high elevation. *Science*, **329**, 75–8.

Yuan, B., Huang, W., and Zhang, D. (2007). New evidence for human occupation of the northern Tibetan plateau, China, during the Late Pleistocene. *Chinese Science Bulletin*, **52**, 2675–9.

Zhang, D. and Li, S. (2002). Optical dating of Tibetan human hand- and footprints: an implication for the palaeoenvironment of the last glaciation of the Tibetan Plateau. *Geophysical Research Letters*, **29**; doi:10.1029/2001GL013749.

Zhao, H. (2002). On the Bangga site, Qugong culture, and prehistoric civilization in Tibet.Paper presented at the International Academic Conference on Tibetan Archaeology and Art, Beijing. (In Chinese)

Zhao, M., Kong, Q., Wang, H., *et al.* (2009). Mitochondrial genome evidence reveals successful Late Paleolithic settlement on the Tibetan Plateau.*Proceedings of the National Academy of Sciences*, **106**, 21 230–5.

Zhao, Y-B., Li, H-J., Li, S-N., *et al.* (2011). Ancient DNA evidence supports the contribution of the Di-Qiang people to the Han Chinese gene pool. *American Journal of Physical Anthropology*, **144**, 258–68.

Zhong, H., Shi, H., Qin, X-B., *et al.* (2011). Extended Y chromosome investigation suggests postglacial migrations of modern humans into East Asia via the northern route. *Molecular Biology and Evolution*, **28**, 717–27.

18

Migration, globalization, instability, and Chinese in Peru

INTRODUCTION

Tradition holds that Chinese were a non-migratory people with a strong ancestor-worshipping, homeland-bound culture. In the past, Chinese generally rarely left home without a compelling, pragmatic reason. They left home primarily to further their family name and fortune and thus honor their ancestors, such as taking the civil examinations and serving as esteemed scholar-bureaucrats, engaged in commerce activities, or seeking refuge in times of war or famine. Furthermore, those who did so most often expected to return – hopefully wealthier and/or with heightened social status – to die and be buried in the fold of family and ancestors (Purcell, 1965:30; Wang, 1966:23). As a Chinese proverb proclaims: Fallen leaves shall return to the roots, wanderers are to return to their place of birth. In Chinese history, imperial governments encouraged migration in the spirit of territorial expansionism only sporadically and typically discouraged or even outlawed migration to all foreign lands. This traditional Chinese migratory-adverse pattern was in distinct contrast to the German – and European – call in favor of crossing oceans as in: "*Amerika Du hast es besser*!" – America you have it better!

In the twenty-first century changes have been swift and dramatic. Not only has the People's Republic of China – and Taiwan – made great strides in "catching up" with the West in general, and the United States specifically, but the Chinese are now leaving the Mainland and Taiwan in ever increasing numbers for overseas. In order to make sense of the twenty-first-century Chinese migratory dynamics it is first necessary to consider some fundamentals for international migration. In the twentieth century world populations underwent dramatic changes.

Causes and Consequences of Human Migration, ed. Michael H. Crawford and Benjamin C. Campbell. Published by Cambridge University Press. © Cambridge University Press 2012.

Billions

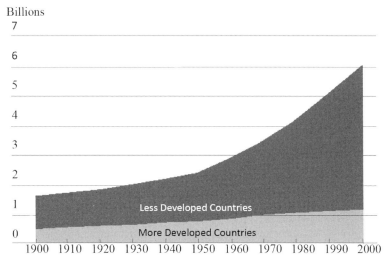

Figure 18.1   Population growth in more developed and less developed
countries, 1900–2000. (Sources: UN, 2003; and Population Reference
Bureau estimates.) Note: Developed countries include Australia, Canada,
Japan, New Zealand, the United States, and all of Europe. All the other
countries are included in less developed.

The century began with some 1.6 billion and ended with some 6.1
billion (PRB Staff, 2004:3). Change was not just in numbers but, more
importantly, in complexity, making the future not only more challenging but substantially more uncertain for ever greater numbers of
individual human beings. Public discourse about population in general
and divergent population shifts in particular grew more contentious.
Whereas populations in the less developed world regions continued
their unrelenting increases, those in the more developed areas experienced persistent decreases (see Figures 18.1 and 18.2). This is largely due
to persistently higher fertility rates in the former and unprecedented
low fertility rates in the latter part of the world (PRB Staff, 2004:7). This
new demographic dichotomy, with its "push–pull" effect (IOM, 2003),
now constitutes the engine for migration where populations flow prin-
cipally for existing or perceived socioeconomic–political advantages.

INTERNATIONAL MIGRATION: CAUSES AND NUMBERS

Migration – people or peoples moving from their native land to
elsewhere – has been omnipresent for all of human existence. Nevertheless, globalization, economic fluctuations, natural disasters,

(in thousands)

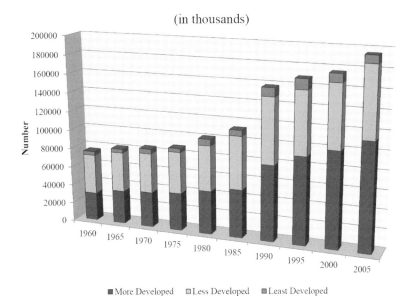

Figure 18.2 Number of migrants in the world by developed regions; 1960–2005 (in thousands). (Source: Population Reference Bureau.)

conflict, genocide, ethnic cleansing, or killing of thousands for one reason or another has measurably accelerated individuals as well as entire populations. In addition, factors such as new technologies, innovation/development of the internet, and air transportation (travel around the globe in less than 48 hours) have become viable push–pull elements for migration.

Evolutionary sociobiology proposes a perspective that suggests that constant movements for individuals and groups of people, that is, migration, is imbedded in our human genetic makeup. The very beginning of our species is associated with the original migration out of Africa. However, whereas migration in search of food is indeed as old as humankind, international migration is of more recent derivation. Only in the early twentieth century did the system of nation states, passports, and visas evolve. Answers and analyses of human migration must then indispensably combine both a biological as well as a cultural/social paradigm. As social values change and are more succinctly influenced by worldly security or economic circumstances, so do human behaviors. Human beings, in an era of accelerated globalization and technological change, do things differently – the future becomes something quite different from the present and the past. Economic globalization is not as new, or different, as are high degrees of uncertainty, that is, international competition, insurgencies of various kinds, and generational warfare. Since World War II, there have occurred over 170 significant conflicts around the globe (Ciment, 2006).

More than 500 years ago, European exploration, conquest, and colonization of far-off continents with rich natural resources were more integrally connected with the growth of a mercantile, capitalist economy. Circumnavigation of the globe was made possible by new knowledge, new technologies, and migration as an important concomitant companion. Today's economic/technology globalization gives new meaning to older phenomena. Developments and evolving growth in communication and transportation, combined with the willingness of states to enter into a variety of binding trade commitments, have resulted in an integration of economies that had previously operated in far more heterogeneous spaces.

Adam Smith reminded us that "Man is all sorts of baggage the most difficult is to be transported" (Martin and Widgren, 2002:4). Migration has been recognized as the most complex and most volatile demographic variable. Migration is selective; it is the educated and more adventurous individuals who are more likely to move than others. Migration is closely linked with the life cycle and people are more likely to move at certain stages of their lives. Migration, as well, is difficult to measure since most countries do not control accurate means to track migratory population movements (McFalls, 2003:14–15). International migration – people moving across national boundaries – most likely represents, aside from uncertainty caused by, for example, fourth or even fifth asymmetric generation warfare, one of the most important global challenges. More than 190 nation states now issue their own passports and visas – and more importantly, regulate who can cross their borders and who can legally stay, or reside, in their country. At least 160 million people were estimated living outside their country of birth or citizenship in 2000, up from an estimated 120 million in 1990 (Martin and Widgren, 2002:3). Such a volume of population flow not only fluctuates but also reflects particular world events on different continents – both economic and political. Wars and other variations of conflict invariably mean greater numbers of people move, including those moving across international borders as illustrated in Figures 18.3 and 18.4.

We would be remiss not to note a paradox in the very nature of migration. A powerful element in human existence is surely inertia accompanied by boredom or passivity-driven action. A great many

(in thousands)

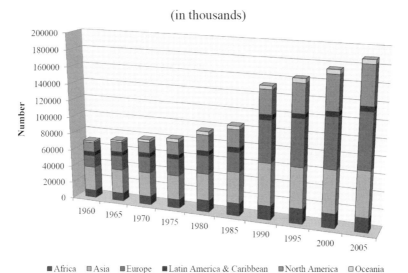

Figure 18.3   Number of migrants in the world by continents; 1960–2005 (in thousands). (Source: Population Reference Bureau.)

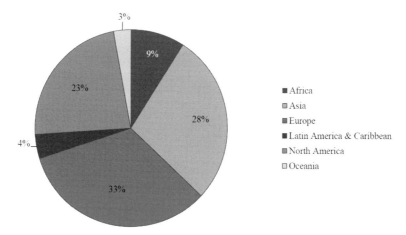

Figure 18.4   Percentage of migrants in the world by continents; 2005. (Source: Population Reference Bureau.)

human beings lack the desire and drive to leave "home" – moving away from the "familiar" places, from family and friends. More recently, and surely in the first decades of the twenty-first century, the movement of people across borders or continents is often no longer controlled – or controllable – by national governments. The complexity of accelerating

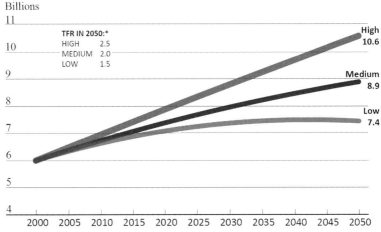

Figure 18.5   World population projections, 2000–2050. (Source: UN, 2003.)
Note: TRF (Total Fertility Rate) is the average number of children
a woman would have under prevailing age-specific rates.

globalization is reflected in a non-viable international effort. Complexity and numbers have become effectively unmanageable. Individuals move, yet their motives are important for understanding the root causes of why migration occurs at all. Socioeconomic–political–cultural forces, are equally, if not more, important precisely because they shape the context in which migration decisions are made. Nevertheless, the management of international migration is likely to become increasingly more controversial, complex, difficult, and urgent in decades to come. Even described in simple terms, distinguishing between voluntary and forced migration, legal, quasi-legal, or illegal is very difficult and more urgent for a most likely 9.5 billion world population more unequally distributed than ever in the twenty-first century, as illustrated in Figure 18.5.

International migrants fall into two broad groups: voluntary migrants and forced migrants (Martin, 2001). Voluntary migrants may feel compelled to search for new homes because of pressing problems at home; whereas forced migrants may chose a particular refuge because of greater security, or enhanced economic or personal opportunity. Furthermore, one form of migration may evolve into another. Perhaps, fundamentally most countries tend to intrinsically discourage emigration. The efforts of the former Soviet Union and its satellites to prevent emigration, symbolized by the Berlin Wall, are a case in point. North Korea continues to prohibit emigration for any reason for its citizens.

Considering twenty-first century globalization, just five major countries, surprisingly, continue openly welcoming international migrants as permanent residents: the United States, Canada, Australia, Israel, and New Zealand. Collectively these countries accept 1.2 million immigrants a year. About 800 000 immigrants each year are officially admitted to the United States, 200 000 to Canada, 75 000 to Australia, 60 000 to Israel, and 35 000 to New Zealand (Martin and Widgren, 2002:4). Clearly these figures account for but a minuscule percentage of the estimated annual migration, which means that most people moving from one country to another are not necessarily accepted as legal immigrants. Instead, numbers of migrants are refugees, guest workers, or in ever greater numbers, undocumented individuals. There are the increasingly unaccounted for "aliens" who enter, work, and settle in defiance of any immigration jurisdiction. It is a fair estimate that by 2010, illegal migrants have far outnumbered legal ones.

By 2010, migration may then well be viewed as a natural, expected, somewhat predictable response to causal conditions and differences in the countries of origin and destination including demography, internal security, instability, and, increasingly, human rights. In the past, significant numbers of people leave their native land to take advantage of and participate in the perceived benefits of globalization and to escape the turmoil of a conflict and/or taking advantage of a plethora of new opportunities. Population may be compared to water: it will flow wherever the terrain – or presumed space and opportunity – permits. In 2002, over 40 million people (16 million refugees and an estimated 25 million displaced persons) fled from their homes because of war, persecution, human rights abuses, or uneven economic development exacerbating generally unstable conditions, as indicated in Figure 18.6.

In 1800, Europe had some 20% of the world's one billion population, while the Americas had but 3%. One century later, millions of Europeans emigrated to North and South America in search of economic and other opportunities. Two centuries later, Europe had just 12% of the world's then 6 billion people, while North and South America together had about 14% (UNPD, 1998). In the twenty-first century, another shift of population is occurring as population growth and loss bifurcate throughout various geographical settings. The 2007 figures from the United Nations Population Division predict a global upheaval without parallel in human history. There will be hundreds of millions more peoples in Africa, Asia, and the Middle East (UNPD, 2008). Of these, it is a fair guess, large numbers will be migrating to Europe and the Americas while the indigenous populations of the most developed, affluent world will either

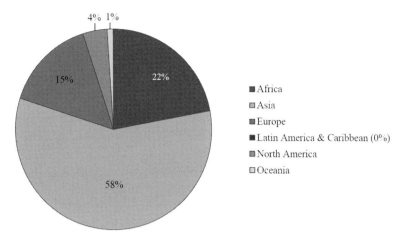

Figure 18.6   Percentage of refugees in the world by continents, 2005.
(Source: Population Reference Bureau.)

stagnate or decline. United Nations' estimates suggest that the world's population will keep growing and reach between 7.4 and 10.6 billion by 2050 (UN, 2003). While some countries will grow exponentially, others will shrink dramatically. As alluded to earlier, such a future increase of 2.5 billion, almost all of which will occur in Africa, Asia, and the Middle East, represents the equivalent of the total global population in 1950! With such a trend of population growth, Asia will continue to be the most populated region, followed by Africa in 2050, as shown in Figure 18.7.

The number of international migrants in more developed countries more than doubled between 1985 and 2005, from almost 55 million to 120 million (Martin and Zürcher, 2008:3). During the next 40 or so years, immigration might well run at more than twice the 1970–80 level and likely will approach more than 2 million every year until 2050 with more than one million individuals coming from Asia. The pressure exerted by rising populations, changing demographic, economic, and political patterns, as well as a variety of assumed opportunities – freedom, spatial and personal mobility – will result in continuing population mobility/migration.

At the beginning of the twenty-first century, the Population Division of the United Nations estimated that there were some 17 million plus people living outside of their country of birth or citizenship. This figure has doubled since 1975 and is now larger than those of all but four countries in 2007. While conflict constitutes a major source of insecurity encouraging migration, the process of economic globalization has a certain potential to increase the volume of migration

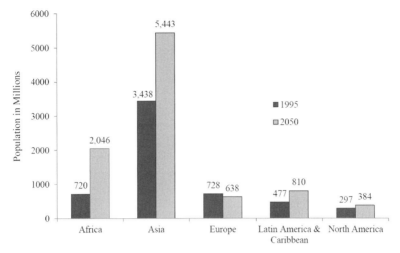

Figure 18.7   Population growth by region, 1995–2050. (Source: UN, 2007.)

worldwide. One major effect of the expansion of international trade is facilitating the movement of capital, goods, services, and labor across borders (DeLung and Jones, 2003).

THE DRAGON IN THE BACKYARD

If all goes according to plan, by 2012, the first shipment of copper from Toromocho, a mine in the Peruvian Andes, will be sent by train and truck to a new $70 million wharf in the port of Callao. From there, the copper will be shipped across the Pacific to the People's Republic of China (PRC). The mine is being developed at a cost of $2.2 billion by the metals giant Chinalco, a Chinese state-owned enterprise with ties to the Communist Party Central Committee. Both it and the wharf will be the most visible symbols of the burgeoning trade and investment that are fast turning the PRC into a leading partner for Peru (The Economist, 2009). So far, Chinese investment has been concentrated in mining and oil. Some 34% of mineral investments in Peru are from China, while 40% of oil production in Peru is owned by Chinese investors through a partnership between China National Petroleum Company (CNPC) and the Argentine firm Pluspetrol (Salazar, 2010; Sanborn, 2011:26).

In September 2009, Peru's Ministry of Foreign Affairs inaugurated a special exhibition to commemorate the 160th anniversary of the arrival of the first Chinese immigrants to Peru, while the Peruvian Postal Service (Serpost) issued a new postage stamp (Andina, 2009a, 2009b). Celebration activities coincided with the first Chinese president's official visit to Peru during the APEC summit (Andina, 2009c). A couple of months later, the Peru Embassy in Beijing held another exhibit of that legacy in the Imperial City Museum of Art to reiterate friendship and economic ties between China and Peru. According to the Embassy, about 15% of the 30 million Peruvian population has Chinese roots, making Peru the country populated by the most Chinese immigrants in South America (People's Daily Online, 2009).

The presence of Chinese migrants in Peru, and Latin America in general, can be traced back to the nineteenth century, preceded by commerce interests (Chang-Rodriguez, 1958). From the 1560s until 1815, a fleet of Spanish galleons made an annual epic voyage from the Mexican port of Acapulco to Manila in the Philippines, carrying silver and supplies and returning Chinese silks and porcelains that were eagerly acquired by the wealthy in colonial Peru and Mexico (Kindleberger, 1990). In November 1849, Peru passed its law for importing Chinese coolies. In fact, as early as the sixteenth century, the Peruvian Amazon region especially has been linked to a world market in need of timber, rubber and quinine. The nineteenth century immigration of some 100 000 coolies, almost exclusively male, resulted in capacious "miscegenation" with local women (Ah, undated; Benavides, 2002; Clayton, undated). This presence of settled Chinese encouraged more Chinese to leave home for Peru. The suddenness and the scale of the twenty-first century link with the PRC are, however, new. This PRC presence is no longer a Cold-War-like race for geostrategic advantage; rather, it is the securing of raw materials for China's manufacturing industries. It establishes reliable access to primary products as well as access for Chinese goods. R. Evan Ellis (2011) has suggested that the Chinese advance on the multidimensional strategic-economic global stage has been primarily through application of "soft power"; he notes that the PRC's economic footprint in Latin America has become enormous. Whereas Cynthia Sanborn (2011) of the Universidad del Pacifico in Lima notes correctly that China has adapted to doing business in Latin America more successfully than its Western counterparts.

No one knows precisely how many ethnic Chinese live outside of China but estimates range from 40 to 50 million – or more. It must be noted that the study of the People's Republic and its people in the twenty-first century is seriously hampered by the effective absence, paucity, and/or the questionable viability of published PRC or Peruvian sources. These overseas Chinese in fact represent the largest ever human diaspora. This migrant population surprisingly, however, rather than being representative of China as a whole, originates primarily in just one province: Fujian (Keefe, 2009:33–4). In the early 1990s, the vast majority of illegal immigrants from China in the United States were from Fujian province as well, estimated to be 2500 per month in the first half of 1992 (Banister, 1993:15). While all Chinese economic initiatives abroad are directed by the Party and the Chinese Central Government and its various agencies as may be expected, some individual Chinese provinces recently have begun to initiate their own economic advances, and encouraged migration, all tolerated by the PRC Central Ministries. For example, Chris Alden noted that Fujian and Zhejiang have been encouraging – and permitting – migration of its citizens as a source of remittances and new jobs (The Economist, 2007).

Peru has considered China more recently as an important economic partner and investor. All the while, Lima has quietly, or not so quietly, become an important, if not the most important, entry point for Chinese to the Americas. The dragon has arrived in the backyard – legally and, recently, more illegally. Unfortunately, precise numbers for various arrival categories (legal, short-term, long-term, tourist, illegal arrivals) remain unavailable from the pertinent government agencies from either of these two countries. Frequently, after procuring a Peruvian residence permit Chinese continue traveling north or apply for a visa to the United States or Canada (personal field notes). Whereas the period between 1880 and 1950 saw an influx of Chinese businessmen who set up stores and managed estates of absentee landlords, the newer arrivals since the 1940s started the by now ubiquitous Chinese restaurants (*chifas*) which soon became most popular throughout Peruvian society. Still more recently Lima's Chinatown has become a major tourist attraction.

Without doubt, the Chinese and their People's Republic continue to be on the move, becoming a leading world power. The question remains: is it simply a continuation of the past with some Chinese leaving their homeland for the "usual" various reasons, or does it represent a dramatically changed migration configuration by a "soft-powered," now 1.3 billion-people-strong People's Republic with dramatically elevated global expectations? As alluded to earlier, China is aggressively expanding its reach into the Americas and the other continents but, now additionally, tolerating – or making it possible – for some of its citizens to migrate through legal, extra legal, and illegal channels to countries of economic, developmental, or political interest to the Motherland. Given the tight control of the Chinese government over any movement of its citizens, substantial illegal immigration cannot possibly take place on the current scale without some acquiescence from the Party and the Central Government. In the light of the history of Chinese government policy for strategic migration into various developing countries including Latin America and Africa, this should not be unexpected. Discussion about movements of Han Chinese populations cannot ignore the role of the Chinese government. In its most recent history, it has systematically encouraged Han Chinese to settle in sensitive regions or areas, with Tibet or Xinjiang as prime examples. Furthermore, clearly the Chinese leadership has concluded that if the PRC is to regain the position it once occupied as the world's largest, and one of its most inventive, economies, it must reach a viable accommodation – including a human component – within an increasingly interdependent but highly competitive global community.

Mainland Chinese immigration to Peru began to gather real momentum in 1971. Prior to that date the Taiwanese dominated the Peru portal into Latin America. As Peru followed the United States adopting a "One China policy" and shifting their diplomatic relations from Taiwan to the People's Republic, the Taiwanese who had up to then flourishing, successful businesses were replaced by arriving Mainlanders. In the mid 1990s (1997) President Alberto Fujimori, known by his fellow countrymen as "*el Chino*," allowed gambling houses to function legally. As a concomitant consequence, with more Chinese and more Chinese capital/investment arriving, many *chifas* diversified and evolved into casinos and, in turn, accumulated more money and more economic influence. At that time a Chinese businessman turned a large office building in Lima's affluent Miraflores District into a hotel and casino catering primarily to Chinese businessmen and tourists while at the same time operating a branch of the Mainland Tourist Agency, illustrating this new reality (personal field notes). In 2000, according to the Chinese Consulate in Lima, there were some 25 000 individuals born in the PRC who had Peruvian resident permits registered, as were 85 000 PRC-born individuals holding Peruvian citizenship, and 1.5 million Peruvian Chinese with one parent or grandparent born in China (Benavides, 2002; People's Daily Online, 2009). These numbers, however, neither include illegal Chinese residents nor Taiwanese. One may also note that in the early twenty-first century, when Lima had a population of some 6 million, it also had some 2000 *chifas* in the city, and the sale of Chinese goods as well as Chinese herbal medicine flourished (Benavides, 2002). Gastronomic attractions aside, the network of *chifas*, especially those in the Chinese quarter, sheltered and provided work for the majority of the new Chinese immigrants (Lausent-Herrera, 2011).

It is a fair estimate that illegal immigration into both South and North Americas has become an integral part of Chinese immigration patterns. Illegal flows of Chinese migrants in particular have drawn attention in the international media. Illegal migrants now constitute a significant part of the overall reach into the Americas. Not surprisingly, there are no published or available data on PRC migration in general, or figures on volume and composition of illegal Chinese immigration. Nevertheless, U.S. authorities have estimated that some 100 000 Chinese a year were entering the United States illegally in the 1990s, while up to 500 000 were poised to move up from the south (Wang, 2001). The significance of this illegal Chinese flow to the West and to the Americas lies as much with the nature of official PRC government acquiescence as with the sheer number of its 2010 population of 1.3 billion.

A most troubling aspect of immigration in general, and of specifically Chinese migration, has been the emergence of professional smuggling and human trafficking – migrant trafficking. Certainly new is the vast scale of this type of smuggling, such that the United Nations General Assembly resolution 55/25 adopted the "Protocol against the Smuggling of Migrants by Land, Sea and Air" in 2000 (UNDOC, 2011a). Smuggling rings now routinely sell, rent, or trade fraudulent documents used in obtaining entry into a country and, as is the case in Peru, even obtaining "eligibility" for residence and employment and gain the freedom for further movement (UNDOC, 2011b). In Peru as elsewhere smugglers may act like legitimate businessmen guaranteeing their services and "legitimately" receiving payments. In the twenty-first century it has unfortunately become quite common for traffickers to do business across international boundaries initiating *narco* and human trafficking as well as transporting migrants across borders – or even oceans – to exploit and abuse their labor. New is the horrific cost of smuggling and the immense profits derived from it and the emerging collaboration between PRC and Latin American criminal organizations.

Migrants smuggled from the PRC's Fujian Province are said to pay upwards of $50 000 per person plus some $4000–$6000 for a Peruvian residence permit enabling the holder to move North towards the United States and Canada – or Europe (personal field notes). Not only does it take years to repay this debt but this migration-based industry has become an estimated 5 to 7 billion dollar global enterprise.

In this new reality one can then only conclude that insecurity, globalization, changing economic dynamics with highly inflated profit expectations in a now 7 billion populated world, has a game changing effect on all migration patterns: voluntary, involuntary, or illegal.

REFERENCES

Ah, X. (undated). Chinese Coolies. Retrieved July 7, 2011 from http://www.imperialchina.org/coolie.html.

Andina (Agencia Peruana de Notician) (2009a). Peru to issue postage stamp commemorating Chinese immigration anniversary. September 7.

Andina (Agencia Peruana de Notician) (2009b). Peru inaugurates exhibition commemorating Chinese immigration anniversary. September 10.

Andina (Agencia Peruana de Notician) (2009c). 160 Anniversary of Chinese immigration to Peru celebrated in Lima. November 10.

Banister, J., Harbaugh, C. W., and Jamison, E. (1993). *Population and Migration Characteristics of Fujian Province, China*. CIR Staff Paper 70. Washington, DC: Center for International Research, U.S. Bureau of the Census.

Benavides, M. A. (2002). Chinese immigrants in Sao Paulo, Brazil, and in Lima, Peru: preliminary case studies. In *Essays on Ethnic Chinese Abroad*, Vol. II: *Women, Political Participation and Area Studies*, ed. T. Chang and S. Tang, pp. 355–76. Taipei: Overseas Chinese Association.

Chang-Rodriguez, E. (1958). Chinese labor migration into Latin America in the 19th century. *Revista de Historia Latino America*, **46**, 375–97.

Ciment, J. (ed.) (2006). *Encyclopedia of Conflicts Since WWWII*, 2nd edn. Armouk, NY: M.E. Sharpe.

Clayton, L. A. (undated). Chinese indentured labour in Peru. Retrieved March 12, 2011 from www.historytoday.com

DeLung, J. S. and Jones, B. (2003). Executive summary: internal migration. Princeton, NJ: Population Resource Center.

The Economist (2007). China in Africa: partner, competitor or hegemon? Book review. November 24, p.89.

The Economist (2009). The dragon in the backyard: Latin America is tilting towards China, Iran and the Global "South" – and away from the United States. September 13.

Ellis, R. E. (2011). Chinese soft power in Latin America: a case study. *Joint Force Quarterly*, **60**, 85–91.

International Organization for Migration (IOM) (2003). *World Migration 2003: Managing Migration Challenges and Responses for People on the Move*. Geneva: IOM.

Keefe, P. R. (2009). Snakeheads and smuggling: the dynamics of illegal Chinese migration. *World Policy Journal*, Spring, 33–44.

Kindleberger, C. P. (1990). *Historical Economics: Art or Science?* Berkeley, CA: University of California Press.

Lausent-Herrera, I. (2011). The Chinatown in Peru and the changing Peruvian Chinese community(ies). *Journal of Chinese Overseas*, **7**, 69–113.

Martin, P. and Widgren, J. (2002). International migration: facing the challenge. *Population Bulletin*, **57**(1).

Martin, P. and Zürcher, G. (2008). Managing migration: the global challenge. *Population Bulletin*, **63**(1).

Martin, S. F. (2001). *Global Migration Trends and Asylum*. New Issues in Refugee Research, Working Paper 41. Geneva: UN High Commissioner for Refugees.

McFalls, J. A., Jr. (2003). Population: a lively introduction, 4th edn. *Population Bulletin*, **58**(4).

People's Daily Online (2009). Exhibition reveals Chinese legacy in Peru. December 7.

Population Reference Bureau (PRB) Staff (2004). Transitions in world population. *Population Bulletin*, **59**(1).

Purcell, V. (1965). *The Chinese in Southeast Asia*, 2nd edn. London: Oxford University Press.

Salazar, M. (2010). *Social Responsibility Missing in Growing Trade Ties*. Retrieved February 3, 2010 from http://ipsnews.net/news.asp?idnews=50206

Sanborn, C. (2011). Conference discussion: China and Latin America: political and economic partners, or competitors? In *China, Latin America, and the United States: The New Triangle*, ed. C. J. Arnson and J. Davidow, pp. 25–34. Washington, DC: Latin American Program, Woodrow Wilson International Center for Scholars.

United Nations (UN) (2003). *World Population Prospects: The 2002 Revision*. World Population Data Sheet.

United Nations (UN) (2007). *World Population Prospects: The 2006 Revision*. Medium projection series. World Population Data Sheet.

United Nations Office on Drug and Crime (UNODC) (2011a). *World Drug Report 2011*. United Nations Convention against Transnational Organized Crime and its Protocols. Retrieved from www.unodc.org/unodc/en/treaties/CTOC/index.htm

United Nations Office on Drug and Crime (UNODC) (2011b). *World Drug Report 2011: Migrant smuggling*. Retrieved from www.unodc.org/unodc/en/human-trafficking/smuggling-of-migrants.html?ref=menuside

United Nations Population Division (UNPD) (1998). *Revisions of the World Population Prospects: Briefing packet*. United Nations Population Division.

United Nations Population Division (UNPD) (2008). *Revisions of the World Population Prospects, Median Variant: Briefing packet*. United Nations Population Division.

Wang, J. Z. (2001). Illegal Chinese immigration into the United States: a preliminary analysis. *International Journal of Offender Therapy and Comparative Criminology*, **45**, 345–55.

Wang, Y. C. (1966). *Chinese Intellectuals and the West 1879–1949*. Chapel Hill, NC: University of North Carolina Press.

19

The great blue highway: human migration in the Pacific

INTRODUCTION

The Pacific region, defined here as the islands of the Pacific Ocean from New Guinea eastwards to Rapa Nui/Easter Island in the west and from Hawai'i in the north to Aotearoa/New Zealand in the south (Figure 19.1), is particularly interesting and valuable for studying human migration. There are a number of characteristics that make migration here unique: the timing of colonization, the varieties of environments that people encountered, the relative isolation compared with most continental regions and, perhaps most importantly, the fact that migration for most of the history of human occupation required crossing vast stretches of open ocean in some form of watercraft. However, both despite and perhaps because of the relative isolation of most Pacific islands, migration has always been a major feature of life.

The Pacific Ocean covers over a third of the earth's surface, with an area of more than 165 000 000 square kilometers stretching nearly 20 000 km east to west. The total land mass of the Pacific Islands, however, is only about 1 262 000 square kilometers and more than half of that is taken up by New Guinea, the second largest island in the world. While many people in the world have and continue to view the ocean as a barrier, for Pacific peoples the open ocean has been the life force, the link to their ancestors and to their neighbors. It was a great highway, which, like many highways, at some times allowed people to move quickly and at other times restricted movement.

The initial human occupation of the Pacific represents one of the earliest major human migrations in the world. Most genetic studies

Causes and Consequences of Human Migration, ed. Michael H. Crawford and Benjamin C. Campbell. Published by Cambridge University Press. © Cambridge University Press 2012.

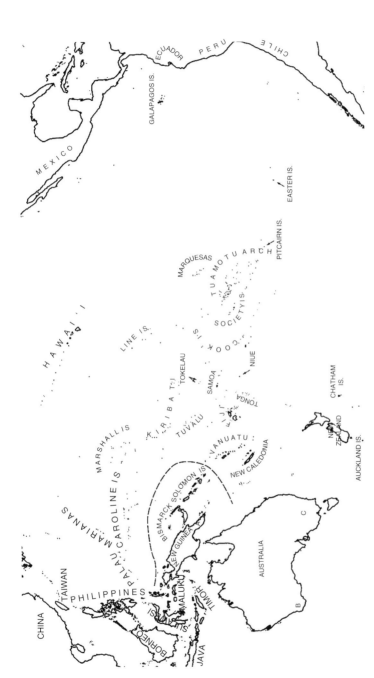

Figure 19.1 Map of the Pacific. Dotted line delineates Near and Remote Oceania. Pleistocene sites: (A) Ivane Valley, New Guinea; (B) Devil's Lair, Western Australia; (C) Willandra Lakes, New South Wales.

suggest the first migration of modern humans out of Africa began sometime around 70 000 years ago. The earliest archaeological evidence for human occupation in the Pacific is dated to around 50 000 years before present (BP), more than 10 000 years before *Homo sapiens* arrived in Europe. At the other end of the time spectrum, the human colonization of the extremes of the Polynesian triangle occurred within the last 1200 years and, therefore, represents the last major human migration that resulted in the discovery of previously unoccupied land.

In colonizing the Pacific Ocean people encountered a range of new environments and associated challenges to which they adapted biologically, socially, and culturally. The island of New Guinea represents a region of particularly high biological diversity and richness, while the many atolls and low islands of the Pacific region are some of the most biologically impoverished and fragile environments on earth. People have had to deal with significant environmental changes in the region ranging from rapidly changing sea levels and tectonic activity to major volcanic eruptions and tsunami, all of which would have had impacts on migrations and population histories. The relative isolation and the low population density of the region meant that, for much of the history of human occupation, people were particularly healthy and free from infectious diseases. Yet this isolation also meant that when infectious diseases were introduced by European explorers and sailors, they had a devastating effect on many Pacific island communities. Unlike continental migrations, which can progress at a slow and steady pace, the movement of peoples across the Pacific Ocean requires relatively rapid movement across vast distances. All of these features of the Pacific environment have shaped the people of the region biologically, socially, and psychologically, both in the past and today, and will, no doubt, continue to do so in the future.

INITIAL OCCUPATION AND PLEISTOCENE MIGRATIONS IN THE PACIFIC

At the time of the earliest migrations into the Pacific region, the Pacific environment looked significantly different than it does today. Lowered sea levels during the Pleistocene (as much as 80–100 meters below current levels) meant that many of the islands of what is now Island Southeast Asia were joined to the greater Asian landmass known as Sunda. The islands of New Guinea and Tasmania were part of the Australian continent, making up a great southern landmass known as Sahul. Sunda and Sahul are separated by the deep water trenches of

Wallacea so the islands there, including Sulawesi, Timor, and the Maluku Islands, remained isolated from either of the two major landmasses. In order for humans to cross from Sunda to Sahul, even during the periods of lowest Pleistocene sea levels, water crossings of distances of 70 km or more were necessary.

Currently, the earliest archaeological dates for the human occupation of Sahul date from 49 000 BP and come from sites in the Ivane Valley, located at an elevation of approximately 2000 m, in the New Guinea Highlands (Summerhayes *et al.*, 2010b). These sites have yielded stone tools, dating to between 49 000 and 36 000 (calibrated) BP, which have residues of endemic *Pandanus* nuts and yams. In addition, tools that the authors argue were used for forest clearance have also been recovered, suggesting not only human arrival, exploration, and utilization of inland resources, but human modification of the environment at this time. Several other sites in New Guinea and across Australia, including Devil's Lair on the southwest coast of Western Australia and the Willandra Lakes in southwestern New South Wales, date to between 45 000 and 40 000 BP (O'Connell and Allen, 2004), indicating that humans rapidly spread across the landscape of Sahul within a few thousand years of arrival. Not only did people colonize Sahul, but they also quickly expanded out to the islands to the northeast of the New Guinea coast. Archaeological evidence of human arrival in the Bismarck Archipelago, specifically on the large islands of New Britain and New Ireland, also dates to about 40 000 BP (Leavesley *et al.*, 2002) with occupation of the nearby Solomon Islands by 28 000 BP (Wickler and Spriggs, 1988). These initial migrants appear to have been small, mobile, foraging groups who were exploiting a full range of marine and terrestrial resources (Allen, 2000; Summerhayes *et al.*, 2010b). This region of the Pacific that has such deep settlement history has been designated Near Oceania, differentiating it from the rest of the Pacific, now often referred to as Remote Oceania, which was settled much later (Green, 1991; Pawley and Green, 1973) (see Figure 19.1).

Molecular evidence from the Pacific is consistent with the archaeological data both in terms of the likely timing of arrival and in suggesting that populations were probably small in size and relatively widely but sparsely distributed across the landscape. Mitochondrial DNA evidence from populations in Near Oceania indicate a large number of ancient and diverse lineages (Friedlaender *et al.*, 2005, 2007). The earliest "Out of Africa" migrations of modern humans are linked to the two deep mitochondrial DNA (mtDNA) lineages, or macrohaplogroups, identified as M and N. Several unique M lineages are found in Near Oceania and these are likely related to those ancient M haplotypes carried by the first migrants that took the southern coastal route from Africa through India and along the coast of South-east Asia (Endicott *et al.*, 2003; Macaulay *et al.*, 2005; Pierson *et al.*, 2006). Interestingly, the mtDNA lineages in Near Oceania and Australia belong to both the deep M and the N branches of the human mtDNA tree, and while some are shared, others are unique to only particular regions. This may indicate that multiple routes were taken to Sahul, but also strongly suggests that once they arrived, the founding populations were relatively isolated during the first 20 000 years of human occupation (Friedlaender *et al.*, 2007). Mitochondrial DNA lineages belonging to haplogroup P (a subgroup of the N branch) are found in both Australia and the islands of Near Oceania. Haplogroups S, O, and M42 are currently found only in Australia (Van Holst Pellekaan *et al.*, 2006; Pierson *et al.*, 2006), whereas haplogroup Q and several unique M lineages, including M27, M28, and M29, have only been reported in Oceanic island populations. The unique M27, M28, and M29 lineages are believed to have originated in Near Oceania, most likely in the New Britain/Bougainville region (Friedlaender *et al.*, 2007). Nearly 90% of the mtDNA lineages found today in New Guinea belong to either the P or Q haplogroups, which are believed to have originated in the region around the time of initial settlement and diversified within Near Oceania. Estimates of the age of these lineages in Near Oceania are consistently in the 30 000–50 000 BP range (Friedlaender *et al.*, 2007).

Numerous unique Near Oceanic Y-chromosome markers also indicate ancient ancestry and *in situ* evolution in Sahul (Hudjashov *et al.*, 2007). Several lineages believed to have origins in Near Oceania and thought to be exclusive to Near Oceanic or their derived populations have been identified including those belonging to haplogroups C-M38, C-M208, M-P34, K-P79, K-M254, and K-M226 (Kayser *et al.*, 2003, 2008; Mona *et al.*, 2007; Scheinfeldt *et al.*, 2006). Again, the Y-chromosome data suggest that the founding population was small, isolated, and quickly became dispersed across the landscape.

The indigenous languages of Australia and New Guinea are both incredibly diverse and unrelated to any other languages outside of the Melanesia/East Indonesian region. This is consistent with the archaeological and genetic evidence for ancient early migration and of small populations who became isolated from one another and from outside influences for a significant period of time. The languages of New Guinea, the northwestern third of the island in particular, have been described as the most diverse in the world (Pawley, 2007). The 800 or so languages of New Guinea belong to as many as 18 unrelated language families and are often grouped together under the term "Papuan," which really only distinguishes them as a group from the Austronesian languages that were introduced much more recently in Near Oceania (Ross, 2005). Papuan languages are also spoken out in the islands of the Bismarck Archipelago and in the Solomon Islands. In terms of their relationship with the languages of the New Guinea mainland, Pawley (2007:52) states: "The Papuan languages of Northern Island Melanesia have probably had separate histories from those of New Guinea since the late Pleistocene and possibly since people first reached Northern Island Melanesia."

Despite the lack of linguistic evidence for lack of or limited interaction between the New Guinea mainland and the islands to the north and east, archaeological evidence suggests that from the period of approximately 20 000 BP onwards mobility and, thus possibly migration, increased in Near Oceania. At this point in time we see the earliest evidence worldwide for the translocation of animal species, resulting in the introduction of the cuscus (*Phalanger orientalis*) from the mainland of New Guinea to the islands of the Bismarck Archipelago and the bandicoot (*Echymipera kalubu*) from the mainland to the Admiralties (Flannery and White, 1991; Leavesley, 2005). Similarly, we see other indicators of mobility, possibly of trade and exchange, in the movement of obsidian (volcanic glass) from west New Britain to New Ireland, which required transporting it for distances of up to 350 km (Summerhayes, 2007). During this time it has also been suggested that seafaring skills of the inhabitants of Near Oceania developed, as is demonstrated by the settlement of Manus Island, which required open ocean sailing for over 200 km. Perhaps more important than the distance covered, however, was the fact that, in reaching Manus, the voyagers had to sail out of sight of land, which until that point had not been the case, as all of the islands colonized until then were intervisible. This would have most likely necessitated not only improved technology but mastery of and confidence in navigation and voyaging skills and, thus, this region of Near Oceania has been identified as a possible "voyaging nursery" (Irwin, 1994).

HOLOCENE MIGRATIONS AND INITIAL SETTLEMENT OF REMOTE OCEANIA

The Holocene brought significant changes to the Pacific region, as it did in most locations (Dickinson, 2000), though identifying the implications

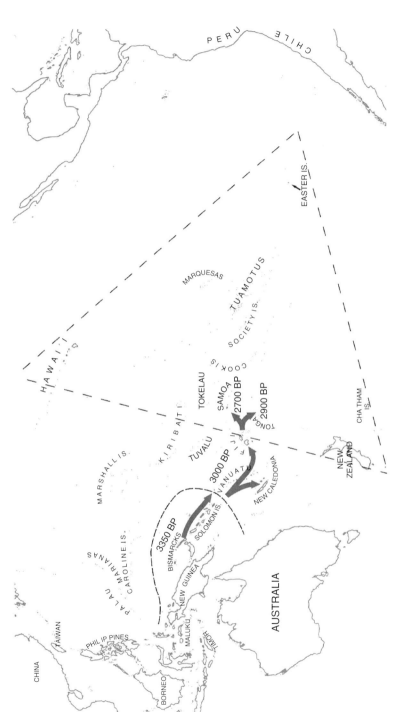

Figure 19.2 The expansion of the Lapita Cultural Complex from the Bismarck Archipelago in Near Oceania out into Remote Oceania to Samoa and Tonga on the western edge of the Polynesian Triangle (shown in dashed lines). Dotted line delineates Near and Remote Oceania.

of these changes in Near Oceania has been quite contentious. Changes in sea levels and climate had huge impacts in the region: New Guinea and Tasmania became separated from the Australian mainland between 11 000 and 8000 BP. Vegetation patterns changed with the warming climate and we see evidence of further land clearance in both lowland and highland environments on the New Guinea mainland and, most notably, the development of agriculture and the domestication of a number of native species including bananas, sugarcane, taro, and possibly yams (Denham *et al.*, 2004; Fullagar *et al.*, 2006). Landscape changes on the north coast of New Guinea also would have caused major migrations as people moved inland in reaction to the rising seas, particularly in the Sepik and Ramu River basins (Swadling and Hide, 2005).

Approximately 3350 years ago, archaeological evidence reveals a significant change in sites located in the Bismarck Archipelago. At this point we see the first appearance of small villages or hamlets made up of stilt houses built out over reef flats. We also see the appearance of a range of new artifacts including new forms of adzes made of stone and shell, fish hooks, shell ornaments, and, perhaps best known, the distinctive dentate stamped pottery that is often used to identify these new "Lapita" sites. This archaeologically defined "Lapita Cultural Complex" first appears in coastal and small, off-shore island sites in the Bismarck Archipelago (Kirch, 2000; Summerhayes *et al.*, 2010a), but within a few hundred years, Lapita sites appear out in Remote Oceania where they clearly represent the first human colonists. The earliest Remote Oceanic Lapita sites date to approximately 3000 BP in the Reef/Santa Cruz Islands, Vanuatu, and New Caledonia (Bedford *et al.*, 2006; Green *et al.*, 2008; Sand, 1997), 2900 BP in Fiji and Tonga (Burley and Dickinson, 2001; Clark and Anderson, 2009) and about 2700 BP in Samoa (Petchey, 2001). Lapita expansion stopped there and the settlement of the rest of the Polynesian Triangle would not commence for at least another 1200 to 1500 years (Figure 19.2). Both the speed of spread and the cultural continuity between the earliest Lapita sites in Remote Oceania and those in the Bismarck Archipelago indicate that this was indeed a widespread migration of a defined cultural group, but what and when was the origin(s) of Lapita and who were the people that transported it?

It has often been suggested that the apparently sudden appearance of the Lapita Cultural Complex represented both the arrival of a new group of people and new languages in Near Oceania. The appearance and spread of Lapita is generally associated with the expansion of the Austronesian languages out of their homeland in Taiwan (Pawley and Ross, 1993). The spread of the Austronesian languages through Island Southeast Asia and into the Pacific is then taken to represent a major population migration which is thought to be driven by the rapid population growth resulting from the Neolithic developments, rice agriculture in particular, in the Asian mainland (Bellwood, 2005). Austronesian languages are spoken through most of Island Southeast Asia, the Pacific, and in Madagascar. Many of the coastal populations in the islands of Near Oceania and most of those living in Remote Oceania speak languages that belong to the Oceanic subgroup of Austronesian languages (Pawley and Ross, 1995). Palauan and Chamorro are the two exceptions; these belong to a higher order subgroup of Austronesian languages and are more closely related to the languages of the Philippines and Indonesia (Pawley, 2002).

While there is general agreement that the first colonists in Remote Oceania carried the Lapita Cultural Complex with them and that they spoke Austronesian languages, the origins of the various components and markers of the Lapita culture and the biological origins of the people associated with the earliest Lapita sites in both Near and Remote Oceania have been topics of much debate. Two extreme models, often referred to as the "Express Train to Polynesia" or the "Out of Taiwan" model (Diamond, 1988) and the "Indigenous Origins" model regularly appear in discussions about Lapita and the settlement of the Pacific. Clearly these types of models are overly simplistic for explaining human behavior and they clearly no longer fit the archaeological, biological, or linguistic data (Hurles et al., 2003a). Alternative models such as the "Slow Boat" model (Oppenheimer and Richards, 2001), which acknowledges a much greater degree of interaction between different "populations," or the "Triple I" (Green, 2000) model, which allows for a range of possible origins for the various components of the Lapita cultural package and acknowledges that human interactions and the creation of culture are both complex, are more realistic. But these too have been criticized as being untestable and not particularly useful (Terrell, 2004b; Terrell et al., 2001). Part of the difficulty of testing models and reconstructing prehistory, of course, is that while the archaeological record is (generally) chronologically controlled and represents particular points in time and through time, it is rather patchy, particularly in some key geographical areas and for some very important points in time. The record in Near Oceania, for example, is not very good for the period just preceding the appearance of Lapita in Near Oceania (e.g. 6000–4000 BP), and while it is improving, the archaeological record for much of Island Southeast Asia, particularly the islands in Wallacea, is still limited. When it comes to trying to reconstruct linguistic expansions and test theories about population migrations, we can really only rely on data obtained from modern populations, and these people and languages, for the most part, are removed by several thousands of years from the events we are trying to reconstruct. A lot can happen in 3000 years and it might not all be archaeologically visible. But until we have access to the necessary ancient human remains from the appropriate sites, and the permission of the descendant communities for destructive DNA and other biochemical analyses, we do our best with trying to reconstruct the past from the present. However, we should always keep in mind that language, biology, and culture do not always move hand in hand. Indeed, it has also been suggested that we are often too focused on the ultimate origins of languages, cultures, and peoples as opposed to their history and are too inclined to treat them as the same thing (Terrell, 2004a).

Over the last 15 years, molecular evidence, and in particular mtDNA data, has been central to the development of the debates about the biological origins of Lapita peoples. Studies of modern populations living in Remote Oceania have shown that in addition to the Near Oceanic mtDNA lineages belonging to haplogroups P and Q, these populations have high frequencies of the Asian-derived mtDNA haplogroup B and, in particular, those belonging to the B4a1a1 and derived haplotypes. The frequencies of the B4a1a1a lineages are particularly high in East Polynesian populations, where it is found above 95% in some locations, leading to the dubbing of the key mutations defining the haplotype as the "Polynesian Motif" (Redd *et al.*, 1995). Based on this high frequency in Polynesia, its distribution in Near Oceania and the ultimately Asian origins of the lineage led many to suggest that the B4a1a1a haplotypes were the marker of the Austronesian expansion through Island Southeast Asia and the Lapita expansion into Near Oceania and out into Remote Oceania (Melton *et al.*, 1995, 1998; Merriwether *et al.*, 1999). It has been suggested that a better name for the combinations of mutations defining the B4a1a1 haplotype might be the "Oceanic" (Terrell *et al.*, 2001) or "Austronesian" motif (Lum and Cann, 2000); however, linking a molecular marker to any particular linguistic or cultural group can be dangerous as these terms often carry significant baggage that may not relate to biology or to current social identity.

In what has become described as the "orthodox view" of Lapita origins and dispersal (Spriggs, 1984), the relatively high levels of Near

Oceanic derived P and Q lineages seen in Remote Oceania, particularly in Vanuatu, New Caledonia, and Fiji, are indicators of post-settlement interaction between "Papuan" populations in Near Oceania and those in Melanesian Remote Oceania. Alternatively, and probably more generally accepted today, the P and Q mtDNA lineages in Remote Oceania are seen as markers of admixture between the Austronesian Lapita peoples and the indigenous inhabitants of Near Oceania which occurred during the 200–300 years they were in the Bismarck Archipelago prior to moving into Remote Oceania.

While the mtDNA data, particularly the distribution of the so-called "Polynesian motif," were generally seen as suggesting that the Lapita people were primarily Asian in origin, when people began studying the Y-chromosome variants in the Pacific, a very different picture emerged. A large percentage of the Remote Oceanic Y chromosomes are of Near Oceanic origin, including 66% of those identified in Polynesian populations (Kayser *et al.*, 2000). While some more recently derived Asian Y chromosomes are found in Remote Oceanic populations, specifically the O-M324 haplotypes, the most common Y chromosomes found in Remote Oceania, belong to the C, K, and M haplogroups that are thought to originate in Near Oceania (Kayser, 2010; Kayser *et al.*, 2006). It has been suggested that this pattern might reflect the matrilineal descent and matrilocal dispersal patterns that are common in the Pacific today and have been reconstructed for proto-Oceanic societies (Hage and Marck, 2003).

It is clear that the B4a1a1 lineages are ultimately Asian derived and are relatively recent arrivals in Near Oceania compared with the P or Q mtDNA lineages; however, more recent analyses of complete mtDNA sequences belonging to the B4 lineages from populations throughout Island Southeast Asia and Near Oceania indicate a history for their origins and dispersals that may challenge the previous hypotheses that seem to fit so well with it being part of the Austronesian Neolithic dispersal story (Soares *et al.*, 2011; Tabbada *et al.*, 2010). Soares *et al.* (2011) argue that, according to their calculations, the immediate precursor to the "Polynesian motif," the B4a1a1 clade, which is absent from Taiwan, is both the most diverse and the oldest in populations from the Bismarck Archipelago. They estimate its overall age there to be approximately 8400 BP and determine that it "most likely either arose from a B4a1a ancestor within the Bismarcks or arrived there from further west in the early Holocene, much earlier than the appearance of Lapita and the putative arrival of Austronesian languages" (Soares *et al.*, 2011:4). This evidence is consistent with Irwin's (1994) concept of a

Voyaging Corridor that extended not only through Near Oceania, but also north into Island Southeast Asia. Significant mid-Holocene inter-action is also argued for based on the distribution of a number of New Guinea plants, which were domesticated there and transferred into Island Southeast Asia (Donohue and Denham, 2010). The pre-Lapita movement of a native wallaby (*Dorcopsis*) from New Guinea to the Maluku Islands with evidence on Halmahera as early as 5500 BP (Flannery, 1995) and from Gebe as early as 8000 BP (Bellwood *et al.*, 1998) also indicate interaction between Near Oceania and Island Southeast Asia prior to the appearance of Lapita. This coincides with changes in the environmental conditions, which between 8000 and 6000 BP would have created rich lagoons and floodplains around much of this area including the north coast of New Guinea. Terrell (2004b) argues that these changes would have awakened the "Sleeping Giant" of New Guinea, making contact between New Guinea and the islands of Wallacea finally possible after the thousands of years of isolation partly driven by the extreme and uninviting coastal conditions of New Guinea during most of the Pleisto-cene and early Holocene. Other Asian-derived mtDNA lineages also likely arrived in Near Oceania at some point in the mid-Holocene such as the E1a and E1b lineages. To date these have not been found in Remote Oceanic populations (Friedlaender *et al.*, 2007) and may indicate further interactions within this corridor, perhaps after the Lapita dispersals to Remote Oceania. Clearly migration across Wallacea in both directions has a long history, and still continues today. Therefore the standard two-migration view so often depicted clearly needs to be reconsidered.

MICRONESIAN ORIGINS AND SETTLEMENT HISTORY

Unfortunately Micronesia, literally meaning "little islands," is often left out of studies and discussions regarding the settlement of the Pacific. The islands that make up Micronesia are clustered into the main archi-pelagoes of Palau, the Mariana Islands, the Caroline Islands, the Marshall Islands, and Kiribati. Like the islands of Melanesia, the culture history of Micronesia is complex and, therefore, the inhabitants of these islands do not fit into any single coherent linguistic, cultural, or biological category (Green, 1991). Most of the islands of Micronesia are atolls, though there are some upraised coral limestone "makatea" islands, such as Nauru and Banaba, and the few high volcanic islands of Yap, Chuuk, Pohnpei, and Kosrae. The earliest dates for Micronesia, not surprisingly, come from western Micronesia with archaeological sites in the Marianas and Palau suggesting that human occupation there dates from about 3300 BP

(Clark, 2004). It has been argued based on changes in the paleoenviron-mental record, however, that human presence may predate this by as much as 1000 to 1500 years (Wickler, 2001).

While the settlement history of western Micronesia may be con-temporaneous with the Lapita expansion into the rest of Remote Oceania, the linguistic and archaeological evidence suggests separate origins, more closely associated with populations in Island Southeast Asia (Pawley and Ross, 1993). Pottery has been recovered from early sites in the Marianas that has been described as red-slipped and thin-walled with some having lime-filled impressed designs. It is generally thought that these are not directly related to the Lapita pots (Butler, 1994) but are more likely related to similar pots from the Philippines (Kirch, 2000).

Archaeological evidence for initial settlement of central-eastern Micronesia is significantly later than the dates in the west, and the settlement of the Carolines, Marshalls, and Kiribati, like the islands of Polynesia, is linked ancestrally to Lapita populations. The timing of settlement of the atolls of central-eastern Micronesia was very much influenced by environmental conditions as they were uninhabitable prior to 2000 BP when sea levels reached the current levels (Dickinson, 2001, 2003). Kirch (2000:167) suggests that the origins of the initial colonists to the high islands came from late Lapita plainware-producing populations located somewhere between the Bismarcks and northern Vanuatu. Linguistic subgrouping suggests connections between these Micronesian languages and the languages of Fiji, Rotuma, and Polynesia (Marck, 2000; Pawley and Ross, 1995).

Pottery has been recovered from the high islands of Chuuk, Pohnpei, and Kosrae, and is dated to approximately 2000 BP; however, its use declines through time (Kirch, 2000). Pottery is, as yet, unknown in the low islands of central-eastern Micronesia. Major landscape changes in western Micronesia and the high islands including the construction of megalithic structures and massively terraced land-scapes are indicative of increased social complexity from about AD 1000. The famous "Yapese Empire," which linked Yap with Palau and the Caroline atolls, demonstrates that long-distance communication, political, and other social interactions were a significant part of the later periods of Micronesian prehistory (Butler, 1994; Hage and Harary, 1996).

Only a few biological studies have focused on Micronesian popula-tions, addressing the issues of their biological origins and similarities to other Pacific populations. Morphological studies consistently group Micronesian and Polynesian populations together with Asian popula-tions and separate from other "Lapita derived" populations in Melanesia

(Pietrusewsky, 1996). Analyses of mtDNA of western Micronesian populations indicate complex origins and are relatively compatible with the
archaeological picture discussed above (Lum and Cann, 2000). Mariana
Islanders and those from the high island of Yap show links with Southeast Asian populations, where Palau has clear genetic links with populations in Near Oceania. Central-eastern Micronesian populations have
high frequencies of the "Polynesian motif" haplotypes (Lum and Cann,
2000) while neutral, biparentally inherited molecular markers link
Polynesian and Micronesian populations to the exclusion of "Melanesian"
populations, including other Lapita-derived populations (Friedlaender
et al., 2008; Lum *et al.*, 2002). It has recently been suggested that the
consistent grouping of some Micronesian and Polynesian populations
based on biological data may be indicative of a more complex history
for the populations of the atolls of central-eastern Micronesia and the
islands of Polynesia than is currently reconstructed (Addison and Matisoo-
Smith, 2010).

THE SETTLEMENT OF THE POLYNESIAN TRIANGLE
AND BEYOND

The last major geographical region of the earth to be settled was the
Polynesian Triangle – identified by the apices of Hawai'i, in the north,
Rapa Nui/Easter Island, in the east, and Aotearoa/New Zealand in
the south. For at least the last 50 years, there has been consensus that
the origins of the Polynesians and the settlement of the Polynesian
Triangle are tied to those Lapita-derived populations who arrived in
Samoa and Tonga some 2900 years ago. What has been described as
the remarkable linguistic, cultural, and biological homogeneity of Polynesians (Houghton, 1996; Howells, 1970) is likely due to their common
and relatively recent origins from Hawaiki, or a common Polynesian
homeland located in West Polynesia (Kirch and Green, 2001). The major
debates within Polynesian prehistory have focused in recent years on
the timing and sequence of settlement and the associated impact of
human arrival on the island ecosystems, the amount of post-settlement
interaction that existed within Polynesia and on the economic and
political transformations of the island societies (Kirch and Kahn, 2007).

For a period of time in the mid 1980s there was a general trend
amongst Polynesian prehistorians to suggest longer periods of settlement history for many Polynesian archipelagos. Many questioned the
"long pause" in West Polynesia and suggested that settlement into
Polynesia was continuous or that only as little as 1000 years may have

separated the earliest sites in Central and East Polynesia from those in Samoa and Tonga (Irwin, 1981, 1994; Kirch, 1986). However, recent years have seen a shift towards a critical evaluation of some of the radiocarbon dates in what has become known as "chronometric hygiene" (Spriggs and Anderson, 1993; Wilmshurst et al., 2011). Today the settlement of most of the central and east Polynesian archipelagos is thought to date to no earlier than AD 800–900, though slightly earlier settlement in the Society and the Cook Islands is still a possibility (Kirch and Kahn, 2007). Hawai'i now has an identified "Foundation Period" dated to AD 800–1200, during which discovery, colonization and establishment of populations on the main islands would have occurred (Kirch and McCoy, 2007). New dates for initial settlement of Rapa Nui/Easter Island at AD 1200 have been suggested (Hunt and Lipo, 2006), and arguments for initial human arrival in New Zealand dating to AD 200 or earlier (Holdaway, 1996; Sutton, 1984) have not been substantiated (Wilmshurst et al., 2008) and settlement is now firmly accepted to have occurred around AD 1250 at the earliest (Walter et al., 2010).

Linguistic and artifactual similarities as well as oral traditions have long suggested that Polynesians maintained contact and interaction spheres across great distances, some for several hundreds of years after initial settlement. While researchers have long been aware of the trade networks involving Samoa, Tonga, and Fiji (Barnes and Hunt, 2005; Dye and Dickinson, 1996) the general lack of pottery in East Polynesia made similar studies difficult. Recent advances in geochemical and other sourcing studies, however, have provided new evidence as to the extent of contact and the distances covered within East Polynesia. For example, trace element and isotope analyses of basalt tools found in the Tuamotu Archipelago have been sourced back to the Marquesas, Austral, Society Islands, and even as far away as Hawai'i, indicating a trade network requiring voyages of over thousands of kilometers of open ocean (Collerson and Weisler, 2007). While such trade and exchange networks were extensive by the time Europeans arrived in the Pacific and, in some cases, such as in New Zealand, such networks had diminished significantly as populations focused on intra-archipelago social developments (Irwin, 1998; Walter, 2004; Weisler and Kirch, 1996).

Another indicator of continued interaction and contact comes from genetic studies of the plants and animals that were transported by Pacific colonists. This "commensal approach" is based on the concept that because these plants and animals cannot self-disperse and were introduced by humans to the islands of the Pacific, genetic studies that identified the origins of island populations of these plants and animals would, by proxy, indicate the origins of the peoples who transported them (Matisoo-Smith, 1994). The model was first applied in the Pacific to studies of extant populations of the Pacific rat (*Rattus exulans*) from throughout Polynesia and identified two distinct interaction spheres in Polynesia: a northern sphere and a southern sphere, both linked to a central-east Polynesian homeland located in the Cook and Society Islands (Matisoo-Smith *et al.*, 1998). Commensal studies have also recently identified evidence of interaction networks and likely origins, migration pathways that conflict with traditional views of the settlement of and interactions within Oceania and beyond (Addison and Matisoo-Smith, 2010; Larson *et al.*, 2007; Matisoo-Smith and Robins, 2004; Matisoo-Smith *et al.*, 2009; Storey *et al.*, 2007).

Most standard histories of the settlement of the Pacific end with the colonization of Rapa Nui/Easter Island and New Zealand, but evidence is accumulating which would suggest that Polynesian voyaging continued beyond the eastern boundary of the well-known Polynesian Triangle (Jones *et al.*, 2011). The presence of charred kumara, or sweet potato, remains in prehistoric archaeological sites in Polynesia (Hather and Kirch, 1991) was a clear indicator that prehistoric contact occurred between Polynesians and South America. The fact that the Polynesians used the term *kumara*, a "Polynesianized" version of the South American name for the tuber, *kumar*, was evidence that it could not have arrived in Polynesia unaccompanied through drift voyaging or other natural means. The discovery, radiocarbon dating and ancient DNA analysis of archaeological chicken bones in the pre-Columbian site of El Arenal, located on the south-central coast of Chile (Storey *et al.*, 2007, 2008), however, renewed interest in studying those interactions and their implications for Polynesian prehistory. The AD 1300 to 1400 dates obtained from the bones clearly indicate that Europeans were not the first to introduce chickens to the Americas. Both the timing of introduction and the fact that the mtDNA sequences obtained from the bones were identical to those from ancient Pacific chicken bones suggest a Polynesian origin. Several studies have now been undertaken identifying additional evidence of contact (Matisoo-Smith and Ramirez, 2010; Ramirez-Aliaga and Matisoo-Smith, 2008) and assesses the likely sources of the voyages and other possible locations for landing and population interactions (Fitzpatrick and Callaghan, 2009).

At about the same time that Polynesian migration commenced from West Polynesia eastwards into Central and East Polynesia, Polynesian peoples also began moving westwards, back into the islands of Melanesia and Micronesia. There are approximately 18 Polynesian societies located in the archipelagos of Vanuatu, New Caledonia, the Solomon Islands, and further afield recognized (Kirch, 2000). Generally, these "Polynesian outliers" are located on small, offshore islands and though they interact with their non-Polynesian neighbors, have remained linguistically and culturally, though not necessarily biologically, distinct from them for hundreds of years. In some cases these Polynesian arrivals were the first long-term inhabitants of the small islands they settled on, but in others the Polynesian settlers were clearly intrusive (Davidson, 1992; Kirch and Yen, 1982).

As discussed previously, the Polynesians are generally seen as a remarkably homogenous population, linguistically, culturally, and biologically (Kirch and Green, 2001; Pawley, 1966; Pietrusewsky, 1996), and while this may be demonstrated in terms of language, culture, and perhaps even skeletal biology, there have been few fine-grained studies of Polynesian populations at a molecular level. Most genetic studies, including and often focused on Polynesians (see for example Kayser *et al.*, 2006), are fairly limited in samples from East Polynesia. Much of what we know about East Polynesian mtDNA and Y-chromosome variation is based on a few samples (often these same samples are analyzed in several studies) of New Zealand Maori and the indigenous population of Rapa Nui. These studies indicate limited genetic variation within Polynesia (Melton *et al.*, 1995; Murray-McIntosh *et al.*, 1998; Whyte *et al.*, 2005) and suggest that this is due to the repeated bottlenecks that must have been experienced in the process of initial colonization. Both of these populations, like many in Polynesia, suffered dramatic postcolonization population bottlenecks as a result of the introduction of European diseases, forced labor recruitment or "blackbirding," and high levels of admixture with European populations, particularly European males (Hurles *et al.*, 1998). A recent study of both ancient and modern populations in the Gambier Islands of French Polynesia (Deguilloux *et al.*, 2011), however, has indicated that the assumption that the near ubiquitous presence of the mtDNA haplotype B4a1a1a in East Polynesia may be incorrect. These authors show not only a higher frequency of mtDNA haplotype Q1 in both the ancient and modern populations, but also identify a number of new haplotypes within the B4a1a1a clade. We anticipate that further fine-grained studies of Polynesian populations focusing on analyses of complete mtDNA genomes combined with a full range of other genetic markers are likely to indicate significantly more genetic variation within Polynesia than currently recognized, as has been demonstrated in similar studies in Near Oceania (Friedlaender *et al.*, 2007). This may have implications for understanding the settlement history and subsequent interaction in the region.

EUROPEAN ARRIVAL, COLONIALISM, AND URBAN MIGRATION
IN THE PACIFIC

As discussed above, European arrival in the Pacific had dire consequences for many Pacific Island communities. Estimates of population
sizes at the time of European contact have been debated widely, yet there
is general agreement that the introduction of European diseases to
Pacific populations with no resistance caused a rapid and dramatic
reduction in the population numbers (McArthur, 1967). It is claimed that
the Marquesas saw the loss of more than 90% of its population as a result
of introduced diseases and while it was probably one of the worst
affected archipelagoes, many Pacific islands would have reduced the
populations by more than half after the first century of European contact due to disease alone (Harrison *et al.*, 1993; Rallu, 1991; Shell, 1999). In
a recent assessment of population growth and collapse in the Pacific
Islands (Kirch and Rallu, 2007), Norma MacArthur's (1967) often cited
estimates for Pacific population sizes at contact were criticized as significantly underestimating likely population size and density at contact in
many archipelagoes including Hawai'i, the Societies, the Marquesas,
Samoa, New Caledonia, and Vanuatu. This means that the impact of
introduced diseases as a result of initial contact was even more severe
than often calculated. Later epidemics such as the 1918 flu epidemic in
Western Samoa (Tomkins, 1992) had further dire consequences for
Pacific Island populations.

The European explorers were quickly followed by missionaries,
whalers, and sealers and a range of European entrepreneurs and other
"colonists" who all had major impacts on the demographic and social
history of the Pacific Islands. While long-distance interactions among
Pacific Island populations diminished in most areas by the time of
European arrival, Pacific Islander mobility increased again during the
eighteenth and nineteenth centuries with the numbers of ships tra-
versing the Pacific Ocean. Pacific Islanders were regular recruits in
whaling and sealing crews; they were recruited as missionaries and
travelled across the Pacific to spread the word of God; and they were
quickly engaged in trade and other economic opportunities that came
as a result of the growing European colonies popping up across the
Pacific.

Unfortunately not all migration at this time was voluntary.
Peruvian slavers looking for workers for the guano mines of the
Chincha Islands off the Peruvian coast visited several Pacific Islands
"recruiting" for labor from 1862 to 1863, once again causing massive

depopulation of up to 80% in some islands (Maude, 1981). In Tokelau an estimated 42% of the population, including almost all able-bodied males, were taken, against their will, to Peru (Green and Green, 2007). Occasionally, the islanders were returned or escaped. In some cases, repatriation meant further disease introductions as was the case in Rapa Nui/Easter Island when the return of 15 men resulted in the introduction of smallpox (Harrison *et al.*, 1993:527). In other cases men were dropped off in archipelagoes other than those from which they were taken and were assimilated. The majority of those taken, however, never returned, having died on the ships or as a result of the poor working conditions they experienced in Peru (Maude, 1981).

The rapid growth of the sugar industry in Hawai'i, Australia, and Fiji in the 1870s and 1880s resulted in further Pacific Islander mobility. Again, while some of this mobility was voluntary, much of the "recruitment" was not. Hawaiian ships picked up recruits from the Gilbert Islands (Kiribati), Rotuma, and the New Hebrides (Vanuatu) and transported them to Honolulu and then on to other islands in the archipelago. Some of these recruits stayed in Hawai'i permanently, some returned to their home islands, but many died – death rates of up to 11% for Gilbertese workers were recorded on the island of Hawai'i (Bennett, 1976). Conditions were worse in the sugar plantations of Fiji and Queensland, Australia, where the Solomon Islands, the New Hebrides (Vanuatu), and Papua New Guinea were major targets for labor recruitment (Corris, 1968). A number of the Solomon Island men who were taken to Fiji stayed there, marrying local women, and as a result a strong Solomon Island Fijian community still lives near Suva on the main island of Viti Levu. Partly in reaction to negative pressure regarding "blackbirding" from the 1890s onwards, the plantation owners in both Hawai'i and Fiji began recruiting non-Pacific Islander workers, from Japan in Hawai'i and primarily from India in Fiji. These new migrants came willingly and in many cases permanently, making major social and biological contributions to the communities they joined.

Eighteenth and nineteenth century colonial expansion in the Pacific resulted in the carving up of the region by the various western powers, with the British claiming New Zealand, Australia, central and southern parts of the Solomon Islands, Fiji, Kiribati and Tuvalu (formerly known as the Gilbert and Ellice Islands), and the Cook Islands; the Germans claiming New Guinea (including the Bismarck Archipelago), the northern parts of the Solomon Islands, western Samoa, the Caroline, Marshall and Marianas Islands (except Guam); the French claiming New Caledonia, the Society, Marquesas, Tuamotu and Austral

Islands, Wallis and Futuna; the Americans claiming Guam, Hawai'i and the eastern part of Samoa, now known as American Samoa; and Chile taking Rapa Nui/Easter Island. Vanuatu (then known as the New Hebrides) was a recognized condominium shared by the French and British. Only Tonga remained unclaimed by western powers (Barcham *et al.*, 2009). This carving up made Pacific Island mobility difficult for many, particularly when archipelagoes were split between different political powers with extended families now isolated from one another due to new political boundaries. By contrast, these colonial connections in many cases opened up new opportunities for migration to the metropolitan centers of the colonizers. While some shuffling of political control of the Pacific Islands changed after the two World Wars, colonial rule continued in many Pacific Islands until relatively recently and in some cases still continues today.

Despite achieving independence, colonial connections are often still maintained for many island communities and migration continues. Large Pacific Island communities are located now on the west coast of the United States, in New Zealand, and on the east coast of Australia, creating what has been described as the "New Polynesian Triangle" (Barcham *et al.*, 2009). This is part of a general trend, which began in the 1950s and 60s, of rural to urban migration by Pacific Islanders in search of work, educational opportunities, and the promise of a better lifestyle. A large number of Pacific Islanders, primarily from Polynesia, came to New Zealand to work in the factories, freezing works, and forestry industry in the 1960s, facilitated by immigration policies that encouraged such migration. Today many particular Pacific Island communities living in New Zealand now outnumber the populations on their islands of origin. Economic reforms and deregulation of trade in both New Zealand and Australia in the 1980s and 1990s, however, led to closure of many of the factories, causing widespread and disproportional unemployment in many resident Pacific Island communities. High levels of unemployment and other urban problems in many Pacific Island nations are also beginning to drive some urban residents back to rural villages and towns and for non-local migrants back to their islands of origin. Out-migration continues to be a problem in many Pacific Island nations, particularly for places like Niue, Tokelau, Tuvalu, and the Cook Islands (Stahl and Appleyard, 2007). The populations of the many atoll islands in the Pacific face numerous challenges in the future, including the possibility of permanent and total migration due to rising sea levels.

CONCLUSION

Migration has always been and probably will always be an important part of Pacific Island life. Reconstructing past migrations in the Pacific has been a major focus of scholars for centuries. Most recently, reconstructing prehistoric Pacific population origins and migration pathways has become something of a hot topic for molecular studies. Unfortunately, most of these scholars have not paid much attention to the complex history of population mobility in the region. While many now acknowledge the fact that the classic division of the Pacific into Melanesia, Polynesia, and Micronesia does not make much sense biologically, the settlement history of the Pacific is still generally told as a story of two migrations: the "Papuans" and the Austronesians. Increasing evidence suggests, however, that the history of the region is much more complex. And while the realization that mtDNA and Y-chromosome data suggested two very different histories has led to consideration of some of the social forces that might explain the data, few studies have focused on other historical events. The severe depopulation and inter-island migration in the last few hundred years make genetic studies of modern populations particularly unreliable for reconstructing population origins unless these factors are taken into account. These relatively recent events may also have had differential impacts on male versus female linked genetic markers, as the work of Hurles *et al.* (2003b), one of the few studies where these events have been considered, has demonstrated. There seems to be the implication in many genetic studies of Pacific peoples that populations are static and unchanging and thus events that occurred thousands, if not tens of thousands, of years ago are easily reconstructed from the DNA of peoples, their languages, and their cultural affiliations today.

I am not suggesting that such attempts to reconstruct past migrations in the Pacific are impossible. Pacific Island communities are becoming increasingly interested themselves in combining the latest evidence from archaeology and molecular biology with their own knowledge of their history. They are not only becoming involved in scientific studies of prehistory, but in many cases are driving that research and the questions being addressed. In the last few years archaeological investigations in the Pacific have uncovered new sites or reanalyzed old sites, many with human remains, that date to critical periods and are found in key locations for addressing important questions regarding past human migrations (Bedford *et al.*, 2009; Bentley *et al.*,

2007; Brooks *et al.*, 2009; McNiven *et al.*, 2011; Shaw *et al.*, 2010). Ancient DNA analyses of these human remains, being undertaken with the expressed permission of and in some cases at the request of the descendant communities, combined with the improved chances for DNA recovery with the use of next generation sequence technology (Lambert and Millar, 2006) are particularly exciting. With such data we can really start to understand and identify the genetic makeup of particular Lapita populations or that of the pre-European populations in Polynesia. By incorporating historical data with molecular data from ancient and modern Pacific populations we can even possibly reconstruct population histories through time.

Many of the causes of Pacific migration in both the past and present are common to all human populations; however, many are also unique. In trying to reconstruct past migrations or study modern migration patterns we need to be aware of the range of factors that affect migration and recognize the historic events that have impacted and shaped the populations living on Pacific Islands today and in the past. One thing that would help is for researchers studying Pacific peoples and cultures to realize that the Pacific Ocean was not just a barrier to interaction but a facilitator of migration – it was, in actuality, a great blue highway.

REFERENCES

Addison, D. J. and Matisoo-Smith, E. (2010). Rethinking Polynesian origins: a West-Polynesian Triple-I Model. *Archaeology in Oceania*, **45**, 1–12.

Allen, J. (2000). From beach to beach: the development of maritime economies in prehistoric Melanesia. In *East of Wallace's Line: Studies of Past and Present Maritime Cultures of the Indo-Pacific Region*, ed. S. O'Connor and P. Veth, pp. 139–75. Rotterdam, Netherlands: Balkema.

Barcham, M., Scheyvens, R., and Overton, J. (2009). New Polynesian triangle: rethinking Polynesian migration and development in the Pacific. *Asia Pacific Viewpoint*, **50**, 322–37.

Barnes, S. S. and Hunt, T. L. (2005). Samoa's pre-contact connections in West Polynesia and beyond. *Journal of the Polynesian Society*, **114**, 227–66.

Bedford, S., Spriggs, M., Buckley, H., Valentin, F., and Regenvanu, R. (2009). The Teouma Lapita site, south Efatem Vanuatu: a summary of three field seasons (2004–2006). In *Lapita: Ancestors and Descendants*, ed. P. J. Sheppard, T. Thomas, and G. R. Summerhayes. Auckland: New Zealand Archaeological Association.

Bedford, S., Spriggs, M., and Regenvanu, R. (2006). The Teouma Lapita site and the early human settlement of the Pacific Islands. *Antiquity*, **80**, 812–28.

Bellwood, P. (2005). *First Farmers: The Origins of Agricultural Societies*. Oxford, UK: Blackwell.

Bellwood, P., Nitihaminoto, G., Irwin, G. J., *et al.* (1998). 35,000 years of prehistory in the northern Moluccas. *Modern Quaternary Research in Southeast Asia*, **15**, 223–73.

Bennett, J. A. (1976). Immigration, 'blackbirding', labour recruiting? The Hawaiian experience 1877–1887. *Journal of Pacific History*, **11**, 3–27.

Bentley, R. A., Buckley, H. R., Spriggs, M., *et al.* (2007). Lapita migrants in the Pacific's oldest cemetery: isotopic analysis at Teouma, Vanuatu. *American Antiquity*, **72**, 645–56.

Brooks, E., Jacomb, C., and Walter, R. (2009). Archaeological investigations at Wairau Bar. *Archaeology in New Zealand*, **52**, 259–68.

Burley, D. V. and Dickinson, W. R. (2001). Origin and significance of a founding settlement in Polynesia. *Proceedings of the National Academy of Sciences of the United States of America*, **98**, 11 829–31.

Butler, B. M. (1994). Early prehistoric settlement in the Marianas Islands: new evidence from Saipan. *Man and Culture in Oceania*, **10**, 15–38.

Clark, G. (2004). Radiocarbon dates from the Ulong site in Palau and implications for Western Micronesian prehistory. *Archaeology in Oceania*, **39**, 26–33.

Clark, G. R. and Anderson, A. J. (2009). Site chronology and a review of radiocarbon dates from Fiji. In *The Early Prehistory of Fiji*, ed. G. Clark and A. Anderson. Canberra: The Australian National University E-Press.

Collerson, K. D. and Weisler, M. I. (2007). Stone adze compositions and the extent of ancient Polynesian voyaging and trade. *Science*, **317**, 1907–11.

Corris, P. (1968). "Blackbirding" in New Guinea waters, 1883–84: an episode in the Queensland labour trade. *Journal of Pacific History*, **3**, 85–105.

Davidson, J. (1992). New evidence about the date of colonisation of Nukuoro atoll, a Polynesian outlier in the eastern Caroline Islands. *Journal of the Polynesian Society*, **101**, 293–8.

Deguilloux, M.-F., Pemonge, M. -H., Dubut, V., *et al.* (2011). Human ancient and extant mtDNA from the Gambier Islands (French Polynesia): evidence for an early Melanesian maternal contribution and new perspectives into the settlement of easternmost Polynesia. *American Journal of Physical Anthropology*, **144**, 248–57.

Denham, T., Haberle, S., and Lentfer, C. (2004). New evidence and revised interpretations of early agriculture in Highland New Guinea. *Antiquity*, **78**, 839–57.

Diamond, J. (1988). Express train to Polynesia. *Nature*, **336**, 307–8.

Dickinson, W. R. (2000). Changing times – the Holocene legacy. *Environmental History*, **5**, 483–502.

Dickinson, W. R. (2001). Paleoshoreline record of relative Holocene sea levels on Pacific Islands. *Earth-Science Reviews*, **55**, 191–234.

Dickinson, W. R. (2003). Impact of mid-Holocene hydro-isostatic highstand in regional sea level on habitability of islands in Pacific Oceania. *Journal of Coastal Research*, **19**, 489–502.

Donohue, M. and Denham, T. (2010). Farming and language in island Southeast Asia reframing Austronesian history. *Current Anthropology*, **51**, 223–56.

Dye, T. S. and Dickinson, W. R. (1996). Sources of sand tempers in prehistoric Tongan pottery. *Geoarchaeology*, **11**, 141–64.

Endicott, P., Gilbert, M. T., Stringer, C., *et al.* (2003). The genetic origins of the Andaman Islanders. *American Journal of Human Genetics*, **72**, 178–84.

Fitzpatrick, S. M. and Callaghan, R. (2009). Examining dispersal mechanisms for the translocation of chicken (*Gallus gallus*) from Polynesia to South America. *Journal of Archaeological Science*, **36**, 214–23.

Flannery, T. F. (1995). *Mammals of the South-West Pacific and the Moluccan Islands*. Sydney, Australia: Reed Books.

Flannery, T. F. and White, J. P. (1991). Animal translocation. *Research and Exploration*, **7**, 96–113.

Friedlaender, J., Schurr, T., Gentz, F., *et al.* (2005). Expanding Southwest Pacific mitochondrial haplogroups P and Q. *Molecular Biology and Evolution*, **22**, 1506–17.

Friedlaender, J. S., Friedlaender, F. R., Hodgson, J. A., *et al.* (2007). Melanesian mtDNA complexity. *PLoS ONE*, **2**, e248.

Friedlaender, J. S., Friedlaender, F. R., Reed, F. A., *et al.* (2008). The genetic structure of Pacific islanders. *PloS Genetics*, **4**, e19.

Fullagar, R., Field, J., Denham, T., and Lentfer, C. (2006). Early and mid Holocene tool-use and processing of taro (*Colocasia esculenta*), yam (*Dioscorea* sp.) and other plants at Kuk Swamp in the highlands of Papua New Guinea. *Journal of Archaeological Science*, **33**, 595–614.

Green, R. C. (1991). Near and Remote Oceania – disestablishing "Melanesia" in culture history. In *Man and a Half: Essays in Pacific anthropology and ethnobiology in honour of Ralph Bulmer*, ed. A. Pawley. Auckland, New Zealand: The Polynesian Society.

Green, R. C. (2000). Lapita and the cultural model for intrusion, integration and innovation. In *Australian Archaeologist: Collected Papers in Honour of Jim Allen*, ed. A. Anderson and T. Murray. Canberra: Coombs Academic Publishing, The Australian National University.

Green, R. C., Jones, M., and Sheppard, P. (2008). The reconstructed environment and absolute dating of SE-SZ-8 Lapita site on Nendo, Santa Cruz, Solomon Islands. *Archaeology in Oceania*, **43**, 49–61.

Green, V. J. and Green, R. C. (2007). An accent on atolls in approaches to population histories of Remote Oceania. In *The Growth and Collapse of Pacific Island Societies: Archaeological and demographic perspectives*, ed. P. V. Kirch and J.-L Rallu. Honolulu, HI: University of Hawaii Press.

Hage, P. and Harary, F. (1996). *Island Networks: Communication, Kinship and Classification Structures in Oceania*. Cambridge, UK: Cambridge University Press.

Hage, P. and Marck, J. (2003). Matrilineality and the Melanesian origin of Polynesian Y chromosomes. *Current Anthropology*, **44**, S121–S127.

Harrison, G. A., Tanner, J. M., Pilbeam, D. R., and Barker, P. T. (1993). *Human Biology: An Introduction to Human Evolution, Variation, Growth and Adaptability*. Oxford, UK: Oxford University Press.

Hather, J. and Kirch, P. V. (1991). Prehistoric sweet potato (*Ipomoea batatas*) from Mangaia Island, Central Polynesia. *Antiquity*, **65**, 887–93.

Holdaway, R. N. (1996). Arrival of rats in New Zealand. *Nature*, **384**, 225–226.

Houghton, P. (1996). *People of the Great Ocean: Aspects of Human Biology of the Early Pacific*. Cambridge, UK: Cambridge University Press.

Howells, W. W. (1970). Anthropometric grouping analysis of Pacific peoples. *Archaeology and Physical Anthropology in Oceania*, **5**, 192–217.

Hudjashov, G., Kivisild, T., Underhill, P. A., *et al.* (2007). Revealing the prehistoric settlement of Australia by Y chromosome and mtDNA analysis. *Proceedings of the National Academy of Sciences of the United States of America*, **104**, 8726–30.

Hunt, T. L. and Lipo, C. P. (2006). Late colonization of Easter Island. *Science*, **311**, 1603–6.

Hurles, M. E., Irven, C., Nicholson, J., *et al.* (1998). European Y-chromosomal lineages in Polynesians: a contrast to the population structure revealed by mtDNA. *American Journal of Human Genetics*, **63**, 1793–806.

Hurles, M. E., Matisoo-Smith, E., Gray, R. D., and Penny, D. (2003a). Untangling Oceanic settlement: the edge of the knowable. *Trends in Ecology and Evolution*, **18**, 531–40.

Hurles, M. E., Maund, E., Nicholson, J., *et al.* (2003b). Native American Y chromosomes in Polynesia: the genetic impact of the Polynesian slave trade. *American Journal of Human Genetics*, **72**, 1282–7.

Irwin, G. (1998). The colonisation of the Pacific plate: chronological, navigational and social issues. *Journal of the Polynesian Society*, **107**, 111–43.

Irwin, G. J. (1981). How Lapita lost its pots: the question of continuity in the colonisation of Polynesia. *Journal of the Polynesian Society*, **90**, 481–90.

Irwin, G. J. (1994). *The Prehistoric Exploration and Colonisation of the Pacific*. Melbourne, Australia: Cambridge University Press.

Jones, T. L., Storey, A. A., Matisoo-Smith, E., and Ramirez-Aliaga, J. M. (eds.) (2011). *Polynesians in America: Pre-Columbian Contacts with the New World*. Plymouth, UK: AltaMira Press.

Kayser, M. (2010). The human genetic history of Oceania: near and remote views of dispersal. *Current Biology*, **20**, R192–R201.

Kayser, M., Brauer, S., Cordaux, R., *et al.* (2006). Melanesian and Asian origins of Polynesians: mtDNA and Y chromosome gradients across the Pacific. *Molecular Biology and Evolution*, **23**, 2234–44.

Kayser, M., Brauer, S., Weiss, G., *et al.* (2003). Reduced Y-chromosome, but not mitochondrial DNA, diversity in human populations from West New Guinea. *American Journal of Human Genetics*, **72**, 281–302.

Kayser, M., Brauer, S., Weiss, G., *et al.* (2000). Melanesian origin of Polynesian Y chromosomes. *Current Biology*, **10**, 1237–46.

Kayser, M., Choi, Y., Van Oven, M., *et al.* (2008). The impact of the Austronesian expansion: evidence from mtDNA and Y chromosome diversity in the Admiralty Islands of Melanesia. *Molecular Biology and Evolution*, **25**, 1362–74.

Kirch, P. V. (1986). Rethinking East Polynesian prehistory. *Journal of the Polynesian Society*, **95**, 9–40.

Kirch, P. V. (2000). *On the Road of the Winds: An Archaeological History of the Pacific Islands before European Contact*. Berkeley, CA: University of California Press.

Kirch, P. V. and Green, R. C. (2001). *Hawaiki, Ancestral Polynesia: An Essay in Historical Anthropology*. Cambridge, UK: Cambridge University Press.

Kirch, P. V. and Kahn, J. G. (2007). Advances in Polynesian prehistory: a review and assessment of the past decade (1993–2004). *Journal of Archaeological Research*, **15**, 191–238.

Kirch, P. V. and McCoy, M. D. (2007). Reconfiguring the Hawaiian cultural sequence: results of re-dating the Halawa dune site (MO-Al-3), Moloka'i island. *Journal of the Polynesian Society*, **116**, 385–406.

Kirch, P. V. and Rallu, J.-L. (eds.) (2007). *The Growth and Collapse of Pacific Island Societies: Archaeological and Demographic Perspectives*. Honolulu, HI: University of Hawai'i Press.

Kirch, P. V. and Yen, D. E. (1982). *Tikopia: The Prehistory and Ecology of a Polynesian Outlier*. Honolulu, HI: Bernice P. Bishop Museum.

Lambert, D. M. and Millar, C. D. (2006). Evolutionary biology – ancient genomics is born. *Nature*, **444**, 275–6.

Larson, G., Cucchi, T., Fujita, M., *et al.* (2007). Phylogeny and ancient DNA of Sus provides insights into neolithic expansion in Island Southeast Asia and Oceania. *Proceedings of the National Academy of Sciences of the United States of America*, **104**, 4834–9.

Leavesley, M. (2005). Prehistoric hunting strategies in New Ireland, Papua New Guinea: the evidence of the Cuscus (*Phalanger orientalis*) remains from Buang Merabak Cave. *Asian Perspectives*, **44**, 207–18.

Leavesley, M. G., Bird, M. I., Fifield, L. K., *et al.* (2002). Buang Merabak: early evidence for human occupation in the Bismarck Archipelago, Papua New Guinea. *Australian Archaeology*, **54**, 55–7.

Lum, J. K. and Cann, R. L. (2000). mtDNA lineage analyses: origins and migrations of Micronesians and Polynesians. *American Journal of Physical Anthropology*, **113**, 151–68.

Lum, J. K., Jorde, L. B., and Schiefenhovel, W. (2002). Affinities among Melanesians, Micronesians, and Polynesians: a neutral, biparental genetic perspective. *Human Biology*, **74**, 413–30.

Macaulay, V., Hill, C., Achilli, A., *et al.* (2005). Single, rapid coastal settlement of Asia revealed by analysis of complete mitochondrial genomes. *Science*, **308**, 1034–6.

Marck, J. (2000). *Topics in Polynesian Language and Culture History*. Canberra: Pacific Linguistics.

Matisoo-Smith, E. (1994). The human colonisation of Polynesia. A novel approach: genetic analyses of the Polynesian rat (*Rattus exulans*). *Journal of the Polynesian Society*, **103**, 75–87.

Matisoo-Smith, E., Hingston, M., Summerhayes, G., *et al.* (2009). On the rat trail in Near Oceania: applying the commensal model to the question of the Lapita colonization. *Pacific Science*, **63**, 465–75.

Matisoo-Smith, E. and Ramirez, J. M. (2010). Human skeletal evidence of Polynesian presence in South America? Metric analyses of six crania from Mocha Island, Chile. *Journal of Pacific Archaeology*, **1**, 76–88.

Matisoo-Smith, E., Roberts, R. M., Irwin, G. J., *et al.* (1998). Patterns of prehistoric human mobility in Polynesia indicated by mtDNA from the Pacific rat. *Proceedings of the National Academy of Sciences of the United States of America*, **95**, 15 145–50.

Matisoo-Smith, E. and Robins, J. H. (2004). Origins and dispersals of Pacific peoples: evidence from mtDNA phylogenies of the Pacific rat. *Proceedings of the National Academy of Sciences of the United States of America*, **101**, 9167–72.

Maude, H. E. (1981). *Slavers in Paradise: The Peruvian Labor Trade in Polynesia, 1862–1864*. Stanford, CA: Stanford University Press.

McArthur, N. (1967). *Island Populations of the Pacific*. Canberra: Australian National University Press.

McNiven, I. J., David, B., Richards, T., *et al.* (2011). New direction in human colonisation of the Pacific: Lapita settlement of South Coast New Guinea. *Australian Archaeology*, **72**, 1–6.

Melton, T., Clifford, S., Martinson, J., Batzer, M., and Stoneking, M. (1998). Genetic evidence for the proto-Austronesian homeland in Asia: mtDNA and nuclear DNA variation in Taiwanese aboriginal tribes. *American Journal of Human Genetics*, **63**, 1807–23.

Melton, T., Peterson, R., Redd, A. J., *et al.* (1995). Polynesian genetic affinities with Southeast-Asian populations as identified by mtDNA analysis. *American Journal of Human Genetics*, **57**, 403–14.

Merriwether, D. A., Friedlaender, J. S., Mediavilla, J., *et al.* (1999). Mitochondrial DNA variation is an indicator of Austronesian influence in Island Melanesia. *American Journal of Physical Anthropology*, **110**, 243–70.

Mona, S., Tommaseo-Ponzetta, M., Brauer, S., *et al.* (2007). Patterns of Y-chromosome diversity intersect with the trans-New Guinea hypothesis. *Molecular Biology and Evolution*, **24**, 2546–55.

Murray-McIntosh, R. P., Scrimshaw, B. J., Hatfield, P. J., and Penny, D. (1998). Testing migration patterns and estimating founding population size in Polynesia by using human mtDNA sequences. *Proceedings of the National Academy of Sciences of the United States of America*, **95**, 9047–52.

O'Connell, J. F and Allen, J. (2004). Dating the colonization of Sahul (Pleistocene Australia-New Guinea): a review of recent research. *Journal of Archaeological Science*, **31**, 835–53.

Oppenheimer, S. and Richards, M. (2001). Fast trains, slow boats, and the ancestry of the Polynesian islanders. *Science Progress*, **84**, 157–81.

Pawley, A. (1966). Polynesian languages: subgrouping based on shared innovations in morphology. *Journal of the Polynesian Society*, **75**, 39–64.

Pawley, A. (2002). The Austronesian dispersal: languages, technologies and people. In *Examining the Farming/Language Dispersal Hypothesis*, ed. P. Bellwood and C. Renfrew. Cambridge, UK: McDonald Institute for Archaeological Research.

Pawley, A. (2007). Recent research on the historical relationships of the Papuan languages, or, What does linguistics say about the prehistory of Melanesia? In *Genes, Language, and Culture History in the Southwest Pacific*, ed. J. S Friedlaender. Oxford, UK: Oxford University Press.

Pawley, A. and Green, R. C. (1973). Dating the dispersal of the Oceanic languages. *Oceanic Linguistics*, **12**, 1–67.

Pawley, A. and Ross, M. (1995). The prehistory of Oceanic languages: a current review. In *The Austronesians: Historical and Comparative Perspectives*, ed. P. S. Bellwood, J. J. Fox, and D. T. Tryon. Canberra: Department of Anthropology, The Australian National University.

Pawley, A. and Ross, M. D. (1993). Austronesian historical linguistics and culture history. *Annual Review of Anthropology*, **22**, 425–59.

Petchey, F. J. (2001). Radiocarbon determinations from the Mulifanua Lapita site, Upolu, Western Samoa. *Radiocarbon*, **43**, 63–8.

Pierson, M., Martine-Zarias, R., Holland, B., *et al.* (2006). Deciphering past human population movements in Oceania: provably optimal trees of 127 mtDNA genomes. *Molecular Biology and Evolution*, **23**, 1966–75.

Pietrusewsky, M. (1996). The physical anthropology of Polynesia: a review of some cranial and skeletal studies. In *Oceanic Culture History: Essays in Honour of Roger Green*, ed. J. Davidson, G. Irwin, F. Leach, A. Pawley, and D. Brown. Auckland, New Zealand: New Zealand Journal of Archaeology Special Publication.

Rallu, J. L. (1991). Population of the French Overseas Territories in the Pacific, past, present and projected. *Journal of Pacific History*, **26**, 169–86.

Ramirez-Aliaga, J. M. and Matisoo-Smith, E. (2008). Polynesians of prehistoric times in Southern Chile: hard evidence, new questions and a new hypothesis. *Clava*, **7**, 85–100.

Redd, A. J., Takezaki, N., Sherry, S. T., *et al.* (1995). Evolutionary history of the COII/tRNALys intergenic 9 base pair deletion in human mitochondrial DNAs from the Pacific. *Molecular Biology and Evolution*, **12**, 604–15.

Ross, M. D. (2005). Pronouns as a preliminary diagnostic for grouping Papuan languages. In *Papuan Pasts. Cultural, linguistic and biological histories of Papuan speaking peoples*, ed. A. Pawley, R. Attenborough, J. Golson, and R. Hide. Canberra: Pacific Linguistics.

Sand, C. (1997). The chronology of Lapita ware in New Caledonia. *Antiquity*, **71**, 539–47.

Scheinfeldt, L., Friedlaender, F., Friedlaender, J., *et al.* (2006). Unexpected NRY chromosome variation in Northern Island Melanesia. *Molecular Biology and Evolution*, **23**, 1628–41.

Shaw, B., Buckley, H., Summerhayes, G., *et al.* (2010). Migration and mobility at the Late Lapita site of Reber-Rakival (SAC), Watom Island using isotope and trace element analysis: a new insight into Lapita interaction in the Bismarck Archipelago. *Journal of Archaeological Science*, **37**, 605–13.

Shell, R. J. (1999). The Marianas population decline: 17th century estimates. *Journal of Pacific History*, **34**, 291–305.

Soares, P., Rito, T., Trejaut, J., *et al.* (2011). Ancient voyaging and Polynesian origins. *American Journal of Human Genetics*, **88**, 239–47.

Spriggs, M. (1984). The Lapita cultural complex: origins, distribution, contemporaries and successors. *Journal of Pacific History*, **19**, 202–23.

Spriggs, M. J. T. and Anderson, A. (1993). Late colonization of East Polynesia. *Antiquity*, **67**, 200–17.

Stahl, C. W. and Appleyard, R. T. (2007). *Migration and Development in the Pacific Islands: Lessons from the New Zealand Experience*. Canberra: Australian Agency for International Development.

Storey, A. A., Quiroz, D., Ramirez, J. M., *et al.* (2008). Pre-Colombian chickens, dates, isotopes, and mtDNA. *Proceedings of the National Academy of Sciences of the United States of America*, **105**, E99–E99.

Storey, A. A., Ramirez, J. M., Quiroz, D., *et al.* (2007). Radiocarbon and DNA evidence for a pre-Columbian introduction of Polynesian chickens to Chile. *Proceedings of the National Academy of Sciences of the United States of America*, **104**, 10 335–9.

Summerhayes, G., Matisoo-Smith, E., Mandui, H., *et al.* (2010a). Tamuarawai (EQS): an early Lapita site on Emirau, New Ireland, PNG. *Journal of Pacific Archaeology*, **1**, 62–75.

Summerhayes, G. R. (2007). Island Melanesian pasts: a view from archaeology. In *Genes, Language, and Culture History in the Southwest Pacific*, ed. F. J. Friedlaender. Oxford, UK: Oxford University Press.

Summerhayes, G. R., Leavesley, M., Fairbairn, A., *et al.* (2010b). Human adaptation and plant use in Highland New Guinea 49,000 to 44,000 years ago. *Science*, **330**, 78–81.

Sutton, D. G. (1984). A paradigmatic shift in Polynesian prehistory: implications for New Zealand. *New Zealand Journal of Archaeology*, **9**, 135–56.

Swadling, P. and Hide, R. (2005). Changing landscape and social interaction: looking at agricultural history from a Sepik Ramu perspective. In *Papuan Pasts: Cultural, Linguistic and Biological Histories of Papuan-speaking Peoples*, ed. A. Pawley, R. Attenborough, J. Golson, and R. Hide. Canberra: Research School of Pacific and Asian Studies.

Tabbada, K. A., Trejaut, J., Loo, J. H., *et al.* (2010). Philippine mitochondrial DNA diversity: a populated viaduct between Taiwan and Indonesia? *Molecular Biology and Evolution*, **27**, 21–31.

Terrell, J. E. (2004a). Introduction: "Austronesia" and the great Austronesian migration. *World Archaeology*, **36**, 586–90.

Terrell, J. E. (2004b). The "sleeping giant" hypothesis and New Guinea's place in the prehistory of Greater Near Oceania. *World Archaeology*, **36**, 601–9.

Terrell, J. E., Kelly, K. M., and Rainbird, P. (2001). Foregone conclusions? In search of "Papuans" and "Austronesians". *Current Anthropology*, **42**, 97–124.

Tomkins, S. M. (1992). The influenza epidemic of 1918–19 in Western Samoa. *Journal of Pacific History*, **27**, 181–97.

Van Holst Pellekaan, S. M., Ingman, M., Roberts-Thomson, J., and Harding, R. M. (2006). Mitochondrial genomics identifies major haplogroups in Aboriginal Australians. *American Journal of Physical Anthropology*, **131**, 282–94.

Walter, R. (2004). New Zealand archaeology and its Polynesian connections. In *Change Through Time: 50 years of New Zealand Archaeology*, ed. L. Furey and S. Holdaway. Auckland: New Zealand Archaeological Society.

Walter, R., Jacomb, C., and Bowron-Muth, S. (2010). Colonisation, mobility and exchange in New Zealand prehistory. *Antiquity*, **84**, 497–513.

Weisler, M. I. and Kirch, P. V. (1996). Interisland and interarchipelago transfer of stone tools in prehistoric Polynesia. *Proceedings of the National Academy of Sciences of the United States of America*, **93**, 1381–5.

Whyte, A. L. H., Marshall, S. J., and Chambers, G. K. (2005). Human evolution in Polynesia. *Human Biology*, **77**, 157–77.

Wickler, S. (2001). *The Colonization of Western Micronesia and Early Settlement in Palau*.

Wickler, S. and Spriggs, M. (1988). Pleistocene human occupation of the Solomon Islands, Melanesia. *Antiquity*, **62**, 703–6.

Wilmshurst, J. M., Anderson, A. J., Higham, T. F. G., and Worthy, T. H. (2008). Dating the late prehistoric dispersal of Polynesians to New Zealand using the commensal Pacific rat. *Proceedings of the National Academy of Sciences*, **105**, 7676–80.

Wilmshurst, J. M., Hunt, T. L., Lipo, C. P., and Anderson, A. J. (2011). High-precision radiocarbon dating shows recent and rapid initial human colonization of East Polynesia. *Proceedings of the National Academy of Sciences*, **108**, 1815–20.

MARÍA DE LOURDES MUÑOZ, EDUARDO RAMOS,
ALVARO DÍAZ-BADILLO, MARÍA CONCEPCIÓN MORALES-
GÓMEZ, ROCÍO GÓMEZ, AND GERARDO PÉREZ-RAMIREZ

20
_____

Migration of pre-Hispanic and contemporary human Mexican populations

There is considerable interest in determining the exact route(s) taken by populations that entered the Americas, which would be expected to be genetically linked to many Asian lineages. However, some of the lineages of these American ancestors that were likely lost by drift through time may be unearthed by mitochondrial DNA (mtDNA) sequencing of the ancient populations that are revealed in a growing body of fossils in America, including Mexico. The most recent common ancestors in America are identifiable because their lineages survived from one generation to the next and have started their differentiation by means of accumulated mutations, defining the founder mtDNA. Consequently, the genetic studies of human Mexican populations is a research area will inform us about genetic markers specific to each population, their movement, and their relationship through time (Davis *et al.*, 2011; Ebenesersdóttir *et al.*, 2011; Martins *et al.*, 2011).

DNA is passed from one generation to the next; most of it is admixture, making each person unique from his or her parents. However, mtDNA passes from the mother to the child with no changes (with few exceptions). Mitochondrial DNA allows men and women to trace their maternal lineages; the non-recombinant region of the Y chromosome that passed intact only from father to son without any modification allows men to trace their paternal lineage. Both Y-chromosome DNA and mtDNA are subject to occasional mutations that become inheritable as genetic markers and then, after several

Causes and Consequences of Human Migration, ed. Michael H. Crawford and Benjamin C. Campbell. Published by Cambridge University Press. © Cambridge University Press 2012.

generations, a particular genetic marker is carried by almost all male and female inhabitants of the region where it arose (Terreros *et al.*, 2011; Wilder *et al.*, 2004). When people leave this region, they carry the marker with them, allowing the tracing of migration patterns of a given person's ancient ancestors. In addition, anthropological studies will complement genetic studies in answering the question of why people migrate. Because of the complexity of choosing every population in our study, we focus on the Mexican population, including the pre-Hispanic populations and the contemporary Mestizo populations. Accordingly, studying mitochondrial DNA will allow us to reveal the pattern of pre-Hispanic population migration. This is of particular importance since the American continent has been populated as a consequence of different migrations through time (Tarazona-Santos and Santos, 2002).

Although the study of autosomal DNA is also important, it is a random admixture of contributions from each parent, making it more complex: genetic recombination impedes the study of lineage as well as the study of the size of a randomly mating population that has the same rate of genetic drift as the population of interest (effective population size). This means that autosomal DNA studies represent a broad picture of an individual's heritage rather than a trail of specific ancestry. However, autosomal DNA should be also considered because this gives an idea of the allele distribution in a specific population and will help to elucidate the population structure demographic and bottleneck events, as well as the linkage disequilibrium patterns of the ancient and contemporary Mexican populations.

The first Paleo-Indians were descendants of Ice Age hunters from Asia (Goebel *et al.*, 2008; Horai *et al.*, 1993) who entered America, giving origin to Amerindians. They were nomadic hunter-gatherers, which is probably the original lifestyle of most indigenous people. The nomad life interfered with population growth and life expectancy was below 20 years of age. Eventually, humans distributed their activities among each other, forming specialized groups gaining experience in the development of tools, which in turn varied according to each specialized group. It is also suggested that they used at least two migration routes, coastal and inland, based on the distribution of two rare mtDNA haplogroups (Perego *et al.*, 2009).

The population composition in the Americas underwent a drastic change during the fifteenth century because of the arrival of Europeans and Africans (Figure 20.1). The admixture of these populations to the American native populations gives the contemporary Mexican populations, so-called Mestizo, an asymmetric admixture of the trihybrid ancestry.

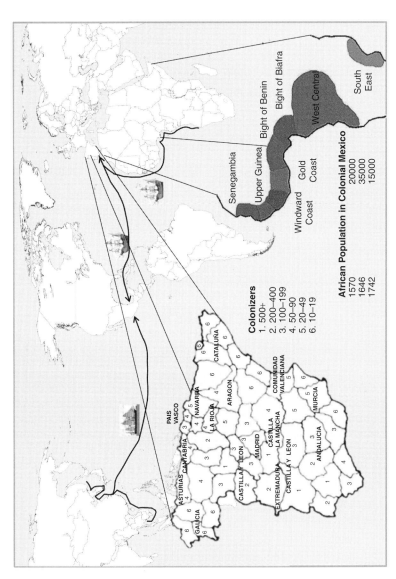

Figure 20.1 Spanish and African immigration to Mexico. The map displays Spaniard migrants and the African slaves that they brought during the Mexican Colonial period.

To understand the focus of our analysis on pre-Hispanic and contemporary human migration, first we will explain how the major pre-Hispanic Mexican populations were distributed and the hypothesis of their migrations.

MEXICAN PRE-HISPANIC POPULATIONS

The earliest civilization in Central America, and possibly in the American continent, was the Olmec civilization, believed to have originated around 1250 BCE. They originally lived in the Gulf Coast region of southern Mexico, but soon the population expanded into Guatemala. The four major Olmec cities were San Lorenzo Tenochtitlan, Laguna de los Cerros, Tres Zapotes, and La Venta, existing from between 1200 to 400 BCE. Around 300 BCE, the Olmec vanished for reasons that vanished with them. However, we do know that much of their culture and social structure was absorbed by other human groups. It is important to mention that this civilization first arose with the local ecology of well-watered alluvial soil, as well as by the transportation network that the Coatzacoalcos river basin provided in San Lorenzo Tenochtitlan. The Olmec were probably first in the chain of development of the Mesoamerican culture. This site was abandoned around 900 BCE, approximately at the same time that La Venta became very prosperous. Around 950 BCE there was an internal uprising; invasions or environmental changes destroyed many San Lorenzo monuments which resulted in the move of Olmec centers to La Venta. Olmec centers at La Venta lasted from 900 BCE until it was abandoned around 400 BCE. This depopulation was probably the result of very serious environmental changes that made the region unsuited for agriculture, in particular changes to the river that the Olmec used for agriculture, hunting, and transportation. The Tres Zapotes site, on the western edge of the Olmec heartland, was occupied beyond 400 BCE. Although people living in the Tres Zapotes site did not maintain all features of the Olmec culture, they were more closely related to post-Olmec culture, frequently labeled as Epi-Olmec, similar to those found at Izapa (550 km to the southeast). Colossal heads are characteristic of Olmec centers and they provide us with some idea of the nature of Olmec ideology and their culture sites (Medel y Alvarado, 1963; Santley, 2007).

After the Olmec civilization vanished, a new civilization began in the second century BCE in the valley of Mexico, which dominated this region for almost a millennium and stands as the most significant cultural influence throughout the history of Central American civilizations. This civilization was centered on the city of Teotihuacan and had over 100 000 people. It was one of the largest cities in the ancient world period (100 BCE). Teotihuacan was the religious center of Mesoamerica, dominated by two enormous pyramids called the Pyramid of the Sun and the Pyramid of the Moon. Around 700 CE, people simply stopped living in the city (Manzanilla-Naim and López-Luján; 1995).

Archaeological studies have suggested that between 10 000 and 6700 BCE, the populations in the Tehuacan Valley were made up of hunters. The years between 6000 and 5000 BCE were marked by an increasing sedentariness and population increase. In the ninth century BCE people from the Tehuacan Valley migrated to Teotihuacan. Thereafter, the city was transformed into a hub of development and attracted people from the surrounding localities. Then the city became cosmopolitan with a strong society and a great political, religious, military, and economic power. Around 900 CE, community life changed and the variety of cultivated plants increased and hunting practices diminished. The consequence of these changes was that human groups settled and exchanged surplus materials, such as food and tools. This was fundamental to their subsistence. Different products were no longer only for their own use – they were exported to other cities. Shells, jade, and turquoise were exported and imported, and these began to appear in funerary offerings.

Teotihuacan was conquered by northern tribes in 700 CE and began to rapidly decline in its influence over the Teotihuacan people. After the decline of Teotihuacan, the region had no centralized culture or political control for approximately one hundred years (Gallegos-Ruiz, 1997).

Toltecs from Tula, Hidalgo, began to dominate Central America by approximately 950 CE. They were a war-like people and expanded rapidly throughout the area of present-day Mexico, Guatemala, and the Yucatán peninsula. On top of their societal hierarchy there was a warrior aristocracy who were the teachers (Toltecatl) of the culture of Teotihuacan. They also expanded the cult of Quetzalcoatl (the Sovereign Feathered Serpent). They believed that Quetzalcoatl, the warrior-god driven out from Tula, was the creator of humanity, which would return some day. Around 1200 CE, their dominance over the region faded. The Toltec also conquered large areas controlled by the Mayan, settled and migrated as far south as the Yucatán peninsula. The culture born out of this fusion was called the Toltec–Maya. They preserved many of the Teotihuacan traditions (Florescano, 2004; Hooker, 1996b).

The Nahua-speaking people in the Valley of Mexico were Aztecs, while the culture that dominated the area belonged to a tribe of the

Mexica (regionally Chichimec) called the Tenochca. Apparently, the Mexica migrated from Aztlan in the northwest to the Valley of Mexico as early as the twelfth century CE, after the close of the Classic Period in Mesoamerica. They were a small nomadic group of people who, after approximately a century, settled in the small islands of the Lake Texcoco. In the year 1325, the Aztecs built their capital city Tenochtitlan (Chimalpain-Cuauhtlehuanitzin, 1998; López-Austin and López-Luján, 1996).

The Mayas, the best known classical civilization of Mesoamerica, built incredible cities on agricultural villages. They originated in Yucatán around 2600 BCE and came to prominence around 250 CE in southern Mexico, Guatemala, western Honduras, El Salvador, and northern Belize. From Olmec inventions and ideas, Mayans developed astronomy, a calendar system, and hieroglyphic writing. Evidence of settled habitation in Mexico, such as corn cultivation, basic pottery, and stone tools, has been found in the archaic period of 5000–1500 BCE. The relationship between the Olmecs and the Mayans is unknown; archaeologists have not established whether Mayans were their descendants, trading partners, or whether they had any other kind of relationship (Manrique-Castañeda *et al.*, 1988). Our genetic studies will contribute to this knowledge. Notably, some studies suggest that the Mayan civilization comprised populations from different origins (Martínez-Cortés *et al.*, 2010). For example it has been suggested that Mayans entered Yucatán from the west. It is believed that Itzammá, considered a sun god for the Mayan civilization, led the first migration from the Far East, beyond the ocean. The second historic migration was led from the west by Kukulcan, a miraculous priest and teacher, founder of the Mayan kingdom and civilization. Under Kukulcan, the people were divided into four tribes: the first one belonged to Kukulcan himself and established his residence at Mayapan, which thus became the capital of the whole nation. The Tutul-xiu held vassal rule at Uxmal, the Itzá at Chichen-Itzá, and the Chelé at Izamal. Later Mayapan was destroyed and split up into a number of independent minor states and part of the Itzá emigrated south to Lake Petén, Guatemala, where they established a kingdom with their capital and sacred city of Flores Island in the lake. After the Classic period, the Mayans migrated to the Yucatán peninsula (De la Garza and Ilia-Nájera-Coronado, 2002).

Chichen Itzá (near Valladolid, Mexico), Uxmal (near Merida, Mexico) and Mayanspán (west of Chichen Itzá) were the three most important cities during the Post Classic period. They lived in relative peace from around 1000 to 1100 CE when Mayanspán overthrew the confederation and ruled for over 200 years. In 1441 CE the Mayans who had previously ruled Uxmal destroyed the city of Mayanspán and founded a new city at Mani. Wars were fought between rival Mayan groups over the territory until the region was conquered by the Spanish (Hooker, 1996a).

Chichen Itzá was first populated between 500 and 900 CE by Mayans and for unknown reasons abandoned around 900 CE. The city was then resettled 100 years later and then invaded by Toltecs from the north. Finally the city was abandoned about 1300 CE. The Spanish killed all the Mayan priests and burned books when they arrived, resulting in much information being lost (Florescano, 2004).

The only period in which the urban centers were important to the Mayans was during the Classic period from 300 to 900 CE. The Maya culture placed an emphasis on urban centers and their structures in the religious life of the Mayas and the expansion of a literary culture. The Mayan urban centers were entirely used as religious centers for the rural populations surrounding them. The decline of the urban centers after 900 CE did not involve immense social change so much as religious change. It is believed that the abandonment of the cities was primarily due to religious proselytizing from the north. After the abandonment of the Classic Mayan cities, the Yucatán peninsula became the principal region of a new, synthetic culture called Toltec/Mayan, formed when Toltecs migrating from the north integrated with indigenous Maya peoples (Hooker, 1996b).

Based on the anthropological studies mentioned above, we are proposing a migration pattern of the major populations based on their culture (Figure 20.2). Because it is possible to trace the path of human

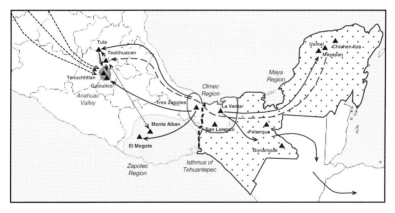

Figure 20.2   Map of pre-Hispanic population migrations. The map shows the Mexican pre-Hispanic population migrations based on archaeological history.

migrations by the bones found, their DNA and artifacts, we are studying genetically pre-Hispanic populations to determine whether each group was closely related or belonged to a different genetic group. Consequently, in our research we are analyzing all available ancient bones from the pre-Hispanic populations. This is important since cultural identity does not equal genetic identity. In other words, an ethnic group does not necessarily correspond to the same genetic origin. Therefore, our focus is on pre-Hispanic and contemporary populations to determine the genetic origin of populations and their migration patterns. This interdisciplinary research focuses on tracing migrations through archaeological, anthropological, and genetic studies. Furthermore, we are giving a picture of the genetic relationships among populations and the allele variability. This study will tell us also how long an indigenous population has lived in a region.

DNA results will also provide information on the sex of ancient individuals when the bones are not well preserved or when they are from children (De La Cruz *et al.*, 2008). A good example of these studies was the sex determination of the Peñon skeleton, where some controversies existed, and where it was determined that the skeleton was from a woman (Martínez-Meza *et al.*, 2005).

New computerized tools have allowed researchers to record the sequence of many human genes, giving us the opportunity to compare and contrast the genes of diverse people within a few months. Scientists are now able to test human migration patterns to attempt to show the distribution of ethnic genetic codes over certain geographic areas in relation to time. We expect that information from our research will help to build the Mexican family tree from its roots in Africa to its branches out to the Americas; also to reveal the secrets of our common ancestry, and to use the similarities and differences to explain susceptibilities to various diseases.

The analysis of DNA from many ancient skeletons and mummies (Bustos-Ríos *et al.*, 2008; Herrera-Salazar *et al.*, 2008; Kim *et al.*, 2010, 2011; López-Armenta *et al.*, 2008; Muñoz *et al.*, 2003; Ottoni *et al.*, 2011) is usually performed on the mtDNA; it offers the best chance of isolating DNA from ancient samples since it is circular and the cell has many copies. In addition, it is known that mtDNA mutates at a higher rate compared with nuclear DNA (approximately one mutation in every 10 000 years).

Wallace and his colleagues (1999) constructed a world female genetic tree based on mitochondrial DNA. They found that nearly all American Indians have lineages belonging to haplogroups named A, B, C, and D. Europeans belong to lineages H through K and T through X. In

Asia the ancestral lineage is known as M, with descendant branches E, F, and G. In Africa there is a single main lineage, known as L, which is divided into three branches. L3, the youngest branch, is common in East Africa and is believed to be the source of the American, Asian, and European lineages.

HUMAN MTDNA STUDIES IN RECENT YEARS

Studies of mitochondrial DNA have made this molecule one of the most extensively investigated in genetic systems because of its abundance in human cells, its non-recombining mode of inheritance, its high mutation rate compared with that of the nuclear genome, and because it is uniparental. Knowledge of mtDNA sequence variation is rapidly accumulating, and the field of anthropological genetics, which initially made use of only the first hypervariable segment (HVS-1) of mtDNA, is currently being transformed by complete mtDNA genome analysis (Pereira *et al.*, 2009). We have sequenced DNA from bones of pre-Hispanic Mexican populations from Monte Albán, Oaxaca, and Teotihuacán, Mexico, and determined their relationship with contemporary populations from Mexico City, Michoacán, and Torreon by using Median Network analysis (Figure 20.3). The size of the circle in the network is proportional to the frequency of each haplotype. All the sequences from the pre-Hispanic populations pertain to haplogroup D. In addition, the two haplotypes of the individuals from Monte Albán survive in the contemporary populations of Mixtecs from Brazil and from the Dominican Republic since the sequences were grouped in the major node (labeled with the star symbol in Figure 20.3) containing sequences from the GenBank (2011) pertaining to those populations (Table 20.1). Mitochondrial DNA haplotypes from the samples from Teotihuacan were different compared with all the haplotypes included in this study. It will be necessary to include more sequences to confirm if these haplotypes are specific to the people from this archaeological site and if they came from Monte Albán since archaeological studies have suggested that they migrated from Monte Albán.

Contemporary combined sources offer approximately 65 000 HVS-I records (Behar *et al.*, 2007) and over 5140 complete mtDNA sequences (Pereira *et al.*, 2009). There are several available sources that offer mtDNA records: GenBank (2011), Mamit-tRNA (2011), MitoMaster (2011), MitoMap (2011), and MtDB (2011). This information will also be useful in our studies.

The origin of indigenous migrations of pre-Hispanic populations was tied to the religious and powerful cities which have not changed

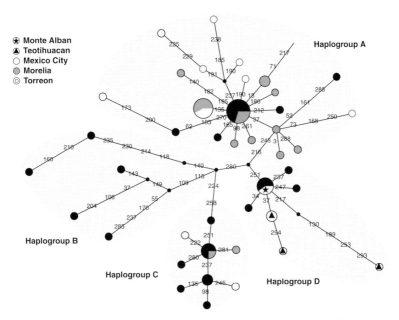

Figure 20.3   Median Network analysis of sequences from pre-Hispanic
and contemporary Mexican populations. Haplogroup and haplotype of the
pre-Hispanic and contemporary mtDNA sequences of the hypervariable
region I were analyzed by Network software. Two samples from Monte
Albán and 4 from Teotihuacan were grouped in the branch of haplogroup
D; 7 and 2 samples from Mexico City were clustered in haplogroups A and
C respectively; 19 and 2 samples from Michoacán were clustered in
haplogroups A and C respectively; and 2 samples from Torreon were in
haplogroup A.

since then. Migration of indigenous people in Mexico now is linked to
industrialization and to the transformation from an agricultural-based
economy to an urban industrialized economy in the 1940s. Table 20.2
shows some of the factors that have affected Mexican populations and
encouraged their migrations. This change lowered the level of agricultural production in the indigenous areas, which became marginalized;
investment was favored in northwestern Mexico, where commercial
agriculture began to rapidly develop. Thus, the indigenous labor force
migrated in the direction of commercial development, especially after
1980 (Table 20.3). The Purepéchas of Michoacán began to migrate to the
United States in the 1940s (Table 20.4). Some indigenous populations,
such as Maya communities from Yucatán, had already acquired the
tradition of migrating as a result of religious feasts. Among Zapotecs

Table 20.1. *GenBank accession number of sequences included in the haplotype network analysis*

Haplogroup	Isolate	Region	GenBank Accession Number
A	As1A	Asian	AY195760
	Cuban A2	Cuba	HQ198250
	Na5A	Native American	AY195786
	Mixe031	Mexico	EU719927
	Huichol56	Mexico	EU719811
	Cora52	Mexico	EU719679
	Mixtec057	Mexico	EU720004
	Zapotec079	Mexico	EU720308
	NahuaCu008	Mexico	EU720078
	Huichol06	Mexico	EU719797
B	M1a1e	USA	EF060333
	Na1B	Native_American	AY195749
	Piman_B	USA	AF347001
	ORA131B	Malaysia	BDQ981472
	TGR87B	Indonesia	DQ981465
C	Asian5C	Asian	AY195772
	Na4C	Native_American	AY195759
	C1b2a	Puerto_Rico	GQ397486
	NahuaAt42	Mexico	EU720071
	NahuaAt64	Mexico	EU720073
	Zapotec055	Mexico	EU720339
	Zapotec046	Mexico	EU720336
	NahuaCu039	Mexico	EU720102
	Pima103	Mexico	EU720202
D	Na2D	Native_American	AY195748
	PilaFor044	Argentina	EU034320
	Tor25	Dominican_Republic	EF079876
	BraSC113	Brazil	GQ449339
	D1-1-10	China	DQ282486
	Mixtec050	Mexico	EU720029

and Mixtecs from Oaxaca, migration was linked traditionally to the commercial activities of the isthmus of Tehuantepec.

Initially, there was at least one member of the household who emigrated, a phenomenon found in all the 56 indigenous groups of the country. This was reinforced through time and slowly began to include brothers, sons, and kinfolk, until it became a mass migration that

Table 20.2. *Motivation of indigenous migration*

	Indigenous group affected
Ecological factors	
Low productivity of lands	Oaxaca, Mountains (Guerrero), the Tarahumara Sierra, Otomi, and Mazahua (Hidalgo)
Climatological phenomena: droughts, frosts, hurricanes	Huasteca region, Tarahumara Sierra, and the coast
Soil deterioration due to the introduction of commercial products	Yucatán, Huasteca, Campeche Petroleum area
Down-time in the rain-fed, traditional agricultural cycle	Affecting all indigenous regions
Land tenure	
Lack of lands and land conflicts due to illegal encroachment	Huasteca (Chiapas) and the Huichol region of Jalisco
Large-scale domestic animal production requiring extensive grasslands	Huasteca (Chiapas) and Totonacas area (Veracruz)
Construction of dams, roads, and industrial plants	Petroleum-producing area of Veracruz, Isthmus of Tehuantepec, the Tarahumara Sierra, and the Papaloapan River
Lower prices of the cash commercial crops	
Coffee, henequen, sugar, tobacco, cocoa, tomato, citric, and others	Chiapas, Huasteca (San Luis Potosí), Northern Sierra of Puebla, Totonaca region (Veracruz), Mazahuas and Otomis (State of Mexico, the Chontals (Oaxaca), Huichol region (Jalisco), Peninsula of Yucatán
Inter-ethnic and armed conflicts and military incursion	Mountain of Guerrero
Resettlement and involuntary relocation	
Due to assignment of lands to new non-indigenous–Mestizo colonizers	Chiapas, Nahuas of Michoacán, Mazahuas and Otomis (States of Hidalgo and Mexico)
Inter-ethnic conflicts, armed conflict and military occupation	Mountain of Guerrero
Social and demographic factors	
Lack of basic social services	Most of the indigenous regions focus on the mountains (Guerrero, Oaxaca, and Chiapas states)
Demographic pressure	Most of the indigenous regions with exception of the northern states
Religious conflicts	Chiapas, Guerrero, and some communities of Oaxaca and Michoacán

Table 20.3. *Attraction poles for indigenous groups and number of migrants*

Indigenous group	Attraction pole	Migrants (number)
Mixteco (Oaxaca)	Ensenada Baja California	12 073
	Tijuana Baja California Norte	3 542
	La Paz Baja California Sur	1 285
	Culiacán, Sinaloa	2 909
	Novolato, Sinaloa	2 805
Zapoteco (Oaxaca)	Ensenada Baja California Norte	2 228
Triqui (Oaxaca)	Ensenada Baja California Norte	1 770
Nahua from different	Monterrey, Nuevo León	1 775
states	Tampico, Tamaulipas	1 560
	Altamira, Tamaulipas	1 321
	Matamoros Tamaulipas	11 296

Table 20.4. *Indigenous groups and areas of attraction*

Ethnic group	Areas of attraction	Job market
Mixtecos Mazahuas Mayas, Yaquis, Huichol	California, Oregon, New York, Los Angeles, Florida, Washington, Watsonville, Livingston County, and San Jose	Agricultural work: strawberry, cucumber, grape, vegetables, tomato. Services: hotels, restaurants, dry cleaning, servants, clothes, factories, construction, gardening.
Purepecha, Zapotec, Triqui, Mazatec	Northern California, San Diego County, San Joaquin Valley, Santa Cruz	Informal market. Sales of flowers, fruits, jewelry, tortillas.

included women as well. The major centers of attraction in the country are Mexico City, Veracruz, and the State of Mexico (National Population Council, CONAPO, 2010). Table 20.5 and Figure 20.4 display states of attraction for the largest indigenous populations. Mexico City has the largest concentration of indigenous people throughout the entire country. Furthermore, the country has received indigenous refugees from Guatemala, especially from the Kanjabal, Ixil, Chuj, Cakchiquel, and Jacalteco groups. Their presence is congruent with solidarity among indigenous peoples, which has enriched the historically important

Table 20.5. *States of attraction of the largest indigenous populations*

State	Number
Distrito Federal	117 760
Veracruz	76 482
State of Mexico	57 638
Sinaloa	18 577
Campeche	17 695
Baja California	17 454
Quintana Roo	10 426
Jalisco	9 508
Tabasco	6 138
Total	**343 863**

Note: This corresponds to 81.7% of the total indigenous internal migration in the country (CONAPO, 2010; Granados-Alcantar, 2005).

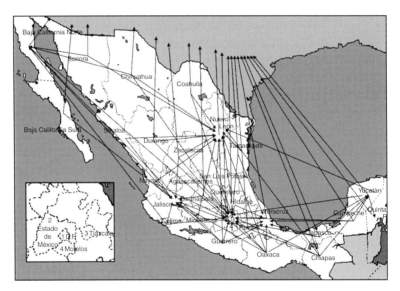

Figure 20.4   Map of contemporary Mexican population migrations. The map shows migrations within Mexico and to the United States of America.

exchange among the indigenous Maya groups and increased Mexico's rich cultural diversity.

Long-term migration (of at least a year) has been detected by analyzing information about birthplace and current place of residence. A total of 450 000 indigenous language speakers lived in a place other than their place of birth in 1990, representing 8.7% of the total nationally. The highest migration percentage was from Oaxaca with over one third of the total and Yucatán with slightly over one sixth of the total. Mexico City is the predominant pole of attraction followed by the State of Mexico and Quintana Roo state. These account for 43% of the total indigenous interstate migration of the country.

The largest migratory flow between two states is that of the Mayas from the state of Yucatán to the state of Quintana Roo. The Maya migration can be attributed to preference to remain in their traditional habitat. In contrast, migrants from Oaxaca are away from their traditional habitat in Mexico City, the State of Mexico and Veracruz. Within Mexico City, the areas with most indigenous migrants are ranked as follows:

Gustavo A. Madero > Cuauhtémoc > Iztapalapa > Miguel Hidalgo > Álvaro Obregón > Xochimilco > Milpa Alta

Some temporary migratory streams go from the center and northwest, starting with the sugarcane harvest in Morelos and Puebla, to the Federal District, continuing to the region of Baja California and from there to Guadalajara. From there migrants proceed to Zacatecas, Durango, and Chihuahua up to Ciudad Juárez, or from Zacatecas move on to Nuevo León and from there to the border region of the state of Tamaulipas, where they are employed in informal and marginal economic activities in the urban area and often cross the border into the United States (Figure 20.4).

Colonization of new lands is also associated with permanent migration and occurs mainly in the southern state of Chiapas and the Lacandon jungle. This region received an influx of internal migrants (Choles, Zoques, Tzotziles, Tojolabales, and Tzeltal) and others from Veracruz, Zacatecas, Jalisco, and Michoacán. Migrants from northern Mexico and Purepécha populations from Veracruz and Michoacán have also settled in the states of Campeche and Quintana Roo. The state of Tabasco also became a pole of attraction for indigenous migrants due to the petroleum industry and to the project of the Plan Chontalpa. In addition, there were a series of new colonies installed permanently in the Huasteca region (National Geographic and Statistical Institute, INEGI, 2010).

Northern Mexico and the United States are of enormous attraction to indigenous migrants because they are sources of secure employment, such as in the ranches of San Quintín in Baja California or in the vegetable farms close to the border. They are usually employed as peons or construction workers, incorporated in the service sector or in the formal economy of cities like Tijuana and Mexicali. From there they go to California via San Diego and are received by indigenous organizations (Mixtecs or Purepéchas) installed in the main cities.

Contemporary migrations can be also tested by sequencing the mtDNA; Figure 20.3 displays the Median Network analysis of individuals from Mexico City, Michoacán, and Torreón. Our study found that some people from Michoacán contained haplogroups A, have the same haplotype as Zapotec, Cona, Mixe, Nahua, and Hichol (Figure 20.3, Table 20.1); and also those from Michoacán with haplogroup C are in the same node (the largest circle in the network, Figure 20.3) as Zapotec and people from Puerto Rico (Figure 20.3, Table 20.1). Furthermore, samples from Mexico City and Michoacán were clustered in haplogroups A and C. The node (colored in white and gray in Figure 20.3) showed that samples from Mexico City and from Morelia in Michoacán had the same haplotype, suggesting migration from Michoacán to México City. Finally, samples from Torreon displayed haplogroup A, but the haplotypes were specific for the individuals from this city (Figure 20.3). These studies will allow a better picture of pre-Hispanic and contemporary population migrations in Mexico when we have more mtDNA sequences representative of all populations.

Temporary migration of indigenous people as agricultural workers is of great importance, since their labor force is critical to the viability of the most important agroindustrial crops.

In conclusion, migrations result from multiple factors (Table 20.2) that make some cities attractive poles to populations due to their economical, political, and religious power.

ACKNOWLEDGMENTS

This work was supported by the "Instituto de Ciencia y Tecnología del D. F. ICYT-DF" PICSA10−189 (01/11/2010−2011). We thank all members of the Multidisciplinary Network of Pre-Hispanic and Contemporary group for their discussions. We want to thank Isabel Mercado-Gonzalez and Ivan I. Hernandez for the critical review of the English language of this manuscript.

REFERENCES

Behar, D. M., Rosset, S., Blue-Smith, J., *et al.* (2007). Genographic Consortium. The Genographic Project public participation mitochondrial DNA database. *PLoS Genetics*, **3**, e104.

Bustos-Ríos, D., López-Armenta, M., Moreno-Galeana, M. A., *et al.* (2008). Purification of DNA from an ancient child mummy from Sierra Gorda, Queretaro. In *Mummies and Science: World Mummies Research/Proceedings of the VI World Congress on Mummy Studies (Teguise, Lanzarote)*, ed. P. Atoche, C. Rodríguez, and A. Ramírez, p. 700. Santa Cruz de Tenerife: Academia Canaria de la Historia Ayuntamiento de Teguise, Cabildo Insular de Lanzarote, Caja Canarias, Fundación Canaria Mapfre Guanarteme, Universidad de las Palmas de Gran Canaria.

Chimalpain-Cuauhtlehuanitzin, D. (1998). *Las ocho relaciones y el memorial de Colhuacan*, ed. R. Tena. Mexico City: CONACULTA (Cien de Mexico).

CONAPO (2010). Migración urbana. www.conapo.gob.mx/publicaciones/sdm/sdm2010/10.pdf.

Davis, M. C., Novak, S. J., and Hampikian, G. (2011). Mitochondrial DNA analysis of an immigrant Basque population: loss of diversity due to founder effects. *American Journal of Physical Anthropology*, **144**, 516–25.

De La Cruz, I., Gonzalez-Oliver, A., Kemp, B. M., *et al.* (2008). Sex identification of children sacrificed to the ancient Aztec rain gods in Tlatelolco. *Current Anthropology*, **49**, 519–26.

De la Garza, M. and Ilia-Nájera-Coronado, M. (2002). Religión maya. In *Enciclopedia Iberoamericana de Religiones*, Vol. 2. Madrid: Editorial Trotta.

Ebenesersdóttir, S. S., Sigurðsson, A., Sánchez-Quinto, F., *et al.* (2011). A new subclade of mtDNA haplogroup C1 found in Icelanders: evidence of pre-Columbian contact? *American Journal of Physical Anthropology*, **144**, 92–9.

Florescano, E. (2004). Quetzalcóatl y los mitos fundadores de Mesoamérica. Tauru, Mexico: Santillana Ediciones Generales.

Gallegos-Ruiz, R. (1997). *Antología de documentos para la historia de la arqueología de Teotihuacán: Proyecto Historia de la Arqueología de Teotihuacan*. México, D.F.: Instituto Nacional de Antropología e Historia.

GenBank (2011). www.ncbi.nlm.nih.gov/Genbank/index.html.

Goebel, T., Waters, M. R., and O'Rourke, D. H. (2008). The late Pleistocene dispersal of modern humans in the Americas. *Science*, **319**, 1497–502.

Granados-Alcantar, J. A. (2005). Las nuevas zonas de atracción de migrantes indígenas en México. *Investigaciones Geográficas, Boletín del Instituto de Geografía, UNAM*, **58**, 140–7.

Herrera-Salazar, A., Bustos-Ríos, D., López-Armenta, M., *et al.* (2008). Mitochondrial DNA analysis of mummies from the North of Mexico. In *Mummies and Science: World Mummies Research/Proceedings of the VI World Congress on Mummy Studies (Teguise, Lanzarote)*, ed. P. Atoche, C. Rodríguez, and A. Ramírez, p. 417. Santa Cruz de Tenerife: Academia Canaria de la Historia Ayuntamiento de Teguise, Cabildo Insular de Lanzarote, Caja Canarias, Fundación Canaria Mapfre Guanarteme, Universidad de las Palmas de Gran Canaria.

Hooker, R. (1996a). The Mayans. In *Civilizations in America*, ed. R. Hooker. Pullman, WA: Washington State University. www.wsu.edu/~dee/CIVAMRCA/MAYAS.HTM.

Hooker, R. (1996b). The Toltecs. In *Civilizations in America*, ed. R. Hooker. Pullman, WA: Washington State University ./www.wsu.edu/~dee/CIVAMRCA/TOLTECS.HTM.

Horai, S., Kondo, R., Nakagawa-Hattori, Y., *et al.* (1993). Peopling of the Americas, founded by four major lineages of mitochondrial DNA. *Molecular Biology and Evolution*, **10**, 23–47.

INEGI (2010). Demografía y población. www.inegi.org.mx/Sistemas/temasV2/Default.aspx?s=est&c=17484.

Kim, A. J., Kim, K., Choi, J. H., *et al.* (2010). Mitochondrial DNA analysis of ancient human bones excavated from Nukdo island, S. Korea. *Biochemistry and Molecular Biology Reports*, **43**, 133–9.

Kim, N. Y., Lee, H. Y., Park, M. J., Yang, W. I., and Shin, K. J. (2011). A genetic investigation of Korean mummies from the Joseon Dynasty. *Molecular Biology Reports*, **38**, 115–21.

López-Armenta, M., Bustos-Ríos, D., Moreno-Galeana, M. A., *et al.* (2008). Genetic origin of a mummy from Queretaro (Pepita). In *Mummies and Science: World Mummies Research/Proceedings of the VI World Congress on Mummy Studies (Teguise, Lanzarote)*, ed. P. Atoche, C. Rodríguez, and A. Ramírez, p. 251. Santa Cruz de Tenerife: Academia Canaria de la Historia Ayuntamiento de Teguise, Cabildo Insular de Lanzarote, Caja Canarias, Fundación Canaria Mapfre Guanarteme, Universidad de las Palmas de Gran Canaria.

López-Austin, A. and López-Luján, L. (1996). *El Pasado Indígena*. Mexico, D.F.: Fondo de Cultura Economica.

Mamit-tRNA (2011). Compilation of mammalian mitochondrial tRNAs. http:// mamit-trna.u-strasbg.fr/.

Manrique-Castañeda, L., *et al.* (1988). Lingüística. In *Atlas Cultural de Mexico*, pp. 56–139. Mexico, D.F.: Secretaria de Educacion Publica, Instituto Nacional de Antrologia e Historia y Grupo Editorial Planeta.

Manzanilla-Naim, L. and López-Luján, L. (1995). *Historia Antigua de Mexico* (3 vols.). Mexico, D.F.: INAH, UNAM, Editorial Porrúa.

Martínez-Cortés, G., Nuño-Arana, I., Rubi-Castellanos, R., *et al.* (2010). Origin and genetic differentiation of three Native Mexican groups (Purépechas, Triquis and Mayas): contribution of CODIS-STRs to the history of human populations of Mesoamerica. *Annals of Human Biology*, **37**, 801–19.

Martínez-Meza, A., Moreno-Galeana, M., Díaz-Badillo, A., Maya, L., and Muñoz, M. L. (2005). Fin de la controversia: El Hombre de Tepexpan es molecularmente una mujer. *Diario del Campo*, **77**, 37–9.

Martins, J. A., de Freitas Figueiredo, R., Yoshizaki, C. S., Paneto, G. G., and Cicarelli, R. M. (2011). Genetic data of 15 autosomal STR loci: an analysis of the Araraquara population colonization (São Paulo, Brazil). *Molecular Biology Reports*, **38**, 5397–403.

Medel y Alvarado, L. (1963). Historia de San Andrés Tuxtla. In *Colección Suma Veracruzana*. Mexico, D.F.: Editorial Citlaltépetl.

MitoMap (2011). www.mitomap.org/.

MitoMaster (2011). http://mitomaster.research.chop.edu/MITOMASTER.

MtDB (2011). www.genpat.uu.se/mtDB/.

Muñoz, M. L., Moreno-Galeana, M., Díaz Badillo, A., *et al.* (2003). Análisis de DNA mitocondrial de una población prehispánica de Monte Albán, Oaxaca, Mexico. In *Antropología y Biodiversidad*, Vol. 2, ed. M. Pilar Aluja, A. Malgosa, and R. M. A Nogués, pp. 170–82. Barcelona, Spain: Ediciones Bellaterra S.L.

Ottoni, C., Ricaut, F. X., Vanderheyden, N., *et al.* (2011). Mitochondrial analysis of a Byzantine population reveals the differential impact of multiple historical events in South Anatolia. *European Journal of Human Genetics*, **19**, 571–6.

Perego, U. A., Achilli, A., Angerhofer, N., *et al.* (2009). Distinctive Paleo-Indian migration routes from Beringia marked by two rare mtDNA haplogroups. *Current Biology*, **19**, 1–8.

Pereira, L., Freitas, F., Fernandes, V., *et al.* (2009). The diversity present in 5140 human mitochondrial genomes. *American Journal of Human Genetics*, **84**, 628–40.

Santley, R. S. (2007). The culture history of the Tuxtlas. In *The Prehistory of the Tuxtlas*, pp. 24–78. Albuquerque, NM: University of New Mexico Press.

Tarazona-Santos, E. and Santos, F. R. (2002). The peopling of the Americas: a second major migration? *American Journal of Human Genetics*, **70**, 1377–80.

Terreros, M. C., Rowold, D. J., Mirabal, S., and Herrera, R. J. (2011). Mitochondrial DNA and Y-chromosomal stratification in Iran: relationship between Iran and the Arabian Peninsula. *Journal of Human Genetics*, **56**, 235–46.

Wallace, D. C., Brown, M. D., and Lott, M. T. (1999). Mitochondrial DNA variation in human evolution and disease. *Gene*, **238**, 211–30.

Wilder, J. A., Mobasher, Z., and Hammer, M. F. (2004). Genetic evidence for unequal effective population sizes of human females and males. *Molecular Biology and Evolution*, **21**, 2047–57.

21

A review of the Tupi expansion in the Amazon

"The Araweté say that the souls of the dead, once they have arrived in the heavens, are devoured by the Maï, the gods, who then resuscitate them from the bones; they then become like gods, immortal." Eduardo Viveiro de Castro, 1992

INTRODUCTION

This chapter discusses the relationship between the largest language stock in the lowlands of South America and its correlation with the archaeological evidence recovered in Amazonia. In spite of many descriptive and ethnohistorical reports, the correlation and association between language and archaeological material still is a difficult problem to solve (Moore and Storto, 2002). Verifying the material culture with the language of extinct societies is a challenge, but advances in archaeological research are improving the resolution of the past view.

During the last two decades research in the region is gaining support from different Amazonian researchers through a mixing of disciplines that is increasing the amount of data related to ancient human occupation in the area. By combining information from ethnohistorical research, archaeological survey, geography, linguistics, and other social sciences, it has been possible to develop an explanation of the center of the origin of the Proto-Tupi languages and other linguistic groups, as well as their expansion through the lowlands of South America (Balée, 1993, 1994; Balée and Erickson, 2006; Caycedo, 2005; Denevan, 2001; Gomes, 2002, 2008; Heckenberger, 2005, 2008; Neves, 1999, 2008; Noelli, 1998, 2008; Pärssinen *et al.*, 2009; Rodrigues, 2005,

Causes and Consequences of Human Migration, ed. Michael H. Crawford and Benjamin C. Campbell. Published by Cambridge University Press. © Cambridge University Press 2012.

2007; Rostain, 1994; Roosevelt, 1991; Schaan, 2004, 2008; Versteeg and Rostain, 1997; Woods *et al.*, 2009). First, a presentation of a background is necessary, followed by the results of the research in the Central Amazon. Details of excavations and associated coring and soil chemical analyses will not be presented here, but indications will be provided of their results.

It is proposed that the success of these skilled agriculturalists resulted in population increases necessitating expansions of members of the societies into the territories of other groups. These outward movements were not peaceful ones, but involved great bellicosity, successes in warfare, and cannibalism against former resident populations across Greater Amazonia (e.g. Carneiro, 2007). The presence of contemporaneous defensive enclosures and rapid changes in both ceramics and settlement forms provide further evidence for these propositions. Continued contact between the various invasive groups strongly suggests expansion and *not* migration as the predominant process.

WHAT IS THE TUPI OR MACRO-TUPI?

The Tupi is actually a stock language with many different families which include many distinct languages. The Macro-Tupi Group (MTG) is the total of them. The main and best detailed family of the MTG is the Tupi-Guarani (Arion, 1958; Lemle, 1971). The languages inside the Tupi-Guarani family are more similar than the other four macro-language groups in Brazil: the Tupi, Carib, Ge, and Arawak, plus the isolated related languages. In comparison with other regions, such as Africa or Australia, Amazonia has the most diversity of stocks and families of languages per unit area (Balée, 2000; Rodrigues, 1984/85). The Tupi languages present ten different families associated genetically with a remote Proto-Tupi: Tupi-Guarani, Tupari, Mondé, Arikém, Ramaráma, Mundurukú, Jurúna, Awetí, Mawé (Sateré), and Puruborá (Rodrigues, 1984/85; 2007:168).

Rodrigues (1986:29) compares the MTG with the Romantic languages inside the Indo-European stock and suggests 2000 years of separation between them. The Tupi-Guarani is one of the ten families of the MTG and it contains 40 languages and represents the largest group among the ten Tupi language families.

Considered the most widespread family in the lowlands of Amazonia and also the meridional portion of South America (Figure 21.1), the Tupi-Guarani languages are mainly distributed (1) in the southern interfluvial zone between the Madeira and Tapajós rivers;

South America

Figure 21.1 The Amazon and adjacent river basins.

(2) in the southeastern interfluvial zone between Xingu and Tocantions rivers; (3) in the Paraguay River drainage (Guarani); and (4) along the northeastern Brazilian coast (Coastal Tupi) (Heckenberger, 2008:947). During the contact period the Tupi-Guarani family languages were spread from the eastern Peruvian lowlands to the Brazilian Atlantic coast and from Venezuela to Paraguay (Brochado, 1989; Rodrigues, 1958).

Therefore, the language similarities shared by the Tupi-Guarani across such a huge territory call for explanation. Languages are considered genetically related when they share structure and lexical characteristics (Rodrigues, 1984/85:34). Language properties: (1) tend to change constantly; and (2) when a community splits apart, with total or partial interruption of communication, a linguistic differentiation starts (Rodrigues, 1984/85:34). The time depth (of the separation of the communities) is responsible for the degree of language distinction; the longer the time of separation the bigger the differences. This begins with a simple dialect distinction, passing to a family, until the proto-language is reached (Rodrigues, 1984/85:34). This chapter is centered on the Tupi-Guarani groups and their significance for the understanding of the precolonial history in the lowlands of South America.

CHARACTERISTICS OF THE TUPI GROUPS

The first explorers to the Amazonian region described the costumes and languages of the peoples they encountered. Some of their accounts presented common characteristics within distinct geographic areas, especially for the extensive Tupi-Guarani family. The most detailed reports came from the Brazilian coast, where the groups had been contacted during the first decades of the colonization process.

Mobility (geographic mobility) is a central characteristic of the Tupi-Guarani language groups, but the linguistic concept cannot say if it was due to ecological or cultural factors. The ecological adaptation was stressed by Meggers (1971, 1973, 1977) as the principal issue for the mobility of the Indians in the lowlands of South America. According to this author, changes in the environment (such as long-term droughts) adversely affected human communities and these coupled with the poor tropical soils forced the Indians into a situation of constant movement (Meggers, 1971, 1973, 1977; 1979). Meggers (1979) also uses the concept of climatic fluctuation during the Holocene to apply a model that explains the precolonial language dispersion and archaeological pattern of mobility (Meggers, 1977; 1979). But, an environmental explanation alone cannot be enough to understand the expansion of the geographical occupation of these groups. What is really surprising when one pays close attention to the domain occupied by the Tupi-Guarani family language is the extensive territory encompassed by these groups. Father Anchieta was the first to record the languages on the Brazilian coast and wrote about the grammar of the most used language. He published his findings in 1595 (Anchieta, 1933), in which he described the similarity of the languages in this region. Currently, through anthropological works in association with ethnohistory it is possible to say that the mobility of the Tupi groups was for other reasons than just ecological adaptations.

In spite of distinct social organizations found in the current societies, there are some geographic inventories of the cultural material of native groups in Brazil. Alfred Métraux identified homogeneous cultural material among these societies such as: manioc, maize, cotton, and tobacco cultivation; bows and arrows; fishing with poison and man-made dams; wooden mortars; hammocks; mantles of plumes; painted ceramics; the collection of trophy heads, and others (Métraux, 1928:301–2). The resemblance between similarities and differences among these societies is intriguing. However, similarities in some material culture items do not correspond with the enormous hetero-geneity in their social morphology. There is distinct variability in their village morphologies, kinship, ceremonies, warfare, and the import-ance of shamanism (Viveiros de Castro, 1992:24). Settlement types range from nomadic hunters' temporary camps (Guajá, Sirionó, Aché) to complex and expanded, semi-permanent to permanent Tupinambá agricultural villages. But, as pointed out by Viveiros de Castro, there is more than linguistics homogeneity as a unifying factor among them. The linguistic homogeneity allowed accessing the commonly held mythology, religion, and institutional vocabulary that continued for centuries (Viveiros de Castro, 1992:26). Through ethnobotanical research, Balée (2000:399) was able to reconstruct the precolonial bio-logical knowledge through comparisons based on historical linguistics and modern ethnology among the varieties of domesticated and semi-domesticated species of plants and the identification of anthropogenic forests formed by palms, bamboo, lianas, and Brazilian nut species in many parts of Amazonia (Balée, 1989).

The variability in the settlement forms might be another example of divergence of associated pressures during the colonization period which was responsible for large numbers of deaths and the virtual extinction of many groups. The deadly influence of the colonization process on indigenous social organization is described in numerous sources and has been summarized by Fernades (1963). But, according to our investigation another reason for the village morphology variabil-ity could be linked with economic issues (and not just ecological or cultural); that is, the use of the fertile soil for food production in areas with Amazonian Dark Earths (ADE) (Rebellato et al., 2009).

During the precolonial period, the distribution of similar pottery assemblages identifies the large amount of territory occupied by the same chronostylistic tradition; that is, that generally related to the polychromic painted and corrugated ceramics (Brochado, 1989; Meggers, 1977, 1979; Noelli, 1998). The question is, why were those groups moving so far, reaching long distances, and settling in different landscapes?

Métraux (1928) analyzed the first chronicled descriptions of the terror engendered by the anthropophagical rituals conducted by native peoples on each other and on captured Europeans. Some of these latter ultimately escaped and provided accounts of their ordeal (Léry, 1990 [1578]; Staden, 1948 [1557]; Thevet, 1978 [1575]). Cannibalism was a characteristic of the Tupi-Guarani family groups and represented a vendetta against their enemies (Métraux, 1928). Viveiros de Castro (1992) pointed out that the association with exocannibalism represented more than warfare and was part of a revenge–conquest system in the strict sense. The cannibalism also was impelling the social machine towards the future (Viveiros de Castro, 1992:274). Through a complex cosmological triad matrix nature/culture/supernature, Viveiros de Castro interpreted the significance of culture (the current world) for the Araweté groups understood as immature and the dead as the final "built" soul. The interpretation of H. Clastres (1975) related the prophetic "land-without-evil" and the political-religion in the groups. Looking for paradise on earth, these groups had to be in movement and it was better to be in the belly of the enemy than buried in the grave, so that they could reach the paradise on earth. Thus, such sacrifice is essential for social reproduction and the relation-to-the-enemy; therefore, cannibalism was (literally) an incorporation of enmity in order to reach the immortality for both eaters and eaten; moreover, the cannibal ritual unified all the Tupinamba (Viveiros de Castro, 1992:286). The system was based in consistent warfare periods that also can be regarded as a mobility-compelling force pushing incursions toward surrounding territories. This population expansion-based mobility was a characteristic that was pushing those societies further and further from their original territory.

Therefore, three different movements of native societies in the lowlands of South America need to be understood: (1) the precolonial; (2) the contact; and, (3) the post-contact. We will focus on the precolonial movements and what the reasons were that forced these populations to spread out over extremely long distances in a relatively short period of time.

MIGRATION OR EXPANSION?

According to Brochado (1984) migration is leaving a place to go somewhere else, so this is not an adequate explanation for the Tupi people. The Tupi speakers spread out of their territory without abandoning the heartland and this has been confirmed by archaeological research. This process was called by Brochado colonization and he felt that the causes of these expansions of territories were due to demographic explosion

(Brochado, 1989). To Noelli (1998), the key thing to understanding the Tupi expansion was territoriality, which enclosed the hunting and fishing areas, the agriculture fields, and the areas of gathering and forestry management. In addition, the territories were expanded by kinship and associated alignments. Brochado and Noelli also highlighted the importance of agriculture for the Tupi expansion. Planting and field management techniques influenced the rhythm of the expansion because new cultigens were introduced into the new territories that they occupied. So, instead of jumps, the expansion was characterized by slow flows and continuous territorial attachments. The late expansion along the east coast made many researchers postulate a split from the Amazonian groups around 2000 to 3000 years ago or even more recently (Brochado, 1989; Lathrap, 1970; Meggers, 1977; Sušnik, 1975). So, if the coast was occupied recently by these groups, where was their starting point?

THE HISTORY, THE LINGUISTIC, AND THE ORIGIN CENTER

The center of origin of MTG is a controversial issue. Linguists, anthropologists, and archaeologists agree, at least on one thing; namely, that the MTG speakers were spread out all over the lowlands in South America during the contact period. Alfred Metraux (1928) placed the center of origin to the isthmus between the Paraná and Paraguay river basins, with a later occupation towards the east coast of Brazil mainly by the Tupi-Guarani languages also called Tupinambá (old Tupi) or Ñeengatu (or modern Tupi) (Rodrigues, 1958). Today, Amazonia is indicated as the origin of these groups; but the coast has more evidence on them due to the historic colonization process in Brazil. The disagreement between the linguistic interpretations and the archaeological record was bigger in the past than currently. Lathrap (1970) and Meggers (1977, 1979) each introduced a hypothetical model for the Amazon occupation and both authors felt that it is possible to identify the links between languages and archaeological remains.

For Lathrap (1970), the Proto-Tupi and Proto-Arawak had started in the Negro River basin above its Amazon River confluence and that the Macro-Tupi developed in the Madeira River basin above the Amazon confluence. According to his model, the languages started to diverge (Macro-Arawak and Macro-Tupi) around 4000–5000 years ago in an environment characterized by innovation which saw a flourishing of agricultural plants and techniques and pottery styles. Through time, more and more languages started to split and take over other regions due to demographic pressures; that is, the competition for the fertile soils on the *várzea* (floodplain) and this evolved into a progressive movement out of the Central Amazon. Lathrap also supposed that these groups were looking for similar regions for their settlements, such as the Madeira River alluvial lands, and also moved further toward the Andean regions. Brochado (1989) and Noelli (1998) highlighted the growth of intensive agricultural systems and a tendency toward sedentism at this time.

By contrast, Urban (1992) proposed that the Tupi groups were the first to move to the Central Amazon lowlands, as they did not originate from there, and also set the first phase of dispersion of the Macro-Tupi around 4000–6000 years BP (before present). According to the author the origin center for Tupi, Carib, and Ge languages was at the head tributaries of the Madeira, Tapajós, and São Francisco rivers (Urban 1992). After some time, those populations started to migrate toward the major rivers in a process Urban called the periphery hypothesis. Rodrigues (1984/85, 2005, 2007) studied the chronological depth of the Proto-Tupi languages through the linguistic analysis of words and pointed out that five of the ten linguistic families are in a region around the Upper Madeira River, currently in the State of Rondônia, Brazil; which from the linguistic point of view is, therefore, the origin center.

During the 1980s Brochado reconsidered the linguistic discussion about the migration of precolonial populations and the archaeological records through the correlation between the Tupi groups with the Amazonian Polychromic Ceramic tradition (APC). J. Brochado and D. W. Lathrap (unpublished manuscript, 1982) proposed the direct association between the APC and Tupi migration using radiocarbon dates to explain the successive migration routes during the precolonial period towards the south, west, and east across the lowlands, and set the origin point of these Proto-Tupi speakers in the Central Amazon.

Some authors report the Tupi pattern of dispersion is more like explosions and radiations, so distant idioms reveal similarities. It is possible to see this relationship between the Chiriguano (Bolivia) and the Potiguara on the Brazilian coast and between groups from the north and south (Urban, 1992:92). At this time though, the archaeological research has not been sufficient to analyze and access all of these theories and the many conclusions derived from the linguistics models.

The controversial issue of making relationships between linguistic and archaeological data is beginning to be resolved, but not completely explained, by a growing amount of multidisciplinary research in the Amazon basin. Currently, some consensus about the Proto-Tupi center of origin in the southwestern portion of Amazonia is being supported by both archaeological and linguistic data (Heckenberger, 2008; Rodrigues, 2007). Thus, the area around the Madeira, Guaporé, and Mamoré river basins is regarded as the center. Due to the linguistic evidence this area presents the most family language diversity (Rodrigues, 2007). The high level of linguistic diversity and minimal geographic dispersion identify it as the center of origin of a proto-language, and Rodrigues (2005) postulates that the region was occupied by Tupi people for more than 5000 years. In contrast, the similarity of the languages spoken in the eastern region led linguists to think that there was a fast movement of expansion along the coast (Brochado, 1989). This movement Heckenberger calls the Tupi-Guarani diaspora, chronologically occurring *c.* 2500–1500 years BP (Heckenberger, 2008:947).

THE AMAZON POLYCHROME TRADITION

During the last 15 years the Central Amazon Project has made some significant input into these questions and this investigation will be accumulating and reporting more details. First, some results show that the Polychrome Tradition ceramics, associated with Tupi groups in the Central Amazon, were not evolving from the "Incised Rim" or "Barracoid" Tradition, associated with Arawak groups, as argued by Lathrap (1970) and Brochado (1984). The relatively late radiocarbon dates refute the hypothesis of a long period of occupation by this tradition (Neves, 2008). Although the polychromic ceramics in the region present complex characteristics and suggest sophisticated formation processes, they did not evolve *in situ,* but rather were intrusive (Heckenberger *et al.*, 1998). A profound change in the ceramic tradition around 1000 years BP is interpreted by Neves as the emergence of a wide cultural patterning through the replacement of sites of the Incised Rim by the Polychromic Tradition over Amazonia and close to the piedmont of the Colombian, Ecuadorian, and Peruvian Andes (Neves, 2008:367).

Diachronic settlement morphology patterns were investigated by the Central Amazon Project in an effort to understand the expansion of Tupi groups associated with the Polychromic Tradition. The physical and chemical soil properties and pottery analyses carried out at the archaeological sites within the Central Amazon have since confirmed this association and showed a circular concentration of organic material and Amazonian Dark Earths (ADE; those anthropogenic fertile soils associated with long-term, nucleated occupations) surrounding a plaza at the Hatahara archaeological site. This settlement form is associated with "Incised Rim" ceramics related to the Paredão phase (Arawak) (Moraes, 2006; Rebellato *et al.*, 2009). This type of ceramics abruptly disappears and is replaced by a linear-shaped village with the Amazonian Polychromic ceramics affiliated with the Guarita phase (Tupiguarani) (Rebellato *et al.*, 2009). The village then occupied the riverside border, facing the Amazon River and backing the areas composed by ADE. Thus, it was possible to confirm precolonial relationships in the Central Amazon area through linguistic, ethnohistoric, and archaeological data; a confirmation of the descriptions made by the first European travelers, who reported continuous, linear villages and dense occupations along the bluffs overlooking the Amazon floodplain; for example, the 1542 account by Friar Gaspar de Carvajal (Carvajal, 1992).

Porro (1996) associated a linear pattern for this population with an economy mainly associated with the water resources, which is completely understandable. Results presented in this chapter also furnish one more reason for this shape: namely, better use of the ADE area for food production. Tupi speakers are generally associated with intensive agriculture as showed in earlier works (Brochado, 1984; Noelli, 1998), so the Tupi expansion could also be related to the conquest of ADE territories.

DISCUSSION AND CONCLUSIONS

The data related to the Hatahara archaeological site reveal a definite change in the settlement patterns around 1000 years BP. Many archaeological sites in the confluence region of Amazon and Negro rivers show an increase of trenches and defensive systems, suggesting a fortification period due to warfare (Neves, 2008). This increase in village protection is associated with the subsequent establishment, at some sites, of peoples with the Amazon Polychromic Tradition. In addition, transition from a circular village shape to a linear pattern was observed. We propose these changes in the village shape and pottery tradition around 1000 years BP are associated with the Tupi expansion in the area. Heckenberger (2008:950) highlighted that during the beginning of the second millennium a macroregional interaction associated with a geopolitical identity and exchange of prestige goods (polychromic ceramics) took place along the Amazon floodplains and many adjacent tributaries.

Before the establishment of these new settlers, as witnessed by the fortifications, a process was caused which involved a period of warfare with the former occupants who were associated with "Incised Rim" Tradition ceramics (Arawak speakers). Our interpretation for those waves of invasions is related to the fertility of the soils of the area. This fertility was associated with both the floodplains of the Amazon River and the ADE. Bellicosity associated with the Tupi groups was one of the characteristics that suggest that the expansion of these groups was not a peaceful one, but rather was aimed at acquiring new territories in the Central Amazon. The linear settlement morphology strongly suggests that the warfare had succeeded in the region for the invaders and that they were not in fear of attack since linear settlement forms are indefensible. The linear form was excellent for expanding food production since it had the dual advantage of ready access to the floodplain and maximizing use of the ADE found within the areas of prior habitation. Indeed, the thick deposits of ADE were so valuable to the Tupi that they spread them out over a wide zone behind their villages in order to enlarge the area covered and thus increase product-ivity. All indications point to a period of stability for these new occupa-tions and interactions within a well-conformed inter-regional system of exchange between related groups across an extensive area. This stability lasted for five centuries until the European encounters which set into play a new history of movements of the native populations across the entire continent.

REFERENCES

Anchieta, J. [1595] (1933). *Arte de grammatica da lingua mais usada na costa do Brasil.* Rio de Janeiro, Brazil: Imprensa nacional, Biblioteca Nacional.
Arion, D. R. (1958). Classification of Tupi-Guarani. *International Journal of American Linguistics*, **24**, 231–4.
Balée, W. (1989). The culture of Amazonian forest. In *Resource Management in Amazonia: Indigenous and Folk Strategies*, ed. D. A. Posey and W. Balée, pp. 1–21. New York: New York Botanic Garden.
Balée, W. (1993). Language, culture, and environment: Tupi-Guarani plant names over time. In *Amazonian Indians from Prehistory to the Present: Anthropological Perspectives*, ed. A. C. Roosevelt. Tucson, AZ: University of Arizona Press.
Balée, W. (1994). *Footprints of the Forest: Ka'apor ethonobotany: The Historical Ecology of Plants Utilization by an Amazonian People*. New York: Columbia University Press.
Balée, W. (2000). Antiquity of traditional ethnobiological knowledge in Ama-zonia: the Tupi-Guarani family and time. *Ethnohistory*, **47**, 399–422.
Balée, W. L. and Erickson, C. L. (2006). *Time and Complexity in Historical Ecology: Studies in the Neotropical Lowlands*. New York: Columbia University Press.
Brochado, J. P. (1989). A expansão dos Tupi e da cerâmica da tradição polícroma Amazônica. *Dédalo, São Paulo*, **27**, 65–82.
Brochado, J. P. (1984). *An Ecological Model of the Spread of Pottery and Agriculture into Eastern South America*. Urbana-Champaign, IL: Department of Anthropology, University of Illinois.

Carneiro, R. L. (2007). Cannabalism: a palatable/unpalatable reality of Amazonia. *South American Explorer*, **84**, 9–13, 41–44.

Carvajal, G. (1992). *Descubrimiento del Río de las Amazonas*. Valencia, Spain: Estudios Ediciones y Medios.

Caycedo, A. O. (2005). *San Jacinto 1: A Historical Ecological Approach to an Archaic Site in Colombia*. Tuscaloosa, AL: University of Alabama Press.

Clastres, H. (1975). *La Terre Sans Mal: Le prophétism Tupi-Guarani*. Paris: Éditions du Seuil.

Denevan, W. M. (2001). *Cultivated Landscapes of Native Amazonia and the Andes: Triumph Over the Soil*. Oxford, UK: Oxford University Press.

Fernades, F. (1963). *Organização Social dos Tupinambá*. São Paulo, Brazil: Difusão Européia do Livro.

Gomes, D. M. C. (2002). *Cerâmica Arqueológica Amazônica*. São Paulo, Brazil: Edusp.

Gomes, D. M. C. (2008). *Cotidiano e Poder na Amazônia Pré-Colonial*. São Paulo, Brazil: Edusp.

Heckenberger, M. J. (2005). *The Ecology of Power: Culture, Place, and Personhood in the Southern Amazon, A.D. 1000–2000*. New York: Routledge.

Heckenberger, M. J. (2008). Identity, interaction, and integration in the tropical forest. In *Handbook of South American Archaeology*, ed. H. Silverman and W. H. Isbell. New York: Springer.

Heckenberger, M. J., Neves, E. G., and Petersen, J. B. (1998). De onde surgem os modelos?: as origens e expansões Tupi na Amazônia central. *Revista de Antropologia*, **41**, 69–96.

Lathrap, D. W. (1970). *The Upper Amazon*. London: Thames and Hudson.

Lemle, M. (1971). Internal classification of the Tupi Guarani linguistic family. In *Tupi Studies*, Vol. I, ed. D. Bendor–Samuel, pp. 107–29. Norman, OK: University of Oklahoma.

Léry, J. [1578] (1990). *History of a Voyage to the Land of Brazil, Otherwise Called America* (trans. J. Whatley). Berkeley, CA: University of California Press.

Meggers, B. J. (1971). *Amazonia: Man and Culture in a Counterfeit Paradise*. Chicago, IL: Aldine.

Meggers, B. J. (1973). A reconstituição da pre-história amazônica; algumas considerações teóricas. *Museu Paraense Emílio Goeldi*, **20**, 51–69.

Meggers, B. J. (1977). Vegetational fluctuation and prehistoric cultural adaptation in Amazonia: some tentative correlations. *World Archaeology*, **8**, 287–303.

Meggers, B. J. (1979). Climatic oscillation as a factor in the prehistory of Amazonia. *American Antiquity*, **44**(2), 252–66.

Métraux, A. (1928). *La civilisation matérielle des tribus Tupi-Guarani*. Paris: P. Geuthner.

Moore, D. and L. Storto (2002). As línguas indígenas e a pré-história. In *Homo Brasilis*, ed. S. D. J. Pena. São Paulo, Brazil: FUNPEC

Moraes, C. P. (2006). Levantamento arqueológico da região do Lago do Limão. Master's thesis, Museu de Arqueologia e Etnologia, Universidade de São Paulo, Brazil.

Neves, E. G. (1999). Changing perspectives in the Amazonian Archaeology. In *Archaeology in Latin America*, ed. G. Politis and B. Alberti. London: Routledge.

Neves, E. G. (2008). Ecology, ceramic chronology and distribuition, long-term history, and political change in the Amazonian floodplain. In *Handbook of South American Archaeology*, ed. H. Silverman and W. H. Isbell. New York: Springer.

Noelli, F. S. (1998). The Tupi: explaining origin and expansions in terms of archaeology and of historical linguistics. *Antiquity*, **72**, 648.

Noelli, F. S. (2008). The Tupi expansion. In *Handbook of South American Archaeology*, ed. H. Silverman and W. H. Isbell. New York: Springer.

Pärssinen, M., Schaan, D. P., and Ranzi, A. (2009). Pre-Columbian geometric earthworks in the upper Purús: a complex society in western Amazonia. *Antiquity Publications*, **83**, 1084–95.

Porro, A. (1996). *O Povo das Águas: ensaios de etno-história amazônica.* Rio de Janeiro, Brazil: Vozes.

Rebellato, L., Woods, W. I., and Neves, E. G. (2009). PreEuropean continuity and change in the Central Amazon. In *Amazonian Dark Earths: Wim Sombroek's Vision*, ed. W. I. Woods *et al.* New York: Springer.

Rodrigues, A. D. I. (1958). Classification of Tupi-Guarani. *International Journal of American Linguistics*, **24**, 231–4.

Rodrigues, A. D. I. (1984/85). Relações internas na família linguística Tupi-Guarani. *Revista de Antropologia*, **28**, 33–53.

Rodrigues, A. D. I. (1986). *Línguas brasileiras: para o conhecimento das línguas indígenas.* São Paulo, Brazil: Edições Loyola.

Rodrigues, A. D. I. (2005). Sobre as linguas indigenas e sua pesquisa no Brasil. *Ciencia e Cultura*, **57**, 35–8.

Rodrigues, A. D. I. (2007). As consoantes do Proto-Tupi. In *Linguas e Cultura Tupi*, ed. D. R. Arion, A. S. A. C. Cabral, B. C. C. da Silva, *et al.* Campinas, Brazil: Editora Curt Nimuendaju.

Roosevelt, A. C. (1991). *Moundbuilders of the Amazon: Geo-physical Archaeology on Marajó Island, Brazil.* San Diego, CA: Academic Press.

Rostain, S. (1994). *L'occupation amérindienne ancienne du littoral de Guyane* (2 vols.). Paris: Université de Paris I-Panthéon/Sorbonne, U.F.R. d'art et d'archéologie, Centre de recherche en archéologie précolombienne.

Schaan, D. P. (2001). Into the labyrinths of Marajoara pottery: status and cultural indentity in an Amazonian complex societies. In *Handbook of South American Archaeology*, ed. C. McEwan, C. Barreto, and N. Eduardo G. Neves. New York: Springer.

Schaan, D. P. (2004). *The Camutins Chiefdom: Rise and Development of Social Complexity on Marajó Island, Brazilian Amazon.* Pittsburgh, PA: University of Pittsburgh.

Schaan, D. P. (2008). The nonagricultural chiefdoms of Marajó Island. In *Handbook of South American Archaeology*, ed. H. Silverman and W. H. Isbell. New York: Springer.

Staden, H. [1557] (1948). *O prisioneiro de Ubatuba.* São Paulo, Brazil: Edições Melhoramentos.

Sušnik, B. (1975). *Dispersión Tupí-Guaraní prehistórica: ensayo analítico.* Asunción, Paraguay: Museo Etnográfico Andrés Barbero.

Thevet, A. [1575] (1978). *As singularidades da França Antártica.* São Paulo, Brazil: Itatiaia/Editora Universidade de São Paulo.

Urban, G. (1992). A história da cultura brasileira segundo as línguas nativas. In *História dos índios no Brasi*, ed. M. C. Cunha, pp. 87–102. São Paulo, Brazil: São Paulo Fundação de Amparo à Pesquisa do Estado de São Paulo; Companhia das Letras; Secretaria Municipal de Cultura.

Versteeg, A. H. and Rostain, S. (1997). *The Archaeology of Aruba: The Tanki Flip Site.* Oranjestad, Aruba: Archaeological Museum Aruba; Foundation for Scientific Research in the Caribbean.

Viveiros de Castro, E. B. (1992). *From the Enemy's Point of View: Humanity and Divinity in an Amazonian Society.* Chicago, IL: University of Chicago Press.

Woods, W. I., Teixeira, W. G., Lehmann, J., *et al.* (2009). *Amazonian Dark Earths: Wim Sombroek's Vision.* New York: Springer.

ANNE JUSTICE, BARTHOLOMEW DEAN,
AND MICHAEL H. CRAWFORD

22

Molecular consequences of migration and urbanization in Peruvian Amazonia

INTRODUCTION

With its rich archaeological and historical record, Peru offers an exceptional opportunity for the study of human migration. While Amazonia comprises nearly 60% of the country's national territory, most studies of Peru's human populations have emphasized the Andean highlands. The *selva baja*, or lowland tropical forested region of Peru's Lower Huallaga Valley, is particularly important for genetic studies on migration. A geographically significant crossroads of migration, the Lower Huallaga Valley is characterized by its degree of ethnic diversity among both indigenous and immigrant populations. Despite centuries of colonization, many contemporary indigenous societies reside in the *selva baja* region surrounding the city of Yurimaguas, including: Quechua-speaking populations (Kichwa Lamista, Kichwa del Pastaza); Jibaroan speakers (Achuar, Awajun, Kandozi, Wampis, and Jibaro); Tupi-Guarani speakers (Kukama-Kukamira); Cahuapanan speakers (Shawi and Shiwilu); Arawakan speakers (Chamicuro); and the Urarina (linguistic isolate).

In light of the region's recent pattern of urbanization, this study evaluates the genetic consequences of migration using mitochondrial DNA (mtDNA) to characterize the maternal genetic structure of residents of the "new urban settlements" (or *barriadas*) enveloping Yurimaguas, one of the *selva baja*'s principal cities (Dean and Silverstein, 2011). Maternal markers were used to infer prominent source population and/or pattern of migration into the provincial capital city of Yurimaguas by comparing the

Causes and Consequences of Human Migration, ed. Michael H. Crawford and Benjamin C. Campbell. Published by Cambridge University Press. © Cambridge University Press 2012.

focus sample with others from South America. By estimating the proportion of non-native maternal admixture and establishing estimates of a past population reduction we provide novel insights for understanding the effects of human migration in the Lower Huallaga Valley.

BACKGROUND

Regional history and population background of the *selva baja*

Yurimaguas is situated at the confluence of the Paranapura and Huallaga Rivers in Alto Amazonas, one of the seven provinces in the Loreto Region of Peru (Figure 22.1). Located in northeastern Peruvian Amazonia, the area surrounding Yurimaguas is distinguished by its diverse terrain – marked by the rolling foothills of the eastern slopes of the Andes, deep valleys forged by an extensive hydrological system, and a vast tropical lowland region known as the *selva baja*. Bisecting the center of the upper Amazon, the Huallaga River has historically served as a primary route of human migration (Buitron, 1948:9; Kernaghan, 2009:121; Villarejo, 1988:46).

The *selva baja*'s geographically strategic location made it an important pre- and post-Columbian crossroads for communication and trade. The *selva baja* borders the lower Andes and what is known as the Peru Flat, a region where there is a shallowing of the angle of subduction of the Nazca tectonic plate. The mountain ranges bordering the *selva baja* are free from volcanoes and lower in altitude compared with other parts of the Andes (Ramos and Folguera, 2009), making the region a popular trans-Andean travel route. Judging from the archaeological record (Myers, 1974), there was significant mixing of indigenous populations both from the Andean highlands and tropical lowlands long before the sixteenth-century European colonial expansion pushed indigenous groups into the *selva baja*. Moreover, prior to 1000 BCE, there was communication between the coastal regions of Ecuador and the lowland Amazonian tropics (Braun, 1982; Bruhns *et al.*, 1990; Myers and Dean, 1999). While scant archaeological research has been conducted on the Lower Huallaga River, archaeological evidence from the nearby Ucayali and Marañón Rivers indicate that the *selva baja* was densely populated prior to Francisco de Orellana's arrival in 1541 (Heckenberger and Neves, 2009). After conquest, the *selva baja* served as a refuge zone for indigenous peoples fleeing the Portuguese from Brazil in the east, and the Spanish from the bordering Andean highlands. The geography of the Huallaga Valley has historically provided humans with a

Figure 22.1 This map of South America includes the collection site, Yurimaguas, Peru, along with the location for comparative populations. The barrier identified by the Monmonier's Maximum Difference Algorithm is highlighted with a black line.

favored migratory path; the lower reaches of the Huallaga River are relatively easy to navigate, inviting communication and commerce long before and after initial Spanish colonization of the area.

In 1533, the Spanish began launching expeditions across the eastern flanks of the Andes into Amazonia. They soon established colonial settlements in the tropical highland forested regions, or *selva alta* (Regan, 1983). As the frontiers of the European colonization expanded into the *selva baja*, violence intensified, and slave raiding became all too commonplace. The resulting fission of the *selva baja*'s indigenous populations in turn gave rise to the region's highly diversified gene pool. Moreover, the so-called "Columbian exchange" (Crosby, 1972, 1986) brought diseases, such as smallpox, influenza, malaria, measles, poxvirus, yellow fever, and possibly hantavirus epidemics that soon drastically reduced the *selva baja*'s indigenous populations. Studies of the effects of infectious diseases on Native American population size indicate that the first wave of smallpox wiped out 25–95% of the local indigenous populace (Cook, 1998; Davies, 1997; Mann, 2005; Riley, 2010).

Beginning in 1567, the Jesuits established mission posts located in the *selva baja*'s riverine areas that could draw on the populations of the interfluvial regions to supply them – by force if necessary – with new converts and catechumens (see Ardito Vega, 1992; Dean, 1990:19; Fritz, 1922; Golob, 1982:13; Marzal, 1984; Stephan, 2000). Between 1700 and 1714 the Jesuits established a mission outpost on the Lower Huallaga River that eventually became known as Yurimaguas (founded in 1709), named purportedly after two indigenous groups, the Yuris and the Omaguas, who sought refuge in the region after escaping Portuguese colonialist violence in Brazil (Rhoades and Bidegaray, 1987). By 1768 the Jesuits had been forced out of the upper Amazon, allowing those indigenous peoples who still lived in the missions to return to their previous ways of life (Chantre y Herrera, 1901:669–83; Dean, 2009; Regan, 1983). Many of upper Amazon's "missionized Indians" fled to the security of refuge zones of the Huallaga Valley or to the inaccessible headwaters of the *selva baja* (Smyth and Lowe, 1836:199).

Indigenous peoples who did not resist the new pressures of traders, plantation owners, soldiers, and priests either were annihilated, or were incorporated into the *selva baja*'s new class of peasantry – the *ribereños* (people of the river). In the most populous and economically vital region of Peruvian Amazonia – the Huallaga Valley – plantation owners usurped indigenous people's lands and enslaved workers (Davies, 1974:26). Following the trails and river ways linking the mission trading posts of Amazonia, merchants began traveling between the Pacific coast and the *selva alta*, and then made their way down to the *selva baja*. The peddlers who worked the northwestern flanks of the upper Amazon were primarily migrants from Quito and the region's major urban center, Moyobamba. By the end of the eighteenth century the majority of the inhabitants of Moyobamba were considered *mestizos* (meaning of mixed European and Indian ancestry), while the presence of free black residents was double the rate found in other areas of Peru (Reyes Flores, 1999:129). The town of Yurimaguas reportedly had about 250 inhabitants by the mid nineteenth century (Herndon, 1952:171). The total population of Loreto was estimated in 1864 between 80 000 and 90 000, with 2600 residing in the entire district of Yurimaguas (Report from Her Majesty's Consuls, 1864:218).

Spurred by the expansion of agro-extractive mercantilism, socio-economic change intensified in Amazonia. Nowhere was this more apparent than in the boom in the rubber industry that led to the influx of foreign capital and immigrants (North Americans, Ashkenazi Jews, Spaniards, Portuguese, Italians, British, Chinese, Barbadians, etc.), and set into motion a series of cataclysmic events that irrevocably changed the environmental, economic, and social contours of Amazonia. Beginning in the early 1870s and lasting until the end of World War II (Haring, 1986), in the regions surrounding Yurimaguas the rubber boom drew thousands of Andean migrants and indigenous and *mestizo* workers from distant lowland Amazonian communities (Stocks, 1983:84; cf. San Román, 1975). The brutal nature of the rubber industry was reflected in increased rates of mortality due to disease, malnutrition, and forced labor migration (Pennano, 1988:100−4, 177). At this time, Alto Amazonas had 9660 inhabitants, while Yurimaguas reportedly had 460 residents (Stiglich Álvarez, 1913:198). The producers of Amazonian wild rubber were eventually pushed out of the international market by a slump in demand, owing to the advent of synthetic rubber in the early 1920s (Dean, 2009; Domínguez and Gómez, 1990; Jackson, 2008; Stanfield, 1998).

In the past, river transport represented the dominant communication network linking the Huallaga's *selva alta* and *selva baja*. This began to change in the 1930s when the Peruvian state started to promote colonization and road construction schemes in Amazonia (Chiro, 1943; Gootenberg, 2009:292). Continued demographic pressures and widespread peasant unrest in the central and southern Andes fueled the migration of highland migrants into Peruvian Amazonia. Throughout the Lower Huallaga region of San Martín and Loreto an ever-expanding network of roads and market opportunities encouraged urbanization. By 1967 the Marginal Highway connected Yurimaguas and the tropical lowlands with the *selva alta*, spurring commercial activity and increasing migration into the Lower Huallaga Valley.

Recognized for its commercial rather than political significance, contemporary Yurimaguas consists of the descendants of migrant populations, many of whom came to the port town during the late nineteenth and early twentieth century rubber boom. Yet continued patterns of extractive production and exploitative labor conditions led to frequent regional population turnover. Linked to major cities by road and to the rest of the Amazon Basin via the Huallaga River, Yurimaguas became a thriving commercial center in the *selva baja* with a relatively large transient population. Over the past 50 years, migrants from throughout Peru have been drawn to Yurimaguas because of the development of various extractive enterprises in the Lower Huallaga Valley. Between 1961 and 1971 Alto Amazonas' urban population more than doubled from 8057 to 17 624 (INEI, 2010). By 1981, the population of the District of Yurimaguas was 36 417 with 63% living in urban areas (Rhoades and Bidegaray, 1987). Most recently (2007), the population of the District of Yurimaguas numbered 63 345, with 77% reportedly residing in urban centers, and 26.5% of the population consisting of new migrants who had arrived in Yurimaguas since 2005 (INEI, 2007).

Many of the recent migrants to the urban settlements or *barriadas* ringing the city of Yurimaguas are indigenous peoples displaced from their rural homes by a combination of neoliberal economic policy and destructive, extractive economies, such as illegal logging, palm-oil production, coca-leaf cultivation, and agriculture (rice, plantains) for the market (Dean and Silverstein, 2011). Due to its proximity to numerous indigenous communities located throughout the surrounding *selva baja* region, the overall demographic makeup of Yurimaguas appears to exhibit a much higher proportion of indigenous residents, especially when compared with other upper Amazonian urban centers, such as the *selva alta* cities of Tarapoto or Moyobamaba.

While they often recognize their indigenous ancestry, many individuals residing in the *selva baja* self-identify as *mestizo*, a term used to describe Spanish-speaking individuals of mixed European and indigenous ancestry. In contrast to other regions of Amazonia, the swath of the Huallaga valley from Chasuta to Yurimaguas has often been noted for the predominance of its *mestizo* (mixed) social identities (e.g. Buitron, 1948; Espinosa, 1995:60; Kernaghan, 2009). Given nearly 500 years since the onset of the colonial encounter, it seems likely that significant biological admixture has taken place among the populations of the Huallaga, which would logically contribute to their local cultural identifications of *mestizo* – a term used in the *selva baja* vernacular in such a way that highlights biological admixture while at the same time erasing indigenous identities (Dean and Levi, 2003). While initial European colonization and subsequent settlement undoubtedly did set the stage for genetic change in the *selva baja*, the region's recent pattern of rural to urban migration appears to have had a much more significant impact on the contemporary genetic makeup of the population residing in Yurimaguas. The apparent incongruity in the genetic structure of Yurimaguas' *barriadas* and their self-identification as *mestizo* proves especially interesting when considering the demographic makeup of the early foreign colonists of the Upper Amazon, who were nearly all males.

MtDNA variation in the Americas

Mitochondrial DNA (mtDNA) is the most studied genetic marker in humans for several reasons. First, mtDNA is almost entirely inherited through the mother, and as such provides a deep maternal history. Mitochondrial DNA has a constant mutation rate and does not undergo any measurable recombination. Any changes in genetic markers seen across generations can assumed to be the result of new mutations, making mtDNA ideal for statistical analyses. Likewise, the rate of mutation is useful for determining the separation of founding and offspring populations. Mitochondrial DNA resides within the cell's readily abundant mitochondria, and hence it is relatively easier to obtain than nuclear DNA. Given its utility for anthropological analysis, mtDNA is often used to reconstruct population histories in the Americas, as well as for determining patterns of genetic diversity within and among Indigenous American populations. Mitochondrial DNA presents distinct haplogroups (inherited groups of genetic markers which represent a discrete lineage) that differ among geographically distant populations. This feature of mtDNA facilitates comparisons among worldwide populations. Differences observed in mtDNA lineages among continents allow researchers to measure the amount of maternal gene flow that is the result of migration (e.g. the proportion of Indigenous American, European, Asians, and African mtDNA haplogroups found in any given region of the Americas).

Five major mtDNA haplogroups characterize mtDNA diversity among Indigenous American populations: A, B, C, D, and X. While all five of these haplogroups are present in Siberian and Asian populations, their specific frequencies vary geographically across the Americas. Haplogroup A has high frequencies in Alaska, Canada, and the eastern portions of the United States and among central Mexican Chibchan speakers. Haplogroup B is found in high frequencies among the indigenous peoples of the Western and Midwestern United States, and is almost absent in Arctic populations. Haplogroup C is rarely found among Native North Americans, but increases in frequency across South America. Haplogroup D has been shown to occur in higher frequencies among Native Alaskans, in lower frequencies in the rest of North America, and in high frequency among South American populations residing in Amazonia (Bonatto and Salzano, 1997; Lalueza-Fox *et al.*, 2001; Merriwether, 1995; Pereira *et al.*, 2005; Rubicz *et al.*, 2003; Salzano, 2002; Schurr and Sherry, 2004; Torroni *et al.*, 1993a, 1993b). Haplogroup X is found in high frequency around the Great Lakes and in Greenland, with moderately lower frequencies found elsewhere in the Americas (Rubicz *et al.*, 2003; Schurr and Sherry, 2004).

Ever since the seminal work of Vigilant *et al.* (1991), the study of mtDNA sequence variability has become commonplace, thus allowing for greater resolution of mtDNA haplogroup relationships. Mutations specific to circumpolar populations and Indigenous Americans for haplogroups A2, C1, D1, and X2a have been found in the hypervariable regions (HVS1 and HVS2) of mtDNA, which, when combined with RFLP analysis, reveal possible founding lineages for the New World (for additional details on American specific mutations see Achilli *et al.*, 2008).

Using patterns of variability in mtDNA haplogroup and sequence variation, researchers have furthered our understanding of the peopling of the Americas, as well the historical relationships among Indigenous American populations. Compared with Europe, Africa, and Asia, Indigenous American populations exhibit decreased genetic variation, especially as one moves from North to South America (Tarazona-Santos *et al.*, 2001; Wang *et al.*, 2007). While controversy surrounds the number and the timing of human migrations into the New World, it is generally accepted that North America was first occupied by peoples who migrated from Siberia sometime before the last glacial maximum ~20 000 years BP (Achilli *et al.*, 2008; Wang *et al.*, 2007), and into South America by ~13 000 years BP (Fuselli *et al.*, 2003). As one travels from west to east in South America a cline becomes evident in both diversity within and variation among indigenous populations. Compared with the rest of South American indigenous populations, Andean populations possess the greatest within-group diversity along with greater homogeneity among the populations. In eastern South America, and especially in Amazonia, relatively little mtDNA diversity is present within populations, and there is greater heterogeneity among populations. This pattern of variation, which is replicated in studies of Y-chromosome and autosomal DNA markers, supports the theory that the Americas were first peopled by migrants who crossed from the Bering Land Bridge, then along the Pacific coastline, and finally eastward across South America (Fuselli *et al.*, 2003; Tarazona-Santos *et al.*, 2001; Wang *et al.*, 2007).

The Lower Huallaga region is of interest to anthropological geneticists precisely because the region flanks an area critically important for understanding the history of the peopling of South America – the border between the Andes and the greater Amazonian basin. Study of the molecular profile of the indigenous populations of the Lower Huallaga may in fact provide further evidence of a clinal relationship between mtDNA variation across South America or, conversely, may reveal the existence of a genetic barrier between Andean and lowland Amazonian populations.

As noted, haplogroups A, B, C, D, and X2a comprise the entire spectrum of Indigenous American mtDNA diversity. Founding lineages are only shared with Siberian populations, so the presence of any other haplogroups is an indication of gene flow. European admixture can be detected through the presence of haplogroups H, I, J, K, T, U, V, W, and X, while African haplogroups are associated with the presence of haplogroups L1, L2, and L3. Studies similar to ours have been performed on putatively "white" Brazilian populations. Using mtDNA, a number of studies have shown that significant admixture among European, Indigenous American, and African populations. The contribution of each parental population varies according to location, with Indigenous American lineages comprising between 22% and 54%, European between 31% to 66%, and African between 15% and 44% (Alves-Silva *et al.*, 2000). While less European and African admixture has been found outside of Brazil, autosomal, mtDNA, and Y-chromosome markers generally show some evidence of European and African gene flow into the Americas (Alves-Silva *et al.*, 2000; Wang *et al.*, 2007). In addition to providing evidence for the impact of European colonization and the slave trade on the genetic makeup of South American populations, such lines of inquiry also yield important insights regarding the dynamics of cultural identity in the Americas.

MATERIALS

The samples we analyzed were collected in 2005 by Bartholomew Dean from various residents of "new urban settlements" or *barriadas* surrounding the city of Yurimaguas (Figure 22.1) many of whom had emigrated from the surrounding countryside to Yurimaguas in hopes of obtaining employment and educational opportunities associated with the city. All 52 participants in our study provided informed oral consent. Since admixture is central to our inquiry regarding the cultural construction of social identity, we made no attempt to exclude individuals who did not claim maternal indigenous ancestry. Likewise, information on family history was limited, so no attempts were made to exclude related individuals. For comparative purposes, mtDNA sequences were used from 22 other South America populations (see Table 22.2 of the Results section).

LAB METHODS

DNA was extracted from buccal cells using the QiaAmp DNA Mini Kit according to the manufacturer's instructions (Qiagen, Valencia, CA). Standard polymerase chain reaction (PCR) was used in this study to amplify regions of the mtDNA for sequencing, while standard restriction fragment length polymorphism (RFLP) analysis was used to confirm haplogroup assignment. A 423 bp fragment of the Control Region of the Hypervariable Sequence Region I (HVS1) of the mitochondrial DNA (mtDNA) molecule was analyzed for 52 samples, from nucleotide position 16000 to 16422. Amplicons were purified using a QIAquick PCR purification kit (Qiagen, Valencia, CA) following the manufacturer's protocol. After purification, samples were sequenced in the University of Kansas DNA Sequencing Laboratory (see Rubicz *et al.*, 2010 for a detailed description of standard protocols).

ANALYTICAL METHODS

To determine the amount of variation within and among populations, Nei and Li's (1979) measure of nucleotide diversity was employed using mtDNA sequence data. Gene diversity was assessed for haplotype data using Nei's (1987) method, which is less affected by recent evolutionary events and stochastic changes in allele frequency. Both tests were performed using Arlequin ver. 3.11 (Excoffier *et al.*, 2005).

In order to highlight the underlying genetic structure of the Yurimaguas sample population as well as to examine the phylogenetic relationship between the focus population and closely related comparative populations, we used median-joining network analysis (Bandelt *et al.*, 1999) for each of the four major Indigenous American haplogroups using mtDNA sequence data. All network analyses were carried out using Network ver. 4.0 (www.fluxus-engineering.com). Kimura-2p distances were calculated using Arlequin ver. 3.11 (Excoffier *et al.*, 2005) and distances were used to create a multidimensional scaling (MDS) plot. All MDS plots were performed in NTSYSpc version 2.02h (Rohlf, 2003).

To assess the effects of gene flow and genetic drift on these populations, an R-matrix analysis (Harpending and Jenkins, 1973) was performed on the haplogroup frequencies to obtain distance from the centroid (r_{ii}) and then plotted against gene diversity. This is similar to Harpending and Ward's (1982) method of examining a regression between r_{ii} and heterozygosity. When no forces of evolution are operating on populations, there is a linear relationship between heterozygosity and r_{ii} (Harpending and Ward, 1982). Consequently, any observed deviations from the theoretical regression line are indicative of a population experiencing either gene flow or genetic drift. Those populations that appear above the theoretical line (expressing more variation than expected) are most likely experiencing gene flow, whereas those populations that fall below the line (having less diversity than expected) are most likely under the influence of genetic drift. In the latter case, gene diversity is replacing heterozygosity as our measure of population variation. MtDNA sequence data were used to conduct a Mismatch analysis (Rogers and Harpending, 1992), which produced a distribution of pairwise differences between individuals within a population. This distribution may provide evidence for population expansion, stability, or decrease. Two tests of neutrality were performed – Tajima's D (1989) and Fu's F (1997) – to reveal any possible effects of natural selection and/or fluctuations in population size.

Lastly, Monmonier's algorithm was employed to test for any possible genetic barriers among the populations compared in this study. Monmonier's algorithm, like other phylogeographic methods, identifies geographical areas in which barriers to gene flow exist by locating areas of rapid change in gene frequency. This method was chosen over others as it has been shown effective in locating the correct genetic barriers when using only one marker, such as mtDNA sequence data (Dupanloup *et al.*, 2002). The computer program Alleles in Space (Miller, 2005) was used to apply Monmonier's algorithm to the sequence data.

RESULTS

The HVS-I region sequences from np 16050–16383 (trimmed to 16363 for MJ network analysis) for 52 of the Peruvian samples from Yurimaguas are presented in Table 22.1. This range was chosen from the original

Table 22.1. *This table displays the polymorphic sites for the mtDNA HVS-I region and 41 haplotypes for the focus population*

f	Haplotype	16051 A	16069 T	16092 T	16093 C	16095 C	16111 T	16126 G	16129 C	16145 C	16162 A	16168 A	16172 C	16183 T	16189 T	16209 A	16213 A	16217 C	16223 T	16224 T	16234 C	16243 A	16245 A	16256 C	16260 A	16261 C	16266 A	16270 C	16278 C	16290 G	16291 A	16294 C	16295 C	16298 T	16304 T	16311 A	16319 G	16325 T	16327 C	16362 T
1	A2-01	.	C	.	.	.	.	.	.	.	.	.	.	.	C	.	.	.	.	.	.	.	.	.	.	.	.	.	.	.	.	.	.	.	.	.	.	.	C	C
1	A2-02	.	C	.	T	.	.	.	.	.	.	.	.	.	C	.	.	.	.	.	.	.	T	.	.	.	.	.	.	.	.	.	.	.	.	A	.	.	.	C
1	A2-03	.	.	.	T	.	.	.	.	.	.	.	.	.	.	.	.	.	.	.	.	.	T	.	.	.	.	.	.	.	.	.	.	.	C	A	.	.	.	C
2	A2-04	.	.	.	T	.	.	.	.	.	.	.	.	.	.	.	.	.	.	.	.	.	T	.	.	.	.	.	.	.	.	.	.	.	.	A	.	.	.	C
1	A2-05	.	.	.	T	.	.	.	.	.	.	.	.	.	C	.	.	.	.	.	.	.	T	.	.	.	.	.	.	.	.	.	.	.	.	C	.	.	.	C
2	A2-06	.	.	.	T	.	.	.	.	.	.	.	T	.	.	.	.	.	.	.	.	A	T	.	.	.	.	.	.	.	.	.	.	.	.	A	.	.	.	C
1	A2-07	.	.	.	T	.	.	.	.	.	.	.	.	.	.	.	.	T	.	.	.	.	T	.	.	.	.	.	.	.	.	.	.	.	.	A	.	.	.	C
1	A2-08	.	.	.	T	.	.	.	.	.	.	.	.	.	C	.	.	.	.	.	.	.	T	.	.	.	.	T	.	.	.	.	.	.	.	A	.	.	.	C
1	A2-09	.	.	.	T	.	.	.	.	.	.	.	.	.	.	.	.	.	.	.	.	.	T	.	.	.	.	T	.	.	.	.	.	.	.	A	.	.	.	C
1	B-01	G	.	.	.	.	C	.	.	.	.	.	.	.	.	C	.	.	.	.	.	.	.	.	.	.	.	.	.	.	.	.	.	.	.	.	.	.	.	?
4	B-02	G	.	.	.	.	.	.	.	.	.	.	.	.	.	C	.	.	.	.	.	.	.	.	.	.	.	.	.	.	.	.	.	.	.	.	.	.	.	?
1	B-03	.	.	.	.	.	.	.	.	.	.	.	.	.	.	C	.	.	.	.	.	.	T	.	.	.	.	.	.	.	.	.	.	.	.	G	.	.	.	C
1	B-04	.	C	.	.	.	.	.	.	.	.	.	.	.	.	C	.	.	.	.	.	.	.	.	.	.	.	.	.	.	.	.	.	.	.	.	.	.	.	.
1	B-05	.	.	.	.	A	.	.	.	.	.	.	.	.	.	C	.	.	.	.	.	.	.	.	.	.	.	.	.	.	.	.	.	.	.	.	.	.	.	C
2	B-06	.	.	.	.	.	.	.	.	.	.	.	.	.	.	C	.	.	.	.	C	.	.	.	.	.	.	.	.	.	.	.	.	.	.	.	.	.	.	.
1	B-07	.	C	.	C	.	.	.	.	.	.	.	.	.	.	C	.	.	.	.	.	.	.	.	.	.	.	.	.	.	.	.	.	.	.	.	.	.	.	C
1	B-08	G	.	.	C	.	.	.	.	.	.	.	.	.	.	C	.	.	.	.	.	.	.	.	.	.	.	.	.	.	.	.	.	.	.	.	.	.	.	?
1	B-09	G	.	.	.	.	.	.	.	.	.	.	.	.	.	C	.	.	.	.	.	.	T	.	.	.	.	.	.	.	.	.	.	.	.	.	.	.	.	.
1	B-10	.	.	.	.	.	.	.	.	.	.	.	.	.	.	C	G	.	C	.	.	.	.	.	.	.	.	.	.	.	.	.	.	.	.	.	.	.	.	.
1	B-11	.	.	.	.	.	.	.	.	.	.	.	.	.	.	C	.	.	C	.	.	.	.	.	.	.	.	.	.	.	.	.	.	.	.	.	.	.	.	.
1	B-12	.	.	.	.	.	.	.	.	.	.	.	.	.	.	C	.	.	C	.	.	.	.	.	.	.	.	.	.	.	.	.	.	.	.	.	.	.	.	.
1	B-13	.	.	.	.	.	.	.	.	.	.	.	.	.	.	C	.	.	C	.	.	.	.	.	.	A	.	.	.	.	.	.	.	.	.	.	.	.	.	.
2	C1-01	.	.	.	.	.	.	.	.	.	.	.	.	.	.	.	.	.	.	.	.	.	T	.	.	.	.	.	.	.	.	.	C	.	.	C	.	.	T	C
1	C1-02	G	.	.	.	.	.	.	.	.	.	.	.	.	.	.	.	.	.	.	.	.	T	.	.	.	.	.	.	.	.	.	C	.	.	C	.	.	T	C
3	C1-03	.	.	.	.	.	C	.	.	.	.	.	.	.	.	.	.	.	.	.	.	.	T	.	.	.	.	.	.	.	.	.	C	G	.	C	.	.	T	C
1	C1-04	.	.	.	.	.	.	.	.	.	.	.	.	.	.	.	.	.	.	.	.	.	T	.	.	.	.	.	.	.	.	.	C	.	.	C	.	.	T	C
1	C1-05	.	.	.	.	.	.	.	.	.	.	.	.	.	C	.	.	.	.	.	.	.	T	.	.	.	.	.	.	.	.	.	C	.	.	C	.	.	T	C
1	C1-06	.	.	.	.	.	.	.	.	.	.	.	.	.	.	.	.	.	.	.	.	.	T	.	T	.	.	.	.	.	.	.	C	.	.	C	.	.	T	C
1	C1-07	.	.	.	.	.	.	.	.	.	.	.	.	.	.	.	.	.	.	.	.	.	T	.	.	.	T	.	.	.	.	.	C	.	.	C	.	.	T	C
1	C1-08	G	.	.	.	.	.	.	.	.	.	.	.	.	.	.	.	.	.	.	.	.	T	.	.	.	.	.	.	.	.	.	C	.	.	C	.	.	T	C
2	C1-09	.	.	.	.	.	.	.	.	.	.	.	.	.	C	.	.	.	.	.	.	.	T	.	.	.	.	.	.	.	.	.	C	.	.	C	.	.	T	C
1	C1-10	G	.	.	.	.	.	.	.	G	.	.	.	.	.	.	.	.	.	.	.	.	T	.	.	.	.	.	.	.	.	.	C	.	.	C	.	.	T	C
1	C1-11	.	C	.	.	.	.	.	.	.	.	.	.	.	.	.	.	.	.	.	.	.	T	.	.	.	.	.	.	.	.	.	C	.	.	C	.	.	T	C
1	C1-12	.	.	.	.	.	.	.	.	.	.	.	.	T	.	.	.	.	.	.	.	.	T	.	T	.	.	.	.	.	.	.	C	.	.	C	.	.	T	C
1	C1-13	.	.	.	.	.	.	.	.	.	.	.	.	.	.	.	.	.	.	.	.	.	T	.	.	.	.	.	.	.	.	.	C	.	.	C	.	.	T	C
1	C1-14	.	.	.	.	.	.	.	.	.	.	.	A	.	.	.	.	.	.	.	C	.	.	.	.	C	.	.	.	.	.	.	C	.	.	C	.	.	T	C
1	D-01	.	.	A	.	.	.	.	.	.	.	.	.	.	.	.	.	.	.	.	.	.	.	G	.	.	.	.	.	.	.	.	.	.	.	.	.	.	.	C
1	D-02	.	.	.	.	.	.	.	.	.	.	.	.	.	C	.	.	.	.	.	.	.	T	G	.	.	.	.	.	.	.	.	.	.	.	.	.	.	.	C
1	D-03	.	C	.	.	.	.	.	.	.	.	.	.	.	.	.	.	.	T	.	.	.	T	.	.	.	.	.	.	.	.	.	.	.	.	.	.	.	.	C
2	D-04	.	.	.	T	.	.	.	.	.	.	.	.	.	.	.	.	.	T	.	.	.	T	.	.	.	.	.	.	.	.	.	.	.	.	.	.	.	C	C
1	D-05	.	.	.	.	.	.	.	.	.	.	.	.	.	.	.	.	.	.	.	.	.	T	.	.	.	.	.	.	.	.	.	.	.	.	.	.	.	.	C

base pair span to maximize the sample size used, as some of the sample sequences were unreliable outside of this range. A total of 41 different haplotypes were observed (listed as A201–D05), characterized by 48 variable sites. All four major founding maternal lineages were represented in the current sample (A2: 21%, B: 33%, C1: 35%, D: 11%). This pattern of haplogroup frequencies differs from that found among Amazonian populations, who tend to possess higher frequencies of haplogroup D, and from Andean populations, which have higher frequencies of haplogroup B.

Sequence diversity and neutrality tests

Table 22.2 contains the results for sequence diversity parameters, Π (nucleotide diversity) and h (haplotype diversity), and neutrality test statistics for the populations used in this study, using the HVS1 fragment from nucleotide position 16051 to 16383. Significant values are shown in bold ($p < 0.05$ for Tajima's D and $p < 0.02$ for Fu's F_S). The Peruvian population ranks the highest for both measures of sequence diversity, with the Quechua populations exhibiting similarly high values for both measures. This is to be expected for mixed populations; however, the Yurimagaus sample has greater diversity than does the San Martín de Pangoa, a mixed indigenous population from the Peruvian highlands. The focus Yurimaguas population exhibits a within-group variation pattern similar to that of highland Peruvian populations rather than Amazonian populations, which exhibit comparatively little within-group variation. The Yurimaguas population displays a negative score for both neutrality tests (although only Fu's F_S is significant). The significantly negative Fu's F_S indicates the presence of a higher number of total nucleotide differences than expected for the number of different haplotypes in the population, which is characteristic of recent population expansion. The Aché and Ijka possess the lowest sequence diversity measures among the comparative populations, as noted in previous studies using larger portions of the control region (Melton *et al.*, 2007; Schmitt *et al.*, 2004).

Mismatch distributions (figure not shown) were generated for the Yurimaguas focus population for each individual haplogroup and pooled haplogroups. When the Yurimaguas sample population is considered as a whole, the distribution is bimodal, indicative of a stable population. However, when each haplogroup is displayed separately, a unimodal distribution becomes apparent, which is indicative of recent population expansion. The average number of pairwise differences is 5.972.

Table 22.2. Sequence diversity parameters, Π (nucleotide diversity) and h (haplotype diversity), and neutrality test statistics for the populations used in this study. Significant values shown in bold ($p < 0.05$ for Tajima's D and $p < 0.02$ for Fu's F_S).

Population	N	n_2	k	% unique	h	Π	Tajima's D	Fu's F_S	Source
Aché	63	3	7	0.04762	0.20380	0.00375	−0.39911	3.08577	Schmitt et al., 2004
Arsario	28	4	10	0.14286	0.72490	0.01242	**1.97578**	**5.74459**	Melton et al., 2007
Cayapa	30	8	18	0.26667	0.83680	0.01816	1.15462	2.87312	Rickards et al., 1999
Emberá	44	20	23	0.45455	0.94190	0.01803	0.45886	−4.37850	Kolman and Bermingham 1997
Gavião	28	7	16	0.25000	0.86240	0.01261	0.08383	1.96936	Ward et al., 1996
Ijka	31	3	12	0.09677	0.18490	0.00460	**−1.58397**	−2.96061	Melton et al., 2007
Kogi	21	3	10	0.14286	0.52380	0.00972	0.58130	**5.39794**	Melton et al., 2007
Kuna	63	7	10	0.11111	0.59190	0.00987	1.51872	2.77500	Batista et al., 1995
Mapuche	39	14	21	0.35897	0.91630	0.01628	0.31621	−0.42613	Ginther et al., 1995
Movima	12	8	12	0.66667	0.89390	0.00880	−1.09342	−2.63182	Bert et al., 2004
Moxo	26	20	32	0.76923	0.97540	0.01995	−0.76654	**−9.05762**	Bert et al., 2004
Peru (Yurimaguas)	52	41	46	0.78846	0.98870	0.02221	−1.12081	**−25.08892**	This study
Quechua (Ancash)	33	27	40	0.81818	0.98110	0.01755	−1.48207	**−19.79057**	Lewis et al., 2005
Quechua (Arequipa)	22	17	25	0.77273	0.96540	0.01494	−1.03124	**−8.83975**	Fuselli et al., 2003
Quechua (Tayacaja)	61	42	48	0.68852	0.96780	0.01799	−1.38925	**−25.26771**	Fuselli et al., 2003
San Martin (Mixed)	22	15	22	0.68182	0.93940	0.01531	−0.57306	**−5.44370**	Fuselli et al., 2003
Shamatari	151	6	14	0.03974	0.63930	0.01097	1.20335	6.89414	Williams et al., 2002
Wayuú	30	6	17	0.20000	0.82530	0.01648	0.96660	4.63394	Melton et al., 2007
Wounan	31	14	29	0.45161	0.91180	0.02008	−0.27329	−1.01317	Kolman and Bermingham 1997
Xavante	24	4	10	0.16667	0.68480	0.00925	0.51418	3.75263	Ward et al., 1996
Yanomamö	129	30	31	0.23256	0.90540	0.01434	−0.47596	−8.63071	Merriwether et al., 2000
Yuracare	15	11	22	0.73333	0.95240	0.02002	−0.04894	−2.22439	Bert et al., 2004
Zoro	29	8	16	0.27586	0.75860	0.01148	−0.20284	0.85041	Ward et al., 1996

Relationship among South American populations

Figure 22.2 displays the MJ network analyses. Figure 22.2a shows the results from only the Yurimaguas sample population, while Figure 22.2b includes all of the Peruvian populations. The other Peruvian populations were chosen for inclusion in the Network due to their geographic and genetic similarities with the focus population. While the Moxos from Bolivia shared the greatest number of distinct haplotypes (four) for any single population, including this population in the figure did not increase interpretability, so the Andean populations stand alone for simplicity. In Figure 22.2a, haplogroups C and D show a star-like cluster resulting from the high occurrence of low-frequency mutations. This would normally be indicative of population expansion; however, the ancestral nodes are either missing or appear in low frequency. In Figure 22.2a, the ancestral nodes for haplogroups B and D are not accounted for in the sample Yurimaguas population. However, in Figure 22.2b, which includes the other Peruvian populations in the study, these ancestral nodes are filled in. There do not seem to be any satellite clusters specific to the Yurimaguas sample in haplogroups A, C, and D, indicating that the Yurimaguas sample represents a transient or recent migrant population from other areas. Haplogroup B shows a satellite cluster that is still missing an ancestral node, so the ancestral lineage for the satellite node in B not present in the comparative samples used is a result of sampling error within the Yurimaguas sample or because of the absence of a parental population within the comparative data. This is surprising since haplogroup B is present in such high frequencies among the Peruvian highland populations.

The result of the multidimensional scaling (MDS) plot is shown in Figure 22.3. This three-dimensional plot illustrates the close relationship among the Peruvian samples, while the other Amazonian sample populations appear dispersed. These results mirror previous studies in which greater variation in distance among populations has been found among Amazonian populations when compared with Andean groups (Lewis *et al.*, 2007). The Yuracare and Moxos from Bolivia also show a close relationship to the samples from Peru. This is not surprising given their close geographic proximity and a greater number of shared haplotypes. The location of the Yurimaguas population is central within the MDS plot, which is due to their great diversity. The stress 1 values for the 2D and 3D MDS plots were 0.13665 and 0.07807 respectively, indicating that these plots are a good fit to the original Kimura-2p distance matrix (Sturrock and Roche, 2000).

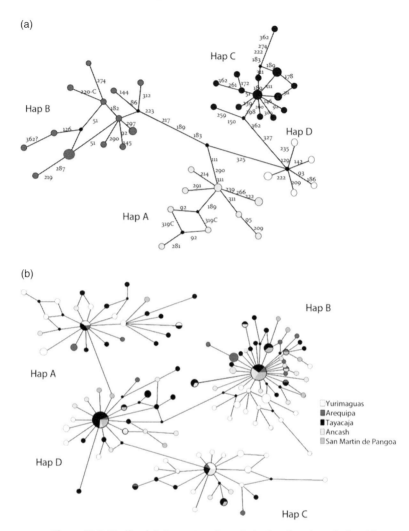

Figure 22.2 Median-joining network analysis showing the relationship among lineages. (a) Displays the network for only the focus population from Yurimaguas. (b) Median-joining network analysis including focus population (white), and the other Peruvian populations (ancestral nodes are marked by pentagons).

The results of the comparison between gene diversity and r_{ii} (plot not shown) place the Yurimaguas, all the Peruvian populations, and the Movima, Moxos, Wounan, Zoro, Gavião, Emberá, as well as the Yuracare populations, above the theoretical regression line ($y = -0.1498x + 0.9613$; $r^2 = 0.3589$), indicating these populations possess higher than expected diversity and are likely undergoing gene flow. While Arasario

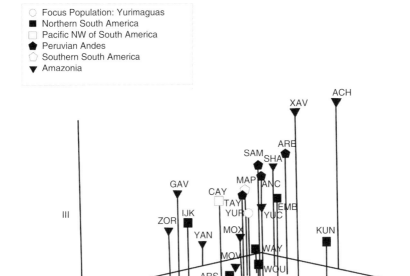

Figure 22.3   Three-dimensional MDS plot for HVS-I sequence data of all populations generated using Kimura-2p distance. Population codes: ACH, Aché; ARS, Arsario; CAY, Cayapa; EMB, Emberá; GAV, Gavião; IJK, Ijka; KOG, Kogi; KUN, Kuna; MAP, Mapuche; MOV, Movima; MOX, Moxo; YUR, focus population (Yurimaguas, Peru); ANC, Quechua (Ancash, Peru); ARE, Quechua (Arequipa, Peru); TAY, Quechua (Tayacaja); SAM, mixed ancestry (San Martin de Pangoa, Peru); SHA, Shamatari; WAY, Wayuú; WOU, Wounan; XAV, Xavante; YAN, Yanomamõ; YUC, Yuracare; ZOR, Zoro.

lies on the regression line, the Mapuche, Wayuú, Cayapa, Shamatari, Kuna, Kogi, Xavante, and Ijka are located below the regression line. These populations possess less diversity than expected from the model, and thus exhibit signs of genetic drift.

Finally, Monmonier's algorithm (results shown on map in Figure 22.1) began its intersection between the northern South American populations and the Amazonian populations, but then creates a loop around the population sampled in this study. This is not surprising given the high genetic diversity within the population sampled. As mentioned previously, most residents of Yurimaguas' new urban settlements or *barriadas* are migrants coming from the surrounding rural areas, and as such the parental populations for the sample are not among the comparative populations. The high variation and the absence of many shared haplotypes with surrounding populations seem to have caused the identification of the Yurimaguas sample as a distinct group (greatest number of shared unique haplotypes is four with the Moxos, followed by three with Ancash Quechua).

DISCUSSION

Our study sets out to characterize the maternal genetic structure of a Peruvian population drawn from the residence of the *barriadas* surrounding the city of Yurimaguas, and then to make inferences about the molecular consequences of migration and urbanization in the *selva baja* region of the Huallaga Valley. Despite more than five centuries of foreign colonization culminating in recent patterns of urbanization and commercialization, and contrary to the self-identification of *mestizo* by most of the participants in the study. 100 percent of the sample from Yurimaguas exhibited an indigenous American maternal DNA lineage (A2: 21%, B: 33%, C1: 35%, D: 11%). So, even with a lengthy history of inter-cultural relations, foreign migration into the *selva baja* region of the Lower Huallaga has not resulted in non-Native maternal gene flow. However, despite the absence of gene flow from Europeans and Africans, the r_{ii} versus h plot indicates significant variation within the population. While there is significant gene flow into this population, it appears to be from other Indigenous American populations. Analysis of the sample data underscores Yurimaguas' history of rapid urbanization. This includes a pattern of massive rural to urban migration, which helps explain the tenfold multiplication in the population of Yurimaguas over the past 50 years.

While our sample revealed no evidence of European gene flow, European migration into the region did in fact affect the genetic structure of the *selva baja*. The population exhibited very high diversity and shared few haplotypes within the sample. High estimates for gene diversity ($h = 0.9887$), along with statistically significant negative values for Fu's F_S (-25.08892, $p < 0.00001$), indicate that the population has undergone a recent population expansion. Given the large population estimates for Amazonia prior to colonization and the discrepancy between the Theta 0 (< 0.001) and Theta 1 (26.328) values resulting from the Mismatch analysis, the Lower Huallaga River Basin experienced a great population decrease post-colonization that has only recently begun to recover. However, as seen in the Network analysis, the Yurimaguas sample does not possess the repetitive ancestral sequences that you would expect of a stable population or one undergoing an endemic population expansion resulting in higher variation (Chakraborty *et al.*, 1988). Accordingly, an alternative explanation is that our molecular results reflect the fusion of formerly isolated populations. The amalgamation of formerly isolated populations results in a sharp increase in variation in a short period of time. However, these newly introduced genetic variants may appear in lower frequency within the context of a highly diverse and large population. Our sample from Yurimaguas is thus representative not of an endemic population, but rather represents a fusion of distinct indigenous peoples, all of whom migrated recently to Yurimaguas in search of improved employment, educational, and social mobility opportunities.

While Yurimaguas is located on the eastern side of the Andes and has historically been inhabited by a number of Amazonian populations, only the Moxos and Yuracare of Bolivia seem to share an appreciable number of unique haplotypes and cluster closely with the Yurimaguas sample in the MDS plots. Instead, the sample under study exhibits a closer relationship to Andean populations including the highland populations of Peru (primarily Quechua), the southern South American Mapuche, and the northern South American Emberá (Figure 22.3). The Quechua populations filled in the missing ancestral nodes in the Network, sharing haplotypes within haplogroups A, C, and D. These factors may indicate that a significant proportion of the individuals moving into Yurimaguas to seek employment have been from the Peruvian highlands. Also, these populations share a more distant relationship as a result of the Huallaga region being long used as a historical trade route between the highlands and the rest of Amazonia. So, these similarities are the result of both shared population history with the other Peruvian populations and indicative of the great genetic and geographic diversity of the Amazonian region.

Despite the centrality of the Yurimaguas sample in the MDS plots, Monmonier's algorithm detects a genetic barrier surrounding this population, clearly separating Yurimaguas from all other populations. This genetic barrier is the result of several factors. First, Yurimaguas shares few haplotypes within haplogroup B with the other Peruvian populations. This exaggerates the distance between them as haplogroup B is the most common haplogroup in the Andean highlands. Additionally, no comparative samples exist for other indigenous populations who traditionally live in and around Yurimaguas, which may explain why ancestral nodes are missing from the Network analysis, especially in the case of Haplogroup B. Finally, Yurimaguas is a unique population within the Amazon, as it is highly diverse and exhibits high frequencies of haplogroup C and low D.

CONCLUSIONS

In spite of nearly half a millennium of colonial contact, not to mention the prevalence of self-proclaimed *mestizo* identity, analysis of the mtDNA of the populations residing in the *barriadas* enveloping Yurimaguas reveals no history of non-native maternal admixture. As noted, Yurimaguas has experienced a recent population expansion due in part to rural to urban migration. Indeed, population expansion in Yurimaguas is not endemic, but rather the result of population fusion from various indigenous Amazonian populations as a result of urbanization, the expansion of extractive enterprise in the Lower Huallaga, as well as the region's increased incorporation into global markets. Indeed, the area in which the samples were collected is under migratory pressures. While European conquest and subsequent colonization resulted in profound genetic change in Peruvian Amazonia, our analysis of the genetic profile of the Yurimaguas sample underscores the significance of more recent indigenous migration and urbanization, which reflect the cyclical nature of the *selva baja*'s extractive industries. This would explain the high occurrence of low-frequency haplotypes within the sample. The Yurimaguas sample's lack of consistent shared haplotypes with other samples indicates that most of the migrants are neither from distant Andean highlands nor remote Amazonian regions. Instead, molecular and ethnographic evidence indicate that most migrants in the Yurimaguas sample population originated from nearby communities in the *selva baja* not previously sampled. Furthermore, we found no evidence of a kin pattern in the migration to Yurimaguas. Since there was no attempt to remove any individuals from the sample that were related, one would expect to have found repeated haplotypes with a kin-structured migration. The apparent fusion of indigenous populations from surrounding *selva baja* populations now residing in Yurimaguas has caused a highly diversified and unique gene pool.

REFERENCES

Achilli, A., Perego, U. A., Bravi, C. M., *et al.* (2008). The phylogeny of the four Pan-American MtDNA haplogroups: implications for evolutionary and disease studies. *PLoS ONE*, **3**, e1764.

Alves-Silva, J., da Silva Santos, M., Guimarães, P. E. M., *et al.* (2000). The ancestry of Brazilian mtDNA lineages. *American Journal of Human Genetics*, **67**, 444–61.

Ardito Vega, W. (1992). La estructura de las reducciones de Maynas. *Amazonía Peruana*, **11**, 93–124.

Bandelt, H. J., Forster, P., and Rohl, A. (1999). Median-joining networks for inferring intraspecific phylogenies. *Molecular Biology and Evolution*, **16**, 37–48.

Batista, O., Kolman, C. J., and Bermingham, E. (1995). Mitochondrial DNA diversity in the Kuna Amerinds of Panama. *Human Molecular Genetics*, **4**, 921–9.

Bert, F., Corella, A., Gené, M., Pérez-Pérez, A., and Turbón, D. (2004). Mitochondrial DNA diversity in the Llanos de Moxos: Moxo, Movima, and Yuracare indigenous American populations from Bolivia lowlands. *Annals of Human Biology*, **31**, 9–28.

Bonatto, S. L. and Salzano, F. M. (1997). A single and early migration for the peopling of the Americas supported by mitochondrial DNA sequence data. *Proceedings of the National Academy of Science of the United States of America*, **94**, 1866–71.

Braun, R. (1982). The Formative as seen from the Southern Ecuadorian Highlands. In *Primer Simposio de Correlaciones Antropológicas Andino-Mesoamericanas*, ed. J. G. Marcos and P. Norton, pp. 41–100. Guayaquil, Ecuador: ESPOL.

Bruhns, K. O., Burton, J., and Miller, G. R. (1990). Excavations at Pirincay in the Paute Valley of southern Ecuador, 1985–1988. *Antiquity*, **64**, 221–33.

Buitron, A. (1948). *Etude ethnographique de la vallée du Huallaga*. Paris: UNESCO.

Chakraborty, R., Smouset, P. E., and Neel, J. V. (1988). Population amalgamation and genetic variation: observations on artificially agglomerated tribal populations of Central and South America. *American Journal of Human Genetics*, **43**, 709–25.

Chantre y Herrera, J. (1901). *Historia de las Misiones de la Compañía de Jesús en el Marañón español 1637–1767*. Madrid: Imprenta de A. Avrial.

Chiro, M. (1943). *Tingo María: Ensayo Monográfico*. Lima: Libería e Imprenta El Competidor.

Cook, N. D. (1998). *Born to Die: Disease and New World Conquest, 1492–1650*. New York: Cambridge University Press.

Crosby, A. (1972). *The Columbian Exchange: The Biological and Cultural Consequences of 1492*. Westport, CT: Greenwood Press.

Crosby, A. (1986). *Ecological Imperialism: The Biological Expansion of Europe, 900–1900*. New York: Cambridge University Press.

Davies, N. (1997). *The Ancient Kingdoms of Peru*. New York: Penguin Books.

Davies, T. (1974). *Indian Integration in Peru: A Half-Century of Experience, 1900–1948*. Lincoln, NE: University of Nebraska Press.

Dean, B. (1990). The State and the Aguaruna: frontier expansion in the Upper Amazon, 1541–1990. M.A. thesis, Harvard University.

Dean, B. (2009). *Urarina Society, History and Cosmology in Peruvian Amazonia*. Gainesville, FL: University Press of Florida.

Dean, B. and Levi, J. (eds.) (2003). *At the Risk of Being Heard: Identity, Indigenous Rights, and Postcolonial States*. Ann Arbor, MI: University of Michigan Press.

Dean, B. and Silverstein, S. (2011). The new urban jungle: contesting territories and identities in the Upper Amazon. *Cultural Survival Quarterly*, **35**, 34–45.

Domínguez, C. and Gómez, A. (1990). *La Economía Extractiza en la Amazonía Colombiana*. Bogotá: COA.

Dupanloup, I., Schneider, S., and Excoffier, L. (2002). A simulated annealing approach to define the genetic structure of populations. *Molecular Ecology*, **11**, 2571–81.

Espinosa, O. (1995). *Rondas Campesinas y Nativas en la Amazonía Peruana*. Lima: CAAAP.

Excoffier, L., Laval, G., and Schneider, S. (2005). Arlequin ver. 3.0: an integrated software package for population genetics data analysis. *Evolutionary Bioinformatics Online*, **1**, 47–50.

Fritz, S. (1922). *Journal of the Travels and Labours of Father Samuel Fritz in the River of Amazons between 1686 and 1723* (trans. and ed. G. Edmundson). London: Hakluyt Society.

Fu, Y. X. (1997). Statistical tests of neutrality of mutations against population growth, hitchhiking and background selection. *Genetics*, **147**, 915–25.

Fuselli, S., Tarazona-Santos, E., Dupanloup, I., *et al.* (2003). Mitochondrial DNA diversity in South America and the genetic history of Andean Highlanders. *Molecular Biology and Evolution*, **20**, 1682–91.

Ginther, C., Corach, D., Penacino, G., *et al.* (1995). Genetic variation among the Mapuche Indians from the Patogonian region of Argentina: mitochondrial DNA sequence variation and allele frequencies of several nuclear genes. In *DNA Fingerprinting: State of the Science*, ed. S. Pena, R. Chakraborty, J. Epplen, and A. Jeffreys, pp. 211–19. Basel, Switzerland: Birkhäuser-Verlag.

Golob, A. (1982). The Upper Amazon in historical perspective. Ph.D. dissertation, City University of New York.

Gootenberg, P. (2009). *Andean Cocaine: The Making of a Global Drug*. Chapel Hill, NC: University of North Carolina Press.

Haring, M. (1986). *Boomtown aan de Amazone: een historisch-sociologische studie over de Peruaanse Amazoneregio en de stad Iquitos, met nadruk op de periode 1880-1980.* Utrecht, Negtherlands: Instituut voor Culturele Antropologie, Rijksuniversiteit Utrecht.

Harpending, H. and Jenkins, T. (1973). Genetic distance among Southern African populations. In *Methods and Theories of Anthropological Genetics*, ed. M. H. Crawford and P. L. Workman. Albuquerque, NM: University of New Mexico Press.

Harpending, H. C. and Ward, R. H. (1982). Chemical systematics and human populations. In *Biochemical Aspects of Evolutionary Biology*, ed. M. H. Nitechi. Chicago, IL: University of Chicago Press.

Heckenberger, M. and Neves, E. G. (2009). Amazonian archaeology. *Annual Review of Anthropology*, **38**, 251–66.

Her Majesty's Consuls (1864). *Commercial Reports Received at the Foreign Office Between July 1st 1863 and June 30*. London: Harrison and Sons.

Herndon, W. L. (1952). *Exploration of the Valley of the Amazon* (ed. H. Basso). New York: McGraw-Hill.

INEI (2007). *Perfiles de Sociodemográficos. Resultados Censos de los Nacionales.* Lima: Instituto Nacional de Estadística e Informática.

INEI (2010). *Censos Nacionales de Población y Vivienda de 1940, 1961, 1972, 1981, 1993 y 2007.* Lima: Instituto Nacional de Estadística e Informática.

Jackson, J. (2008). *The Thief at the End of the World: Rubber, Power, and the Seeds of Empire*. New York: Viking Publishing.

Kernaghan, R. (2009). *Coca's Gone: Of Might and Right in the Huallaga Post-Boom*. Stanford, CA: Stanford University Press.

Kolman, C. J. and Bermingham, E. (1997). Mitochondrial and nuclear DNA diversity in the Choco and Chibcha Amerinds of Panama. *Genetics*, **147**, 1289–302.

Lalueza-Fox, C., Calderon, F. L., Calafell, F., Morera, B., and Bertranpetit, J. (2001). MtDNA from extinct Tainos and the peopling of the Caribbean. *Annals of Human Genetics*, **65**, 137–51.

Lewis, C. M., Lizarraga, B., Tito, R. Y., *et al.* (2007). Mitochondrial DNA and the peopling of South America. *Human Biology*, **79**, 159–78.

Lewis, C. M., Jr., Tito, R. Y., Lizarraga, B., and Stone, A. C. (2005). Land, language, and loci: mtDNA in Native Americans and the genetic history of Peru. *American Journal of Physical Anthropology*, **127**, 351–60.

Mann, C. C. (2005). *1491: New Revelations of the Americas Before Columbus*. New York: Alfred A. Knopf.

Marzal, M. (1984). Las reducciones indígenas en la amazonía peruano. *Amazonía Peruana*, **5**, 7–45.

Melton, P. E., Briceño, I., Gomez, A., *et al.* (2007). Biological relationship between Central and South American Chibchan speaking populations: evidence from mtDNA. *American Journal of Physical Anthropology*, **133**, 753–70.

Merriwether, D. R. and Ferrell, R. E. (1995). Distribution of the four founding haplotypes in indigenous Americans suggests a single wave of migration for the New World. *American Journal of Physical Anthropology*, **98**, 411–30.

Merriwether, D. A., Kemp, B. M., Crews, D. E., and Neel, J. V. (2000). Gene flow and genetic variation in the Yanomama as revealed by mitochondrial DNA. In *America Past, America Present: Genes and Languages in the Americas and Beyond*, ed. C Renfrew, pp. 89–124. Cambridge, UK: McDonald Institute for Archaeological Research.

Miller, M. P. (2005). Alleles in space: computer software for the joint analysis of interindividual spatial and genetic information. *Journal of Heredity*, **96**, 722–4.

Myers, T. (1974). Spanish contacts and social change on the Ucayali River, Peru. *Ethnohistory*, **21**(2), 135–57.

Myers, T. P. and Dean, B. (1999). Cerámica prehispánica del río Chambira, Loreto. *Amazonía peruana*, **13**, 255–88.

Nei, M. (1987). *Molecular Evolutionary Genetics*. New York: Columbia University Press.

Nei, M. and Li, W. H. (1979). Mathematical model for studying genetic variation in terms of restriction endonucleases. *Proceedings of the National Academy of Sciences of the United States of America*, **76**, 5269–73.

Pennano, G. (1988). *La Economía del Caucho*. Iquitos, Peru: CETA.

Pereira, M., Socorro, A., Fernandez, I., *et al.* (2005). Phylogenetic information in polymorphic L1 and Alu insertions from East Asians and Indigenous American populations. *American Journal of Physical Anthropology*, **128**, 171–84.

Ramos, V. A. and Folguera, A. (2009). Andean flat-slab subduction through time. *Geologic Society*, **327**, 31–54.

Regan, J. (1983). *Hacia la tierra sin mal: estudio sobre la religiosidad del pueblo en la Amazonía*. Iquitos, Peru: CETA

Reyes Flores, A. (1999). *Hacendados y Comerciantes: Piura-Chachapoyas-Moyobamba-Lamas-Maynas (1770-1820)*. Lima: Juan Brito.

Rhoades, R. E. and Bidegaray, P. (1987). *The Farmers of Yurimaguas: Land Use and Cropping Strategies in the Peruvian Jungle*. Lima: International Potato Center.

Rickards, O., Martinez-Labarga, C., Lum, J. K., De Stefano, G. F., and Cann, R. L. (1999). MtDNA history of the Cayapa Amerinds of Ecuador: detection of additional founding lineages for the Native American populations. *American Journal of Human Genetics*, **65**, 519–30.

Riley, J. (2010). Smallpox and American Indians revisited. *Journal of the History of Medicine and Allied Sciences*, **65**, 445–77.

Rohlf, F. J. (2003). *NTSYSpc: Numerical Taxonomy System, ver. 2.11s*. Setauket, NY: Exeter Publishing.

Rogers, A. R. and Harpending, H. (1992). Population growth makes waves in the distribution of pairwise genetic differences. *Molecular Biology and Evolution*, **9**, 552–69.

Rubicz, R., Schurr, T., Babb, P. L., and Crawford, M. H. (2003). Mitochondrial DNA variation and the origins of the Aleuts. *Human Biology*, **75**, 809–35.

Rubicz, R., Zlojutro, M., Sun, G., *et al.* (2010). Genetic architecture of a small, recently aggregated Aleut population: Bering Island, Russia. *Human Biology*, **82**, 719–36.

Salzano, F. M. (2002). Molecular variability in Indigenous Americans: widespread but uneven information. *Anais da Academia Brasileira de Ciências*, **74**, 223–63.

San Román, J. V. (1975). *Perfiles Históricos de la Amazonía Peruana*. Lima: Ediciones Paulinas.

Schmitt, R., Bonatto, S. L., Freitas, L. B., *et al.* (2004). Extremely limited mitochondrial DNA variability among the Aché Natives of Paraguay. *Annals of Human Biology*, **31**, 87–94.

Schurr, T. and Sherry, S. (2004). Mitochondrial DNA and Y chromosome diversity and the peopling of the Americas: evolutionary and demographic evidence. *American Journal of Human Biology*, **16**, 420–39.

Smyth, W. and Lowe, F. (1836). *Narrative of a Journey from Lima to Para, Across the Andes and Down the Amazon: Undertaken with a view of ascertaining the practicability of a navigable communication with the Atlantic, by the rivers Pachitea, Ucayali, and Amazon*. London: J. Murray.

Stanfield, M. E. (1998). *Red Rubber, Bleeding Trees: Violence, Slavery and Empire in the Upper Amazon, 1850-1933*. Albuquerque, NM: University of New Mexico Press.

Stephan, J. (2000). Jesuiten am Amazonas: spanische Herrschaft und Mission in der Grenzprovinz Maynas 1619-1768. Doctoral thesis, Katholische Universität.

Stiglich Álvarez, G. (1913). *Diccionario Geográfico del Perú*. Lima: Imprenta Torres Aguirre.

Stocks, A. (1983). Native enclaves in the Upper Amazon: a case of regional non-integration. *Ethnohistory*, **30**(2), 77–92.

Sturrock, K. and Roche, J. (2000). A multidimensional scaling stress evaluation table. *Field Methods*, **12**, 49–60.

Tajima, F. (1989). Statistical method for testing the neutral mutation hypothesis by DNA polymorphism. *Genetics*, **123**, 585–95.

Tarazona-Santos, E., Carvalho-Silva, D. R., Pettener, D., *et al.* (2001). Genetic differentiation in South Amerindians is related to environmental and cultural diversity: evidence from the Y chromosome. *American Journal of Human Genetics*, **68**, 1485–96.

Torroni, A., Cabell, M. F., Brown, M. D., *et al.* (1993b). Asian affinities and continental radiation of the four founding American Native mtDNAs. *American Journal of Human Genetics*, **53**, 563–90.

Torroni, A., Schurr, T. G., Starikovskaya, Y. B., *et al.* (1993a). mtDNA variation of Aboriginal Siberians reveals distinct genetic affinities with Indigenous Americans. *American Journal of Human Genetics*, **53**, 591–608.

Vigilant, L., Stoneking, M., Harpending, H., Hawkes, K., and Wilson, A. C. (1991). African populations and the evolution of human mitochondrial DNA. *Science*, **253**, 1503–7.

Villarejo, A. (1988). *Así es la Selva*. Iquitos, Peru: CETA.

Wang, S., Lewis, C. M., Jakobsson, M., *et al.* (2007). Genetic variation and population structure in Native Americans. *PLoS Genetics*, **3**, e185.

Ward, R. H., Salzano, F. M., Bonatto, S. L., *et al.* (1996). Mitochondrial DNA polymorphism in three Brazilian Indian tribes. *American Journal of Human Biology*, **8**, 317–23.

Williams, S. R., Chagnon, N. A., and Spielman, R. S. (2002). Nuclear and mitochondrial genetic variation in the Yanomamo: a test case for ancient DNA studies of prehistoric populations. *American Journal of Physical Anthropology*, **117**, 246–59.

CARLOS EDUARDO GUERRA AMORIM, CAROLINA
CARVALHO GONTIJO, AND SILVIENE FABIANA DE OLIVEIRA

23

Migration in Afro-Brazilian rural communities: crossing historical, demographic, and genetic data

INTRODUCTION

In this chapter we present a general overview of the causes and consequences of migration in Brazilian Afro-derived rural communities. These communities, known in Brazil as *Remanescentes de Quilombos*, present some important characteristics that make them ideal models to study human migrations on a local scale, such as a distinct genetic constitution and also some degree of isolation. They were mainly formed by fugitive and freed African slaves and their descendants (Reis and Gomes, 1996). For this reason, African ancestry is predominant in their genetic composition (Bortolini *et al.*, 1999) in contrast to other Brazilian populations, in which the European contribution is more preeminent (Godinho *et al.*, 2008). Moreover, these communities were usually located at a considerable distance from urban centers, as a strategy for resisting slavery during colonial times (Reis and Gomes, 1996); nowadays, this confers them a certain degree of isolation (Souza and Culpi, 2005).

Our study seeks to relate the socioeconomic causes of the migratory behavior observed in these communities to the evolutionary consequences of gene flow at the population level, in order to understand the role of migration as an agent in the evolution of smallholder populations. We start this chapter by unraveling the history behind the first migrations of Africans to the Americas and then explain the current situation of the African descendants in Brazil, before a brief description

Causes and Consequences of Human Migration, ed. Michael H. Crawford and Benjamin C. Campbell. Published by Cambridge University Press. © Cambridge University Press 2012.

473

of the communities here employed as models (*Mocambo*, *Riacho de Sacutiaba e Sacutiaba*, and *Rio das Rãs*). Next, there is a detailed description of the observed migratory patterns in these communities, followed by an analysis of admixture with uni- and biparental genetic markers. Finally, demographic and genetic data are crossed in order to propose new insights into the study of migrations in rural smallholder populations. We believe this might serve as a primary source for comparative studies of migration, providing guidance for assessing models of past and current human population mobility.

THE CONSTITUTION OF THE BRAZILIAN POPULATION: A GENERAL OVERVIEW AND THE AFRICAN SLAVE TRADE TO THE COUNTRY

The Brazilian population was formed by an intense admixture process including three main parental groups: Amerindians, sub-Saharan Africans, and Europeans (mainly Iberians). The admixture between these groups over the last 500 years in Brazil was not homogeneous, nor was their dispersion into the different regions of the country. This heterogeneity is also reflected in the differential phenotypic distribution observed nowadays. According to the last Brazilian census, conducted in 2010 by the *Instituto Brasileiro de Geografia e Estatística* (Brazilian Institute of Geography and Statistics, free translation; IBGE, 2010), half of the over 190 million Brazilians have indications of African ancestry (people who were self-identified as "black" or "admixed," using the terminology applied by IBGE). However, the percentage of the self-identified in the categories defined by IBGE varies among the Brazilian regions, and the highest "admixed" and "black" proportion is found in the Northeastern region (IBGE, 2010) as shown in Figure 23.1.

Godinho *et al.* (2008) have estimated the contribution of the Amerindian, African, and European parental groups to the five Brazilian regions (North, Northeast, Center-West, Southeast, and South) based on autosomal STR data. Parental contributions to the current Brazilian population estimated by autosomal STRs (Figure 23.2) have shown different proportions from those indicated by self-identification (Figure 23.1). Other estimates based on genetic markers belonging to different chromosomes have yielded different results (Figure 23.2): Brazilian male lineages – Y-chromosome markers – are mainly European whilst female lineages – mitochondrial DNA (mtDNA) – belong to the three parental groups in similar proportions among them.

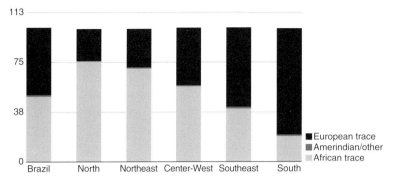

Figure 23.1 Percentages of individuals with European (self-identified as "white"), Amerindian/other (self-identified as "indigenous" or "other"), and African traces (self-identified as "black" or "admixed") according to the last Brazilian census in all five Brazilian regions (IBGE, 2010).

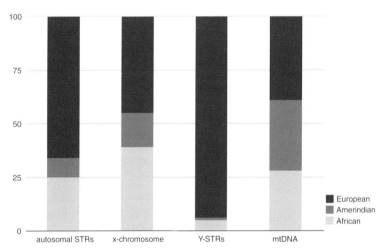

Figure 23.2 Admixture estimates based on autosomal STRs (Godinho *et al.*, 2008), X chromosome (Monteiro, 2007), Y chromosome (Grattapaglia, 2005), and mtDNA (Alves-Silva *et al.*, 2000) for the Brazilian population.

Comparing self-identification according to the groups defined by IBGE (Figure 23.1) with ancestry affiliations obtained by genetic marker analyses (Figure 23.2), it becomes evident that, in general, Amerindian and European contributions are underestimated by self-identification, while the African is overestimated. It is likely that this is due to the great number of people self-identification as "admixed," because this group comprises people of multiple ancestries, but is usually considered together with those self-identified as "black." Affirmative actions, intending to promote equal opportunities for people of African ancestry, have been being implemented in Brazil over the last few years and have led to an increase in self-esteem and, consequently, an increment in the number of people self-identified as "black" and "admixed." Again, these categories are taken together by IBGE, even though they include multiple ancestries. Furthermore, it is very improbable to find Brazilians of exclusive African ancestry with no contribution from any other parental group, but it is quite possible to find Brazilians with exclusive Amerindian or European ancestry (see Wang *et al.*, 2008, for examples).

The European flow to Brazil began in 1500 with the arrival of the first Portuguese caravels. Portugal was the main source of European migrants to the country, but later the influx of people from different nations, especially Italy, was intensified due to governmental incentive to migration. This second wave of European migrations to Brazil lasted from the mid nineteenth century until the beginning of the twentieth century. These new migrants were mainly settled in Southern and Southeastern Brazil in both urban and rural areas, but even though Italian migration became very important, it never outnumbered Portuguese migration (Fausto, 2002).

When the first Europeans arrived in the region, the Amerindian population was estimated at one to ten million people (FUNAI, 2011), most belonging to Tupi-Guarani groups (Fausto, 2002). Contact with the Portuguese, sometimes peaceful, but more often hostile, led to admixture and a drastic decrease in the Brazilian Amerindian population to the currently estimated 460 000 individuals (around 0.25% of the Brazilian population) living in 225 Amerindian societies and another 100 000 to 190 000 living outside these lands, including urban areas. There are also groups currently waiting for official acknowledgment by FUNAI and there are also indications of the existence of around 63 isolated groups that have never been contacted (FUNAI, 2011). Many Amerindian groups became extinct, but their genetic contribution to the Brazilian gene pool, caused by admixture with both Europeans and Africans, is still significant.

There are estimates that 40% of the African slaves brought to the Americas (3.6 to 10 million people) had Brazil as their destination. Historical records from the slave trade and trafficking period are full of gaps, partly due to the fact that old documents were frequently imprecise and rarely standardized, but also because there were no registers, and the harbors used for shipping and receiving slaves were constantly changed to avoid surveillance when the slave trade became illegal. Still, the existing records state that most slaves brought by the Portuguese were Bantu and Sudanese captured on both east and west sub-Saharan coasts (Sudanese here refers to proximal sub-Saharan peoples, not necessarily from Sudan; Salzano and Freire-Maia, 1967). Throughout the centuries during which they were brought to Brazil, enslaved Africans were captured and shipped from different regions (Mello e Souza, 2006). In the early sixteenth century, their main origins were the harbors in the Congo and, less importantly, Angola, both in West Africa (Mello e Souza, 2006; Schwartz, 1988). With the growing Dutch influence and domination, the Portuguese Crown established harbors and trade in regions farther south, mainly in Angola, at Luanda and Benguela harbors. During the eighteenth century, two places located in the Gulf of Guinea – the Bight of Benin and the *Costa da Mina* – gained importance for the slave trade. Nevertheless, about one fourth of all slaves brought to Brazil still came from Angola, even during the nineteenth century (Schwartz, 1988).

At the beginning of the eighteenth century, as a consequence of the intensification of the slave trade and changes in the political scenario, slaves were captured in more inland regions, closer to the African Great Lakes. The predominance of the ethnic groups captured, enslaved, and traded varied over time, because of the alliances formed, accessibility, and control over harbors, and also due to political issues determining the places and kingdoms where slaves were sought. The Congo and Angola, for instance, traded predominantly Bantu people, whilst Benguela traded different groups (Mello e Souza, 2006).

The opening and consequent intensification of the Atlantic slave trade were influenced by external politics, as mentioned above, but also by internal politics in Africa. Variation in the internal scenario depended greatly on the fluid participation of the Portuguese, who made alliances with local chiefs of small and large kingdoms (Ferreira, 2006b). Thus, many different African peoples acted as *pumbeiros* – those who captured slaves – even though they were also subjected to slavery. Among the main ethnic groups who participated in this were the Jaga, Umbundo, Imbangala, Ovimbundu, and Yoruba (Mello e Souza, 2006).

The Congo and Angola held the harbors from where the largest number of African slaves was shipped to Brazil. These regions, which are nowadays a reference for understanding African–European interactions during the colonial time, are still predominantly, yet not exclusively, peopled by Bantus. Around 40% of all slaves brought to the Americas are estimated to have been shipped from these regions and might, therefore, have belonged to the Bantu group (Miller, 1988). The captured slaves belonged mainly to the kingdoms of Cabinda, Dongo, Congo, Daomé, Kazembe, Luba, Lunda, and Lozi (Mello e Souza, 2006).

According to Nina Rodrigues (2004), most studies on the African slave trade to Brazil have prioritized Rio de Janeiro harbor, Vacongo, as a reference, and so Bantu groups were frequently considered the only – or almost exclusive – ethnic group brought to the country. Another distortion generated by giving Vacongo harbor such priority is the assumption that the state of Bahia (northwards in relation to Vacongo) received only Sudanese slaves. However, because of bilateral agreements between Brazilian states and African harbors, it can still be said that certain ethnic groups were predominant in different Brazilian regions.

Internal African migrations and the availability of slaves from different ethnic groups at distinct moments must also be taken into account. The harbor of Salvador, Bahia state, for instance, received mostly Sudanese slaves, who were sold to southern Bahia and to states located at inner land Brazil, such as Minas Gerais and Goiás (Schwartz, 1988), where therefore Sudanese ethnic groups and their enslaved descendants were present in a large number. However, because Bantus were, and still are, the predominant ethnic group in Africa, they also represented an important number of slaves and consequently contributed to the gene pool of the Northeastern region, where the states of Bahia and Pernambuco are situated.

As previously mentioned, Brazil received a large number of enslaved Africans. According to the 1849 census, this number was so significant that in this year the freed and enslaved people in Rio de Janeiro represented 43.5% of the local population (Karasch, 2000). During the seventeenth century, when the slave trade to the country intensified, the flow from Angola reached an annual mean of 6000–9000 slaves (Alencastro, 2000). During the nineteenth century, between 1838 and 1839, over 40 000 slaves were brought to Brazil (Alencastro, 2000), 70–90% of them through the harbor of Rio de Janeiro (Schwartz, 1988), and between 1846 and 1850, the average annual number of slaves entering Brazil came close to 50 000 people (Florentino, 2002), indicating the great importance of these people for the constitution of the Brazilian populations, yet their history and organization during early times is still not fully understood.

THE CONTEMPORARY 'QUILOMBO' COMMUNITIES

In Brazil, African slaves resisted slavery in different ways like suicide, aggression to their masters and, especially, escaping and hiding in remote and difficult to reach places. This gave rise to geographically isolated communities known as *Quilombos* (Reis and Gomes, 1996). Over 1500 Brazilian rural communities, spread over every part of the country, descend from old *Quilombo* communities (Palmares, 2011). These populations are currently known as *Remanescentes de Quilombos* or simply as contemporary *Quilombos* and include communities presenting a wide range of religious, economic, and demographic characteristics (Arruti, 2006; Brasileiro and Sampaio, 2002; Reis and Gomes, 1996; Silva, 2000; Véran, 2000). Despite being heterogeneous, the *Remanescentes de Quilombos* present a common feature: their existence is linked to the presence of African slavery in Brazil. Brazilian legislation recognizes them as belonging to an ethnic group, which is defined by self-identification, with presumed black ancestry associated with a specific historical trajectory and territorial relationships, and related to resistance against historical oppression. Some of the *Remanescentes de Quilombos* are in fact the heirs of the old *Quilombos* and exist in the same territory, but others are freed slaves to whom the land was given after the abolition of slavery (Silva, 2000).

According to Brazilian regulations, the certification of a community as a *Remanescente de Quilombo* allows its inhabitants to request ownership of the land they live in. This process usually takes a long time, beginning with the self-recognition of the community as being mainly composed of the descendants of slaves; this stage is followed by a series of anthropological studies that aim to evaluate the traditional use of the land by its inhabitants and to analyze the genealogical relationships. The ownership of land can then be regulated and its inhabitants may gain the right to live in the community.

Better understanding of the demographic and genetic characteristics of these communities is essential for reconstructing the history of Africans and their descendants in Brazil, especially because there is a lack of documents about the early life of *Quilombos* (Funari, 1996; Reis and Gomes, 1996; Silva, 2000). The great majority of the available documents are those used for search warrants, written by military personnel that aimed to destroy the *Quilombos* (Reis and Gomes, 1996; Silva, 2000). These documents can be used to check the existence of some of these communities, but not for a better understanding of the *Quilombos'* life, politics, and social organization. Furthermore, less than 10% of the *Quilombos* have been studied with genetic markers (Abe-Sandes *et al.*, 2004; Bortolini *et al.*, 1999; Carvalho *et al.*, 2008; Gontijo *et al.*, 2010; Ribeiro-dos-Santos *et al.*, 2002; Silva *et al.*, 2006; Souza and Culpi, 2005) and even fewer have been demographically characterized (Amorim *et al.*, 2011; Novion *et al.*, 2004; Oliveira *et al.*, 2008).

Quilombos are known to have been formed mainly by African slaves from different African nations or their descendants, but there were also people from other ethnic and geographic backgrounds, such as Europeans and Amerindians (Silva, 2000). The latter were also enslaved in colonial Brazil and, therefore, also joined the *Quilombos* in order to resist slavery (Funari, 1996; Reis and Gomes, 1996). Kidnapping of Amerindian women was also a common phenomenon in the *Quilombo* life, especially in those places where gold-mining was a common practice. In such cases, female slaves were left to do housework in farms or urban centers as well as in agricultural areas; while male slaves were supposed to mine, having therefore more opportunities for escape (Karasch, 1996). The Europeans were mainly Portuguese men. As they had free passage to metropolitan areas, they made it possible to exchange goods and information between the *Quilombos* and the cities (Reis and Gomes, 1996).

Since 1998, our research group has been conducting investigations with some of these communities (e.g. Amorim *et al.*, 2011; Gontijo *et al.*, 2010; Novion *et al.*, 2004; Oliveira *et al.*, 2004, 2006, 2008; Ribeiro *et al.*, 2009, 2011), including three populations located by the São Francisco River in Northeastern Brazil (Figure 23.3): *Mocambo*, *Riacho de Sacutiaba e Sacutiaba* (from now on referred to as *Sacutiaba*), and *Rio das Rãs*. These populations have all been certified by the Brazilian government as *Remanescentes de Quilombos* (Palmares, 2011). The choice of subjects for this research was based on the fact that they all have this certification and the ownership of the land is already regulated.

In 1998, we visited these three communities and interviewed over 500 individuals. At that time, *Mocambo* had an estimated population of 500 inhabitants. This community is located in the State of Sergipe, close to an indigenous reserve, the *Xocó*, with whose inhabitants they keep contact, and sometimes contract marriages. The first reports of the existence of slaves in the region are about 200 years old. In 1825 slaves reached around 7% of the municipality population (Arruti, 2006).

The remaining communities are located in the State of Bahia, approximately 1100 km from *Mocambo*, and 246 km apart. *Sacutiaba* has approximately 200 inhabitants. It is organized in approximately 35 domestic groups representing an extended family centralized around the leadership of a matriarch. It is believed that this population has been settled in the region for 200 years (Brasileiro and Sampaio, 2002).

Rio das Rãs is one of the largest Brazilian *Quilombos*, despite having been established by only a small number of families in the first half of

Figure 23.3 Geographical location of the three analyzed Afro-Brazilian communities.

the nineteenth century. The first inhabitants of this land were a group of Amerindians, who were then replaced by the *Quilombo* population (Véran, 2000). At least 230 families now live in this community (Véran, 2000) and are spread along a wide area of 38 000 ha (Silva, 2000). The region where *Rio das Rãs* is located was once important for inland slave trade routes, after overseas slave trade had been forbidden (Silva, 2000).

These three populations are located in rural areas and, like other Brazilian contemporary *Quilombos*, they maintain a lifestyle based on subsistence agriculture and livestock farming. This is a source of products they exchange with neighboring metropolitan populations, establishing therefore a certain degree of contact with people from distinct ethnic backgrounds (Arruti, 2006; Brasileiro and Sampaio, 2002; Reis and Gomes, 1996; Véran, 2000).

MIGRATION AND MATRIMONY IN BRAZILIAN 'QUILOMBOS'

In order to understand the causes and consequences of migration in Afro-Brazilian rural communities, we first conducted a demographic characterization of the three target populations, seeking associations between sociocultural features and migratory patterns. Migration is known to be one of the main factors influencing population size and composition (Mielke and Fix, 2007). It is also an important evolutionary force that shapes genetic diversity, introducing new variants, possibly leading to the homogenization of populations (Fix, 1999). Mobility patterns may be determined by sociocultural factors, by the environment, and also by genetic variation (Marlowe, 2004; Mielke and Fix, 2007). Among the sociocultural factors, matrimony and economics are the most common determiners (Fix, 1999; Marlowe, 2004; Mielke and Fix, 2007).

The characterization of the demographic profile of the three *Quilombos* was based on information about migration, age, gender, and marriage structures, using questionnaires filled out during the interviews conducted in 1998. These questionnaires included data on sex, age, place of birth, and marital status of the respondents and their children, spouses, parents, and grandparents. We interviewed 171 respondents in *Mocambo*, 70 in *Sacutiaba*, and 278 in *Rio das Rãs*.

For a better visualization of age information, age pyramids with intervals of five years were constructed, in which the extant offspring of the respondents were also included and male and females were separated. These respondents were classified either as "migrants," defined as *Quilombo* inhabitants that were not born in the community, thus making them first-generation migrants; and "locals," that is, people born in the *Quilombo*, thus autochthonous individuals. Additionally, we estimated the proportion of migrants separated by sex in the assessed generation. Marriages were classified according to the place of birth of each member of the couple as (a) endogamous, when both members were born in the community; (b) exogamous, when only one member was born in the community; and (c) between migrants, when both members were born outside the community. The three different types of marriage were quantified for the generation directly accessed (F2), as well as for the previous two generations (F1 and P). Only the parents of locals were included in the analysis of the corresponding preceding generation. Thus, if an exogamous patrilocal couple was detected in F2, the parents of the woman would not be included in the analysis conducted for F1, and so forth. The number of patrilocal exogamous marriages (a local man married to a migrant woman) were then compared with the number of matrilocal ones (a migrant man married to a local woman) by using a ratio ($P{:}M$) calculated between the number of patrilocal marriages (P) divided by the number of matrilocal marriages (M). If $P{:}M > 1$, then the number of patrilocal matrimonies is larger than matrilocal ones and vice versa.

The age pyramids revealed the classical form observed in developing or fast-growing countries (Cohen, 2003), with a wide base and a narrow top, representing high fecundity rates and few elderly individuals. They also revealed a gap in the category of men aged between 20 and 30 years. This gap suggests out-migration of men in this age range. A similar pattern was described by Woortmann (1990), who defined it as the "trip." According to this author, the "trip" is a common practice among Brazilian rural communities and is driven by the search for better economic conditions in metropolitan areas. After a few years, migrated men return to their hometown. Although Woortmann's research reveals a wider age range, the data presented here indicate that the "trip" is also a common behavior among the three populations we studied.

The proportion of migrants in the generation of respondents in *Mocambo*, *Sacutiaba*, and *Rio das Rãs* was 16.1%, 30.0%, and 20.2% respectively, among whom 60.7%, 66.7%, and 63.5% respectively were females. Marriages classified as endogamous predominated in all generations (Table 23.1), while marriages between migrants were the least common among them, except for generation *P* in *Rio das Rãs*. Among exogamous marriages, patrilocality was more frequent in generation F2 (Table 23.1), which means that for this generation local men more often married non-local women than the other way round.

The proportion of migrants in these *Quilombos* seems to be high, especially considering that the direction of migration is primarily from rural to urban areas (Fix, 1999; Woortmann, 1990), the phenomenon known as the "rural exodus." The reasons for this high proportion of migrants among the *Quilombo* inhabitants could be related to marriage,

Table 23.1. *Proportions of marriage types*[a] *among three generations of the three Afro-Brazilian rural populations and corresponding ratio of patrilocal and matrilocal exogamous marriages (P:M)*

Population	Generation	Sample size (couples)	Proportion (%) of marriage classes			P:M ratio
			EN	EX	BM	
Mocambo	P	188	76.6	15.4	8.0	0.7
	F1	143	66.4	25.9	7.7	1.1
	F2	80	55.0	40.0	5.0	1.1
Sacutiaba	P	59	45.8	42.4	11.9	0.09
	F1	46	56.5	39.1	4.4	0.64
	F2	46	43.5	34.8	21.7	7
Rio das Rãs	P	161	76.4	10.5	13.0	6.2
	F1	160	67.5	25.0	7.5	1.5
	F2	166	49.4	41.6	9.0	1.6

[a] Marriages were classified according to the place of birth of each member as endogamous (EN), exogamous (EX) and between migrants (BM).
Source: Amorim *et al.* (2011).

since it is often the primary determinant of migration in sedentary human societies around the world (Fix, 1999). However, it could also be associated with land-owning opportunities, because the legal ownership of land in Brazilian *Quilombos* is guaranteed to those living within their territories since the 1988 legislation. Apparently, this has propelled migration towards such communities, as many inhabitants reported during our fieldwork. In order to evaluate whether the high migration rate observed among these populations was caused by marriage or by any other factor – such as the ownership of land – we compared the share of exogamous marriages with the share of couples formed by two migrants. A higher proportion of the former might indicate a predominance of marriage-driven migration, as observed among generations F1 and F2 (Table 23.1). Thus, marriage seems to be a more important cause of migration in these generations, rather than land-owning opportunity.

It is important to note that in the two largest populations, the ratio between the proportion of exogamous marriages and marriages between migrants increased down the generations (1.9, 3.3, and 8 for *Mocambo*; and 0.8, 3.3, and 4.6 for *Rio das Rãs* in generations P, F1, and F2 respectively). In this regard, the importance of each factor – marriage and ownership of land – might have changed over the course of history.

In fact, during the land-owning regulation process, access to the land becomes more controlled and the population boundaries become less permeable, in order to prevent the entrance of opportunistic migrants aiming to gain ownership of the land (Véran, 2000). Therefore, if there has been an actual population boundary impermeability emerging in the last years, we expect to see a decrease in the proportion of migrant couples over time, as is observed in these two populations. The same phenomenon could not be observed in *Sacutiaba*, where this ratio is estimated as 3.6, 8.9, and 1.6 for generations P, F1, and F2 respectively. Still, the proportion of exogamous marriages is higher than the proportion of married migrants, indicating that the effects of land regulation might also be important in *Sacutiaba*. Surprisingly, we do not see an increase in endogamy down the generations. Apparently, the land-owning regulation process may hamper the entrance of migrants, hence preventing the entrance of migrant couples, but it has no effect on migration propelled by marriage.

In comparison to other populations, these *Quilombos* are intermediately endogamous, analogous to the !Kung in South Africa, but less endogamous than the Maya in Mexico or the Oxford villagers, and more endogamous than the Yolgnu in Australia (Fix, 1999). *Sacutiaba*, the smallest population among all, presents the lowest proportion of endogamous marriages (Table 23.1), which may suggest that endogamy and population size could be associated in human populations. Apparently, there is an evolutionary advantage to avoiding endogamy, as explained by Fix (1999). According to his observations, out-migration and consequent decrease of endogamy would prevent populations from experiencing genetic depression. The prevention of this phenomenon could be stronger in smaller communities, as suggested by the comparison between *Mocambo*, *Sacutiaba*, and *Rio das Rãs*.

The larger share of females among migrants is apparently associated with the marriage-driven migratory pattern expected for these communities, suggesting that men meet their wives during their "trip" and later return with them to the *Quilombos*. The predominance of patrilocality over matrilocality gives further support to this hypothesis (Table 23.1). A higher female mobility is also observed among other populations worldwide (Chaix *et al.*, 2007; Fix, 1999; Wilkins and Marlowe, 2006). This behavior in agricultural and pastoral societies is believed to be associated with patrilinear wealth inheritance (Marlowe, 2004). According to this hypothesis, sedentariness promotes territorial defense and control of resources. When land is inherited patrilocally, residence is more likely, since males can convert their inheritance into much greater reproductive success. In this case, parents will preferentially pass resources to sons rather than to daughters, and this will favor patrilocality.

There is no evidence, however, that this behavior is characteristic of the contemporary *Quilombos*, where no difference regarding gender-based inheritance priorities exists, and particularly in *Sacutiaba*, where a matriarchal cultural component is evident (as described in the previous section). Véran (2000) declares that in the history of *Rio das Rãs*, it has been observed that women exchange places among the villages that compose the community, indicating that higher female mobility can also be observed inside this community.

To summarize our findings, the three Afro-Brazilian communities reveal similar demographic characteristics in the current generation, defined by (a) a gap in the age pyramid for men aged between 20 and 30 years; (b) a high proportion of migrants (16% to 30%); (c) the predominance of female migrants; (d) a predominance of endogamous marriages; (e) a predominance of patrilocality over matrilocality. Moreover, matrimony seems to be the most important cause of migration and population size is inversely proportional to endogamy. To understand the consequences of this migratory pattern a genetic comparison was conducted, as described in the following sections.

GENE FLOW AND ADMIXTURE

Gene flow, caused by spatial mobility, has been acting on the Brazilian population throughout its history, especially during the colonial period, when Brazil received huge numbers of migrants from different continents. At that moment, the impact of migration on the genetic composition of the inhabitant populations may have been very significant, as the populations involved in the process presented quite different genetic compositions. As a consequence of this process, intense admixture among autochthonous people and the many different migrants, especially the Portuguese colonizers and sub-Saharan Africans, took place in the country. As stated before, admixture and dispersion was not homogeneous across Brazilian territory and led to the great diversity in phenotype and culture that is observed in the country today.

The contemporary *Quilombos* are an example of this diversity. Aiming to describe the genetic constitution of the *Quilombo* populations of *Mocambo*, *Sacutiaba*, and *Rio das Rãs* and to evaluate the impact of migrations on their gene pools through the course of history, unrelated individuals from these communities, both locals and migrants, were analyzed for genetic markers located in the nuclear genome and mtDNA. To assess the historical phenomena that have occurred in the past, one must resort to tools that, like genetics, allow indirect inference. In this regard, looking at the genetic variation found in contemporary populations, it is possible to understand aspects of their formation and the changes that have subsequently taken place.

The genetic characterization of *Mocambo*, *Sacutiaba*, and *Rio das Rãs* was carried out according to uni- and biparental genetic marker variation in a sample of unrelated individuals. For the purposes of this chapter, we used data for ten autosomal Ancestry Informative Markers (AIMs; Amorim *et al.*, 2011); that is, those presenting large frequency differential among populations (Shriver *et al.*, 2003); X- chromosome (Ribeiro, 2009) and Y-chromosome (Ribeiro *et al.*, 2009) markers; and polymorphisms in the mtDNA HVS-I region (Ferreira, 2006a). All AIMs (APO, D1, ECA, FXIIIB, PV-92, Sb19.3, TPA-25, GC, RB2300, and DRD2/*Taq*I) are either SNPs or indels with no evidence of physical linkage between them. In the mtDNA HVS-I region, 24 polymorphisms, which characterize the main Amerindian (A, B, C, D, X), African (L, L0a, L1b, L1c, L2a, L2b, L2c, L2d, L3b, L3d, L3e), and European (H, J, K, T) haplogroups were analyzed. Finally, we employed data from 12 Y-STRs (PowerPlex Y kit) and six X-chromosome indels (RS16460, RS17394, RS2307707, RS5743760, RS2307741, and RS621). *Sacutiaba* was not analyzed for the Y chromosome due to technical problems.

Admixture-weighted estimates, generated for AIMs and X and Y chromosomes, were determined by the gene-identity method described by Chakraborty (1985), using the Admix95 software (available at www.genetica. fmed.edu.uy). Based on Brazilian history, a trihybrid model was assumed, where Amerindians, sub-Saharan Africans, and Europeans were used as putative parental populations, for which allele frequencies were obtained from the literature (see for more details: Amorim *et al.*, 2011; Ribeiro, 2009; Ribeiro *et al.*, 2009). The analyses of the mtDNA markers provided another estimate of the parental contribution to the populations analyzed: haplogroup frequencies. Taken together, these estimates provided an overview of the genetic composition of the populations under analysis.

The considered trihybrid admixture model was adequate for estimating parental contributions to all analyzed populations. Even though estimates for the different classes of markers yielded different results (Figure 23.4), they were all consistent with Brazilian history.

The estimates for autosomal ancestry indicated a large African contribution to the three *Quilombos*: they all presented over 40% of this

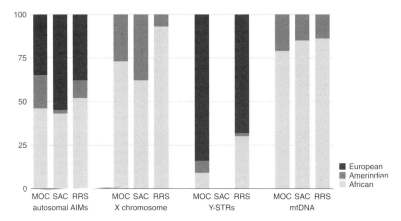

Figure 23.4 Admixture estimates based on autosomal AIMs (Amorim *et al.*, 2011), X-chromosomal markers (Ribeiro, 2009), Y-STRs (Ribeiro *et al.*, 2009) and mtDNA (Ferreira, 2006a) for the populations of *Mocambo* (MOC), *Sacutiaba* (SAC), and *Rio das Rãs* (RRS).

parental group in their constitutions, even though Europeans have contributed more significantly to the *Sacutiaba*'s pool in comparison with the other populations. The Amerindian contribution was more important in *Mocambo*, followed by *Rio das Rãs*. These analyses indicated the same picture as that provided by autosomal ancestry in other *Quilombos*: a high African contribution, with significant European participation (Bortolini *et al.*, 1999).

This result concurs with historical data, given *Mocambo*'s long history of contact and exchange with the *Xocó* Amerindians (Arruti, 2006) resulting from their geographic proximity and the recent demographic flow observed in the questionnaires filled in by the volunteers during our fieldwork (two exogamous marriages between a local man and a *Xocó* woman). This is the population that might have undergone the most significant influence from people of genetic backgrounds other than African, as indicated by the largest admixture estimate for parental populations other than Africans.

According to admixture estimates from X-chromosome marker data (Figure 23.4), the main parental contribution in the three populations is African, and Amerindian contribution was also important, in contrast to what has been observed in the Brazilian population as a whole, for which the European contribution was the most important (Figure 23.2). The difference observed between female and male X-chromosomal contribution (Figure 23.5) shows that the European contribution was observed in the male sample only in *Rio das Rãs*, where

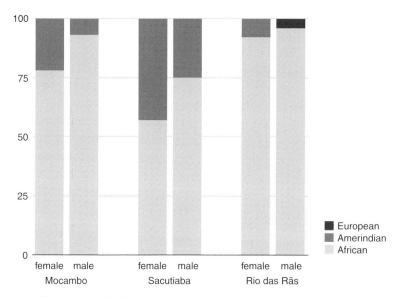

Figure 23.5 Admixture estimates based on X-chromosome markers (Ribeiro, 2009) for three *Quilombo* populations, considering male and female samples separately.

no Amerindian contribution was detected. By contrast, in *Mocambo* and *Sacutiaba* the European contribution to males was not detected, whilst the Amerindian contribution was detected. In the female share, no European contribution could be detected in any population. Furthermore, the African contribution to females was lower than in the male share, especially in *Mocambo* and *Rio das Rãs*.

The estimates obtained from Y-STR data (Figure 23.4) indicate a relatively high African contribution to the constitution of the *Rio das Rãs*, when compared with that observed in urban Brazilian populations (Figure 23.2), but not for *Mocambo*. In both cases, the European contribution was the most significant.

The haplotypic frequencies obtained from the mtDNA data were quite different from those obtained from the Y-STR data (Figure 23.4): the former indicated a higher African contribution, and the latter a higher European contribution. The absence of female European contribution to the gene pool of these populations was also observed in other *Quilombos* previously analyzed (Abe-Sandes *et al.*, 2004; Carvalho *et al.*, 2008; Ribeiro-dos-Santos *et al.*, 2002; Silva *et al.*, 2006). In other *Quilombos*, a very low European contribution was detected (Ribeiro-dos-Santos *et al.*, 2002), although in some communities low estimates have been detected and, in other *Quilombos*, estimates as high as 15% have been observed (Bortolini *et al.*, 1999).

Admixture estimates suggest that Africans and their descendants were the main – although not the only – contributors to the gene pools of these populations. The admixture estimates indicate a tri-hybrid (African, Amerindian, and European) origin for Afro-Brazilian rural communities. This might be due to individuals of different ancestries having joined these communities (as occurred in some populations; Reis and Gomes, 1996), or to the founders of the *Quilombos* having already been admixed, as at least some of them were slaves born in Brazil.

African, Amerindian, and European men and women have not contributed equally to the gene pools of the three *Quilombos* under analysis, as reflected in the haploid genome studies conducted among them (Figure 23.4), reflecting different migration patterns among them with different importance of each parental population through the course of history. Y-STR analyses point out a predominantly European male contribution. By contrast, mtDNA analyses indicate a predominance of African haplogroups, followed by Amerindian ones. No European haplogroup has been detected in samples from these populations. It is noteworthy that, with the exception of *Sacutiaba*, the Amerindian contribution evaluated by specific lineages was low. The high Amerindian contribution estimated with X-chromosome markers reflects the same history: Brazilian *Quilombos* maintained intense economic and social bonds with Amerindian tribes and, consequently, maintained gene flow. This picture has indicated that men were mainly responsible for the insertion of European alleles in the *Quilombos* and women for the insertion of Amerindian ones. Both men and women have contributed to the insertion of African variants.

The hypothesis that European men were among the founders of these populations is plausible, since there are historical records indicating that this group participated in the foundation of *Quilombos*. These men were in charge of exchanging information and goods between the *Quilombos* and urban centers (Reis and Gomes, 1996). Likewise, the presence of Amerindian women might be due to their presence among the founders of the *Quilombos*, but might also have been a consequence of later contact: *Quilombos* were known to have had social and economic bonds with indigenous tribes, and Amerindian women were sometimes abducted from their tribes and incorporated in the *Quilombos* (Karasch, 1996; Reis and Gomes, 1996). A third explanation is that the *Quilombos* might have been founded by individuals of multiple ancestries born in

Brazil: it is well established that European men, especially the Portuguese, bred with Amerindian and African women – sometimes by raping them. These children were often rejected by their fathers and raised by their mothers alone, being kept as slaves.

CROSSING DEMOGRAPHIC AND GENETIC DATA

Mutation is the basic evolutionary mechanism for variability, both within and between populations. However, mutation alone cannot lead to significant changes in a population over a short period of time, especially when neutral genetic markers are considered. When it comes to introducing variability into a population or changing its structure, gene flow is the most important evolutionary mechanism, as in a short period of time its impact might be considerably higher than that caused by genetic drift (Wang and Whitlock, 2003).

The impact of gene flow in population evolution depends on two parameters: migratory flux and the differences existing between the populations taking part in the process. In the short term, its impact might be the insertion of genetic variation that is new to the population receiving the migration. If it is maintained for a longer time its main product is the homogenization of the populations participating in the migration (Futuyma, 2005).

To further understand the impact of the observed migratory dynamics upon the genetic diversity of these communities and the importance of gene flow as an evolutionary mechanism, we crossed the demographic and genetic data obtained for *Mocambo*, *Sacutiaba*, and *Rio das Rãs*. This analysis allowed us to assess the consequences of recent migratory movements, as well as allowing us to understand certain features of these populations more thoroughly.

For these purposes, migrants and locals were compared according to their allelic and genotypic distributions and also according to the admixture proportions for biparental genetic constitution, as previously described (Amorim *et al.*, 2011). Linkage-disequilibrium (LD), observed and expected heterozygosities, and inbreeding coefficients were estimated for each population, considering a significance level of 0.05 for each analysis or a 95% of confidence interval. The population structure was analyzed according to a Bayesian framework (Pritchard *et al.*, 2000) with 1000 iterations for the burn-in period and 1000 additional iterations to obtain the estimates. In addition we sought the insertion of X- and Y-chromosomal haplotypes due to recent migration.

Table 23.2. *Genetic admixture proportions for three Afro-Brazilian communities. Estimates were generated for locals and total (migrants and locals) according to autosomal AIM variation*

	Parental contribution (%)					
	Mocambo		Sacutiaba		Rio das Rãs	
Parental population	Locals	Total	Locals	Total	Locals	Total
African	0.50	0.46	0.51	0.43	0.43	0.52
European	0.28	0.35	0.36	0.55	0.34	0.38
Amerindian	0.22	0.19	0.13	0.02	0.23	0.10

Source: Amorim *et al.* (2011).

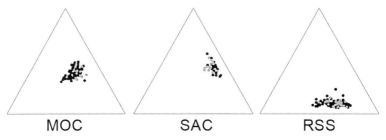

Figure 23.6 Population structure triangle-plots for *Mocambo* (MOC), *Sacutiaba* (SAC), and *Rio das Rãs* (RRS) based on ten autosomal AIMs (Amorim *et al.*, 2011). Darker dots represent local individuals and lighter ones represent migrants.

No statistically significant allelic or genotypic differentiation was observed between locals and migrants. Between 1.0% and 3.4% of the loci were in LD for each population analyzed. Mean expected and observed heterozygosities were 0.51 and 0.49 for *Mocambo*, 0.49 and 0.49 for *Sacutiaba*, and 0.49 and 0.50 for *Rio das Rãs* respectively. The inbreeding coefficient (F_{is}) for *Mocambo*, *Sacutiaba*, and *Rio das Rãs* and corresponding confidence interval (in parenthesis) was estimated as 0.053 (−0.0243–0.127), −0.005 (−0.082–0.079), −0.013 (−0.124–0.082). We can observe that population structure did not change significantly after the inclusion of migrants (Figure 23.6). The inclusion of migrants in the admixture estimates resulted in an increase in the European contribution and a decrease in the Amerindian one, while the African contribution decreased in *Mocambo* and *Sacutiaba*, but not in *Rio das Rãs* (Table 23.2).

The impact of migration upon the genetic composition of these populations appears to have been limited. No significant population differences between locals and migrants were observed in terms of allelic and genotypic distribution, and population structure remained similar even when migrants were included (Figure 23.6), suggesting homogeneity between donor and recipient gene pools. Although *Quilombo* populations might have been isolated for a certain time in the past, it seems that gene flow has already been an important evolutionary mechanism operating in the homogenization of these communities and their neighboring populations for a certain time. Indeed the low proportion of loci in LD among the three populations indicates that the admixture model of "continuous gene flow" seems to be more adequate than the "hybrid-isolation" model (Long, 1991; Pfaff *et al.*, 2001), considering that these populations were founded approximately eight generations ago as previously described. Therefore, although genetic isolation seems to be a characteristic of certain *Quilombos* (Souza and Culpi, 2005), migration has been strongly active in *Mocambo*, *Sacutiaba*, and *Rio das Rãs*. In fact, Véran (2000) reports the presence of migrants in *Rio das Rãs* since early times. These migrants were jobless male peasants and poor nomadic families looking for better living conditions. According to this author, they were constantly integrated in the *Quilombos* up to the time when the community's boundaries became less permeable due to the land regulation process.

In spite of it, admixture analysis indicates an influx of European alleles due to migration into these three populations. This phenomenon is probably linked to the predominance of European autosomal contribution in the Brazilian gene pool and, more specifically, in the region where these *Quilombos* are located, in Northeastern Brazil (Godinho *et al.*, 2008). The decrease in the proportion of Amerindian alleles due to migration might be associated with the contribution of this parental group in this region of Brazil, which is the lowest among the three parental populations (Godinho *et al.*, 2008). Although *Mocambo* lies close to an Amerindian *Xocó* reserve, there was a decrease in the proportion of Amerindian contribution in this population with the inclusion of migrants. Indeed, only two couples out of 36 that were not endogamous had a *Xocó* member, showing that the relationship between *Mocambo* and the *Xocó* might not have the great importance that it had through the course of history (Arruti, 2006).

Newly arrived migrants carried new X and Y haplotypes. For the X chromosome, six haplotypes have been recently incorporated into *Mocambo*'s and *Sacutiaba*'s gene pool through migration, and two into that of *Rio das Rãs*. That means that, of all the X-chromosome haplotypes that have been analyzed, 6.74% were introduced via migration in

Mocambo, 23.08% in *Sacutiaba*, and 1.83% in *Rio das Rãs*. Such a high percentage might be due to the small population size in *Sacutiaba*, which could lead to allele fixation caused by drift. Moreover, all migrants analyzed brought new Y chromosomes to the pools of *Mocambo,* and half of them into those of *Rio das Rãs*.

Despite the predominance of endogamous marriages, the non-significant F_{is} values and similarities between expected and observed heterozygosities suggest an absence of population inbreeding. It should be remembered, however, that local endogamy (the practice observed among these populations) is not necessarily associated with inbreeding (indicated by significant positive F_{is} values). Thus the F_{is} values estimated in our study may indicate that a couple classified as endogamous might not represent individuals with biological kinship.

CONCLUSION

A thorough description of migration patterns in three Afro-Brazilian rural communities was carried out in this chapter. The causes and consequences of the observed patterns were inferred by using demographic and genetic data.

A common migration pattern could be observed among the three Afro-Brazilian rural communities: men of approximately 20 years old left their communities and returned when they reached the age of 30; around a fifth of the population consisted of immigrants, most of them women; among the current generation endogamous marriages were predominant, followed by those between a local and a non-local; patrilocal marriages were more frequent than matrilocal ones. Among the current generation, marriage appeared to be the main cause of migration, although other causes could not be excluded.

This study confirms historical data, which indicate both the predominance of African alleles in the gene pools of Brazilian *Quilombos*, and admixture between Africans and people from other ancestry, such as European men and women from all ethnic backgrounds. Comparing these three populations to the Brazilian urban population as a whole, some similarities and dissimilarities can be observed. The male European contribution is most often high. The female contribution, in contrast, is much more markedly African and Amerindian in *Quilombo* populations. This observation is further reinforced by X-chromosome analyses, which detected little or no European contribution. When autosomal markers are considered, a complex and yet similar picture arises: the three parental populations are detected. In spite of it, the proportions are quite different between *Quilombos* and the Brazilian population.

The impact of migration upon the genetic composition and structure of the three populations was low for the current generation, possibly due to the genetic similarity between them and the populations from which migrants originated. These *Quilombos* might have been isolated sometime in the past, but nowadays the barrier to gene flow has already become quite permeable. Our data indicate that the three *Quilombos* analyzed have recently received migrants that altered their genetic compositions and might also have incorporated migrants and the genetic variants they brought during their histories.

Further investigation is necessary to increase our understanding of the cultural background that rules migration in smallholder populations and the biological consequences of these phenomena. In this regard, we believe that this work serves as a primary source for comparative studies of human migrations.

ACKNOWLEDGMENTS

We would like to thank the *Fundação Cultural Palmares*; the population of *Mocambo*, *Rio das Rãs*, and *Riacho de Sacutiaba e Sacutiaba*; Aguinaldo L. Simões, Francisco M. Salzano, Gabriel Falcão-Alencar, Rafaela C. P. Toledo, Rogério S. Campos, Raquel C. Gontijo, Marcelo R. Luizon, Maria Angélica F. Pedrosa, Maria de Nazaré Klautau-Guimarães, and Neide M. O. Godinho for their assistance during the development of this work.

This research was approved by Brazil's National Ethical Committee for Research (CEP-FS/UnB 151/07) and was funded by Conselho Nacional de Desenvolvimento Científico e Tecnológico, Fundação de Empreendimentos Científicos e Tecnológicos, and Coordenação de Aperfeiçoamento de Pessoal de Nível Superior, Brazil.

REFERENCES

Abe-Sandes, K., Silva, W. A., Jr., and Zago, M. A. (2004). Heterogeneity of the Y chromosome in Afro-Brazilian populations. *Human Biology*, **76**, 77–86.

Alencastro, L. F. (2000). *O Trato dos Viventes: A formação do Brasil no Atlântico Sul*, 1st edn. São Paulo, Brazil: Companhia das Letras.

Alves-Silva, J., da Silva Santos, M., Guimarães, P. E., *et al.* (2000). The ancestry of Brazilian mtDNA lineages. *American Journal of Human Genetics*, **67**, 444–61.

Amorim, C. E. G., Gontijo, C. C., Falcão-Alencar, G., *et al.* (2011). Migration in Afro-Brazilian rural communities: crossing demographic and genetic data. *Human Biology*, **83**, 509–21.

Arruti, J. M. (2006). *Mocambo: Antropologia e história do processo de formação quilom-bola*. Bauru, Brazil: Edusc.

Bortolini, M. C., Da Silva, W. A., Jr., De Guerra, D. C., *et al.* (1999). African-derived South American populations: a history of symmetrical and asymmetrical matings according to sex revealed by bi- and uni-parental genetic markers. *American Journal of Human Biology*, **11**, 551–63.

Brasileiro, S. and Sampaio, J. A. L. (2002). Sacutiaba e Riacho de Sacutiaba: uma comunidade negra rural no oeste baiano. In *Quilombos: Identidade Étnica e Territorialidade*, pp. 83–108. Rio de Janeiro, Brazil: Fundação Getúlio Vargas and Associação Brasileira de Antropologia.

Carvalho, B. M., Bortolini, M. C., Santos, S. E. B., and Ribeiro-dos-Santos, A. K. C. (2008). Mitochondrial DNA mapping of social-biological interactions in Brazilian Amazonian African-descendant populations. *Genetics and Molecular Biology*, **31**, 12–22.

Chaix, R., Quintana-Murci, L., Hegay, T., *et al.* (2007). From social to genetic structures in central Asia. *Current Biology*, **17**, 43–8.

Chakraborty, R. (1985). Gene identity in racial hybrids and estimation of admixture rates. In *Genetic Microdifferentiation in Man and Other Animals*, pp. 171–80. Delhi, India: Indian Anthropological Association.

Cohen, J. E. (2003). Human population: the next half century. *Science*, **302**, 1172–5.

Fausto, B. (2002). *História do Brasil*, 10th edn. São Paulo, Brazil: Editora da Universidade de São Paulo.

Ferreira, L. B. (2006a). Diversidade do DNA mitocondrial de populações brasileiras ameríndias e afrodescendentes. Ph.D. dissertation, Faculdade de Medicina de Ribeirão Preto, Universidade de São Paulo, Brazil.

Ferreira, R. (2006b). Biografia, mobilidade e cultura atlântica: a micro-escala do tráfico de escravos em Benguela, séculos XVIII–XIX. *Revista Tempo*, **20**, 33–59.

Fix, A. G. (1999). *Migration and Colonization in Human Microevolution*. Cambridge, UK: Cambridge University Press.

Florentino, M. (2002). *Em costas negras. Uma história do tráfico de escravos entre a África e o Rio de Janeiro*. São Paulo, Brazil: Companhia das Letras.

FUNAI (2011). Fundação Nacional do Índio, Brasília, DF, Brazil. www.funai.gov.br (viewed May 29, 2011).

Funari, P. P. A. (1996). A arqueologia de Palmares: sua contribuição para o conhecimento da história da cultura afro-americana. In *Liberdade por um fio*, pp. 26–51. São Paulo, Brazil: Companhia das Letras.

Futuyma, D. (2005). *Evolution*, 1st edn. Sunderland, MA: Sinauer Associates.

Godinho, N. M. O., Gontijo, C. C., Diniz, M. E. C. G., *et al.* (2008). Regional patterns of genetic admixture in South America. *Forensic Science International: Genetics Supplement Series*, **1**, 329–30.

Gontijo, C. C., Amorim, C. E. G., Pedrosa, M. A. F., *et al.* (2010). Estimates of parental genetic contribution to the constitution of Brazilian populations of African descent. In *Diversidad Humana y Antropología Aplicada*, ed. A. Gutiérrez-Redomero, A. Sánchez-Andrés, and V. Galera Olmo, pp. 107–115. Alcalá de Henares, Spain: Universidad de Alcalá.

Grattapaglia, D., Kalupniek, S., Guimarães, C. S., *et al.* (2005). Y-chromosome STR haplotype diversity in Brazilian populations. *Forensic Science International*, **149**, 99–107.

IBGE (2010). Instituto Brasileiro de Geografia e Estatística – Censo 2010, Brasília, DF, Brazil. www.ibge.gov.br/home/estatística/população (viewed September 24, 2010).

Karasch, M. (1996). Os quilombos de ouro na capitania de Goiás. In *Liberdade por um fio*, pp. 240–62. São Paulo, Brazil: Companhia das Letras.

Karasch, M. (2000). *A Vida dos Escravos no Rio De Janeiro, 1808–1850*. São Paulo, Brazil: Companhia das Letras.

Long, J. C. (1991). The genetic structure of admixed populations. *Genetics*, **127**, 417–28.

Marlowe, F. W. (2004). Marital residence among forages. *Current Anthropology*, **45**, 277–84.

Mello e Souza, M. (2006). *Reis Negros no Brasil Escravista: História da Festa de Coroação de Rei Congo*, 1st edn. Belo Horizonte, Brazil: Editora UFMG.

Mielke, J. H. and Fix, A. (2007). The confluence of anthropological genetics and anthropological demography. In *Anthropological Genetics: Theory, Methods, and Applications*, pp. 112–40. Cambridge, UK: Cambridge University Press.

Miller, J. (1988). *Way of Death. Merchant Capitalism and the Angolan Slave Trade, 1730–1830*. Madison, WI: Wisconsin University Press.

Monteiro, E. H. G. (2007). Desenvolvimento e aplicação de polimorfismos de inserção/deleção do cromossomo x em genética forense. Master's thesis, Departamento de Ciências Genômicas, Universidade Católica de Brasília, Brazil.

Novion, H. P., Nogales, A. M. V., and Oliveira, S. F. (2004). Estimativas de fecundidad en poblaciones afro-descendientes rurales brasileñas. In *Biologia de Poblaciones Humanas: Diversidad, Tiempo, Espacio*, ed. J. E. Egocheaga, pp. 885–95. Sociedad Española de Antropologia Física conference. Oviedo, Spain: Ediciones de la Universidad de Oviedo.

Oliveira, S. F., Amorim, C. E. G., Diniz, M. E. C. G., *et al.* (2008). Evaluación demográfica de los Kalunga, una población brasileña de origen africano. In *Genes, Ambientes y Enfermedades en Poblaciones Humanas*, ed. J. Amada, J. Nogués, and S. Pinilla, pp. 565–72. Sociedad Española de Antropologia Física conference. Zaragoza, Spain: University of Zaragoza Press.

Oliveira, S. F., Pedrosa, M. A. F., Ribeiro, G. B. L., *et al.* (2004). Uni- and bi-parental analyses of the genetic contribution in an Afro-descendent community in central Brazil. In *Biología de Poblaciones Humanas: Diversidad, Tiempo, Espacio*, 1st edn., ed. J. E. Egocheaga, pp. 609–16. Sociedad Española de Antropologia Física conference. Oviedo, Spain: Ediciones de la Universidad de Oviedo.

Oliveira, S. F., Ribeiro, G. G. B. L., Ferreira, L. B., Klautau-Guimarães, M. N., and Simões, A. L. (2006). Reconstrucción histórica de poblaciones afro-descendientes aisladas de Brasil: el contraste entre las contribuciones masculina y femenina. In *Diversidad Biológica y Salud Humana*, ed. A. Martinez-Almagro, pp. 203–210. Sociedad Española de Antropologia Física conference. Múrcia, Spain: Fundacion Universitaria San Antonio.

Palmares, Fundação Cultural (2011). Brasília, DF, Brazil. www.palmares.gov.br (viewed April 29, 2011).

Pfaff, C. L., Parra, E. J., Bonilla, C., *et al.* (2001). Population structure in admixed populations: effect of admixture dynamics on the pattern of linkage disequilibrium. *American Journal of Human Genetics*, **68**, 198–207.

Pritchard, J. K., Stephens, M., and Donnelly, P. (2000). Inference of population structure using multilocus genotype data. *Genetics*, **155**, 945–59.

Reis, J. J. and Gomes, F. S. (1996). Introdução – uma história de liberdade. In *Liberdade por um fio*, pp. 9–25. São Paulo, Brazil: Companhia das Letras.

Ribeiro, G. G. B. L. (2009). Análise genética de marcadores do tipo STR e indel em cromossomos sexuais humanos em populações remanescentes de Quilombos. Ph.D. dissertation, Instituto de Ciências Biológicas, Universidade de Brasília.

Ribeiro, G. G., Abe-Sandes, K., Barcelos, R. S., *et al.* (2011). Who were the male founders of rural Brazilian Afro-derived communities? A proposal based on three populations. *Annals of Human Biology*, **38**, 237–40.

Ribeiro, G. G., De Lima, R. R., Wiezel, C. E., *et al.* (2009) Afro-derived Brazilian populations: male genetic constitution estimated by Y-chromosomes STRs and AluYAP element polymorphisms. *American Journal of Human Biology*, **21**, 354–6.

Ribeiro-dos-Santos, A. K., Pereira, J. M., Lobato, M. R. L., *et al.* (2002). Dissimilarities in the process of formation of Curiau, a semi-isolated Afro-Brazilian population of the Amazon region. *American Journal of Human Biology*, **14**, 440–7.

Rodrigues, N. (2004). *Os Africanos no Brasil*, 8th edn. Brasília, Brazil: Editora Universidade de Brasília.

Salzano, F. M. and Freire-Maia, N. (1967). *Populações Brasileiras*. São Paulo, Brazil: Companhia Editora Nacional.

Schwartz, S. B. (1988). *Segredos internos: Engenhos e escravos na sociedade colonial*. São Paulo, Brazil: Companhia das Letras.

Shriver, M. D., Parra, E. J., Dios, S. (2003). Skin pigmentation, biogeographical ancestry and admixture mapping. *Human Genetics*, **112**, 387–99.

Silva, V. S. (2000). Rio das Rãs à luz da noção de quilombo. *Afro-Ásia*, **23**. (Electronic-publication viewed May 17, 2011) www.afroasia.ufba.br/pdf/afroasia_n23_p267.pdf.

Silva, W. A., Jr., Bortolini, M. C., Schneider, M. P., *et al.* (2006). MtDNA haplogroup analysis of black Brazilian and Sub-Saharan populations: implications for the Atlantic slave trade. *Human Biology*, **78**, 29–41.

Souza, I. R. and Culpi, L. (2005). Valongo, genetic studies on an isolated Afro-Brazilian community. *Genetics and Molecular Biology*, **28**, 402–6.

Véran, J. (2000). Rio das Rãs: memória de uma "comunidade remanescente de quilombo". *Afro-Ásia*, **23**. (Electronic-publication viewed May 17, 2011: www.afroasia.ufba.br/pdf/afroasia_n23_p297.pdf)

Wang, J. and Whitlock, M. C. (2003). Estimating effective population size and migration rates from genetic samples over space and time. *Genetics*, **163**, 429–46.

Wang, S., Ray, N., Rojas, W., *et al.* (2008). Geographic patterns of genome admixture in Latin American Mestizos. *PLoS Genetics*, **4**, e1000037.

Wilkins, J. F. and Marlowe, F. W. (2006). Sex-biased migration in humans: what should we expect from genetic data? *BioEssays*, **28**, 290–300.

Woortmann, K. (1990). Migração, família e campesinato. *Revista Brasileira de Estudos de População*, **7**, 35–53.

LORENA MADRIGAL, MONICA BATISTAPAU,
LOREDANA CASTRÌ, FLORY OTÁROLA, MWENZA BLELL,
ERNESTO RUIZ, RAMIRO BARRANTES,
DONATA LUISELLI, AND DAVIDE PETTENER

24

Indentured migration, gene flow, and the formation of the Indo-Costa Rican population

INTRODUCTION

Few regions in the world have seen as many human population upheavals as has the Caribbean region broadly defined (including the Atlantic coast of Central America). While it has been well established that the Caribbean region was inhabited by large human populations before the European invasion, it is difficult to estimate exactly how many people died after the Europeans arrived. In his book *Born to Die* (1998), Cook details the earliest stages of the European-Amerindian contact in the Caribbean. The sad conclusion to Cook's account is that after a quarter century of contact the *Taino* and their circum-Caribbean neighbors were approaching extinction. Since the native populations of the Caribbean essentially died off (Cook, 2002; Kiple and Ornelas, 1996), the Europeans turned to African sources of labor to sustain their expansion into the region (Klein, 1978).

In this chapter we discuss the history of Caribbean human population migratory movements. We begin by taking a macro perspective which considers large migrations. We finish with a micro perspective focusing on a small population derived from East-Indian workers who settled in the Atlantic coast of Costa Rica. We argue that the human migratory history of the Caribbean is evident in the genetic makeup of this small group of Indo-Costa Ricans.

African slaves participated in the earliest stages of the New World European invasion, as members of the various *Conquistador* teams (Klein,

Causes and Consequences of Human Migration, ed. Michael H. Crawford and Benjamin C. Campbell. Published by Cambridge University Press. © Cambridge University Press 2012.

1978; Yelvington, 2004). Indeed, African slaves began arriving to the Americas as soon as the European conquest started (Conniff, 1995; Morrissey, 1989). In Costa Rica for example, African slaves were initially brought during the early 1500s as members of exploration teams, which focused their efforts in the North-Central Pacific areas of the country, specifically *Guanacaste* and *Puntarenas* (Blutstein, 1970). There are several African-derived populations in the Caribbean and in Latin America that descend from these early African slaves, quite apart from those that descend from the slaves brought in the Trans-Atlantic trade during the 1600s to 1700s. The former slaves, called *ladinos* by the Spanish and Portuguese, were Christian and actual members of the invading parties. The latter, called *bozales* by the Spanish and Portuguese, were non-Christian, non-Portuguese or Spanish speakers, and were taken directly from Africa (Klein, 1986).

The slave trade during 1600–1700 in the Caribbean resulted in a total transformation of the human population in the region from what the earliest European colonizers found. The establishment of the sugarcane monoculture, supported by a plantation economy, resulted in the forced migration of millions of people from Africa (Madrigal, 2006). After the abolition of the slave trade (1807 to 1824, depending on which European government) and the emancipation of slaves in the Caribbean (beginning in 1793 in Haiti, continuing in 1833 in the British colonies), many former slaves continued working in the same plantations as when they were slaves, but others left the plantations and established peasant villages. Starting in this period (1860s and 1870s), indentured workers were brought to the Caribbean from India, China, and to a lesser extent from Europe (Vertovec, 2000). Indentured servants were brought to the New World with the promise of a free passage back home and a lump sum at the end of their contract.

Some of these indentured workers from the Indian subcontinent formed large communities in Trinidad, Suriname, and Guyana, dramatically changing the human genetic landscape of these regions. These three Indo-Caribbean communities in particular have received a great deal of attention from cultural anthropologists because the groups have been able to maintain their own religious practices and music, and have become important political actors in their countries (Angrosino, 1974; Klass, 1961; Speckmann, 1965; van der Veer, 1995; van der Veer and Vertovec, 1991; Vertovec, 1992, 1994, 2000). In 1990, people of East Indian descent constituted the largest ethnic group in the twin island Republic of Trinidad and Tobago (Jayaram, 2006).

In contrast with the wealth of cultural anthropological research on Indo-Caribbean groups, there is a dearth in biological anthropology work on these populations. Indeed, we could find only a few citations on the population genetics of Indo-Caribbean groups (Carrington *et al.*, 2002, 2003).

The Atlantic province of Limón in Costa Rica was affected by the Caribbean population extinctions and movements described in the previous paragraphs more than by those experienced by the country at large. Just like the rest of the Central American coast, Limón proved a privileged site for the expansion of malaria, which contributed to the decimation of Amerindian groups, forcing them to retreat to the highlands. Indeed, malaria was the main reason the Costa Rican Atlantic coast was not developed by the Spanish colonial government or by the young Costa Rican republic government through the seventeenth, eighteenth, and most of the nineteenth centuries.

In the late 1800s, however, the Costa Rican government started the construction of a railroad from the central part of the country to the Atlantic coast. Consequently, a large inflow of foreign workers, the large majority of whom were descendants of African slaves from Jamaica, migrated to the area. These workers came to work on the construction of the railroad line and on a young banana industry, and permanently changed the ethnic composition and culture of Costa Rica (Harpelle, 1993; Herzfeld, 2002; Purcell, 1993).

Just like the rest of the Caribbean, the Limón region also received immigrants from China and from India, who were part of the indentured servant migration of the 1860s and 1870s previously discussed. Although the Chinese and Afro-*Limonense* groups of Limón have received attention from anthropologists and others (Duncan, 1981; Grillo-Rosanía, 2003; Madrigal, 2006; Purcell, 1993), the presence of descendants of the East-Indian migrants has been ignored until recently by scholars.

In the rest of this chapter we present a summary of a research project which has spanned several years and which has implemented a biocultural approach to the study of the Indo-Costa Rican community residing in Westfalia Limón (Castri *et al.*, 2007; Madrigal *et al.*, 2007; Otarola-Duran, 2007). Our project was inspired in great part by the community's interest in demonstrating that they were descendants from South Asian migrants, ethnically distinct from the Jamaican-derived Afro-*Limonense* community which has been so well researched by Costa Rican anthropologists. When our project concluded in 2007 we visited each participant household and we delivered to each a copy of the scientific papers (Castri *et al.*, 2007; Madrigal *et al.*, 2007) we had published and a research summary written in colloquial English and in Spanish.

MATERIALS AND METHODS

Our project was approved by the committee on bioethics from the University of South Florida and the *Universidad de Costa Rica*. Our cultural anthropologist (FO) visited the community and determined by interviews of key informants which families were considered to be part of the group. By interviewing community members, our cultural anthropologist was able to reconstruct genealogies of the families which helped us understand the marriage patterns which had been practiced across several generations (Madrigal *et al.*, 2007). In the early 2000s we estimated that the population of the Indo-*Limonense* community was no more than 100 people.

Sampling for DNA extraction took place over two field seasons. In the first one, we collected hair follicles from 44 participants (20 females and 24 males) and in the second one we collected buccal swabs from 24 individuals who had been sampled previously but whose hair follicles did not yield amplifiable Y-chromosome DNA. All community families are represented in our sample, including members from Westfalia and the other places where Indo-*Limonense* families have relocated. Based on the community's genealogy, we are confident that we have multiple copies of each and every one of the mitochondrial and the Y-chromosomal lines of the group. For details on the genetic analysis, please see Castri *et al.* (2007).

RESULTS

Genealogical analysis

Our study of the families' genealogies showed that they could all be linked into a single tree (Madrigal *et al.*, 2007). Our analysis led us to conclude that the Indo-Costa Ricans avoided any form of consanguineous marriage. Since the community was so small and since relatives were not considered acceptable marriage partners, marriages took place with members of the neighboring Afro-*Limonense* community. We could determine this because in Limón most Afro-*Limonense* individuals carry English last names while members of the wider Spanish-speaking community or the Native Amerindian groups carry Spanish surnames. All individuals who married into the community from the earliest generation until the most recent generation had English last names. Therefore, our analysis of the community's genealogy leads us to conclude that the Indo-Costa Rican population had engaged in relatively frequent gene flow with its Afro-*Limonense* neighbors. This is a rather unusual practice when compared with the marriage practices of other Indo Caribbean groups (Madrigal *et al.*, 2007).

Mitochondrial DNA analysis

In contrast with other Costa Rican populations previously studied, the Indo-*Limonense* population shows a preponderance of East Indian and African mitochondrial lineages. Indeed, the Native American lineages represent only 11.4% of the Indo-*Limonense* mtDNAs, a value substantively lower than that observed in other Costa Rican populations (Table 24.1). It is important to note the absence of European specific lineages, which have been found at high frequencies in other Costa Rican groups (Segura-Wang *et al.*, 2010). The major components of the Indo-Limonense mtDNA gene pool are African and Indian lineages. The former are present at frequencies of 31.8%, a relatively high value if compared with that observed in New World groups with the exception of Afro-Colombians from Choco and Garífunas from Honduras. The highest contribution to the Indo-*Limonense* mtDNA gene pool is due to Indian lineages with a frequency of 56.8%. These lineages have not been demonstrated in other Central or South American population, with the exception of some sporadic occurrence (Alves-Silva *et al.*, 2000). Moreover, the low number of haplotypes (one in the case of haplogroups U2a, R6 and MD) belonging to each Indian lineage points out to a strong founder effect, evident also for the Native American and African components (Table 24.1).

Y-chromosome analysis

When compared with those of other Central and South American populations our Indo-Costa Rica sample shows higher frequencies of African (E3a-M2 and E3b-M35) lineages and dramatically lower frequencies of Native American lineages (P-M45 and Q-M3; Table 24.2). On the contrary, lineages of Indian origin (H1-M52), virtually absent in other New World populations, have very high frequencies, suggesting a strong contribution to the Indo-Costa Rican population. Nevertheless, Y-chromosome microsatellite haplotype diversity is lower than in other Native American population, with a dramatic reduction of diversity when considering the Indian fraction separately. The presence of at least two (R1-M173

Table 24.1. *Frequencies of continent-specific mtDNA haplogroups in some Central and South America populations*

	Total	Native American		African		European		Indian		Reference
		n	%	n	%	n	%	n	%	
Mexico	223	199	89.10	10	4.50	12	5.38	0	0.00	Green et al., 2000
Garifunas	44	7	15.91	37	84.09	0	0.00	0	0.00	Salas et al., 2005
Costa Rica	59	49	83.00	nd	nd	nd	nd	nd	nd	Carvajal-Carmona et al., 2003
Limón	44	5	11.36	14	31.82	0	0.00	25	56.82	present study
Puerto Rico	800	489	61.30	220	27.20	91	11.50	0	0.00	Martínez-Cruzado et al., 2005
Chocó	49	8	16.33	41	83.67	0	0.00	0	0.00	Salas et al., 2005
Antioquia	113	102	90.00	nd	nd	nd	nd	nd	nd	Carvajal-Carmona et al., 2003
Colombia	230	96	41.74	58	25.22	61	26.52	0	0.00	Rodas et al., 2003
Brazil	247	81	33.00	69	28.00	96	38.87	0	0.00	Alves-Silva et al., 2000

nd, not determined.

Table 24.2. *Frequencies of Y-chromosome lineages in some Central and South America populations*

	Total	P-M45		DE		Y(xDEQ)		H1-M52		Reference
		n	%	n	%	n	%	n	%	
Mexico	29	27	93.10	2	6.90					Lell et al., 2002
C. America	60	56	93.33			4	6.67			Lell et al., 2002
Panama	15	12	80.00			3	20.00			Ruiz-Narvaez et al., 2005
Costa Rica	78	59	75.64			19	24.36			Ruiz-Narvaez et al., 2005
Costa Rica	60	30	50.00	7	11.67	23	38.33			Carvajal-Carmona et al., 2003
Limón	24			10	41.67	4	16.67	10	41.67	**present study**
Antioquia	80	48	60.00	6	7.50	26	32.50			Carvajal-Carmona et al., 2003
Oriente	92	69	75.00	5	5.43	18	19.57			Bedoya et al., 2006
Colombia	102	92	90.20	4	3.92	6	5.88			Bortolini et al., 2003
Brazil	200	108	54.00	57	28.50	35	17.50			Carvalho-Silva et al., 2001

and E3b3a), and probably three (Y*) lineages of possibly European origin, and the absence of Native American lineages is noteworthy, in contrast with the mtDNA data where no European haplogroup was observed and Native American lineages represent 11.36% of the gene pool (Table 24.2).

DISCUSSION

In this chapter, we report results of an anthropological project in a recently described Indo-Costa Rican population (Castri *et al.*, 2007; Madrigal *et al.*, 2007; Otarola-Duran 2007). The group was keenly interested in participating in the genetic aspect of the project, as it wished to know where (or even if) in pre-partition India their ancestors came from. Thus, our study fills an important gap in the anthropological study of the Costa Rican and wider Caribbean region, but most importantly, it is a service to the community itself. Our study is unique in its biocultural approach. Although other Indo-Caribbean communities have been researched by cultural anthropologists (Jayaram, 2006; Jayawardena, 1980; Jha, 1974; van der Veer, 1995; van der Veer and Vertovec, 1991; Vertovec, 1992, 1994, 2000; Weller, 1968), the Indo-Costa Rican community is the only one which – to the best of our knowledge – has been researched from a cultural and biological perspective, asking questions about its origin and evolution, as well as about its culture.

We acknowledge the small size of our sample, but note that if the entire population of Indo-*Limonenses* is fewer than 100 people, our initial sample of 44 individuals included close to half of the population and our second subsample of 24 males included about a quarter of the group. It is hard to imagine that genetically unrelated individuals may have escaped sampling, thus leading us to underestimate the genetic diversity of the Indo-*Limonense* population.

Although the maternal and paternal markers both agree on the overwhelmingly Indian origin of the community, they paint a very different picture of its evolution by gene flow. Whereas the Indo-*Limonense* mtDNA gene pool has a substantial African component (31.82%) and a minor Amerindian component (11.36%), lacking evidence of European admixture, the Y-chromosome gene pool lacks any Amerindian marker, while having a large African (37.5%) and a moderate European component (20.8%). We do not know if the mtDNA Amerindian markers were a result of gene flow with local Costa Rican Amerindians or if they came to the Indo-*Limonense* population via the Afro-*Limonenses* who married in with the Indo-*Limonenses*, whose ancestors might have mated with Amerindian Jamaican or Costa Rican women. However, the most likely explanation is that the Amerindian markers were brought by Afro-Limonenses, given that most individuals who married in the community had English surnames. Local Amerindians, in contrast with Afro-*Limonenses*, usually have Spanish names (Madrigal *et al.*, 2001).

At the same time, the absence of European mtDNA markers suggests that gene flow with the Spanish-speaking *Limonense* community and of African slaves with European females in Jamaica was either non-existent, or left no traces in the Indo-*Limonense* group. Our community's pedigree certainly supports the first point, as Spanish names enter into the pedigree only in the last generation. Additionally, the paucity of European females in the plantations of the Caribbean is a well-known fact. Thus, it is very unlikely that European females in Jamaica would have contributed to the mtDNA gene pool of the slaves. In contrast, it is well known that European males frequently produced offspring with their African slaves, thus contributing Y-chromosomal markers to the Afro-Jamaican ancestors of the Afro-*Limonense* community.

The fact that the indo-Costa Ricans married with their neighbors is a departure from the cultural practices said to be observed by other and larger Indo-Caribbean groups such as those of Trinidad and Guyana. In these larger groups consanguineous marriages were avoided while still taking place within the Indo-Caribbean group. There are even some reports of brides being brought from India (van der Veer, 1995; van der Veer and Vertovec, 1991; Vertovec, 1992, 1994, 2000).

Our results, together with those of previous researchers, strongly indicate that human populations which arise as a result of admixture do not necessarily include paternal and maternal representatives of the parental groups. Rather, whereas a parental population may supply males, another parental population may supply females. In the wider context of the evolution of Caribbean and Latin American living populations, our results confirm previous studies of African-derived, *Creole* and "*mestizo*" populations in these regions, which indicate that whereas male Amerindians were largely eliminated upon the invasion of the Europeans, female Amerindians were kept as wives of European and African males. Similar results have been found in Afro-Uruguayan (Bravi *et al.*, 1997) and Afro-Brazilian samples (Abe-Sandes *et al.*, 2004; Bortolini *et al.*, 1997a, 1997b). In the same manner, the presence of European paternal, but not maternal, markers in Afro-Jamaican groups indicates that male Europeans contributed to the formation of the Afro-Jamaican gene pool, whereas female Europeans did not (Parra *et al.*, 1998). These studies indicate that gene flow in humans is gender-mediated, and that the precise historical context in which the gene flow took place must be taken into consideration.

If anything, the story of the Indo-*Limonenses* is a mirror of the story of many Caribbean communities. This group is part of massive migrations of indentured servants who filled the void left by the out-migration of former African slaves away from the sugar plantations. In their new land, the Indo-*Limonenses* maintained a strict avoidance of close-kin marriage and married with their neighbors, who descended from Afro-Jamaican workers, and whose ancestors were forcefully brought as slaves to the Caribbean by the European powers. The evolution of the Indo-*Limonense* gene pool cannot be considered separately from that of Afro-Caribbean communities, which received mtDNA markers from Amerindian but not from European females, and Y-chromosomal markers from European but not Amerindian males. The formation of the Indo-*Limonense* group is a result of migration which affected the human populations in the Caribbean: the invasion of Europeans, slavery of African slaves, and indentured servitude of East-Indian workers. Gene flow among these three groups with the defeated Amerindians resulted in the current Caribbean human gene pool.

REFERENCES

Abe-Sandes, K., Silva, W. A., and Zago, M. A. (2004). Heterogeneity of the Y chromosome in Afro-Brazilian populations. *Human Biology*, **76**, 77–86.

Alves-Silva, J., M. Santos, P. Guimaraes, *et al.* (2000). The ancestry of Brazilian mtDNA Lineages. *American Journal of Human Genetics*, **67**, 444–61.

Angrosino, M. (1974). *Outside is Death: Community Organization, Ideology, and Alcoholism Among the East Indians of Trinidad*. Winston-Salem. NC: Overseas Research Center, Wake Forest University.

Bedoya, G., Montoya, P., Garcia, J., *et al.* (2006). Admixture dynamics in Hispanics: a shift in the nuclear genetic ancestry of a South American population isolate. *Proceedings of the National Academy of Sciences of the United States of America*, **103**, 7234–9.

Blutstein, H. (ed.) (1970). *Area Handbook for Costa Rica*. Washington, DC: US Government Printing Office.

Bortolini, M. C., Salzano, F. M., Thomas, M. G., *et al.* (2003). Y-chromosome evidence for differing ancient demographic histories in the Americas. *American Journal of Human Genetics* **73**, 524–39.

Bortolini, M. C., Salzano, F. M., Zago, M. A., DaSilva, W. A., and Weimer, T. D. (1997b). Genetic variability in two Brazilian ethnic groups: a comparison of mitochondrial and protein data. *American Journal of Physical Anthropology*, **103**, 147–56.

Bortolini, M. C., Zago, M. A., Salzano, F. M., *et al.* (1997a). Evolutionary and anthropological implications of mitochondrial DNA variation in African Brazilian populations. *Human Biology*, **69**, 141–59.

Bravi, C. M., Sans, M., Bailliet, G., *et al.* (1997). Characterization of mitochondrial DNA and Y-chromosome haplotypes in a Uruguayan population of African ancestry. *Human Biology*, **69**, 641–52.

Carrington, C., Kondeatis, E., Ramdath, D., *et al.* (2002). A comparison of HLA-DR and -DQ allele and haplotype frequencies in Trinidadian populations of African, South Asian, and mixed ancestry. *Human Immunology*, **63**, 1045–54.

Carrington, C., Norman, P., Vaughan, R., *et al.* (2003). Analysis of Fc γ receptor II (CD32) polymorphism in populations of African and South Asian ancestry reveals east-west geographic gradients of allele frequencies. *European Journal of Immunogenetics*, **30**, 375–9.

Carvajal-Carmona, L. G., Ophoff, R., Service, S., *et al.* (2003). Genetic demography of Antioquia (Colombia) and the Central Valley of Costa Rica. *Human Genetics*, **112**, 534–41.

Carvalho-Silva, D. R., Santos, F. R., Rocha, J., and Pena, S. D. J. (2001). The phylogeography of Brazilian Y-chromosome lineages. *American Journal of Human Genetics*, **68**, 281–6.

Castri, L., F. Otarola, M. Blell, *et al.* (2007). Indentured migration and differential gender gene flow: the origin and evolution of the East-Indian community of Limon, Costa Rica. *American Journal of Physical Anthropology*, **134**, 175–89.

Cook, N. (1998). *Born to Die: Disease and New World Conquest, 1492–1650*. Cambridge, UK: Cambridge University Press.

Cook, N. (2002). Sickness, starvation and death in early Hispaniola. *Journal of Interdisciplinary History*, **32**, 349–86.

Conniff, M. L. (1995). Afro-West Indians on the Central American isthmus: the case of Panama. In *Salve and Beyond: the African Impact on Latin America and the Caribbean*, ed. D. J. Davis. Jaguar Books on Latin America 5. Wilmington, DE: Scholarly Resources.

Duncan, Q. (1981). El negro antillano: inmigracion y presencia. In *El Negro en Costa Rica*, 8th edn, ed. C. Melendez and Q. Duncan, pp. 99–147. San José, CR: Editorial Costa Rica.

Green, L. D., Derr, J. N., and Knight, A. (2000). mtDNA affinities of the peoples of North-Central Mexico. *American Journal of Human Genetics*, **66**, 989–98.

Grillo-Rosanía, R. (2003). Chinos en Costa Rica: víctimas de abuso y racismo. *Crisol. Suplemento de ciencia y tecnología*, **11**, 63–4.

Harpelle, R. N. (1993). The social and political integration of West Indians in Costa Rica: 1930–50. *Journal of Latin American Studies*, **25**, 103–20.

Herzfeld, A. (2002). *Mekaytelyuw. La Lengua Criolla*. San José, Costa Rica: Editorial de la Universidad de Costa Rica.

Ho, C. G. (1999). Caribbean transnationalism as a gendered process. *Latin American Perspectives*, **26**, 34–54.

Jain, R. (1998). Indian diaspora, globalization and multiculturalism: a cultural analysis. *Contributions to Indian Sociology*, **32**, 337–60.

Jayaram, N. (2006). The metamorphosis of caste among Trinidad Hindus. *Contributions to Indian Sociology*, **40**, 143–72.

Jayawardena, C. (1968). Migration and social change: survey of Indian communities overseas. *Geographical Review*, **58**, 426–49.

Jayawardena, C. (1980). Culture and ethnicity in Guyana and Fiji. *Man*, **15**, 430–450.

Jha, J. (1974). Indian heritage in Trinidad (West-Indies). *Eastern Anthropologist*, **27**, 211–34.

Kiple, K. K. and Ornelas, K. C. (1996). After the encounter: disease and demographics in the Lesser Antilles. In *The Lesser Antilles in the Age of European*

Expansion, ed. R. L. Paquette and S. L. Engerman, pp. 50–67. Gainesville, FL: University Press of Florida.

Klass, M. (1961). *East Indians in Trinidad: A Study of Cultural Persistence*. New York: Columbia University Press.

Klein, H. S. (1978). *The Middle Passage: Comparative Studies in the Atlantic Slave Trade*. Princeton, NJ: Princeton University Press.

Klein, H. S. (1986). *African Slavery in Latin America and the Caribbean*. New York: Oxford University Press.

Lell, J. T., Sukernik, R. I., Starikovskaya, Y. B., *et al.* (2002). The dual origin and Siberian affinities of native American Y chromosomes. *American Journal of Human Genetics*, **70**, 192–206.

Madrigal, L. (2006). *Human Biology of Afro-Caribbean Populations*. Cambridge, UK: Cambridge University Press.

Madrigal, L., Ware, B., Hagen, E., Blell, M., and Otarola, F. (2007). The East Indian diaspora in Costa Rica: inbreeding avoidance, marriage patterns, and cultural survival. *American Anthropologist*, **109**, 330–7.

Madrigal, L., Ware, B., Miller, R., *et al.* (2001). Ethnicity, gene flow, and population subdivision in Limon, Costa Rica. *American Journal of Physical Anthropology*, **114**, 99–108.

Martinez-Cruzado, J. C., Toro-Labrador, G., Viera-Vera, J., *et al.* (2005). Reconstructing the population history of Puerto Rico by means of mtDNA phylogeographic analysis. *American Journal of Physical Anthropology*, **128**, 131–55.

Morrissey, M. (1989). *Slave Women in the New World: gender Stratification in the Caribbean*. Lawrence, KS: University Press of Kansas.

Otarola-Duran, F. (2007). Un gajo de Limón: los coolíes, un grupo olvidado en la construcción de la historia nacional costarricense. Ph.D. thesis, Universidad de Costa Rica, San José.

Parra, E. J., Marcini, A., Akey, L., *et al.* (1998). Estimating African American admixture proportions by use of population-specific alleles. *American Journal of Human Genetics*, **63**, 1839–51.

Purcell, T. W. (1993). *Banana Fallout. Class, Color and Culture among West Indians in Costa Rica*. Los Angeles, CA: Center for Afro-American Studies Publications, University of California.

Rodas, C., Gelvez, N., and Keyeux, G. (2003). Mitochondrial DNA studies show asymmetrical Amerindian admixture in Afro-Colombian and Mestizo populations. *Human Biology*, **75**, 13–30.

Ruiz-Narvaez, E. A., Santos, F. R., Carvalho-Silva, D. R., *et al.* (2005). Genetic variation of the Y chromosome in Chibcha-speaking Amerindians of Costa Rica and Panama. *Human Biology*, **77**, 71–91.

Salas, A., Richards, M., Lareu, M. V., *et al.* (2005). Shipwrecks and founder effects: divergent demographic histories reflected in Caribbean mtDNA. *American Journal of Physical Anthropology*, **128**, 855–60.

Segura-Wang, M., Raventos, H., Escamilla, M., and Barrantes, R. (2010). Assessment of genetic ancestry and population substructure in Costa Rica by analysis of individuals with a familial history of mental disorder. *Annals of Human Genetics*, **74**, 516–24.

Speckmann, J. (1965). *Marriage and Kinship Among the Indians in Surinam*. Assen, Netherlands: Van Gorcum.

van der Veer, P. (1995). *Nation and Migration: The Politics of Space in the South Asian Diaspora*. Philadelphia, PA: University of Pennsylvania Press.

van der Veer, P. and Vertovec, S. (1991). Brahmanism abroad – on Caribbean Hinduism as an ethnic religion. *Ethnology*, **30**, 149–66.

Vertovec, S. (1992). *Hindu Trinidad: Religion, Ethnicity and Socio-economic Change.* Hong Kong: Macmillan.

Vertovec, S. (1994). Official and popular Hinduism in diaspora: historical and contemporary trends in Surinam, Trinidad and Guyana. *Contributions to Indian Sociology*, **28**, 123–47.

Vertovec, S. (2000). *The Hindu Diaspora: Comparative Patterns.* New York:Routledge, Taylor and Francis.

Weller, J. (1968). *The East Indian Indenture in Trinidad.* Rio Piedras, Puerto Rico: University of Puerto Rico.

Yelvington, K. (2004). African diaspora in the Americas. In *Encyclopedia of Diasporas: Immigrant and Refugee Cultures Around the World*, Vol. 1, ed. C. R. Ember, M. Ember, and I. Skoggard, pp. 24–35. Hingham, MA: Kluwer.

25

Causes and consequences of migration to the Caribbean Islands and Central America: an evolutionary success story

INTRODUCTION

The Caribbean Islands of the Lesser Antilles were originally settled by Native American Arawak populations approximately AD 100 (Haag, 1965). From the 1200s, until the time of European contact, Carib Indians began to diffuse into the Lesser Antilles from Venezuela replacing or intermixing with the original Arawak population (Rouse, 1976; Taylor, 1977). Africans began arriving in the Americas during the time of the trans-Atlantic slave trade between the fifteenth and nineteenth centuries. This forced migration over vast geographic distances dramatically changed the genetic landscape of the Caribbean.

COLONIALISM AND ITS IMPACT IN THE CARIBBEAN

In the late fifteenth century Spain entered the Caribbean as the first European country with colonizing intent. As the Spanish expanded into neighboring Caribbean islands from their original settlement on Hispaniola (today's Dominican Republic and Haiti), imperialist views resulted in enslavement of the native populations along with the Africans who had arrived along with the Spanish explorers and colonists. Realizing that more labor force was needed for economic exploitation, Spanish King Charles V, in 1518, sanctioned the direct shipment of Africans to the Caribbean, thus beginning the trans-Atlantic slave trade. By the seventeenth century, French, Dutch, and English influences had begun intruding into the Spanish-American

Causes and Consequences of Human Migration, ed. Michael H. Crawford and Benjamin C. Campbell. Published by Cambridge University Press. © Cambridge University Press 2012.

world of the Caribbean (Knight, 1990). Along with their imperialism, these European powers introduced a host of diseases to which the native populations of the islands had no resistance, including smallpox, typhus, and measles. Smallpox in particular decimated or extinguished entire civilizations, the knowledge of which was used at a later date in 1763 by a British military colonel with insidious purpose by suggesting that smallpox-infected blankets be given to Native Americans to precipitate an epidemic (Jobling *et al.*, 2004; Stearn and Stearn, 1945). Malaria was introduced into the Americas by Africans who were already infected with the disease at the time of their arrival and the presence of suitable malarial vectors in the Americas sustained the disease (CDC, 2009). The combination of disease imports from both Europe and Africa, such as smallpox, malaria, yellow fever, chickenpox, whooping cough, diphtheria, plague, typhoid fever, and cholera, proved disastrous for the susceptible Native American population (Crawford, 1998).

GARIFUNA ETHNOGENESIS

The origins of the Black Carib or Garifuna population can be traced to St. Vincent Island in the Caribbean. This population arose from the admixture of the original Native American population and newly arrived Africans in the form of runaway and/or shipwrecked slaves from European-held islands (Crawford, 1983). Raiding Caribs would also return to St. Vincent with African slaves taken from neighboring European plantations (Palacio, 2001). In 1797, the British forcibly removed the majority of the Black Caribs from St. Vincent and relocated them to Roatan Island off the coast of Honduras (Gonzalez, 1988). From Roatan, the Spanish transferred the majority of the Black Caribs to Trujillo, Honduras, and from there the displaced population settled the coast of Central America from Belize to Nicaragua (Gullick, 1976). Figure 25.1 traces the migration pattern of the Caribs, the second Native American population after the Arawak to enter the Caribbean Islands from South America, and later the arrival of African individuals and the subsequent relocation of a portion of the admixed population from St. Vincent to the Central American coast, where the Garifuna established 54 villages from Belize to Nicaragua (Davidson, 1984).

It is estimated that 4338 individuals were initially deported from St. Vincent to Baliceaux Island, where many people perished, and eventually 1465 people arrived upon the shores of Trujillo in Honduras on September 23, 1797 (Gonzales, 1988). The Central American populations refer to themselves as Garifuna while those remaining on St. Vincent are known as Black Caribs.

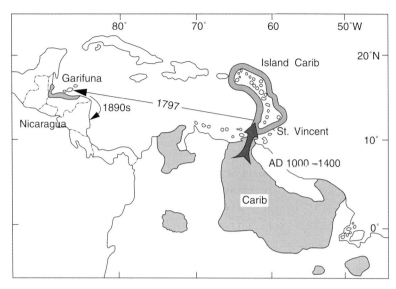

Figure 25.1 Map representing the Carib migrations and relocations of the Garifuna (Black Carib). (Adapted from Crawford, 1983.)

The genetic composition of the Garifuna has been of anthropological interest due to their unique population history and successful colonization of the Central American coast. From the small number of founding individuals in Central America, the population has expanded to well over 200 000 at present (Palacio, 2001; Paz-Bailey *et al.*, 2009). The highest reported birth rate in the Americas belongs to the first generations of Garifuna with an average of 10.9 children per woman (Brennan, 1983). Living in an environment along the Central American coast where malaria is endemic, their African genetic heritage may indeed impart resistance to disease severity, giving them an advantage over those of non-African descent.

CONSEQUENCES OF MALARIA

Genomic adaptations have taken place in recent human history, which are directly related to the strong selective pressures exerted on humans living in a malarial environment. Adaptation to this devastating disease has allowed the differential survival of individuals with certain advantageous genetic mutations. Natural selection against malaria operates through diseases such as sickle-cell, thalassemia, glucose-6-phosphate-dehydrogenase deficiency, and other red blood cell defects (Kwiatkowski, 2005; Madrigal, 2006). It has been estimated that in 2002 there were 2.2 billion people worldwide at risk of exposure to *Plasmodium falciparum* malaria, resulting in an estimated 515 million clinical attacks attributable to this parasite. Africa is the region with the largest affected population, followed by Southeast Asia, the western Pacific, the eastern Mediterranean, and the Americas (Snow *et al.*, 2005). Generally, *P. falciparum* causes the most severe form of malaria, but there are also hundreds of millions of cases due to other malarial parasite species: *P. vivax*, *P. malariae*, and *P. ovale* (Kwiatkowski, 2005).

Where malaria is endemic, hemoglobinopathies have evolved which offer protection against the disease. The most common hemoglobinopathies are the alpha and beta thalassemias where there is deficient synthesis of globin protein, and three polymorphic structural mutations of the beta-globin chain, hemoglobin S (HbS), hemoglobin C (HbC), and hemoglobin E (HbE). The worldwide distribution of these hemoglobinopathies coincides with that of malaria, and molecular characterization and haplotype analysis of these hemoglobin variants reveals the mutations are regionally specific and have all increased in frequency within the last 5000 years (Flint *et al.*, 1998). The HbS allele, for example, is found across a large region of sub-Saharan Africa as well as parts of the Middle East. The corresponding HbS protein, hemoglobin S or sickle hemoglobin, tends to polymerize at low oxygen concentrations, causing the red blood cell to deform into a sickle-like shape. HbS homozygotes have sickle-cell disease, which is debilitating and often fatal due to these erythrocyte deformities. The heterozygous state, HbAS, is not usually associated with any clinical abnormalities and confers an average tenfold increase in protection from life-threatening forms of malaria (Kwiatkowski, 2005). The hemoglobin S mutation is one of the best examples of heterozygote selective advantage in humans.

GENETIC CONSEQUENCES OF MIGRATION

Numerous studies have been conducted examining the genetic ancestry of the Black Caribs and Garifuna. In the recent past, studies have utilized classical genetic markers, such as blood groups, proteins, and immunoglobulins to gain insight into the ethnic diversity and history of the population (Crawford, 1983). More recently, mitochondrial DNA, Y-chromosome, and autosomal markers have been employed to elucidate more information on the ancestry of this unique population.

Mitochondrial DNA

Mitochondrial DNA (mtDNA) is particularly useful in the reconstruction of the maternal ancestry of a population due to its non-recombining, uniparental inheritance pattern. The human mitochondrial genome was completely sequenced in 1981 and is a circular, double-stranded DNA molecule, consisting of 16 569 base pairs (bp). The molecule contains two main domains: a control region (also called the d-loop) of about 1000 bp, subdivided into two hypervariable segments (HVSI and HVSII), which are spaced by a more conservative segment, and a coding region of about 15 000 bp (Francalacci *et al.*, 1999; Jones *et al.*, 1992; Passarge, 2001). The energy-generating process of oxidative phosphorylation takes place within the mitochondria: the reason this organelle is commonly called the "power-house" of the cell. The number of mitochondria present in a cell varies with cell type. Cells requiring large amounts of energy, such as nerve and muscle cells, contain thousands of mitochondria, each containing 2 to 10 copies of mtDNA, while other cell types may contain only a few hundred (Jobling *et al.*, 2004). This high copy number of mtDNA is particularly useful when applied to genetic studies where the sample has undergone degradation and nuclear DNA may not be retrievable, as is many times the case with ancient DNA studies. Mutations accumulate faster in mtDNA, at about 5 to 10 times the rate of nuclear DNA, because the mtDNA molecule lacks the DNA repair mechanisms present in the nuclear genome (Francalacci *et al.*, 1999; Jones *et al.*, 1992). The non-coding mtDNA control region has an even higher mutation rate than the coding portion of the mitochondrial genome since it has none of the evolutionary restrictions of the coding region, which requires encoding functional products. This elevated rate of mutation is advantageous when applied to anthropological studies since it allows for the successful examination of evolutionary relationships through the passage of time (Sykes, 2001). In addition to the high mutation rate, the many attributes of mtDNA include high copy number per cell, relatively small genome, and because it is inherited primarily through the maternal line, this genetic material can be used to reconstruct evolutionary history unencumbered by the limitations presented by recombination. Mitochondrial DNA has been an invaluable tool employed by the scientific community to study a broad range of questions, from the origins of modern humans, to the diversity we see in present populations worldwide.

Y chromosome

The human Y chromosome is a useful anthropologic tool employed in reconstructing the evolutionary history of a population through the paternal line. The non-recombining portion of the Y-chromosome (NRY) in particular, which constitutes about 90% of the chromosome, is useful in evolutionary studies (Jobling *et al.*, 2004). The Y chromosome has an abundance of DNA repeat elements. These include microsatellites or short tandem repeats (STRs), which comprise a core unit or motif of 1–6 base pairs tandemly arranged, with the total repeat unit usually less than 350 base pairs. STRs are spread throughout the Y. The Y chromosomal polymorphisms most widely used in anthropological genetics studies include STRs, and slowly evolving biallelic markers. The biallelic markers include single nucleotide polymorphisms (SNPs) and insertion/deletion events (indels), which are believed to have occurred only once in humans, and are sometimes referred to as unique mutational events (UMEs). Biallelic markers can be used to construct Y-chromosome haplogroups (paternal lineages), while the STRs can be used to characterize the diversity within haplogroups and aid in the resolution of phylogenies (Rubicz, 2007). The Y chromosome, in essence, does for the paternal lineage what mitochondrial DNA does for the maternal lineage; it allows for the examination of evolutionary history through an individual path without recombination.

Autosomal markers

Although not free from the confounding factors of recombination, autosomal markers are useful tools in the examination of populations and can be used to assess admixture. Genetic variability between ethnic groups allows for estimation of genetic contribution in an admixed population. The growth of forensic databases has increased the practical application of autosomal marker use in the anthropological setting by providing comparative data. Commercially available forensic kits, which are designed to examine unique autosomal allelic variations present at different rates in different ethnic groups, can be used to examine population genetic structure.

GENETIC STUDIES

In 1984 immunoglobulin marker Gm data were published for Central American Garifuna from Stann Creek and Punta Gorda, Belize, and St. Vincent Island Black Caribs from Sandy Bay and Owia, to assess gene flow in these hybrid populations. At that time, immunoglobulin allotype frequencies provided the most sensitive serum genetic markers for the study of admixture. Based on the frequencies of these immunoglobulin markers, 76% of the genes in the Central American gene pool were African, the Native American component was about 20%, and 4% of the genes were attributed to European admixture. As for St. Vincent, the African component of the population was 46%, the Native American contribution was 38%, and 16% corresponded to European genes (Schanfield et al., 1984).

Monsalve and Hagelberg (1997) examined the mtDNA of 28 samples taken from the Garifuna of Belize in the 1970s to assess maternal ancestry of the population. The HVSI region was sequenced from nucleotide position 16 067 to 16 344 and samples were also screened for the presence of markers that define the four major haplogroups in Native Americans through Restriction Fragment Length Polymorphism (RFLP), as well as direct visualization of the polymorphic region which may contain the 9-bp deletion in the intergenic region between cyto-chrome oxidase II and lysil transfer RNA. None of the samples were classified as belonging to Native American haplogroups A, C, or D. One sample exhibited probable Native American ancestry (haplogroup B), while the remaining samples were identified as belonging to an African ancestral lineage.

Their results correlate with the historical record that suggests high levels of admixture of the original Island Caribs with West African people. They also assert that the Garifuna sample showed high genetic affinity with the African Yoruba people (Monsalve and Hagelberg, 1997). The Yoruba are from Nigeria and belong linguistically to the eastern group of South-Central Niger-Congo, a branch of the Niger-Kordofanian family, which comprises most West African languages (Cavalli-Sforza et al., 1994).

Mitochondrial DNA was again employed in 2005 to ascertain maternal ancestry of the Garifuna population. Salas et al. (2005) analyzed DNA obtained from 44 maternally unrelated individuals from the Atlantic Honduran coast. HVSI and HVSII sequences were obtained as well as RFLP data on ten diagnostic sites in order to distinguish major African and Native American mtDNA haplogroups. All of the individuals analyzed were classified as belonging to either Native American or African lineages, with no European lineages detected. Native American mtDNA comprised 16% of the population and 86% belonged to a typically African haplogroup. The four major conclusions asserted by the authors are as follows: there is a major African component in the

Garifuna population, but the Native American component is also significant; the Native American component is characteristic of Central
and northern South America; the main African contribution is from
West Africa, but a number of types can also be assigned a Southeast
African origin; and the Garifuna carry the imprint of a major founder
effect (Salas *et al.*, 2005).

Mitochondrial and Y-chromosome diversity in the English-
speaking Caribbean was investigated in 2007 by Torres *et al.* (2007).
In this study, 314 DNA samples were collected from the Caribbean
islands of Dominica, Grenada, St. Lucia, St. Kitts, St. Vincent,
and Trinidad, along with a supplemental 187 blood samples from
St. Thomas and Jamaica. The participants in this study were self-
identified as African-Caribbean. Mitochondrial HVSI was sequenced
and select RFLP sites were utilized to aid in haplogroup assignment.
A total of 12 loci were typed from the non-recombining region of the
Y chromosome (NRY).

With respect to the maternal ancestry of the study populations
86.3% of the Caribbean samples were of African descent. Native American
mtDNA lineages were present in Dominica, Trinidad, and St. Vincent
samples, with the highest percentage of 28 found in Dominica. Of the
non-African and non-Native American mtDNA sequences in the entire
Caribbean sample, 4.1% were classified into Eurasian macrohaplogroups.
Admixture estimates based on Y STRs for the pooled Caribbean sample
identified 72.6% African contribution.

The Caribbean study populations and comparative African populations had similar ranges in average gene, nucleotide, and haplotype
diversity values for both the mtDNA and Y-chromosome loci, indicating there was no loss of genetic diversity as a result of the forced
migrations of Africans to the Caribbean. This observation remained
consistent after the non-African mitochondrial sequences were
removed from the Caribbean group, which suggests that gene flow
from Eurasians and Native Americans is not the sole cause of the high
diversity observed in the Caribbean groups, but likely reflects the
high degree of genetic variation present in the parental African populations. It could also be reflective of the admixture of multiple African
groups once in the Americas (Torres *et al.*, 2007).

Autosomal short tandem repeat (STR) loci were used to access
allelic frequency distributions in Garifuna populations of the Honduran Caribbean coasts in 2010 by Herrera-Paz *et al.* Thirteen genotyped
markers of the pooled Garifuna sample were compared with populations from Africa, the Americas, and Europe. Signatures of founder

events were present in the Garifuna sample at alleles 46.2 and 25.2 at the FGA locus of the CODIS (Combined DNA Index System) autosomal STR loci. When these relatively high allele frequencies in the Garifuna sample were compared with those present in the worldwide population, both alleles were found to be present in very low frequencies in only a few populations. The Garifuna also exhibited a low average expected heterozygosity when compared with other populations, indicating low genetic variability despite their multi-ethnic origin, which correlates with the mtDNA analyses of Salas *et al.* in 2005 (Herrera-Paz *et al.*, 2010).

Currently, ongoing research being conducted at the University of Kansas aims to further identify genetic relationships between Central American Garifuna and their ancestors on St. Vincent Island. In the spring of 2004, I collected DNA samples from participating individuals on St. Vincent Island and during the winter of 2005, I traveled to Belize and collected samples from study participants there as well. I employed mitochondrial DNA markers to examine maternal lineages present in the populations of interest. From St. Vincent Island, individuals from the Black Carib villages of Sandy Bay, Owia, Fancy, and Greiggs participated in the study; from Belize individuals from the Garifuna town of Punta Gorda and Barranco village participated. Mitochondrial DNA RFLPs, along with additional HVSI sequence data, classified individuals into major haplogroups, namely the African haplogroups L0, L1, L2, and L3, as well as Native American haplogroups A, B, and C. Samples from both Belize and St. Vincent display mtDNA haplogroups indicative of both African and Native American maternal ancestry. St. Vincent shows approximately 44% Native American and 47% African ancestry. Belize displays a much higher African component at 92% with only 4% attributed to Native American ancestry.

INTERPRETATION OF PREVIOUS STUDIES

The genetic variability of Caribbean populations of African descent is greater than that of the Garifuna population of Central America. During the time of their deportation from St. Vincent Island, before their eventual arrival on Roatan, they were deposited on the small island of Baliceaux, where almost half of the people perished from disease and hunger. From the original group of approximately 4338 individuals, only 2248 survived to endure the remainder of the journey to Roatan, where 2026 people disembarked. From Roatan 1465 Black Caribs were transported to their final destination along the Central

American coast (Gonzalez, 1988; Gullick, 1976). These events of significant human loss and the resulting smaller founding Central American group likely explain the founder effect signature observed in the genetic structure of the Garifuna. It stands to reason that during such a time of population decimation, genetic variability was decreased and is reflected in the higher diversity measures found in the Caribbean islands compared with those of the Central American Garifuna. From devastating loss, the population rebounded, in part due to their unique genetic constitution, along with adaptive cultural strategies taken from their Native American and African roots.

CONCLUSIONS

The genetic structure of the Garifuna has been created through gene flow of African and Native American populations and the forced migration of this admixed group from St. Vincent Island to the Central American coast. During the time of deportation a loss of genetic diversity occurred through the significant loss of human life, and after arriving at their destination, further partitioning of the gene pool resulted from kin migration and the formation of separate villages. Assisting this displaced population in their successful colonization of the coastal regions of Central America was their African genetic ancestry: specifically, genetic mutations which provided a selective advantage in a malarial environment.

When addressing the origins of the Garifuna population of Central America, historical records relating to the forced migration patterns of this population add valuable information for optimal interpretation of resulting data from genetic studies. Displaced from their original homeland on St. Vincent Island, the Garifuna have become known to be one of the most successful colonizing populations, settling the coast of Central America and expanding in record numbers. Today this adaptive population remains firmly entrenched along the Central American coast and immigration continues to bring individuals to countries such as England, the United States, and other parts of the world.

REFERENCES

Brennan, E. R. (1983). Factors underlying decreasing fertility among the Garifuna of Honduras. *American Journal of Physical Anthropology*, **60**, 177.
Cavalli-Sforza, L., Menozzi, P., and Piazza, A. (1994). Africa. In *The History and Geography of Human Genes*, pp. 158–94. Princeton, NJ: Princeton University Press.

Centers for Disease Control and Prevention (CDC) (2009). *CDC Health Information for International Travel 2010.* Atlanta, GA: U.S. Department of Health and Human Services, Public Health Service.

Crawford, M. H. (1983). The anthropological genetics of the Black Caribs (Garifuna) of Central America and the Caribbean. *Yearbook of Physical Anthropology*, **26**, 161–92.

Crawford, M. H. (1998). Population size and the effects of European contact. In *The Origins of Native Americans: Evidence from Anthropological Genetics*, pp. 32–62. New York: Cambridge University Press.

Davidson, W. V. (1984). The Garifuna in Central America: ethnohistorical and geographical foundations. In *Current Developments in Anthropological Genetics*, Vol. 3: *Black Caribs. A Case Study in Biocultural Adaptation*, ed. M. H. Crawford, pp. 13–35. New York: Plenum Press.

Flint, J., Harding, R. M., Boyce, A. J., and Clegg, J. B. (1998). The population genetics of the haemoglobinopathies. *Bailliere's Clinical Haematology*, **11**, 1–51.

Francalacci, P., Montiel, R., and Malgosa, A. (1999). A mitochondrial DNA database: applications to problems of nomenclature and population genetics. In *Genomic Diversity: Applications in Human Population Genetics*, ed. S. S. Papiha, R. Deka and R. Chakraborty, pp. 103–119. New York: Kluwer Academic/ Plenum Publishers.

Gonzalez, N. L. (1988). *Sojourners of the Caribbean: Ethnogenesis and Ethnohistory of the Garifuna*, pp. 15–38. Urbana, IL: University of Illinois Press.

Gullick, C. J. M. R. (1976). *Exiled From St. Vincent: the Development of Black Carib Culture in Central America up to 1945.* Malta: Progress Press.

Haag, W. G. (1965). Pottery typology in certain Lesser Antilles. *American Antiquity*, **31**, 242–5.

Herrera-Paz, E.-F., Matamoros, M., and Carracedo, A. (2010). The Garifuna (Black Carib) people of the Atlantic coasts of Honduras: population dynamics, structure, and phylogenetic relations inferred from genetic data, migration matrices, and isonomy. *American Journal of Human Biology*, **22**, 36–44.

Jobling, M. A., Hurles, M. E., and Tyler-Smith, C. (2004). *Human Evolutionary genetics: Origins, Peoples and Disease*, pp. 300–28. New York: Garland Publishing.

Jones, S., Martin, R., and Pilbean, D. (1992). *The Cambridge Encyclopedia of Human Evolution*, pp. 316–21. Cambridge, UK: Cambridge University Press.

Knight, F. W. (1990). *The Caribbean: The Genesis of a Fragmented Nationalism*, 2nd edn, pp. 22–65. New York: Oxford University Press.

Kwiatkowski, D. P. (2005). How malaria has affected the human genome and what human genetics can teach us about malaria. *American Journal of Human Genetics*, **77**, 171–92.

Madrigal, L. (2006). Population genetics of Afro-Caribbean populations. In *Human Biology of Afro-Caribbean Populations*, pp. 108–24. New York: Cambridge University Press.

Monsalve, M. V. and Hagelberg, E. (1997). Mitochondrial DNA polymorphisms in Carib people of Belize. *Proceedings of the Royal Society of London: Biological Sciences*, **264**, 1217–24.

Palacio, J. (2001). A re-consideration of the Native American and African roots of Garifuna identity. *Caribbean Amerindian Studies (Occasional Papers of the Caribbean Amerindian Centrelink)*, **3**.

Passarge, E. (2001). *Color Atlas of Genetics*, 2nd edn., pp. 124–31. Stuttgart, Germany: Thieme.

Paz-Bailey, G., Morales-Mirands, S., Jacobson, J., *et al.* (2009). High rates of STD and sexual risk behaviors among Garifunas in Honduras. *Journal of Acquired Immune Deficiency Syndromes*, **51**, S26–34.

Rouse, I. (1976). Cultural development on Antigua, West Indies: a progress report. *Actas del XLI Congreso Internacional de Americanistas*, **3**, 701–9.

Rubicz, R. (2007). Evolutionary consequences of recently founded Aleut communities in the Commander and Pribilof Islands. Unpublished dissertation, University of Kansas, Dept. of Anthropology, Lawrence, KS.

Salas, A., Richards, M., Lareu, M.-V., *et al.* (2005). Shipwrecks and founder effects: divergent demographic histories reflected in Caribbean mtDNA. *American Journal of Physical Anthropology*, **128**, 855–60.

Schanfield, M. S., Brown, R., and Crawford, M. H. (1984). Immunoglobulin allotypes in the Black Caribs and Creoles of Belize and St. Vincent. In *Current Developments in Anthropological Genetics*, Vol. **3**: *Black Caribs: A Case Study in Biocultural Adaptation*, ed. M. H. Crawford, pp. 345–63. New York: Plenum Press.

Snow, R. W., Guerra, C. A., Noor, A. M., Myint, H. Y., and Hay, S. I. (2005). The global distribution of clinical episodes of *Plasmodium falciparum* malaria. *Nature*, **434**, 214–17.

Stearn, E. W. and Stearn, A. E. (1945). *The Effect of Smallpox on the Destiny of the Amerindian*. Boston, MA: Bruce Humphries.

Sykes, B. (2001). *The Seven Daughters of Eve*. New York: W.W. Norton.

Taylor, D. (1977). *Languages of the West Indies*. Baltimore, MD: Johns Hopkins University Press.

Torres, J. B., Kittles, R. A., and Stone, A. C. (2007). Mitochondrial and Y chromosome diversity in the English-speaking Caribbean. *Annals of Human Genetics*, **71**, 782–90.

Section 3 Overview

26

Why do we migrate? A retrospective

INTRODUCTION

The scientific study of migration, and of migrants, has a long history in
anthropology, genetics, and medicine (Boas, 1912; Chakraborty and
Szathmary, 1985; Crawford, 1976, 1984; Morton *et al.*, 1982). Yet in
anthropological genetics it has been a decade since the publication
of Goldstein and Chikhi's (2002) review of the relevance of human
migration and population structure studies and even longer since
the appearance of Fix's (1999) volume on migration, colonization, and
microevolution. The time is ripe for a re-examination of human migration in the context of new methods of molecular analysis, a re-
examination of historical, economic, and ecological motivations for
migration, as well as continuing refinements and extensions of the
archaeological and paleoecological records that inform our understanding of past population movements. This volume successfully provides
such an updated perspective on the field, and serves as a valuable
adjunct to the historical-economic examination of modern migration
by Goldin *et al.* (2011) and the recent anthropological perspective on
migration by Cabana and Clark (2011). These new treatments, along
with the current volume, highlight the growing perception of migration not only as an evolutionary mechanism, but as a primary
agent of structure and change in the deep past that echoes in the
contemporary world.

The multidisciplinary conference upon which this volume is
based was a gathering of over 100 scholars who engaged in spirited
debate and discussion over the course of the meeting. It was an exciting

Causes and Consequences of Human Migration, ed. Michael H. Crawford and
Benjamin C. Campbell. Published by Cambridge University Press. © Cambridge
University Press 2012.

and gratifying experience. The timeliness of the discussions is reflected in the chapters in this volume, and those initial discussions have been enhanced by the perspectives provided by several chapters that were not represented at the original meeting (noted in the Preface). It would be a disservice to the authors of the chapters to attempt a detailed summary and review of their contributions. They present a daunting array of data (both new and old), analysis, and inference on migration in diverse contexts far more eloquently than any brief summary could capture. Some concluding thoughts regarding alternative approaches to the study of migration, what has been done, and what might yet be done, seems worthy of some retrospection, however.

Migration, literally the relocation of people(s) from one place to another, is the stuff of history and human evolution. In most documented cases of migration, migrants become imbedded in the local population of which they have elected to become a part. Occasionally, migrants arrive in such numbers that they overwhelm the local population in the area to which they have relocated, an event often referred to as colonization. In either case, and both may be seen in various chapters in this volume, the result is that migrants and residents interbreed, resulting in a hybrid descendant population (Crawford, 1984; Currat and Excoffier, 2011; Hammer et al., 2011). The economic, social, and ecological forces that motivate human migration also affect the genetic structure of human populations. In this way, migration as a process links the natural and social sciences. The genetic result of migration, gene flow, is intimately tied to our understanding of the evolution and demographic structure of populations (Wright, 1951, 1978). The social and economic drivers of migration are often framed in similar theoretical terms within the field of behavioral ecology, where individual decisions on when and where to move are linked to resource acquisition or economic opportunities or efficiencies that enhance individual fitness (Fix, 1999).

Given the multiplicity of drivers of migration (Black et al., 2011; Goldin et al., 2011), the characterization of migration can take many forms, and be called by many names, for example dispersal, diaspora, colonization, as well as migration. As the chapters in this volume illustrate, the context of individual migration events usually makes clear the scale of movement implied by different terms, but it is worth emphasizing that the terms used to describe migration are not necessarily always synonymous. The distinction between colonization and migration is illustrative, since all colonizations are migrations, but not all migrations are colonizations. Drivers of true colonization events are as often ecological as they are economic. Groups migrating to new, uninhabited lands select routes and locations of settlements that permit adequate resource procurement and continuation of the group.

In a recent study, Ramachandran and Rosenberg (2011) examined patterns of population differentiation in Eurasia and the Americas relative to lines of latitude and longitude. The result of their analyses indicated that while both latitudinal and longitudinal distances were important in predicting population differentiation in the Americas, only latitudinal distance was significantly associated with genetic distance between Eurasian populations. This result implies a reduced level of gene flow among Native American populations since founding and a corresponding increase in genetic differentiation between populations. In fact, genetic differentiation between indigenous American populations is greater per unit of latitudinal distance than similar measures of divergence along measures of latitudinal distance in Eurasia (Ramachandran and Rosenberg, 2011). Thus, the pace of migration and gene flow in a general north–south orientation is slower than comparable rates in Eurasia, which is oriented east–west. The implications for the spread of people and domesticates late in prehistory is obvious. Indeed, Hunley and Healy (2011) observed that, at least in the Americas, genetic diversity is hierarchically structured and that gene flow among adjacent populations has had little impact on observed patterns of geographic diversity, irrespective of the impact of historical admixture with non Native American genomes. This result suggests that population structure at colonization is as important as later migrations and admixture in establishing the observed patterns of modern geographic structure, at least in the Americas (Hunley and Healy, 2011; Raff *et al.*, 2011). Taken together these results suggest that we should be very careful in formulating colonization models of population migration further back in prehistory, where movement along lines of latitude may be more readily accomplished, as ecological zones correlate with latitude and require fewer adaptations for change than movement along lines of longitude. Such inferences have significant effects on our views not only of the pace and direction of colonization events, but also the sizes of populations involved in early colonizations.

The new ecological areas exploited by colonizing populations have substantial demographic implications for subsequent generations, for example carrying capacity, population growth rates, and speed of subsequent movement of communities. For migrants moving into new areas that are already occupied by native populations, the same concerns with viability and sustainability exist, but the ecological drivers are likely supplanted by economic trade-offs against the existing populations already occupying the region. The "language" of migration has implications for the demography of both the migrant and recipient populations, as well as temporal and/or spatial implications, and it is important to be precise in characterizing individual migration events.

Because much of the recent literature on migration stems from large historical population movements – for example, European migration and colonization in the sixteenth century or the Irish migration following the mid nineteenth century potato famine – we often associate migration with some appreciable population density in the source population. This is certainly true of the two examples noted, or in the myriad cases of urbanization or military expansion. But the anthropological perspective taken in this volume emphasizes that low population density populations of hunters/gatherers/foragers also are often sources of migrant groups.

The recent sequencing of the Neandertal genome (Green *et al.*, 2010) has provided dramatic insights into human evolution and the nature of migration and admixture. Although the complete sequencing of the Neandertal mitochondrial genome yielded no evidence for Neandertal–modern human admixture (Green *et al.*, 2008), the sequencing of the Neandertal nuclear genome did provide evidence of low-level admixture between these two early populations. This observation has resulted in a dramatic change in perspective on the relationship between populations of Neandertals and modern humans in the geographic regions where they appear to have coexisted. It is no longer tenable to postulate a complete replacement of Neandertals by modern humans. Rather, the evolutionary and demographic story is one of migration, intersection, and admixture. The rate of admixture, however, is still somewhat unresolved. The Neandertal genomic sequence suggests an admixture rate of 1–4% between Neandertals and modern humans. Currat and Excoffier (2011) modeled the admixture in a spatially expanding population (modern humans) and found that the level of admixture reflected in the Neandertal genome could be accounted for by less than 200 total admixture events for a 1% rate of admixture, and just over 400 total admixture events if admixture was approximately 3% between Neandertals and modern humans. Their modeling estimates suggest that the data are most likely consistent with admixture rates < 1%. These rates imply an admixture event only once in every one or two generations during the time the lineages were in geographic contact. This low level of admixture is also consistent with the absence of Neandertal mtDNA in modern humans as a result of genetic drift (Currat and Excoffier, 2011).

Basing demographic models on such sequence data indicates that the majority of admixture events occurred at the wave front of the expanding modern human population during its migration out of Africa and into Eurasia (Currat and Excoffier, 2011); that is, in geographic locations far removed from the later geographic positions associated with Neandertals or modern European populations. Thus, the conjunction of the newer genomic data and statistical modeling provides a framework from which to assess the time and place of admixture during migration events. Such demographic models based on genomic data provide linkages to other streams of data and analysis that begin to converge on several lines of inference. For example, genealogical analysis of the Canadian population of Saguenay Lac-Saint-Jean indicate a selective advantage to being on an expanding, colonizing, wave front via a heritable increased fertility rate that does not exist in the core area away from the wave front (Moreau *et al.*, 2011). Such a selective advantage on an advancing wave front in admixing populations may also relate to the inference of "adaptive introgression" of archaic alleles into the human immune system (Abi-Rached *et al.*, 2011). In this latter case, genomic sequences from both Neandertals and a sister species identified from aDNA sequences, Denisovans (Reich *et al.*, 2010), suggest the archaic contribution of specific immune response alleles into the modern human genome. Finally, the genomic sequences defining the Denisovans, along with modern genomic sequences of an Australian Aboriginal male (Rasmussen *et al.*, 2011) indicate a more complex migration and pattern of archaic admixture during the colonization of South Asia, Australia, and New Guinea (Reich *et al.*, 2011). From the original colonization of Eurasia by low population density groups moving out of Africa, to the colonization of Australia, Oceania, the Americas, or even the more recent migrations of Aleuts south from Alaska, of Thule whalers across the North American Arctic, or of Numic-speaking groups migrating into the Great Basin in prehistory, small, low population density groups are frequent migrants.

The study of migration events that occurred in the remote past emphasizes the need for high resolution archaeological information, direct dating of early sites, and a robust and high resolution paleoecological record with which to frame the timing and transit of colonizing populations. While climate change in the contemporary world is often associated with migrations and relocations (Piguet *et al.*, 2011), more ancient climate events may also have been associated with migrations.

D'Andrea *et al.* (2011) present evidence that abrupt temperature changes over the past 4500 years in West Greenland are coincident with Paleo-Eskimo and Norse settlement and abandonment. A number of prehistoric migrations have been hypothesized to be related to periods of climatic instability and dramatic ecological change, including the colonization of the western hemisphere at the close of the last glacial cycle.

An aspect of colonizing populations that is not dealt with directly in the volume, but that is implicit in some chapters, is the potential for migration to act as a selective agent (Black *et al.*, 2011). As populations move long distances, and traverse multiple ecozones, genomes are subject to selective screening across environmental gradients (longitudinal transects). And as noted above, presence on the wave front of a migrating population may enhance selective intensity (Moreau *et al.*, 2011), complementing the study of the end result of migrant populations adapting to new environments, both culturally and biologically (Hancock *et al.*, 2008). A related approach is the use of proxies for human behavior and migration. The study of human pathogens and the biogeography of human diseases provide proxies for human movement across broad geographic areas. Moodley *et al.* (2009) demonstrated that lineages of *Helicobacter pylori* characterized populations of Australia and New Guinea (hpSahul) and Melanesia and Polynesia (hspMaori). Both sets of lineages were of Asian origin, but the *H. pylori* lineage characterizing Australian and New Guinean populations split from the Asian ancestral form over 30 000 years ago, while the hspMaori clades have a more recent origin. In both instances, the timing and distinctiveness of the pathogen lineages associated with specific populations are consistent with the colonization history inferred from archaeology and patterns of human genetic variation. Similarly, Ghose *et al.* (2002) documented Asian strains of *H. pylori* in Native American populations, suggesting indigenous American groups possessed this pathogen at colonization of the hemisphere, augmenting evidence for the Asian origin of early American colonists.

Polyomavirus JC (JCV), the pathogen responsible for progressive multifocal leukoencephalopathy, benignly infects a large portion of the world's population, and its various lineages have been used as a proxy for reconstructing human migrations (Sugimoto *et al.*, 1997), including linking Asian-derived genotypes in Native American and Pacific Island populations (Agostini *et al.*, 1997) – although care must be exercised in using such proxies to infer population origins and migrations as some pathogen lineages may result from recent introductions (Major and Neel, 1998).

A final example comes from documenting the range expansion of *Coccidioides immitis*. Fisher *et al.* (2001) found that *C. immitis* genotypes were highly geographically structured in North America, but lacked variability in South American samples. This latter observation was consistent with a single colonization event from a Texas lineage in the time frame most anthropologists assume that South America was colonized by humans. However, the estimated time range for the *C. immitis* colonization of South America was so broad as to preclude confirmation of its introduction to South America by a single colonizing human population. Nevertheless, the reduced genetic variation in South American *C. immitis* but variation and geographic structure in North American *C. immitis* lineages, genetic patterns of variation that parallel those seen in modern Native American populations of the continents, are suggestive. If further analyses ultimately confirm the link between *C. immitis* introduction to South America by early colonists, it provides another avenue for modeling the timing, dispersal pattern, and rates, as well as population sizes of early migrants to South America. Of course, such inferences remain speculative until additional research on this pathogen, its pattern of genetic variation, and association with human colonists can be firmly established.

The study of aDNA or stable isotopes from archaeologically recovered domesticates or prey items also can be informative of prehistoric migrations and relocations (Coltrain *et al.*, 2004). Such approaches require a close reading of the archaeological and paleoenvironmental records. This perspective is well represented in several chapters in the volume.

As noted earlier, migrant studies have a long history in anthropology and genetics, but employing modern refugee populations as sources for genetic sampling is novel. Given the large number of refugee populations across the modern world, this approach may well be more fully exploited in future studies. The presentations at the conference included a wide variety of "migration" maps based on various genetic systems, historical records, etc. These are somewhat less in evidence in the current volume. The assumptions inherent in the creation of such maps, and the deterministic models they are based on, have been refined and streamlined in the final written versions included here. This is to be expected. Authors are increasingly making explicit the assumptions of statistical models employed and the effects that violation of these assumptions have on inferences drawn; from time-dependency of mutation rates to coalescent time estimates, to starting values of demographic parameters such as population size and growth rates. As evident in a number of chapters, the greater robusticity of new data on population variation, especially genetic variation, permits asking more insightful questions about the process of migration, population histories, and evolution – questions worthy of the resolution of our embarrassment of data riches.

A significant issue in all studies that attempt to reconstruct historical dynamics, whether from archaeological, genetic, or historical documents, is sampling. As data richness increases, and it certainly will continue to do so for genomic data, the problems of sampling may appear to decrease in importance. This is unlikely to be true in general, as modern, observable patterns of genetic variation may be the result of a variety of alternative selective or demographic processes (Goldstein and Chikhi, 2002; Pannell and Charlesworth, 2000). Indeed, one of the strengths of this volume is in demonstrating the value of integrating diverse streams of data and information – genetics, archaeology, paleo-ecology, patterns of health and illness – in order to more accurately reconstruct population histories, and to permit testing of rational hypotheses relating to the formation of those histories. The need to strive for concordance between genomic, linguistic, and archaeological inference, the accurate dating of prehistoric material, as well as accurate reconstructions of paleoecology, are clearly required in interdisciplinary efforts to reconstruct "deep history" (O'Rourke, 2011). This is perhaps especially true when basing such reconstructions primarily on genetic or genomic data. The need for greater articulation between researchers in different specialties is clearly demonstrated by the synthetic, multidisciplinary investigations that comprise the chapters in this volume.

REFERENCES

Abi-Rached, L., Jobin, M. J., Kulkarni, S., *et al.* (2011). The shaping of modern human immune systems by multiregional admixture with archaic humans. *Science*, **334**, 89–94.

Agostini, H. T., Yanagihara, R., Davis, V., Ryschkewitsch, C. F., and Stoner, G. L. (1997). Asian genotypes of JC virus in Native Americans and in a Pacific Island population: markers of viral evolution and human migration. *Proceedings of the National Academy of Sciences of the United States of America*, **94**,14 542–6.

Black, R., Bennett, S. R. G., Thomas, S. M., and Beddington, J. R. (2011). Migration as adaptation. *Nature*, **478**, 447–9.

Boas, F. (1912). *Changes in the Bodily Form of Descendants of Immigrants*. New York: Columbia University Press.

Cabana, G. S. and Clark, J. J. (2011). *Rethinking Anthropological Perspectives on Migration*. Gainsville, FL: University Press of Florida.

Chakraborty, R. and Szathmary, E. J. E. (eds.) (1985). *Diseases of Complex Etiology in Small Populations: Ethnic Differences and Research Approaches*. New York: Alan R. Liss.

Coltrain, J. B., Hayes, M. G., and O'Rourke, D. H. (2004). Sealing, whaling, and caribou: the skeletal isotope chemistry of Eastern Arctic foragers. *Journal of Archaeological Science*, **31**, 39–57.

Crawford, M. H. (ed.) (1976). *The Tlaxcaltecans: Prehistory, Demography, Morphology and Genetics*. Publications in Anthropology 7. Lawrence, KS: University of Kansas.

Crawford, M. H. (ed.) (1984). *Current Developments in Anthropological Genetics*, Vol. 3: *Black Caribs. A Case Study in Biocultural Adaptation*. New York: Plenum Press.

Currat, M. and Excoffier, L. (2011). Strong reproductive isolation between humans and Neanderthals inferred from observed patterns of introgression. *Proceedings of the National Academy of Sciences of the United States of America*, **108**, 15 129–34.

D'Andrea, W. J., Huang, Y., Fritz, S. C., and Anderson, N. J. (2011). Abrupt Holocene climate change as an important factor for human migration in West Greenland. *Proceedings of the National Academy of Sciences of the United States of America*, **108**, 9765–9.

Fisher, M. C., Koenig, G. L., White, T. J., *et al.* (2001). Biogeographic range expansion into South America by *Coccidioides immitis* mirrors New World pattern of human migration. *Proceedings of the National Academy of Sciences of the United States of America*, **98**, 4558–62.

Fix, A. G. (1999). *Migration and Colonization in Human Microevolution*. Cambridge, UK: Cambridge University Press.

Ghose, C., Perez-Perez, G. I., Dominquez-Bello, M-G., *et al.* (2002). East Asian genotypes of *Helicobacter pylori* strains in Amerindians provide evidence for its ancient human carriage. *Proceedings of the National Academy of Sciences of the United States of America*, **99**, 15 107–11.

Goldin, I., Cameron, G., and Balarajan, M. (2011). *Exceptional People: How Migration Shaped our World and Will Define Our Future*. Princeton, NJ: Princeton University Press.

Goldstein, D. B. and Chikhi, L. (2002). Human migrations and population structure: what we know and why it matters. *Annual Review of Genomics and Human Genetics*, **3**, 129–52.

Green, R. E., Malaspinas, A -S., Krause, J., *et al.* (2008). A complete Neandertal mitochondrial genome sequence determined by high-throughput sequencing. *Cell*, **134**, 416–26.

Green, R. E., Krause, J., Briggs, A. W., *et al.* (2010). A draft sequence of the Neandertal genome. *Science*, **328**, 710–22.

Hammer, M. F., Woerner, A. E., Mendez, F. L., Watkins, J. C., and Wall, J. D. (2011). Genetic evidence for archaic admixture in Africa. *Proceedings of the National Academy of Sciences of the United States of America*, **108**, 15 123–8.

Hancock, A. M., Witonsky, D. B. H., Gordon, A. S., *et al.* (2008). Adaptations to climate in candidate genes for common metabolic disorders. *PLoS Genetics*, **4**, e32.

Hunley, K. and Healy, M. (2011). The impact of founder effects, gene flow, and European admixture on Native American genetic diversity. *American Journal of Physical Anthropology*, **146**, 530–8.

Major, E. O. and Neel, J. V. (1998). The JC and BK human polyoma viruses appear to be recent introductions to some South American Indian tribes: there is no serological evidence of cross-reactivity with the simian polyoma virus SV40. *Proceedings of the National Academy of Sciences of the United States of America*, **95**, 15 525–30.

Moodley, Y., Linz, B., Yamaoka, Y., *et al.* (2009). The peopling of the Pacific from a bacterial perspective. *Science*, **323**, 527–30.

Moreau, C., Bhérer, C., Vézina, H., *et al.* (2011). Deep human genealogies reveal a selective advantage to be on an expanding wave front. *Science*, **334**, 1148–50.

Morton, N. E. (1982). *Outline of Genetic Epidemiology*. New York: S. Karger.

O'Rourke, D. H. (2011). Contradictions and concordances in American colonization models. *Evolution: Education and Outreach*, **4**, 244–53.

Pannell, J. R. and Charlesworth, B. (2000). Effects of metapopulation processes on measures of genetic diversity. *Philosophical Transactions of the Royal Society of London: B*, **355**, 1851–64.

Piguet, E., Pécoud, A., and de Guchteneire, P. (2011). Migration and climate change: an overview. *Refugee Survey Quarterly*, **30**, 1–23.

Raff, J. A., Bolnick, D. A., Tackney, J., and O'Rourke, D. H. (2011). Ancient DNA perspectives on American colonization and population history. *American Journal of Physical Anthropology*, **146**, 503–14.

Ramachandran, S. and Rosenberg, N. A. (2011). A test of the influence of continental axes of orientation on patterns of human gene flow. *American Journal of Physical Anthropology*, **146**, 515–29.

Rasmussen, M., Guo, X., Wang, Y., *et al.* (2011). An Aboriginal Australian genome reveals separate human dispersals into Asia. *Science*, **334**, 94–8.

Reich, D., Green, R. E., Kircher, M., *et al.* (2010). Genetic history of an archaic hominin group from Denisova Cave in Siberia. *Nature*, **468**, 1053–60.

Reich, D., Patterson, N., Kircher, M., *et al.* (2011). Denisova admixture and the first modern human dispersals into Southeast Asia and Oceania. *American Journal of Human Genetics*, **89**, 516–28.

Sugimoto, C., Kitamura, T., Guo, J., *et al.* (1997). Typing of urinary JC virus DNA offers a novel means of tracing human migrations. *Proceedings of the National Academy of Sciences of the United States of America*, **94**, 9191–6.

Wright, S. (1951). The genetical structure of populations. *Annals of Eugenics*, **15**, 323–54.

Wright, S. (1978). *Evolution and the Genetics of Populations*, Vol. 4: *Variability Within and Among Natural Populations*. Chicago, IL: University of Chicago Press.

Index